INSTRUMENT OF WAR

Volume 1 of
The Austrian Army in the Seven Years War

With the support of the Austrian Army Museum
(Heeresgeschichtliches Museum), Vienna

Christopher Duffy

Helion & Company

Helion & Company Limited
Unit 8 Amherst Business Centre
Budbrooke Road
Warwick
CV34 5WE
England
Tel. 01926 499 619
Email: info@helion.co.uk
Website: www.helion.co.uk
Twitter: @helionbooks
blog.helion.co.uk

Published by Helion & Company 2020
Designed and typeset by Mach 3 Solutions Ltd (www.mach3solutions.co.uk)
Cover designed by Paul Hewitt, Battlefield Design (www.battlefield-design.co.uk)
Printed by Gutenberg Press Ltd, Tarxien, Malta

Text and maps © Christopher Duffy 2000, 2020
Illustrations © as individually credited

Cover painting: Silesia in the late summer of 1762. View from the Eulen-Gebirge to the Zobten-Berg and to the fortress of Schweidnitz, under siege by the Prussians. To the right we see the guileful Austrian field marshal Leopold Joseph Daun, escorted by a platoon of the Staff Infantry in their distinctive blue coats. The general officer in the background is Franz Moritz Lacy, who founded the Austrian General Staff. The sound of a exploding magazine or mine has carried across the plain, and Lacy has drawn the attention of an officer of the regiment of Alt-Colloredo (No. 20) to a plume of smoke rising from Schweidnitz. (Painting by Peter Dennis © Helion & Company 2020)

Every reasonable effort has been made to trace copyright holders and to obtain their permission for the use of copyright material. The author and publisher apologize for any errors or omissions in this work, and would be grateful if notified of any corrections that should be incorporated in future reprints or editions of this book.

ISBN 978-1-912390-96-0

British Library Cataloguing-in-Publication Data.
A catalogue record for this book is available from the British Library.

All rights reserved. No part of this publication may be reproduced, stored in a retrieval system, or transmitted, in any form, or by any means, electronic, mechanical, photocopying, recording or otherwise, without the express written consent of Helion & Company Limited.

For details of other military history titles published by Helion & Company
Limited contact the above address, or visit our website: http://www.helion.co.uk

We always welcome receiving book proposals from prospective authors.

Contents

List of Maps		v
Introduction		vii
	Austria's War In Outline	x
Part I	The Foundations	13
1	Austrian Beginnings	15
2	The Heart Of The Monarchy	20
3	The Territorial Base	36
4	Finance	110
5	Diplomacy	121
Part II	The Army	129
6	The Army as a Whole	131
7	The Rosenkavalier Goes to War – The Austrian Officer	156
8	Adam Bauer – The Austrian Private Soldier	213
9	The NCOS and the Regimental Staffs	251
10	The Infantry	259
11	The Cavalry	278
12	The Artillery	299
13	The Engineers and Other Technical Support	322
14	The Croats	333
15	Logistics	349
16	Body and Soul	364
Part III	Waging War	381
17	Strategic Dimenions	383
18	Operational and Tactical Dimensions	416
Conclusions		460
List of Regiments (Designations as of 1759)		463
Appendices		
I	Military Representation of Hungarian Counties and Transylvania	469
II	Religion in Hungary and Transylvania by Location	471
III	Origins of Netherlands Private Soldiers	473
IV	Origins of German Private Soldiers	474

iii

V	Wastage	475
VI	Regimental Officers by Nationality	477
VII	Age and Service of the Regimental Officer	479
VIII	Recruiting *Rayons* Designated for the Cavalry	481
IX	Civilian Trades by Category	482
X	Age and Service of Private Soldiers	483
XI	Losses through Desertion	489
XII	Background of the Personnel of the Field Artillery	491

Notes	493
Bibliography	528
Index	544

List of Maps

1	Central and Western Europe.	46
2	The Habsburg Possessions in Central and Southern Europe.	49
3	Bohemia, Moravia and Northern Austria.	59
4	Hungary, with Eastern Austria	71
5	The Austrian Netherlands.	84
6	The German Reich.	94

Dedication
To Johann Christoph von Allmayer-Beck

The Empress-Queen Maria Theresa.
(Courtesy of the curators of the Schönbrunn Palace)

Introduction

Austria in the 1750s was already acquiring the music, the architecture, the cuisine and the styles of living which have added not a little to the happiness of the human race. Perhaps the notion of Austria as a military power does not occur so readily. All the same, the leaders of that society were the first to confront an historical process which ran its full and damaging course only towards the end of the 20th century. This was the rise of militaristic Prussia, which shook Habsburg Austria almost to its foundations in the 1740s, and went on to unite Germany under its leadership in 1871 – and so consolidated the base on which Germany in its turn went to war in 1914, 1939 and 1941. Through stupendous efforts the armies of Soviet Russia held the last great German offensive in 1943, and fought their vengeful way into the heart of Central Europe in 1945, where Soviet control remained paramount until the collapse of the Marxist-Leninist political system in the late 1980s.

All of this lends point to the striving of the Austrian Empress Maria Theresa and her foreign minister Kaunitz to overthrow the youthful Prussian military state in the Seven Years War (1756–63). They failed in this immediate objective, but their efforts were rewarded indirectly, for they had begun to promote a distinct Habsburg state consciousness, and in this respect their 'Austria' was strengthened.

As the 20th century merges into the 21st another historical perspective comes to mind. Sixty or so years ago 18th-century bodies politic like the Habsburg Empire or the old multi-state German *Reich* appeared as primitive and unformed creatures, doomed to be overtaken entirely by progress. Since then, the emergence of supra-national bodies and influences has opened the possibility of new insights into Central Europe at the time of Maria Theresa, when she, her statesmen and her soldiers worked, not indeed in the environment of a failed nation state, but in a framework of customs and values which deserve respect and study in their own right. The multi-national Habsburg army must occupy a central place in any such review.

The 'Austrian' army was in fact an association of men who sprang from environments as diverse as Belgian cities, Alpine meadows, Irish bogs and Transylvanian forests – in other words as complete a cross-section of 18th-century Europe as you are likely to find. The kind of military history which concerns itself with nothing but the fighting will therefore miss much which is of value to the study of humankind in a particular stage in its evolution. At the same time my present book will prove abhorrent to those practitioners of the New Military History who interest themselves in everything BUT the fighting. Armies, if they are not employed for internal repression, exist primarily to deter and if necessary combat external enemies, and their fighting ability and record is the conclusive standard by which they must be judged.

The coming-together of accumulated insights and new methodologies has helped to reclaim a place for the Seven Years War in the eyes of discerning historians and public, and it is probably a good thing that answers have been so long to arrive to the challenge that was set by Theodor von Bernhardi as long ago as 1881. He was disappointed to learn that the Austrian General Staff's programme of histories of Austrian wars placed the study of the Seven Years War in such a distant prospect (so distant, in fact, that Staff and Austro-Hungarian Empire disappeared before their historians came within striking-distance of the enterprise). Meanwhile the continuing silence of the Austrian historians seemed to him to represent an injustice to what their army had achieved in that war (*Friedrich der Grosse als Feldherr*, Berlin 1881, II, 626–7).

My contribution bears the overall title of *The Austrian Army in the Seven Years War,* and is arranged in two volumes. The first, *Instrument of War,* presents the environment in which the Austrian army operated, its organisation and identity, and its ways of fighting. The second volume, *By Force of Arms,* takes the form of a military and diplomatic narrative, supported by studies of strategic geography, the leading commanders and the individual regiments.

On reading the next-but-final text of *Instrument of War,* I was at first puzzled by the harsh tone of many of its judgements on the Theresian Army. On reflection I believe I can identify three reasons. The first is the sheer mass of detail preserved in the Austrian archives on all that army's doings, for good or ill. A record of this quality is very rare indeed. Few armed forces in any period have laid themselves so open to posterity, and I suspect that many a 'glorious' record would not survive such a narrow scrutiny as is possible in this case.

Inevitably the historian writes backwards, in the knowledge of what became of all the works and hopes of the people he or she is investigating in the safety and quiet of a study. In fact the issue of the war remained entirely in doubt until early in 1762, and it is possible that I had forgotten that if, as could so easily have happened, Frederick had strayed into the path of a cannon shot, or Elizabeth of Russia had lived a few weeks longer, then historians would now be taking Field Marshal Daun's 'finely-measured prudence' as an established fact, and afflicting their students with questions like: '"Charles XII of Sweden and Frederick of Prussia – merely different paths to the same destruction" (John Keegan). Discuss.'

Third, although I have devoted every spare moment of the last 15 years to the present study, my interest in the theme goes back very much further, to the time when, as a lad of six or so, I opened an encyclopaedia at an illustration which showed Old Fritz standing aghast at the door of his lodgings in Hochkirch, while his grenadiers streamed past him in flight. I thought that was good. Another page showed a blonde and buxom Maria Theresa appealing to her Hungarian nobles, who were brandishing their swords in response. That was even better. To a degree which is probably inadmissible in a professional historian I have remained a devotee of Maria Theresa, and I suspect that I am outraged unduly by the shortcomings which held back the Austrians from doing even better in their war than they did. I can only regret the gap of six or seven generations which has prevented me from contributing to her cause in a way more direct than this book.

I can scarcely begin to acknowledge all the help I have received in writing *Instrument of War* – help which makes this study in many ways a joint enterprise. In the first place I must thank Dr Manfried Rauchensteiner (now Director of the Austrian Army Museum) and his wife Marianne for many years of hospitality and support. The good cheer and shrewd advice of Dr Lothar Höbelt, Dr Erwin Schmidl and Roland Starrach have for many years been a further reason to look forward to visits to Vienna.

An ancient tradition of the Austrian War Archives (*Kriegsarchiv*) is expressed in a sign in their library which reads: 'Researchers are the reason for our work, not its interruption.' A project such as mine would have been unthinkable without the active help of its present Director, Dr Rainer Egger, Dr Peter Broucek (who has an unrivalled knowledge of the ranges of documents consulted most frequently by me), Dr Christoph Tepperberg (master of the muster lists), Dr Erich Hillbrand (manager of the map collection), Karl Rossa (my first line of reference), and Christine Röllig whose technical skill made it possible for me to take back to Britain perfect copies of documents by the thousand. I still count myself as the pupil of Dr Johann Christoph von Allmayer-Beck, from his time at the *Kriegsarchiv,* and I am delighted that he has accepted the dedication of this work.

Vienna is also the home of the Haus-Hof und Staatsarchiv, where Dr Leopold Auer and Dr Christina Thomas pointed me to important runs of documents of diplomatic and strategic interest. Informed Austrian perspectives were also to be had from the formidably energetic Dr Grete Klingenstein of Graz University, Dr Michael Hochedlinger (who is doing work of fundamental importance on the recruitment of the Austrian army in the 18th century), and Professor Franz Szabo who (although technically a Canadian) combines high historical expertise with the living traditions of a line of Habsburg gunners.

Through the kind offices of Lieutenant-Colonel Professor Joszef Zachar I was introduced to the very substantial holdings of the Hadik papers in the Hungarian Military Institute and Museum in Budapest, and to the facilities and hospitality that were extended by Dr Jósef Kun, and by Major-General Dr Ervin Liptai, Lieutenant-Colonel Dr Laszo Bence, and Kottra Györgyi Csákváriné. It was an historian's dream to have the unlimited time to peruse the papers of the old hussar, and look up and see Hadik's bulky form represented in the bronze equestrian statue a few yards away in the Kapisztrán Square.

Thanks to a friend of long standing, Dr Miroslav Mudra, I was able to pass a profitable period of study at the State Archives in Bratislava (the old Pressburg, and now in Slovakia), which holds the extensive papers of Rudolph Pálffy, stray correspondence of Field Marshal Daun, and the memoirs of the old general Wöllwarth. Much otherwise inaccessible information on Bohemian and Moravian topography was transmitted by Jaromir Hanák, the Director of the Austerlitz Battlefield Museum.

The observations of foreign attachés with the Theresian army are of particular interest. Those of the French observers were accessible through the kindness of the *Service Historique de l'Armée de Terre* at Vincennes, and the massive report of Fromhold Armfeldt through the Swedish *Krigsarkiv*. The good offices of Dr Anders Karlson yielded the voluminous dispatches of the Swedish envoy Nils Bark, held in the Swedish *Riksarkiv*, while Dr Jurgen Kloosterhuis as Director of the *Geheimes Staatsarchiv Preussischer Kulturbezitz* gave me access at short notice to the reports of the Prussian spymaster Winterfeldt and his agents. Colonel Manfred Gansdorfer kindly provided photographs of the magnificent run of portraits in the Theresian Military Academy at Wiener Neustadt.

I am also grateful to the staff of the *Archives de l'État* at Arlon (de Bryas papers), the *Archives de la Ville de Bruxelles* (Pesser papers), and the Northumberland County Record Office (unpublished papers of Horace St. Paul).

Over the years I have had fruitful contact with Dr Johannes Kunisch, who has done so much to sustain academic interest in the period of the Seven Years War. I had a most useful conversation with Professor Peter Dickson, while Claudio Donati, Marco Gioannini and Fabrizio Daví alerted me to valuable Italian published sources. Fabrizio is a fellow-member of the Seven Years War Association, where the companionship (especially that of Neil and Valerie Cogswell, Paul Dangel, Paul Petri, Jim Purky, Alister Sharman and Brian Vizek) provided essential moral support for the present enterprise.

Two further members, Jim Mitchell and Dean West, assisted greatly in the preparation of the present text. However the responsibility for errors and misjudgements remains entirely my own.

Austria's War In Outline

1756
Maria Theresa's diplomats had been striving to put together a coalition that would enable Austria to recover the province of Silesia from Frederick of Prussia, and reduce his kingdom to the status of a minor power. The process was still incomplete when Frederick took the initiative by overrunning the Electorate of Saxony, which he believed (wrongly) to be a partner in the alliance. A Prussian incursion across the border into Bohemia led to the little battle of Lobositz (1 October), which was a technical victory for Frederick, but showed the Austrian army had improved greatly since the last war with Prussia (1744–5).

1757
The blatant breach of peace by Frederick helped the Austrians to put together their system of alliances, culminating in the Second Treaty of Versailles (1 May) with France. However Frederick had already launched a full-scale invasion of Bohemia, and by beating the main Austrian army at Prague (6 May) he seemed to shake the foundations of Habsburg rule. The situation was saved by Field Marshal Daun, who assembled a second army, and defeated the king at Kolin (18 June). This victory was hailed as 'the Birthday of the Monarchy,' and was the first time the Austrians had ever got the better of Frederick in open battle. By late November the Austrians had regained nearly all Silesia, but Frederick, having routed an army of French and allied Germans at Rossbach (5 November), turned back east and defeated the Austrians in the hard-fought battle of Leuthen (5 December).

1758
In the spring and early summer Frederick for the last time took the offensive into Austrian territory, when he invaded Moravia and laid siege to Olmütz. By brilliant manoeuvring the Austrians forced him out again, and thenceforward the war was to be conducted mostly to the north of the Habsburg borders – in Saxony and Silesia. Daun surprised and beat Frederick at Hochkirch (14 October), but was unable to exploit his success.

1759
The campaign was slow to get under way, for the combatants were unable to keep up the furious pace of the early stages of the war. An Austrian corps under Loudon contributed to the spectacular defeat of Frederick by the Russians at Kunersdorf (12 August). Frederick faced ruin in the face, but the Austrians and Russians were unable to summon up the will to combine their main forces and grasp the prize that was within their reach. In the subsequent campaigning in Saxony the Austrians captured the corps of the Prussian general Finck at Maxen (20 November).

1760
There was much encamping and manoeuvring on the plains of Silesia and Saxony and the fringes of the border hills. A chapter of accidents enabled Frederick to beat the Austrians at Liegnitz in Silesia (15 August), and thus escape a dangerous trap. He won again at Torgau in Saxony (3 November) – a great and bloody battle that left the armies stalemated in this theatre.

1761
Frederick was thrown on the defensive, and the Austrians and Russians were for the first time able to bring together powerful forces in Silesia. Frederick survived a virtual siege in his entrenched camp at Bunzelwitz, but on the night of 30 September he lost the key fortress of Schweidnitz to a brilliant coup de main by Loudon.

1762

Frederick had been about to sue for peace when he learned that Empress Elizabeth of Russia had died on 5 January. The anti-Prussian alliance began to break apart, and for a time a Russian corps actually joined Frederick's army in Silesia, which helped the king to beat Daun at Burkersdorf (21 July). A further Austrian defeat at Reichenbach (16 August) signalled the end of the attempts to relieve the besieged Austrian garrison in Schweidnitz, which fell on 9 October after a gallant defence. Silesia was lost irretrievably to the Austrians. Frederick's brother Prince Henry defeated a force of Austrians and *Reichsarmee* Germans at Freiberg (29 October), which saw a similarly unhappy end to the war in Saxony.

1763

At the Peace of Hubertusburg (15 February) the Austrians gave up their claim on Silesia. Maria Theresa, her statesmen and her military men had failed to gain their declared objective, but their efforts had consolidated the Austrian military and civil institutions, and prompted a supra-national Habsburg state which survived in a recognisable form until 1918.

Note

It should be mentioned that the standard 'Austrian' currency was the florin, or *Gulden*. The florin was made up of 60 *Kreutzer*, each of which had very roughly the purchasing power of an United States dollar in the year 2000. Eight florins made a ducat.

Part I
The Foundations

1

Austrian Beginnings

'Austria' and *'Austrian'* – most historians still argue about when we can first begin to apply these names to that empire which, at its greatest extent, bestrode Europe from the sands of Ostend to the Transylvanian Carpathians, and from the headwaters of the Elbe, the Oder and the Vistula to the rocky spine of Italy in the distant south.

The word 'Austria' sprang from the *marchia orientalis* or *Ostmark,* a territory which was established by peoples of Bavarian stock who pushed down the Danube under the leadership of the House of Babenberg (946–1246). Austria survived as an independent and sovereign duchy after the Babenbergs died out, and in 1283 the land passed to the Habsburgs – a line of nobles who had their base of power in Swabia and northern Switzerland, where their white limestone castle of Habichts-Burg ('Castle of the Hawk') rose to the east of Basel. The Habsburgs were a particularly tough and acquisitive breed, and the leader of the house, Duke Rudolph (1218–91) had already been elected Emperor of Germany in 1273. This was a title which the Habsburgs (with one short interval) went on to claim as a matter of course from 1438.

Germany, or the *Reich,* was an assemblage of principalities, duchies, knightly fees and free cities. Although the Habsburgs had no direct sovereign power over this association of states, they succeeded so well in identifying the Imperial dignity with their family that they were able to extend a degree of legal and moral authority over their fellow-Germans for centuries to come. So it was that the Imperial German device (the black double eagle on its yellow field) became as much a part of Habsburg heraldry as the white-red-white shield of Austria.

We return to the Austrian heartland. Having gained the vacant duchy of Austria, the Habsburgs at once began to expand their domains beyond the basin of the upper Danube. Their first direction of aggrandisement lay south across the Alps, and it was accomplished not by force of arms, but through the wit of lawyers and scheming Habsburg parents. In the celebrated phrase: 'Let others wage wars; you, fortunate Austria, go forth and marry!' Styria came to the Habsburgs in the same year as Austria, in 1283; Carinthia and Carniola followed in 1335, and the Tyrol from 1363. A second series of accessions carried Habsburg rule over the Alps and into the borderlands of the Italians and south Slavs (County of Istria 1382; Fiume 1466; Görz by 1518).

The Habsburg authority assumed continental or even potentially global dimensions when the house inherited Aragon and Castile in 1496. However the affairs of Spain, the Netherlands and other concerns of this great empire were of marginal interest to its Austrian component, which now faced the advance of the Ottoman Turks, who had overrun the Serbs, and were now marching west across the central plain of Hungary. The Ottoman Turks were at once a mortal threat to the Austrian Habsburgs, and the instrument which elevated them into a great power in their own right.

This paradox was illustrated most tellingly by the battle of Mohács (29 August 1526) and its consequences. Louis II, the last of the Jagellon kings of Hungary, was killed by the Turks along with his leading nobles. The crown of Hungary was due to revert to the Archduchy of Austria, and a few weeks later the noble assemblies of Hungary, Croatia, Silesia, Moravia and Bohemia proclaimed Archduke Ferdinand of Austria as their legitimate king. The rule of the Austrian Habsburgs now extended east and south-east into Hungary and Croatia (or whatever parts of those territories could be secured against the Turks), and across the Sudetens into the north German plain.

Emperor Charles V abdicated in 1555, and he divided the Habsburg domains among the Spanish and Austrian branches; his younger brother Ferdinand not only retained in full sovereignty all the recent and enormous accessions of territory, but inherited the family claim to the Imperial dignity of the German *Reich*. The struggle against the Turks continued, and its needs produced two of the distinguishing features of the Habsburg war machine, namely the military settlements of the Croatian military border, which took shape from 1552, and the *Hofkriegsrath* (Court Council of War), established in 1556 to manage military administration.

In the plain of the Danube the line of equilibrium with the Turks approximated the course of the river Leitha, which ran uncomfortably close to the Austrian heartland – a circumstance that was emphasised when the Ottomans laid siege to Vienna in 1529, and again in 1683. A volunteer of princely Italian blood, Eugene of Savoy, contrived to distinguish himself even in the great multi-national army of relief which broke the second of these sieges, and Emperor Leopold I singled out this ugly young man for his thanks. Leopold was repaid many times over when the Christian forces pushed down the Danube in the following campaigns, and in 1697 Eugene, who was now commander-in-chief, smashed a Turkish army in the great battle of Zenta. Two years later the Turks had to sign away the Principality of Transylvania, all the ground they had once held in Hungary, and large parts of Croatia and Slovenia.

Eugene in his prime displayed a mastery of all the levels of war. He was at once a fiery and charismatic leader on the battlefield, a commander who grasped the essential issues in a campaign and followed the necessary measures through to the end, however bold and unorthodox they might be, and lastly a farseeing soldier-statesman who was alive to the long-term strategic interests of the monarchy.

Scarcely had Eugene's first Turkish war finished before his masters had need of him in what was to be the protracted War of the Spanish Succession (1701–14), in which a European coalition fought to prevent Louis XIV from uniting France and Spain under the Bourbon dynasty as a super-state. Eugene himself campaigned in Italy, and in a famous partnership with Marlborough in Germany in 1704, and again in the Spanish Netherlands from 1708 to 1714. However British support for the war fell away, and this, linked with a Bourbon military revival, enabled the armies of Louis XIV to gain the upper hand in final campaigns in the Netherlands, along the Rhine and in eastern Spain. On balance the Austrians emerged with net gains from the peace settlements of 1713 and 1714. If Emperor Charles VI (who set great store by symbols) could never reconcile himself to losing the historic Habsburg land of Spain, he gained the former Spanish Netherlands, which were another part of the Habsburg inheritance, and he won Lombardy, Naples and Sicily. France and Spain were to remain separate, albeit under Bourbon kings.

Eugene crowned his last Turkish campaigns (1716–18) by capturing Belgrade, and the subsequent peace broadened the Austrian holdings on either side of the Danube to embrace the Bánát of Temesvár and Little Wallachia to the north, and Serbia with Belgrade well to the south-east.

The map of Europe now suggested that 'Austria' was in almost equal measures a Central European, a Northern European, a Balkan and a Mediterranean power. The Habsburg lands had certainly expanded in a remarkable way, but the trouble was that the internal consolidation had not kept pace. Even in the oldest Hereditary Lands the Habsburgs exercised authority only through negotiation and partnership with the local noble assemblies (*Stände*) in a kind of commonwealth. State consciousness, as far as it existed, was the indirect product of the alliance that was forged between the dynasty and the Counter-Reforming Catholic Church in the Baroque period. All the time the recent, covert or open practice of Protestantism remained an alienating force among the nobility of Hungary and Bohemia.

'Austria' could so easily have gone Protestant. In the summer of 1619 Vienna had been under threat from converging armies of heretical Bohemians and Hungarians, while Archduke Ferdinand was beset in the Hofburg palace by a clamorous crowd of Lower Austrian nobles. The pious Ferdinand was confident of divine help, and his trust was justified when on 19 June a trumpet blast and a clatter of hooves announced the arrival of a force of 400 cavalrymen, sent from the Tyrol by his brother Leopold. Building on this success the Catholic forces were able to secure the election of Ferdinand as Emperor a matter of weeks later, and they formed the army which repressed the Bohemian rebels at the Battle of the White Mountain (8 November 1620), which closed the first significant episode of the Thirty Years War in Central Europe.

Dampierre's force of 'Florentine Troopers' survived to become the senior regiment in the Austrian army (appearing in the Seven Years War as the Erzherzog Ferdinand Cuirassiers), with the privilege of riding through the Hofburg with sounding trumpets and flying standards, while their commander had the right to present himself unannounced before the Emperor, booted and spurred. All the same it had taken force of arms to enforce Habsburg authority, and four or five generations later events were to show that only about half of the Bohemian nobles identified their interests with those of the Habsburgs. Rebellion in Hungary (1703–11) was a matter of recent memory, and the lenient Treaty of Szatmár (1 May 1711) served to confirm the Magyar nobles in their prickly sensibilities of independence.

Charles VI (ruled 1711–40) attempted to give his domains their first legal cohesion by grouping them as a *Fideikommiss,* or an indivisible and inalienable possession of the Habsburgs under the principles of family law, and an entity that would pass through the female line if (as was thought unlikely) he failed to produce a male heir. These provisions were enshrined in a document called the Pragmatic Sanction (1713), and it was a genuine gain for the Habsburgs when the Hungarian nobles accepted it as fundamental state law ten years later. However, Charles had to bargain away tangible state interests to gain guarantees of the Pragmatic Sanction abroad. The price exacted by the British and Dutch (1731) was the dissolution of the Ostend Company, which deprived the Habsburgs of much of the benefits of ruling the Netherlands, while leaving them with heavy responsibilities for the defence. Although the British and Dutch were going to stick by their word, the same did not hold true of the French, who gained the sovereignty of the Duchy of Lorraine, a prime piece of Franco-German borderland. Duke Francis Stephen of Lorraine (son-in-law of Charles VI and future Emperor) was consoled by being given the reversion of the Grand Duchy of Tuscany, which even then was to remain separate from the Habsburg domains proper.

By now Prince Eugene of Savoy had outlived his best days, and his inertia contributed to the generally dismal performance of the Austrians in the War of the Polish Succession (1733–5). The settlement of 1735 and the definitive peace of 1738 deprived the Austrians of Naples and Sicily and part of the state of Milan, and compensated them only in a very inadequate way by the acquisition of Parma and Piacenza. Eugene died in 1736, and the crowning conquest of his career, the fortress-town of Belgrade, was lost to the Turks in a new and disastrous eastern war (1737–9). These reverses were at once a cause and symptom of the decay of the army in this period.

Charles VI died without warning on 20 October 1740. He was aged 55, which was fairly young by the standards of European monarchs, and until 15 or so years earlier he had retained the hope that his late wife (née Princess Elisabeth of Brunswick-Wolfenbüttel) would provide him with a male heir. By the year of his death he was a widower, but still hoping to remarry and beget sons. This is probably why he had given so little thought to providing a political training to his eldest daughter Maria Theresa, who was born in 1717. From the age of 11 this sensible, warm-hearted and exceptionally pretty fair-haired and blue-eyed girl received a sympathetic education from Countess Charlotte Fuchs (*die Füchsin*), who promoted her genuine love-match with the exiled Duke Francis III Stephen of Lorraine, who was one of her companions at court.

However it never occurred to Emperor Charles to encourage Maria Theresa to sit in on important conferences, or give her the opportunity to judge the worth of the leading men of state.

Maria Theresa succeeded her father on 21 October 1740, most immediately as Archduchess of Austria. She learned soon enough how little confidence could be placed in all the elaborate provisions which her father had made for the inheritance. Another young monarch, Frederick II of Prussia, had his eyes on the rich and populous northern province of Silesia, and with scarcely a pretence of lodging a legal claim he brought his army across the Silesian border on 16 December. Not many years later it was possible to romanticise the first and most heroic period of Maria Theresa's reign, but she makes it clear that her circumstances at the time were desperate:

> Such was the state in which I found myself – without money, without credit, without an army, without experience or knowledge of my own, and ultimately without advice, for every minister's priority was to investigate how things would turn out. That was the state of affairs when I was attacked by the King of Prussia.[1]

This explains why Frederick of Prussia was able to gain possession of Silesia within six weeks.

Early in 1741 Field Marshal Neipperg led an army across the snowy hills to try to reclaim Silesia for Maria Theresa, but he was surprised and beaten by the Prussians on 10 April. This battle confirmed what many observers suspected, that the Austrian army was in very bad way, and only a few months passed before some of the major powers of Europe, as well as a number of the smaller ones, were arrayed in a disreputable league which aimed to dismember the Habsburg inheritance. Frederick had already established his interest in Silesia; Elector Charles Albert of Bavaria claimed Vorder-Österreich, the Tyrol, Upper Austria and Bohemia, which together amounted to the most significant part of the Hereditary Lands, and he was determined to break the centuries'-old Habsburg monopoly of the Imperial title; the Austrian possessions in northern Italy seemed likely to fall to the Spanish, while the Austrian Netherlands were open to invasion by the French.

The theme of our story will be the Seven Years War, which was to be the crucial episode in the confrontation between Maria Theresa and the Prussians, but it would be wrong to forget the immediate danger which the French and Bavarians presented to her survival at the outset of her reign, and what their efforts revealed concerning the weaknesses of the Habsburg body politic.

Prague fell to the French and Bavarians on 26 November 1741 and on 19 December Charles Albert received the homage of the Bohemian *Stände* as King of Bohemia. The human and material resources of this kingdom were vital to the credibility of 'Austria' as a military power, which made it all the more disturbing that the invaders were able to assemble a working majority of the Bohemian noblemen in their cause, including representatives of families as prominent as the Chotek, Czernin, Gallas, Kinsky, Kollowrat, Sternberg and Waldstein.

Likewise the Bavarians and French challenged the Habsburg standing in the German *Reich,* where they persuaded or coerced the majority of the Electors to choose Charles Albert as Emperor on 24 January 1742.

In this crisis the House of Habsburg-Lorraine had a pledge of at least family continuity in the person of Maria Theresa's first son Joseph, who was born on 13 March 1741. She left him behind when she went to Pressburg to ask the Hungarian magnates for help, but the Hungarians responded no less warmly to the appeals of the bereft young mother, and they drew their swords and affirmed their support with the cry: *Moriamur pro Rege nostro Maria Theresia!* ('We offer our lives for our King, Maria Theresa!')

She had gained an important accession of legal authority, and the Hungarian hussars and the newly-raised regiments of Hungarian infantry proved to be of welcome assistance in her military needs. These needs were as pressing as ever, since Frederick (after a short period of truce) again declared his support for her enemies, and in February 1742 a combined force of Prussians, Saxons and French made for the Danube by way of Moravia. Prussian hussars came within sight of the spires of Vienna, and the capital became too vulnerable for Maria Theresa to linger there for the birth of her next child, the Archduchess Christine.

The Austrians rallied under the leadership of reliable old soldiers like Field Marshal Ludwig Andreas Khevenhüller, and with the help of the Hungarians and new foreign allies they were able to regain much of what had been lost. Prince Charles of Lorraine (Maria Theresa's brother-in-law) cleared the French and Bavarians from Bohemia before the end of 1742. In 1743 a combined army of Austrians, Hanoverians and British beat the French at Dettingen (27 June), and in the following year Charles was able to carry the war for a time across the Rhine and into Alsace.

The Austrians concurrently regained symbolic ground by having Maria Theresa crowned as Queen of Bohemia on 12 March 1743, and ensuring the election of Francis Stephen as Emperor of Germany on 13 September 1745. While the distant Netherlands proved to be indefensible against the French, the Austrians won the upper hand in northern Italy, thanks to an agreement with the British and Sardinian-Piedmontese on 13 September 1743, and the conclusive victory gained by Prince Liechtenstein over the French and Spanish at Piacenza on 16 June 1746. Thus the threat from the French and their historic allies gradually fell away.

The continuing danger from Frederick of Prussia stood out all the more starkly on two accounts: his success in hanging onto Silesia, and an unbroken series of Prussian victories. On 17 May 1742 Frederick had beaten Prince Charles of Lorraine at Chotusitz in northern Bohemia, and in the definitive peace of Berlin (28 July) the Austrians had to confirm his sovereignty over Lower Silesia, the County of Glatz, and most of Upper Silesia. These territories increased the area of Prussia by one-third, and left the Austrians holding just one-seventh of the disputed province.

In the late summer of 1744 Frederick invaded Bohemia with 80,000 troops, and reduced Prague after a short siege. Prince Charles returned at speed from chasing the French, and on the advice of the veteran Field Marshal Traun he avoided battle, struck at the enemy communications, and finally manoeuvred the Prussians from Bohemia with the loss of 30,000 of their men. Buoyed up by his success, Prince Charles strode into Silesia in the early summer of 1745, and experienced an almost predictable defeat at Hohenfriedberg on 4 June. A string of further actions (Soor, 30 September; Hennersdorf, 23 November; Kesselsdorf, 15 December) confirmed that the Prussians were superior at this kind of war. The Peace of Dresden (25 December 1745) confirmed Frederick as master of Silesia and Glatz, and the Austrians renewed their guarantee in the all-embracing Peace of Aix-la-Chapelle (18 October 1748) which wound up the War of the Austrian Succession.

2

The Heart Of The Monarchy

Maria Theresa And The Imperial Family

The Austrian effort in the Seven Years War was directed by a partnership between two disparate but complementary individuals – the Empress-Queen Maria Theresa, who was prompted by instinct and by deeply-held beliefs, and her *Staatscanzler* (foreign minister) Wenzel Anton Kaunitz, the shrewd, self-possessed man of the world, who prided himself on acting from rational calculation.

Maria Theresa was a person of integrity in the strict sense of the word, in that her life, her principles and her conduct were all of one piece. She bore line upon line of pompous and ancient titles, but was still able to fashion something fresh and original from old materials. She showed a regal presence on state occasions, yet was never happier than when presiding over her brood of children in unassuming chambers tucked away in the Schönbrunn and Hofburg palaces. Maria Theresa spoke for preference in the sing-song dialect of Vienna, and she shared the Viennese *Hausfrau's* disinclination towards anything that was abstract, doctrinaire or dehumanising.

Here is an explanation for the at first sight disconcertingly matter-of-factness of some aspects of Theresian Austria. The Schönbrunn was a working palace which had been adapted from a hunting lodge, and it disappointed visitors who expected to find a residence as grand as Versailles, or as elegant as Nymphenburg or Sans Souci. Musicians, versifiers, architects and painters were hired as necessary to create pleasing effects, and not to disturb the conscience or challenge the intellect. The corps of ceremonial household troops (the *Arcieren-Garde,* the *Trabanten-Garde,* and from 1760 also the Hungarian noble *Leibgarde*) amounted to no more than about 300 officers, and the Austrian army proper was remarkable for having no royal Guard as such. Garrison service in Vienna was done by the regiments of the army by rotation, and it was not especially welcome, for the units were on public show all the time, and it was expensive to have to keep up appearances. The infantry regiment of Deutschmeister (No. 4) as yet had no particular links with the city, and no reputation of any note (except perhaps for its high rate of desertion). In no other major army of Europe were the troops dressed so simply.

Maria Theresa's fifth son and last child, Archduke Maximilian, was born on 8 December 1756, a few weeks after the Seven Years War had broken out. She typically refused to allow the event to interfere with the conduct of affairs, even though 'she suffered considerably, for the baby was amazingly big and strong'.[1] Again, from the public history of the times we might have been aware that smallpox twice swept through the Imperial family during the war, threatening the life of Archduke Joseph in 1757, and carrying away the 15-year-old Archduke Charles on the night of 17 January 1761.

A sense of family and religion informed Maria Theresa's dealings with her subjects. If some of her preoccupations were open to ridicule (regarding, for example, her affront at the short skirts worn in the Tyrol), she showed moderation and a concern for the sensibilities of others even in the most necessary reforms. She took her son Joseph to task for some harsh words he had spoken concerning the old general Joseph-Charles d'Ayasasa: 'Why do you judge him so harshly and damn him out of hand? I am very much afraid that you hold a very poor opinion of humankind in general, and antagonise the few honourable men by throwing them together with the others'.[2]

When Frederick of Prussia and Charles Albert of Bavaria attacked the Austrian domains, they found that Maria Theresa defended her patrimony with the determination of a mother tigress. Charles Albert wilted under the ordeal, which left Frederick isolated as a 'bad man,' a 'wicked neighbour' and a 'monster.' She believed that nothing worse could happen to her subjects than to fall under Prussian rule, and she considered that she had a special responsibility to save them from that fate. Maria Theresa did not know that Frederick in private repaid this enmity with unstinted admiration. He recognised the strength of her religious principles (even if he did not share them), he believed that her work for the army was worthy of a great man, and when things were going badly for him he drew inspiration from the courage she had shown at the outset of her reign.

Maria Theresa's dedication to public affairs could be impressive. On working days she rose at four or five in the morning in summer, and at six during the winter. She heard Mass, then at once got down to her papers, pausing every now and then to dip a *Kipfel* (croissant) in her cup of coffee. She loved fresh air (her one unViennese trait), and when she resided at Schönbrunn in the summer months she worked variously by an open window, on the terrace overlooking the park, in Jadot's new summer house (*Volière*) in the centre of the Menagery, or under a tree with a box of papers strapped to her waist. The lunch was solitary and hurried, and after a couple of hours' relaxation she worked through until about seven in the evening. She allocated her ministers specific days on which to make their reports, and at least once in the week she called them together in one or other of the types of conferences (below). The most secret talks were held in the small and richly-decorated *Cabinett* in the Schönbrunn, a chamber which was provided with food from a table which rose from the floor below, so that the discussions could continue in privacy and without interruption. The *Staatscanzler* Kaunitz had lodgings in a penthouse suite above, and he could come and go as he wished by means of a private staircase.

Maria Theresa took an active and informed part in state business of every kind, as is shown by the minutes of the conferences, and the comments she scribbled in the margins of reports and memoranda. However nobody could doubt her particular dedication to military affairs: 'This branch of state administration was the only one in which I had a personal interest'.[3] At the great Kolin manoeuvres in July 1754 it was noted that Maria Theresa inspected the magazines and field bakeries, while her spouse went off hunting. Frederick exclaimed: 'wouldn't you think that the woman has passed herself off as a man, and her man as a woman?'[4]

Other Prussians commented that:

> This great princess was active in encouraging her troops. It was her habit to be present in person whenever regiments marched past Vienna on their way to join the army. She spoke to the men in the most gracious way you could imagine, calling them her children, and she laughed with delight when the words 'our mother!' resounded along the ranks like a *feu de joie*'.[5] On this account... she is beloved by her troops, and their regard is strengthened by the resolution she displayed under the heaviest blows of fate. We know that for a considerable time she harboured the serious intention of commanding her army in person'.[6]

Leadership of this kind had its own power, and the French brigadier Montazet declared to her that at the battle of Torgau in 1760 'your troops fought as if you had been at their head'".[7]

For Frederick of Prussia his soldiers were a human resource that was to be hoarded or expended, praised, encouraged or beaten as the occasion demanded. Maria Theresa could not harden herself to such a degree of detachment. She invariably attended the Masses that were being said for the good of the souls of her dead soldiers, and nearly every day during the campaigning season she prayed for the common cause in the parish church at Hietzing just outside the Schönbrunn palace, or at the church of Mariahilf on the way to Vienna. As a further proof of her concern Maria Theresa and the court ladies made up bandages for the wounded, thus encouraging a fashion that reached ridiculous proportions (see p. 371).

Frederick's ambassador in Vienna told him after the Silesian Wars that:

> she singles out the military for particular distinction, and there can be no doubt that the army stands in higher esteem than under the late Emperor. She has said repeatedly that only through the sword will a man be able to make his name during her reign. When officers are on duty at court, she invites them to dine at her table regardless of birth – much to the displeasure of the high nobility.[8]

By an *Hofkriegsrath* directive of 23 March 1741 all the orders to army commanders and other important personages had to be submitted to Maria Theresa for her instruction and signature, and during the Seven Years War she required the commanders in their turn to keep her briefed constantly on the course of the campaigns. This was an onerous obligation, as the busy generals had not only to set aside time to write their reports, but arrange for the couriers to carry the correspondence to and from Vienna.[9]

All of this is much to Maria Theresa's credit, but we must resist the temptation to exaggerate the degree of control she could exercise over her military machine. The Swedish attaché Fromhold Armfeldt concluded that 'setting all differences in military talents aside, the distinction between the Austrians and the Prussians lies in the fact that the king [Frederick] is answerable for his intentions to nobody but himself. He is bound by no set plan of operations; he marches, breaks camp and acts without lengthy cogitation, and punishes and rewards as he sees fit'.[10] With the best will in the world Maria Theresa could not see everything that was going on in her vast monarchy, and depended heavily on advisers: 'she often follows the first impressions which such people choose to give her – and they are folk who might well be motivated by selfish aims, jealousy and other considerations'[11].

Maria Theresa's management of the army and its operations was indeed for the most part indirect. Frederick, by way of contrast, proved and selected all of his senior commanders individually, and inspected each of his regiments almost every year. He commanded in the field in person, as Armfeldt indicated, and he subjected his army to a constant and direct process of training through parades, manoeuvres, and formal and informal instructions.

As for Maria Theresa's advisers, she was looking for good men who would come to her with a well thought-out 'system' of reform, such as she found in Liechtenstein for the remaking of the artillery, Haugwitz for the finances, Hildburghausen for the military borders, Kaunitz for foreign affairs, and Felbiger after the war for education. Counsel of this quality was not always at hand.

Frederick was ruthless in the way he purged and disciplined bad servants, and even punished some excellent ones, just in case they were inclined to take his goodwill for granted. Maria Theresa found it virtually impossible to free herself from a sense of obligation to anyone who had ever earned her gratitude. She tolerated old Harrach at the *Hofkriegsrath* long after he had outlived his usefulness, and she was unable to advance promising young commanders without instituting a general round of promotions to console the disgruntled incompetents. In such an atmosphere the spirit of faction raged unchecked. One of her Italian officers wrote that:

> During the Seven Years War nothing was more deplorable than to see the way the most able Austrian commanders were frustrated at every turn by all the other generals. Since time immemorial democracies like these have been ravaged by jealousies of the most pernicious and inexplicable kind. It seems to me that envy is rather like gout – once it gets into the

bloodstream it is impossible to get rid of it; the slightest thing can cause a recurrence, and often when you expect it the least.[12]

Denied the possibility of following her instinct to command in the field, Maria Theresa was forced to wait for the tidings of the war in a state of almost hysterical anticipation. The reports of the defeats provoked floods of tears and invocations of the Almighty, while the news of a victory could inspire her to rouse the members of the Imperial family from their chambers in various states of deshabille to celebrate the great event.

Frederick gave his all to the war, and in a manner 'deserved' to win, or at least survive it. Maria Theresa was a princess of the Austrian Baroque, and could still devote time and treasure to entertainments appropriate to her status. At the height of the campaigning season of 1760 Kaunitz had to write apologetically to *FZM*. Loudon. He was aware that his protégé had to correspond with the court four times a week – a tiresome business – and he regretted that he now had to lay a further burden on him. This was now the hunting season, which took Maria Theresa away from Vienna for days on end, and the only way to save precious time was for Loudon to be so good as to send additional reports direct to Kaunitz in the capital.[13]

The refurbishment of the Schönbrunn palace went on apace during the war, and the artist Gregorio Gugliemi spread a painted army of Theresian soldiers over the ceiling of the Grosse Galerie at the same time as the real army in the field was short of necessities. Professionally-minded officers were scandalised in particular by the extravagant expenditure on the marriage of Archduke Joseph to Infanta Isabella of Parma, which was celebrated on 6 October 1760. *FZM*. Lacy wrote to Daun from Vienna that:

> here they are throwing themselves into the preparations for the marriage festivities. They are making a new highway from the Line Wall to Schönbrunn. The cost is said to come to 100,000 florins, and just when my regiment writes to me that the authorities have abolished the six creutzer which used to be held at the regimental depots for every reconvalescent arriving there from the hospitals. Your Excellency is aware how important it is that these men should be given every help to rebuild their strength. I would ask Your Excellency to do everything possible to remedy this misplaced economy, which is a trick worthy of Martin Luther.[14]

Prince Liechtenstein duly set off with a great train to collect the bride in Italy. She arrived in Vienna in a cortege of 100 coaches, and the final union was celebrated by banquets, theatrical performances and illuminations. The final cost was put at 3,000,000 florins. Prince Albert of Sachsen-Teschen confided his

bitterness to his diary, where he pointed up 'the striking contrast between our situation out here… exposed appalling weather, spending our time up to the knees in mud, or in combat, and the life of the idle nobility in the capital, who deployed an

Prince Albert of Sachsen-Teschen, 1738–1822. (Austrian Army Museum)
By no means as stupid as he looks, Prince Albert was a trenchant critic of the extravagance which was displayed in Vienna at the height of the Seven Years War, and his diary is a valuable source for the later campaigns. He went on to marry Maria Theresa's favourite daughter Marie Christine, and founded the Vienna Albertina, which is one of the world's finest collections of graphic art.

extraordinary measure of luxury and magnificence on this occasion'.[15]

Contradictions like these seem incomprehensible until we try to penetrate the baroque mentality, which allowed a seemingly bizarre compartmentalisation of roles. Thus in the previous war Francis Stephen as Austrian sovereign had required the British Royal Navy to maintain an effective blockade of Genoa, while in his capacity as Grand Duke of Tuscany he had protested when the British intercepted innocent ships on their way from Tuscan ports to the same city. Again he was reputed to have supplied fodder and flour to the Prussians through his network of contractors in 1756 and 1757, and to have made a profit on the coupons in which the Austrian army was forced to take some of its pay later in the Seven Years War.

At the same time Maria Theresa's husband and co-regent was in many ways an attractive character – dignified but rarely on his dignity, generous, easily-pleased, drawn to women and the theatre, and one of the century's foremost connoisseurs of objets d'art. Francis Stephen was a shrewd judge of character, responsible for introducing both Haugwitz and

Prince Charles of Lorraine. (Liotard)

Kaunitz to Maria Theresa, and his financial acumen brought benefits both to the state and to the private fortune of the House of Habsburg-Lorraine.

Maria Theresa loved Francis Stephen dearly, and bore him 16 children, but their differences in habits and temperament were so extreme as to impede an effective working partnership. It seemed to one of the senior courtiers that 'we have two masters, the Emperor and the Empress, and both wish to reign.' Francis Stephen would have liked to direct the army and the finances, but he was too easy-going to follow up his inclinations: Maria Theresa, on the other hand, was fiery and impatient. 'The heads of department are aware of these respective shortcomings, and they have exploited them in a most skilful way to hold up or advance affairs as their interest suggests'.[16]

Family ties linked the credit of Francis Stephen to that of his younger brother Prince Charles of Lorraine, who was recognisably of the same stock, though more coarsely grained. He was personally brave, militarily experienced, and he was capable of showing the enterprise which made his forcing of the Rhine in 1744 a fine thing, as Frederick admitted. All the same his red face and his loud voice betrayed a lack of self-confidence, which he tried to redress by resorting to the bottle and the company of a notoriously dissolute set of cronies. Charles lost his standing with the public through his showing in the campaign of 1745, when he was 'blamed for spending a great part of the daytime at table, and the evenings in all sorts of debaucheries. When the morning came he was usually incapable of working, for he would be labouring under a hangover from his excesses of the night before'.[17]

Considerations of dynastic prestige sustained Charles in command until early in 1758, but he was already excluded from Maria Theresa's innermost counsels. Negotiations with the French were at a critical stage when he happened to blunder into a secret meeting on 4 March 1757. Charles had intended to pass the time of day with his brother Francis Stephen, but the presence of Maria Theresa and the ministers told him that something important and secret was afoot. He retreated in some embarrassment and shut the door behind him.

It was clear that Maria Theresa would have to look beyond her family circle for the assistance she needed to manage her state.

Kaunitz

Wenzel Anton Count von Kaunitz-Rietberg (1711–94) was born into a house of Moravian nobility closely associated with the rebellion of the Bohemian nobles (1618–20) which had launched the Thirty Years War. Thereafter the family succeeded in winning its way back to favour with the Habsburgs, and had risen steadily in their service.

Wenzel Anton received a comprehensive grounding for his administrative and diplomatic career. He studied law at Leipzig, which was the leading university of Germany, and after a Grand Tour through the Netherlands, Italy, Germany and France he returned to Vienna in 1734 as a young man of the world, fluent in at least four languages. In the capital he made his first acquaintance with the public service through some not particularly demanding appointments in local and legal administration.

In 1736 Kaunitz married Maria Ernestine von Starhemberg, which was a match linking him with one of the grandest houses of Austria, and through the influence of his new father-in-law he was able to acquire his first diplomatic experience, on a mission to Piedmont-Sardinia in 1741. Kaunitz represented Austria at Turin as full ambassador from 1742 until 1744, at a time when Piedmont became an active theatre of war. Later in 1744 he joined the administration of the Austrian Netherlands as minister, and he acquitted himself so well that he was appointed minister plenipotentiary in 1745. This too was a scene of operations, for the French were in the process of reducing the Barrier Fortresses by sieges. Kaunitz witnessed the allied defeat at Fontenoy in 1745, and early the following year he negotiated the surrender of Brussels to the French. It is reasonable to suggest that these experiences told him that the Austrian Netherlands were difficult to defend, and that the French had a very effective army. Kaunitz represented Austria at the subsequent peace congress of Aix-la-Chapelle in 1748, and came to know the workings of international politics on the grandest scale.

In October 1750 Kaunitz arrived in Paris as ambassador. This was a prestigious posting, and yet for more than two years Kaunitz experienced little but frustration. He was convinced that Austria's best interests lay in an alliance with the French, but he was unable to persuade them to re-orientate their politics in such a fundamental way. He had nevertheless gained the full confidence of Maria Theresa, and she now appointed him *Staatscanzler* in place of the deaf and near-senile Corfiz Anton Count Ulfeld. Kaunitz took up his new post on 13 May 1753, after he returned from Paris.

Maria Theresa valued in Kaunitz the ability to put forward a rationale for action, and the will to pursue that action through to the end. Add to this the bureaucratic and presentational skills of Kaunitz, and his excellent everyday working relationship with Maria Theresa, and we have a man whose authority was ultimately unchallengeable.

In 1756 and 1757 the emergency of the first campaigns of the Seven Years War permitted Kaunitz to consolidate his standing in the innermost counsels, which became more and more secretive and exclusive. The responsibilities of *Staatscanzler* already extended beyond diplomacy to all affairs which had a bearing on the policy and power of the state, and in 1758 Kaunitz tested the waters to see whether Francis Stephen and Maria Theresa would be open to the idea of appointing him as a prime minister. Their Imperial Majesties were unreceptive. Kaunitz bided his time, and returned to the charge in December 1760, when he argued successfully that it was important to establish a *Staatsrath,* or overall consultative body, to keep all the internal business of the Hereditary Lands under review (below). The sittings of the *Staatsrath* began on 26 January 1761, and Kaunitz inevitably had the leading voice. He was now in a position to exercise a decisive influence on all the affairs of the monarchy.

Kaunitz was a remarkably balanced man, if we are willing to extend this term to an equilibrium of opposites. As the Prince de Ligne noted, through believing himself to be the greatest man in the world, Kaunitz made great progress towards actually becoming so.[18]

Nothing makes him more laughable [commented a Prussian diplomat] than the three brushes he employed. I really must describe them. The first of them served to brush his teeth shortly before he rose from the table; he took it from his container, asked for a glass of water, scoured out his mouth, and spat onto his plate… The second brush was for polishing his diamonds. He had three sets of the regalia of the Golden Fleece, and every 15 minutes he buffed up the one he happened to be wearing to show it to the best advantage… The third and last brush was for his snuff box. He had a great quantity of them, all adorned with the miniatures of ladies. When he opened a box he made sure that it was possible to gain a glimpse of the picture, and when he was naturally asked to show it he replied: 'One moment, dear sir!' This was the cue for him to take out the brush, clean the picture and hand it over to be admired.[19]

Kaunitz was already foreign minister before the Seven Years War (which he did so much to bring about), and by the end he had won control of policy making overall. The portrait was executed after the war, and shows Kaunitz wearing the insignia of the new Order of St. Stephen. The long coat is in the style of a much earlier generation, while the wig defies description.

Perhaps it was important for Kaunitz to show forth such a parade of eccentricities in order to clear his mind of what he called the *Nebenumstände* (secondary considerations) – prejudices, passions and private interests – which he believed must be set aside in order to arrive at a rational evaluation of the interests of the state. He made due allowance for the influence of such *Nebenumstände* on foreign powers and lesser intellects – the way the English public associated itself with Protestant Prussia, for example, or the hatred which the Pompadour, Empress Elizabeth of Russia and her chancellor Bestuzhev bore for Frederick – but he believed that he himself could not go far astray if he looked at Austria's interests dispassionately and took them as his guide. Kaunitz did not shrink from the inevitable consequences, when the light of reason revealed that an old enemy (France) must be made into a friend, that a lost province (Silesia) must be regained at the cost of a new war, or that an existing province (the Netherlands) could if necessary be bargained away.

Kaunitz approved in others the same consistency of principle he believed he could see in himself. In 1758 he admired the elder Pitt as the man who guided the British ship of state, and 'whose conduct has now furnished convincing proof that he is not the kind of man who exists from one day to the next, but goes to work in a systematic fashion, and directs the British counsels towards a single stated objective'.[20] It was of a kind with the enthusiasm of Kaunitz for neo-classical modes of music and architecture, and fundamentally just as contrived.

Kaunitz wrote so much, and wrote so very well, that it would be easy to reconstruct a history of Austria's part in the Seven Years War entirely from his viewpoint and to his entire credit. This is a temptation to be resisted. He set goals for Austrian policy which surpassed the capabilities of the Austrian army to meet, and he likewise attached too much importance to the 'objective' advantages of the anti-Prussian alliance in the Seven Years War. He was the most bellicose of Maria Theresa's ministers until he learned of the damage which the war was doing to the Austrian finances, and he then instituted a notorious reduction which left the Austrian army at a crucial disadvantage in the field. He put his support behind the Croats, whose best days belonged to the past, but, for all his genuine technical military expertise (below), he did not comprehend the usefulness of the new Staff services and technical arms. He was right to be alarmed at the dangers which Prussia presented to the Habsburg body politic, but the world 'alarmist' probably best describes the threats he now perceived from Ottoman Turkey and from Russia as leader of an Orthodox 'Illyrian' (Slavonic) world.

When the Seven Years War was over, a chastened Kaunitz concluded that warfare must have changed in fundamental ways since the last century, for battles no longer determined which party gained what at a final peace. Everything now hung on outlasting the enemy, and this depended 'alone and exclusively on the greatest possible conservation of one's resources in time of peace'.[21]

We shall encounter the activity of Kaunitz in so many military contexts during his great war that it will perhaps be convenient to draw them together here in an overview.

In late June 1757 Kaunitz confided to a French military attaché that:

> the confidence which the Empress reposes in my devotion and zeal has persuaded her to entrust me not only with determining the course of operations, but making the projects and plans as well. I confess to you that such a task demands talents considerably more distinguished than those at my command, but I am not altogether a novice at this kind of thing, and I have followed the course of a number of campaigns with some attention.[22]

This might seem a remarkable kind of authority for Maria Theresa to invest in a civilian. In fact the military qualifications of Kaunitz extended well beyond those of an interested amateur. Among the campaigns which he had followed with particularly 'close attention' were those which he had witnessed at least from a distance in north Italy and at first hand thereafter in the Netherlands. There is at least indirect evidence that Kaunitz reinforced his observations of military events with a study of theory, and notably Puységur's *Art de Guerre par Principes et par Règles* (Paris 1748).[23] This work presented by far the most comprehensive, realistic and balanced survey of the contemporary way of war, and the title alone would have appealed to Kaunitz's structured way of thinking.

The memoranda of Kaunitz, and his contributions to the conferences were the means by which the *Staatscanzler* influenced the internal management of the military machine. They showed that he had an expert knowledge of the relevant issues, and that he was willing to attend to the detail of subjects as recondite as maladministration in the forwarding of recruits[24] or the state of foraging in Saxony.[25]

Still more impressive was Kaunitz's grasp of the potentialities and ethos of the Habsburg service. He was the consistent advocate of the Croats, and he was regarded by them in turn as their protector. He maintained that the Croatian light infantrymen were over-exploited, in the sense that they were in constant contact with the enemy in the field, and yet were denied adequate material and tactical support, or any recognition of their courage and endurance. They were simultaneously under-exploited, in the sense that the Croatian Military Borders offered a reserve of hardy and loyal manpower which, he argued after the war, could furnish the best base for expanding the army.

It was due to Kaunitz that the Austrian army and state were spared the extremes of Prussomania which were to be encountered in other monarchies in the second half of the 18th century. Kaunitz was consistent in his views as to what should, and should not, be taken over from the military practice of Frederick II of Prussia. He admired and commended the facility with which Frederick moved his armies on the theatre of war and on the battlefield (after all, he and Old Fritz had probably read the same books). At the same time he recognised that Austria had her own military traditions, and could only harm herself by adopting Prussian ways without discrimination.

Something that was present in the Prussian order of things, but almost completely absent in the Austrian, was the existence of a sociopolitical class like the Junkers, dedicated to the service of the state. Kaunitz recognised this shortcoming, and he had a substantial part in shaping the character of the Military Order of Maria Theresa, which was instituted in 1757, and which was made accessible to suitably brave or ingenious officers regardless of their birth, rank or age. Kaunitz typically manoeuvred himself into the position of true power in the Order's Chapter as Chancellor, while leaving the position of Grand Master to Emperor Francis Stephen. The family politics of the House of Habsburg-Lorraine dictated that the discredited Prince Charles of Lorraine must lead the first Promotion, on 7 March 1758, ahead of the deserving Field Marshal Daun. There was potential for great embarrassment, but the speech of Kaunitz on this occasion was recognised as 'a masterpiece of eloquence and tact,' for he emphasised the part which Charles had played in the victory at Breslau on 22 November 1757, while saying nothing about the prince's share in the disaster at Leuthen on 5 December.[26]

The diplomatic and military knowledge at the command of Kaunitz fitted him to speak with some authority on matters of strategy, the level at which war interacts most immediately with politics. Here the most fundamentally important advice that can be tendered by an individual or body must relate to 'security,' which is the business of identifying a state's interests, the possible threats to those interests, and the appropriate responses.

Although the word as such would probably not have been recognised by Kaunitz, he kept Austria's 'security' under constant review, and he summed up his assessments every now and again for the benefit of Maria Theresa. Among some particularly impressive surveys we may cite the celebrated memorandum which he presented on 24 March 1749 before he came to power, and the reviews of 30 December 1760 (which looked beyond the end of the war), 24 November 1762 and 3 March 1763. Kaunitz was not blind to the long-term dangers of the expansion of Orthodox Russia, but again and again he insisted on the multiple threats presented by Frederick of Prussia – as the conqueror of Silesia with its rich resources and strategic position, as a rival in the *Reich,* and the representative of a despotic and militaristic state. As long as Prussian power remained intact, Kaunitz believed that Austria's best security lay in a close understanding with the French.

The operational level of war – the conduct of individual campaigns – was also of close concern to Kaunitz, who was by no means ignorant of such affairs, as we have seen. He travelled to the headquarters of the main army only once, which was in May 1757 in the crisis immediately after the Austrians had been defeated at Prague, but he was already in a position at the heart of Austria's military counsels. In this sphere at least Kaunitz was too much of a pragmatist to bind himself to any one 'system' of war, but he had a secure grasp of military geography and the meaning of concentration of effort.

Kaunitz believed that the Austrian army needed bold and charismatic commanders in order to put forth its full potential. He was confident that he had found one such man in Field Marshal Maximilian Browne, who commanded the main army at the outset of the Seven Years War. Browne in his turn warmed to Kaunitz, in whom he found someone who possessed 'great insight… and has gone on campaign in person'.[27] Another fellow spirit was one of Browne's friends, the cavalry general Joseph Lucchese d'Averna.

Neither Browne nor Lucchese survived the bloody year of 1757, and it was not until 1760 that Kaunitz was able to cement a new personal alliance, this time with Gideon Ernst Loudon, who had been promoted with unprecedented speed to the rank of full general (*Feldzeugmeister*), and entirely on the strength of his 'luck' and fitful flashes of enterprise. Kaunitz had made the first démarche by inviting Loudon to comment on the plan for the forthcoming campaign. Loudon duly sent his observations, and on 7 March he wrote to Kaunitz asking him to arrange for three of his staff officers to be appointed adjutants, and for leave to correspond with him directly on military affairs. Loudon had occasion to apply to Kaunitz again on 15 May, this time with a request for pontoons for his campaign in Silesia.[28] Thereafter the two remained in constant contact, and Kaunitz gave Loudon every conceivable support in his work of commanding the independent corps in Silesia. Just as the general looked to Kaunitz to circumvent the bureaucratic ways of the *Hofkriegsrath,* so Kaunitz hoped for dramatic deeds on the part of his protégé in Silesia. Later in the war a comparable figure emerged on the Saxon theatre in the person of *G.d.C.* Andreas Hadik, who took over the Austrian command in 1762, and won the plaudits of Kaunitz for the energy he brought to operations in that part of the world.

Less happy were the relations between Kaunitz and Field Marshal Daun, who directed the main Austrian army from the spring of 1758 until the end of the war. The *Staatscanzler* constantly spurred the cautious and pessimistic Daun into the kind of action that would secure decisive results in the field, or at least convince the allies that Austria was shouldering her fair burden of the war. On his side Daun believed that Kaunitz was ill-informed, and that a commander who rushed headlong into battle on disadvantageous terms would put the monarchy at risk.

It would be anachronistc to identify ourselves overmuch with Kaunitz and his assorted favourites, who indeed represented a more 'modern' style of war. The attractions of offensive operations have a way of growing in proportion to the time and distance which separates one from a theatre of war; to Kaunitz they held a strong appeal, and to historians writing centuries later they might well appear irresistible. It is worth pointing out that Loudon had notorious shortcomings as a commander, and that the objections of the other generals to his rapid promotion were not due just to envy. Both Browne and Lucchese came to bad ends, and in a remarkably similar war – by leading dramatic counterattacks (at Prague and Leuthen) which ended in disaster.

How Policy Was Formulated And Implemented

Frederick of Prussia weighed up and determined the fundamental questions of state with little or no reference to any other individuals or bodies – on his walks, perhaps, on rides, or (as one observer suspected) when he was feeding his dogs.

At the time of the Seven Years War the Austrian debates and decision-making involved one or more of five or six organs. At one extreme the *Hofkriegsrath* was an elaborate and firmly-entrenched bureaucracy. Other bodies amounted to little more than informal meetings, with no permanent secretariat. The names of most of them are singularly uninformative, and difficult to carry in the head for more than a few seconds at a time. It is no help to adhere to the English translation, once it has been explained, for then we lose contact with the original altogether.

Geheime Conferenz *(Privy Council)*
This was the survivor of a consultative body which had been set up in 1670, and was attended by the heads of the departments of state and the leading courtiers as a matter of right. As the senior and the most conservative of the councils, it was the one least accessible to the influence of Kaunitz, who made sure that it became increasingly marginalised.

Conferenz
A product of the pressing need to prepare the army for the new war, the *Conferenz* was first called together on 8 July 1756 as a *Rüstungs Commission* (Mobilisation Commission) to bring together the necessary human, animal and material resources. Thereafter it met once a week under the chairmanship of Kaunitz and on home ground in his *Staatscanzley,* and assumed the character of a war cabinet in which he inevitably had the leading voice. Maria Theresa was usually present in person, and the meetings typically included the heads or deputy heads of:

> the *Hofkriegsrath* (Court Council of War, below)
> the *Directorium in Publicis et Cameralibus* (Ministry for Internal Affairs), President Friedrich Wilhelm Count Haugwitz, Vice-Present Johann Count Chotek
> the *General Kriegs-Commissariat* (Department of Military Supply), which was absorbed into the *Directorium* in November 1757 (below).

Individual generals or other officials were summoned in person if they were required to make specialised contributions. Not all the meetings were equally productive, since the *Conferenz* was racked by internal divisions. There was a notable period of upheaval late in 1757 when the *Commissariat* was swallowed up by the *Directorium,* with dire effects.

Conferenz In Mixtis

A short-lived body, the *Conferenz in Mixtis* was formed on the initiative of Maria Theresa in May 1757 after the defeat at Prague, with the intention of bringing together the old *Geheime Conferenz* and the new *Conferenz* to consult every Thursday. Kaunitz disliked the arrangement, since it threatened the independence of the *Conferenz,* and by December he contrived to kill it off, by postponing the meetings for weeks at a time, and finally excluding the members of the *Geheime Conferenz* altogether. This measure was aimed in particular against Rudolph Count Colloredo-Waldsee (the *Reichs-Vizecanzler*) who got on badly with Kaunitz.

Military Conferenz

This was a gathering of generals and officials of the *Hofkriegsrath,* who met at irregular intervals to consider matters of narrower military concern, like recruiting or the provision of fodder. Kaunitz was present at the sessions, and made some important contributions to the deliberations.

The Reichscanzley *(Chancellery Of The German Empire)*

The *Reichscanzley,* which managed Austrian relations with the *Reich,* occupied one of the grandest wings of the Hofburg palace in Vienna. The *Reichs-Vizecanler* Colloredo was admittedly excluded from the ministerial conferences outlined above, but he corresponded directly with the current commanders of the *Reichsarmee* and the supporting Austrian forces, and the allied ambassadors found him more accessible than the increasingly reclusive Kaunitz. Colloredo was therefore able to exercise a significant influence on the conduct of war on the Saxon theatre, and quite independently of Kaunitz, who does not seem to have been fully aware of what was going on.

The Staatsrath *(Council Of State)*

The meetings of this body were not related directly to military operations, but they were highly relevant to the ability of the Austrians to sustain their effort in the last years of the war. After prolonged discussions with Kaunitz, Maria Theresa wrote to him late in 1760 to ask him what remedies he had in mind for the desperate state of the internal affairs of the monarchy. He replied that the finances were exhausted, and the departments of state were in disorder, and the reason was that 'everything is done without regard to principles of system, without having been discussed properly, in a piecemeal fashion, and from day to day without liaison or concert.' A prime ministership would be unconstitutional and unfitting (above), and so Kaunitz recommended that Maria Theresa should set up a standing council of state, where experienced men could meet on a regular basis, and so bring harmony to the management of affairs.[29] Maria Theresa gave the idea her enthusiastic approval on 14 December, and the body first came together on 26 January 1761.

The *Staatsrath* was a consultative body that kept all the domestic affairs of the Austrian and Bohemian lands, Hungary and Transylvania under review, and scrutinised all the sources of revenue, all the directions of expenditure, and all the documents which came to Maria Theresa from the departments of state. The Empress-Queen attended one of the two regular weekly meetings, and she was free to accept or reject the advice of the members without constraint.

Kaunitz stipulated that all the members of the *Staatsrath* must lay down their other appointments. He made an immediate exception in his own case, on the technical grounds that his *Staatscanzley* was concerned with foreign and not domestic affairs. Kaunitz therefore kept his independent base of power intact, and in addition he retained his control of the affairs of the Austrian Netherlands and Austrian Italy, whose councils had been absorbed into the *Staatscanzley* in 1757.

The Staatscanzley *(Chancellery Of Foreign Affairs)*
We are probably beginning to suspect that any continuity and purpose in the direction of the Austrian effort in the Seven Years War must be identified largely with the person of Kaunitz. The institutional basis of authority has been outlined already – in essence he kept full control over foreign affairs through his *Staatscanzley,* while he extended his influence through the councils, of which the last and the most important was the *Staatsrath.*

It will probably be useful to trace a typical cycle of decision-making. We may take it for granted that Kaunitz was already apprised of the relevant issues through the dispatches which came to him from the ambassadors, and by reports which reached him from the field; his protégé Loudon wrote to him direct, but more commonly the letters from the generals reached him by way of Maria Theresa or the *Hofkriegsrath.* Having formed his opinions, Kaunitz made his initial demarche to Maria Theresa through a *Vortrag* (memorandum). This was a lengthy but clearly-argued essay which set out the facts of the case, and recommended a course of action; it was all the more persuasive because it was set out in the excellent German which gave Kaunitz an inherent advantage over people like Daun or Francis Stephen, who had little grasp of spelling or grammar in any language. Having talked over the matter in hand with Maria Theresa, Kaunitz and his private secretary Friedrich Binder von Kriegelstein prepared the instruction (*Cabinet-Schreiben*) which was to be sent to the relevant commander or diplomat. Maria Theresa read the draft, and after Kaunitz had incorporated any corrections or amendments Binder worked up the final version for her approval and signature, and the document was carried on its way by one of the couriers of the *Staatscanzley.*

Kaunitz and the staff of the *Staatscanzley* likewise set the agenda for the conferences. The meeting usually began with the reading of the minutes of the last conference, and the more important of the reports from the heads of department or commanders in the field. If Francis Stephen were present, he almost invariably gave his *placet* ('it is pleasing') without more ado. Maria Theresa took a more active part, and whether verbally or in writing she delivered her opinions of the last conference, and drew the attention of her advisers to the matters which should be addressed next; she disliked working through secretaries, and preferred to dash down her comments (innocent of captions or punctuation) on slips of paper or in the margins of the documents. Kaunitz then asked Neipperg, Haugwitz or other heads of departments for progress reports, and they in turn noted any further matters which they had to bring up with their officials. The staff of the *Staatscanzley* were responsible for drawing up the conference minutes, which further reinforced the position of Kaunitz at the heart of Austrian counsels.

The Hofkriegsrath *(Court Council Of War)*
The *Hofkriegsrath* was the most celebrated and the most maligned of the Austrian military organs of government. It was not a policy-making body as such, but was concerned primarily with the business of military administration. This was of enormous extent, and concerned matters as diverse as the appointment of all generals and senior regimental officers, recruiting, troop movements, hospitals, plague cordons, supply and military justice (except during the periods when these were managed by separate organs), and both the military and civilian affairs of the 'Croatian' military borders.

Even at the height of the Seven Years War by far the greatest part of the work of the *Hofkriegsrath* had nothing to do with the campaigns, but was taken up as before by the multifarious internal affairs of the regiments, and by the problems of maintaining and exchanging prisoners – which was its largest single category of business. It was some alleviation that it could devolve the labour of procuring weapons and ammunition almost entirely to Prince Joseph Wenzel Liechtenstein.

The potential for disorder was still very great. Regiments and individual officers had the right to circumvent the chain of command by appealing directly to the *Hofkriegsrath*.[30] Moreover the offices and papers of the department were scattered between seven locations in the Inner City of Vienna and the rampart casemates, which put it at a disadvantage in relation to Kaunitz, who had all the staff and documents of the *Staatscanzley* concentrated in its splendid new building right next to the Hofburg palace.

Whereas the *Staatscanzley* had come into existence only in 1742, the *Hofkriegsrath* had been founded by Ferdinand I in 1556, and was burdened by history and institutionalism. Prince Eugene became President in 1705, and brought the *Hofkriegsrath* to a pinnacle of power and prestige. When Eugene's faculties declined the *Hofkriegsrath* decayed also, and by the time of the War of the Austrian Succession this august institution was in a dismal state. Favouritism was rampant, and affairs were directed without co-ordination and were subject to inordinate delays. Authority slipped from the increasingly senile president, *FM.* Johann Joseph Harrach, and power was disputed between the cantankerous vice-president, *FM.* Ludwig Andreas Khevenhüller, and the able but self-willed first *Referendar* August Thomas Wöber, who headed the civilian counsellors (*Räthe*).

An *Instruction* of 23 March 1745 launched a first and largely unsuccessful period of reform. The intention was to have business conducted more expertly and promptly by depriving the *Hofkriegsrath* of two of its most important responsibilities, namely supply and military justice. Thus the *General-Kriegscommissariat* was taken away in 1747 (and ultimately absorbed in the all-embracing *Directorium*), and in 1753 the *Justizabtheilung* became a *Justizcollegium* responsible directly to Maria Theresa.

On balance it was probably a good thing to have separated justice from the core of the *Hofkriegsrath,* since this was a function which changed little in essentials in time of peace and war. The same did not hold true of the *General Kriegscommissariat.* The successive campaigns of the Seven Years War confirmed Daun in his opinion that the work of military supply was too important to be lost to sight in a civilian ministry where the head inevitably lacked the necessary experience and influence, 'and especially in a monarchy like ours, where the sovereign concedes too much of her sovereignty and thus of her authority, and thereby gives too much of a free rein to people who are motivated by envy and jealousy'.[31]

In October 1755 *FM.* Reinhard Wilhelm Neipperg had been appointed Vice-President and effective head of the *Hofkriegsrath*. The process was attended by typical fictions and intrigues. By now old Joseph Philipp Harrach was incapable of tottering out of his house, but Maria Theresa allowed him to keep his title and salary 'out of regard for his past services, but still more through the influence and power of his supporters'.[32] Neipperg had to be content with the title of deputy, but he demanded the dismissal of Wöber, with whom he would otherwise have been in direct competition. Maria Theresa was reluctant to lose such an accomplished public servant, and so she moved Wöber to the new department of military justice as a lieutenant-general (*FML.*), which was a strange rank for a civilian, but one which assured that Wöber retained his right to military honours and the 'entry' to the Imperial departments.

Dionys Ferdinand Grolier proved to be a poor replacement for Wöber as the first *Referendar,* and Neipperg himself was a slowwitted and pedantic individual, who owed his eminence chiefly to some long-standing connections with Francis Stephen. He had been tutor to Francis Stephen when the future Emperor first came to Vienna, and a further link was established when Francis Stephen took Neipperg's young daughter (Maria Wilhelmina Josepha, Princess of Auersperg) as a mistress.

Francis Stephen and Neipperg formed a conservative alliance which, as Daun pointed out to Maria Theresa, allowed the regiment of Kaiser to stand out as an anomaly in the reformed army: 'Everything about the regiment of His Majesty the Emperor shows the way he thinks about military affairs. The more it resembles the [French] regiment of Champagne the more it will be to his liking, without regard to order, cleanliness or exactitude. These things are the soul of the service, but according to our bad old principles (for there is nothing good about them) they are dismissed as being of no account'.[33]

Only someone as confident as Kaunitz, and as secure in his support from Maria Theresa, could have challenged authority as heavily entrenched as this. In the midsummer of 1757 Maria Theresa gave him a wide remit to manage military affairs, even some which lay within the purview of Neipperg. Thereafter Kaunitz seems to have emerged the winner every time he and Neipperg were at odds. 'How fortunate we are,' commented Haugwitz, 'that Kaunitz had finally broken the chains'.[34]

The war had entered its last year of active operations when Daun was at last given the opportunity to reform the *Hofkriegsrath,* replacing Harrach as President on 30 January 1762. Five days before he was appointed, Daun had outlined a programme which set the *Hofkriegsrath* goals which extended well beyond administration, and would have anticipated some of the features which distinguished the Prussian General Staff under Helmuth von Moltke from 1857. Daun argued that once the *Hofkriegsrath's* affairs had been put in order, it must address itself to various needful tasks, the first of which was the further training of the officers. The *Hofkriegsrath* must:

> bring forward and encourage both generals and officers by holding out advantages and rewards of all kinds, so that in peacetime they will study the art of war, and devote themselves to military, historical and mathematical reading. A commander must display his competence not only in the management of the various arms, but by knowing his way around books, maps and topographical sketches. He must have the powers of insight to see through to the fundamental principles of military knowledge.[35]

This new-born *Hofkriegsrath* should draw up plans in advance for campaigns and sieges, organise a standing intelligence service, bring back military justice and supply under its control, and take its direction (under Maria Theresa) from qualified generals.

Although Daun's proposals for advanced officer training and contingency planning proved altogether too revolutionary for Maria Theresa to accept, the new articles for the *Hofkriegsrath,* as set out in a Resolution of 30 January 1762, still amounted to a comprehensive and salutary reform.

Maria Theresa established the principles of the *Hofkriegsrath* as being to:

1 Uphold religion,
2 Conduct business in a serious and urgent way,
3 Improve the military establishment as was indicated by changing circumstances,
4 Co-ordinate its work with that of the civilian economy in general, so as to promote and improve native industry,
5 Work in harmony with the other departments of state,
6 Gather intelligence in war and peace (one of Daun's original proposals).

As regards the personnel, the civilian *Kriegs-Räthe* were abolished, and their authority invested instead in a panel of senior generals. The civilians now took second place as *Hof-Räthe,* of whom there were ten. Their number included the energetic and highly-regarded *General-Kriegscommissar* Johann Georg Baron Grechtler, whose department was again made answerable to the *Hofkriegsrath* for matters relating directly to military supply.

In the days of the *Hofkriegsrath's* decadence old *FM.* Khevenhüller had boxed Wöber's ears in front of witnesses, and the new Articles laid down rules of procedure which were clearly designed to avert scenes of this kind. All members were to behave towards one another in a courteous and relaxed way, and all thorny questions of detail were to be referred to specialised committees.

For all its continuing defects the *Hofkriegsrath* had been put on a much sounder footing, and the new structure survived Daun's death in 1766. The Swedish attaché Armfeldt noted that Daun must have enjoyed a great deal of support from Maria Theresa in order to carry his changes through, and 'we can only express the wish that other powers may follow the Austrian example, for nothing could be more rational than for a College, which is dedicated to military affairs, to be directed by military men, while employing as many civilians as are necessary to keep the minutes, manage the accounts, and dispatch and register the documents'.[36]

We turn finally to the quality of the Austrian military direction as it affected the commanders in the field. The proceedings were inevitably slow and indirect, for an exchange of correspondence between Vienna and an army in Silesia could scarcely be effected in less than five days, and with an army in Saxony in less than six or seven. Were these processes also unnecessarily slow and indirect?

At first sight the evidence is contradictory. The fashion of fastening the blame on the *Hofkriegsrath* for intervening in military operations was already an article of faith among some officers during Maria Theresa's reign,[37] and for a century the legend grew in the telling until it was challenged by the great historian Alfred von Arneth, who declared outright that it was 'conjured out of thin air, and devoid of all foundation. It is paradoxical but true that the *Hofkriegsrath* at that time had nothing to do with the direction of military operations'.[38]

This was going too far. In the first place all the commanders of the armies and the independent corps of any size were expected to render account of their doings to the *Hofkriegsrath* through their reports and journals. The *Hofkriegsrath* was free to allocate praise or blame ('*approbatur*' and *clisapprobatur*' are some of the most frequent words to be found in its documents), and at the height of the campaigning season of 1759 it brought home to Daun the fact that the Prussian army had been knocked about very badly by Saltykov and Loudon at Kunersdorf (12 August), 'and is unlikely to be able to offer any serious resistance; the *Hofkriegsrath* is therefore of the firm opinion that you must not allow the army in question to escape from your view and grasp, but pounce on it with all the energy you can muster, and so accomplish its complete destruction'.[39]

In no sense, however, was the *Hofkriegsrath* a war cabinet which pondered strategy and operations as a matter of routine, and sent the appropriate instructions to the field. Advice was tendered when it was asked (a facility appreciated by the generals, including that allegedly free spirit Loudon), but very rarely did the *Hofkriegsrath* urge a course of action on a high-ranking commander on its own initiative, and it is significant that the example just quoted was a spur to positive measures, and no kind of restraining order.

As the commander of the main Austrian army for most of the war, Daun complained to Maria Theresa not about the *Hofkriegsrath* as such, but the fact that the directions he received from Vienna were the product of competing interests. 'How is it possible,' he asked, to decide on the best course of action in a monarchy like the Austrian, 'where everyone is at liberty to criticise, intrigue and contradict, and for no better reason than envy, jealousy or some other private motive? They can frustrate the finest plan, and so the general must be engaged in a process of constant negotiation in order to put his point across, meanwhile laying himself open in a way that will end in his ruin'.[40] This destructive power (continued Daun) was exercised by people who were badly informed. Just as an excellent tailor would be at a loss to make a good shoe, or a shoemaker a good coat, 'so all paper schemes are incompatible with the service, for there is a great difference between an economic plan and a military one. A sovereign is unfortunate when she has to preside over a realm where every province, every minister, and every private individual is at liberty to enter representations and protests in a way that will end up like an assembly of Polish nobles. The King of Prussia avoids that kind of thing in a masterly fashion'.[41]

Experience taught Daun that the state of the Austrian monarchy was so defective that it needed double the strength of the Prussians to bring them down.[42]

Through wastage, an Austrian army of a nominal 70,000 effectives would have only 50,000 men fit for service, and an army of 90,000 troops was required if the Austrians were to put 70,000 into the field. Daun believed that such realities were not understood by Kaunitz, who therefore put the Austrians at a political disadvantage vis-a-vis the allies, who asked why Austria was not living up to her promises. He wrote to Maria Theresa in June 1760 that:

> I must admit that my only hope resides in the ancient saying: 'Our good old God is still alive.' Your Majesty of all people is justified in putting your trust in Him, but the trouble is that your ministry invariably exaggerates the streagth of your armies, as in the present plan which has been sent to the Russians, in which the total of the army is put at 192,000 men, and the combatants at 158,000, when they cannot number as many as 110,000.[43]

He returned to the charge the following year, when he argued that the ministers must not meddle in plans of campaign, and that once the generals had been chosen on the grounds of their merits, they should be given full support instead of being made the target of intrigues.[44] On campaign, Daun did not complain of individual directives as such (indeed he often begged for guidance) but of a continuing pressure to give battle in circumstances that would put the monarchy as well as the army at risk. Daun's charges carry weight, even after we take into consideration his pessimism and his lack of trust in himself.

The way the Austrians ran their war was a model of speed, efficiency and selflessness when set alongside that of their French, Russian and Swedish allies. However the only comparison which counted was with the practice of the King of Prussia. One of Maria Theresa's advisers pointed out that:

> his power is founded directly on his personal military government. Everything that concerns that power is set in motion by a single word that brooks no obstruction or delay. I am aware that the constitution of Your Majesty's states is such as to preclude a similar arrangement, but why is it not possible to furnish the military establishment with an absolute chief who has unlimited authority over everything that concerns the army?... The arm that has rendered the greatest service to Your Majesty during this war is the artillery. And why? Because it has a head who commands, dispenses, punishes and rewards on his own account.[45]

3

The Territorial Base

Demography

At the eve of the Seven Years War the lands of the Habsburg Monarchy supported some 15,800,000 souls. The populations, and especially those of the central and eastern domains, were expanding in accordance with the continental-or even world-wide phenomenon of the 'Demographic Revolution.' The Austrian Netherlands (76 people per sq. km.) and Austrian Italy (about 180) had the highest densities of population in Europe. Elsewhere in the monarchy the overall settlement was heaviest in Bohemia, Moravia, Austrian Silesia and Lower and Upper Austria (over 50). The poor southeastern provinces of Austria were sparsely inhabited in comparison (28–40). Hungary had a large overall population, but the great expanses of the kingdom were settled unevenly; tracts of uninhabited waste and forest contrasted with areas like the highly-cultivated County of Ödenburg (70), which extended along the Austrian border not far from Vienna.

If we except the urban societies of the Netherlands and northern Italy, the peoples of the monarchy were overwhelmingly country-dwellers, who accounted for about 90 percent of the populations of the German and Hungarian lands, as compared with the 80 percent of France at that time, or the 73 percent of Prussia. The town-dwelling peoples of Lower Austria (including Vienna), Bohemia and Carniola all stood at about 20 percent of their provincial totals; Upper Austria, Carinthia and Moravia at about 12 percent, and Styria at only 5 percent.

The same marked disproportion is noticeable in the spread of populations even among the urban areas. Vienna with its 175,400 inhabitants accounted for 22 percent of the entire population of Lower Austria, and embraced nearly all the town-dwellers of that archduchy.

The population of Prague (51,000) amounted to less than one-third that of Vienna, but the place was incomparably the largest settlement in Bohemia. Graz, the capital of Styria, was ranked third to Vienna and Prague in size of population, but was altogether smaller (still only 35,000 in 1780), and all the other centres of local life – Linz, Innsbruck, Klagenfurt, Pressburg, Pest and the like – may be regarded as little more than large market towns, however important they were to their regions.

Nationality and Language

Well over half of the citizens of Prague were Germans, and ethnic Germans not only made up the basic stock of Lower and Upper Austria, but were to be found across the central lands of the monarchy, whether in the towns, or in coherent and long-established settlements in Transylvania and along the peripheries of Bohemia and Moravia, or in 'language islands' like those of Budweis in Bohemia, Iglau and Brünn in Moravia, Gotschee in Carniola, or in the colonies of the Donauschwaben in the Bánát of Temesvár. German culture was itself highly diverse. While Kaunitz and Lacy could write in an elegant and purified style which anticipated the language reform of the 19th century, the official decrees and documents deployed a baroque extravagance of titles and honorifics, and were couched in a highly-evolved *Canzleydeutsch* which borrowed heavily from the French and Latin.

At the time of the Seven Years War the Habsburg lands were made up of the following entities:

	Population in 1754	as proportion of Monarchy	area in square km	as proportion of Monarchy
Austrian Hereditary lands				
Lower Austria	929,576	5.74 %	19,829	3.81 %
Upper Austria	430,371	2.66	11,769	2.26
Styria	696,606	4.30	22,459	4.32
Carinthia	271,924	1.68	10,376	1.99
Carniola	344,564	2.13	10,394	2.00
Görz & Gradisca	102,337	.63	2,781	.53
Trieste & Littoral	Not recorded		2,166	.42
Tyrol	384,955	2.38	20,480	3.94
Vorder-Österreich	299,788	1.85	2,849	.55
Bohemian Hereditary Lands				
Bohemia	1,971,613	12.16	51,968	9.99
Moravia	886,974	5.47	22,235	4.27
Austrian Silesia	154,782	.95	5,149	.99
Lands of the Hungarian Crown				
Hungary	4,657,503	28.74	208,778	40.14
Transylvania	1,037,655	6.40	54,928	10.56
Croatia & Slavonia	465,918	2.87	39,255	7.55
Austrian Italy in 1769	1,300,000	8.02	7,172	1.38
Austrian Netherlands in 1784	2,273,000 approx.	2.87	27,571	5.30
Totals	16,207,000 approx.		520,159	

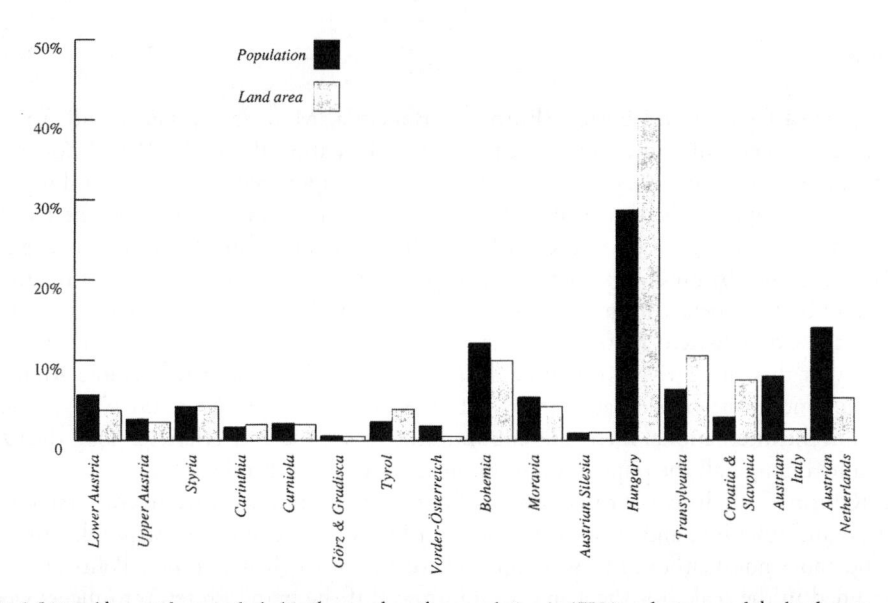

Trieste & Littoral has not been included in the graph as the population in 1754 is unknown, and the land mass neglible. The populations of the Austrian Netherlands and Italy have been included though only approximations.

The international servants of the monarchy brought their own peculiarities and inadequacies to the German language. We find one of the Piedmontese Guasco brothers writing in French to the Hungarian Hadik: 'if there happens to be something in my representations which displeases you, I would ask you to consider that I do not have a full grasp of the force of the German language, and I therefore have to use a translator, who has perhaps given more weight to one or other expression than I intended'.[1]

Hadik himself was thoroughly Germanised. There exists not a scrap of paper in his hand in Hungarian, nor was there a single book in the Hungarian language to be found in the great library of Prince Nicolaus Esterházy the Magnificent.

Through practice Prince Charles Joseph de Ligne (from the Franco-Celtic south-eastern Austrian Netherlands) acquired a mastery of

> what they call 'army German,' which works well when it is spoken by proper generals and officers... It must resound in a way that is inspiring and to the point: the soldiers are shrewd judges of their superiors, and they often frame their verdict by this standard... It is good to have the service expressed as it is now, in a single language, and it is proper that German should be the language in the army of the head of the *Reich*. It is an extraordinary fact, however, that 150,000 of the men do not understand it... the most general language in our army and in Europe as a whole is the Slavonic... it is easy, simple and harmonious.

A few phrases learned parrot-fashion from the Hungarian were useful when you addressed Magyar troops, and something more coherent could be conveyed if the men understood Latin, which survived in Hungary as a living language. 'You just have to be careful about the pronunciation. They speak it in the same way as their own charming language, which through a harmonious combination of metre and syllable imitates the galloping of their horses'.[2]

Religion

A great part of Central and Eastern Europe – Bohemia, Moravia, Hungary and Austria itself – would almost certainly have succumbed to the Reformation if Charles V had not set himself against Martin Luther on 19 April 1521, and generation upon generation of Habsburgs had not followed his example in their own time. In the German Hereditary Lands and the Lands of the Hungarian Crown the position of the Catholic Church was reinforced not only by the favour of the Habsburgs, but by great (if sometimes exaggerated) reserves of property, treasure and landed wealth, and by legal persecution of non-Catholics. By the 1750s, however, both the mass-proselytism of the Counter-Reformation and the campaigns of coercion had largely run their course, and heresy or dissent survived in scattered Lutheran communities in the remote Alpine valleys of Austria, among the considerably greater numbers of the 'crypto-Protestants' in Bohemia and Moravia, in the international merchant communities of Vienna and Trieste, among the Orthodox Croats, and among half the population of Hungary and Transylvania.

The 'Reform' Catholicism of the second half of the 18th century turned to conversion by means of witness and teaching, and even in the German Hereditary Lands a *de facto* toleration allowed more and more non-Catholics to worship undisturbed with their families. Political calculation also weighed in the scale, for the army would unravel if the many Protestant officers were made to feel themselves unwelcome, and it was important to keep on good terms with heretical allies if Frederick were not to present himself as the champion of persecuted Protestantism.

In Vienna itself Maria Theresa called on the skills of the Swiss Calvinist banker Johann Fries to help to process the French subsidy, while reasons of diplomacy allowed Protestants access to the chapels of the Swedish, Danish and Dutch ambassadors. In 1762 Kaunitz prised the 18th volume of the *Oeuvres de Voltaire* from the grasp of the censor of forbidden books, and restored it to the Russian ambassador over the protests of Gerhard Van Swieten, who pointed to the 'frightful obscenities' it contained.[3]

It was nevertheless against the will of Maria Theresa that Jews were so much as allowed to remain in the monarchy: 'This nation is the worst imaginable pestilence to have afflicted the state. They reduce people to beggary through their tricks, their usury and their money dealing, and they engage in all those dishonourable trades which are shunned by decent men. We must therefore do everything possible to keep them out of our lands and reduce their numbers'.[4] Jews retained the right of residence only in Vienna, and (more openly) beyond the Alps in Trieste, Görz and Mantua. The community of some 10,000 Jews in Prague had been tainted by its alleged sympathies for the Prussian forces of occupation in 1744, and after her troops returned Maria Theresa ordered the Jews to be expelled from both the city and the kingdom. Only under pressure from the *Stände*, the Archbishop of Prague and the guilds did she allow the Jews to return to Prague, and then only on payment of a special tax.

Through repeated orders the authorities sought to exclude the Jews from the life of the army. Jews, along with Turks and gypsies, were not to be taken on as recruits.[5] In January 1761 Kaunitz received a reminder from the Saxon minister in Vienna that King Augustus III had received no reply to his demand for the Austrians to expel the Bohemian and Moravian Jews who had descended on the ruins of Dresden after the Prussian bombardment, and who were now selling plundered goods in the Austrian camp. While all of the inclinations of Kaunitz were towards toleration, he could not ignore a representation from this source, and by 5 September all the Jewish stallholders had been banned from the army, leaving only the contractors who supplied provisions and other necessities.

Class and Condition

Outside the Tyrol and parts of Upper and Lower Austria, the German Hereditary Lands and the Lands of the Bohemian Crown were characterised by marked differences in income and condition as between the classes – contrasts which become more pronounced as we progress from west to east.

At the top of the scale the Austro-German Bohemian grandees and the Hungarian magnates made up by far the most politically and socially important grouping of the monarchy. In the German Hereditary Lands it was possible to identify leadership largely with the houses of Abensberg-Traun, Attems, Althann, Colloredo, Czernin, Daun, Dietrichstein, Fürstenberg, Harrach, Herberstein, Hohenems, Kaunitz-Rietberg, Kinsky, Königsegg, Kollowrat, Khevenhüller, Leslie, Liechtenstein, Lobkowitz, Podstatsky, Salburg, Starhemberg, St. Julian Wallsee, Taaffe, Thün, Trautson, Trautmannsdorf, Waldstein (Wallenstein), Wallis and Wurmbrand. Comparable dynasties in Hungary were those of the Esterházys and Batthyánys. Their annual incomes ranged typically from 100,000 to 700,000 florins, and were derived from rents, the product of the unpaid labour of serfs (who amounted to tens of thousands at a time on the estates of the Esterházys, Batthyánys, Liechtensteins and Kinskys), and increasingly also from timber, wine and the 'proto-industry' developing on their estates.

The Dietrichsteins, Kaunitz-Rietbergs, Liechtensteins and Nostitz were among the houses which in addition held territories in individual sovereignty beyond the Habsburg lands, and the authority of the class as a whole was so well entrenched that families could survive with prestige intact while holding themselves largely aloof from public service, or having their names associated with heresy, treason or rebellion in times past. A Habsburg high aristocracy certainly existed in the social sense, but it was not *ipso facto* devoted to the interests of the Habsburgs as a dynasty.

The instruments of the great lords' political power were the provincial assemblies – the *Stände* (Estates) in the German Hereditary Lands, and the comparable *États* of the Netherlands and the county meetings of the Hungarian magnates. The clergy and townsmen were represented also, but seldom displayed any independent political will. In their dealings with the central government the *Stände* and their counterparts displayed some of the attributes of sovereign powers. They maintained offices in Vienna almost in the capacity of embassies; they bargained with the royal representatives when those gentlemen presented Maria Theresa's *Postulata* (demands) for taxes, loans, recruits, foodstuffs and other needs of the central government; finally their standing bureaucracies managed the business of the *Subrepartition,* or how the requirements were to be allotted and met. When Maria Theresa came to the throne she found that the *Stände* had even been able to carry their power into the heart of the central government, for every minister identified himself with the interests of the leaders of the province where he had most of his estates. The confident and authoritative Maria Theresa of the Seven Years War was willing to employ threats of double taxation or even military execution against such provinces as proved *morosus* (recalcitrant), but in the absence of a large and strong central bureaucracy she was ultimately powerless to exact her needs from the Habsburg lands against the will of the entrenched aristocracy.

Altogether 747 readily-identifiable titled regimental officers (from colonel commandant downward) appear in our selected muster lists. They were distributed among the commissioned ranks as follows:

Ensign, cornet and second lieutenant:	6.91%
First lieutenant:	5.05
Captain:	23.43
Major:	33.07
Lieutenant-colonel:	30.42
Colonel commandant:	54.80

From captain onwards the correlation between nobility and military rank is clear. No single arm of the service may be counted as particularly 'fashionable' until we reach the rank of major, when the cuirassiers account for 66.66 percent of the noble officers of that rank, a lead they sustain as lieutenant-colonels (53.84 percent) and colonels commandant (65.00).

Of these officers 409 were born in Habsburg territories:

Netherlands	17.84%
(with Luxembourg	20.77)
Bohemia	10.02
Vienna	9.04
Austrian Italy	8.80
Styria, Görz and Gradisca, Hungary	7.82 each
Tyrol	6.60
Carinthia	4.64
Moravia	4.40
Carniola	4.15
Upper Austria	3.17
Transylvania	1.71
Lower Austria (excl. Vienna)	0.97
Austria unidentified	0.73
Austrian Silesia, Croatia, Slavonia	0.48 each

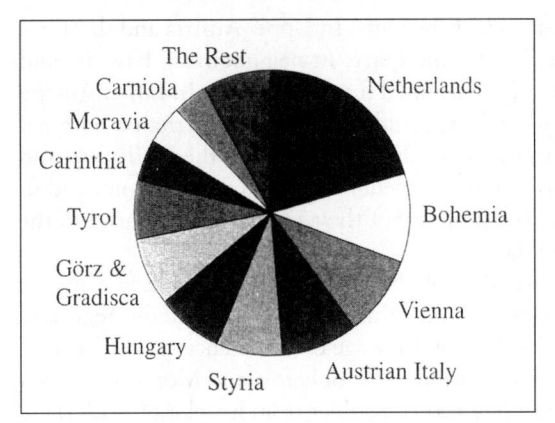

Nobles of all conditions were present in the high representation from the Austrian Netherlands. Many of the nobles born in Vienna were of well-known families, who had the means to maintain some kind of establishment in the capital. The relatively high proportions of nobles from Austria's mountain provinces and Görz and Gradisca is striking, and is made up almost exclusively of middle- and lower-ranking nobles. Otherwise the Habsburg dominions held no equivalent of the poor country landowners who formed the backbone of the officer corps of the Prussian army. The reason was that the ranks of the gentry (*Ritterschaft*) had been whittled away over the generations by two processes – either through falling on bad times and being subsumed among the peasants, or by having risen in the Habsburg service and favour. (See the table in Part II, Chapter 2 for the detailed interrelation between social class and military rank.)

A well-nigh unbridgeable gap therefore existed between the grandees and the peasant masses. The proto-industrial revolution of the middle of the 18th century took root on the great estates rather than in the towns, and outside the Netherlands and Italy the monarchy possessed no well set-up bourgeoisie capable of generating the capital needed for new enterprises. The approximately 10,000 Viennese courtiers and officials listed in the census of 1762 were paid functionaries who were devoid of economic power, while the 100 or so merchant bankers (*Niederleger*) were shadowy people of foreign origin, unlike the high-living contractors who scandalised Berlin during the Seven Years War.

Maria Theresa granted patents of nobility to deserving officials and military officers at a rate of about 36 a year. In the long term this nobility of service became a valued resource of the monarchy, but even in the 19th century it in no way constituted a counterweight to the landed aristocracy of the grandees and magnates. In the time of Maria Theresa about three-quarters of the elevations were to the *Edelleute,* the lowest rank of the nobility, and very few of the newly-minted nobles had the means to live in an aristocratic style. The old aristocracy stood apart not only on account of its wealth, pedigrees and connections, but by its jealously-conserved power to grant the *Indigenat*, or *Incolat*, which alone gave admission to the ranks of the *Ständische* nobility who sat in the provincial assemblies.

Not until the salon culture of Mozartian Vienna developed in the 1780s was there common ground where some of the more intelligent and open-minded of the grandees were willing to meet fellow-spirits from commerce, the professions and the public service. Meanwhile the pretensions of all newcomers were to be resisted to the utmost. Great offence was occasioned on 29 November 1759 when the *Banco-Präsident* Rudolph Chotek and *FZM*. Antonio Clerici were numbered among the 12 new knights of the Golden Fleece, the highest order in the gift of the Habsburgs, 'for it is well known that neither Chotek nor Clerici are sufficiently qualified by their lineage. It must be a cause of universal regret that the first stain has thereby been attached to this exalted order'.[6]

The peasants of the Austrian Netherlands, Austrian Italy, the Tyrol, Vorder-Österreich and much of Upper Austria could be counted among the best set-up of Europe. Elsewhere the rural peoples of the Habsburg lands were to a greater or lesser degree the victims of historical processes. The second series of Theresian domestic reforms, which eventually brought education and alleviation of serfdom to the peasantry, were instituted only after the Seven Years War. In the 1750s the peasants of most of Central and Eastern Europe still laboured under what historians call the 'Second Enserfment,' whereby these regions assumed the condition of a colony, exporting grain in bulk to Western Europe, and importing their needs in manufactured goods; almost all of the proceeds of the deal went to the landowners, who had every incentive to exact additional days of

Robot (compulsory labour) from their peasants, as well as the rents. In Upper Austria and the Tyrol the peasants enjoyed many of the freedoms of their counterparts in neighbouring Bavaria, and *Robot* stood at a mere 14 days a year, and was usually commuted for cash anyway. In Lower Austria the lords had the right to exact 104 days of work, which could amount to more than a nominal burden even when it was required only in part. In the poor Alpine provinces of the south-east, and in Bohemia and Moravia the *Robot* and the restrictions on freedom amounted to serfdom, and in Hungary the peasants on the grand estates were the property of their masters and reduced to the condition of slaves, to the outrage of Maria Theresa.

The age of the great plagues was past, but not that of the great hungers. There is evidence to suggest that standards of nutrition in the German and Hungarian lands actually regressed between 1750 and 1850,[7] and, when whole peoples lived on the edge of subsistence, a succession of poor harvests was enough to reduce a province to starvation, as in Bohemia and Moravia between 1770 and 1772. While a peasant might still coax a few scanty eatables from his plot of land, there was little insurance for the craftsman, who could buy little or nothing in times of famine.

The conditions of the rural poor, as re-created by an historian of Styria, applied over wide areas of the monarchy:

> Let's follow the 18th-century doctor into the huts of the south Styrian peasants. As soon as he set foot over the threshold he would be gripped in the throat by the dense smoke and the intolerable stench. Hens, lambs, calves and pigs had the run of the chambers with their earthen floors, befouling the accommodation with their droppings, and filling the huts with their cries throughout the winter. Everything was dirty and musty, and even the animals were rarely in good health... while sick people were often just planted on the stoves and left to their fate.[8]

Conditions like these need to be borne in mind when we consider the style of life of the ex-peasants in the military service.

The Lands of the Monarchy

(N.B. unless otherwise stated, all figures of a military nature from now onwards are estimates of the field forces of the army, derived from muster lists of the period of the Seven Years War. See the note 'The Muster Lists' in the Bibliography. It should be mentioned here that national origins are entered strictly by place of birth, regardless of origin of family).

The German Hereditary Lands

The Austrian Hereditary Lands
The Archduchies of Lower and Upper Austria as a whole with Vienna

Population 1754: 1,359,947 = 8.40% of the monarchy
Area: 31,598 sq. km. = 6.05% of the monarchy

Military Representation
1. Other Ranks: 10.35% of the total.
   Dragoons 23.93; cuirassiers 16.92; pioneers, miners and sappers 14.93; German infantry 10.35; artillery 8.82; Hungarian infantry and hussars 1.25 each; Italian infantry 1.00

2. NCOs, Corporals and *Gefreyten:* 9.02
3. Non-combatants: 6.33
4. Officers: 9.46
5. Professionals: surgeons 6.61; chaplains 6.02; provosts 12.30.

Of the above totals the following were born in Vienna:
1. Other Ranks: 9.44
2. NCOs, Corporals and *Gefreyten:* 29.3
3. Non-combatants: 50.30
4. Officers: 40.29

Former Civilian Trades of Military Personnel as Proportion of Monarchy as Whole (Vienna considered separately)

Textile:	Austria	10.82
	Vienna	0.46
Clothing & Footwear:	Austria	7.80
	Vienna	0.46
Building & Furnishing:	Austria	13.62
	Vienna	4.15
Food Processing:	Austria	11.17
	Vienna	2.41
Metal:	Austria	8.81
	Vienna	1.18
Mining:	Austria	0.84
	Vienna	0.84
Transport:	Austria	0.11
	Vienna	2.40
Manufacturing & Processing:	Austria	11.48
	Vienna	5.30
Medical:	Austria	10.38
	Vienna	7.79
Students:	Austria	5.06
	Vienna	5.56
Service:	Austria	9.30
	Vienna	5.13

It is not possible to distinguish between personnel born in Lower and Upper Austria on a systematic basis, because many of the individuals are entered on the muster lists by their parishes, the names of which were common to the two Austrias. Austria as a whole contributed heavily to the cavalry, and especially to the dragoons. The Swedish military attaché Armfeldt's knowledge of the Austrian soldiers came mostly from the infantry, and he describes them as being the 'craftiest' of the monarchy's soldiers, but at the same time 'the most attached to their fatherland and their sovereign'.[9]

Austrian Officer Families
Just as the ambiguity of the parish names makes it difficult to establish the native province of the Austrian soldiers, so the drawing-power of Vienna distorts the origins of the officers. Among the military families of Austria, or those which had strong connections there, we may cite:

Abensberg-Traun, Andlern, Auersperg, Canto, Clam, Colloredo, Fischern, Gastheim, Goes, Hackelberg, Harrach, Herberstein, Heyden, Hohenfeld, Khevenhüller, Knorr, Koch, Kollonitz, Lagelberg, Lasperg, Leysser, Mienizky de Rothendorf, Perlas, Plettenberg, Saffran, Salburg, Schaffgotsch, Schwarzenberg, Starhemberg, Spritzenstein, Stockhammer, Thürheim, Wachtenberg, Weissenwolf, Wöber.

The Archduchy of Lower Austria (Österreich unter der Enns)

Population 1754: 929,576 = 5.74% of the monarchy
Area: 31,598 sq. km. = 3.80% of the monarchy
Predominant Languages 1914: German 96%; Czech 4% (probably much lower in the 1750s).

Lower Austria lay at the heart of the Habsburg monarchy, 'and it is not only a great and extensive territory, but one which is blessed and fertile in all its elements'.[10]. It was the most prosperous of the German Hereditary Lands, for it benefited alike from the proliferation of trades in Vienna, the income brought to the city by the court and government, and the position of Vienna at the centre of the land or water routes from Germany, Poland, Hungary, Turkey and Italy, and by the produce of the fertile Marchfeld. It was noted that

> the peasants are powerfully built, and uncommonly diligent and industrious, and agriculture is therefore in a flourishing state; there are very few patches of ground left uncultivated… the natives' way of speaking… has a pronounced singing intonation. A common expression is *I may ni* for *Ich kann nicht* ('I cannot'). The women, especially among the peasants, wear a distinctive costume, and short and round skirts – so short indeed among the girls of the Danube valley that they have had to be banned by law.[11]

Some of Lower Austria's contributions to the army were not in proportion to its general wealth. 'In this respect the ground is infertile. It is the Walloons, the Hungarians, the Italians – and in earlier times the Spanish, Lorrainers and Irish – the foreigners as a whole and some officers from the *Reich,* who in every rank and in every war have done the greatest honour to our army'.[12] Great houses like Auersperg, Harrach, Schwarzenberg and Starhemberg were certainly present in the army in the Seven Years War, but not to a degree which corresponded with their social status, or their contribution in other generations.

Significantly, perhaps, a high proportion of the 'Viennese' Knights of the Military Order of Maria Theresa were men of comparatively low birth, who made their way though merit alone. Such were the distinguished gunner *GFWM*. Walther von Waldenau, or the infantry regimental officers Jacob Brockhausen, Karl Balthasar Sauer, and Carl Joseph Sterndahl. Anton Ravizza, who earned the Order as a major of cavalry, was the son of a common soldier, and began his career in the Cordua Cuirassiers. The ordinary citizens of Vienna passed for being so deficient in the military qualities that it was considered remarkable when conscripts from the city showed themselves to be good soldiers in Revolutionary Wars.[13]

The Lower Austrian *Stände* had their seat in the capital, and to some degree acted as standard bearers for the provincial estates as a whole. Thus in the summer of 1759 the landed nobles of Lower Austria led the chorus of protest which claimed that Lower Austria, along with Upper Austria, Inner Austria and the mining towns of Bohemia were incapable of meeting Maria Theresa's latest *Postulatum* for recruits.[14] Maria Theresa and the *Hofkriegsrath* relented to the extent of allowing the obligation to be bought off in part or in whole at the rate of 40 florins' *Reluition* (substitution money) per recruit, the proceeds being used by the state to support voluntary recruiting in the *Reich*. These exemptions were granted to:

Lower Austria for 1,000 of its obligation in recruits
Two-thirds of the recruits due from Upper Styria
One-third of the recruits due from Carinthia and Carniola
All the recruits due from the three Upper Austrian manufacturing towns of Steyr, Gmünd and Vocklabruck.
All the recruits due from the Bohemian mining towns of Bleistadt, Eule, Kamkow, Kuttenberg, Platten, Berg Reichenstein, Sebastiansberg and Sonnenberg.

The second of the *Postulata* demanded in 1762 found the German Hereditary Lands short of 7,388 recruits, even after the *Reluition,* and this time Maria Theresa ordered the Bohemian-Austrian *Hofcanzley* (civil administration) to ensure that the obligation was to be 'exacted in a most vigorous way, and that those who are recalcitrant are to be subject to a process of judgement and penalty.[15]

The Archduchy of Upper Austria (Osterreich ob der Enns)

Population 1754: 430,371 = 2.66% of the monarchy
Area: 11,769 sq. km. = 2.25% of the monarchy
Predominant Languages 1914: German 99%, others 1%

Upper Austria extended westwards on both sides of the Danube towards Bavaria and the independent bishoprics of Salzburg (not yet incorporated in Austria) and Passau. In general character it was the part of the monarchy which most resembled Lower Austria, and it shared the same Bavarian-German population base. However both the geography and the economy were more varied. The Danube lowlands were hemmed in to the north by the wooded hills of the Bohemian border, and to the south by the Alps. While the archduchy was predominantly agricultural, it was already renowned for the export of iron goods, and for the large and growing woolen industry which had its main centre in the provincial capital at Linz, where the state-privileged factory enjoyed a short-lived revival during the Seven Years War.

Inner Austria

Styria, Carinthia, Carniola, Görz and Gradisca (Friaul, Friuli), Trieste, Istria and Fiume.

The diverse territories which made up Inner Austria sprawled across the Alps from the borders of the two Austrian archduchies and Hungary to the plain of the Po and the coastlands of the Adriatic. The populations comprised Germans, Slavs, Italians and the descendants of the Romanised Alpine tribes. They were classed at the time along the Tyrolese as being unsuited for regular warfare: they had little resistance against infection, they suffered from goitre, they were stricken with homesickness for their remote upland valleys, and as herdsmen they were supposed to lack some of the endurance and manual skills of the lowland labourer. *FZM.* Lacy commented that:

> the men from Carniola and Carinthia speak a language which is incomprehensible in the army, and they have an excessive attachment to their homelands, which makes them subject to a dangerous nostalgia *[Heimweh,* seen as a distinct mental illness at the time]. In order to prevent it we ought to detach from the army a number of officers and private soldiers who are acquainted with their language and way of life, and set up a militia in which the young men can be accustomed gradually to the military existence, and so furnish willing and suitable recruits to complete the regiments.[16]

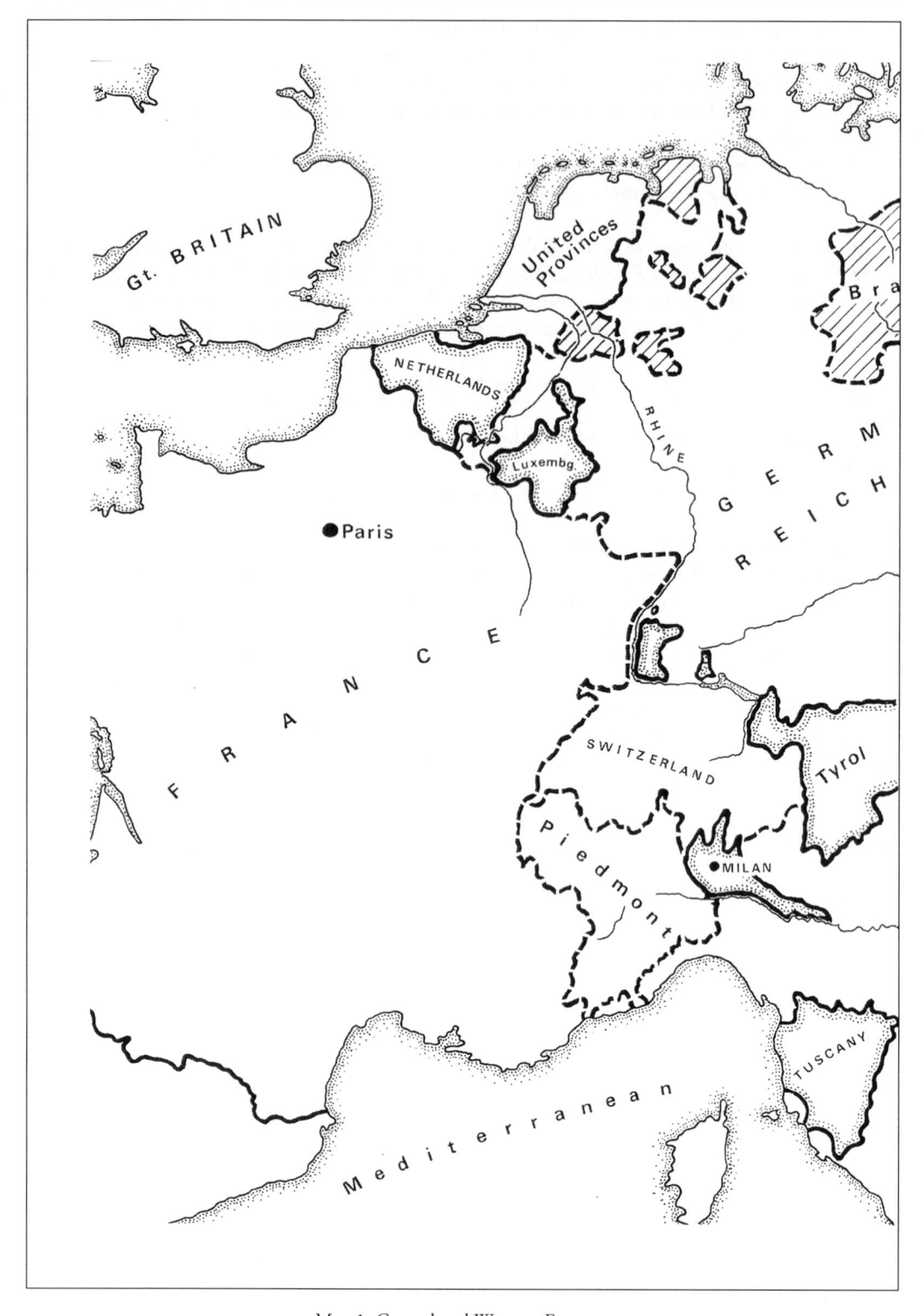

Map 1 Central and Western Europe.

THE TERRITORIAL BASE 47

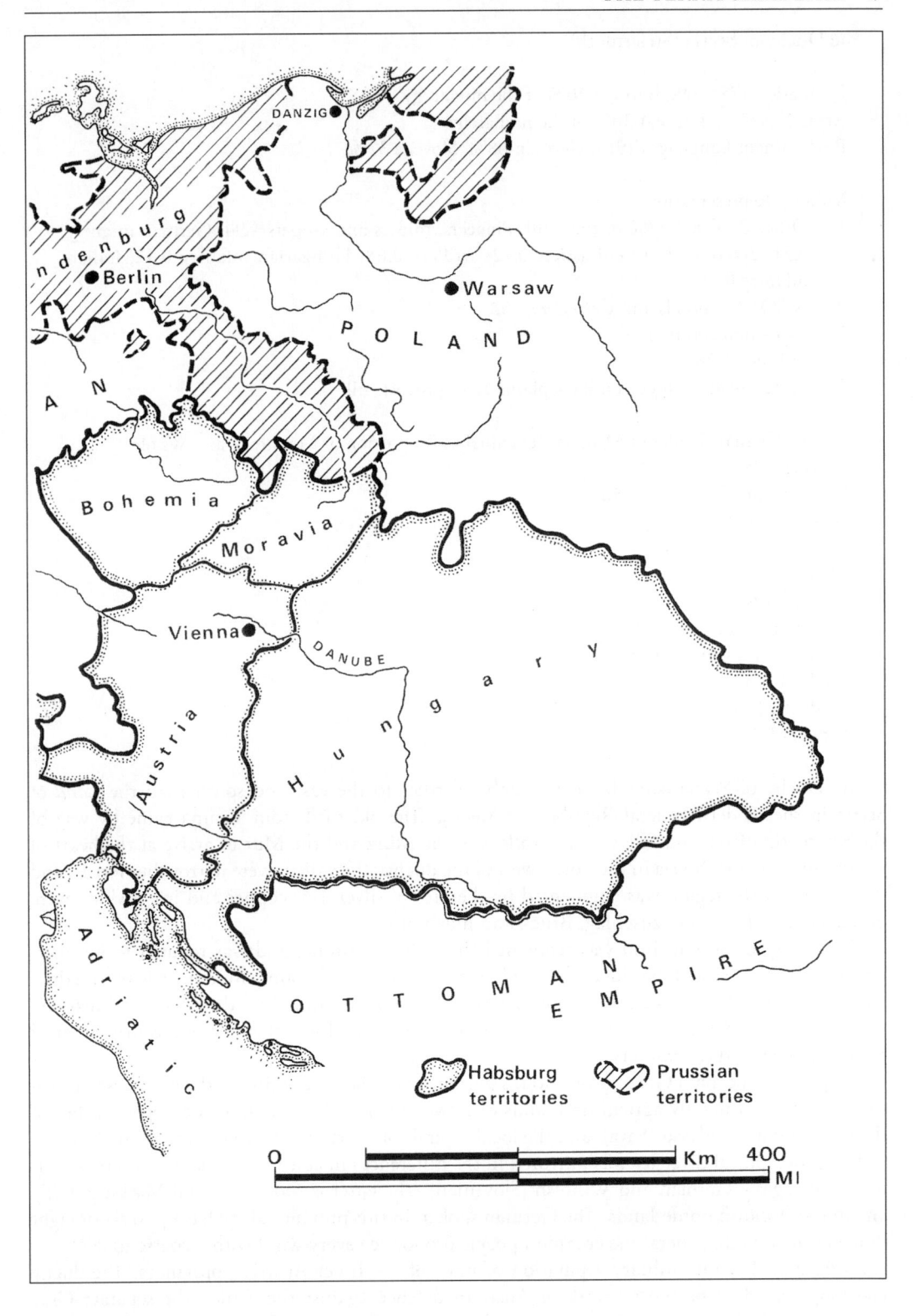

The Duchy of Styria (Steiermark)

Population 1754: 696,606 = 4.40% of the monarchy
Area: 22,459 sq. km. = 4.30% of the monarchy
Predominant Languages 1914: German 68%, Slovene 32%

Military Representation
1. Other Ranks: 2.27% of the total. Pioneers, miners and sappers 4.94; German infantry 3.71; dragoons 1.26; cuirassiers 0.72; artillery 0.68; Hungarian infantry 0.42; Italian infantry 0.28
2. NCOs, Corporals and *Gefreyten:* 1.52
3. Non-combatants: 1.26
4. Officers: 1.28
5. Professionals: surgeons nil; chaplains 1.20; provosts nil.

Former Civilian Trades of Military Personnel as Proportion of Monarchy as a Whole
Textile: 1.84
Clothing and Footwear: 3.36
Building and Furnishing: 2.56
Food Processing: 1.78
Metal: 2.80
Mining: 1.68
Transport: 2.40
Manufacturing and Processing: 2.44
Medical: 1.55
Students: 1.61
Service: 1.28

The Duchy of Styria extended considerably further to the east and south than the *Land* of Styria in the modern Federal Republic of Austria. The old road from Vienna came by way of the Semmering Pass, and followed the valleys of the Mürz and the Mur to arrive at the heart of mountainous Upper Styria in the north-west of the duchy. The valleys were narrow but fertile, and the income of the region was augmented by the ores of silver, tin, copper and iron, which were processed mainly at Mürzzuschlag, Bruck and Judenburg.

The quality of Styrian iron was renowned throughout Europe, and was reputed to be finer-grained than the Swedish product. The wool seems to have served mainly for domestic production, and it was worked up in the areas adjoining Salzburg and Carinthia into the coarse and densely-woven cloth called *Loden*. 'Such cloth is often dyed green, and it is therefore a favourite wear of the young men and the hunters'.[17]

The provincial capital Graz lay one hour's journey from the mountains, and gave access in turn to the flatter and mainly agricultural lands of Lower Styria, which took in the upper reaches of the Drau (Drava) and Sau (Sava), and the local capitals of Marburg (Maribor) and Cilly (Celja).

This geographical diversity was mirrored in the differences in culture. 'Styria has two predominant languages – German and Windish [Slovenian]. The latter is spoken around Marburg, Cilly and in the Windish borderlands. The German spoken in this province alone has up to six or eight different dialects. In general the common people pronounce every word with a coarse tone'.[18]

Styria shared the unmilitary reputation of most of the Inner Austrian provinces. The duchy had long ceased to be the bulwark of Austrian defence against the Turks; the separate Graz *Hofkriegsrath* had ceased to exist in 1743, and it was significant that the great *Zeughaus* (Arsenal)

Map 2 The Habsburg Possessions in Central and Southern Europe.

in Graz was stuffed with antique or obsolescent weapons which had never been replaced. The *Münz- and Bergwesens-Hof Direction* (Mint and Mining Department) asked in vain for Styria to be exempted completely from the conscription, which was damaging to the production of metals and salt, while the *Stände* protested that it was unfair to calculate the levy on the basis of the numbers of houses, when so many of the buildings consisted of uninhabited *Weinzierin* (vintners' huts).

As some alleviation of the burden, the *Stände* petitioned Vienna to relax the standards regarding the maximum age and the minimum height of the recruits, and to admit men who would normally have been rejected as unfit, 'for experience shows that most of the men furnished by Upper Styria are afflicted with thick and puffy necks resulting from the fatty diet, while the Lower Styrians have foot trouble on account of their boots'.[19] The *Stände* were confident that the stout army shoes would protect the feet better than the soft boots of Lower Styria, and that the military food would remedy the defective diet of the highlanders (the influence of iodine deficiency being unknown).

Between 1755 and 1763 Styria contributed altogether 23,806 recruits to the army; between 85 and 90 percent of them were single men, and they must have amounted to a significant proportion of the 58,531 single male natives of the military age group of the duchy, even when allowance is made for the admission of Croats, Hungarians and deserters. A large shortfall in the male population of that age group was identified after the war,[20] and the Styrian historians, like the Styrians of that time, considered that their province was badly done by. It appears paradoxical that the number of the Styrians appearing in the muster lists of the field battalions is much smaller than Styria's place in the monarchy's population; the discrepancy almost certainly arises from the notoriously high rates of wastage among the mountain men.

Styrian Officer Families

As was the case in most of Inner Austria, the unsoldierly ways of the common folk of Styria contrasted with the existence of a military tradition among the gentry and nobles, among whom were numbered the families of:

> Abfaltern, Adelsfein, Colloredo, Frischenschlager, Gabelkoven (four barons serving simultaneously), Gaisruck, Caller (four counts), Herberstein (three counts), Karlstetten, Klebersberg, Königsbrunn, Rauber von Plankenstein (a name deriving from an ancient feudal right to rob), Reissig, Rindsmaul (lit. 'Ox-Mouth'), Strassoldo, Stubenberg (one baron and one count) and Windischgrätz.

The Duchy of Carinthia (Cärnten)

Population 1754: 271,924 = 1.68% of the monarchy
Area: 10,376 sq. km. = 1.98% of the monarchy
Predominant Languages 1914: 72% German, 28% Slovene

Military Representation
1. Other Ranks: 0.80% of the total.
   German infantry 1.42; pioneers, miners and sappers 0.32; artillery 0.25; dragoons 0.18; Italian infantry 0.14; cuirassiers 0.07.
2. NCOs, Corporals and *Gefreyten:* 0.43
3. Non-combatants: 0.33
4. Officers: 0.63
5. Professionals: Surgeons nil; chaplains nil; provosts 1.53.

Former Civilian Trades of Military Personnel as Proportion of Monarchy as a Whole
Textile: 1.68
Clothing & Footwear: 1.18
Building & Furnishing: 1.70
Food Processing: 0.87
Metal: 1.61
Mining: 2.52
Transport: 1.20
Manufacturing & Processing: 2.58
Medical: 1.55
Students: 1.43
Service: 0.64

Carinthia was bordered to the north by the ranges of the Hohe Tauern and the Niedere Tauern, and to the south by the Carnic Alps and the Karawanken. Between these rocky walls the fertile plain of Lower Carinthia extended around the provincial capital of Klagenfurt, while the valleys of the Gail, the Schwarzach and the upper Drau snaked into the mountains of Upper Carinthia to the west.

Illiteracy was high in western Carinthia even in the last days of the monarchy. In the 1750s hardly any of the Carinthian lower orders could read at all, even if they had an eloquence of their own: 'like their country and climate, the Carinthians are wild and coarse, much inclined to robbery, and also to cursing and swearing'.[21]

Remote and backward in some respects, Carinthia had enjoyed some prosperity through mining and a very large export of wool. However the burden of the war pressed heavily on all classes, and a British diplomat reported afterwards that the land tax, together with the extraordinary contributions made during the war, had 'brought them so low, that, I have been assured, there is scarce now a gentleman in that country, that can give his daughter 500 florins for her marriage portion, or afford to send his sons to school'.[22]

Carinthian Officer Families
Christalnig (three barons and two counts), Eichelburg, Flednig, Frohmüller (two barons), Hallerstein, Mandorf, Rehbach (three barons), Rosenberg, Stampfer, Strasser von Waldegg, Tattenbach, Thum, Willz, Windischgrätz.
One of the three Rehbachs (Baron Maximilian, 1706–64) captured the Prussian lieutenant-general Tresckow at Kolin, and he was advanced by rapid promotions to the rank of *FML.* in 1763.

The Duchy of Carniola (Crain)

Population 1765: 344,564 = 2.13% of the monarchy
Area: 10,384 sq. km. = 1.99% of the monarchy
Predominant Languages 1914: Slovene 94%, German 6%

Military Representation
1. Other Ranks: 1.13% of the total.
   Pioneers, miners and sappers 24.40; Italian infantry 4.08; German infantry 1.56; dragoons 0.16; artillery 0.07; cuirassiers 0.03; Hungarian infantry 0.02
2. NCOs, Corporals and *Gefreyten*: 0.37

3. Non-combatants: 0.24
4. Officers: 0.61
5. Professionals: surgeons 2.53; chaplains nil; provosts nil

Former Civilian Trades of Military Personnel as Proportion of the Whole
Textile: 2.68
Clothing & Footwear: 1.21
Building & Furnishing: 1.03
Food Processing: 0.43
Metal: 0.59

Mining: not enough to register (an obvious underreporting; see below)
Transport: 1.86
Manufacturing & Processing: 0.75
Medical: 1.03
Students: 1.43
Service: 0.51

Carniola was almost identical in area to neighbouring Carinthia, but more densely populated, due partly to the fertility of the plains of the Sau (Sava) in the east of the duchy, which were capable of bearing a second harvest. Mountainous Upper or western Carniola was barren in comparison, but the people supported themselves with the help of a thriving domestic industry. Travellers commented that when they were not cultivating their plots, all the members of the peasant families were at furious work spinning and weaving.[23]

The capital Laibach [Ljubljana] was a lively and attractive place, and an important staging post on the monarchy's communications. The road from Vienna through Graz, Marburg and Cilly arrived from the north-west, and it continued to the seaport of Trieste by way of Adelsberg and the desolate limestone plateau of the Karst.

Slovene was the most common language of all classes in Carniola, though there were concentrations of archaic German in some locations, and French was cultivated among the nobles and merchants.

When Maria Theresa demanded a first and modest levy of 502 recruits in 1755, the Carniolan *Stände* protested in vain that their people had neither aptitude nor inclination for the military life. Carniola, like the rest of Inner Austria, nevertheless had to submit to the successive *Postulata* for recruits. A contingent of 243 of these men reached the regiment of Andlau on 16 June 1758, 'and out of all of these people we had scarcely 87 left by the end of the campaign! The Carniolans succumb to any other climate but their own, and die from what the French call *mal de pays* and the Germans *Heimweh*. And yet the Carniolans who manage to hold out against it become the finest soldiers you could imagine'.[24] In terms of percentage Carniola's most significant contribution to the war effort was among the pioneers, miners and sappers, where natives of the duchy made up nearly one quarter of the personnel. Very few of the Carniolans have their civilian trade entered as 'miner' on the muster lists, though the contrary must have been the case; possibly there was a need to conceal the drain on this reserved occupation.

Carniolan Officer Families
Abfaltern (two barons), Barbo, Eichelburg, Benaglia (two barons), Bittoni, Christalnig (three counts, one baron), Flednig, Lazarini, Lichtenberg (three counts), Oberburg, Palenfels, Rasp, Raunach (two barons), Widerstein, Zetschker.

The Princely County (gefürstete Graffschaft) of Görz (Gorizia) and Gradisca

Population 1754: 102,337 = 0.63% of the monarchy
Area: 2,781 sq. km. = 0.53% of the monarchy
Predominant Languages 1914 (with Istria and Trieste): Slovenian and other Slavonic 52%;
   Italian 46%; German 2%

Military Representation
1. Other Ranks: 0.36% of the total.
   Italian infantry 27.1; German infantry 0.08; dragoons 0.03, cuirassiers 0.01
2. NCOs, Corporals and *Gefreyten:* 0.14
3. Non-combatants: 0.05
4. Professionals: surgeons nil; chaplains 1.20; provosts nil

Former Civilian Trades of Military Personnel as Proportion of the Whole
Textile:	0.61
Clothing and footwear:	0.40
Building & Furnishing:	0.40
Food Processing:	0.17
Metal:	0.25
Mining:	nil
Transport:	0.24
Manufacturing & Processing:	nil
Medical:	nil
Students:	0.53
Service:	nil

Görz and Gradisca were an historical and geographical anomaly, which projected Austrian territory on both sides of the winding Isonzo river to the plain at the head of the Adriatic near Trieste. Although the northern and eastern parts of the county were mountainous, the valleys were fertile, and together with the black earth of the coastal plain they were capable of bearing rich crops of cereals, flax and wine. 'It is all the more regrettable that the people almost everywhere are unduly given to drink, and this, together with the yoke under which most of the peasants labour, produces a great inclination towards idleness and an immoral way of life'.[25] The capital Görz and the nearby town of Gradisca were agreeable and busy places in the manner of Laibach, though built in the Italian style rather than the German.

The county's contribution to the army was small in number, even in proportion to the modest size of the territory. However the natives formed a significant element in the regiments of 'Italian' infantry, while the gentry played a disproportionately large part in the Austrian officer corps and the life of the state in general:

> The reason lies principally in the nobles' standard of education, which gives them a considerable advantage over many of their counterparts elsewhere. They are happy to send their sons to distant academies, and do not fear that any harm might befall their beloved offspring in such places. We could also enumerate a number of gentlemen who have dispatched their sons to Stuttgart, Gottingen and other locations. However most are educated in Vienna. The nobility have very close connections with the nobility in Vienna and other cities, mainly through family liaisons. They show taste in their manner and the way in which they dispense

their wealth, though we must enter some reservations concerning those who live towards the border with Venetia.[26]

The Thurn-Valsassinas (cousins to the German Thum and Taxis) originated in the county, as did the probably equally prolific Colloredos. Rudolph Joseph Count Colloredo (1706–88) was *Reichs-Vizecanzler* at the time of the Seven Years War, and two of his eight children, Joseph and Wenzel, rose to become Field Marshals. The Lanthieris of Görz produced a full general of cavalry in the person of Johann Friedrich, while their many-branched Strassoldo neighbours were probably the most thoroughgoing military family of the monarchy, comparable with Prussian military clans like the Kleists, Manteuffels and Mansteins. Altogether the nobles of Görz and Gradisca accounted for nearly 8 percent of the titled regimental officers of the field army, which put them on a par with those of Styria and Hungary.

Officer Families of Görz and Gradisc
Attems (four counts), Corini/Coronini, Cossio, Edling/Etling, Formentini, Kheul, Lanthieri, Marmiajjo, Neuhaus, Pithoni, Rasp, Sauren/Saurau, Strassoldo (eight counts), Terzi (two barons), Varenzi

The Austrian Littoral – Trieste, Istria, Fiume and Dalmatia

Population in 1754: Not recorded
Area: 2,166 sq. km. = 0.42% of the monarchy

Military Representation
1. Other Ranks: 0.007% of the total. Italian infantry 0.57
2. NCOs, Corporals and *Gefreyten:* nil
3. Non-combatants: nil
4. Officers: 0.04
5. Professionals: nil

Former Civilian Trades as Proportion of Monarchy as Whole
None recorded in any category

Arriving at the edge of the limestone plateau of the Karst the traveller found himself

all at once with a view over the Adriatic Sea, the wide bay of Trieste with all its inlets, and part of the town itself; Istria extends to the left, and to the right, along the northern borders of Venetia, stretches a long row of high Alpine peaks which are still entirely covered with snow. Directly under your feet you look down on a little green world, an artificial garden created by industrious hands from naked rocks and precipitous slopes. What a contrast to the land we have just left!

Here for the first time and all at once the traveller from Northern Europe could see cypresses, figs, peaches, and almond and olive trees growing happily in the open air.[27]

By the time of the Seven Years War the Littoral was important to the Austrians almost entirely on account of the cosmopolitan port of Trieste, which offered the heartland of the monarchy its only direct outlet to the sea. This facility kept the commerce of the port alive, even though the Trieste Company had been abolished at the outset of the reign, and it helped to compensate for the severe geographical disadvantages – the long and difficult land communication with Vienna, and the inadequate roadstead, which was improved only marginally after a great and expensive mole was built in 1750.

The Littoral was scarcely represented in the Austrian army, if we except the commentator Jacob Cogniazzo (born in Hungary, but probably to a Dalmatian family), and the families of Ferretti (Trieste), Gregorini (Dalmatia), Grisoni (Istria) and Varenzi (Trieste).

The Princely County of the Tyrol

Population 1754: 384,955 = 2.38% of the monarchy
Area: 20,480 sq. km. = 3.92% of the monarchy
Predominant Languages 1914: German 62%, Italian 38%

Military Representation
1. Other ranks: 0.58% of the total.
   Feld-Jäger 95.00; Italian infantry 4.30; German infantry 1.01; cuirassiers 0.92; dragoons 0.76; pioneers, miners and sappers 0.41; artillery 0.39; Hungarian infantry 0.01; Netherlands infantry 0.01
2. NCOs, Corporals and *Gefreyten:* 0.52
3. Non-combatants: 0.85
4. Officers: 1.28
5. Professionals: surgeons nil; chaplains 1.20; provosts nil

Former Civilian Trades of Military Personnel as Proportion of the Whole
Textile:	0.23
Clothing & Footwear:	0.92
Building & Furnishing:	1.81
Food Processing:	0.83
Metal:	1.44
Mining:	6.72
Transport:	0.72
Manufacturing & Processing:	1.74
Medical:	1.29
Students:	0.53
Service:	3.65

Geographically the Tyrol was divided by the Alps into two parts. North Tyrol looked inwards towards the valley of the Inn and the capital, Innsbruck. South Tyrol lay beyond the Brenner Pass, and extended down either side of the Adige; German predominated in the upper reaches, Italian further south, and the archaic tongue of the Ladinen survived in the remoter valleys.

Apart from a little industry in the Italian south, the economy of the Tyrol was based on forestry, agriculture, and the mining of silver, copper, iron, semi-precious stones, rock salt (at Hall near Innsbruck) and mercury. According to a British account:

> There is more general affluence in Tyrol, than in almost any other part of the Empress's German dominions. The Court has more than once showed a desire to increase their taxes... But the Tyroleans are a shrewd sturdy people, who are not easily dealt with, and know very well how to avail themselves of the advantage of their situation, which makes them hard to be come at, and have more than once insinuated, that if they are ill-used, they would throw themselves under the protection of the Swiss.[28]

The German Tyroleans showed their warlike potential when they put up a stout resistance against the Bavarians in the War of the Spanish Succession, and again when they revolted against the French in 1809, and went on to fight in the ranks of the *Kaiserjager* against the enemies of Franz Josef. In the Seven Years War the Tyrolean military spirit was best represented by the *Feld-Jäger Corps,* which was formed as a single battalion in 1758. In February 1760 Colonel Ebner reported that a new recruiting drive was going well, 'contrary to the initial claims of the *Directorium*',[29] and the corps was able to take the field that year in the strength of 1,000 men and an establishment of ten companies.

The common folk of the Tyrol discovered no such appeal in the life of the *Tyroler Land- and Feld-Regiment,* which was reformed from an old and ineffective battalion of militia. Vienna was therefore forced to try to make up the deficiencies by recruiting in the *Reich,* and by exerting pressure on the *Stände* to enlist natives by force.[30] In the event most of the rank and file were recruited from dubious elements in the *Reich,* and the unit was consigned to garrison service for most of the Seven Years War. The natives of the southern Tyrol showed no inclination to serve in any kind of German regiment at all, but made their presence felt in the regiments of Italian national infantry.

In the absence of any system of *Robot,* many of the Tyrolean nobles were little better off than their peasant labourers, and they lacked the time and effort to make themselves into proficient officers. The colonel commandant of the *Land- and Feld-Regiment, FML.* Sigismund Maguire, reached the sensible conclusion that the regiment must be led by the best officers he could find, regardless of their place or origin. A whole round of promotions became necessary after Lieutenant-Colonel Baron Teuffel had been killed at Leuthen, and Maguire unwittingly precipitated a crisis when he submitted the names of three suitable candidates direct to the *Hofkriegsrath,* rather than to the *Landeshauptmann* (local head of administration) Count Wolckenstein, whose whereabouts were unknown, though Maguire asked the *Hofkriegsrath* to contact Wolckenstein if the great man happened to be in Vienna. Wolckenstein took offence at the perceived slight to his privileges, and complained to Neipperg that Maguire's list had ignored the fact that the regiment had been set up 'so as to bring forward the numerous Tyrolean nobility… so that it will thereby be encouraged to embrace the military service'.[31]

For the important post of First Major, Maguire had favoured Captain Theodorus de Furst, who wrote in his turn to Neipperg that he feared that he would be passed over in favour of a junior captain from another regiment, Baron Rossi, who had bought his captaincy and was being pushed forward by Wolckenstein; de Fürst therefore applied to Neipperg to 'accord me your gracious protection, as a foreigner who has no other patronage, but one who over the course of many years have given loyal and conscientious service to the most esteemed Hereditary House of Austria.[32]

This instructive episode came to an end on 16 March 1758, when the *Hofkriegsrath* suggested to Maria Theresa that the promotions to major and some of the other vacancies should be resolved in favour of Maguire; for the other posts, however, due regard must be paid to the contention of Wolckenstein that 'the regiment has been overloaded with such a quantity of unknown foreign cadets that it is difficult to accommodate the numerous sons of the Tyrolean nobility, for whose advancement the regiment had been set up; the result must be the complete frustration of the object of the [religious] foundations and the *Stände* when they established the regiment.' Maria Theresa decided the issue by penning the comment: 'I am of Wolckensteirt's opinion'.[33] Such was the power of entrenched local privilege.

Tyrolean Officer Families

> Arco (two counts), Arzt, Barteler, Bollaus, Bud, Criss, Füchs, Fugger, Khün von Belasi, Lodron (three counts, all born in the Italian Tyrol), Megerle/Majerle (two counts), Migazzi, Pizzini von Thyrenberg, Quarienti, Saracini, Taxis, Thaunn, Wolckenstein (two counts).

Vorder-Österreich and the German Enclaves

Population 1754: 299,788 = 1.85% of the monarchy
Area: 2,849 sq. km. = 0.54% of the monarchy

Military Representation
1. Other ranks: 0.27% of the total.
    Dragoons 0.64; German infantry 0.37; cuirassiers 0.15; Netherlands infantry and Italian infantry, 0.14 each; artillery 0.10; Hungarian infantry 0.001
2. NCOs, Corporals and *Gefreyten:* 0.38
3. Non-combatants: 0.57
4. Officers: 0.89
5. Professionals: surgeons 5.05; chaplains nil; provosts 3.06

Former Civilian Trades of Military Personnel as Proportion of the Whole
Textile:	0.38
Clothing & Footwear:	0.73
Building & Furnishing:	0.74
Food Processing:	1.17
Metal:	nil
Mining:	nil
Transport:	1.20
Manufacturing & Processing:	0.81
Medical:	1.03
Students:	1.43
Service:	0.44

(N.B. The above lists exclude all personnel entered merely as having been born 'in the Black Forest,' which inevitably embraced some Austrian enclaves).

Vorder-Österreich was the collective name for the Austrian territory of the Vorarlberg, which projected north-west from the Tyrol to Lake Constance, and for the enclaves of Austrian sovereign territory which lay beyond – the city of Constanz towards the western end of the lake, Breisgau with the city of Freiburg at the edge of the Rhine plain, and a number of lordships.

In the Vorarlberg the military traditions lived on in the family of Hohenems, and in the person of the leading gunner *FZM.* Anton Ferdinand Baron Feuerstein von Feuersteinsberg, who was an associate of Liechtenstein, and commanded the artillery at the battle of Prague. As for the Black Forest enclaves, there was 'nothing finer in Germany than the little holdings of the House of Austria in Swabia'.[34] VorderOsterreich as a whole had no specific military reputation, though the figures show that it made a disproportionately high contribution to the ranks of the military surgeons and the provosts.

Officer Families of Vorder-Österreich
Duran, Feuerstein, Giradi von Castell, Hohenems, Hohenzollern, Löhr, Ried, Schonau, Weichenhauer.

The Bohemian Hereditary Lands

The Kingdom of Bohemia

Population 1754: 1,971,613 = 12.16% of the monarchy
Area: 51,968 sq. km. = 9.96% of the monarchy

Military Representation
1. Other Ranks: 28.28% of the total.
    Artillery 62.68; German infantry 38.58; cuirassiers 33.59; dragoons 29.55; pioneers, miners and sappers 24.70; Hungarian infantry 0.98; Italian infantry 0.64; Netherlands infantry 0.56; Netherlands dragoons 0.51; hussars 0.27
2. NCOs, Corporals and *Gefreyten:* 24.42
3. Non-combatants: 25.18
4. Officers: 10.03
5. Professionals: surgeons 5.76; chaplains 31.32; provosts 15.38

Former Peacetime Trades of Military Personnel as Proportion of the Whole
Textile:	46.89
Clothing & Footwear:	35.42
Building & Furnishing:	46.65
Food Processing:	43.61
Metal:	35.76
Mining:	25.29
Transport:	35.42
Manufacturing & Processing:	41.74
Medical:	31.16
Students:	44.88
Service:	49.13

Bohemia was the foundation of the economic power of the Austrian monarchy, and furnished the basic stock of Maria Theresa's artillery and her 'German' infantry. It provided the monarchy with its most direct access to northern Europe, after Frederick had captured Silesia, and in terms both of resources and strategic position it had to do service for that lost province.

Although Bohemian chronology was punctuated by the violent episodes of the armed Hussite heresy and the Thirty Years War, Bohemian society was formed by processes of long-term evolution. From the 14th-century onwards Germans came to Bohemia and neighbouring Moravia not as conquerors, but as miners, glass and textile workers, and peasant settlers. Bohemian families still outnumbered the German among the lines raised to the gentry (*Ritterschaft*) by the Habsburgs in the first century of their rule; conversely, Catholics and the bearers of German names joined the Protestant Bohemian nobles in the great revolt of 1618. Out of the 27 nobles executed by the victorious Habsburgs in Prague in 1621, most were from German-speaking families, and only three represented the old stock of the Bohemian high nobility. Such were the effects of integration and continuity.

While large numbers of Protestant nobles were indeed evicted by the Habsburgs, the greatest single re-distribution of lands followed on the assassination of the over-mighty Wallenstein (Waldstein) and his associates Adam Trĉka and Vilim Kinsky in 1634. Some of the richest lands of north Bohemia were now at the disposal of Emperor Ferdinand II, and the lavish way he distributed the estates had the effect of bringing into Bohemia the German families of Auersperg,

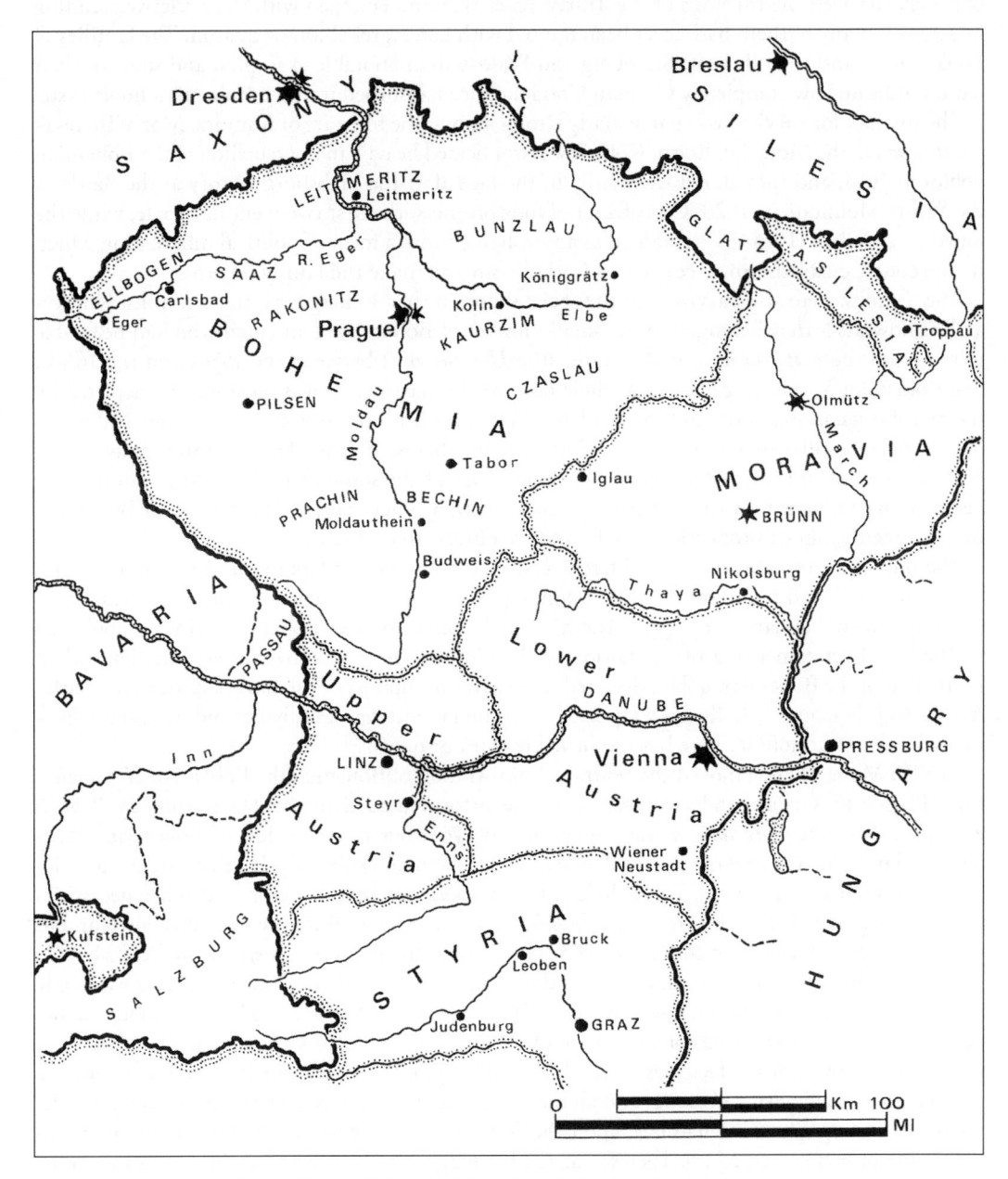

Map 3 Bohemia, Moravia and Northern Austria.

Fürstenberg, Haugwitz, Herberstein, Hohenlohe, Khevenhüller-Metsch, Löwenstein and Nostitz. However some of the lines already established in Bohemia (Clam-Gallas, Clary-Aldringen, Collalto, Colloredo) shared in the bounty, and a circle of Bohemian-Moravian dynasties of the old stock survived the turmoils of the Thirty Years War and emerged with their relative standing intact, as if many of them had never been tainted with heresy, rebellion or treason. The families of Lobkowitz, Kinsky, Kollowrat, Sternberg and Waldstein are notable examples, and some of their names indicate how completely German blood had been absorbed into the Bohemian noble caste.

The instinct for survival was particularly strong among the forbears of Kaunitz, Maria Theresa's *Staatscanzler*. The Moravian line of Kounic was implicated heavily in the rebellion of the Bohemian nobles in 1618, and ruin stared the family in the face after the Habsburg victory at the Battle of the White Mountain in 1620. Out of a set of four brothers, the first two went into exile, while the fourth, Lev Vilem (1614–55) remained as an orphan child – a form of political hibernation which in due course enabled him to convert to Catholicism and make the family fortune.

The Kaunitz were also survivors in the social sense, in that – along with the Czernins, Kinskys and Kollowrats – they belonged to the small number of Bohemian gentlemen who had been able to rise from the *Ritterstand* to lordly status (the *Herrenstand*) between the 1550s and the 1660s. The Bohemian-Moravian gentry as a whole became the class which was most heavily depleted by the Habsburg confiscations, and the burdens of taxation, and so it was that only about 100 of the old knightly families survived into the 1750s. As the Theresian army depended so heavily on the resources of Bohemia and Moravia, the disappearance of the squierarchy from these lands had a determining influence on the character of the Austrian officer corps. The army had Bohemian troops a-plenty, but disproportionately few native officers to lead them.

The higher aristocracy was in a different case, for it was both adaptable and well dug-in, and was therefore able to retain social and economic power independently of the successive Habsburg challenges to Bohemian sovereignty. The historical constitution of Bohemia had been abolished in 1627, and yet something of the notion of the old elective monarchy survived in 1741, when nearly half of the Bohemian nobles declared themselves in support of the Bavarian usurper Charles Albert. In July Count Schaffgotsch reported to Vienna that it was 'totally beyond my comprehension why the great nobility here have so little love for our queen'.[35]

In 1745 Maria Theresa moved the central administration of Bohemia (the Bohemian *Hofcanzley*) from Prague to Vienna, and two years later she incorporated it in the *Directorium in Publicis et Cameralibus;* the *Directorium* was broken up in 1761, but the direction of Bohemian affairs remained in Vienna as part of the new Austrian and Bohemian *Hofcanzley*. To that extent authority was centralised in the capital. Nevertheless, the *Postulata* for recruits, cash and other necessities had to be negotiated with the provincial *Stände,* which could not refuse the demands outright, but still managed the business of collection. The nobles found an ally in the Austro-Irish Field Marshal Maximilian Browne, who had married into the old Bohemian family of Martinitz, and was ready to identify himself with the narrower interests of his neighbours. In the period of tension just before the Seven Years War he asked for a regiment of hussars to be sent from Moravia to Chrudim 'so as to give better cover for the factories there'.[36] At a military conference in the following year Browne was able to persuade Prince Charles and all the others present to ask Maria Theresa to postpone the double recruiting quota she had laid upon the Bohemian *Stände* for having been behindhand in the raising of manpower. Maria Theresa entered her judgement in a few terse lines: 'this cannot be conceded, for it would mean the negligent going unpunished and ranked with the zealous'.[37]

In terms of annual income as declared in 1756, the Bohemian aristocracy was headed by a group of six magnates who all acknowledged incomes of more than 100,000 florins, namely Prince Schwarzenberg at 329,000, Count Kinsky at 165,000, Count Czernin at 156,000, Prince Lobkowitz at 154,000, Count Waldstein at 120,000, and Count Trautmannsdorf at 115,000, and by 40 or more landowners who declared incomes of at least 50,000 florins.

Bohemia undeniably produced officers who were at once wealthy and accomplished in their work. On 22 April 1756 the Austrian ambassador in St. Petersburg identified the cavalryman Franz Carl Count Trautmannsdorf as a general who would be suitable to go on mission with the Russian army, on account of both his military talents and his command of the Bohemian language (the differences between the Slavonic tongues were assumed to be questions of dialect). Among his fellow magnates in the Seven Years War were numbered the intelligent and active *GFWM.* Joseph Maria Carl Prince Lobkowitz, and two members of the great house of Kinsky von Chinitz and Tettau – the brilliant young dragoon officer Joseph, and the Franz Ulrich who played a decisive part in stemming the Prussian attack at Kolin, and who as *FML.* commanded the artillery at Torgau in 1760. The Kollowrats represented the wealthy upper nobility, and were *Inhaber* (colonels proprietor) of two of the finest regiments in the Austrian service. *Rittmeister* (captain of horse) Ignaz Ferdinand Kautsch, Major Franz Count Kokorzowa and *GFWM.* Joseph Franz Zedtwitz were worthy representatives of the small class of the Bohemian gentry, and were all decorated with the Military Order of Maria Theresa.

With exceptions like these, the military contributions of the Bohemian nobles did not correspond with their positions in society. An officer of the regiment of Andlau recollected that since the time of Homer military service had justified the privileges of the aristocracy, and yet proper warlike instincts seemed to be scarce among the nobles of Bohemia, and particularly those of the Circle of Saaz, where he had spent some time in winter quarters. 'There were very few of them to be found in our army, sharing our dangers and exertions. As for the ones who stayed on their estates, they received us in a cold way which showed clearly enough that they held us in contempt'.[38]

The wealth of the Bohemian nobles derived at least as much from the burgeoning protoindustry on their estates, as from the natural produce of fine lands such as the plains of the Elbe, the Iser valley and the Eger. Budweis, Eger town, Königgrätz, Pilsen and Pisek were scarcely more than large villages, and Prague with its population of 51,000 souls was the only town of consequence. The proportions of Bohemian military personnel born in Prague came to:

1. Other Ranks: 1.51%
2. NCOs, Corporals and *Gefreyten:* 4.85
3. Non-combatants: 11.08
4. Officers: 29.04

Outside Prague probably the only resemblance to a Bohemian middle class was to be found among the *Verleger* who acted as middle men between the domestic outworkers and the factories, and millers like the Jan Guelich (reported to be worth 30,000 florins), with whom Lieutenant Gorani lodged at Kosteletz on the Adler in 1758.

In the absence of a large and prosperous bourgeoisie the aristocracy was the class best placed to establish breweries, paper mills, glassworks, and textile mills such as the factory of the Waldsteins at Oberleutensdorf, between Teplitz and Kaaden in north-west Bohemia, which produced some of the finest woollen cloth in Central Europe. As a great landowner in his own right, Emperor Francis Stephen helped the process by founding a woolen mill at Kladrub near Pardubitz in 1749, and a linen factory not far away at Pottenstein. Kaunitz himself owned textile factories on his Moravian estates at Austerlitz and Krizanow.

Industry and mining were associated largely with the areas of German settlement along the perimeters of Bohemia and Moravia, and especially in the northern border hills, where the dense population, the cheap and hardworking labour, and the minerals, forests and rushing streams all favoured economic activity. In part these efforts were driven by the needs and opportunities created by the fact that Hirschberg, Landeshut and other centres of Silesian industry had been lost to the Prussians.[39]

The muster lists of the artillery *Haupt Corps* are the only ones in the army which specify the origins of the Bohemian military personnel by *Creis* (lit. 'circle,' administrative area), and therefore provide a rough guide as to the locations of economic activity. On the face of it most of the gunners with peacetime trades hailed from western Bohemia, though we must make allowances for the probably dis-proportionate recruiting in the north-western *Creise,* and in the *Creis* of Bechin which contained the artillery school, depot and ranges.

Key Former Civilian Trades of Bohemian Artillerymen, by *Creise*

Textile (total 128)
Bechin:	34.4%
Leitmeritz:	12.50
Saaz:	9.37
Königgrätz:	7.81
Prachin:	7.03
Pilsen:	6.25
Czaslau:	5.46
Bunzlau:	3.12
Beraun, Chrudim, Prague city, Rakonitz:	2.34 each
Eger, Elbogen, Kaurzim:	1.56 each

Metal and Mining (total 50)
Saaz:	30.00%
Pilsen:	26.00
Bechin:	12.00
Beraun:	10.00
Bunzlau, Eger, Leitmeritz, Prachin:	4.00 each
Kaurzim, Prague city, Rakonitz:	1.00 each

Manufacturing and Processing (total 144)
Bechin:	19.43%
Saaz:	12.50
Leitmeritz, Pilsen:	8.33 each
Prague city:	7.63
Prachin:	5.55
Koruiggratz:	4.16
Bunzlau, Rakonitz:	3.47 each
Beraun, Elbogen:	2.77 each
Eger:	2.08
Budweis, Chrudim, Czaslau:	1.38 each
Kaurzim:	0.69

The Bohemians of the middle of the 18th century were aware of distinctions in language and nationality to about the same degree as they were about differences in height, dress, station, age or other personal characteristics, but they had yet to find in these any motives for antagonism. The nobility were for the most part multilingual, 'and many of the highest-born ladies speak a mish-mash of Bohemian [Czech] and German'.[40] A large number of the nobles who used Bohemian for preference resented the Germanising influence of the Viennese bureaucracy as an intrusion on their freedom, rather than a nationally-inspired assault on their culture as such. The common people of the two traditions were content to lead their separate lives, and at that time there were few of the German or Czech communities who could understand one another's language.⁴¹

Ethnic Preponderance of Bohemian Military Personnel by Identifiable Types of Surname		
Rank	Slavonic	German
Other Ranks:	+31.79	
NCOs, Corporals & *Gefreyten*:	+13.47	
Non-combatants:	+17.61	
All officers:		+17.61
Ensigns, Cornets, Second Lieutenants:		+7.75
First Lieutenants:		+17.53
Captains:		+37.59
Majors:		+43.65
Lieutenant-Colonels:		+66.67
Colonels-Commandant: (too few to sample)		

The relationship between rank and ethnic origin emerges clearly, and in a way which is most disadvantageous to the Slavs.

Gorani's Miller Guelich was a Protestant, one of many such folk who had survived persecution in Bohemia and Moravia. In this case the muster lists are wholly misleading, for they indicate all Bohemian and Moravian military personnel as Catholics, which was clearly not the case. The Hungarian recruits were at much greater liberty to speak their minds, as we shall see later. Lieutenant Gorani discovered some Hussite literature which the Guelichs had been careless enough to leave on a table, but he assured his hosts that they had nothing to fear from him. 'These unfortunate Hussites have to keep themselves hidden, along with their books of devotion, and they have to attend the parish church lest the priest should take offence, and make them liable for punishment by denouncing them'.⁴²

In the 1740s Frederick had been able to recruit willing spies from among the Bohemian Protestants as well as the Prague Jews, and in the 1770s the Protestants in Moravia began to hope that the king might come to their help. Treasonable inclinations of this kind were in abeyance during the Seven Years War, and most probably on account of the brutal behaviour of Prussian armies and raiding parties. Moravian peasants offered both active and passive resistance to the Prussian invaders in 1758,⁴³ and in his commentary on Frederick's *General-Principia vom Kriege, FM.* Daun told Maria Theresa that she could be confident that 'the king recognises that there is not a single man in Bohemia or Moravia who is open to a bribe'.⁴⁴

GFWM. Joseph Maria Carl Lobkowitz, 1725–1802 (M. Militz, Military Academy, Wiener Neustadt). Although born to one of the greatest families of Bohemia, the young Lobkowitz proved to be a dedicated, brave and perceptive commander in the Seven Years War, and came to the aid of Brentano during a critical phase of the action at Meissen (21 September 1759). After the war Lobkowitz took up a diplomatic career, and became Austrian ambassador at St. Petersburg.

Endurance as well as loyalty was a distinctive feature of the Bohemian peasant, and therefore by extension of the 'Austrian private soldier. The condition of the Bohemian and Moravian serfs was marginally better than that of their counterparts in Poland, Hungary or even France,[45] but still shocking in absolute terms:

> Not only do they live in utter subjection, but they are treated with an extremity of harshness which makes no allowance for their total destitution[46]... they have hovels to live in, little better than those of Westphalia; being loose stones laid on another for the walls, and the crevices filled with mud, and the covering some strong poles, with turf spread on them, and a hole at the top in the middle is all the chimney that any of them have; adjoining is their barn, built of the same materials'.[47]

Conditions like these nevertheless produced uncomplaining, biddable men who made the foundation of the army. Armfeldt noted that few of their officers were familiar with the Bohemian language, which produced a relationship that reminded him of the connection between Swedish officers and their Finnish soldiers.[48] Habits of command nevertheless proved a workable substitute for genuine communication, and the Bohemian peasant-soldier was aware that his condition was easier than one spent labouring for a lord in the fields. 'Generally speaking their heads are rather large, though not strikingly so in comparison with their broad shoulders and generally very thickset bodies. Out of all the Imperial subjects they undoubtedly make the best soldiers, as the ones who can withstand the hardships of the military life for the longest time without going under'.[49]

Bohemian Officer Families
Bechenie von Lazan, Benedict, Bubna, Clary von Aldringen, Coenem, Colloredo, Deym von Stritetz, Fleissner von Wostrowitz, Gefellner, Grezl, Herberstein, Hilprandt von Ottenhausen, Hirzan, Hrobschitzky, Kapaun von Swogkow, Khuen, Kinsky von Chinitz and Tettau, Klebsberg/ Klebersberg (two counts), Klenau (three counts), Kokorzowa, Kotz von Dobr, Kutz, Lobkowitz, Mallowez (two barons), Morzin, Otto von Ottenfeld, Pachta, Pecenia, Pergler von Perglas, Radetzky, Ruaski, Ridzan, Stadl, Thun, Trautmannsdorf, Walderode, Wantzura, Worazitzky, Wratislau (three counts), Zedtwitz.

The Marquisate of Moravia

Population 1754: 886,974 = 5.47% of the monarchy
Area: 22,234 sq. km. = 4.26% of the monarchy
Predominant Languages 1914: Czech 70%, German 29%, other 1%

Military Representation
1. Other ranks: 11.06% of the total.
   Cuirassiers 25.29; dragoons 24.74; German infantry 11.27; artillery 8.27; pioneers, miners and sappers 4.94; Hungarian infantry 1.94
2. NCOs, Corporals and *Gefreyten:* 7.07
3. Non-combatants: 6.63
4. Officers: 3.16
5. Professionals: Surgeons 5.06; chaplains 13.25; provosts 1.30

Former Civilian Trades of Military Personnel as proportion of Monarchy as a Whole
Textile:	11.58
Clothing & Footwear:	12.00
Building & Furnishing:	13.29
Food Processing:	12.81
Metal:	14.52
Mining:	3.36
Transport:	11.80
Manufacturing & Processing:	11.31
Medical:	10.12
Students:	11.49
Service:	13.66

Moravia shared most of its history and institutions with Bohemia, its larger western neighbour. Geographically Moravia had a more uniform character. It was set between rugged hills to the west, the prolongation of the Riesengebirge to the north, and the first ridges of the Carpathians towards Hungary in the east. The highway from Poland and Prussian Upper Silesia came from the northeast by way of the Moravian Gate, and entered the extraordinarily fertile region of the Hanna-the tract of well-watered black earth which extended around Olmütz, Littau, Wischau, Kremsier and Leipnik. The road continued across the rolling estates of Kaunitz and other noblemen to reach the fortress town of Brünn, which was separated by only a couple of days' journey from the Danube plain and Vienna.[50]

The prosperous agriculture, the estate industries, and the cloth factories of the German 'language islands' of Iglau and Zwittau in the west combined to make the marquisate one of the most economically valuable lands of the monarchy, and created an impression of general well-being. In fact the inequalities were still more startling than in Bohemia, for the Liechtensteins and Dietrichsteins between them owned one-quarter of Moravia, and a large proportion of the rest was in the hands of the families of Althann, Blümegen, Cobenzl, Daun, Haugwitz, Herberstein, Kaunitz, Mittrowski, Podstatsky, Wallis, Wratislau and Wrbna.

The spirit of public service was more evident than among the comparable classes in Bohemia. As the director of the artillery, Joseph Wenzel Prince Liechtenstein devoted his fortune without reserve to his guns and gunners, and contributed more than any other individual to the Austrian military effort in the Seven Years War. The diplomacy and much else besides lay in the hands of the *Staatscanzler* Wenzel Anton Count Kaunitz.

However the underlying resemblance to conditions in Bohemia are evident in the muster lists, which show the same predominance of personnel of German surnames in the higher ranks:

Ethnic Preponderance of Moravian Military Personnel by Identified Types of Surname:
Rank	Slavonic	German
Other Ranks:	+45.33	
NCOs, Corporals & *Gefreyten*:	+14.01	
Non-combatants:	+12.33	
All Officers:		+34.33
Ensigns, Cornets, Second-Lieutenants:		+33.63
First-Lieutenants:		+11.11
Captains:		+53.77
Majors:		+100.00
Lieutenant-Colonels: (too few to sample)		
Colonel-Commandants: (too few to sample)		

Moravia's most distinctive military contribution was in the 'German' cavalry, where its representation among both the cuirassiers and dragoons was (proportionate to population) the highest in the monarchy.

Moravian Officer Families
Althann, Cavallery, Chorinsky, Freyenfels (two barons), Fürstenberg, Herberstein, Leslie, Liechtenstein, Mittrowski, Mingwitz, Oppersdorf, Podstatzky, Roden, Rzikowsky von Dobrzics, Schauerfeld, Stain, Wallis, Wurmbrand.

The Duchy of (Austrian) Silesia

Population 1754: 154,782 = 0.95% of the monarchy
Area: 5,149 sq. km. = 0.98% of the monarchy
Predominant Languages 1914: German 47%, Polish 30%, Czech 23%

Military Representation
1. Other Ranks: 0.57% of the total.
   Cuirassiers 1.83; dragoons 0.99; German infantry 0.54; artillery 0.35; pioneers, miners and sappers 0.30; husssars 0.02; Hungarian infantry 0.01
2. NCOs, Corporals and *Gefreyten:* 0.38
3. Non-combatants: 0.53
4. Officers: 0.48
5. Professionals: Surgeons 1.26; chaplains 2.40; provosts nil

Former Civilian Trades of Military Personnel as Proportion of Monarchy as a Whole
Textile: 0.61
Clothing & Footwear: 0.48
Building & Furnishing: 0.59
Food Processing: 1.36
Metal: nil
Mining: nil
Transport: 0.48
Manufacturing & Processing: 0.58
Medical: 0.77
Students: 1.97
Service: 0.44

This little corner was all that was left to the Habsburgs of the great Silesian lands which they had lost to the Prussians militarily in 1741, and signed away in 1745. It stretched from the border hills with Moravia and Hungary into the northern plain, and represented in miniature many of the characteristics of the lost territories. While the estates of the Liechtensteins bulked proportionately larger still than in Moravia, Austrian Silesia was distinguished by the good condition of the peasants, and the large numbers of its freeholders and small landowners.

Austrian Silesian Officer Families
Hennberg, Orlick

The Lands of the Hungarian Crown

The Kingdom of Hungary

Population 1754: 4,657,503 = 28.74% of the monarchy
Area: 208,777 sq. km. = 40.20% of the monarchy
Predominant Languages (including Transylvania) 1914: Magyar 49%, Romanian 17%, German 13%, Slovak 13%, Serbo-Croat 4%, Ruthenian 2%, others 2%

Military Contribution (with Transylvania)
1. Other Ranks: 15.10 of the total.
   Hussars (excl. *Grenz Husaren*) 90.43; Hungarian infantry 70.50; dragoons 2.51; pioneers, miners, sappers 2.47; cuirassiers 1.64; Italian infantry 1.21; artillery 1.14; German infantry 0.79; Netherlands dragoons 0.12; Netherlands infantry 0.07
2. NCOs, Corporals and *Gefreyten:* 14.57
3. Non-combatants: 7.12
4. Officers: 18.02
5. Professionals: Surgeons 3.79; chaplains 20.58; provosts 12.30

Former Civilian Trades of Military Personnel as Proportion of Monarchy as a Whole (with Transylvania)

Textile:	14.58
Clothing & Footwear:	22.29
Building & Furnishing:	8.53
Metal:	25.26
Mining:	46.21
Transport:	18.55
Manufacturing & Processing:	17.60
Students:	20.82
Service:	13.59

The first home of the Magyar people was in the Ural borderlands of Europe and Asia. Linguists have established connections with the fellow 'Ugric'-speaking Finns and Basques (which only adds to the mystery of Magyar origins), and little is known except through legend about the King Arpad who led his peoples to the Hungarian plains in about the year 900.

The royal line of Arpad died out in 1301. The succeeding Angevins became extinct in 1382 (leaving the fleur de lys which still features in the coat of arms of Bosnia). The reign of the Jagellonians, and with it a 150-year struggle against the Ottoman Turks, was terminated when Louis II and his companions were killed on the field of Mohács in 1526. The Hungarian lands proper then coalesced into three elements: 'Habsburg Hungary' – an arc of territory in the northwest, extending along the borders with Austria, Moravia, and Galician Poland; central Hungary with the plain of the Great Alföld, which was completely under Ottoman domination; and finally the Principality of Transylvania in the east, which enjoyed a large measure of independence under the Turks, and was seen by the anti-Habsburg party as the guardian of Magyar traditions.

The Reformation made rapid progress through the Hungarian lands, and converted most of the Magyars to Calvinism, and the German townspeople to Lutheranism. People like these were not to be reduced to the status of Austrian vassals. National and religious unrest grew in 'Habsburg' Hungary when the Austrian authorities violated Magyar freedoms and the Catholic clergy proselytised among the heretics, and the tensions were racked up by the very success of the Austrian armies in their counteroffensive of 1683–99, which extended the antagonisms across wide tracts of historic Hungary and Transylvania. The dissident Hungarians responded violently, and Vienna itself came under threat during the rebellion or rather war (1703–11) which was waged against the Austrians by the followers of Prince Ferenc Rakoczy II.

While the Habsburgs finally gained the military superiority, the new Emperor Charles VI brought the unrest to an end through the well-considered Treaty of Szatmár on 11 May 1711, which proved to be probably the most statesmanlike and enduring achievement of his reign. It was a settlement between partners, rather than a rebel surrender, and it confirmed the Hungarian nobles in their constitutions and freedoms.

The militancy of the Rakoczy era was already a fading memory when Charles VI died in 1740, and one of Rakoczi's lieutenants, the Calvinist Alexander Count Károly joined with the Esterházys and other avowedly 'Habsburg' magnates at the celebrated Diet of 1741. The Hungarian Insurrection and the newly-raised Hungarian regiments now gave the Habsburgs a timely accession of force (comparable with the arrival of the Siberian divisions at beleaguered Moscow in 1941). It was as 'King' of Hungary as well as Archduchess of Austria that Maria Theresa began to free her northern and western lands of the Prussians, French, Bavarians and Saxons.

Maria Theresa ruled Hungary with the lightest of reins. The nobles retained their personal freedom from taxes, their religious liberty, their almost untrammelled powers over their serfs, and the right to gather in the *Comitat* (county) assemblies and in the grander and much rarer Diets. Shortly before the Seven Years War one of the meetings of the Conference in Vienna agreed that it would be inherently wrong, as well as politically unwise, to infringe Hungarian freedoms, and that the government policy must be based on the principle of eradicating the must blatant abuses, while preserving established custom: *'ut tollantur abusus et maneat usus'*.[51] The Swedish attaché Armfeldt noted that 'out of all her [Maria Theresa's] subjects none have been more devoted to her than the Hungarians, once she assured them that she would maintain their privileges relating to religion and other matters.' The need of the Court of Vienna to cultivate the good opinion of the Hungarians would last 'as long as it has anything to fear from the King of Prussia'.[52]

Hungary's contribution to the Habsburg effort in the Seven Years War characteristically took the form of putting into the field regiments of hussars and specifically Hungarian infantry, which could therefore be identified with the spirit of the nation and the enthusiasm of individual magnates, rather than forwarding money – which would have touched on privilege, and would have been lost from sight in a common pool. The monarchy raised altogether 260 million florins to meet the extraordinary expenditure of the war, and of this Hungary accounted for only 8 million, or 3.07 percent.

By the middle of the 18th century sedition and dissent appeared to have become marginalised, in that they were linked with particular foreign influences. The most immediately hostile of these was that of Prussia, which took advantage of the right which the Peace of Westphalia (1648) had given to Protestant states to intercede on behalf of Protestants in the Austrian Hereditary Lands. Frederick extended the right of intervention to Hungary, where he sought to undermine Habsburg authority through agents, spies and the encouragement of desertion. During an interlude of peace in 1743 a party of Prussians under Colonel Bornstedt accompanied the Austrian campaigns on the Danube and the Rhine as 'volunteers,' and inveigled a number of disgruntled officers of hussars into betaking themselves to Prussia along with their followers. The renegades Johann Theodor Rüsch and Michael Székely rose to become Prussian generals and *Chefs* of regiments of hussars, but they were surpassed in vindictiveness by the Johann Paul Werner who served in the Habsburg Czaky (later Nádasdy) Hussars until 1748, but went over to the Prussians in the conviction that his Protestant faith had stood in the way of his promotion. 'Pride, hate and vengeance came together… to urge him to show the enemies of Prussia (who were also his own) his great worth, and what they had thereby lost. Nádasdy was his particular target, and his dearest wish was to take him prisoner'.⁵³ In April 1762, as a Prussian lieutenant-general, no less, he was commissioned by Frederick to join the Tartars in ravaging the country around Vienna.

The Austrians were able to limit the damage from this source. Just before the battle of Kolin in 1757 Frederick instructed his envoy in Nuremberg to 'find some cunning means to establish contact with the Hungarian Lutherans. This year we intend, with the grace of God, to advance our forces to within a short distance of the Hungarian borders. You must therefore assure the Hungarians that, if they beat their way through to us and take our side, we shall not make peace until the Austrians concede and confirm their religious freedoms in perpetuity'.⁵⁴ Field Marshal Daun shattered the scheme by defeating Frederick in the great battle of 18 June 1757, and later in the same year the Austrians were able to carry the war into the north European plain. Among the prisoners they took in Lusatia was the Hungarian gentleman Révay – a spoiled Franciscan brother, who had deserted his monastery at Neutra, wandered about various Protestant universities in Germany, and had now been captured as a cornet in the Prussian hussars. Révay was now consigned to the Archbishop of Prague for punishment under ecclesiastical law⁵⁵.

The great majority of the Hungarians were proof against the Prussian blandishments, and experience told Frederick that Hungarian deserters had a way of making their way back to the Austrians at the first opportunity, together with their horses and saddles. Lieutenant-Colonel Baboczay of the Baranyay Hussars resisted every offer to take service with the Prussians, and when he finally came to Berlin it was as an officer in Hadik's raiding corps. Sad to tell, he was shot dead by a Prussian musketeer, and so became one of the very few casualties sustained on this expedition.

In some ways it was more difficult to prevent Hungarians from being poached by Maria Theresa's friends. Refugee Hungarians had found a welcome in France since at least the days of Rakoczy, and in November 1756 Kaunitz was embarrassed to receive a request from Versailles to permit Lieutenant-General d'Estrées to go recruiting in Hungary for the 1,100 men who were needed to bring up to strength the three regiments of hussars in the French service. Kaunitz suggested to Francis Stephen that the French should be told that the competition for recruits would be unwelcome, and that the Austrians would be helping them out anyway by sending a body of hussars to support their promised auxiliary corps⁵⁶.

Similarly, when Kaunitz became *Staatscanzler* in 1753 he discovered that one of the most intractable problems facing him was the way the Russians were striving to attract ethnic Serbs from the Habsburg dominions. The Austrian authorities had issued prohibitions against Serbian emigration from Lower Austria on 23 January 1743, from the Hereditary Lands in general on 19 June 1752, and from the Bánát of Temesvár on 21 July the same year, and special provision had been made against the practice in the 14th article of the Austro Russian treaty of alliance in 1746.

Matters came to a head from 1752, for the scale of the emigration threatened to denude the Serbian population of the Theiss-Maros region of southern Hungary and the Bánát of Temesvár, and the Sultan was taking fright at the build-up of the immigrant population in the Russian settlement of New Serbia, which was located threateningly close to the Turkish border. A new Turkish war would present the Austrians with dilemma upon dilemma: they were anxious to keep on good terms with the Sultan and his Grand Vizier, yet they could not leave their Russian allies in the lurch if the Russians became embroiled with the Ottomans; such a war would not only turn a benevolent neutral into an enemy, but give the opportunity for the French and Prussians to ingratiate themselves at Constantinople.

The only measure open to Kaunitz was to do what he could to hinder the Serbian emigration, and measures to this effect were instituted in March 1754. Kaunitz told the Russian ambassador that the Austrians had been left with no alternative, since the long and costly wars had left Maria Theresa without enough hands to cultivate her fertile and extensive territories.

The Serbian issue offers a reminder that the Magyars, although the undoubted leaders of society, constituted only a minority in Hungary, amounting to about 40 percent of the population in

BRÜNN
TRENTSCHIN
ARVA
LIPTAU
TURÓCZ
Trentschin
Neusohl
Kremnitz
NEUTRA
SOHL
GÖMER
UPPER
LOWER
AUSTRIA
Schemnitz
Melk
St. Pölten
Vienna
Pressburg
BARS
HONT
NEOGRAD
BOR
Neuhäusel
WIESELBURG
Komorn
HEVES
Wr. Neustadt
Gran
ÖDENBURG
RAAB
KOMORN
Jász-Berény
Bruck
Buda
Leoben
Weiz
EISENBURG
VESZPRÉM
FEHÉRVÁR
Danube
PEST
SZOLNOK
STYRIA
GRAZ
ZALA
Klein-
Kumanien
Kecskemét
Mur
Marburg
Pettau
Drau
TOLNA
SOMOGY
CSONGRÁD
Cilli
Warasdin
WARASDINER
Laibach
CARNIOLA
Sau
Agram
St. Georger
Creutzer
BARANYA
Drau
BÁCS
Theiss
CIVIL CROATIA
Peterwardein
SLAVONIAN
Fiume
Carlstadt
Szluiner
BANAL
Oguliner
Broder
CARLSTÄDTER
Sau
Peterwardeiner
Ottocaner
Belgrade
OTTOMAN

Map 4 Hungary, with Eastern Austria

the middle of the 18th century. The predominantly Lutheran Slovaks formed the majority of the population of the northern counties (Trentschin, Neusohl etc.) of the old Habsburg Upper Hungary, and they had significant settlements in the counties of Békés, Szatmár, Arad, Csanád, Bács, and the countryside of the county of Pest.

While the urban population of Hungary as a whole was tiny, the towns of the north-west Kremnitz, Schemnitz, and so on – were home to populations of the so-called 'Sachsen,' who made up the older-established German communities of Hungary and Transylvania. When the progress of the Christian reconquest opened up the Great Alföld and the Bánát of Temesvár to settlement from every direction, the Habsburgs put a special value on immigration from the *Reich*, on account of the industry, skills and levels of culture of the German newcomers. Charles VI therefore initiated the settlement of the southern *Comitat* of Sacs and the adjoining Bánát of Temesvár. These settlers were characteristically drawn from Austria, Bohemia, the middle Rhine and the Palatinate, and most of them were Catholics, which made them doubly desirable. The name of the 'Swabians' is attached more specifically to the second wave of German settlement, which was fostered by Maria Theresa from 1748, and brought immigrations from Vorder-Österreich, Bavaria, Franconia, the Rhine, Lorraine and Luxembourg as well as from Swabia proper.

The neat white German settlements represented islands among the Orthodox Serbs who predominated in the south-western Bánát, southern Bács and areas of the *Comitat* of Baranya, and who represented the chief competitors to the Magyars, now that the central plain (the Great Alföld) was being repopulated. In the eastern Bánát, and all along Hungary's borders with Transylvania the basic stock of the population was Wallachian (Romanian). The ethnic mix of the kingdom was compounded by Croats, Bulgars, Ukranians, gypsies, and the tribes of the Cumanians (who arrived in the wake of the Tartar invasion of 1241), and the once-free warrior castes of the Jász-Kun and the Hajdú towns.

In general, however, the counties of the north-west (with the exception of Wieselburg [Sopron], Pressburg [Pozsony, Bratislava] and Neutra [Nyitra]) were inhabited almost exclusively by Slovaks and Germans. The Magyars predominated in the counties of the Alföld and the lands beyond the Danube,[57] and had a way of 'Magyarising' the newcomers that eventually suppressed their diversity. Traditions were distorted beyond all recognition, and so it was that the rhythmic music (Terebonkos' = 'Werbung' = 'Recruiting') of the recruiting parties of Maria Theresa's army became associated with gypsy bands, and later still (and just as unhistorically) with Hungarian folk music as a whole.

The first Hungarian census was carried out only in 1787, and is therefore of limited use for our present purposes, but it shows a number of counties of the centre and north-west so heavily in the lead in terms of population (Pest, Neutra, Pressburg, Bács, Trentschin and Szabolcs together accounting for 47.81 percent or nearly half, excluding Transylvania), that something of the sort probably also held true in the 1750s.

We are on firmer ground with the muster lists of the period of the Seven Years War (See Appendix I: Military Representation of Hungarian Counties and Transylvania), which includes the person lel from Transylvania, and indicates that the most important recruiting areas of the Hungarian infantry were to be found in three groups of counties, distributed along a northwest to south-east axis, namely:

> The counties of Trentschin, Neutra and Pressburg along the borders with Moravia and Lower Austria (15.42 percent)
> The central counties of Borsod, Heves, and Pest (11.59)
> A heavy representation in the east from Transylvania and the neighbouring county of Bihar (12.64)

Broadly similar conditions are shown in the origins of the hussar troops, though the weighting is shifted to the west:

The counties of Neutra, Pressburg, Ödenburg and Eisenburg (23.25)
County of Pest (7.50)
Transylvania and county of Bihar (12.64).

Among the officers of the Hungarian infantry altogether 30.51 percent hailed from six of the western counties (Pressburg, Neutra, Eisenburg, Ödenburg, Raab, Trentschin), and a still significant 17.79 from Transylvania (but only 2.05 from Bihar) and 9.86 from the counties of Pest and Heves in the centre. The representation of hussar officers sinks to 7.58 from Transylvania, 7.86 from Pest and Heves, but rises to an altogether preponderant 40.43 from the same six counties which furnished so many officers to the infantry (in this case, in descending order, from Eisenburg, Pressburg, Neutra, Raab, Ödenburg and Trentschin). All of this suggests the perpetuation of a military elite based in old Habsburg Upper Hungary. Political allegiance rather than social rank appears to have been the determining influence, for there was a disproportionate concentration of the nobility and gentry in the north-eastern counties, where in Szabolcs they made up 13 percent of the population, in Szatmár 14 percent, and in Borsod 15.2 percent.

The Hungarian magnates and upper aristocracy as a whole were well educated, and many of them could speak and write fluently in German, French and Latin. Most could speak Magyar (Hungarian), though for many of them it hardly counted as a written language, let alone a literary one. Outside their circle, the problems of communication were not easy to resolve. A knowledge of Hungarian was needed to engage the full respect of Magyar soldiers, 'and for this reason,' wrote the Prince de Ligne, 'they are the only troops among whom I would never wish to see a foreign officer. Moreover the language is both essential in itself, and too difficult for the Germans, who are in any case loathed by the Hungarian infantry and hussars alike'.[58] The confidential reports of the crack Hungarian infantry regiment of Erzherzog Carl (No. 3) nevertheless reveal a very uneven command of the language. The 19-year-old Lieutenant Antonijs Kokics is singled out for praise, for 'he possesses a particular skill and facility in everything which concerns the military profession, and speaks Hungarian, German, French, Latin and Slavonic. He is a nephew of Colonel Siskovics, who spares nothing which is needed to acquire a noble education and the learning of languages and the arts'.[59] Lieutenant Jacob Cogniazzo (later the celebrated commentator) was a native of Fiume on the Adriatic littoral, but a young officer of great intelligence who also spoke fluently in Hungarian. However Captain Franz Stredoni from Moravia, and even his Hungarian-born comrades the captains Carl Rebl and Johann Hopffern were totally ignorant of the language. After the Seven Years War, *G.d.C* Andreas Hadik, a Germanised Hungarian of Slovak ancestry, actually set himself against translating the hussar *Reglement* into Hungarian, 'since it appears to me essential to promote the learning of German in the hussar regiments, among the senior and junior officers alike, and, as far as possible, among the ordinary troopers. It is uncommonly useful to be able to understand the speech of the local people when we are campaigning in German lands. I therefore express the hope that such officers who wish to distinguish themselves in the service will apply themselves to this language, by which I mean German'.[60]

Both practical convenience and the power of tradition kept the politically-neutral Latin alive in Hungary longer than in any other part of Europe. It was the language of law and political debate, 'though the Latin of the common people is nothing special, as we may hear from the lips of the hussars serving with the German armies. One of them asked the whereabouts of a saddler to make him a pair of pistol holsters: *"Ubinam est ille home, qui facit chirothecas bombardarum?"* When they find themselves embroiled unexpectedly with enemy infantry they give vent to the cry: *"Fuge, fuge! hic infanteria est!"'*.[61]

Religious adherence in the Hungarian lands was as diverse as the variety of nationalities and languages might suggest. Catholicism was the faith of most of the leading Hungarian magnates, most of the newer German settlers, and of the Croats proper – who were at daggers drawn with their Orthodox Serbian kinsmen. The Orthodox tradition was itself divided into three branches: the Greek Church, the Russian Church, and the Uniats of Transylvania and north-eastern Hungary who had embraced Catholicism at the end of the 17th century, while retaining the Orthodox liturgy and usages. The Unitarians of Transylvania (quite distinct from the Catholic Uniats) were an extreme Protestant sect and scarcely counted as Christians at all. The Lutheranism was associated with the Slovaks of northern Hungary, and the Germans of Transylvania and the old towns of 'Habsburg' Hungary. Calvinism was professed as the distinctively Magyar faith of a few of the magnates and almost all of the 75,000 noble families.

The muster lists identify 19,486 military personnel of Hungarian birth by religion throughout the army, and furnish the following perspectives (see chart on following page).

It is evident that the relative position of real or avowed Catholics improved with status, though not to the same degree as with the Lutherans. The standing of the Calvinists deteriorates with ascent in rank, and markedly so among the officers, while the Orthodox and the small sects disappear altogether.

When religion is related to geography (See Appendix II: Hungarian Religion by Location), it emerges that Catholicism was most firmly established in the regions of Hungary most accessible to Austrian influence, namely in the north-west, though there was an isolated concentration of Catholic soldiers recruited from the *Comitat* of Csongrád in the south centre. Another anomaly is shown by the presence of a large number of Catholic officers hailing from the north-central counties of Abauj and Liptau.

Liptau was otherwise the stronghold of the Lutherans, who were clustered in a number of counties of the centre and north, though they were very thin on the ground in the east. That part of the world was the land of the Calvinists, who had their spiritual centre at Debreczen in the *Comitat* of Szabolcs, and predominated generally in the counties towards Transylvania. The Orthodox rank and file were a small minority and were recruited principally from the northeast, though (another anomaly) the southern counties of Bács and Baranya produced most of the few officers of that faith, probably through Serbian influence.

Hungarian economic development, such as it was, had been associated with a spread of northern counties, and more specifically with mining (the counties of Máramaros and Szabolcs in the northeast, and those of Bars, Hont and adjacent areas in the central Tatras), and textile production (counties of Zepes and Saros), and Trentschin, Liptau, Turócz and Arva in the northern Tatras towards Poland. However the nature, pace and location of Hungarian economic life underwent important changes in the course of the 18th century, for the expulsion of the Turks opened up 18,000 square kilometres of central and eastern Hungary for settlement, and the Tariff System of 1754 discriminated against Hungary in terms of manufactured goods, but favoured the export of Hungarian agricultural products. The expanses of the Great Alföld were now available for livestock rearing and grain production, and the existing landed families were the people best placed to avail themselves of these opportunities; the peasant population was young and growing, but its relative condition of life probably declined, for the lords now had the incentive to exploit their estates for the rewards promised by the market economy. The Seven Years War gave a boost to the process, for Hungarian grain, fodder, cattle and horses were much in demand for the army.

The muster lists give some indication of the state of economic affairs at the time of the Seven Years War. When ranked alongside the other lands of the monarchy, Hungary and Transylvania came fourth to Bohemia, Moravia and Lower and Upper Austria in the soldiers who came from the building trades, and second only to Bohemia in every other type of employment except mining, where the 46.21 percent gave Hungary and Transylvania a clear lead over Bohemia's 25.29. When the Hungarian and Transylvanian ex-miners are considered together, the great majority (67.79 percent) are found to have come from the County of Hont, with that of Sohl second at 11.62 percent, and all the others below 7 percent.

Students are to be found more frequently among the Hungarian and Transylvanian troops than in any other element of the army except the Bohemian gunners. The largest contingent (as a proportion of the Hungarian and Transylvanian total) originated in the county of Pressburg (11.62 percent), with those of Eisenburg and Neutra second at 9.30 each, then Ödenburg and Pest (8.13 each), Raab and Transylvania at 5.81 each, Komorn at 4.65, and Baranya, Bihar, Heves, Neograd and Zemplen all at 3.48 each, and the rest nowhere.

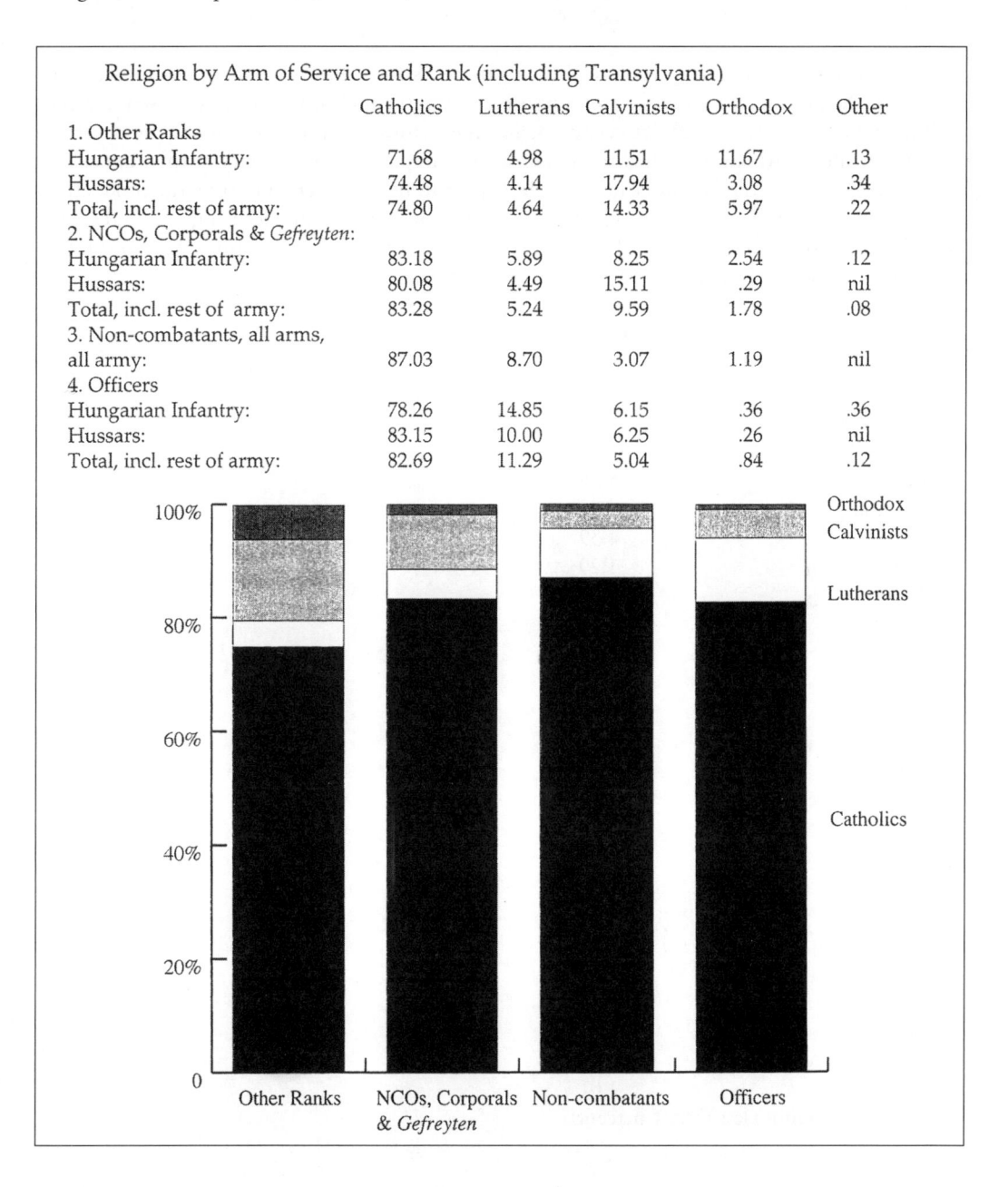

Religion by Arm of Service and Rank (including Transylvania)					
	Catholics	Lutherans	Calvinists	Orthodox	Other
1. Other Ranks					
Hungarian Infantry:	71.68	4.98	11.51	11.67	.13
Hussars:	74.48	4.14	17.94	3.08	.34
Total, incl. rest of army:	74.80	4.64	14.33	5.97	.22
2. NCOs, Corporals & *Gefreyten*:					
Hungarian Infantry:	83.18	5.89	8.25	2.54	.12
Hussars:	80.08	4.49	15.11	.29	nil
Total, incl. rest of army:	83.28	5.24	9.59	1.78	.08
3. Non-combatants, all arms, all army:	87.03	8.70	3.07	1.19	nil
4. Officers					
Hungarian Infantry:	78.26	14.85	6.15	.36	.36
Hussars:	83.15	10.00	6.25	.26	nil
Total, incl. rest of army:	82.69	11.29	5.04	.84	.12

The figures of former textile workers indicate the following leading centres of textile manufacture, again expressed as a percentage of the combined Hungarian and Transylvanian totals:

Transylvania:	9.26
Trentschin:	8.88
Eisenburg:	8.12
Neutra:	6.65
Ödenburg:	6.17
Saros:	4.24
Komorn, Pest, Pressburg:	3.47 each

Economic development as a whole is difficult to assess from the evidence of the muster lists. As always, the presence of ex-workers of a particular group could just as likely represent a recent decline in a trade as its current prevalence; again, the figures give no indication of the contribution of agriculture, which happened to be increasingly important in Hungary at this time, as we have seen. Otherwise the key indicators would appear to be those relating to textile production, mining and metal working (taken together in this instance), and manufacturing and processing. By adding former workers from the three sectors we arrive at the following figures, again expressed as percentages of the Hungarian and Transylvanian total:

Transylvania:	10.52
Trentschin:	6.37
Neutra:	5.84
Pressburg:	5.49
Saros:	5.31
Ödenburg:	5.04
Eisenburg:	4.84
Pest:	4.39
Bihar:	4.29
Hont:	3.87
Sohl:	3.57
Raab:	3.39
Heves:	2.93
Borsod:	2.62
Komorn:	2.90
Abauj:	2.49
Zemplen, Zepes:	1.92 each
Veszprém:	1.90
Neograd:	1.82
Féhérvar:	1.51
Corner:	1.30
Bács:	1.21
Zala:	1.15
Tolna:	1.13
Somogy:	1.10
Szatmár:	1.08
Ung:	1.01

(All other counties less than 1 percent).

Land remained the foundation of the Hungarian economy. The Magyar nobility was the manifestation of a ruling nation rather than a class in Hungarian society, and great and growing disparities of wealth and condition existed between the mass of the noble smallholders (which formed a large minority of the population in some of the eastern counties), and the ten or a dozen magnates, who held lands or rather private kingdoms in Upper Hungary, the plain of the Little Alföld, and parts of northern Croatia. Wealthiest by far was the principal branch of the family of Esterházy (declared income 450,267 florins), followed by the Batthyány (190,898), the Károly (150,532), the Grassalkovich (60,363) and the Erdödy (50,496). Together with the remaining magnates and the 25 or so significant landowners, these people formed the true aristocracy of Hungary.

Austrians remained alien and abhorrent creatures to the common folk of Hungary,[62] however most of the magnates identified their wider interests with those of the Habsburgs to a degree which was remarkable, and which contrasted notably with the behaviour of some of the leading landowners of Bohemia. By the 1870s the Esterházys were to contribute more than 20 field officers to the army, including five Field Marshals, and they gained four crosses of the Military Order of Maria Theresa. During the Seven Years War the grandest of the line, Nicolaus Joseph Prince Esterházy (1714–90) won the Theresian Order for his prowess as brigade commander, and rose to *FML*. (*FM*. in 1768); his younger brother Paul Anton died in 1762 as a *FML*.

The Principality of Transylvania (Siebenbürgen)
Population 1754: 1,037,655 = 6.40% of the monarchy
Area: 54,928 sq. km. = 10.53% of the monarchy

Military Representation
1. Other Ranks: 2.20% of the total.
    Hungarian infantry 15.38; hussars 7.49; pioneers, miners and sappers 0.72; Italian infantry 0.21; artillery 0.14; German infantry 0.11
2. NCOs, Corporals and *Gefreyten*: 2.34
3. Non-combatants: 7.19
4. Officers: 1.98
5. Professionals: Surgeons 1.26; chaplains 1.20; provosts nil

Former Civilian Trades of Military Personnel as Proportion of Monarchy as a Whole Incorporated in 'Kingdom of Hungary', above
Religion as Represented in the Muster Lists (all arms, whole army)

	Other Ranks	Officers
Catholics	72.86	62.86
Calvinist	17.87	20.00
Lutherans	8.44	15.55
Orthodox	0.83	0.11
Sects	*	1.11

* None entered as such

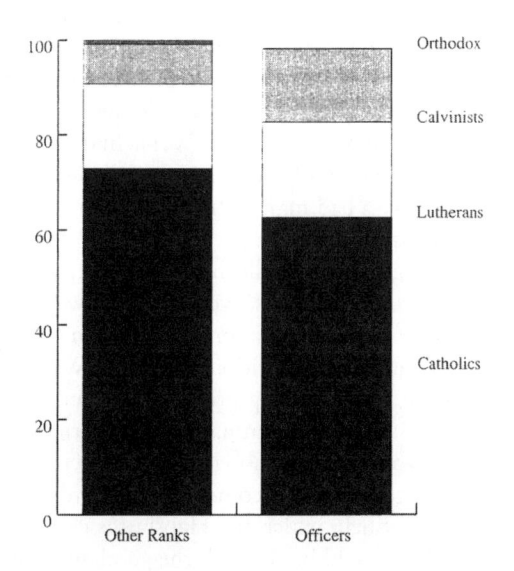

Transylvania (lit. 'The Land Beyond the Forests') was formed of the basins of the Maros and the Szamos rivers, and the flanking ranges of the Transylvanian Alps, which projected deep into Turkish Europe. For the Magyars, Transylvania was no small cousin of Hungary proper, but a repository of the values of their nation. Under Ottoman rule the principality had been spared the depopulation and destitution which had overtaken the Great Alföld, and the local authority was retained by the representatives of the Three Nations:

1. The Magyars
2. The closely-related Szeklers or Székely (claiming descent from the Huns who had arrived in the A.D. 376)
3. The 'Saxons,' whose ancestors came from Flanders and the Rhine, and were settled by King Geza II of Hungary in 1141. Their dialect was an amalgam of German, Flemish and Luxembourgeois, and befitted their origins, and they survived as a recognisable community until they emigrated *en masse* to Germany in the 1990s.

Without the help of the Three Nations Emperor Leopold I would scarcely have been able to expel the Turks from the principality, and the Austrians acknowledged their debt in the Leopoldine Diploma of 1691, which confirmed the Nations in their privileges.

The religious affiliations of the Transylvanians, as represented in the muster lists (above) is certainly unrepresentative of the balance between the religions in the principality as a whole, where Calvinism was the national faith of the Magyars. Catholics were to be found more frequently among the Szeklers, who lived mainly in eastern Transylvania. The Lutheran Saxons, who were the best farmers, and dominated crafts, industry and the life of the towns, constantly refreshed their links with the homeland of Luther by sending their best young men to study at Leipzig, and by inviting Protestant Germans to settle in the *Gau* of Mühlenbach, where the *Stände* accorded them citizenship much more freely than to the native Catholics. The family of Haller (which originated in Nuremberg) was one of the few Catholic lines which figured prominently in public life. The majority population, the Orthodox Wallachians, were for the most part bound to the soil in abject serfdom.

The Austrian authorities kept a vigilant eye on the frictions between the communities, and on their connections with like-minded people outside the principality. Thus the comings and goings of the Lutherans between Transylvania and Germany was a matter for suspicion, as was the fact that the young men of the neighbouring Hungarian *Comitat* of Bihar frequented the high schools in Clausenburg – a stronghold of Saxon Lutheranism.

During the Seven Years War a bogus Orthodox priest from Poland, one Soffronius, was found to be stirring unrest among the Wallachians and the nearby counties of Hungary. He was disowned by the Orthodox Metropolitan of Carlowitz, who declared that he knew nothing of him, except that he was 'a bad man, a drunkard, and a bigamist if not a trigamist',[63] and his deluded followers were put down by force.

The plight of the Wallachian community was otherwise viewed sympathetically by the Austrian Commanding Generals, even if their power to help them was circumscribed by the political domination of the Three Nations. As Commanding General from 1749 to 1751, *FZM.* Maximilian Browne noted that petitions from the Wallachians were being ignored by the *Stände,* which at that time were granting privileges to German immigrants in the way mentioned above. One of his successors, *FML.* Immanuel Voghtern, found that Wallachian areas were being depopulated of their young men, who were fleeing to the forests to escape the forcible conscription which was being targeted at their community towards the end of the Seven Years War.

The only help which the Habsburgs could expect to receive from the principality in the Seven Years War would be through the goodwill of its leading circles, and in the event this proved to be considerable. Through collective action or the initiative of magnates Transylvania furnished the army with two regiments of infantry (Bethlen and Gyulai), and four regiments of regular hussars (Bethlen, Hadik, Kálnoky and the Székely) in addition to contingents of *Grenz-Husaren*.

GFWM. Adam Joseph Count Bethlen represented one of the foremost Calvinist families, and was esteemed highly by Loudon (who was no lover of unearned privilege). As a colonel of infantry, Samuel Count Gylau von Maros-Németh and Nadaska accompanied Hadik on his raid on Berlin in 1757, and went on to distinguish himself in the final Austrian victory in the open field, at Teplitz on 2 August 1762. Nearly the last notable Austrian action of any kind was the brilliant sortie executed from Schweidnitz on 27 September of that year by First-Lieutenant Michael Waldhütter, who was born in Schassburg and represented the German community. This retiring and elegant young man was rewarded with the *Ritterkreuz* of the Military Order of Maria Theresa, and ennobled with the suffix 'von Minenburg.'

Hungarian and Transylvanian Officer Families (in this case a selection of many)
Allvintzi, Batthyány, Bereny (Neutra), Bethlen (Transylvania), Dessewffy, Draskovich, Eötvös (Szatmár), Erdödy (Eisenburg), Esterházy de Galantha, Festetics, Forgách de Ghymes, Grassalakovich, Gyulai, Grosz, Haller, Károly, Kerekes, Kiss (Neutra), Koháry, Luzinsky (Zepes), Morocz, Nádasdy, Pálffy ab Erdöd, Révay (Turocs), Siskovich (Csongrád), Soro (from Spain), Splényi (Saros), Széchenyi (Ödenburg), Török (Veszprém), Vecsey (five barons, Gömer), Veldner (two barons, Ödenburg), Wulffen.

Croatia and Slavonia

Population 1754: 465.918 = 2.87% of the monarchy
Area: 39,255 sq. km. = 7.52% of the monarchy

Military Representation
(N.B. excluding that of the Military Borders)
1. Other Ranks: 0.57% of the total.
   Hungarian infantry 4.71; Italian infantry 0.42; pioneers, miners & sappers 0.40; hussars 0.36; German infantry 0.14; dragoons 0.06; cuirassiers 0.019
2. NCOs, Corporals and *Gefreyten:* 0.91
3. Non-combatants: 0.39
4. Officers: 0.95
5. Professionals: Surgeons 1.26; chaplains 2.40; provosts nil

Former Civilian Trades of Military Personnel as Proportion of Monarchy as a Whole (N.B. again excluding Military Borders)

Textile:	0.23%
Clothing & Footwear:	0.88
Building & Furnishing:	0.14
Food Processing:	0.08
Metal:	1.44
Mining:	1.68
Transport:	1.92
Manufacturing & Processing:	0.81
Medical:	0.25
Students:	0.71
Service:	0.25

Croatia and Slavonia counted technically as south-western lands of the Hungarian Crown. Their military contribution was significant, but expressed almost entirely in the regiments of 'Croatian' infantry and *Grenz-Husaren* which were raised in the Military Borders – the long strip of land which stood under the immediate direction of the military authorities in Vienna and was kept out of Hungarian control. The percentages of military personnel entered above refer to the presence in the rest of the army, which was negligible, except in the regiment of Simbschen and the Hungarian infantry.

Austrian Italy – The Duchies of Milan and Mantua, and the Principalities of Castiglione and Sabbioneta

Population 1769: 1,300,000 = 8.02% of the monarchy
Area: 7,172 sq. km. = 1.37% of the monarchy

Military Representation
1. Other Ranks: 0.41% of the total.
   Italian infantry 27.67; German infantry 0.08; dragoons 0.03; cuirassiers, Netherlands infantry, Hungarian infantry, hussars, all 0.01
2. NCOs, Corporals and *Gefreyten*: 0.91
3. Non-combatants: 0.05
4. Officers: 3.81
5. Professionals: Surgeons 2.50; chaplains 1.20; provosts 1.53

Former Civilian Trades of Military Personnel as Proportion of Monarchy as Whole
Textile:	0.61
Clothing & Footwear:	1.18
Building & Furnishing:	1.00
Food Processing:	0.17
Metal:	0.59
Mining:	nil
Transport:	1.92
Manufacturing & Processing:	0.46
Medical:	5.45
Students:	0.53
Service:	0.25

Outside the little towns and the noble mansions, scarcely one house in Theresian Hungary owned so much as a pane of glass. It is difficult to conceive that the kingdom formed part of the Habsburg dominions along with the Austrian possessions in northern Italy, with their intensive agriculture, industry and trade, and ancient urban cultures. The Milanese was 'one of the finest and most fertile lands of Italy, in which one encounters not only many beautiful and great cities, but also redoubtable and large fortresses. Moreover the commerce is in a flourishing state, the climate is reasonably temperate and healthy, and the people industrious. For this reason it represents proportionately the most productive of the lands of the Imperial House'.[64] The very small representation of peacetime trades among the soldiers of Austrian Italy merely shows that the folk of that prosperous land had better things to do than enter the army.

By the time of the Seven Years War the Austrian presence in Lombardy still had a century to run, but it had yet to make an impact on regional life comparable with that in the Netherlands, where Austrian rule had arrived just as recently (1714). The Spanish had longstanding connections with this part of the world, which were reinforced when they reoccupied the Milanese in the War of the Austrian Succession, and they enjoyed the support of a significant party among the high aristocracy. The Austrian victory at Piacenza (15 June 1746) assured the military conquest of Lombardy for Maria Theresa, but the task of consolidating Habsburg authority in the wider sense fell to *FZM*. Johann Lucas Count Pallavicini-Centurioni.

Pallavicini's right-hand man was Beltrame Count Cristiani, who was appointed minister plenipotentiary in 1753. He was born to a poor family of Varese, but he gained the patronage of the late *FM*. Traun, who employed him to administer the conquered lands of Parma and Modena, and thus gave him the opportunity to display his outstanding ability. His talents 'not only carried him to the highest positions of honour, but spread his reputation through Italy to such an extent that he became the virtual arbiter of the whole land'.[65] Cristiani undertook a comprehensive tax survey (*cadastre*) of the Austrian territories in Italy, and, after setting up an effective system of provincial and local administration, he co-operated with Kaunitz in transferring the responsibilities of the central Italy *Staatsrath* to the *Hofcanzley* in Vienna. Cristiani died on 3 July 1758, regretted greatly by Maria Theresa.

The Italian troops at their best were 'ambitious and lively, capable of doing excellent service, but they are worthless if they are badly led'.[66] At the outset of her reign Maria Theresa found that Lombardy was represented only by the regiment of Vasquez (No. 48, Luzan from 1755). She therefore commissioned Pallavicini to recruit ten regiments of infantry and three of cavalry, and maintain them from local resources. Pallavicini made virtually no progress, for the genius of the nation was of a different kind, and it is probable that not a single new unit would have taken the field if Antonio Giorgio Marquis Clerici had not been seeking to win favour at court in 1744, and offered to raise a regiment of infantry at his own cost. Within a month he had succeeded in recruiting his regiment (Clerici, No. 44) to a strength of 2,300 men, mostly from a riff-raff of deserters, bandits and the unemployed. Further experience showed that neither Luzan nor Clerici could be recruited from conventional sources, and in December 1757 the two regiments were given the then unique freedom to enlist men for short-term contract service, whether for six years, or for the duration of the war.[67] This arrangement became the prototype for the *Capitulations* whereby almost all recruits were enlisted for the whole army later in the Seven Years War.

However the muster lists show that out of the 1,416 soldiers of the two regiments with identifiable origins, just 27.67 percent were born in Austrian Italy (Lombardy 10.87, Milan city 9.95, Mantua 6.85), almost as many in Görz and Gradisca at 27.18 percent, 4.73 percent in adjacent Austrian territories (Tyrol, Dalmatia, Istria, Trieste), 24.15 percent from the rest of Italy, 2.33 percent from Spain, and the remaining 13.91 percent from a great variety of locations.

The proportions from the 326 qualifying NCOs, corporals and *Gefreyten* show 26.98 percent hailing from Austrian Italy, only 6.13 percent from Görz and Gradisca, 5.52 percent from adjacent Austrian territories, 32.51 percent from the rest of Italy, an interestingly high 17.17 percent from Spain, and 11.65 percent from remaining countries.

The comparable figures relating to 96 officers of the same regiments shows a much higher proportion born in Austrian Italy (39.57 percent, made up of 28.12 from Milan city, 10.41 from Lombardy, 1.04 from Mantua), just 1.04 percent in the adjacent Habsburg territories, 11.45 percent in Spain (again worthy of investigation), and 25.00 percent in the rest of Europe.

All the same, the two Italian national regiments held much less appeal for the gentry of Austrian Italy than did the army as a whole, where natives of Austrian Italy made up 3.81 percent of the officer corps as a whole (that of the two Italian regiments included). 'For the Milanese patrician class, in the Spanish era and the first period of Austrian rule, a military career was considered mostly as an avenue and springboard to a good post in the homeland. In other words, merit acquired in war went towards securing a peaceful niche in the administration of the Duchy of Milan'.[68]

82   INSTRUMENT OF WAR

Military motivation at its lowest was to be found in Pietro Verri, who contrived to have himself appointed a captain in the regiment of Clerici, but complained of his cold reception by Neipperg when he was on his way through Vienna. He believed that the bad manners of the Austrians were due to the influence of the climate, for 'the Italians who stay there any length of time likewise become coarsened. I have also noticed that the men who come from Austria to Lombardy are pretty rough-hewn to begin with, but then become domesticated and civilised in the environment of our country.' Verri then joined the army in the field, and during his brief experience of campaigning he discovered that

> sensibility in general was totally lacking. One day Captain Collin entered my quarters beside himself with mirth. And why? He could scarcely speak for laughing... 'I came across a woman camp follower,' he explained, 'She was carrying a boy child in the barrel on her back, she was leading another by the hand, and she was hanging onto a third which had died when sucking her tits. You'd think the stupid woman would be glad not to have to carry it around any more. But do you know what? That dim-witted creature was so upset she wanted to kill herself!' Now [continues Verri] I ask you, what fine feelings can you expect from someone like that?... You see human nature at its worst among this scum of society, who combine all the brutality of a savage tribe with all that is false and demeaning about a decadent civilisation'.[69]

Against these indictments we may set the extended testimony of Giuseppe Gorani, a young officer of the regiment of Andlau, who had a genuine vocation to the military life, and whom we shall have frequent occasion to quote.

FZM. Octavius Aneas Prince Piccolomini died in 1757, which left *G.d.0* (*FM.* From 1759) Giambattista Serbelloni as the foremost representative of the Italians in the officer corps, and probably the most incapable and disliked of Maria Theresa's generals. Serbelloni retained the command of the army in Saxony until nearly the end of the war, and almost certainly owed his charmed life to his political value to the Habsburgs, as a member of a high noble family of the Milanese.

Lombardy's most positive contribution to the Austrian war effort was at the upper middle level of command. *GFWM.* Bettoni was a more than competent cavalryman, and came from a prosperous bourgeois family which set itself up in some style beside Lake Garda. Two neighbours from the area of Lake Como were notable for their activity and intelligence alike. *FML.* Cajetan Count Stampa, a high noble from Chiavenna, was prized by Prince Charles and the Field Marshals Browne and Daun for his skills in staff work and the handling of cavalry; his reconnaissances contributed greatly to the capture of Finck's corps at Maxen, and he distinguished himself again in the agreeable little victory at Teplitz in 1762. As a man of bourgeois origins *FML.* Joseph Brentano-Cimarolli of Como town did not have the same advantages of birth, and he had to make his name as a colonel of the Warasdiner St. Georger Croats before he became a valued associate of Lacy, and ultimately an almost indispensable corps commander.

Men like these represented the last prominent generation of Lombards in the Austrian service. The *Schema sammentlicher Hohen Generalität* of 1747 had listed 271 field officers, of whom, seven or 2.58 percent, originated in the Milanese. By 1797 there was just one Lombard to be found among the total of 422 generals, and the main reason, as identified by Claudio Donati, was the centralisation of the duchy's administration, which no longer offered an agreeable new career to ex-officers.

Officer Families of Austrian Italy
Allemany, Arese, Barbiano di Belgiojoso, Barbiano di Belgiojoso Este, Boss, Bettoni, Brentano-Cimarolli, Brivio, Brusati, Caznedi, Clerici, Cravenna, Garzia, Guenieri (Mantua), Lanthieri (Mantua), Litta, Luzon (from Spain?), Melza, Messerati, Minutillo, Mugiasco, Novati, Odaleschi, Origo, Orsini, Paggi, Peney (Mantua), Peneralli, Perelli,

Pertusati, Pestalozzi, Pusterla, Roma, Riviera (Mantua), Rusca, Sarti, Serbelloni, Sfontrati, Sommariva, Stampa, Terzago, Trivulzio, Verga, Visconti.

The Austrian Netherlands

Population 1754: No figures available, though it is known that the population was increasing rapidly, and that in 1784 the total stood at 2,272,892, and was distributed among the regions as follows:

Region	%
Flanders:	35.20%
Brabant and Malines:	29.10
Hainault and Tournai:	16.20
Luxembourg:	9.90
Namur:	4.10
Others:	about 1.00

The size of the population in the middle of the 1750s can only be conjectured, but if we put it at about 2,000,000 it would have amounted to about 12.60 percent of that of the monarchy. About 65.20 of the population lived in predominantly Flemish-speaking areas (including Brussels), about 31 percent in predominantly Francophone areas, and 6.5 percent in predominantly German-speaking areas.

Area: 27,571 sq. km. (including Luxembourg at 9,185 sq. km.) = 5.30% of the monarchy.
Military Representation
1. Other Ranks: 5.41% of the total.
   Netherlands dragoons 91.69; Netherlands infantry 84.17; artillery (incl. Netherlandish) 8.49; pioneers, miners and sappers 1.64; German infantry 0.50; Italian infantry 0.28; dragoons (other) 0.19; Hungarian infantry 0.02; cuirassiers 0.01.
2. NCOs, Corporals and *Gefreyten:* 4.60
3. Non-combatants: 5.80
4. Officers: 8.85
5. Professionals: Surgeons 2.52; chaplains 6.02; provosts nil

Former Civilian Trades of Military Personnel as Proportion of Monarchy as Whole

Trade	%
Textile:	6.75
Clothing & Footwear:	8.17
Building & Furnishing:	5.60
Food Processing:	2.93
Metal:	5.18
Mining:	0.84
Transport:	8.91
Manufacturing & Processing:	4.43
medical:	4.41
Students:	1.70
Service:	1.66

The duchies and counties which made up the Austrian Netherlands sprawled in irregular groups from the North Sea eastwards as far as the Rhineland and the Eifel Mountains. These territories corresponded only in part with the territory of the later Belgian state, and were divided into two groups. The western lands comprised the Duchy of Brabant, the counties of Flanders, Hainault (Hennegau) and Namur, the region of Tournai, and the 'free lands' along the coast. The Bishopric of Liège and the Principality of Stavelot-Malmedy were then independent states, and they separated the western territories just mentioned from the eastern group, which consisted of the Duchy of Limburg (extending north-east towards Aachen), the tiny territory of Austrian Guelders, and the extensive Duchy of Luxembourg, which took in the area of the present Grand Duchy, most of the modern Belgian province of Luxembourg, and the fringes of the German Eifel.

Austrian rule as such dated only from the peace settlements of Utrecht in 1713, and Rastatt and Baden in 1714. However the association with the Habsburgs sprang from the reign of Emperor Maximilian I (1493–1519), and Maria Theresa regarded herself as the inheritor of the historic Netherlandish authority of the Spanish Habsburgs,[70] and thus of military traditions engendered by continuous warfare since the beginning of the Eighty Years War in 1565. The old Francophone military aristocracy of the southern Netherlands responded in kind, and their allegiance to Maria Theresa was only strengthened by the depredations of the French in the period of their conquest and occupation (1744–9). The first of the 'Austrian' troops to reenter Brussels in 1749 were those of the Netherlands national regiments, and Prince Charles of Lorraine made his entry as *General Statthalter* (governor-general) on 23 April, to the acclamation of the crowds.

Every province of the Netherlands regarded itself as a semi-independent entity, defended by its powerful *États* and its jealously-guarded privileges. Kaunitz knew the temper of these people from his time as *ministre plénipotentiare,* and under his guidance the Austrians respected the prickly sensibilities

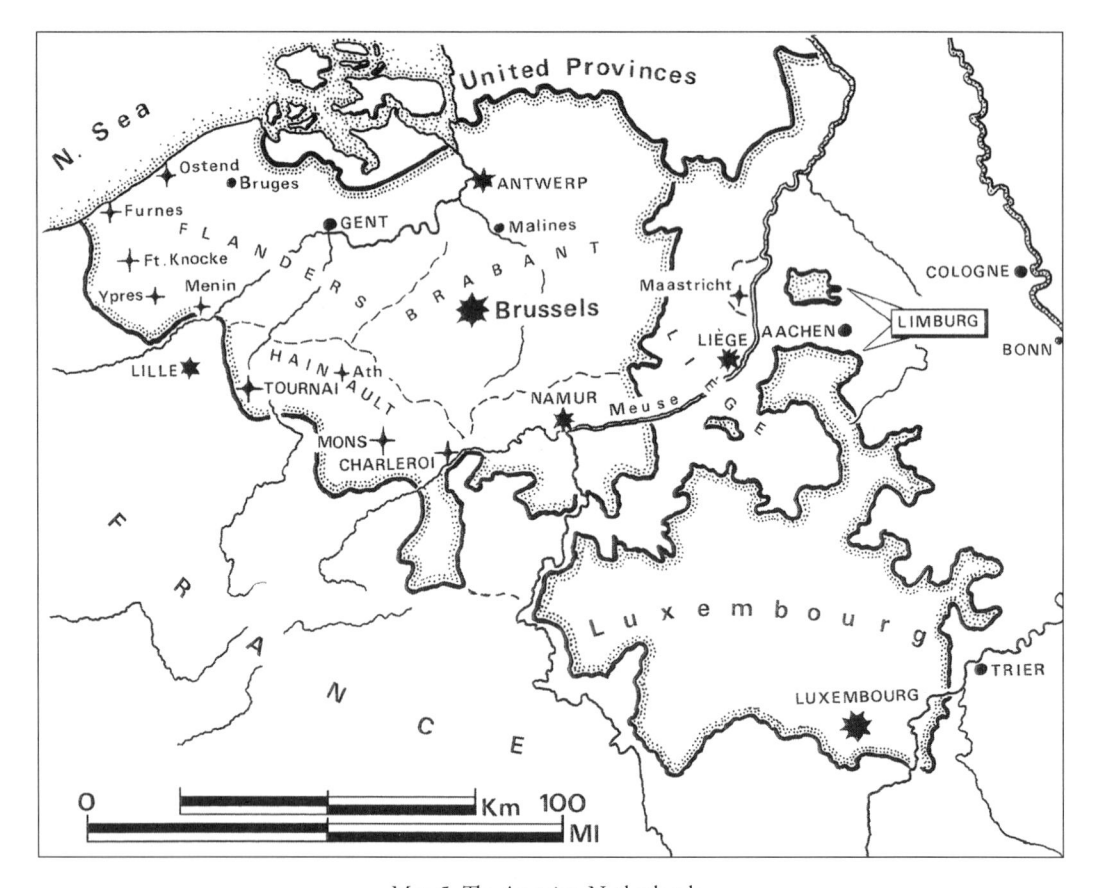

Map 5 The Austrian Netherlands.

of the Netherlanders, and dealt with them through sympathetic and long-serving intermediaries. The affable Prince Charles proved far more successful as Netherlandish *General-Statthalter* (1744–80) than as commander in the field, and he could happily leave the hard work to the successive presidents of his *Conseil-Privé* (A. De Steenhalt [1739–58] and the outstandingly able Irishman Patrick Francis de Neny [1758–83]), and to the overall head of administration, the Austrian *minstre plénipotentiare* Johann Carl Philipp Cobenzl [1753–70]). The Austrians had been spurred into new action when they found how efficient the French had been at managing the Netherlands during their occupation, and this territory soon became a showpiece of Habsburg administration.

The Netherlandish contributions to the cause of Maria Theresa were on balance far more substantial than those of Austrian Italy, and in terms of finance exceeded those of Hungary. Kaunitz reckoned the peacetime revenues accruing to Austria from the Netherlands at five million florins per annum, or enough to maintain 25,000 troops,[71] an interesting equation which equates 200 florins to one man. The Netherlands contribution to the extraordinarily expenditure reached 53 million, in revenues, loans, gifts and processed subsidies, which was the equivalent of nearly half the sum of 115 million raised from the German Hereditary Lands. The Netherlands contribution in terms of manpower was at least as impressive, and it will be outlined shortly.

In the War of the Austrian Succession the French had broken through the belt of the Netherlands Barrier Fortresses in 1744–6, and progressed triumphantly into Dutch territory in 1747 and 1748. In the Seven Years War, however the French became active allies of Maria Theresa, and took over much of the burden of the defence of the Netherlands against possible British attack.

All of this – the contributions which the Netherlands made to the House of Austria in terms of money, credit, financial expertise and troops, and the support now being received from France – was still not enough to make up for the geographical gulf which yawned between the Netherlands and the core area of the Austrian state. As early as 1732 a travel writer remarked that the French and the Dutch were so situated that they would have been able to derive full benefit from the possession of the Netherlands. The Austrians, on the other hand, were forced to assert their authority by maintaining the *Statthalter* in vice-regal style. The distance also gave rise to 'the very costly and very inconvenient business of marching regiments to the Netherlands from, for example, Bohemia, Austria or Hungary. It is in addition more expensive to maintain troops there than in Austria, Bohemia or so on, on account of the higher allowances and pay – which are still scarcely enough to allow the troops to subsist'.[72]

These arguments were given weight by the events of the 1740s, when the Barrier Fortresses fell so easily to the French, and when Prussia emerged as Austria's most deadly enemy. In May 1756, when the Netherlands regiments were hard at work drilling, *FM.* Carl Joseph Batthyány argued that on balance the Netherlands constituted a source of weakness, whereas 'the situation of Silesia means that its reconquest would consolidate and concentrate the inner strength of the monarchy. Silesia is the nursery of the army's best recruits; once in our hands it would free us of constant anxiety concerning our most dangerous enemy, and alleviate the endless inconveniences and damage relating to the commerce of all the Hereditary Lands'[73]. Kaunitz was therefore not alone when he maintained that the possession of the Netherlands must be of secondary importance compared with the confrontation with Prussia, which concerned 'the maintenance of the Catholic religion, the Imperial authority in Germany, the constitution of the *Reich,* the welfare – and I make bold to say – the future existence of the exalted House of Austria'.[74] These words did not come easily, for Kaunitz had served in Brussels as *ministre plénipotentiare* in the 1740s, and he knew that the Netherlands were 'a most precious jewel' of the House of Habsburg.[75]

The Netherlands were by far the most urbanised and proto-industrialised of the possessions of Maria Theresa. About one-quarter of the population lived in towns, of which the most significant were Brussels (population in 1784 about 75,000), Antwerp (just over 50,000), Ghent (45,000) Bruges (30,000) and Tournai (the largest Walloon town, at 26,000).

Textiles were still the most significant of the industrial products. Of these linen (employing about 80 percent of the textile workers) comprised the largest single sector, and flourished in Flanders in particular. The processing of cotton was growing fast, and received new impetus from the development of cotton printing at Ghent from 1750, and the foundation of a royal factory at Tournai in 1760. The silk industry was small, and confined to Antwerp, while the historic strength of wool in Flanders and Hainault was undermined by competition from Britain and elsewhere.

The transition to the next stage of the Industrial Revolution, from the proto-industrial (where most of the basic processes were farmed out to domestic workers) to the centralised and truly industrial, was already advanced in the south-eastern provinces, where it was promoted not only by the sources of iron ore, water power and timber, but very significantly by the exploitation of seams of coal in the region of the *Borinage* around Mons. By the middle 1750s 60,000 tons of coal per annum were being exported along the Haine, and it provided a cheap and virtually inexhaustible substitute for wood, which was consumed at a rate of 5.9 cubic metres for every ton of iron produced. Luxembourg specialised in the production of pig-iron, while manufactured goods were worked up in the forges of Charleroi.

The evidence from the muster lists must be treated with the usual caution, for the most active trades were probably under-represented. Thus very few soldiers are entered as former coal miners, whereas we know that mining for coal was flourishing in regions of Hainault.

Former Civilian Trades of Netherlands Soldiers (key trades only)

1. Textiles: 22.84% of the monarchy as a whole Representation by Region of the Netherlands Total

Flanders:	32.71
Limburg:	24.88
Hainault and Tournai:	15.20
Luxembourg:	7.87
Brussels:	6.45
Brabant and Malines (excl. Brussels)	4.60
Namur:	0.92

2. Metal & Mining: 5.39% of the monarchy as a whole Representation by Region of the Netherlands Total

Luxembourg:	42.30
Hainault and Tournai:	21.15
Brabant and Malines (excl. Brussels)	15.38
Flanders:	9.61
Limburg, Namur:	3.84 each
Brussels, Antwerp:	1.92 each

3. Manufacturing and Processing: 5.81% of the monarchy as a whole Representation by Region of the Netherlands Total

Flanders:	23.21
Luxembourg:	19.64
Hainault and Tournai:	16.07
Brussels, Namur:	10.71 each
Brabant and Malines (excl. Brussels), Antwerp:	7.14 each
Limburg:	5.35

Even in the Netherlands most people lived in the country and laboured principally on the land. The condition of the ordinary countryfolk was in decline, though there were signs of prosperity among their betters: 'Nowadays when you take a walk through a number of the rural areas in our country you notice that most of the surviving older buildings go back to the 18th century; moreover the quality of the construction, even in relatively modest buildings, shows a care and refinement which can only derive from the material prosperity of those for whom they were built'.[76] The historians of Belgium look back on the 18th century as a golden age, which still counts for something, even if the picture has been over-romanticised.

In the Seven Years War the Netherlands furnished the Austrian army with four regiments of national infantry (d'Arberg, de Ligne [Claude], Los Rios and Sachsen-Gotha), one regiment of dragoons (de Ligne [Ferdinand]), and a corps of artillery. According to our selected muster lists the total of other ranks came to 5,250 men, or 5,416 if we include the Netherlanders serving throughout the army. Out of these 5,416 the provinces and cities were represented as follows:

Luxembourg:	32.69
Flanders:	16.80
Hainault and Tournai:	16.00
Brabant and Malines (excl. Brussels):	13.60
Brussels:	7.90
Limburg:	4.76
Antwerp:	4.46
Namur:	3.74

These figures give little clue as to the considerable variations to be found between the Netherlandish national regiments and corps as such (See Appendix III: Origins of Netherlandish Private Soldiers). Thus the artillery corps and the infantry regiments of Claude de Ligne and Sachsen-Gotha turn out to be strongly Luxembourgeois in character, d'Arberg less so, Los Rios as Brabancon, and the de Ligne Dragoons a regiment of Hainault and Tournai. In proportion to the population it transpires that Luxembourg, Hainault with Tournai and Limburg were over-represented in the army, and Flanders, Brabant and Namur under-represented.

Drawing on detailed local knowledge, and a wider spread of muster lists across the century, Belgian historians have established that about two-thirds of the soldiers were recruited from towns, which would make the Netherlands troops by far the most urbanised of the monarchy. This process was probably swollen by the existence of pockets of unemployment, as among the textile workers of Brussels and Antwerp. Economic hardship may not necessarily be the whole story, for the existence of garrisons in the towns of this heavily-militarised region was probably an incentive to local recruiting, as was the case in France at the same period. Military values must also be allowed a place. The textile industry was suffering from competition in Limburg as well as Flanders, but in the latter case the population was reckoned to lack *l'esprit militaire,* and less inclined to consider the option of armed service than the Germanic population of Luxembourg, or the Celto-Belgic Walloons of Hainault, Tournai, Limburg, Namur and western Luxembourg.

Our figures reinforce the conclusion of Joseph Ruwet that in absolute terms, and still more in terms of proportion, the stock of the 'Netherlands' private soldiers was drawn more heavily from Luxembourg than any other region. Ruwet further establishes that soldiers from the German-speaking districts (eastern Luxembourg and eastern Limburg) were much less inclined to desert than were the Flemings, and that in 1786–7 the stature of the troops from the south-eastern Netherlands as a whole (Luxembourg, Limburg, Namur, Hainault and Tournai) was considerably greater than of those from Flanders'.[77]

When all remotely doubtful cases have been excluded, it is possible to identify 3,984 private soldiers of the national regiments and artillery in our chosen muster lists by place of birth as well as type of surname, as in the table below.

'Netherlands' private soldiers by place of birth and type of surname

Place	Type of Surname: French	Flemish	German	Italian/Spanish
Brabant and Malines (excl. Brussels):	38.44	59.07	1.15	1.32
Flanders:	27.85	70.89	0.13	1.11
Hainault and Tournai:	81.50	16.78	0.71	0.99
Limburg:	61.93	32.38	5.68	nil
Namur:	87.95	10.84	0.60	0.60
Luxembourg:	66.41	16.60	16.88	0.09
Brussels:	36.47	59.11	1.17	3.23
Antwerp:	18.55	79.63	nil	1.80

The Prince de Ligne liked to think that the ordinary Netherlands soldiers combined the cheerfulness of the French in a happy association with the steadiness of the Germans under fire. The Swedish observer Armfeldt was distinctly less complimentary. He allowed that they were exceptionally brave, 'but that is the only good thing you can say about them, for they are probably unequalled in the business of plundering. They set a bad example in this respect to entire armies at a time, and they are much given to arguing against orders'.[78]

Everything therefore depended on the Netherlanders' response to the tone and example of their commanders. The Hungarian general Nádasdy became their *'Papa Moustache'*,[79] while the Netherlands dragoons at Hochkirch exacted a terrible revenge on the Prussian Gensd'armes, after the enemy regimental commander had killed their colonel Jacques de Thiennes by a pistol shot.[80] In the camp at Schurz on 2 May 1759 the de Ligne infantry were brigaded with one regiment each of Hungarians, Italians and Germans, and Charles-Joseph de Ligne records that 'General Siskovics frequently drilled this collection of four nations in their four different languages, which he spoke with great fluency. The field marshal [Daun] saw the units of the army pass in successive review under his eyes, and when it was our turn he seemed very pleased. I make bold to say that the Walloons surpassed all the others in the speed and accuracy of their deployments and their marching in general.[81]

It is perhaps worth noting that the regiment of de Ligne nevertheless had a relatively high rate of desertion, coming 13th out of the 56 infantry regiments of the army, and only just ahead of the disreputable regiment of Clerici. The regiment of d'Arberg showed up well, coming joint 41st with Waldeck, while the regiments of Los Rios and Sachsen-Gotha must have been excellent units, for they had the lowest rates of desertion in the entire army.

Foreigners made up about 15 percent of the effectives of the 'Netherlands' private soldiers. In our muster lists they were represented in the following proportions:

    French: 38.25%
        (including 14.55 of the total from Lorraine)
    German: 37.52
        (including 10.70 of the total from Trier)
    Liège: 14.86
    Italy: 3.32

Stavelot:	2.70
Switzerland:	2.59
Avignon:	0.72

When we turn to the other grades of the Netherlanders, we find that men from the larger south-eastern provinces likewise predominate.

Altogether 388 Netherlands non-combatant supporting staff may be identified throughout the army, and they came from the following provinces and cities:

Hainault and Tournai:	28.09%
Luxembourg:	26.03
Brussels:	13.65
Flanders:	12.88
Brabant and Malines (exc. Brussels)	8.24
Antwerp:	3.60
Limburg:	3.09

Of these men, 280 are identifiable by type of surname, namely:
French:	60.71%
Flemish:	31.42
German:	6.07
Italian/Spanish:	1.78

In the army as a whole we encounter 754 Netherlands NCOs, Corporals and *Gefreyten* who may be identified by place of birth:
Luxembourg:	22.01%
Hainault and Tournai:	20.68
Flanders:	16.97
Brussels:	13.92
Brabant and Malines (excl. Brussels):	13.39
Namur:	5.70
Antwerp:	3.84
Limburg:	3.44

Five-hundred-and-seventy-six of these people are identifiable by surname:
French:	63.36%
Flemish:	31.94
German:	3.64
Italian/Spanish:	1.04

By applying the same criteria to the Netherlands regimental officers of the entire army we find 346 individuals who are identifiable by birth:

Hainault and Tournai:	33.81%
(of whom 18.49 of the total born in Mons)	
Brussels:	18.20
Luxembourg:	17.05
Flanders:	10.40
Brabant and Malines (excl. Brussels):	9.53

Antwerp: 5.20
Namur: 4.04
Limburg: 1.73

Officers (all army) identifiable by type of surname:
French: 58.02%
Flemish: 23.72
German: 12.04
Italian/Spanish: 6.20

Thus the Dutch-speaking Flemings held themselves largely at a distance from the officer corps. The nobles of Luxembourg were divided by bitter antagonisms between the German-speakers and the Francophones, and between the old and the new nobility. The Luxembourgeois contingent among the officers was respectable enough, but it represented only 66 percent of the duchy's noble families which happened to have had men in military service; all the other families, or 34 percent, had officers in foreign services, of which the French was reckoned to be the most attractive.

More revealing in their way are the numbers of Netherlands officers with noble titles in relation to the noble officers from elsewhere. Netherlanders made up 9.77 percent of the noble officers of the army as a whole (second only to those of the *Reich,* at 22.08), but a very considerable 17.84 percent of the noble officers from the Habsburg territories by themselves, and they were thus well in the lead over their nearest competitors, the Bohemian nobles at 10.02 percent. Here it is worth mentioning that the Netherlanders not only supplied almost the entire officer corps of their 'national' regiments, but were to be found throughout the army, as witness the careers of *GFWM.* Carl Amadei, Lieutenant-Colonel Emanuel Alexandre Franquet, Major Wilhelm Joseph comte Coswarem de Nyel, Lieutenant-Colonel Philipp Baron Souhay, and Colonel Franz Carl Nesse.

The Netherlanders had their grandees who matched in proportion to those of the other lands of the monarchy. *GFWM.* Charles-Elizabeth duc d'Ursel (1717–75) was a big man in the land of Brabant, where he was Hereditary Marshal, but had little claim to military fame apart from commanding (not very well) a column at Hochkirch. The d'Arenbergs of Château Enghien were more important, both as ducal grandees and 'dukes' in the old warlike sense, as leaders of armies. *FM.* Leopold-Philippe-Charles-Joseph was famed as the victor at Dettingen (1743), but insisted that his son Charles-Marie-Raymond (1721–78) must undergo a programme of rigorous and systematic military training, which included an instructive spell as supervisor of a hospital. The younger d'Arenberg repaid this investment by becoming *FML.* in 1755, *FZM.* in 1758, and gaining the *Grosskreuz* of the Military Order of Maria Theresa for his part in the storm of Schweidnitz in 1757; his standing in his homeland was recognised by his appointments as governor of Mons and captain-general of Hainault. These d'Arenbergs are easily confused with the d'Arbergs de Valenzin, whose leading representative at the time of the Seven Years War was *FZM.* comte Charles (1705–68), *Inhaber* of one of the regiments of Netherlands infantry.

FZM. Charles Duke of Arenberg, 1721–78 (Military Academy, Wiener Neustadt).

FM. Daun had a number of talented Netherlanders in his entourage, among whom *G.d.C.* Joseph-Charles comte d'Ayasasa (1713–79) kept him up to date with the state of intrigues in Vienna. Jean-Pierre baron Beaulieu de Marconnay (1725–1819) of Judoigne in Brabant is remembered in history as the 71 year-old *FZM.* who was beaten by Bonaparte at Lodi (1796), but he did service in the prime of his life to Daun as captain then (from 1760) lieutenant-colonel in the General Staff, and accompanied his chief to most of the actions of the Seven Years War. Beaulieu was a talented artist (a useful accomplishment in a staff officer), and he furnished the sketch after which Johann Christian Brand (1722–95) painted his famous battlescape of Hochkirch.

However the Netherlands officer corps is remarkable not so much for its well-placed or well-connected individuals as for the mass of its noble officers, who represented a warrior squierarchy comparable with that of Prussia. It is remembered chiefly through the writings of Charles-Joseph prince de Ligne (1735–1814), 'the last flower of the Walloons.' He was born on 12 May 1735 to a princess of the family of Salm, and the tough *FM.* Claude-Lamoral Prince de Ligne. As a child Charles-Joseph heard the battle of Fontenoy from the family chateau of Beloeil, and he was taken to see the sieges of SaintGhislain and Ath. His formal education was entrusted to a series of eccentric tutors, who only succeeded in sharpening his dislike of physics, chemistry and mathematics, but his passion for writing was finally awakened by a Jesuit.

At the age of 20 de Ligne obeyed instructions to marry the 14-year-old Françoise Princess of Liechtenstein, and he deserted his bride in the course of their wedding night in order to go hunting: 'In those times it was not fashionable to be a good husband or father'.[82] Charles-Joseph was already an ensign in the family regiment, and he remained with it in the campaigns of the Seven Years War. He was the only captain of the regiment to survive the battle of Leuthen in 1757, he rose to major before the end of the year, lieutenant-colonel in 1758, and in 1759 to colonel-commandant. His father was unimpressed: 'Sir, to have you as my son should have been misfortune enough. Now I have the further misfortune of having you as colonel'.[83]

The Prince de Ligne spent the second half of his life mostly in Vienna, where his wit, ostentation and hospitality made him a leading member of society. He died on 13 December 1814. People said it was as if he had arranged the event to cause a sensation at the Congress of Vienna, and in due course his military funeral eclipsed the official entertainments which had been arranged for the delegates.

Netherlands Officer Families
Antwerp: Peter, de Piza
Brabant: Beaulieu de Marconnay, Bergeick, Bryas (Pryas), Cuistele, Cuukel van Moulandt, Herrisem, Looz-Coswarem (two counts), d'Ursel, Villers *Brussels:* Battin, Castelli Sempietro, Clavet, Comptich, Dalsaie, Draeck, Dysseparth, Gavre, Kerpen, Lannoy, Mercy d'Argenteau, Niccolaerz, Spangen, Stain, Vanderstegen, Werde, Wontier/Woutier
Hainault: d'Arenberg, d'Argout, d'Aubleux, d'Ayasasa, Baillet de Latour, Blas/Blais, Blaregnies, Bournonville, Clerfayt, Colins de Ham, Desandrouins, Fassignies de Gaillard, Genimi-Mole, Lahamayde, de Lathe de la Motte, Ligne, Mentem, Murray de Melgum, Robaul de Beaurieux, Sousleموustiez, Spangen, Trouvain, Vinchant de Gontroeul
Flanders: d'Ankerhielm, Bleckhem, Bouquet, Gheus, de Grass, de Lalaing d'Audenarde, Liederkerke, Moitelle, Nieulandt, Postelberg, Riesse, Thiennes, Wilsdorf
Limburg: d'Arberg
Luxembourg: Althann (two counts), Alcaini, Bryas, Conti, Deneufmanil, Duplessis, Hauden, Mohr von Waldt, Moncheux, Rouvroy, Sebottendorf, Soulevre, Saint-Ignon
Namur: Bibaus de Harsin, Ferrare, Lamede, Louberville d'Ermeton
Other Netherlands noble officers, places of birth to be identified: Feichsem, Flope/Flopen, Floen de Adelscron, Los Rios, Puebla

(N.B. Charles Gobert comte d'Aspremont-Lynden, Baron de Froidecourt (1689–1772) was not technically a Netherlander, having been born at Château Froidecourt in Liège. After spells in the Dutch and Spanish service he entered the Austrian army in 1722, rising to *FM.* in 1754. He was much respected and much consulted).

Further Empires

The Reich *(German Empire)*

Military Representation
1. Other Ranks: 11.95% of the total.
German infantry 18.94; pioneers, miners and sappers 9.98; dragoons 6.69; cuirassiers 6.05; artillery 5.66; Netherlands infantry 5.07; Netherlands dragoons 4.98; Italian infantry 3.37; Hungarian infantry 0.77; hussars 0.15
2. NCOs, Corporals and *Gefreyten:* 22.93
3. Non-combatants: 24.12
4. Officers: 17.84
5. Professionals: Surgeons 29.11; chaplains 10.84; provosts 27.69

(N.B. For the purposes of this section, the above figures include the small representation from Freiburg and the German enclaves, but not those from the 'Austrian' part of Vorder-Österreich. Prussian Silesia is excluded, and will be treated separately).

The perspectives of historical hindsight are particularly distorting when we try to gain an overview of Austria's relations with the states of Germany in the middle of the 18th century. Talk of 'Austria's German mission' (which undoubtedly existed) is likely to conjure up a vision of the Heldenplatz in Vienna in 1938. It is probably just as misleading to imagine the *Reich* as a flawed precursor of the united Germany which was called into existence in 1871. After all the *Reich* enjoyed a long and successful life in its own right as a loose supra-state community, and was the setting of the first half of the 'great German century' (1750–1850), a time of unprecedented cultural, intellectual and scientific advance.

In geopolitical terms, the most significant consequence of the rivalry between the Prussian Hohenzollerns and the Habsburgs was to push the centre of gravity of the Austrian state to the east, and thus away from Germany. In the 1750s the Austrian body politic, and, to a greater extent still, the Austrian army nevertheless wore a predominantly German character. Maria Theresa could laugh at the antique trappings of the *Reich,* but she called the expulsion of the French from Germany and Italy in the last war as a *vaterländisch* mission, and she told her children that they must never forget their German language and ways at foreign courts.

Although Germany was notoriously fragmented into more than 200 states of disparate size and constitution, the idea of a common Empire and a leading role for an elected Emperor still held force in the middle of the 18th century. The Emperor appointed commissioners to represent him whenever the central *Reichstag* was convened, and at the regular meetings of the *Creise* – the collections of states which had been grouped together by Emperor Maximilian I for purposes of convenience. Intractable legal matters were still being referred to the *Reichshofrath* in Vienna, and Austria's dealings with the Empire were still managed by the *Reichs-Vizecanzler* Rudolph Joseph Colloredo.

In the Seven Years War German armed support for the Austrians took the following forms:

1. The joint *Reichs-Executions Armee* (*Reichsarmee* for short), constituted in virtue of the declaration of a *Reichsexecution* against Frederick by the Regensburg *Reich*stag on 17 January 1757;
2. Six regiments of Saxon cavalry, which had escaped from enforced Prussian service after the capitulation of the Saxon army in 1756;
3. The battalion of Anhalt-Zerbst, and three regiments of auxiliary infantry (Mainz, and Blau-and Roth-Würzburg) which were maintained on the Austrian establishment. A number of contingents from further states which were provided on a temporary and subsidised basis;
4. Finally, and most importantly, the German officers and troops who served as organic personnel in the Austrian army.

In most essentials the states of the *Reich* remained sovereign entities, and, lacking any means of compulsion except the crude and unreliable instrument of the *Reichsarmee,* the Emperor (Francis Stephen from 1745) could get his way only through persuasion and moral authority. The loose construction of the *Reich* therefore offered prime opportunities for foreign powers to intervene in the affairs of Germany.

In times past the French had formed working alliances with the Bavaria, Saxony, Cologne, the Palatinate and smaller states, and with Prussia the 1740s, and so established a countervailing force to the Austrians within the Empire, bolstered by France's position as a guarantor (with Sweden) of the Peace of Westphalia (1648). In the Seven Years War the French were using their influence in favour of the Austrians, but by then Prussia was presenting a challenge far more serious than any which had been offered by Louis XIV, because Frederick was threatening to sunder the community along religious lines. Frederick's base of power was considerable in its own right, consisting of East Prussia (not part of the *Reich*), a large central core formed of Brandenburg, Pomerania, Magdeburg and newly-conquered Silesia, and Minden, Ravensburg, Mark, East Frisia and other enclaves in north-western Germany.

The new Austrian connection with France was bought at the heavy price of alienating Hanover. Not only did this considerable electorate now stand in the ranks of the enemies of the alliance, but northern Germany was opened to the power of British finance, which was able to create an effective force of British, Brunswick, Lippe-Bückeburg and Hessen-Cassel troops around the core of Hanover's fine little army. Old Landgraf Wilhelm III of Hessen-Cassel had needed little enough prompting, for his son the Erbprinz Friedrich had converted to Catholicism in 1749, and to compound his crime he had succeeded in keeping it secret until 1754; Kaunitz tried to detach the Landgraf from his British paymasters in the middle of the war, but the enterprise collapsed early in 1759, for well-meaning people had gone behind the Landgraf's back to open negotiations, and the British had renewed their contract for the hired Hessian troops on favourable terms'.[84]

Religious friction, combined with the comings and goings of Austrian troops, aggravated the tensions between Vienna and a group of smaller German states on the approaches to Bohemia. The Principality of Bayreuth was ruled by a branch of the Hohenzollerns, and the dynastic connection with the Berlin line had been cemented when Markgraf Friedrich had married Wilhelmine, the favourite sister of Crown Prince Frederick of Prussia. The Austrians paid less and less regard to Bayreuth sensibilities as the war went on, and in September 1762 the margrave was moved to complain that Major Otto and his corps of 145 Austrian Jäger had descended on the little town of Bayersdorf at the express command of Johann Wenzel Baron Widmann, the Imperial minister to the Circle of Franconia, and the band had proceeded to exact bread and fodder without payment. It was, claimed the margrave, 'particularly painful to a prince of the Empire who has on every occasion demonstrated his devotion to the Imperial Court'.[85]

94 INSTRUMENT OF WAR

Map 6 The German Reich.

The Austrians were at first full of tact and consideration in their dealings with Margrave Carl Wilhelm of Brandenburg-Ansbach, for Ansbach had it in its power to combine with Bayreuth to check the Bishop of Würzburg (who was offering a corps of auxiliaries to the Austrians), and it was important to have a Protestant prince as a friend, 'and so reinforce the principle already established in the agreement [with Würzburg], namely that we have no religious ambitions in view, but wish only to promote our security and the maintenance of the Imperial authority in the *Reich*'.[86] The margrave's own troops were not particularly good, but for wider political reasons the Austrians signed an agreement to subsidise a corps of Ansbach auxiliaries on 2 April 1757. Two years later operational considerations were more important, and Widmann went to Nuremberg to ask the Circle of Franconia to supply the local Austrian forces with flour, and to furnish the necessary transport. Widmann was aware that the margrave would prove recalcitrant, but he also knew that Austria would command the majority of votes in the Circle, and so force him to give way.[87]

The Austrians meted out the same treatment to the lands of Duke Friedrich of Sachsen-Gotha. Friedrich calculated that from the middle of January to the end of September 1761 the Austrian exactions from his two principalities of Gotha and Altenburg amounted to the equivalent of 176,417 florins. He was unable to meet further Austrian demands, and so on 1 December an Austrian *Executions-Commando* of 150 cavalry set about ransacking the stores at Camburg, Eisenburg and in the princely *Residenz-Schloss* at Altenburg (see p. 359).[88]

Inside the German states the causes of Maria Theresa, her allies, and Frederick were being argued with some passion. In the princely house of Dessau the 'Prussian' Prince Dietrich was at odds with his brother the 'Saxon' Prince Eugen, just as the family of young Goethe in Frankfurt was riven by the bitter feud between his father and grandfather. The kind of language which was employed on such occasions came to light in 1758, after the retired Austrian officer Behm had written to Maria Theresa to tell her that he had served the House of Austria for 33 years, and risen in the regiment of Browne from private soldier to captain, until ill-health had compelled him to retire in 1755, when she had been good enough to allow him to sell his company and leave the army with the rank of lieutenant-colonel. Behm had duly settled in his native Bayreuth, but instead of being allowed to live out his days in peace, he had been subjected to a bombardment of insults from one of the margrave's officials, Heinrich Nicolaus Bischoff. This individual disparaged the quality of the Austrian troops, gloated over their defeat at Prague, and explained away Daun's victory at Kolin by saying 'the blind hen has been pecking around, and now at last she's found a pea.' Behm encountered Bischoff again at a dinner party laid on by a mutual acquaintance, and when Behm was taking his leave the official rounded on him: 'Now listen here, you dog, you *Scheisskerl*, if I meet you somewhere else I'll hit you so hard they will have to carry you away!' Maria Theresa took the threat seriously enough to pass the letter to the *Reichshofcanzley*, which intervened to extend its protection to Behm.[89]

It was contrary to the Austrian interests to see the *Reich* split along religious lines, 'for then Your Imperial Majesty would be in danger of losing a good number of your officers and generals, or at leastbe unable to trust the majority of them'.[90] The muster lists reveal the extent of the peril.

Among a total of 846 regimental officers from the *Reich* (from colonel-commandant downwards) the Catholics numbered 70.92 percent, Lutherans 27.65 percent, and Calvinists 1.47 percent, which brings the non-Catholic representation to nearly one-third. Altogether 798 German regimental officers are identified clearly by both religion and place of birth, and (measured as a percentage of the total Lutheran and Calvinist presence in this group), the largest numbers of Protestant officers were put forth by:

Saxony:	7.04%
Breisgau (Austrian territory):	5.13
Swabia:	4.26
Franconia:	4.13
Bavaria:	3.88
Bayreuth, Mainz:	3.63 each
Westphalia:	3.88
Ansbach, Thuringia:	3.00 each

Among the 1,807 non-combatant supporting staff from the *Reich* 83.42 percent were Catholics, 16.18 percent Lutherans, and just 0.38 percent Calvinists.

The total of the German other ranks stood at 13,659, and the religions were represented as follows:

Arm of Service	Catholics	Lutherans	Calvinists
Infantry:	75.52	22.22	2.25
Cuirassiers & Dragoons:	93.77	5.95	0.27
Rest of Army:	91.02	8.16	0.81
Grand Total:	77.75	20.22	2.22

The cuirassiers and dragoons were not only the most 'Austrian' of the arms of service, but also, on this evidence, the most Catholic of the troops recruited in the *Reich*.

When the Austrian representative attended the election of the Bishop of Salzburg in 1753, he was under instructions to offer general support to the Salzburg authorities in their ambition to rid the land of heresy, but impress that 'this aim would be achieved all the more rapidly by discreet and skilled missionaries, who would wean the people from their errors through endless patience, love, and mature reflection'.[91]

For that reason the Austrians were more embarrassed than pleased by the appeal which baroque Catholicism held for the full-blooded princes of Germany. Elector Friedrich August ('Augustus the Strong') of Saxony had succumbed to Jesuitical wiles in 1697, unabashed by the fact that his state was the cradle of the Lutheran Reformation. Hereditary Prince Friedrich of Hessen-Cassel converted in 1749 without the knowledge of the Austrians (above), who did what they could to repair the damage when the deed became public five years later. The Hanoverians took fright, and relations between Landgraf Wilhelm and his apostate son were so strained that Vienna decided to send General Johann Franz Bretlach, a recent convert to Catholicism, to Cassel on behalf of the Emperor to act as intermediary.

Bretlach's mission was in vain. However an agreeable number of Protestant princes or Protestant states gave active support to the Habsburgs, or at least refused to be drawn into the Prussian-Hanoverian nexus. The Duchy of Holstein maintained its independence, with the moral support of the Russians. The neighbouring duchy of Mecklenburg declared against Frederick, and as a result was subject to ravages far more ruthless than anything essayed by the Austrians in the Protestant states of Franconia. The eccentric Prince Friedrich August of Anhalt-Zerbst (father of Catherine the Great) conducted a personal vendetta against Frederick, and was *Inhaber* of a good regiment of cuirassiers (No. 25) in the Austrian service, and a not very good battalion of infantry. Duke Carl Eugen of Württemberg committed his troops to Maria Theresa's cause enthusiastically, even if he was unable to guarantee the goodwill of his men, 'since, as Your Majesty is aware, all the people here – with the signal exception of me as their master – are good Prussians'.[92]

More valuable in every way was the support given to the *Reich* and the Habsburg cause by Landgraf Ludwig VIII of Hessen-Darmstadt, who was a Protestant of impeccable credentials, but also firmly *Kaisertreu*. His second son, Prince Georg Wilhelm, was recalled from the Prussian service, and was the best general of the *Reichsarmee*.

Saxony was in more than one respect the key state of Germany in the Seven Years War. It was large (21,000 sq. km.), heavily populated (two million), economically advanced, and it was an active theatre of operations throughout. For most of the time the greater part of Saxony was in the grip of the Prussians, who plundered the electorate ruthlessly for its rich resources of cash, fodder, cattle, horses and recruits, and yet never lost the fundamental support of the people, who were fellow-Lutherans. The same did not necessarily apply to the Saxon troops, who remained loyal to their exiled sovereign August III (king of Poland and elector of Saxony), and bore a grudge against the Prussians for the massacre of the Saxons at the battle of Hohenfriedberg on 4 June 1745; most of the Saxon units escaped from enforced Prussian service after the capitulation of Pirna in 1756, and the cavalrymen at least were happy to pursue their blood feud alongside the Austrians.

Maria Theresa and her generals were inhibited in their dealings with the Saxons out of regard for the sensibilities of their Lutheran allies, and also because they needed to remind the Germans that it was Frederick who had broken the peace of the *Reich* by invading Saxony in 1756. Maria Theresa told Prince Charles of Lorraine that in operational matters he must accede as far as possible to the wishes of the Saxons, 'and in this respect I must ask you to bear in mind that the more the King of Prussia's career of violence in Saxony has drawn down a general disapprobation, and served to multiply the ranks of his enemies, the more the interests of my service demand that we must on every occasion demonstrate an active commitment to liberating the land in question'.[93]

The Saxon authorities therefore felt free to torment the Austrians with complaints of a kind that they would never have dared to address to the Prussians. They took offence at crimes as modest as poaching, and the cutting of firewood by Austrian soldiers in the Poisten-Wald, the Dresdener Heide and the Moritzburger-Wald.[94]

Maria Theresa nevertheless retained the assistance or at least the fundamental goodwill of most of the *Reich* – a support which was based variously on traditions of service and loyalty, religious affinity or political expediency. Historic French connections inside the *Reich,* and with Bavaria in particular, now worked in favour of the Austrians; likewise the ecclesiastical states, the Teutonic Order and the great land-owning monasteries looked to Austria for protection against 'secularisation' by their neighbours. Through such assistance the Austrians were able to dominate the Circle of Franconia. 'Once any proposition is supported by the Imperial Minister, you may be sure that it will never be turned down by the assembly of the Circle. The reason is that the ecclesiastical princes will not – and the Imperial cities dare not – ever argue to the contrary, which guarantees a majority in every debate'.[95]

FML. Reinhardt Baron Gemmingen auf Hornberg and Treschklingen, 1710–75 (Military Academy, Wiener Neustadt). This horrible man was one of the more unfortunate representatives of a famous Swabian military family. He was a brave and experienced officer, who gained the Knight's Cross of the M.M.T.O for his performance at Hochkirch (14 October 1758). He was also noted for his brutality, and became possibly the most disliked general in the army next to Serbelloni.

Friendly states like these helped to secure the approaches to Bohemia and Saxony from the west, and enabled the Austrians to draw on the human resources of the *Reich*. Drafts of recruits for the Austrian regiments came throughout the war from the fruitful grounds of the lower Rhine, and in addition a treaty of 16 September 1756 with Bishop Adam Friedrich of Würzburg permitted the Austrians to take into their pay the two regiments of Blau- and Roth-Würzburg, which were as fine as any troops in Europe. A similar agreement was signed with the Bishop of Mainz on 27 November, and yielded the regiment of Mainz or Lamberg.

The Austrians counted themselves as Germans, and a common German language (albeit with regional variations) and living connections with the *Reich* gave Maria Theresa's officer corps a predominantly German colouring. The German officer at his best was 'a stickler for order, and he is outstandingly skilful in the way he preserves the alignment of his troops, whether of infantry or cavalry. He takes a great deal of trouble over this point, and in addition he possesses sound judgement, he is patient, he is obedient to his superiors, and he stays calm in action'.[96] After the war Jacques-Antoine de Guibert, who was no lover of Teutons, was compelled to admire the dignity which obtained in the household of the old general Wenzel Mathias Kleefeld at Carlstadt in Croatia. Dining was accompanied by the saying of grace and other simple domestic ceremonies of the Germans; after the meal the daughter of the house kissed the hands of her parents, and the guests kissed the hands of Kleefeld's wife before they too took their leave'.[97]

Prince Albert of Sachsen-Teschen wrote of the armies of Maria Theresa as being forces 'in which the first houses of Germany reckon it is an honour to serve'.[98] German princes or princelings were *Inhaber* of numbers of Austrian units, as witness the Anhalt-Zerbst battalion, the infantry regiments of Baden-Baden, Baden-Durlach, Bayreuth, Hildburghausen, Sachsen-Gotha and Alt- and Jung-Wolfenbüttel, or the cavalry regiments of Prinz Albert, Anhalt-Zerbst, Hessen-Darmstadt, Löwenstein, Sachsen-Gotha and Württemberg. The names of Wolfenbüttel and Bayreuth are a reminder of the enduring power of the tradition of German service to the Emperor, a force which was capable of overriding family ties or political allegiance. Thus Prince Ernst of Mecklenberg, who was at once an ally of the Austrians, and the brother-in-law of George Prince of Wales (King George III from 1760) remained in the Austrian employ almost until the end of the war. The Prince of Sachsen-Hildburghausen wrote to Queen Charlotte of England on 2 March 1762 that her brother deserved further promotion, but that Maria Theresa had been told that the queen had formed the 'wise decision to withdraw her brother from a service which is quite incompatible with the weak and delicate state of health with which God has endowed him.' Maria Theresa had therefore given the prince permission to retire, and she had remarked to Hildburghausen that she had been 'delighted to make known my regard for the queen by promoting her brother, and I am now pleased to be able to furnish further proof by returning the brother she wishes to have close to her'.[99]

There were princes of Württemberg to be found in the services of both Austria and Prussia, while Austria's own 'Prussians' formed a varied element in the officer corps. Colonel Ernst Baron Normann (1717–70), a courageous leader of grenadiers, hailed from a famous military family of Pomerania, and it was known that both the 'Croatian' colonel Friedrich Ludwig Count Donhoff (1724–78) and the dour *GFWM*. Reinhardt Gemmingen had fathers who were generals of Frederick the Great. Indeed the Gemmingens father and son found themselves almost literally face to face on opposite sides at Kolin in 1757.

Nobody could doubt the loyalty of another of the Prussians, Philipp Elmpt (1724–94), who was a captain on Loudon's staff in the Seven Years War, and died as a *FML*. after having survived 16 campaigns, 36 battles and seven major sieges. Daun was wrongly dismissive of the Prussian born Wilhelm Baron Schroder, and advised Maria Theresa against making him as regimental commander: 'He is a sound man, but nothing more, and to appoint him would cause endless and very considerable discontent in this regiment [Neipperg]. Moreover many people believe that he is too much of the Prussian, however much of a slander that allegation might be'.[100] Schroder was made colonel-commandant, in spite of this intervention, and a Captain Gottfried Johann Schroder (born in Berlin, and possibly a relation) received the *Kleinkreuz* of the Military Order of Maria Theresa for his part in the defence of Schweidnitz in 1762. Maria Theresa's trust was betrayed only by *GFWM*. Konrad Emanuel Count Brunyan (1705–87), who was discovered to be in unauthorised correspondence with the enemy (see p. 194).

Prussian Silesia was a special case, as a former Habsburg territory the loss of which was regretted bitterly, and its peculiar contribution will be examined shortly.

Saxony was the home of the Lutheran Reformation, but it furnished excellent officers in the person of the 'partisan' leaders *FML*. Franz Maximilian Baron Jahnus von Eberstädt (1711–72) and *FZM*. Wenzel Matthias Baron Kleefeld von Hnogek (c. 1713–1779), the staff officer Georg Sigismund Baron Rothschiltz (1730–74), and the stalwart old *FM*. Ernst Dietrich Count Marschall von Biberstein (1692–1771) who defended Ohnütz so doggedly in 1758.

The contributions of individual German states to the Habsburg officer corps emphasises that the relationship with the Catholic religion was neither strong nor consistent. After excluding officers from Prussian Silesia and Swedish Pomerania, but including those from Freiburg and the Swabian enclaves, it is possible to identify 798 German regimental officers by place of birth, who were represented as follows:

Saxony:	7.04%
Breisgau:	5.13
Swabia:	4.26
Franconia:	4.13
Bavaria:	3.88
Palatinate (Lower):	3.75
Bayreuth, Mainz:	3.63 each
Ansbach, Thuringia:	3.00 each
Württemberg:	2.85
Würzburg:	2.63
Baden-Baden, Salzburg:	2.50 each
Trier:	2.38
Bamberg:	2.13
Palatinate (Upper), Brunswick:	2.00 each
Hessen-Darmstadt:	1.87
Speyer:	1.75
Brandenburg:	1.62
Mecklenburg:	1.50
Cologne:	1.37
Baden-Durlach, Hessen-Cassel:	1.25 each
Frankfurt, Nuremberg:	1.12 each
All other locations less than 1 percent.	

The number of German other ranks identifiable by place of birth amounts to 12,156 – or 10,676 infantry, 1,278 cuirassiers and dragoons, and 202 from the other arms. The proportions (again excluding Prussian Silesia and Swedish Pomerania, but including Freiburg and the Swabian enclaves) shows a narrower recruiting base than that of the officers, with Bavaria and the ecclesiastical principalities represented more strongly, and (in relation to population) significant contributions from the middling and small states fringing Franconia – possibly because they lay on the march routes to and from the Netherlands. Würzburg would have appeared higher in the scale if our calculations had included the Blue and Red regiments, which were auxiliary units and not organic parts of the Austrian army (See Appendix IV: Origins of German Private Soldiers).

> German Officer Families
> *Anhalt-Bernburg:* Adelsheim
> *Ansbach:* Egloffstein, Eichler, Eyr, Knöbel, Mohr, Voghtern, Voit von Salzburg
> *Baden-Baden:* Löwenstein-Wertheim
> *Baden-Durlach:* Gemmingen auf Hornberg und Treschklingen, Mynzesheim, Ziegesar
> *Bamberg:* Bubenhoffen
> *Bavaria:* Dursch, Frierenberger, Fugger, Leubelfink, Leuwen, Pömler, Rummel von Waldau, Spretti, Winkelhoffer von Wilkelsburg
> *Bayreuth:* Kotzau, Oberlender, Reizenstein, Rusworm
> *Brandenburg-Prussia:* Bory (Geldern), Brunyan (Pomerania), Copens (Jülich), Elmpt, Grevenitz, Kleist, Moltke (East Frisia), Normann (Pomerania), Quitzau, Saamen, Schenchel, Schroder, Tinobelsdorf (Geldem), Zigwiz
> *Cologne:* Kleist, Mylius, Nagel
> *Erbach:* Erbach
> *Erlangen:* Winckler
> *Franconia:* Berlichingen, Bettendorf, Bobenhausen, Jaxheim, Löbenstein, Neipperg, Riedesel, Stetten
> *Frankfurt-am-Main:* Feldern, Humbracht
> *Hamburg:* Corbey
> *Hanover:* Buccow, Hanxleiden
> *Isenburg:* Isenburg
> *Hessen-Cassel:* Buttler, Trais
> *Hessen-Darmstadt:* Hessen-Darmstadt
> *Löwenstein-Wertheim:* Löwenstein-Wertheim
> *Mainz:* Braubach, Schorlemmer, Weeveld
> *Mecklenburg:* Blüschkow, Bülow, Kahlden, Lützow, Rieben, Vogelsang
> *Memmingen:* Reichlin
> *Münster:* Elemendorf, Höflinger, Loen, Schorlemmer
> *Palatinate (Lower):* Berg, Egg, Fett von Muntzenberg, Messina, Schütyter, Staell, Wartenberg, Wunsching
> *Palatinate (Upper):* Fronau, Hautzenberg, Stein, Wenckheim
> *Regensburg:* Blassenburg, Blettenburg, Lerchenfeld
> *Rheinfelden:* Truchsess
> *Rhön und Werra:* Tiemar
> *Saxony (undifferentiated):* Beichlingen, Feillner, Ilten, Jahnus von Eberstädt, Kleefeld, Lüttichau, Marschall, Pöllnitz, Rittrich, Stain, Thürnel, Zittenhofen
> *(Sachsen-Hildburghausen):* Hildburghausen
> *(Sachsen-Meiningen):* Baumbach
> *(Thuringia):* Biela, Broskirchen, Esmond, Phull, Huirschlingen
> *(Vogtland):* Hiller
> *Salzburg:* Arco, Ducker, Lasser, Motzel, Prank, Platz, Rölingen
> *Swabia:* Fugger, Fornstein, Gemmingen, Hiller, Stain, Worbeer
> *Trier:* Gressenich, Lichtenberg, Moskopp
> *Westphalia (undifferentiated):* Brabeck (three barons), Brettlach, Dettichen, Moltke, Ohtmann, Plettenberg, Rassfeldt, Salm-Salm, Schleppenquill, Spittaell, Wengen
> *Wolfenbüttel:* Winterfeldt

Württemberg: Seeger, Welser
Würzburg: Aussess, Hutten, Seydherdiz, Voit von Salzburg
(N.B. Many families owned branches in different parts of the *Reich*).

Further regions of Europe may be counted as members of a still wider Austrian military world, whether through historical association, or the numbers or significance of the officers they supplied:

The Alienated Lands

Prussian Silesia

Military Representation
1. Other Ranks: 5.18% of the total.
   Cuirassiers 12.06; dragoons 7.19; pioneers, miners and sappers 4.32; artillery 1.75; Hungarian infantry 0.68; Italian infantry 0.14; Netherlands infantry 0.09
2. NCOs, Corporals and *Gefreyten:* 6.81 (incl. 8.85 in German infantry)
3. Non-combatants: 5.64
4. Officers: 5.34
5. Professionals: Surgeons 5.06; chaplains nil; provosts 13.84

The loss of Silesia rankled with Maria Theresa so deeply not just on account of the forfeiture of revenues and manufactures, but because the predominantly German northern province was considered, in the words of *FM.* Batthyány, 'the nursery of the best recruits of the army'.[101] In the 1730s Silesia could be ranked with Bohemia as the foundation of the infantry, and it is not fanciful to suggest that by the time of the Seven Years War the veterans had hardened into the excellent men who made the backbone of the corps of Austrian NCOs. Some of the best retired NCOs in their turn became provosts (chiefs of the regimental police), and it is not surprising that Silesians made up nearly 14 percent of these fearsome creatures. In 1757 the Austrians were still ready to draw a distinction between enemy prisoners from the historic Prussian provinces, and those from Silesia, who could still be re-made into useful Austrian soldiers.[102]

Many of the Silesian nobles had remained loyal to Maria Theresa in the Prussian invasion of 1740, and they accommodated themselves unwillingly, if at all, to Prussian rule. After the little action of Colonel Jahnus at Landeshut on 14 August 1757 he praised the contribution made by Count Taaffe, a former Austrian captain of Irish descent, who had left his nearby estates at the outbreak of the war, and put his local knowledge at the disposal of the Austrians.[103] Another Silesian gentleman, Count Warkotsch, proposed the coup de main whereby the Austrians nearly captured Frederick in 1761.

A classic example of the Silesian serving officer was Franz Ludwig Baron Neugebauer (1731–1808), whose grandfather had been ennobled by Ferdinand II for services against the Swedes. As captain and *Flügel-Adjutant* he led three regiments of cuirassiers in a decisive attack against the Prussian right wing at Maxen; promoted to major, he brought up three regiments to plug a gap in the line at Torgau, and was rewarded with the *Kleinkreuz* of the Military Order of Maria Theresa. He died as a *FML.* and Commanding General of Lower Austria.

Among other Silesians to gain the Theresian Order we discover the majors Silvius Alexander Count Bojanowsky (1724–99), Karl Baron Rolke, Karl Baron Hocke (1714–91) and Carl Huff von Kandersdorf (1734–98). Adam Ferdinand Krammer von Obereck (1698–1779) began service as a private soldier, but as a colonel led five companies of grenadiers in the successful action at Moys in 1757, which won him the *Kleinkreuz* and promotion to *GFWM.*

Silesian Officer Families
Abschatz, Belrupt, Bojanowsky, Brougglach, Cellari, Culmar, Geisler, Gersdorf, Giannini (from Modena), Henckel von Donnersmarck, Hochberg, Hocke, Hohenhausen, Hujm, Karwinsky von Karwin, Kalckreuth, Karnasky, Köstlitz, Krammer von Obereck, Larisch, Lestwitz, Materni, Neugebauer, Reibnitz, Ripplar, Rolke, Rosenberg, Roth, Rothkirch, Salisch, Schönborn, Stockmann, Taaffe (from Ireland), Warkotsch, Waffenberg, Zedlitz.

Alsace
   Military Representation:
   1. Other Ranks: 1.41% of the total
   2. NCOs, Corporals and *Gefreyten:* 0.69
   3. Non-combatants: 0.48
   4. Officers: 0.13
   5. Professionals: nil

Alsace had been an historic land of the *Reich,* which was gobbled up bit by bit by the French and lost definitively in 1697. Older traditions of service lingered, and they were perpetuated in the Seven Years War by a handful of officers. Lieutenant-Colonel August Zorn von Plobsheim (d. 1774) signalled himself at the storm of Schweidnitz in 1757, while Joseph Baron Preiss (1704–97) made his reputation as a staff officer, and was promoted in the field to *GFWM.* for his part in managing the retreat from Torgau in 1760.

Alsatian Officer Families
   Preiss, Ried, Schindler, Zorn von Plobsheim.

The Duchy of Lorraine
   Military Representation:
   1. Other Ranks: 0.36% of the total
   2. NCOs, Corporals and *Gefreyten:* 0.52
   3. Non-combatants: 0.40
   4. Officers: 2.68
   5. Professionals: Surgeons 1.26; chaplains nil; provosts nil

In human terms the Austrian connection with Lorraine was surprisingly strong and enduring. This historic territory of the *Reich* was militarily indefensible against the French, for it was situated only 150 kilometres from Paris, and riddled with Metz, Toul and other French enclaves or encroachments. Duke François III had scarcely married Maria Theresa before the Treaty of Vienna (1737) put an definitive end to the War of the Polish Succession, and forced him to renounce his homeland in favour of the French. The duke (later Emperor Francis Stephen) received the Grand Duchy of Tuscany as a personal compensation, but in addition he was able to take with him from Lorraine the allegiance of some of the foremost military families.

FML. Charles-François comte de Dombasle (d. 1775) and Colonel Jean-Joseph comte de Ferraris (1726–1814) both had connections with the family regiment of Carl Lothringen, while *G.d.C* Charles Marquis de Ville de Camon (1705–92) was believed, perhaps wrongly, to owe his eminence solely to the favour of Francis Stephen. The same did not apply to Captain Jean Edmond comte de Ruttant (1737–94) or the active cavalryman *G.d.C.* François Baron de Bosfort (1715–75) – two knights of the Theresian Order who gained promotion and honours with no obvious benefit from patronage.

The Stainvilles, like other families of the Franco-German borderlands, had representatives in both the Austrian and French armies. A predilection for the Habsburg cause lingered in some lines which otherwise became committed entirely to the French service, and this residual attachment was embodied as late as the 20th century in the person of the French marshal Lyautey, who opposed the designs of his prime minister Clemenceau, bent on destroying the Habsburg Empire.

Lorraine Officer Families:
Le Becque, Bietagh (from Ireland), Busselot, Blainville, Bosfort, Coustine, Desallis, Detressi, Dienze, Dombasle, Dumesnil, d'Hoville, Etrepy, Ficquelmont, Fontoy, Gourcy, d'Harnoncourt, d'Hauteville, d'Hennezel (three *chevaliers*), Herbel, Marschall d'Arcla, Poincare, Ravinel, Richecourt, Ruttant, Sailly, Sincere, Stainville (Choiseul), Toussaint, Valdenaire, de Ville.

France
France was an historic enemy of the Habsburgs, and it is not surprising to find that its representation in the Austrian army was virtually non-existent, once we deduct the contributions from Alsace and Lorraine. The one exception relates to the French military surgeons, who made up 3.79 percent of their profession with the Austrians.

Liège
The Archbishopric of Liège had so far escaped incorporation in either the French or Habsburg territories. Its highest numerical contribution to the Austrian army was in the non-combatant personnel, at 0.31 percent, but its natives made up only 0.13 percent of the officer corps. The most prominent of the Liège military families were those of d'Aspremont-Lynden and Souhay.

Spain
The Spanish branch of the Habsburgs had once eclipsed the Austrian both in fame and in the extent of its domains. The last of the Spanish line died out in 1700, and the ensuing contest between the Bourbon pretender and the Austrian branch gave rise to the War of the Spanish Succession, which terminated to the disadvantage of the Habsburgs in 1714. Spanish exiles and Spanish influence had been prominent at the court of Emperor Charles VI, who could never resign himself to the loss of the Spanish crown, but Spanish military families were represented in the reign of Maria Theresa only by a scattering of individuals, who are not always easy to distinguish from Spanish lines which had long been settled in the Netherlands. The only significant contribution of the Spanish to the Austrian army at the time of the Seven Years War was to the Italian national infantry, where Spaniards made up 2.33 percent of the rank and file, 17.17 percent of the NCOs, Corporals and *Gefreyten,* and 11.45 percent of the officers. The majority of these people were born in Spain's eastern provinces – Catalonia, Aragon and Valencia.

Spanish Officer Families
Barco (settled in Hungary), Cordoba (Cordua), Escalar, Los Rios (settled in Netherlands), Montoja, Navarra, Puebla (settled in Netherlands), Vasquez-Ninez von Lowenthal, Velasco, Vemeda, Villegas.

Non-Austrian Italy

    Military Representation
1. Other Ranks: 0.38% of the total (but 23.24 of the Italian national infantry)
2. NCOs, Corporals and *Gefreyten:* 1.00
3. Non-combatants: 0.47
4. Officers: 3.31
5. Professionals: Surgeons 3.79; chaplains nil; provosts 1.53

For centuries Italy had been known as a nursery of active and intelligent officers, who were now represented throughout the Theresian army. *FZM.* Lacy noted in 1761 that the colonel of Jung-Modena *Chevaulegers* had reported to him that 'he had an enormous number of Italian officers in his regiment. He must therefore send in a return of all the officers of his regiment by nationality'.[104]

FML. Ernst Friedrich Giannini (1717–74), Count of the Holy Roman Empire, represented an assimilated family of Modena which had settled in Silesia, and received the *Incolat* of the landed aristocracy. He himself made his name as Loudon's chief of staff from 1759 until 1762, and Armfeldt observed that he possessed 'a fundamental grasp of all the necessary branches of knowledge; he has a penetrating and comprehensive intelligence, uncommon accuracy in all his ideas, and knows all the routes and passes of Moravia, Silesia and Bohemia'.[105] After war the beaky-nosed Giannini became a famously ferocious Director of the Wiener Neustadt Military Academy.

A patrician family of Genoa, the Bottas d'Adorno had broken with their native city and thrown in their lot with the Austrians, to the extent that Maximilian Browne was able to install Antonio Botta after he had conquered Genoa in 1746. Botta ruled so harshly that he provoked a rebellion among the citizens, which upset the whole Austrian plan of campaign. The infantry regiment of Botta was however known as one of the finest in the army, and never performed better than at Kolin in 1757, when it succeeded in holding the line at a critical moment.

The Piedmontese, the northern neighbours of the Genoese, had strong and deep military traditions. Among the natives who came into prominence with the Austrians during the Seven Years war was Colonel Joseph Maximilian Baron Tiller (1728–88, to be distinguished from the 'Swiss' *FML.* Johann Anton Tillier, 1723–61) who had begun his career with the notorious Pandours of Trenck, but paradoxically made his name in the 1750s as a trainer and disciplinarian; his day of glory was at Adelsbach on 6 July 1762, when he commanded an Austrian corps as acting brigadier. Colonel Carl Count Caramelli di Castiglione Fallet (1716–88) caught the attention of Loudon as a leader of cavalry, and he fought under that general's command at Domstadtl, Kunersdorf and Landeshut.

Most celebrated of all the Piedmontese were the two brothers Guasco, namely *FML.* Peter Alexander (d. 1780) and the *FML.* Franz, who defended Schweidnitz with such obstinacy and skill in almost the last episode of the war. There was something of the adventurer about them both (Franz had served for several campaigns with the Russian army), and Armfeldt commented that 'the two of them made their fortune through gambling'.[106]

The subtleties of old Venice were embodied in the person of Lieutenant-colonel Dominik Tomiotti di Fabris, conte de Cassano (1725–89), whose skills as a staff officer were valued by both Daun and Loudon. Uncomplicated soldierly skills were to the fore in another noble Venetian, Lieutenant-Colonel Anton Graf Seriman (1714–89), who gained the *Ritterkreuz* of the Military Order of Maria Theresa for his work at Hochkirch and Maxen.

The Neapolitan tradition in the Austrian service went back to the time when the Two Sicilies were disputed between Austria and Spain. The foremost of the 'Austrian' Neapolitans at the outbreak of the Seven Years War was *G.d.C.* Joseph Graf Lucchese d'Averna, who was a bold cavalryman and a friend and associate of *FM.* Browne. He outlived his patron for only a few months, being killed while leading the desperate attack of the Austrian cavalry at Leuthen.

The one 'foreign' Italian regiment which fought as such in the Austrian pay was that of Toscana, which acquitted itself well in its first trial, at the bloody battle of Liegnitz in 1760.

> Italian Officer Families
> *Genoa:* Botta, Gentili
> *Ferrara:* Fiaschi
> *Modena:* Giannini (settled in Silesia), Martiano, Melza, Poculari
> *Piedmont:* Caramelli di Castiglione Pallet, Colli (Sardinia), Goaquis, Guasco, Margeri, Pernigotti, Promniz, Roche, St. Amos, Tillier
> *Naples:* d'Anna, Campitelli, Caraccioli di S. Eramo, Ferrer (Sicily), Grenada (Sicily), Lucchese d'Averna, Mansuel, Munarini, Nasselli (Sicily), Posta, Pugneti (Sicily), Torres, Zamboni (Sicily)
> *Tuscany* (a Habsburg family possession, but not part of the Austrian dominions): Castelles, Ceretani, Falconini, D'Orlandini
> *Venice:* Buri, Gergorini, Tomiotti di Fabris, Gregorini, Justi, Piatti, Pellegrini, Seriman
> *Locations still unplaced at time of writing:* Porporati, Radicati.

Smaller Elements

It is strange to find scarcely a single Dutchman who found his way into the Austrian army, even in the ranks of the Netherlandish regiments. The chief Swiss of note was *FML.* Johann Anton Baron Tillier (1723–61), who enjoyed a distinguished military and diplomatic career, and was sent on important missions to the Russian army in the Seven Years War.

By a statistical quirk natives of Swedish Pomerania (technically part of the *Reich*) made up 1.57 percent of the Austrian army's majors. Mainland Sweden contributed a scattering of officers and 'Danish' Denmark likewise, but Norway provided the excellent gunner Adolph Nicolaus Alison (d.1779), who became one of the most significant associates of Liechtenstein, and commanded the artillery at the defence of Olmütz in 1758.

In the first half of the 19th century it was to become fashionable for English *milords* to see service with the Austrian army. They were much rarer birds in the period of the Seven Years War, when we encounter isolated individuals like the Northumberland gentleman Horace St. Paul, who served as a volunteer, and two officers of cavalry from old families of Catholic recusants – chevalier Charles Jerningham of Costessey in Norfolk, who is listed as a captain in the de Ligne Dragoons, and John Dormer (1730–95), second son of John the Seventh Lord Dormer (information courtesy of Michael Dormer Esq.).

The great days of the 'Austrian' Scots lay in the past, and it is characteristic that the Scottish knights of the Theresian Order were few in number and junior in rank, typified by Captain Franz Baron Nangle of Rothsay (1720–81) of the mounted grenadiers, and the soldier of fortune Captain Jakob Count Lockhart (1718–90), who had served Nadir Shah of Persia, and undergone further adventures before he threw in his lot with the Austrians in 1752. Towards the end of the Seven Years War he is to be found back in Scotland, from where he kept Daun informed of political developments in Britain. The Scots were otherwise eclipsed by the far greater numbers of the 'Austrian' Irish, which whom they were so easily confused – to the extent that the Scottish Ogilvys saw their name converted by false analogy to 'O'Gilvy.'

The English and Scottish private soldiers are so few that they fail to register even to a second decimal point among the Austrian army's other ranks. Their voices are however transmitted in the names of the places of birth as they were noted by the Commissaries. Thus: 'Annavarnes' (Inverness), 'Glosgau' (Glasgow), 'Hamsher' (Hampshire), 'Klauster' (Gloucester), 'Nordhemden'

(Northampton). All of these pairings are reasonable suppositions. With a little imagination if is possible to match 'Krane with Kent, and 'Wolfscanton' with Wincanton or Wolverhampton, but 'Hohenstatf in Scotland, and 'Speilenberg' in England are places which still defy identification.

'To dwell in the Court of Kings'—The Catholic Irish

In the Seven Years War the Irish were represented in the other ranks of the Austrian army by a dozen private soldiers. In contrast Irishmen made up 2.11 percent of the active officer corps, including 3.84 of the lieutenant-colonels, and they established a distinctive presence in the high command. In this respect it is enough to cite the examples of the stout *FZM.* Johann Sigmund Maguire von Enniskillen (d. 1767) who beat Frederick back from Dresden in 1760, the elegant and flute-playing *G.d.C.* Carl Claudius O'Donnell (1715–71) who took command of the army after Daun had been wounded at Torgau, and Franz Moritz Lacy (1725–1801) who was Austria's first Chief of the General Staff (1758), and became Field Marshal and President of the *Hofkriegsrath* after the Seven Years War. In the course of the history of the Habsburg monarchy Irishmen provided the army with three Presidents of the *Hofkriegsrath,* 13 Field Marshals, and eight of the Knights of the Military Order of Maria Theresa whose portraits hang on the walls of the Military Academy at Wiener-Neustadt.

The Irish had first come to the Allemanü and Bavarians as missionaries or wandering holy men in the seventh and eighth centuries, and they are commemorated today in the Central European personal names of 'Fridolin', 'Killian,' and 'Kalman' – after the Colman who rests somewhere beneath the great abbey church which towers above the Danube at Melk. The Irish presence fell away in the following centuries, and in the Middle Ages it was perpetuated only in isolated institutions like the community of the Schottenkirch, which scandalised the citizens of Vienna by its violent games of football.

For more than 200 years, from the middle of the 16th century to the second half of the 18th, the leaders of Catholic Irish society looked to Catholic Europe for sanctuary, and for the opportunities of life which were being denied to them in their homeland. Old *FML.* Nicholas Taaffe, Sixth Earl of Carlingford, might have been speaking for all these generations when he declared to Francis Stephen and Maria Theresa that he had left Ireland:

> because he was afraid that his descendants pressed by the Penal Laws would not resist the temptation of becoming Protestants. He therefore took refuge to a Catholic country where his ancestors were well known by the military services they had rendered at different times to the House of Austria. He had abandoned his relations and his state and the rank and liberty he had in his country to prevent his descendants deserting a religion to which Their Imperial Majesties so fervently adhered.[107]

The Irish first established themselves in quantity in the Austrian service from the late 1620s, when they arrived as semi-mercenary bands under their own officers, and often in association with the Scots. The first identifiable Irish regimental *Inhaber* was the Jakob Butler who raised a regiment of infantry in 1630; this unit was wiped out by the Swedes in the following year, and Jakob himself was taken prisoner. However Jakob's brother Walter became *Inhaber* of a regiment of dragoons, mostly raised from Irishmen, and this Walter Butler achieved notoriety, if not fame, when he joined the Scots John Gordon and Walter Leslie to assassinate Wallenstein at Eger in 1634. In 1635 the Emperor raised no less than eight regiments from troops (many of them Irish and Scots) who had been released from Polish employ, and from then until 1648 the Irish were present in the Imperial service in quantities that were probably never reached again. Most of these people were birds of passage, who died in the wars, wandered off again after the Peace of Westphalia, or were absorbed without trace in the local communities.

The numbers of the Irish fell off sharply in the third quarter of the 17th century. There was obviously less need for their services after the Thirty Years War. Moreover very few Irishmen emigrated to Central Europe during the Cromwellian wars, while the ensuing restoration of the Stuart dynasty in Britain in 1660 seemed to promise better conditions at home – which thinned the ranks of the Austro-Irish still further. This period is nevertheless important for the story of the Irish in Austria, for it saw the emergence of something of a class of Irish grandees. The first of the kind was *FZM*. Olivier Wallis, Baron Carighmain (1600–67), whose sons founded the two most important branches of that fertile family in Austria. One of his great-grandsons of the Büdwitz line, Michael Johann (1730–98) served in the Seven Years War as a lieutenant-colonel, and headed the *Hofkriegsrath* as President from 1791 to 1796.

The Taaffes were another leading Irish family which struck firm roots in Austria at this time. Viscount Francis, Third Earl of Carlingford (1639–1704) contrived to capture the baggage of the Grand Vizier Kara Mustafa outside Vienna in 1683, while Nicholas the Sixth Earl (1677–1776), whose words have already been quoted, distinguished himself as an 83-year-old *FML.* when he rallied the cavalry at Kolin.

FML. Johann O'Donnell, 1712–84 (Military Academy, Wiener Neustadt). Johann was the elder brother of the more famous Carl, and belonged to the Larkfield branch of the prolific Austro-Irish family. He fought brilliantly as a cavalry commander at Kolin (18 June 1757), and again at Leuthen (5 December 1757), when he was wounded and captured in hand-to-hand fighting.

The year 1683 had in fact inaugurated more than three decades of warfare against the French and Turks, and created a demand for manpower in the Austrian service that was comparable with the one which had obtained during the Thirty Years War. This period happened to coincide with the 'Glorious Revolution which evicted the Stuart king James II from Britain, and the consolidation of the Penal Laws (in force from 1693 to 1829), which barred Catholics from the army and other professions, and burdened them with humiliating restrictions in everyday life. New attempts were made to introduce specifically Irish units to the Austrian service, but they all failed, which confirmed the impression that the distinctive contribution of the Irish was to be to the officer corps.

In 1705 Ulysses Browne of County Limerick (1659–1731) followed his younger brother George to the Austrian service, and so founded another of the Austro-Irish dynasties. *FML.* George acted as Prince Eugene's right-hand man in the campaign of Belgrade in 1717, and in the same year he completed his manuscript *Kriegs-Exercitium,* which became one of the models for Daun's infantry regulations of 1749.

Maximilian Ulysses Browne (1705–57), son of Ulysses, made his name as the most fiery and charismatic Austrian commander of his generation. He conducted important holding actions against the Prussian invasions in 1740–1 and 1756, and after a catastrophic misjudgement at the start of the campaign of 1757 he redeemed himself by an heroic death, leaving the reputation of 'a brave man and a good commander' (Frederick). By then his young protégé and kinsman Franz Moritz Lacy was launched on his eminent career.

The two decades from 1750 to 1770 stand as the foremost age of the Irish in the Austrian service, and lest Irish historians should be accused of exaggeration it is worth quoting the Austrian scholar who has stated that 'at that time the quantity of Irish officers was huge. But more striking than their numbers was the position they occupied in the Austrian service. We may almost speak of a dominating role of the Irish in the leadership of the army'.[108]

On her side Maria Theresa called on the Irish to help her to build up her military caste, which scarcely existed outside the Bohemian gunners, the Silesian NCOs, the nobles of Görz, Gradisca and the southern Netherlands, the Knights of her new Military Order, the other recently-ennobled officers, and individual German families with a tradition of service to the Habsburgs. The 'Austrian' Irish of the middle of the 18th century were well placed to help to supply the need. Through their numbers, their connections, their wealth or their activities a number of families (Browne, D'Alton, Maguire, Nugent, O'Donnell, O'Kelly, Taaffe, Wallis) had won themselves a place in the esteem of the Austrians, and by its example and influence the men of this generation facilitated the arrival of the young Catholic Irish gentry who were now forbidden by the British authorities to seek their fortunes in France.

Daun and Loudon spoke in amused terms of the habits of the Irish in clubbing together. Their young men were brought up in such establishments as the monastery school of Ettal in Bavaria, the Parma Noble College, the *Ritterakademie* at Liegnitz in Silesia, or the medical schools at Prague or Padua. Although Irish regiments no longer existed as such, Irish regimental officers congregated in some units rather than others:

Number of Officers per Regiment	Regiments (infantry unless stated otherwise)
9	Browne, Loudon
7	Bayreuth, Wied
5	Königsegg, Wallis, *Jäger-Corps*
4	Andlau, Baden-Durlach, Botta, Alt-Colloredo, Marschall, Mercy, Pallavicini, Puebla, Sincere, Trautmannsdorf Cuirassiers, Jung-Modena Dragoons/*Chevaulegers*

The regiment of Browne was unique, in that Maria Theresa made a special arrangement whereby the proprietorship passed from the late Maximilian Ulysses Browne to his son Joseph, and this element of continuity almost certainly accounts for the high Irish presence among its officers. The regiment of Wallis was another unit with Irish connections, while the patronage of Lacy may have influenced the officer recruiting of Alt-Colloredo and the *Jäger*. The other regiments listed here represent a cross section of the army, and furnish no obvious explanations for their concentrations of Irish.

The house of the Irish Franciscans near the Powder Tower in Prague served as a post box for communications between the 'Austrian' Irish and their relations and friends in Ireland, and for generations a number of the wealthier families (the D'Altons, the Magauleys, the O'Kellys and Taaffes) travelled freely between the Habsburg dominions and their native land. The Austro-Irish bore no particular grudge against the English, and indeed they probably benefited from the cult of Anglomania which beset Vienna in the later part of the 18th century: in such a way FM. Lacy's park at Neuwaldegg in the Vienna Woods introduced the entranced Austrians to the English style of 'natural' landscape gardening.

Irish officers were just one manifestation of an entire society which had been transplanted to the Habsburg lands. Leading academic reputations were established by the orientalist brothers Peter and Thomas Herbert of Rathkeale, by the Michael Lynch who was made Professor of History at the reconstituted University of Vienna in 1753, and indirectly by the polymath administrator of the Austrian Netherlands Patrice-François Neny, who reformed elementary education and Louvain University, and founded the *Académie Royale* in Brussels. At least 56 Irishmen studied at the Prague School of Medicine, mostly between 1720 and 1760, and they were encouraged and supported by their countrymen Dr. Jacobus Smith von Balroe (Professor of Physiology and Rector of the university) and William Hugh McNeven O'Kelly ab Aghrim.[109]

Many of these Irish therefore existed in three worlds – their own ancient culture, that of the demeaning conditions of life in Ireland under the Protestant Ascendancy, and that of their Austrian environment. These experiences were encapsulated in the life of Ellen O'Leary, née O'Connell, who ran from her family home to marry the wild Arthur O'Leary, who became a colonel in the Austrian service. O'Leary returned to Ireland on a visit, and fell into a dispute with a rich Protestant neighbour, Mr. Morris, who made the contemptuous offer to buy his fine horse for £5 – which was the highest value allowed to a horse owned by a Catholic. O'Leary struck out, but instead of demanding satisfaction in a duel, Morris had him declared an outlaw. O'Leary was a fine marksman, and aided by Ellen (who re-loaded for him) he drove off the soldiers who tried to lay siege to his house of Raleigh. Not long afterwards, on 4 May 1773, he was shot dead by an unknown hand beside a gorse bush at Carrigaminma. It was not as Ellen, but as the vengeful Eileen Dhuv ('Dark Eileen') that his widow mourned her 'rider of the dark eyes' in an improvised verse which became possibly the most famous lament in the Gaelic language. She recalled the sight of Arthur when he rode into the square at Macroom:

> My love and my darling
> The first day I saw you
> By the market-house gable
> My eye was watching you,
> My heart adoring you
> I fled from my father with you
> Far from my house with you…

In a later stanza Ellen mourned the absence of her sister Abigail, 'the lady of 26 summers who crossed the wide ocean to dwell in the court of kings.' The Abigail in question had married a Captain O'Sullivan who was in the Austrian service. Abigail was discovered weeping by Maria Theresa in a corridor outside one of the palace chapels in Vienna, and explained that she feared that the child she was bearing would be just the first of very many. Maria Theresa took her under her wing, and stood as godmother when the infant duly appeared. Abigail was described as being 'vastly well pleased with the military way of living' and learning the German language,[110] though she and all her children were finally swept away by smallpox – the plague which decimated the Imperial family itself.

> Irish Officer Families
> Bietagh (by way of Lorraine), Brady (McBrady) von Longthen, Browne de Camus, Caldwell, Cruise, D'Alton, Everard, Fitzpatrick, Fitzgerald, Hamilton, Hussey, Kavanagh von Ballybrack, Lacy, Lacy-Billingarri, MacCaffry, MacElligot, MacDermott, Maguire von Enniskillen, Nugent von Westmeath, O'Brien, O'Byrne, O'Donnell, O'Flanagan, O'Kelly, O'Leary, O'Mulrian, O'Neillan, Plunkett, Purcell, Smith von Balroe, Sullivan, Taaffe, Wallis.

4

Finance

The most vulnerable flank of the Austrian army was not to be found on any battlefield, not even at Leuthen, but in the ability of the Austrian state to meet its military objectives.

Thanks to the efforts of Friedrich Wilhelm Count Haugwitz, Maria Theresa had been able to secure reliable funding to support a peacetime army of 108,000 troops. A refugee from Silesia, Haugwitz was alive both to the benefit which the Prussians were deriving from that conquered province, and the threat which the bellicose King Frederick still posed to the Austrian monarchy. He laid his case before a sitting of the Conference on 29 January 1748, claiming that the crown and Christendom were now at stake, and that Bohemia and Moravia would surely go the same way as Silesia unless the Hereditary Lands could be persuaded to finance a respectable force over the long term at the cost of 14 million florins per annum. He could argue that this was little more than the provinces were already paying in one form or another, and that the *Stände* would probably welcome the chance of commuting for cash the burdensome obligations to support the peacetime army by provisions, accommodation and transport.

Maria Theresa was convinced by the reasoning of Haugwitz, and she forced his proposals through the Conference. When it came to negotiating with the individual provinces, the *Stände* of Bohemia, Moravia, Lower Austria and Upper Austria – all territories which were exposed to Prussian attack – agreed without demur to make over the increased contributions for a span of ten years; Styria and Carniola assented only to an initial three years, while Carinthia refused altogether – which compelled Maria Theresa to enforce her new taxation there on 15 November 1749 by executive authority (*jure regio*). Local resources were available to maintain 25,000 troops in the Austrian Netherlands and another 25,000 in Austrian Italy, and Hungary would be addressed through separate negotiations. The system lasted well, until war arrived to make altogether unprecedented demands on the resources of the monarchy.

Income

Overview

Austria's total military expenditure during the Seven Years War amounted to 391,848,959 florins. According to the most generally accepted calculations this sum was raised (in approximate percentages) from the following sources:

Taxes and loans from the *Stände*:	33.0
The regular 'Contribution' from the German and Hungarian Hereditary Lands:	29.0
Loans raised by the Wiener Stadt Banco:	15.0
Contributions, gifts and loans from the Austrian Netherlands:	15.0
Various loans:	2.5

Dutch and Italian loans:	2.5
Contribution from the *Reich:*	2.0

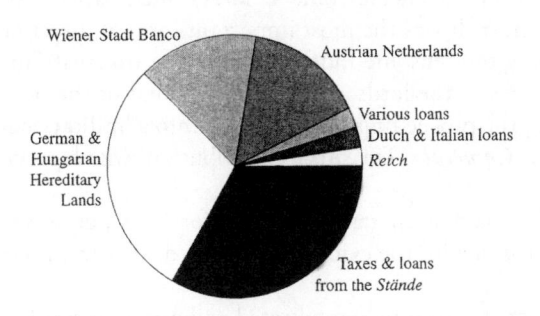

Somewhere in these figures are hidden the income from unconventional sources like the French subsidy (processed in the Austrian Netherlands, and forwarded by way of the *Staatscanzley*), the exactions in conquered territories, and the domestic contributions which were commuted for their value in *Naturalien*. The arrangements year-by-year were inevitably more tangled than the outline might suggest. Thus the income expected for the military year of 1758 was put at 28,667,169 florins, and was made up of:

Contributions proper:	49.58%
As percentage of the 28,667,169 fl.	
German Hereditary Lands	34.68
Austrian Silesia	6.97
Hungary	4.18
Transylvania	2.52
Bánát	1.23
French subsidy via the *Staatscanzley:*	34.88
Enforced loans (including arrears from 1757) from Lower, Upper and Inner Austria and Vorder-Österreich:	6.9
Loans via the Vienna Stadt-Banco:	4.18
Voluntary loan from the Lower Austrian *Stände:*	4.18
Collection from the Church;	0.28[1]

We shall have to look at some of these sources more closely.

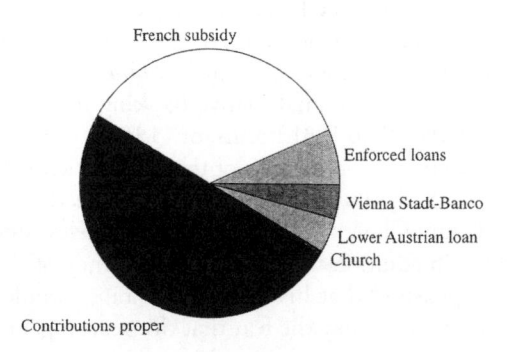

Taxes

The 'Contribution' was a levy on net income at rates which varied from one province of the Hereditary Lands to the next. It was the most important form of direct taxation, it was enforced vigorously, and it was very burdensome indeed, amounting (in Austrian Silesia for example) to 27.2 percent of the revenues of the lords, 35.0 percent of that of the peasants, and 41.2 percent of that of the townsmen. The proceedings were divided into a 'military contribution' which went towards the army, and a *'Cameral'* (Treasury) Contribution' which serviced the interest on the state debt.

The Church in addition paid a separate collection (for 1758 put at 83,000 florins) which did not seem much in comparison with the evident wealth on display in the ecclesiastical buildings of baroque Austria.

The remaining taxes were short-term, complicated and not particularly productive levies which were demanded from the German Hereditary Lands from the middle of the war. They comprised a Supplementary War Tax (*Kriegsbeysteuer,* first levied 1759) in the form of a poll tax; a tax on interest from loans (*Capitaliensteuer*), interest from the Vienna Stadt Banco remaining exempt; an inheritance tax (*Erbsteuer*) on legacies passing out of the direct line. The citizens of Vienna (unlike the *Stände*) owned no powerful collective voice, and on 13 October 1761 they became the target of a daunting combination of almost every conceivable form of taxation, embracing a new poll tax, a supplement on rental payments, and levies on interest and official salaries.

Borrowings and Paper Money

The general character of Austrian war finances was determined at the first meetings of the *Rüstungs-Commission,* on 8 and 9 June 1756, when it was recognised that no modern state was capable of meeting the demands of a war from its ordinary revenues; the Commission rejected expedients like stopping the payment of official salaries, for they would have smacked of desperation, 'our greatest resource therefore consists in domestic and foreign credit, and we simply cannot have enough of it'.[2]

By 'credit' was meant simply borrowing, and it was based on the notion that debts incurred during a war emergency could be paid off over the longer or shorter term after hostilities had ended. Credit in its manifold forms – voluntary or compulsory advances in cash or kind from the Hereditary Lands, loans raised on the commercial market, and the various types of paper money – contributed altogether 64.31 percent of the total extra cost of 160,101,986 florins incurred by the war, or 42.68 percent of the total military expenditure of 391,848,959 florins. This made borrowing the most significant form of war finance, and its relative importance increased still further in the course of the war when the French subsidy ceased.

The Hungarian Hereditary Lands made over a useful seven million or so florins in voluntary loans, or double the 3.5 million forthcoming from the *Stände* of the German Hereditary Lands. The *Hofjuden* (Court Jews') and other small native banking houses raised 2,243,000 florins, a figure which was eclipsed by the 59,207,831 florins, or 15.10 percent of the total military expenditure of 391,848,949 florins, raised on the credit of the city of Vienna by the semi-official Vienna Stadt Banco. Founded in 1705, the Banco was supported discreetly by Emperor Francis Stephen, and directed by Rudolph Count Chotek as President; it nevertheless stood at a useful remove from the state, and when Chotek in addition took over the presidency of the *Hofcammer* (Treasury) at the end of 1759, it was emphasised that his new responsibility would have no influence on the management of the Banco, so as to 'allay the fear that this rearrangement was nothing more than a device for the *Hofcammer* to grab the bank's funds'.[3]

With this, the resources of the Hereditary Lands in voluntary credit were exhausted, except for the kinds of paper money which will be mentioned shortly. There remained the instrument of forced loans, which in the course of the war raised 51,852,757 florins from the Hereditary Lands, over and above the proceeds of the Contributions and the voluntary loans. This was the equivalent of 13.23 percent of the total military expenditure (391,848,959 florins).

The entrepreneurial class of the core area of the monarchy was small (which makes the achievement if of the Stadt Banco all the more remarkable), and from the time of the mobilisation in 1756 Maria Theresa's advisers knew that they would have to go looking for loans beyond the Hereditary Lands. The Habsburg possessions in north Italy and the Low Countries now proved their worth as bridgeheads to some of the most economically and culturally advanced regions of Europe, and they gave the monarchy ready access to a number of the leading bankers of Amsterdam, Genoa and Leghorn (Livorno), as well as the services of a number of prominent native houses such as that of Giuseppe Tamzi of Lombardy, or Madame Louise Barbe Nettine of Brussels (which also processed the French subsidy). Kaunitz first mentioned the widow's name in this connection in 1757, and Maria Theresa wrote in reply: 'I approve. I am an ignoramus in matters financial, but I know from experience that Nettine keeps her own advantage very much in mind in her dealings with the court, and always rates her services very highly'.[4]

The total raised by these means amounted to 31,742,994 florins between 1756 and 1763,[5] with the Austrian Netherlands contributing 70.36 percent directly, Italy 23.60, and the Amsterdam banks 6.02.

'Manipulation' was the generic term for schemes to substitute paper currency for metal coinage. This too was a form of borrowing by the state, for the supposition was that the bearers would be repaid sooner or later in 'real' money, and with interest on top. The most celebrated of the manipulations was the brainchild of the *Directorial- and Commercian Hof-Rath* Ludwig Count Zinzendorf, a protégé of Kaunitz, who believed that readily-negotiable interest-bearing papers would be successful in raising cash when every other expedient appeared to have failed. Kaunitz outlined the proposals to Maria Theresa in March 1759,[6] but the scheme languished until he presented it to the *Staatsrath* two years later. This new supervisory body was under his thumb, and the issue was launched on 1 July 1762.

The scale exceeded the original proposals, in that the total paper value of the issue came to 18 million florins and was offered in two forms. *Zahlungs-Obligationen* to the worth of 7 million were issued in denominations of 25 and 100 florins, and were redeemable for cash on 1 July 1766 and bore a guaranteed annual interest of 6 percent. The remaining 11 million of the float were represented by large-denomination loan certificates (*Darlehens-Obligationen*) that were intended to be weighty financial instruments, as opposed to the everyday substitute currency of the *Zahlungs-Obligationen*.

The *Zahlungs-Obligationen* passed as swiftly through, and out of the populace, as some indigestible object might be conveyed through the alimentary tract. The notes passed rapidly into circulation, because they were forced upon the army officers and other public servants as pay; but the civilian recipients got rid of the notes as soon as they could, usually by using them to pay their taxes, and the result was that they sank rapidly below face value. The big *Darlehens-Obligationen* remained unsold.

On 15 June 1762 the Vienna Stadt Banco pledged its considerable credit to launch *Banco-Zettel* (bank notes) in denominations of 5,10, 25, 50 and 100 florins and to an initial value of 12 million florins. They obeyed the same principles as Zinzendorf s flotations, and the issue flagged for the same reasons. In November Kaunitz had to tell Maria Theresa that this existence of 10 or 12 million florins in paper money was not enough to meet the immediate costs of the campaign of 1763, which might amount to 22 million.[7] That campaign was never fought, for Austria was forced to make peace early in the spring, and not least because the monarchy was financially exhausted.

Who Furnished What?

The story of the Manipulations completes the review of the sums which were raised directly or indirectly from the resources of the Habsburg lands. Who contributed most? In taxes and loans the German and Hungarian Hereditary Lands supplied 243,034,687 florins, or 62.02 percent of the total war expenditure of 391,848,959. In detail the taxes and domestic loans for military purposes were furnished in the following percentages by:

Bohemia:	31.90
Hungarian lands as a whole;	17.36
Lower Austria:	16.07
Moravia:	11.82
Styria:	6.65
Upper Austria:	5.54
Carinthia:	3.14
Carniola:	1.94
Vienna:	1.71
Austrian Silesia:	1.64
Vorder-Österreich:	1.02
Görz and Gradisca:	0.48[8]

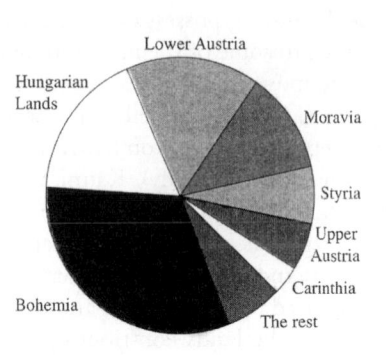

A list of receipts for the military funds in 1759 gives some notion of the sources of monies from within the lands of the Hungarian Crown, namely:

Hungary proper:	67.40%
Transylvania:	19.48
The Bánát:	9.58
'The Military Towns':	0.80[9]

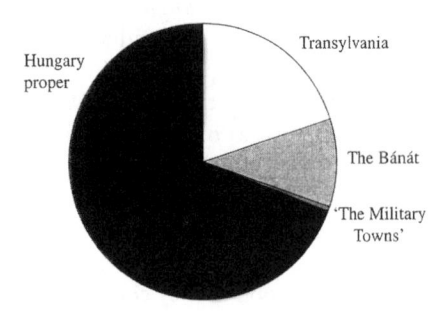

The proceeds from mining were an important feature of the Hungarian revenues, and Hungary proved to be a more generous source of voluntary loans than the German Hereditary Lands. In other respects the Hungarian contribution was niggardly. The kingdom was rich in grain, but time and time again the authorities had to send *Executionscommandi* into the countryside to raise the prescribed *Naturalien* by military action.[10]

Some 55,000,000 florins, or about 14 percent, of the total military expenditure came from the Austrian Netherlands in the form of taxes, loans, *dons gratuits* and the processed French subsidy (below). This was far more than had been expected at the time, and the substantial scale of this support remained unknown until it was uncovered by Professor Peter Dickson.[11] Even if the French subsidy has to be deducted at the full rate, the Netherlanders still contributed a very respectable 8 percent or so to the war costs.

Kaunitz was so impressed that after the war he was inclined to reassess the value of the various lands of the monarchy. The core area represented by the Hereditary Lands now appeared in a reduced state, having been weakened by war, over-exertion and natural disasters like the failure of the harvest. The peripheries, namely the Netherlands and Austrian Italy, had been spared from hostile armies, and had made significant and highly-valued contributions to the war in the form of credit and financial expertise. Only under the most compelling circumstances could they now be traded away to foreign powers, for they had qualified as the 'main supports' of the House of Habsburg-Lorraine, without which it would have been impossible to meet the huge costs of the war.[12]

Help from Outside

In the course of the war the *Reichstag* at Regensburg was able to raise 7,848,611 florins in contributions for the Austrian war effort. This supplied just 2 percent of the total military expenditure (391,848,959 florins), but the gesture of solidarity was not unimportant on its own account, and showed that there was still a glimmer of life in the institution of the *Reich*.

The French subsidy was of considerable value, both financially and politically, and it was paid in virtue of three treaties:

> The First Treaty of Versailles (1 May 1756) pledged French support in the shape of 3,456,000 florins per annum, or a corps of 24,000 troops in lieu;
>
> The Second Treaty of Versailles (1 May 1757) increased the promised subsidy to 12,000,000 florins per annum;

A third Versailles treaty of 31 May 1758 reduced the sum to a more realistic 3,000,000 florins, but bound the French to what was still owing from the earlier agreement. The arrears continued to accrue, because France was slipping into financial crisis, and before long the payments stopped altogether. They nevertheless amounted in all to 24,356,000 florins, and were of roughly the same order as the British subsidy to Prussia.

A review of the likely financial balance for 1758 expressed the hope that the Austrians would derive a 'rewarding' revenue from the conquered Prussian provinces in north-western Germany.[13] In the event the resources from these lands were lost to the French, after a prolonged and bad-tempered correspondence, and the Austrians were able to raise a total of only 497,698 florins in forcible 'contributions' from all the conquered Prussian territories. The worth of fodder and other military supplies captured from the Prussians amounted to a more useful 5,119,387 florins. It would seem that a combination of the two sums accounts in large part for the 6,343,536 florins entered mysteriously as the contribution 'from the military operations.'

Expenditure

In the early 1750s Kaunitz committed Austria to policies which were likely to lead to a new war, but the fact that hostilities broke out as early as they did, in the summer of 1756, overtook the monarchy before Maria Theresa and her advisers had scarcely begun to consider how they could finance a wartime army. All the accepted scales of comparison were overthrown, for the famous 'System' of Haugwitz had been designed only to support a peacetime army, and even before the fighting started the *Rüstungs-Commission* declared that this was no time for false economies, for 'even if a few million florins are wasted just now, this is nothing when we consider that the welfare and survival of the monarchy are at stake'.[14]

When the figures were added up after the war it was found that the total extra military expenditure, or the costs incurred as a result of the war, amounted to 260,101,986 florins, of which 92,824,963 were raised by contributions in cash or kind, and the remaining 167,277,023 by loans. The total military expenditure during the war years, including that which would have had to be paid anyway in peacetime, came to 391,848,959 florins. By 1763 the total state debt stood at a daunting 284,963,042 florins.

It is not easy to establish what costs had been incurred year by year, though Peter Dickson has made a useful extrapolation from the number of men entered on the establishments and suggests the following direct expenditure on troops for each full year of war, namely:

1757:	36,072000 florins
1758:	36,208,000
1759:	36,376,000
1760:	36,308,000
1761:	36,750,000
1762:	32,387,000[15]

At the time of the Seven Years War it was rare for any two sets of figures to be reckoned on the same basis. If, however, we accept the various calculations at their own worth, some of them can tell us a great deal about the spread of expenses among the various items of military expenditure.

A particularly informative set of calculations estimated that 46,904,172 florins were needed to put the army in a state to take to the field in 1758. What might be called the 'normal' costs amounted to 37,320,000 florins, which corresponds closely to Peter Dickson's projection of 36,208,00 from military establishment for that year. It comprised:

Infantry:	8,509,711 florins	= 22.80%
Cavalry:	3,809,574	= 10.20
Field artillery & pontoons:	1,315,246	= 3.52
Subsistence:	21,168,611	= 56.72
Hospitals, extraordinary expenses, and 100 mules for the infantry tents:	1,631,164	= 4.37

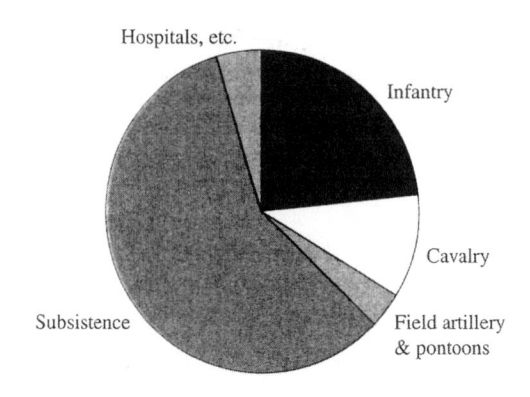

FINANCE

'Subsistence' therefore made up by far the largest single item of expenditure, and most of that would have gone on fodder for the horses. In addition the costs of replacing what the Austrians had lost at the battle of Leuthen (5 December 1757) and thereafter amounted to 9,584,116 florins. The report concludes by pointing out that 'these sums do not cover the transport [of provisions] from the depths of Austria, Hungary and even from the Bánát of Temesvár all the way to the magazines in Bohemia'.[16]

None of the other estimates single out 'subsistence' quite so informatively, but they are still worth quoting on their own account. A comprehensive forecast of all military expenses for 1761 groups the items under a number of broad headings. Out of an anticipated total of 41,466,000 florins the cost were expected to amount to:

Field armies:	18,809,217 florins	= 31.20%
Garrison troops, ordnance and other weapons, recruiting, remounts:	26,000,000	= 43.13
Interest and repayment of capital:	3,000,000	= 4.97
Army wagon train (*Fuhrwesen*), bakeries, magazines, purchase and transport of provisions:	12,466,400	= 20.68[17]

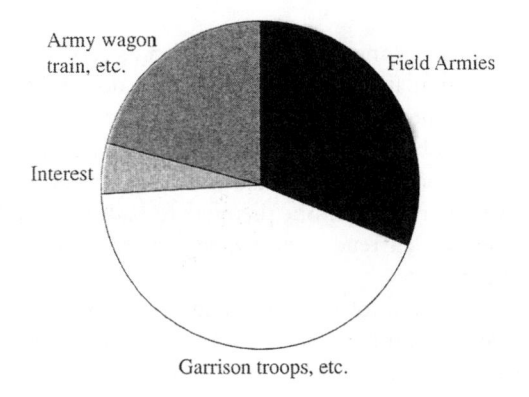

In November 1761 the Lower Austrian *Regierungsrat* Rabenbach compiled a set of costings which focused on the likely expenditure of the field armies for 1762. The total is pitched low at 13,235,294 florins, but it is less interesting than the way it was divided up, which Rabenbach presents in unusual detail:

Infantry:	37.93%
Cuirassiers, dragoons and hussars:	32.97
Croats:	3.64
Loudon 'Green' Grenadiers, Beck free battalion, Palatinal hussar regiment:	1.31
Artillery Fusilier Regiment:	0.78
Saxon cavalry:	4.40
Sapper companies:	0.11
Field Artillery and *Haus Artillerie*:	5.60
Netherlands Artillery:	0.15
Generals:	2.02

Engineer Corps:	0.17
Feld-Kriegs Expedition (HQ clerical staff):	0.05
Feld-Kriegs Commissariat (administrative expenses only):	0.22
Generals' adjutants and staffs:	0.19
General Staff:	0.11
Accountants:	0.01
Physicians and surgeons:	0.19
Field post:	0.01
Invalid convoy battalion:	0.14
Bridging and pontoons:	0.08
Contract with Pieter Dietrich for artillery horses:	0.49
Other teams for artillery and pontoons:	3.13
1,900 hired mules:	.65
Field bakeries (evidently including actual cost of bread):	5.18
Admin. costs of supply contracts:	0.07
Extraordinary expenses:	0.25[18]

These figures emphasise that anything to do with horses was very expensive.

Much of the money was re-circulated within the Habsburg dominions, and was therefore 'lost' at only one remove. All the time, however, cash was being eroded in a way that was permanent and particularly damaging. In September 1758 Maria Theresa alerted her authorities in Bohemia to the fact that money dealers were flooding the land with suspect German and Prussian coinage, and making off with the solid Austrian variety.[19] She therefore forbade her public treasuries in Bohemia to accept payment in the debased currency, and her soldiers to bring the objectionable currency back with them from campaign.

This was at best a partial solution, for it did not address the problem of what was happening to her 'good Imperial money' beyond the borders. The Austrian florin was a 'strong' currency which derived its worth from its metal content, and even at the lowest normal commercial rates it ought to have led to considerable savings when the army was buying provisions in Silesia or Saxony. All the profit, however, was being taken by the unscrupulous dealers, and the fraud was compounded by the fact that when the Austrian soldiers came to change their pay for the local currency, they were being repaid in debased coins at their fictional face value. In April 1759 Kaunitz supported a proposal from the *Directorium* to set up an official exchange that would take over the conversion. This scheme seems to have come to nothing, for a matter of weeks later the *Hofkriegsrath* had to tell Daun and the other commanders that Austrian currency was still flooding to the Prussian mints.[20] The Austrians must therefore insist that the sums dispensed in foreign territory must command their true local worth, and take Prussian currency only at a discount of 25 percent.

Behind all of this stood the malevolent figure of Frederick, for only a man free of scruple would have derived such benefit from debasing his own currency. Whenever his interests were served – as when paying his soldiers, public officials and his debts – he ordered the wretched recipients to take the coins at face value. He expected his soldiers to make up the difference by plundering and living at free quarter in conquered territories. On the other hand the 'good Imperial money' was taken in payment or exchange at no premium, and any resistance was overcome by the money dealers (Frederick's allies in this form of economic warfare), or by applying superior force. *GFWM*. Ernst Friedrich Giannini emphasised in 1761 how this appallingly debased currency permits the king to feed and sustain about 100,000 men from the same quantity of silver as Her Majesty has to pay for 40,000. If we suppose the war to last over any length of time, and if this abuse is not remedied, the result will be that the Austrians will furnish this cunning enemy with the best means to continue the contest, and hand him the dagger with which he can inflict repeated blows, each more deadly than the last.[21]

The Crisis of 1761/2 and its Outcomes

By the close of the sixth year of hostilities it was evident that the expanded *Directorium* was incapable of managing its dual burden of civilian and military administration, and that another of the creations of Haugwitz – the financial system of 1748 – intended to meet the needs of a peacetime army – had collapsed under the demands of war. As Kaunitz put it in his great memorandum of 9 December 1760: 'Most of Your Majesty's lands have been reduced to a state of exhaustion. Their finances are at an end, and we have hardly anything to cover the capital repayments or even the interest on the debts – which have shown a great and inevitable increase in the course of this war'.[22] Maria Theresa was persuaded by the eloquence of Kaunitz that she could no longer allow her state to be run by day-to-day expedients, and she sanctioned the creation of an overviewing *Staatsrath* (see p. 30).

The problem of paying for the war remained, and Kaunitz addressed it in a further substantial paper on 17 October 1761. He recalled to Maria Theresa that he had been at work for several months to see how it might be possible to provide for the campaign of 1762. Every thinkable source of income had been tapped, and every expedient explored, and yet the expected shortfall stood at an irreducible 15 million florins (see p. 141). Serious consideration had been given to confiscating the plate of the churches and monasteries, and turning the silver into coinage, but that measure would yield only 2 or 3 million florins, and create an impression of desperation that would make loans even harder to raise.

> Now that we have such convincing proof of the impossibility of meeting the deficit of 15 million through measures of extreme compulsion, or loans or any other kind of financial manipulation, we are left with the choice of either reducing the military establishment and its accompanying expense, or exposing the Most Illustrious House to something which will be both fatal and unavoidable, namely finding at the outset of the next campaign that we are no longer able to provide for the maintenance of the army. In that case everything will jar to a halt, the machine will collapse, and we will have to submit ourselves totally to the mercy of the enemy.

After much debate and taking of advice Kaunitz had concluded that the state could save 8 million by abolishing the army's perquisites of free rations and extra pay, reducing the regiments of infantry and hussars by two depot companies each, cutting the regiments of cuirassiers to 850 men and horses apiece, and doing away with all the 'new corps' – the regiment of Artillery Fusiliers, the Staff Infantry and Dragoons, the pioneers and the *Jager-Corps,* the Loudon 'Green Grenadiers, the Beck free battalion and the battalion of Anhalt-Zerbst. Kaunitz considered the saving of that 8 million as an essential minimum, for the state would otherwise be staring bankruptcy in the face. Kaunitz pointed that even then a deficit of 7 million would remain, hinting plainly enough that any softening was out of the question.

Almost any other measure (continued Kaunitz) would have been preferable to reducing the army in the middle of a war, since it would create a bad impression internationally, tempt the 'reduced' personnel to seek service with the Prussians, and demoralise the men who remained with the colours. He was therefore open to any realistic suggestions for combating the deficit by other means. However the reduction was the lesser of two evils, and:

> if a power finds that it must continue a war with 150,000 troops rather than 170,000, that is certainly unfortunate, but it does not compare with seeing the whole military machine decay. Let us look at the example of the King of Prussia. He does not have as many troops on foot as at the beginning of the war, but he gets by as best he can. If we set about reducing the newly-raised companies... we will still have a considerable military force with which we may conduct our operations to good effect, especially if the numbers will be strengthened by something not available to us before, namely a corps of at least 15,000 Russian troops.[23]

It will be evident that Kaunitz showed a regard for the conventional and established military order, while singling out for destruction the 'new' corps and units which were showing themselves of the most utility in modern war. Although Kaunitz did not entirely get his own way, the regiment of Staff Infantry was reduced from 16 companies to four, the regiment of Artillery Fusiliers and the corps of Sappers reduced, and the *Pionier* corps and the Staff Dragoons disbanded. The more general reductions affected the reserves and the mounted troops, but were still very damaging.

One of the reasons was that those 15,000 or more Russians, instead of being assigned to the Austrians, as Kaunitz presupposed, were actually put at the disposal of the Prussians (see p. 146). The consequent imbalance of forces, together with the loss of some of the most mobile elements of the army, put the Austrians at a disadvantage in the last and the decisive campaign of the war. It remains an open question whether state bankruptcy, as feared by Kaunitz, would have precipitated an equally damaging collapse.

Why was Frederick able to sustain the war financially, and why were the Austrians unable to do likewise? Their respective subsidies from their allies were approximately the same, but Frederick enjoyed the reliable income from his extensive and intact royal domains (the Habsburgs had given away most of theirs), as well as the revenues of his excise (*Accise*), and the products of the ruthless way he debased his currency and plundered Saxony, Mecklenburg and other German states – all of which builds up a picture of a man who commanded habits of obedience and a well-established bureaucracy, and who set no limits on the exercise of his will. The Theresian monarchy, by way of contrast, was a new creation which was overtaken by a war for which it was not fully prepared. Its authority came from the principle of consent, which (with a few marginal lapses) was observed within the Habsburg domains, and extended to Saxony (which the Austrians were trying to liberate) and in Silesia (which they claimed as their own).

5

Diplomacy

THE OLD SYSTEM

By the 1750s the structure of alliances termed 'The Old System' was in its seventh decade. Although the word 'system' is unduly rigid, the component parts of the league – Austria, Britain and the United Provinces – had come together often enough to show that its foundation was their common interest in containing France. The system was first expressed in the War of the League of Augsburg (1689–97), when the states in question first combined to check the aggrandisements of Louis XIV, but long before then it had been part of the policy of the Habsburgs to link themselves with useful partners to carry on the contest with the French in the German Empire and the Mediterranean Lands. For the British, in their turn, the connection with Austria enabled them to limit their commitments to the European mainland, and devote all the more resources to the colonial and maritime campaigns against the French.

A number of 'sub-systems' had come into being in the process. Just as the French sought to outflank the Old System politically and militarily by agreements with Sweden, the Turks and individual states of the *Reich* (Bavaria by tradition, and more recently Saxony and Brandenburg-Prussia), so the Austrians found in Russia an ally who helped to counter the French machinations in the Baltic, Poland and south-eastern Europe.

The fundamental connection between Austria and the Maritime Powers was reinforced by the peace treaties (1713–14) at the end of the War of the Spanish Succession, which put the Austrians in possession of the Netherlands, and thus gave the Habsburgs a direct responsibility for countering the northward expansion of the French. The terms of the subsequent Barrier Treaty (1716) bound the Austrians to subsidise Britain and the United Provinces to the tune of 1½ million taler per annum, and to pay the cost of the 11–12,000 Dutch troops who garrisoned the Netherlands fortresses.

Through an initially unrelated development Elector Georg of Hanover was welcomed to the throne of Britain by the Protestant Ascendancy after Queen Anne died in 1714. In that way the British acquired an interest in upholding a state of north Germany, just as the Austrians now had a stake in the security of north-western Europe.

KAUNITZ THE DIPLOMAT

The story of how the Old System was replaced is notoriously complicated, but it may be simplified to some degree by relating it to the career of Wenzel Anton Kaunitz. Austria's future *Staatscanzler* was the second son, and the sixth of 16 children of a middle-ranking Moravian noble. The family history told Wenzel Anton how political realities had persuaded his ancestors to renounce Protestantism in the last century, and how his mother, Maria Ernestine, née Countess von Ostfriesland and Rietberg, had inherited a claim to a number of lordships in East Frisia, a duchy situated in the remote north-western corner of Germany.

We have noted already (see p. 25) how Kaunitz was launched on a diplomatic career in 1741, and that it was not long before he saw at first hand how the French were able to run the Austrians, British and Dutch out of virtually the whole of the Austrian Netherlands. All the same, his attention was increasingly caught by the danger that was now presented to the monarchy by Frederick of Prussia, who allied ambition with a lack of scruple, and commanded an army of unexpected excellence.

Frederick's brief and successful First Silesian War (1740–2) had won him the former Austrian territories of the Duchy of Silesia and the County of Glatz. In June 1744 Frederick rejoined the ranks of Austria's enemies by invading Bohemia, and Kaunitz was struck by the fact this time that the king scarcely bothered to justify his resort to arms by legal arguments. In the same year the old reigning house of East Frisia died out, and Frederick ignored the claims of the Kaunitz-Rietbergs and other pretenders by taking possession of the duchy for himself. The Peace of Dresden (1745) confirmed Frederick as master of Silesia and Glatz, and by that time East Frisia had been absorbed into his domains.

Experience of international politics on the grandest scale came to Kaunitz in 1748, when he was dispatched to negotiate on Austria's behalf in an overall peace congress at Aix-la-Chapelle (Aachen). The Austrians intended to keep up a show of support for their British allies, at the same time as extending feelers to the French. The French representative Saint-Severin proved willing to chat, and both Kaunitz and Maria Theresa were encouraged to believe that the French would support an Austrian bid to recover Silesia, if, in return, the Austrians ceded territory in the Netherlands. Kaunitz was being too clever for his own good, for it transpired that the French were interested in conducting serious negotiations only with the British, and their talks led in turn to a definitive treaty of peace in October.

Early in 1749 Maria Theresa appointed Kaunitz as a permanent member of the *Conferenz,* and she invited him and her other leading statesmen to submit their ideas as to the direction for Austrian foreign policy. Her advisers came together on 24 March, and Kaunitz put forward the first and probably the most important of the memoranda (*Vorträge*) of his career.

Kaunitz (like Frederick) had read and admired Christian Wolff's *Vernünftige Gedanken vom gesellschaftlichen Leben der Menschen* (1721), which had rejected the religious formulae of the older political scientists, and looked for guidance instead to what was 'natural' and 'rational' in the secular world. Kaunitz deduced that it would thereby be possible to construct a 'system' that gave an intelligent and consistent direction to the affairs of state. Policy was now to be formulated by identifying the 'true interests' of the state; passions, sentiments and prejudices were to be set aside, except as far as they were known to influence less rational people. Such ways of thinking, allied with an acute intelligence and a way with words, enabled Kaunitz to cut through to the heart of a matter. He believed that the art of foreign negotiation consisted in selecting the single most cogent argument, and putting it across in a few well-chosen words to the people who mattered; this first favourable impression must then be reinforced in writing.

The paper of 24 March opened with a typical *tour d'horizon,* outlining the recent history and present state of diplomatic relations. Kaunitz then broached his specific recommendations. He did not deny that France was an historic enemy, or that many French and Austrian interests were likely to remain in contradiction, but he maintained that the Austrians must now attend to the immediate emergency which had been created when Frederick of Prussia had snatched away Silesia. The loss was intolerable in itself, and the king had shown himself to be 'the most dangerous and implacable enemy of our most gracious House... Not only must the king's hostile enterprises command our first, principal and unwavering attention, but we must devise means to weaken him, confine his superior force once more within acceptable bounds, and thus win back what we have lost'.[1] Austria could rely on the active help of the Russians, and probably draw in a number of smaller states by holding out the prospect of territorial gains. No less importantly, France must be detached from her connections with Prussia, and persuaded (by the offer of territory in the Netherlands) to support the Austrian effort by making over subsidies, and by guaranteeing Maria Theresa in possession of Silesia and Glatz when those lands had been recovered from the Prussians.

In the political sense these proposals were somewhat less than revolutionary. Maria Theresa was already looking to permanent friendship with France, while Kaunitz sought to adapt, rather than abandon, the old connections with the Maritime Powers; indeed, he hoped that Hanover might be drawn into the alliance. Kaunitz's choice of the military option was however startling, and went beyond anything yet entertained by Maria Theresa, or by the old *Staatscanzler* Corfiz Anton Count Ulfeld, who was the only other minister of the *Conferenz* to argue that the threat from Prussia was more urgent than that from France. Maria Theresa was won over by what Kaunitz had to say, and she commended his ideas to the other ministers.

First Overtures and Frustration

For almost seven years the 'Diplomatic Revolution' made no recognisable progress. Maria Theresa appointed Kaunitz as her envoy to Versailles in June 1749, which was a clear sign that she intended to put relations with France on a new footing. His departure was delayed for 13 months, until the French sent an ambassador of their own, and he finally made his entry in a splendid train of coaches in October 1750. The spectators were impressed by the man's style, but Kaunitz did not have the money to keep up the show, and he found that the French ministers were unwilling to be moved from their friendship with Prussia. Kaunitz appeared to have little to show for the two years he spent in France, apart from a knowledge of the workings of the court, and the good opinion of the Pompadour and a number of further individuals.

Meanwhile Austria's 'traditional' diplomats had made a successful demarche to Spain, the other major Bourbon power, and concluded the Treaty of Aranjuez (18 April 1752), which settled historic differences in Italy. Piedmont-Sardinia acceded a few days later. Although the Piedmont-Sardinians were notoriously opportunistic and unreliable, these deals amounted to a useful clearing of the Austrian flank in the Mediterranean, and they had been reached quite independently of Kaunitz.

In April 1753 Kaunitz was appointed *Staatscanzler* in succession to the cold and slow Ulfeld. This was at a time when two wars were in the making – not just from the rivalry of Austria and Prussia, but that arising from the competition between the British and French in North America, which was certain to precipitate hostilities in Europe as well. Rejected by the French, Kaunitz now sought to restore relations with the Maritime Powers, or effectively with the British, since the Dutch were retreating into neutrality. British and Austrian interests touched in the Austrian Netherlands, and again in the *Reich,* where Hanover was exposed to attack by the Prussians. These connections were now reassessed, and in the event they were unable to withstand the strains of definition.

The Austrians objected that the Maritime Powers were strangling the trade of the Netherlands, and, although they proved to be poor guardians of the Barrier, they still required Austria to pay for the upkeep of the Dutch garrisons, and for repairing the fortresses, which had been wrecked by the French in the last war. It did not help the arguments of Kaunitz that the Austrians had put themselves technically in the wrong by defaulting on the recent instalments of the Barrier subsidy, and so the negotiations entered a state of deadlock.

Hanover was isolated geographically from Britain, but the electorate was of great importance to the men in power. The Protestant Ascendancy in Britain rested constitutionally on their joint sovereign George, of the Hanoverian family of Guelph; moreover a French or Prussian army which controlled Hanover would also be master of Oldenburg and the whole German coastline on the North Sea, jeopardising British commerce in northern waters. The British therefore looked to

Austria for military help – a demand which related the Hanoverian issue to that of the Austrian Netherlands, and with that of Austria's political relations and security as a whole.

Kaunitz and Maria Theresa had given priority to fighting the Prussians, and they were willing to divert precious troops to defend the Netherlands and Hanover only if the British would provide an equivalent, by subsidising 60,000 Russians to attack Prussia, and by funding a corps of several thousand German auxiliaries.

The British opened the appropriate talks with the Russians in March 1753, and the negotiations were prolonged in a sporadic way until September 1755, when the envoy Sir Hanbury Williams finally concluded a treaty of subsidy. This agreement was disowned in London (below), and it was in any case overtaken by events.

By the high summer of 1755 the clashes at sea and in North America made a war between the British and French imminent. Since no agreement had yet been reached on the questions of the Netherlands or the Russian subsidy, the Vienna *Conferenz* decided on 16 August 1755 to stand aside from the conflict, and put up not so much as a token resistance if the French invaded the Netherlands. Kaunitz therefore returned to the old idea of a rapprochement with France.

It did not prove difficult to interest the French in a straightforward exchange of territories, whereby a substantial part of the Austrian Netherlands would be consigned to Don Philip (son of the Bourbon King Philip V of Spain); Austria would receive in return Philip's duchies of Parma, Piacenza and Guastalla, which adjoined Austria's existing territories in Lombardy. With his cold-eyed view of statecraft Kaunitz was not troubled at the thought of consigning Netherlanders to foreign rule. He had written that the welfare of the loyal Netherlanders was important to the well-being of the monarchy, but 'since it is impossible to sustain both objectives, the general good must to that extent be preferred to the private advantage'[2] – the 'private advantage' in this case being that of the Netherlanders.

The talks ended there. Louis XV had a personal commitment to an alliance with the Austrians, but the ministry as a whole was not willing to proceed to what Kaunitz considered was the heart of the matter, which was for the French to detach themselves from Prussia, and agree not only to the Austrian reconquest of Silesia and Glatz from the King of Prussia, but to 'pen him up in such narrow confines as to put Prussia in the condition in which it existed before the Thirty Years War, and thereby incapable of exacting any revenge in the future'.[3]

THE BREAKTHROUGH

Providence, as Kaunitz saw it, now took a hand. Frederick was alarmed at warlike noises from Russia, and he took advantage of George II's concerns for the security of Hanover to join the British in concluding a Convention of Westminster (16 January 1756). The parties saw it as a limited and defensive arrangement, which secured their respective strategic hindquarters, but they left out of account entirely the effects which the deal might have on their other relationships. For the Austrians and Russians it constituted a blow to the already tottering Old System. Versailles was outraged beyond measure, since the French had rebuffed loyally every Austrian attempt to detach them from the Prussians, and a French envoy was even now working in Berlin to re-negotiate the Prussian alliance.

Kaunitz exploited his opening with caution and skill. He instructed Georg Adam Count Starhemberg, the Austrian ambassador in Paris, to bend his immediate efforts to preventing the French from renewing their alliance with Frederick (which proved easy enough). A Franco-Austrian defensive alliance was the next realistic goal, since Kaunitz did not yet call on the French to take an active part in the war against Prussia; however it would be useful if the French were to station a corps of observation in friendly territory in Westphalia, so as to keep Hanover and smaller

Protestant states in awe, and he insisted that any cession of territory in the Netherlands must be contingent on the reconquest of Silesia and Glatz by the Austrians, which would give the French a stake in the defeat of Prussia.

The result was a defensive agreement which became known as the First Treaty of Versailles (1 May 1756). The Austrians and French pledged support in the shape of 24,000 troops (or a suitable subsidy in lieu), if the European territories of either came under attack. Among the secret clauses, probably the most important bound the French to abandon the Prussian alliance. The exchange of territories was to be negotiated later (and the French soon put in a bid for the entire Netherlands). The treaty as it stood was ratified by Maria Theresa with unbounded pleasure.

If we have heard little so far about the Russians, it was because the connection between the courts of Vienna and St. Petersburg rested on the foundation of an alliance of 1726, as renegotiated 20 years later, and on a perceived unity of interests. Maria Theresa wrote to Daun in the middle of the Seven Years War that the court of Russia had never wavered in its determination to cut Frederick down to size, being aware that he had doubled the number of his troops, and was intriguing with his sister, Queen Ulrike of Sweden, to 'play the master in northern Europe'.[4]

The Austrians could therefore repose near-absolute trust in Russian support in the event of hostilities, though the manner of such help was difficult to predict, since Empress Elizabeth governed in a notoriously unsystematic way. Austria's connection with Britain was also of long standing, and at first Kaunitz hoped that Britain's concern for Hanover would generate enough English money to set substantial Russian forces in motion when war arrived. On 30 September 1755 (as we have seen) Hanbury Williams negotiated such a treaty with the Russians. On the strength of this agreement Elizabeth and her ministers resolved on 7 October to reduce Prussia to its old boundaries by supporting the enforced return of Silesia and Glatz to the Austrians. As a first step the Russians would establish magazines sufficient to provide for 100,000 troops along the Baltic coast, East Prussia being the obvious target. The arrangement with Hanbury Williams, which had been the incentive for these heroic resolutions, nevertheless fell apart within a matter of weeks.

Hanbury Williams had made the deal in good faith, but the British ministry declined to ratify the treaty, and instead looked to Prussia to provide the immediate security for Hanover. For her part, Empress Elizabeth could only regard the Anglo-Prussian Treaty of Westminster as a betrayal by the British, and on 16 February 1756 Hanbury Williams learned that the Russians considered his agreement as null and void.

The old Russian chancellor Aleksei Petrovich Bestuzhev fell from grace, for he had been associated with the now-defunct Old System. His influence was supplanted by that of the brothers Shuvalov and the 'French' party led by the vice-chancellor Mikhail Ilarionovich Vorontsov. However Russian policy was consistent as far as it concerned hostility against Prussia, and the new men were bent on war. A supreme agency, the Conference at the Imperial Court, came into being on 25 March 1756, and over the short term at least it brought surprising energy and order to the conduct of affairs. As early as 29 April the Russians were able to propose an offensive alliance to Vienna, with full details as to how it might be implemented. Russia would mobilise 80,000 troops for an attack on Prussia simultaneously with the Austrians, and sustain her efforts until Silesia and Glatz had been returned to Maria Theresa, and East Prussia had fallen to the Russians. Elizabeth would than hand over East Prussia to the Poles in return for Kurland, Semigallia and a number of territories along the existing Russo-Polish border; invitations were to be issued to Sweden and Saxony, with the bait of further pieces of Prussian territory.

Matters were actually proceeding too fast for the liking of Kaunitz, for he feared that the Russians were stampeding him into war before he was ready. On 22 May 1756 he therefore sent word to St. Petersburg to ask the Russians to postpone the attack until the following spring, for the recent treaty with the French fell short of an offensive alliance, and he still had to allay French fears about the ambitions of Austria and Russia. Four days later Kaunitz learned that the Austrian army was in no state to take to the field, which confirmed that he had been right to ask the Russians to stay their hand. The Russian Conference gave way with regret, and reminded the Austrians that the slowness of their preparations would act to Frederick's advantage.

The Prussians indeed began to mobilise on 10 June 1756, and in July the Austrians threw themselves into a full-scale mobilisation in response. On 26 July the Prussian envoy Klingenberg asked for an explanation of Austria's warlike preparations, and was fobbed off with a vague answer. He was back again on 22 August, this time with a written demand, and was told that the Austrians were only responding to what the Prussian were doing already, and that Austria had no threatening alliance with Russia. 'But as to what might happen in the future,' Kaunitz commented in private, 'that's something we can pass over in silence without too much violation to the truth'.[5] Maria Theresa and Kaunitz sent word to Starhemberg in Paris that the answer was calculated to leave Frederick in a dilemma, for he must now either wait on events that were unfolding dangerously for him, or do something that would brand him as an aggressor. Such an act would play into the hands of the Austrians, because Kaunitz reasoned that Austria could survive a first blow, and then be able to call with every justification on the help of the Russians and French in the following year.

On 2 September 1756 news arrived that the advance guard of a Prussian army had broken across the border of the Electorate of Saxony. Frederick had been misled by false intelligence to the effect that Saxony was a member of the league that was forming against him, and he had determined to seize the initiative by striking at the nearest and most vulnerable partner of this supposed alliance. Vienna was delighted on three accounts, for the Austrian army (which was far from ready) would be spared the main weight of the first attack, and Frederick had not only broken the peace, but had done so at the expense of innocent Saxony, the first Protestant state of Germany.

Kaunitz concluded that many remaining political obstacles could now be overcome, and he at once urged his envoys in Paris and St. Petersburg to seize the opportunity. All of the negotiations were now pushed through with a new impetus, and by the early summer of 1757 Austria, Russia, France and a number of smaller states had been brought into an active wartime partnership. To that extent the Diplomatic Revolution was complete.

The Tying-Together of the Alliance

Russia

Kaunitz had consigned a particularly bulky set of instructions to Esterházy in St. Petersburg on 13 November 1756. The long-standing French connections with Turkey imposed some delay on the negotiations which followed, but on 11 January 1757 Elizabeth acceded to the first, or defensive, Austro-Treaty of Versailles. A secret treaty of 2 February was more positive and specific, for it set out the scale and nature of the Austrian and Russian efforts, and laid the ground rules for their military co-operation. The empresses each promised to maintain at least 80,000 troops in the field for the duration of hostilities, and not to lay down arms until Prussia had been confined within bounds that would guarantee the public peace. In addition the Austrians promised to pay the Russians a subsidy of 1 million roubles per annum (an obligation later taken over by the French), while the Russians undertook to fit out a fleet of up to 20 sailing warships and up to 40 galleys. Each power was to furnish the other with accurate enumerations of its forces, and to allow the other's military attachés a seat and voice in councils of war in the field.

The military clauses were thus even-handed, and matched very closely the original proposals which the Russians had put forward on 20 April 1756. There was, however, a lack of reciprocity in the political arrangements. Whereas the Russians pledged themselves to continue hostilities until a treaty of peace should secure Maria Theresa in possession of Silesia and Glatz, the Austrians promised only to use their good offices to support the Russian ambition to exchange East Prussia (once it had been conquered) for the Polish territories in Kurland and Semigallia. Kaunitz feared that anything more would frighten off the French and Turks.

Sweden

Austria's démarche towards Sweden was favoured by a particularly auspicious political constellation. As an ally of France, Austria could now benefit from the long-established connection between France and the northern power. Domestic arrangements also worked in Austria's favour. The prolonged and exhausting Great Northern War (1700–21) had left Sweden with just one-quarter of its former holdings in northern Germany, namely western Pomerania (Vorpommern) and the port of Wismar, all the rest having been lost to Hanover and Prussia. The militant 'Hat' party among the nobles (see p. 406) looked for revenge, and their antagonism towards Prussia was sharpened by the knowledge that their queen, Luise Ulrike, a sister of Frederick of Prussia, was working with the rival 'Caps' to terminate what later became known as the 'Era of Liberty' – the noble predominance which had been introduced by a constitution in 1720.

On 21 March 1757 representatives of Sweden, Austria and France signed a Convention of Stockholm, whereby Sweden would work with France to uphold the provisions of the Peace of Westphalia (1648), which was the historic guarantee of the liberties of Germany. For the time being any Swedish gains in Pomerania would be conditional on the Swedes coming under attack by Prussia, but there could be no doubt that Sweden now counted as a working partner of the alliance. The Swedish Senate was under the control of the Hats, and on 22 September the Swedes went on to commit 20,000 troops to the war. If Kaunitz was disappointed in the size of the force (he had hoped for up to 40,000 men), he prized the political connection with Protestant Sweden in its own right, as a means of representing to the states of north Germany that he was not engaged in a war of religion.

France

Once Frederick had invaded Saxony, it was realistic for the Austrians to hope that they could persuade the French to move from the defensive alliance of 1 May 1756 to an offensive one. The appropriate instructions were sent to Starhemberg on 10 October 1756.

Month succeeded month without the resourceful Starhemberg being able to report any progress. In December the negotiations threatened to stick fast on the issue of 'reciprocity,' whereby the French insisted that any efforts to weaken Prussia must be matched by a striving to weaken Britain. This did not suit the Austrians, who wished to avoid any entanglement in the Franco-British hostilities, and Starhemberg argued that 'reciprocity' was always relative, and that any French effort against Prussia would be more than repaid by gains in the Netherlands, and would in any case be eclipsed by Austria's commitment of troops and treasure.

On 5 January 1757 the madman Damiens made an attempt on the life of the French king. Louis XV was not badly injured, but this episode reminded French politicians that the connection with Austria rested on a very narrow personal base, and for a time the Pompadour was deserted by all but her inner circle. There was a further upset on 1 February, when the ministers of War and Marine – d'Argenson and Machault – were sacrificed to placate the Paris *Parlement*.

In the middle of March, however, the French military envoy d'Estrées was back from some productive talks in Vienna, and the acting foreign minister Abbé Bernis was under special instructions from Louis to push the negotiations forward. Events now moved with unexpected speed, and the 18 months of talks, representations and conferences culminated in the signing of the Second Treaty of Versailles on 1 May 1757.

The preamble stated the need to confine the King of Prussia 'within such boundaries as to render him incapable of disturbing the public repose.' The partners would maintain their cooperation until a treaty of peace put Austria once more in possession of Silesia and Glatz, together with 'the principality of Crossen and suitable stretch of territory.' This would bring the Austrian border to within immediate striking range of Berlin.

The French committed themselves to further heavy obligations, promising to maintain 10,000 Württemberg and Bavarian troops as auxiliaries of the Austrians, and to put 105,000 of their own men into the field. France would pay the Austrians an annual subsidy equivalent to 12 million florins, to be made over every 1 March, and backdated to 1 March of the present year. France would also subsidise the Swedes and Saxons, who would be further rewarded by territories wrested from Prussia – with Magdeburg and Halle going to Saxony, and the lost land in eastern Pomerania (Hinterpommern) being returned to Sweden.

Starhemberg managed to disassociate Austria from any direct action against British or Hanoverian interests, and, while the French pledges to Austria were real and binding from the start, the greater part of the Austrian concessions would take effect only after Maria Theresa had regained Silesia and Glatz. The only exception was the clause whereby the French could place garrisons in Ostend and Nieuport immediately after the treaty had been ratified. Otherwise the French would have to wait until after the victory over Prussia before they could take over their promised gains along the southern borders of the Austrian Netherlands. These were the territories of Chimay and Beaumont, Fort de la Knocque, and the towns of Ostend, Nieuport, Furnes, Ypres and Mons. Luxembourg and the rest of the Netherlands would go to Louis' son-in-law the Infant Don Philip, who would make over his Italian duchies to Austria – the arrangement again being conditional on the victory of the alliance.

The Reich

On 10 January 1757 the states of the *Reich* assembled in diet at Regensburg, under heavy pressure from the Austrians to take armed action against Frederick. Seven days later a formal resolution (*Beschluss*) authorised Francis Stephen as Emperor and Supreme Judge to take measure to restore the Saxon lands to their rightful owner, and to gain satisfaction for the further wrongs which had been done against himself and against Maria Theresa, as Queen of Hungary and Elector of Bohemia. The voting in favour of the resolution had been 60 to 25, and the majority had comprised not only the Catholic states, but Protestant ones like Mecklenburg, Pfalz-Zweibrücken, Hessen-Darmstadt and Ansbach, whose rulers aligned themselves variously out of respect for the institutions of the *Reich,* antagonism against Prussia, the hope of reward, or simply because they were hemmed in by Austrian or pro-Austrian territory.

(N.B. See the chapter 'Strategic Dimensions' in Part III *Waging War* for the further history of the alliance, and the interests, aims and military performance of the partners).

Part II

The Army

6

The Army as a Whole

MILITARY REFORM

The Programme and its Achievements

After Maria Theresa had survived the crisis of the first years of her reign, she set herself the task of bringing her army to compete with the awesome military power of Prussia. When she appointed Count Thurn as the tutor of Archduke Leopold in 1761 she told him that her son must be taught the science of arms, as 'the one and only way in a which a prince of his birth may prove of use to the monarchy, excel in the eyes of the world, and endear himself to me. For that reason you, as a soldier, have been selected for this mission'.[1]

Already in 1734 Prince Eugene, who was himself fading fast, had drawn the attention of Emperor Charles VI to the effects of a prolonged peace, 'during which much disorder and many abuses have crept in among the regiments, and many officers have forgotten elements of the service'.[2] Nothing had been put right before the army was overtaken by successive reverses in the Turkish war of 1737–9, and the campaigns of 1741 in Silesia and Bohemia. When he looked back on those events Kaunitz observed that:

> it was all the more difficult to cast about for a remedy, because nearly all the borders were totally devoid of fortresses. Terrifying masses of Turks could break in from the one side, while from the other the King of Prussia could sweep over the Hereditary Lands with a picked and well-drilled army. The welfare, security and peaceful possession of those lands would therefore have been exposed to the arbitrary will of those turbulent neighbours if we had not been able to confront them with a powerful and fitting military force.[3]

A multitude of obstacles stood in the way of creating such a 'powerful and fitting military force.' Maria Theresa exclaimed in her *Political Testament* that 'you would scarcely have believed it, but not the slightest attempt had been made to establish uniformity among our troops. Each regiment went about marching, drilling and taking up alarm stations in its own fashion… The same words and commands were expressed by the regiments in different ways. Is it any wonder that the Imperial troops were invariably beaten during the ten years before I came to the throne?'.[4] We shall encounter the details of the various military reforms in due course, but here would seem to be a convenient place to set out the main features of this enterprise, and take stock of its achievements and limitations.

The process of reform as a whole probably began in 1742, when the direction of foreign policy was separated from the *Hofcanzley,* and entrusted to the new officer of the *Hof- and Staatscanzler* – the base from which Kaunitz was to formulate grand strategy. In the next year the *Innerösterreichische Kriegsstelle* was abolished, and the Vienna *Hofkriegsrath* took over the control of the 'Croatian' Military Borders. Joseph Prince of Sachsen-Hildburghausen (an unlucky soldier but an able administrator) assumed the management of the Military Borders in 1744, and, with the full support of

Vienna, carried out a programme of reform over the next five years. He established the regiment as the common unit of military and civil administration in the Borders, and he made one-third of the Croatian manpower available for service in the field by annual rotation.

Equally comprehensive were the achievements of Joseph Wenzel Prince Liechtenstein. He took up the post of *Artillerie General-Director* in 1744, and by the outbreak of the Seven Years War he was able to furnish the army with a corps of thoroughly professional gunners, together with a train of excellent new pieces of artillery.

The early months of 1748 were a particularly creative period of Maria Theresa's state. Kaunitz explained afterwards that 'contrary to all reasonable hope, she, through her maternal care, for her lands, succeeded in consolidating a system where the necessary funds could be found to support 108,000 troops in the Hereditary Lands in time of peace… there the men were properly maintained, drilled in the use of arms, and received their pay on the nail. The costs of the court, the civil administration and the embassies in foreign parts were also defrayed, along with meeting the interests on the state debt when they fell due'.[5] The necessary financial base had been worked out by Friedrich Wilhelm Count Haugwitz, and approved by the *Conferenz* on 29 January 1748. In essence the *Stände* were to provide long-term funding for the army by agreeing to *Rezesse* whereby they would make over their taxes ('Contributions') for spans of several years at a time. These revenues, together with the income from the royal lands, were to be administered by a new all-embracing administrative department, the *Directorium in Publicis et Cameralibus*.

Ten days later, on 8 February 1748, a Military Reform Commission met for its first session. Prince Charles of Lorraine attended as President, and old Johann Joseph Harrach as head of the *Hofkriegsrath*, but the real initiative lay with *FM*. Liechtenstein, *FZM*. Leopold Daun, and the *General-Kriegscommissar* Franz Ludwig Count Salburg as head of the army supply branch, and the busy little *Hofkriegsrath* counsellor Augustin Wöber as manager of the Commission's business. By the end of its 20 sessions the Commission had amongst other things determined the peacetime establishments of the regiments, worked out measures to eliminate abuses in army accounting, and regularised the raising of recruits.

The Reform Commission was however unwilling to concede that failures in the high command might have had anything to do with the defeats in the last war. Everything was said to have been the product of the disorder among the troops, and their ponderous tactical procedures. These were to be remedied by matching the drills and discipline which had made the Prussians so formidable. As Daun described it, 'I would compare the way the Prussians win their battles with the methods of the Swedes before them, who brought a new way of making war to Germany… It is the same with the Prussians nowadays. They excel in the management of their weapons, they manoeuvre with miraculous skill, they shoot extremely fast, and they are equipped with a lavish artillery'.[6] Daun accordingly published an infantry *Regulament* in 1749, and companion sets for the German cavalry and the hussars appeared between then and 1751.

Frederick had devised Europe's first-ever battle-scale manoeuvres in 1743, which gave his generals invaluable peacetime experience in directing large bodies of troops. By 1752 the Austrians were ready to do the same, and in August of that year they carried out their first essay in contested manoeuvres, when *FZM*. Browne assembled his command on the heights of Skalka near Kolin, and pitted one force against another. Realism was carried to an excess when two of his brigade commanders had become befuddled by drink, and forgot to assign the 'attackers' a line on which to halt their advance, or the 'defenders' a position on which to fall back. Cogniazzo described what happened next: 'Nobody believed that he could give way without losing face … The Hungarians began to shoot off their buttons, which were shaped like bullets, while the Germans answered by discharging their ramrods. I can still picture that major of the regiment of Haller who was skewered by a ramrod before my eyes'.[7]

The manoeuvres of 1753 passed off without mishap, and in July 1754 Maximilian Browne, who had just been promoted to Field Marshal, was able to entertain Their Imperial Majesties at Kolin with a programme of demonstrations, parades and festivities. Frederick learned that the Austrians were now marching in cadenced step in the Prussian style, though they still had to settle on a comfortable length of pace.

Otherwise the drills and manoeuvres 'improved our marching both in line and column. They taught us how to deploy, how to traverse, and countless other technicalities, which had been unknown to our old procedures. They gave our generals the opportunity they had been seeking to try out tactical principles on a large scale, and manoeuvre their forces according to the nature of the terrain'.[8]

> Now, when we brought out troops together, our ears were no longer assailed by that confusion of languages which had brought to mind the Tower of Babel. Now the German word of command exercised its miraculous force, and the Slavonians, the Hungarians, the Italians and the Walloons became as familiar with it as with their native tongue. No more did we hear the old Gothick orders: *Schlagt an! Gebet Feuer!* Instead the young officer gave vent to a clear, short and penetrating *An!* Then exploded in a full-throated *Feuer!* – like Homer's Stentor. Now we saw the generals return smiling and inwardly satisfied from their peaceful battle-fields… where they gazed on their troops with a martial eye and timed them with watches in their hands, observing to their own great astonishment just how many rounds these new Austrians could fire in a minute.[9]

Through public statements and private attentions Maria Theresa showed her peculiar regard for the military condition. She founded the Military Academy at Wiener-Neustadt in 1752, she allowed officers in uniform free access to court, and she instituted her Militär-Maria Theresien-Orden, which was open to brave and resourceful officers without regard to rank or pedigree.

In October 1755 the Commissary Lutter, *FML*. Buccow of the cavalry and the infantry *GFWMs*. Wied and Wolfersdorff carried out an exacting muster inspection of the 12 infantry regiments and the three cavalry regiments – 28,122 men in all – which were quartered in Bohemia. Their report remains the most complete assessment of the moral and material condition of the army before the outbreak of the Seven Years War. They investigated the state of the weapons, and found that 'all the infantry regiments quartered here are… now furnished with new muskets on the regulation calibre, the only exception being the regiment of Kaiser, which still carries its captured French muskets, and its own design of bayonet.' The uniforms were complete, the recruiting had been going ahead in an orderly fashion, the regimental books were in good order, any damp or dark accommodation was being rebuilt or demolished, the pay was being made over without any unauthorised deductions, the rations of bread were ample and palatable, and meat and vegetables were available at cheap prices.[10]

The work of military reform continued throughout the war, when its achievements included the setting-up of a corps of sappers, and (in 1758) the creation of a first-class General Staff. Frederick's secretary noted towards the end of 1760 that 'after the close of every campaign our enemies take due note of their oversights and mistakes. They put them right, and they are therefore in a condition to bite us all the harder when the next campaign comes around'.[11]

At its best the new Austrian army was a being 'full of vigour and life'.[12] The most convincing testimonies as to the achievement of the reformers come from Frederick himself. A British military observer noted that the king was 'very far… from having a contempt for the Austrians, but the contrary; and I have heard himself several times call to his officers and bid them take notice of what the enemy did well'.[13] As a consequence of the loss of Finck's corps at Maxen Frederick had to write to Ferdinand of Brunswick to require the return of the ten squadrons of Prussian dragoons from western Germany, explaining that the prince was contending merely with the French, 'whereas I am at grips here with the Austrians, who keep much better order, and are militarily more proficient than my other enemies'.[14]

The undeniable improvements in the quality of the Austrian troops and horses, their clothing, equipment and provisioning, their supporting artillery, all bear witness to some fundamental institutional strengths. *FM*. Daun was able to uphold discipline among the common soldiers in the main Austrian army until the end of the war, while Frederick had to allow his troops the freedom to plunder if he was to persuade them to remain with the colours.[15]

The Limitations of Reform

Such an army ought to have been able to overcome the forces of Prussia, which were weakened by years of war, 'but experience showed the contrary. There were occasions when we could see one corps of the enemy army confronting two of our own in perfect safety, regardless of the overwhelming odds against it – and what is more, that force would sometimes go over to the offensive. This came as a surprise to many people, but not to soldiers like us, and especially those who looked beyond appearances, and considered the matter more carefully in the light of their military judgement'.[16]

What had gone wrong? A variety of explanations suggest themselves. The Austrians had put at least as much work into their drilling as the Prussians, and yet they had failed to derive equal benefit, for they wasted time on elaborations and ceremonial niceties (while Frederick concentrated on the bare essentials), and it was notorious that the Austrian peacetime garrisons, and especially those of the cavalry, were scattered widely over the dominions. The Austrians were certainly capable of putting on large-scale exercises, as at Kolin, but their troops had been denied the opportunity of drilling together in large bodies as a matter of everyday routine.[17]

By the time the army entered the Seven Years War the new Austrian system had still to settle down as a coherent whole. The military reformers had been labouring for only eight years, whereas decades of work had gone into building up the proficiency of the Prussian army, and Frederick had dedicated himself to this mission with an almost fanatical zeal and attention to detail.[18]

Mastery of the new drills was considered an important qualification by Austrian officers who put themselves forward for promotion,[19] or by seniors who were reporting on the performance of their juniors. Conversely many officers were genuinely overtaxed by the quantity and complexity of the recent changes. In 1757 the *Rangs- and Conduits-Lista* of the infantry regiment of Erzherzog Carl details the sad case of Captain Petrus Kyss, who was 'afflicted with what they call "gout," and has therefore not attained a complete grasp of the new drill.' Captain Antonius Hertelendy was another veteran who had proved himself in action, but was 'not very well schooled in the new drill.' The superannuated Second Lieutenant Andreas Jacobuska 'strives zealously to make himself at home with the new drill, but does not have the talent to master it'.[20]

The Austrian cavalry actually declined in performance when measured against the Prussian horse, and *FM*. Carl Paul Pálffy was inclined to think that 'a considerable part has probably been played by the dismissal and release of so many old but still serviceable cavalrymen – ordinary troopers, NCOs, officers and senior regimental officers of all grades. The loss could well be due to the recently-introduced drill, which is all too extreme'.[21] *FM*. Neipperg had already complained that the infantry had lost experienced officers who had been unable to accommodate themselves to the novelties.[22]

Many of these were probably genuine cases, but we are now beginning to touch on deliberate non-compliance and wilful obstruction. Scarcely had Daun's new infantry *Regulament* made its appearance in 1749 when it seemed that almost every colonel took pleasure in finding excuses and objections that would excuse him from departing from it.[23]

A report of the Prussian ambassador Podewils[24] in 1747 confirms what Maria Theresa already suggested, that her ambition to raise her army to Prussian standards would be opposed by all the officers who had an interest in maintaining the present abuses. One day at a parade she remarked that the soldier's long coats must prove inconveniently warm on hot days, and inconveniently soggy on wet ones. She therefore proposed that the troops should have short coats in the Prussian style. The generals objected that the Prussians could survive in their short coats only because their tents had canvas floor coverings. When Maria Theresa desired to have these as well, officialdom exaggerated the cost to such a degree that the whole project fell through.

Towards the end of the war one of Maria Theresa's officers exclaimed that every useful initiative was still being set at naught by the ministers and great lords, who frustrated every measure which challenged their revenues, comforts, or systems of favourites:

> *FM.* Daun, as master of his trade down to its fundamentals, has by dint of great effort and great skill succeeded in bringing somewhat more discipline and order to the army which stands under his command. But the same does not hold true of the other corps, which together make up more than half the Austrian armed forces. Their commanders are deterred for various reasons – whether through weakness of character, the fact that they have been promoted only recently (which means that they must have recourse to the good offices of the ministers), from the false principle that they must turn a blind eye to irregularities, or just because they subscribe to the maxim that 'we must live and let live'.[25]

Title page of the infantry *Regulament* of 1749.

One of the naive illustrations to the manuscript draft of the 1749 *Regulament*.

The Theresian reforms of the 1740s and 1750s, were directed mostly at building up a military ethos over the long term, and effecting improvements in weapons, supply, and the mechanics of moving and fighting. Such good progress was made towards the more specific ends that it was tempting to think that the great work was complete, but the programme failed to strike at the heart of the culture of privilege, favouritism, irresponsibility and private gain. The more astute critics could still point to the lack of drive" in the *Hofkriegsrath,* the cabals among the ministers, and the ponderous and hesitant execution of measures in the field – which itself proceeded from envy and a spirit of faction among the generals.[26]

The Size of the Army

The Evidence

It is not easy to determine the precise numbers of the troops who were capable of being brought against the enemy on campaign. There is a foundation of sorts in the wartime Establishments of the regiments of infantry and cavalry:

Wartime Establishment, 1757–63
German Infantry	Hungarian Infantry	Italian Infantry	Netherlands
39 regts.	10 + Simbschen	2	Infantry 4
Cuirassiers	Dragoons	Hussars	
18	13	12	

However the Establishment took no account of the gunners, engineers, the specialised technical troops, the free battalions, the Croats, the *Grenz-Husaren,* the civilian drivers, or of the important reductions decreed within regiments as a result of the economies that were implemented in the winter of 1761/2.

The numbers of the regiments and their regulation strengths by themselves tell us little, for we must deduct the garrison battalions and depot squadrons detached for service in the rear, and the losses among the field units through sickness, desertion and casualties. The officials and clerks further complicate the business of showing strengths at a particular time because they present the numbers under four different headings:

1. *Completter Stand:* The paper strength, as if every regiment and branch of the army were completely up to establishment
2. *Effectiver Stand:* Actual numbers present in a theatre of war overall
3. *Loco Stand:* Number of men physically present on individual locations, excluding personnel on detachment, or languishing in rearward service
4. *Dienstbarer Stand:* Numbers of the above personnel actually capable of doing service.

The field strengths of the regiments in the Seven Years War are best shown from the evidence of the muster lists, which correspond principally with the *Loco Stand:*

Average Field Strengths of Regiments in the Seven Years War
	Other ranks	NCOs, corporals & *Gefreyten*	Non-combatant personnel	Officers	Total
Infantry					
1 German:	1,354	227	98	55	1,734
2 Hungarian:	1,160	202	81	46	1,489
3 Italian:	655	166	73	30	924
4 Netherlands:	1,334	228	95	57	1,714
Cuirassiers	702	44	56	37	839
Dragoons	694	49	57	37	837
Hussars	759	59	40	35	893

(N.B. The Hungarian Infantry are shown excluding the anomalous regiment of Simbschen [656 personnel in the chosen muster list], the Dragoons excluding the *Staabs-Dragoner,* and the Hussars the *Grenz-Husaren*).
From the field strengths it is possible to suggest:

Approximate Wartime Strengths of Field Army
Infantry
1. German: 67,600 personnel of all ranks
2. Hungarian: 14,900 (+ Simbschen 656)
3. Italian: 1,850
4. Netherlands: 6,860
Infantry Total   c. 91,900
Cuirassiers Total   15,100
Dragoons Total   10,880 (excl. *Staabs-Dragoner*)
Hussars Total   10,700 (excl. *Grenz-Husaren*)
Grand Total   c.129,300

The figure of 129,300 does not include the men of the artillery and its specialised fusilier regiment, or the staff troops, the free battalions, the engineers, pioneers, miners and sappers, the Croats and the *Grenz-Husaren,* or the civilian drivers. Altogether more comprehensive, consistent and detailed sets of figures are provided by Lieutenant-Colonel Gomez, who was faced in the early 1790s with the task of establishing the relationship between the size of an army, and its requirements in ration and transport. As he used as his basis the statistics he collated from the Seven Years War, we shall have frequent occasion to refer to this particularly useful evidence.[27]

The Army Year by Year

1755

In the last full year of peace the *Completter Stand* of the army amounted to 126,272 regular infantry, and 30,678 cuirassiers, dragoons and regular hussars, or a total of 156,750 regular troops. The numbers of Croats liable to service stood at 46,740, of whom one-third were liable to be called up in any given wartime year.

The numbers of serviceable troops were considerably less, which persuaded Vienna to take urgent measures now that war was approaching. In the autumn of 1755 the Prussian major-general Kyau visited northern Bohemia on the excuse of taking the waters at Carlsbad, but really to sound out the state of the military preparations. On the basis of Kyau's reports the Prussian spymaster Winterfeldt concluded that 'what we ought to do is attack first, and early enough to prevent them completing the intended build-up of their forces'.[28]

1756

On 22 July 1756, not long before the outbreak of hostilities, Neipperg reckoned that the Austrians would soon be able to assemble 57,320 infantry (including 12,000 Croats and the Simbschen battalion of 600 troops), 14,400 cuirassiers and dragoons, and 3,000 hussars, or a total of 75,000 men, excluding the artillery. In September the infantry approached their anticipated totals, though the dragoons were falling short, and the hussars could muster only half of their men and fewer still of their horses.

1757

Cornpletter Stand of all Armies in the Field, with Drivers and all other Civilians (Gomez no. 1)

Men:	164,070
Horses:	55,805

Dienstbarer Stand of Army of FM. Browne and Corps of Serbelloni, February (Gomez No. 5)

Men:	112,258
Horses:	23,944
Field Artillery:	366 pieces
Furhwesen (army transport):	856 carts
Hired civilian transport:	1,331 carts

Dienstbarer Stand of Main Army under Prince Charles, September (Gomez No. 5)

Men:	114,131
Horses:	3,027

A contemporary analysis[29] of the *Haubt Tabella* for the end of September 1757 shows that the nominal total of the forces in Bohemia and Silesia amounted to more than 170,000 troops, and yet the *Dienstbarer Stand* of those in Silesia (the active theatre of war) never quite reached 80,000,

> from which it follows that half the army, namely 80,000 men (including the more than 23–24,000 sick and wounded) remain behind in the Kingdom of Bohemia. This state of affairs is prejudicial and burdensome to the service of Her Majesty, for these men have to be paid just like the ones who are on active service in the field; I except only those small detachments amounting to between 700 and 1,000 men, which the *Hofkriegsrath* has deployed under Colonel Simbschen to counter the threat to Moravia… These facts are beyond dispute… it is easy to see how in the last campaign it was possible for 60,000 men, excluding the genuine sick, to be left behind to no use whatsoever, and at the cost of the Treasury. These men – whether on detachment, or marauding or sick… were scattered so widely over Bohemia that not a single colonel of infantry or cavalry knew, or was capable of knowing, where they were to be found.

It was good in principle to send some of the troops for rearward service in Bohemia, so as to alleviate the problems of supply in Silesia, but it would be better to detach them in a controlled way by entire battalions or squadrons at a time. The root of the problem was, however

> the excessive size of the individual armies… the practice of all the great captains – Montecuccoli, the comte de Saxe and others – shows that an army which amounts to between 70,000 or 80,000 men can be neither supervised nor controlled, and is quite impossible to furnish with supplies when those supplies are most needed.

The same document expressed the hope that the Austrians would be able to put into the field 92,635 of their regular infantry, 6,400 Bavarians, along with further auxiliary infantry, 28,000 regular cavalry and hussars (including 2,400 Saxons), 18,000 Croats, and 12,000 *Grenz-Husaren* (making a total of some 157,000 troops).

1758
Completter Stand of all Armies in the Field, with Drivers and all other Civilians (Gomez No. 1)

Men:	232,634
Horses:	64,843
Fuhrwesen:	2,020 carts
Civilian transport:	1,816 carts
Field Artillery:	366 pieces

For this year Gomez does not set out the size of armies or corps in particular months, but instead provides a remarkably detailed *Completter Stand der im Jahr 1758 im Feld gestandenen Kaiserl. Königl. Armeen* (No. 2)

Infantry
112 grenadier companies	11,648 men
816 fusilier companies	116,116
Staabs-Infanterie-Regiment	2,000
Two *Jäger* companies	327
Loudon Free Corps	1,632
Beck Silesian Free Corps	816
18 Croat grenadier companies	1,872
136 Croat fusilier companies 28,466 (this figure must include those still at home)	
Auxiliary troops (6 grenadier and 40 fusilier companies)	7,436

Cavalry
18 cuirassier regiments	18,378 men ditto horses
13 dragoon regiments	13,260
1 sq. *Staabs-Dragoner*	334
12 husssar regiments	12,040
21 coys. *Grenz-Husaren*	2,357
Saxon auxiliary *chevaulegers*	4,465

Specialised Corps Generals, General Staff
Genie-Corps	249
Artillery	3,788
Sappeurs-Corps	252
Pontoniere and *Schiffamt*	192
Commissariat & other HQ personnel	187

Transport
Infantry supply carts	910 men 1,820 horses 910 carts
Infantry tent carts	225 250
Cavalry supply carts	324 648
Pontoon drivers	15
Artillery teams	1,996 3,500
Furhwesen and field bakery	3,441 8,080

The following figures may be extracted for easier comparison with some of the earlier lists:
Completter Stand

Infantry (excl. Croats and foreign auxiliaries)	130,091
Cuirassiers, dragoons, regular hussars, Saxon *chevaulegers*	48,485
Artillery	3,788

1759

Completter Stand on the War Establishment	154,460
Completter Stand of all Armies in the Field, with Drivers and all other Civilians (Gomez No. 1)	
Men:	227,974
Horses:	68,007
Fuhrwesen	2,070 carts
Civilian transport	1,965 carts

According to a *Nota* dating from before the campaign opened, 'counting the infantry regiments actually with the army, and those ordered to join it, at 1,832 men each, according to the present field strengths, we arrive at a total of 54,960 troops. The garrison battalions of these regiments, at only 500 each, amount to 14,000 men. We have 15 regiments of cuirassiers and nine of dragoons at 800 men each, and nine regiments of hussars at 600, making a total of 24,600. To these we must add the Hungarian [i.e. Croatian] national troops of all kinds'.[30]

At the time of the campaign the *Dienstbarer* totals were about one-third less than the *Completter* paper establishments, and *FZM*. Lacy wrote to Daun on 17 June that 'all the people in Vienna have such a monstrously exaggerated notion of the size of the army that to hear them speak you would think that we had the hosts of Xerxes at our disposal. On this supposition they rage so furiously against the King of Prussia that they claim that we must not only crush him and his army with him, but extirpate him from the face of the earth together with all the forces he might possibly raise'.[31]

1760

Completter Stand on the War Establishment	201,960
Completter Stand of all Armies in the Field, with Drivers and all Civilians (Gomez No. 1)	
Men	228,570
Horses	71,323
Fuhrwesen	2,303 carts
Men	69,358 (*Loco* 77,958)
Horses	13,483 (*Loco* 20,568)
Loco Stand of Main Army under Daun in Saxony, December (*Dienstbarer* not available) (Gomez No. 5)	
Men	63,236
Horses	15,199

Daun returned to an old theme when he wrote to Lacy on 4 March: 'They suppose our forces to amount to 156,000 troops, but I find the subject so disagreeable that I am unwilling to talk about it'.[32]

1761

This was the last year in which the Austrian army appeared in something like its full strength, and the figures are therefore of some importance.

Completter Stand on the War Establishment
154,560 regular infantry, 46,751 regular cavalry
(including the Saxon *chevaulegers*), grand total
201,311 (unchanged since 1758).

Completter Stand of all Armies in the Field, with Drivers and all Civilians (Gomez No. 1)
Men:	218,053
Horses:	59,664
Furkwesen:	2,303 carts
Civilian transport:	1,839 carts

Dienstbarer Stand of Field Armies (Gomez No. 5) Daun in Saxony, May
Men:	72,965
Horses:	20,745

Daun in Saxony, September
Men:	55,925
Horses:	13,717

Loudon in Silesia, May
Men:	74,461
Horses:	18,882

Loudon in Silesia, September
Men:	80,701
Horses:	20,749

The Reduction of 1761/2

As early as January 1760 Austria's intractable financial problems threatened to undermine the achievements of her armies in the field. We find Maria Theresa writing that 'the circumstances are unfortunately such that we must resort to extreme measures of every kind… I can scarcely begin to describe to you how painful it is to me to take anything away from my exhausted but valiant army. You know how dear the army is to me, and therefore how much this resolution goes against my instincts. Only the greatest necessity could have forced it from me'.[33]

Maria Theresa and her counsellors agreed economies were inevitable, and that they should therefore be instituted as soon as possible. They were likewise at one when they singled out the mounted troops as their main target, though they differed as to the mode of execution. Maria Theresa, Batthyány, Haugwitz, the two Choteks and Blümegen were for abolishing four regiments of cuirassiers, and leaving the rest of the cavalry intact, while Francis Stephen, Kaunitz, Neipperg and Carl Paul Pálffy were for the more comprehensive measure of cutting every regiment of cuirassiers by one squadron, reducing the regiments of hussars to 1,200 men and horses each, and converting four of the regiments of dragoons to *chevaulegers* which could do outpost duty alongside the hussars. Maria Theresa had nothing against the second set of proposals in principle, but she still believed that the cuirassiers 'had not been of much use in this war,' and that it was better to convert four of the 18 regiments of cuirassiers to the versatile dragoons, and keep the remaining cuirassiers better up to strength in big men and horses. No firm decision was taken in favour of either party.

By the late summer of 1761 the talk of economies extended well beyond the cavalry. On 28 September Maria Theresa asked Daun for his opinion concerning a new programme of savings. The Field Marshal replied that he feared that the proposed measures would lead to the 'complete ruin of the monarchy.' The Staff Infantry Regiment and the Loudon and Beck free battalions performed essential services, and if they were abolished, their work would have to be taken over by units of the line. He found it 'likewise incomprehensible that we should be contemplating further reductions at the expense of our cavalry, when the enemy is so superior to us in this branch of the service.' Maria Theresa must also bear in mind the impression that any such economies would make on her enemies, who would be encouraged to make further extortionate demands, while her friends would be reduced to despair.[34]

On 17 October Kaunitz submitted an elaborately-argued paper which leaves little doubt that he was the driving force behind the retrenchments. On Maria Theresa's instructions he had been working for several months to provide for the needs of the next campaign, presuming that negotiations for peace came to nothing. When bankruptcy stared the monarchy in the face he could, with the greatest reluctance, see no alternative to a scheme of drastic reductions that would curtail the field establishments of the mounted regiments, reduce the reserves of both infantry and cavalry, and abolish outright a number of the specialised units which had been established since the beginning of the war (see p. 119).

Officer and trooper
of cuirassiers.
(Ottenfeld, 1898)

The memorandum made no reference to having consulted Lacy, whose pet creation of the Staff troops was threatened most directly by these proposals, and as a kind of afterthought Kaunitz discovered objections to reducing the Loudon and Beck free battalions, since they were recruited from Prussian renegades who would otherwise desert back to their old masters, a development that would run counter to the principle that 'our own subjects are to be spared as much as possible.' The equivalent economies could be made at the expense of the Croats, which was a remarkable volte-face on the part of Kaunitz as their erstwhile champion.

Kaunitz concluded by admitting that 'it will not be possible to avoid occasioning some astonishment by this reduction, but a great deal will depend on the way in which it is presented to the public.' The Staff troops and the other units concerned should therefore not be abolished outright, but allowed to wither on the vine by being denied recruits and remounts.[35]

Maria Theresa wrote to Daun on the same 17 October that the proposed reductions were so unpalatable that she had asked her ministers for a second time if they stood by their opinion, and they had replied that they were still of the same mind. She enclosed a copy of the memorandum from Kaunitz, and asked Daun yet again to tell her how the economies could be carried out with the least damage.[36]

Daun replied on 23 October that Vienna should think of building up the army for the next campaign, instead of reducing it, and that he would have consulted his generals if he had not been ordered to keep the affair secret. He expressed his surprise that 'it has been found quite impossible to raise anything from the great numbers of wealthy monasteries and private individuals in the various provinces, or through other financial operations. Many of those monasteries and individuals have incomes of 80,000 florins a year, and still more incomes of 100,000 – sums which are matched by few people in foreign lands – and we can find no evidence that they have been forced to make any economies whatsoever in the course of this extremely costly and long drawn-out war.' Otherwise he did not know enough about the state of the monarchy to be able to offer an alternative to the proposed reduction, or to proceed other than by the suggested tactic of letting the affected units die out through wastage.[37]

The cuts, as finally determined, were instituted in the winter of 1761/2, and their main features may be summarised as follows:

Infantry
Two companies reduced from the six-company strong garrison battalion of each regiment, and 'instead of recruiting for these [garrison] battalions the *Stände* were to pay a certain sum to the Treasury in place of each recruit'.[38] The NCOs and men from the affected companies were to be sent up to reinforce the two field battalions of the regiment, the clerks and medical orderlies dismissed from the service, and the officers held on half pay pending possible reassignment at the discretion of the field commanders. In the event the authorities actually encouraged the Spanish ambassador to go recruiting among the reduced officers on behalf of his king.

Cavalry
Regiments of cuirassiers reduced to 850 men and horses each, and those of the dragoons and hussars each to 1,000 men and 850 horses.

Staff and Technical Troops
Staabs-Infanterie-Regiment reduced from 16 companies to four, the *Staabs-Dragoner-Regiment* wasted out in the course of 1762, the *Artillerie-Füsilier-Regiment* reduced from 24 companies to 18, the *Sappeurs-Corps* reduced from three companies to two, and the *Pionier-Corps* disbanded.

When the cuts became general knowledge they created just the commotion which Kaunitz had intended to avert. 'The whole public cried out against these proceedings. Perhaps the judgement of unreliable and incompetent people that like is not worth very much, but the generals too with few exceptions disapproved of this measure thoroughly, and some of them were honest enough to make their opinion known in public. Once when the *Parole* [password] was being issued, that noble warrior Prince Löwenstein, impelled by his patriotic instincts, gave vent to the cry: "Great, pitiable monarch! How badly you are advised!"'[39]

Speculation raged unchecked, and it concerned the motives of the authors, as well as their identity. Emperor Francis Stephen wrote to his brother Prince Charles of Lorraine on 8 December that he had entered a strong protest but had been overruled. Daun was blamed for having given his silent assent to the cuts, and thus for failing to capitalise on the unique trust which Maria Theresa reposed in his judgement.[40] That was unfair, because Daun had protested to the limits of the confidentiality which had been imposed on him by Maria Theresa. The Swedish attaché Armfeldt knew that Daun had employed all his credit to bring home to the Empress the damage that would be done, and that in an attempt to assuage his feelings she appointed him President of the *Hofkriegsrath* in 1762 in place of the old and incompetent Harrach.[41] The same perceptive observer pointed out that in this vast monarchy Maria Theresa depended on the counsel of others, which was not always of the best, and he cites as proof the critical decision concerning the reductions, which was taken on the advice of ministers without the leading generals having been sounded for their opinion. There were few immediate effects, for the reductions in the line regiments were being carried out at the expense of the garrison and depot units, and the *Stände* were being allowed to compound for money, instead of supplying actual recruits.[42] When, however, the monarchy was overtaken by the military crisis of 1762, it had no means of reinforcing the field units as in previous years, 'which puts it beyond any doubt that the damage outweighed the good that was derived from the savings brought by the reduction. I mention this as a striking example of the weakness inherent in a government in which the sovereign herself is incapable of knowing everything that is going on'.[43]

Cogniazzo states that when one of the best generals protested against the cuts to a member of the *Hofkriegsrath,* he was asked "since when have you been so afraid of the Marquis of Brandenburg" [i.e. Frederick]. The reply was short and to the point. "Sir, it is since you were given a seat and voice in the *Hofkriegsrath*.[44]

This general would have been at one with *FZM.* Lacy who, unlike Loudon, had not been privy to the consultations, but delivered his verdict on 4 December 1761. He told Maria Theresa's Cabinet Secretary that some of his officers deduced that Vienna regarded the Russian auxiliary corps as a substitute for Austrian troops, while others thought that the army was being reduced in proportion to the declining strength of the Prussians, who were worn down by years of war. He himself held with those who believed that Maria Theresa had been brought to this pass by the exhaustion of her finances. However Lacy regarded the savings, as actually carried out, as being more theoretical than real, and stated that genuine and effective economies would enable the army to hold out at least one more campaign:

> The soul of an army is compounded of the love for the sovereign, honour, glory, and everything that is calculated to excite ambition. When a sovereign is confident of having warriors who are moved by these principles, she may he sure of commanding everything that humane exertion is capable of putting forth. It takes an infinity of effort to plant these great principles in the heart of an army. It does not take much to sustain them, but it is the work of a moment to destroy them.

Maria Theresa should have put her case squarely before the army, and can you doubt that in such a case every military man would have offered cheerfully to serve on half pay? I speak with all the more confidence because, as is well known, we have already served on such terms for an entire campaign, when we were paid in debased currency which was only one half the value of our own coinage, and which was nevertheless paid out at face value. It needed only a single order to put into effect, and everyone submitted without demur.

Here Lacy passed over the hardship thereby inflicted on the less well-off officers. He argued with more credibility when he outlined the damage inflicted on the quality of the officer corps, as we shall see.[45]

1762 and the Results of the Reduction

The statistical effect of the reduction was to lower the *Cornpletter Stand* of the troops from the 201,311 of 1761 to the 177,497 of 1762, and the personnel as a whole to 186,630 including all the supporting civilians (Gomez No. 1).

Completter Stand on the War Establishment, with Percentage Reductions
All regular infantry reduced by 12.06 percent to:
German:	94,653
Hungarian:	26,697
Italian:	4,854
Netherlands:	9,708
Total:	135,912

All regular cavalry (cuirassiers, dragoons/*chevaulegers* and hussars) reduced by 11.05 percent,
Total:	41,585
Grand Total of Regular Infantry and Cavalry representing reduction of 11.82 percent.	177,497

Dienstbarer Stand of Field Forces (Gomez No. 5)
Daun's army in Saxony, April
Men:	62,242
Horses:	15,519

Loudon's army in Silesia, April
Men:	47,479
Horses:	11,236

Daun's army in Silesia, July
Men:	78,754
Horses:	18,264

Daun's army in Silesia, 31 September
Infantry:	59,930
Cavalry:	16,995
Total:	76,925

A summary of the returns for July puts Daun's army in Silesia at 84,657 men and 17,519 horses, and the Austrian forces in Saxony at 45,483 men and 10,952 horses.[46]

Some of Lacy's officers had been right to suspect that the cuts had been carried out on the assumption that the Austrians could rely on the support of the Russian auxiliary corps. On this point Cogniazzo adds that Vienna also set store by the role of the main Russian army, which was poised to break into the heart of the Prussian state.[47]

The results of this miscalculation gathered force with geometric speed. When Peter III came to the throne of Russia in 1762 he not only deprived Maria Theresa of the help of the Russian auxiliaries, which actually reached the number of 20,000 troops, but put these men at the disposal of Frederick, which left the Austrians relatively worse off by 40,000 troops at a decisive stage in the new campaign. The Prussian ranks were swelled still further when their various detached corps returned from facing the Russians and Swedes, when their prisoners of war came back from Russian and Swedish captivity, and when recruits could be raised from the areas which had been occupied by the Russians and Swedes.

The way the cuts were implemented was just as damaging as their size. The weeding-out of the officers was effected on the principle of 'last in, first out', and Lacy had to tell Maria Theresa that the economies therefore hit the officers who had risen in recent campaigns through their genuine merit, but spared the mass of incompetents who had been appointed in a hurry to make good the losses at Leuthen in 1757, and who were now sheltered by their relative seniority.[48] Lacy also argued against the reductions among the hussars, 'who deserve all possible attention as things stand now, if the King of Prussia is not to gain the upper hand over Your Majesty's light troops'.[49] He was ignored, 'and the damaging effect of this reduction in the subsequent operations… will be familiar to anyone who accompanied the campaign in Silesia.' Once Schweidnitz had fallen the Austrians were driven back into the border hills with Bohemia and hemmed in by the superior Prussian cavalry from all sides'.[50]

Final Accounting

After the end of the Seven Years War a remarkably helpful document[51] set out the total losses of all ranks from all course in every unit in the course of that conflict. We shall turn to many of the details in due course, but the salient points were these:

Grand Total	303,595
Causes (percentage of the grand total)	
Captured:	78,360 = 25.81%
Killed in action:	32,622 = 10.74
Died in hospital of sickness or wounds:	93,408 = 30.76
Deserted:	62,222 = 20.49
Missing:	19,595 = 6.45
Invalided out:	17,388 = 5.72

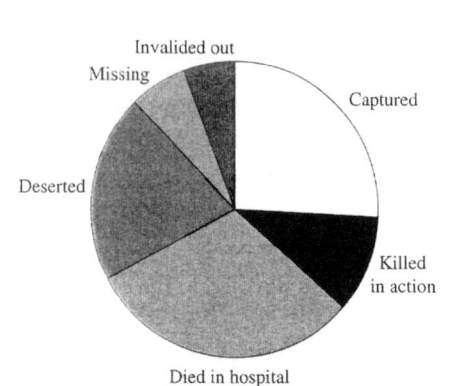

Losses by Arm of Service
Generals:	40 = 0.01
Staff:	16 = 0.001
Regular infantry:	210,560 = 69.29
'New Corps' (Staff troops, Artillery Fusiliers, free bns., Anhalt-Zerbst bn.):	12,593 = 4.14
Auxiliaries (Mainz, Würzburgers, Modena):	12,442 = 4.09
Croatian infantry:	19,723 = 6.49
Feld-Artillerie Corps:	4,314 = 1.42
Ingenieur-Corps:	32 = 0.01
Sappeurs-Corps:	65 = 0.02
Cuirassiers:	10,965 = 3.61
Dragoons:	14,316 = 4.71
Regular hussars:	17,706 = 5.83
Grenz-Husaren:	833 = 0.26

Altogether 47,169 horses were killed, disabled, or sold out of the service.

Losses of Horses by Year
1756:	1.33%
1757:	14.37
1758:	22.66
1759:	15.75
1760:	19.65
1761:	11.09
1762:	15.12

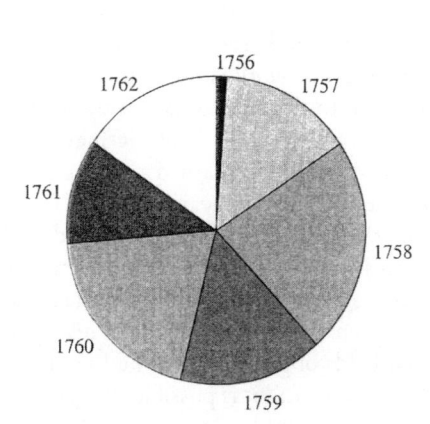

The surprisingly heavy losses for 1758 were almost certainly due to the disorder and epidemics which reigned for several months after the battle of Leuthen.

The numbers killed in action provide a rough guide to the intensity of combat in any one year:

Killed in Action, as Proportion of Annual Losses from all Causes
1756:	18.73
1757:	22.24
1758:	10.70
1759:	8.07
1760:	11.16
1761:	5.42
1762:	6.03

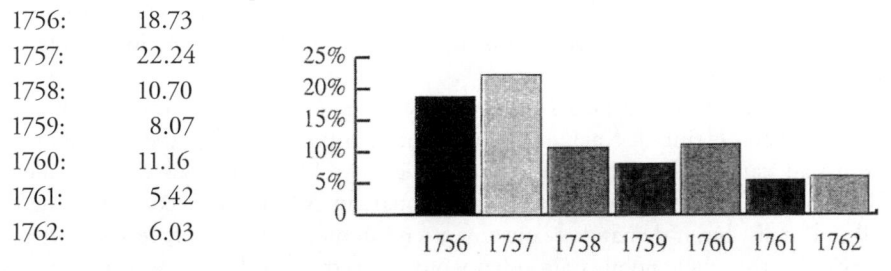

(N.B. See also Appendix V: Wastage, for losses as projected from the muster lists)

Ethos

The Austrian military style was evident most immediately in its heraldry and uniforms. With a single intermission between 1742 and 1745, the House of Habsburg had been associated with the Imperial dignity of Germany, and therefore with the device of the black double-headed eagle on the golden or yellow field, which derived from Ancient Rome by way of Byzantium. In the reign of Maria Theresa we find the double eagle on the colours borne by the regiments, and the gold interwoven with threads of black on the sashes of her officers.

White coats were associated with Catholic armies in general – Frane and Spain, as well as Austria – but the combination of white with red (the most common colour of the Austrian facings) was linked more particularly with the archduchies of Austria, and with the Austrian army as a whole. Commentators from Protestant Europe could not understand the attachment of the Austrians to the white coat, but the officers of Maria Theresa proclaimed that 'white is our colour, and so it must remain… Other countries have blue, green or red as the predominant colours in their armies, so why should we not be fond of white and red in ours, just as our Court is attached to black and yellow'.[52]

White stood out well in the field, when one of the functions of the military garb in that period was to make a good show. In the course of time coats of blue faded badly, those of pike grey turned a dirty ashen colour, and those of green assumed a tinge of yellow, while repairs were all too evident on dyed coats of any kind, and added to a general look of shabbiness.[53] Coats of white, on the other hand, could always be worked up with chalk to make them look 'new and brilliant'.[54] The white coat was retained into the second half of the 19th century, and when the Austrian and Prussian garrisons marched out of the Federal German fortress of Rastatt in 1866 a laundress asked a Bohemian soldier why his coat remained an immaculate white, when his shirts were always so dirty. 'Stupid woman,' he replied, 'how can I possibly work up my shirts with chalk?'.[55]

The infantry *Regulament* of 1749 sanctified another old tradition when it laid down that 'on all parades, public appearances and in action with the enemy, green insignia are to be worn in the hats'.[56] The original purpose had been to distinguish the Austrians from the French and Spanish, but the practice persisted when the Austrians had to turn against other enemies. An order of 1743 (soon rescinded) ordained fields of grass green for all regimental colours except the *Leibfahne*, for the Emperor was now a Bavarian, and it is possible that green was being held in reserve as a 'house' colour in case the Austrians were unable to recover the Imperial dignity over the long term. On the evidence of the 'Bautzen Manuscript' green cockades were worn on the left-hand side of the hats of the officers of infantry, but not on the hats of the private soldiers.

Maria Theresa decreed in 1748 that 'all uniforms must be in conformity, and every superfluous ornamentation abolished'.[57] Individual colonels were fond of introducing variations, but the Austrian army indeed remained probably the most simply dressed of any in Europe. It is all the more odd to find that the Austrian drills by way of contrast were almost uniquely elaborate. The Austrian cavalry *Regulament* of 1749–51 set out nearly 15 pages on the ceremonies attending the presentation of a new standard – which was the same span as the entire section devoted to the conduct of the regiment in battle.

Kaunitz made some astute comments on the more general character of the Austrian service in October 1761, when Heinrich Kajetan Count Blümegen proposed that the Austrians should adopt the Prussian 'cantonal' system of recruiting, whereby soldiers were raised by regiment and company from assigned conscription areas of the monarchy. Kaunitz conceded that the device worked well in Prussia, but it demanded constant attention on the part of Frederick, and an obligation of service on the whole nobility; in other words everything in Prussia was 'interconnected as if in a chain, from which you cannot extract any one link without seeing the whole fall apart'.[58] Kaunitz was unwilling to import the kind of tyranny which the Prussian captains exercised in their conscription areas, and he believed that domestic industry in the Habsburg lands was too backward to allow families to support themselves-when their menfolk were away with the army.

The Prussian model would also force the Austrians to abandon two features of their military culture which Kaunitz regarded as distinct assets, namely those of the multinational units and the practice of rotating them through the various lands of the monarchy.

Whereas the locally-recruited conscripts formed the core of the Prussian units, the Austrian tradition (at least among the 'German' regiments) was founded on multi-national units, 'and so we find that it would be difficult for the [predominantly] Bohemian regiments to do away with their Austrian and Silesian NCOs, just as the Austrian regiments need the firm foundation provided by the Bohemian private soldiers'.[59] On this issue the Prince de Ligne asserted that 'the Austrian army is the only national army, although made up of several nations'.[60]

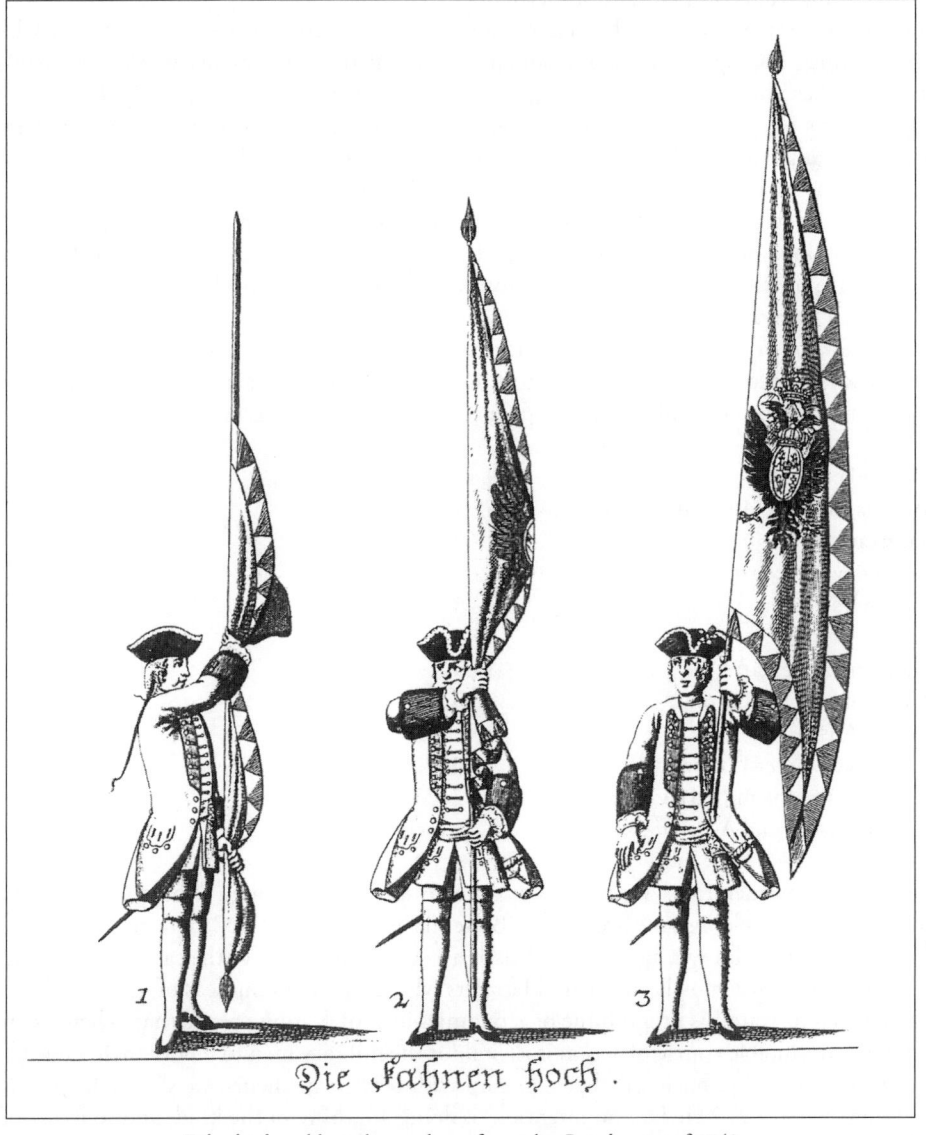

Fähndrich and battalion colour, from the *Regulament* of 1749.

Unlike her ancestors, Maria Theresa was not content to live with the fact that the 'Austrian' army was constituted out of elements which were literally unable to understand one another. She therefore introduced a policy of linguistic Germanisation, not indeed to turn all of her soldiers into imitation Teutons, but to familiarise them with basic commands as delivered the 'army German'[61] (see p. 38). In 1758 the *Hoflcriegsrath* told Daun that Maria Theresa had decided that enlistment in the German Hereditary Lands was to be carried out by individual contract (*Capitulation*) and that would-be recruits from Bohemia and Moravia were to be accepted 'only if they are German, or fluent in the German language, in the hope that in the course of time their progress in the service, along with their other talents will qualify them to be promoted to NCO or higher still'.[62]

There was still a call for bluff, when the gift of tongues failed, and a commander could hardly go wrong if he galloped along the ranks, cursing unfortunate officers for no particular reason, and yelling *Orvat! Przezina! Schmidt! Wagner!* or *Zimmermann!* at the soldiers, as if he recognised individual Hungarians, Bohemians or Germans.[63]

Kaunitz had touched on another characteristic of the Austrian military tradition when he opposed Blümegen's suggestion of introducing locally-planted regiments in the Prussian style, pointing out that 'the Austrian military spirit is maintained in peacetime principally by the practice of marching the regiments from one province to another, and thus keeping them in perpetual movement. That spirit would therefore be destroyed in an instant by the [proposed] new system'.[64] Historians term the principle 'extraterritoriality,' and it was familiar to the Romans. Few people in authority in Austria would have contested the underlying motive, which was to prevent the regiments from striking deep roots among the local population, though it was admittedly hard on the officers to have to remove themselves, for example, from Bohemia to Hungary, and then, after a short time, all the way back again.[65]

When the *Hofkriegsrath* decided where to station the troops, it also had to take into account how well the local economy was able to accommodate and support the men and horses. Before the mobilisation in 1756 the regular forces happened to be distributed as follows:

Bohemia:	19.44%
Austrian Italy & Austrian Netherlands:	15.95 each
Hungary:	14.69
Moravia:	9.47
Transylvania:	4.75
Styria:	4.48
Bánát of Temesvár:	3.49
Carniola and the Littoral:	2.98
Lower Austria:	1.99
Tyrol and Vorder-Österreich:	1.89
Slavonia and the military villages:	1.87
Upper Austria and Austrian Silesia:	1.49 each

Operational considerations were not borne in mind. Only through a happy chance did the highly-developed arable agriculture enable Bohemia to garrison 22.22 percent of the infantry, which was convenient for war against the Prussians; conversely 60.69 of the cavalry was tucked out of the way in Hungary, mostly in isolated hamlets which stood among seas of grass.

When he put forward his programme of economies in 1761 Kaunitz wrote that 'when it comes to taking the most suitable course of action it is vital for the military men to tender their advice, for we wish to avoid harmful publicity. If they come up with better expedients, we should be prepared to accept them cheerfully'.[66] He had no intention of doing anything of the kind, and to many officers the relationship between the military and the rest of society in any case appeared to be an unequal one, which inclined heavily in favour of the civilians. The Prince de Ligne complained that 'those wretched civilians have nothing civil about them, and they give us a thoroughly bad time. The bureaucrats are against us. We are oppressed by trickery, injustice, officiousness and favouritism. If a quarrel arises in a town you may be sure that the citizens will be in the right, but the officers put under arrest, the soldiers assigned to the provost and the colonel of the regiment hauled up for a reprimand'.[67] This contention is borne out by a number of otherwise insignificant episodes.

On 25 July 1759 a hot midsummer had baked the wooden roof shingles of the Leopoldstadt of Vienna to tinder dryness, and a fire spread rapidly along the narrow Ankergasse. The civilian *Vize Stadt Halter* Baron de Mannagetta stated that a large number of citizens hastened up to help, but were held back by the soldiers, who were alleged to have run riot and beat up people at random. As head of the Vienna garrison General Engelshoffer was forced to discipline the designated offenders, headed by First-Lieutenant Mahler of the regiment of Botta, who was put under arrest for 24 hours.

A *Gefreyter* of the regiment of Waldeck was punished by 20 blows of the cane, and an investigation was mounted against a company *Feldscher* (medical orderly) of the Batthyány Dragoons who 'went about pretending to be variously an official of the fire brigade or a military officer, and who was impudent enough to deal a number of individuals some heavy blows with his cane, and draw his sword and injure the servant of the Clerk of the Imperial Household, von Kollhofen'.[68]

In somewhat higher circles a dispute of precedence broke out in Transylvania in1762 between the wife of *FML.* Count Montoja , and the wife of one Major Haller, who, although much junior in military rank, enjoyed an important position in the civil administration. *FM.* d'Aspremont-Lynden forwarded the relevant documents to Maria Theresa, and commented that 'in other lands, especially Italy, the wives (regardless of birth) of generals are accorded an undisputed and marked preference in public assemblies over the wives of the province in question.' Maria Theresa nevertheless ruled that she was 'always concerned to see the military enjoying every possible distinction on all occasions, because they sustain the state, and so Montoja's wife must retain her rank as before. But she must concede precedence to the wife of Haller, because he has become a Privy Councillor, and has obtained a senior post in the provincial administration'.[69]

The Reformed Austrian Army and Prussian Espionage

How much did Frederick know about Austria's military potential when he precipitated war in 1756? He was apparently well served when we look at the number and variety of his sources (see the section *The Brain of the Army* in Part III, Chapter 18, *Operational and Tactical Dimensions*) – namely foreign travellers, his ambassadors in Vienna, the 'sleeping' agents in the same city, and the spymaster Lieutenant-General Winterfeldt and his stable of informants – the long established Gellhorn, Lieutenant-Colonel Rebentisch (recruited in 1750), the hussar captain Paul Werner (1742), and Lieutenant Haude (1755).

From these reports Maria Theresa emerges as a somewhat isolated figure. She is represented as being on such bad terms with her husband Francis Stephen that a break between the two seemed imminent. The Emperor was securing himself against this eventuality by building up his great commercial fortune to support his younger sons against the eldest, Archduke Joseph, 'whom he regards as the heir of the Empress'.[70] Gellhorn noted in December 1749 that Maria Theresa's first domestic reforms on the 'Haugwitz' system had made her widely unpopular in the Hereditary Lands, though he was willing to revise his opinion in her favour by August 1751:

> the Empress has gained greatly thereby, and she now enjoys and accurate and comprehensive overview of her affairs. She knows exactly what the army costs her year by year, as also what

must be allowed for the annual expenditure of the Court. She owes this to Count Haugwitz, because before his time nobody could work out the income or outgoings… The lords complain loudly, and have been forced to curtail their former expenditure, but the peasants are happy, and especially those who live under the authority of the royal towns or the fairer-minded lords, who forbid their officials to enrich themselves by sucking their vassals dry.

Gellhorn nevertheless adds that there was something arbitrary about the process of reform, and he cited the case of the reduction of the fees which had been levied by the clergy for conducting funerals. Maria Theresa had been impelled to act by the widowed Countess Herberstein, who complained that she had been charged 400 florins for her husband's funeral. 'This is entirely typical of the cases which come to her attention. The people who carry the most weight with her are self-seeking or ambitious women, who hail form a wide variety of backgrounds. This limits what the Empress can do, for all her intelligence and good intentions.' Thus the wealth of the great monasteries remained beyond her reach and intact.[71]

Winterfeldt met a number of Austrian generals in the course of his visits to Carlsbad spa in June 1750, and they spoke in the same vein. They were unstinting in their praises of Frederick and his army, and they pointed out 'although the Empress puts forward every conceivable effort, she will never achieve her ambitions.' Winterfeldt ventured to reply that she would go down as one of the greatest women in history, but the generals rejoined that that was the root of the problem, 'the fact that she is a woman, and can never see things through to their proper conclusion.'[72]

The Austrian ministry as it existed in 1749 is described as being bitterly divided, and much under the influence of trouble-makers like the priests and the women. 'Count Kaunitz is sustained only by the support of the ladies. The ministry is absolutely against him, and will go to any lengths to bring about his downfall.'[73] Haugwitz too was uncertain of his position, for Maria Theresa was singing the praises of Count Münchow, Frederick's administrator of Silesia, and she regretted that she did not have a man of that calibre in her employment.[74]

It was not long before the efforts of Haugwitz were rewarded, as we have seen. One of his protégés, Count Blümegen, was doing excellent work as administrator (*Minister Präsident*) of Moravia. Winterfeldt met him in Carlsbad in June 1750, and noted that he was being ostracised by the nobles who were taking the waters there. 'Blümegen mentioned their behaviour to me himself, but he shrugged it off, saying that it only made him all the more determined to serve the interests of the Empress.' Count Blümegen's counterpart in Bohemia, Count Nettolitzky, was also making good progress, supported by a small team of capable officials.[75]

At the beginning of 1754 Haugwitz was still regarded as the most important single minister at Court. All the same he was losing his confidence in his ability to complete his work, 'and it is asserted on good authority that Count Kaunitz and his associates are planning a reorganisation of the dominions, and that he thereby hopes to overthrow Count Haugwitz and his system; the counts Chotek will do all they can to aid him in this enterprise.' This had some foundation, but Gellhorn was badly astray when he asserted that 'even the great men pronounce that, as long as the present King of Prussia lives, the House of Austria on its side will do everything possible to avoid a war.'[76]

Count Salburg had the chief voice in the deliberations on military reform, as he was a 'civilian' general with no regiment in his proprietorship, and was therefore seen as impartial.[77] Winterfeldt had at first singled out Daun as the leading military man among the reformers, but he added in July 1750 that he harbored 'a less favourable opinion of General Leopold Daun than I once did. The reason why the Empress is willing to give so much time to him is not his capacity for hard work, but the fact he has married a lady called Fuchs, who is her favourite.[78] Gellhorn identified Liechtenstein, Seckendorf and Batthyány as the generals who were also seen to have great influence, and Browne as the one best fitted to command the army in the field, 'though they add that he is self-seeking in the extreme.'[79]

Otherwise the Prussian intelligence on the Austrian generals must be regarded as neither accurate nor comprehensive. Much of the information was derived from the tainted source of renegade malcontents who were paying off grudges, such as those borne by Rebentisch against Colonel Unruh of the regiment of Browne, Werner against Nádasdy, and Captain Wiedemann against Liechtenstein. Winterfeldt's character sketches of the officers he encountered at Carlsbad were intended as much for the king's amusement as his edification. Thus he represented the cavalry lieutenant-general Stampach as a good-hearted man, an excellent rider, and totally inarticulate: 'I cannot describe him other than in the terms you would apply to a good cart horse: "That's a sound animal!" Lieutenant-General Kollowrat of the infantry was a courteous individual who was known throughout the Austrian army as the 'Grandfather of the Rosary.' His favourite company was that of the old countesses in Vienna, and he never suspected that they were cheating him at cards. 'Colonel von Gemmingen, commandant of the regiment of Gaisrugg, is a man of considerable geniality. He also passes as a painstaking officer, though this come chiefly from having his men beaten unmercifully at drill, even though he doesn't why he does it.'[80]

At the same time Prussians kept an eye on up-and-coming officers who might bulk large in the future. Such a man was Major Friedrich Caspar Elmendorf of the regiment of Botta (who in fact became a major-general in 1760). Another was the colonel commandant of the regiment of Alt-Colloredo, Franz Moritz Lacy, whose state of mind indicated he might be won over for the Prussian service. He was a stickler for order in his regiment, but received little thanks for his pains, for the Court believed that he was carrying things too far. In October 1754 Winterfeldt learned that Lacy had a new cause for dissatisfaction. Field Marshal Neipperg had once been willing to allow him to marry his daughter, 'but he now wishes to give her away to Lacy's rival the young Prince Auersperg, who has just inherited one million florins. Although his daughter is still inclined towards Lacy, the father hopes to bring her around by persuasion, being very fond of her, he has renounced force.'[81] The outcomes were disappointing for all parties. The Prussians never succeeded in suborning Lacy, and history records that the daughter in question, Wilhelmine (a chestnut-haired and entrancing beauty) indeed married Prince Auersperg, but became the mistress of the Emperor before her early death. Lacy remained unmarried.

Concerning the body of the army, the Prussians had some good words for the Austrian grenadiers, but they described the fusiliers as runtish creatures, who were maltreated by their superiors and liable to be thrown into irretrievable confusion by the slightest upset. The troops went on guard with loaded muskets, and rarely bothered to renew the charges between their spells on duty, and that was one of the reasons why scarcely 30 muskets out of every 100 were able to fire at drill. 'Nobody concerns himself with whether the musket is in good working order with a functioning lock – in fact the spring is so fierce that in order to cock the weapon the soldier has to seat the butt on his chest and haul back on the hammer.'[82]

The lack of purposeful order made a nonsense of the infantry *Regulament* of 1749 by which the Austrians set such store.[83] Gellhorn identified the chief influence on that document as being that of the ex-Prussian captain Doss or Thoss, who was much in favour with Francis Stephen, and who briefed relays of regimental majors who were ordered to report to him in Vienna. Winterfeldt agreed that the *Regulament* had nothing to do with Daun, but claimed that the true author was 'a certain Captain Honig of his regiment, who had been nothing more than a company derk a few years before; he then rose to sergeant-major, and was finally advanced to captain, having been recommended to Daun as an intelligent fellow. All that the general [Daun] had to do was to strike out a number of expressions… the reason being that they sounded too "Prussian," and the document was supposed to contain nothing which smacked of Your Majesty's service.'[84]

Gellhorn claimed the new regulations only perpetuated the historic ponderousness of the Austrian infantry. The Austrians were obsessed with the manual drill of arms, but executed it poorly. 'Whether standing or marching they observe a considerable distance between the files, so as to have the elbows free, with the result that they are unable to keep a straight line or chosen direction, for they either crowd together towards the centre or pull out towards the wings.' They raised their feet high off the ground and set them down again by the heels, 'which means that their steps are very short, and they make little forward progress.' When they had to draw off to the left or right, they did so by the snake-like and vulnerable countermarch.[85]

Just as the Austrian infantry was still being drilled in setting up antiquated chevaux de frise of boar spears for use against the Turks, so the cavalry still practised fire from the saddle by files. Attacks were simple frontal affairs, ending in a hard gallop, while the lines were still being formed from column by the conventional two successive quarter-wheels by fours, fives, sixes, platoons and half or full squadrons – the 'processional' manoeuvre which had the inherent disadvantage of presenting the flanks to the enemy. The Prussian diagonal deployment remained unknown. The remounts were undeniably better than before, but they were still small animals which would be overthrown by the fast and well-proportioned 'Polish' horses of the Prussians.

As regards the Austrian artillery, Gellhorn provided no detail, and recorded without comment Liechtenstein's claim that it was superior to anything in the world in the accuracy and speed of its fire. However, Frederick, Winterfeldt and their technical adviser Lieutenant-Colonel Balbi were taken in by the arguments of the renegade Austrian artillery lieutenant Wiedemann, who claimed that he and his father had forged a compound 12-pounder cannon barrel of iron, brass and copper. At test (so claimed Wiedemann) their piece had proved to be both lighter and longer-ranged than its competitor, Captain Gallot's cannon, which was of conventional cast construction. Gallot nevertheless enjoyed the favour of Liechtenstein, and so his piece was accepted for the Austrian service. Wiedemann could now assure Frederick that the existing Prussian 12-pounder cannon was 'incomparably better than the new Austrian 12-pounder piece.'[86] Frederick authorised Wiedemann to proceed with his work at royal expense.

The Prussians came to believe that all the Austrian attempts to better themselves were being undermined by poor morale. The Austrian commanders were convinced of the superiority of things Prussian, and their own inability to effect any real improvement. Again, nothing much was to be expected from the body of the officer corps: 'When somebody is so rich that he can afford to gamble away 100 *louis d'or* with the ladies in Vienna, he can demand without any inhibition where he wishes to be placed in the army. The vacancies are therefore filled in the same way as before.'[87]

Among the cavalry, the cuirassiers were demoralized at having been reduced to the same ration scales as the dragoons, and, from what Gellhorn was able to judge from the Gelhay Cuirassiers the troopers found their uniforms uncomfortably tight and short. The infantryman had lost the freedom of being quartered among the population, for they were now lodged in prison-like barracks, and Winterfeldt reported that 'the good discipline of the regiments consists merely in keeping them confined like convicts, drilling them twice a day to the accompaniment of cruel beatings, and having an officer inspect their quarters daily. He verifies that the soldier has not lost small items of equipment like his comb, the wax for his moustache, the pricker for his priming pan, or his flask of oil, and that he keeps his musket barrel rubbed down with sand (for they have no other cleaning material).[88]

The desertion from the foot soldiers was therefore massive, and First Lieutenant Warnery (later a celebrated military writer) reported in 1754 that every Austrian regiment he saw was as bad as the last:

> the fusiliers are, and will be, what they were 20 years ago. They are treated like galley slaves, and are lodged and beaten in the same style. Positive motivation has been extirpated, and all the men want to do is desert… Their barracks are old barns dating from the time of Zizka [the medieval Hussite leader], and they are heaped up in the chambers 30 at a time on mattresses.

At Saaz I saw them in broad daylight holding their breeches in their hands, and waging war on those lice who are their constant companions.[89]

What are we to make of all this? Frederick's information on the Austrian army came chiefly from what Winterfeldt saw on his fleeting visits to Bohemia, and otherwise mostly from frustrated men who had an interest in denigrating their old masters, and ingratiating themselves with their new ones. Much of the detail was credible, but taken together it denied Frederick useful insights into the progress that was being made by the Austrian army as a whole. He therefore embarked on war in 1756 with an imperfect knowledge of the risks he was running.

7

The Rosenkavalier Goes to War – The Austrian Officer

Origins

The leadership of the Theresian army was remarkably diverse, and presented greater contrasts in social and national character than were to be found in any other of the major belligerent forces in the Seven Years War.

Social Class

Princes and Grandees

In the Habsburg domains the higher aristocracy could be defined as those families which owned ancient noble birth, landed wealth, and the right to represent their class in the provincial assemblies. You did not have to be a purblind defender of privilege to find good reasons to place men of such qualifications in positions of military authority. The regard for birth at that time was such that an aristocratic regimental commander did not have to say, in effect, 'respect me just because I am a colonel'.[1] It was a natural transfer of the relationships which existed in civil life, and nobody would have been comfortable at the sight of a prince who was thrown among the company of private soldiers, who might be his own peasants.[2]

It was right to make due allowance for the sons of the high aristocracy, the generals and the princes of the *Reich*, and 'indeed these men should be particularly inclined towards the army, for the titles and estates of most of them were bestowed through the grace of the sovereign as a reward for military service; moreover they own a further important qualification in that their upbringing will have inculcated fine sentiments, learning, and right ways of living and thinking. It is given to them in particular to command and lead others'.[3]

Prince Charles Joseph de Ligne spent ungrudgingly more than 200,000 florins of his private fortune on the welfare of the officers under his command, and not much short of another 600,000 on his own military expenses, and even these sums were eclipsed by the 10 million which Joseph Wenzel Prince Liechtenstein devoted to the reform and upkeep of the artillery. Such officers were matched in their way by *grande seigneurs* of the families like the Esterházys and Pálffys who raised regiments largely at their own cost. Members of the lines of Bethlen, Colloredo, Herberstein, Kinsky, Königsegg, Kollowrath, Lobkowitz, Trautmannsdorf and Wallis were represented prominently in the army in the middle of the century, and the commitment of the best of the kind is exemplified by the high court official Johann Joseph Count Khevenhüller-Metsch, who was glad to see his second and third sons enter the service, and proclaimed with pride that 'not only is this condition uncommonly well suited to the nobility, who may be said to have made it their own, but in the present circumstances it offers the easiest and most fitting career for a young nobleman…'[4]

Joseph Esterházy, Joseph Lobkowitz, and Rudolph Pálffy were at once members of famous grandee families, and highly professional officers by any standard.

The absence of some names is striking. We hear little in the Seven Years War about the great houses of Dietrichstein, Schwarzenberg, Waldstein or Auersperg (whatever their contribution in other generations), and nothing of the Czernins – the owners of 91 estates. What dedicated officers found objectionable in the grandees was not their presence on the army as such, but the fact that they were not represented by enough men of the right kind.

Few of the older landed families owned traditions of continuous military service which were powerful enough to combat the attractions of a career in the civil bureaucracy, or in the Church, which in Catholic lands was seen as an excellent field of advancement for the younger sons of influential families. At the age of 18 or 20 a nobleman in the civil service would be dignified by the title of *Rath,* and already launched on a lucrative career, whereas in the army 'he must put in 10 or more years of service, and endure great hardship and personal risk, before he becomes a major or a lieutenant-colonel, and then only if he is lucky and has the support of a powerful patron. His counterpart in civilian life may attain an equivalent rank in two or three years'.[5]

Probably fewer still of the grandees' sons would have been willing to endure the kind of schooling which the young nobles underwent in the Prussian army, where they had to learn and prove themselves in the responsibilities of every rank. Frederick's chief of intelligence Lieutenant-General Hans Carl Winterfeldt made a study of the Austrian army before the Seven Years War, and concluded that 'as long as the cantonal system of recruiting [for private soldiers] is not introduced into the army, along with an obligation on the Bohemian counts to serve as free corporals or ensigns, nothing good can be made of them, and everything will stay as it was'.[6]

If the young Austrian officer of great or influential family came to the army with unrealistic expectations of advancement, and this promotion was not forthcoming, it would require unusual dedication on his part if he were to apply himself to his duties any further. He knew that recommendations for promotion were 'usually coloured with favouritism, intrigue and money. This state of affairs will continue as long as the regimental commanders are not called to account for the men they push forward… They regard promotion only as an instrument whereby they may secure patrons and friends for themselves… It is not just a question of advancing a minister's son every now and then, which might be tolerable, but the brother-in-law, brother and cousin demand to be promoted as well.'

The figures below show how firmly privilege was entrenched at the level of Field Marshal and colonel-proprietor:

	German Sovereigns & Habsburg princes	Austrian princes & higher nobility	Counts & equivalent	Barons	Lesser Nobility
FMs. promoted 1725–55, & serving 1757	34.27%	25.00	37.50	3.12	
FZMs. promoted 1740–54, & serving 1757	9.52	7.06	47.60	30.95	4.76
Regimental proprietors 1757					
Infantry	25.85	10.34	48.27	12.06	3.44
Cuirassiers & Dragoons	46.87	6.25	31.25	15.62	
Hussars	8.33	8.33	41.66	41.66	
Colonel Commandants 1757					
Infantry	–	8.00	26.66	38.46	26.66
Cuirassiers & Dragoons	–	8.69	50.00	21.73	30.95*
Hussars	–	21.42	35.71	42.85	

* including commoners
(Adapted from Hochedlinger, Michael, 'Mars Enobles. the Ascent of the Military and the Creation of a Military Nobility in Mid-Eighteenth-Century Austria,' *German History*, XVII, no.2, London 1999, 145–8)

The author of these lines, an anonymous Austrian officer, was no enemy of aristocratic privilege as such, but he condemned those powerful men who used their positions for personal and family advancement:

> It is true that they occasionally send their children and relations into the field, but they do not wish them to know the discipline and hardship to which the others are subject. They desire to see them promoted speedily to high command, without the young men having to bother overmuch with acquiring knowledge or anything else which demands patient application. They let their protégés know all too early that it is within their power to secure them promotion. The favourites in their turn devote most of their time to gambling, guzzling and other diversions. 'Why,' they ask themselves, 'why should I be stupid enough to give myself a bad time by studying until my brain hurts?' It is enough for them to be able to turn a polished argument; their imaginations do not extend beyond the table and conversation, and they make no effort beyond that required to reproduce what they have heard in a witty and elegant way... Is that the way to form great captains – on whose judgement depends crown and sceptre, the prosperity or ruin of entire lands, the welfare or the ruin of thousand upon thousands of men?[7]

The Gentry, the New Nobility and the Parvenus

The Prince de Ligne idealised the military qualities of the minor squierarchy – 'that class of poor and honourable gentlemen, whose ancestors attained that status through some warlike deed. Their sons are countrymen and hunters, inured to hardship from the age of 12, sleeping in thickets alongside their dogs, arresting poachers, and every now and then fighting the son of a neighbour for the possession of a hare they have taken'.[8] Such people certainly formed the backbone of Frederick's army, and gave the Prussian officer corps its social cohesion, but they were scarcely to be found in the Habsburg lands outside Hungary, the region of Görz and Gradisca, and de Ligne's own Hainault.

Maria Theresa and her advisers were aware of the need to draw the best kind of nobles into the army. The Military Reform Commission of 1748–9 recognised that the state could not possibly afford the great sums that would have been needed to make the military life enticing in the material sense, 'and thus we have to appeal to them by endowing them with special privileges, distinctions and things of that kind'.[9]

The poorer nobles could in turn be encouraged by being granted access to Court as officers, and free education for the sons whom they destined for a military career. The relevant measures – notably the right of entry to the Court granted in 1751, the opening of the Military Academy at Wiener-Neustadt in the following year, and the institution of the Military Order of Maria Theresa in 1757 – call for closer examination in their more immediate contexts (below). Cumulatively they enjoyed some success, and Franz Moritz Lacy later found reason to congratulate Maria Theresa declaring that her ancestors had been forced to recruit:

> all possible foreigners to fill the vacancies in the army, for the officers occupied the lowest status of all in the realm... after the peace of 1748, however, Your Majesty established order in place of the chaos and irregularities which reigned in the army. Military schools were founded, and the nobility began to embrace the military service, because our sovereign had succeeded in making it attractive to them. Through the work of Your Majesty the nobility of your lands is genuinely drawn to the army, while the rewards attached to the military service have brought in a great number of foreigners: the result has been a productive rivalry between the two elements, which must bring forth able officers and good generals.[10]

In the longer perspective we can see that the magnates as a class were not to be drawn into the life of the state so easily. However Maria Theresa's efforts had an important and positive outcome, which was to begin the process of filling the gulf which had yawned between the grandees and the rest of Austrian society. When he was besieging Prague in 1757, Frederick commented to one of his commanders that 'I hope more than ever that this Austrian race of princes and rabble will be forced to lay down its arms',[11] The Prince de Ligne explained that 'with us, you descend all at once from the great lords to the parvenus'.[12].

It was to the credit of some very eminent personages that they were glad to see that the Austrian officer corps offered a home for men who were well below them in social rank.[13]

Maria Theresa was determined to give noble status to officers who had put in long and creditable service. In 1752 she declared that officers who had served for 10 years should be regarded as ennobled. Nothing was done to put her good intentions into specific effect until early in 1757, when the *Hofkriegsrath* all of a sudden promised free elevation to the *Ritterstand* to all officers who could show they had put in 30 years' distinguished service. This measure was opposed by the *Directorium,* which pointed out on 4 April 1757 that the individuals so elevated would be encouraged to aspire to membership of the provincial *Stände,* thus encountering 'manifold objections'.[14] Maria Theresa issued an amended *Rescript* on 12 April, and all the candidates were told to reapply. Altogether 122 elevations to the 'simple nobility' were made between 1757 and 1764. In terms of rank the chief beneficiaries were the captains, at 71.3 percent of the total, and in terms of arms of the service (significantly enough) the Croats, at 26.5 percent.

The *Directorium's* distinction was important, for it established a clear difference between the entrenched aristocracy, with its pedigrees, lands and political influence, and Maria Theresa's new nobility of service. Although the newly-minted nobility therefore failed to offer an avenue into the aristocracy, it soon established a character in its own right, and over the course of the generations it created a class which identified itself more directly than any other with the service of the monarchy.

The new titles were hereditary, and the men thus honoured were given the freedom to devise a resounding suffix, which generally referred to a place of birth or the scene of some distinguishing action, or it might be an allusive artifice compounded with elements like *Feld*, *Berg* (hill), *Burg* (castle), or *Fels* (rock). Thus the young Lieutenant Waldhütter earned the suffix 'von Minenburg' through his desperate sortie against the Prussian mine craters at Schweidnitz in 1762.

'Upstarts' ('*Aufkommlinge*') were officers who tested social tolerance to its limits. Pietro Verri found that 'very few of the officers are men of good birth, and those few are usually penniless younger sons who, incapable of following any other profession, don the white and red coat out of necessity'.[15] A number of individuals at the various headquarters liked to represent themselves as officers, but turned out to be clerks, medical orderlies or servants. Many of the authentically-commissioned officers were sons of merchants, middle-men or household functionaries who 'hear nothing of noble sentiments at home, and learn from their parents only how to deceive and rob their masters, enrich themselves, make shady deals, clip coins and swig glasses of fine wine'.[16]

The corps of NCOs was the most fertile single nursery of the commissioned upstarts. From his experience of the Hungarian infantry Cogniazzo observed that the ambitious and able NCO was content to see two or three noblemen become officers over his head, in accordance with a deal sanctioned by Charles VI to give employment to the numerous Hungarian gentry, but he was right to feel aggrieved if he were passed over again. Cogniazzo adds that the commissioning of deserving NCOs was 'desirable, indeed very nearly essential, for the success of the voluntary recruiting… if we are to attract not just the scum of the lower orders, but the sons of burghers, among whom education and knowledge is often cultivated to a higher degree than among the nobility'.[17] In general, however, the commissioned former NCOs had a bad reputation, for they were alleged to become idle and addicted to drink, while they continued to treat their soldiers in the same brutal and boorish way they had acquired in their previous existence.[18]

These comments are borne out by the details of the *Rangs and Conduits Lista* (one of the most complete of the kind), of Cogniazzo's own regiment, that of Erzherzog Carl (10 March 1757). First-Lieutenant Adam Kovesdy stood out, for he had spent 15 years with the regiment as a private soldier before he had advanced even as far as NCO, but he was now esteemed 'an able and intelligent officer, whose good conduct gained him his [first] promotion from *Feldwäbel* to Second-Lieutenant.'[19] The risks of over-promoting a man from a humble background were nevertheless exemplified by the case of Captain Anton Hertelendey, a former trooper of dragoons, who 'can neither read nor write, who does not understanding the meaning of military discipline, and is totally ignorant of the drill.' The reporting officer also expressed his doubts concerning the alcoholic Second-Lieutenant Thomas Havlik (another ex-NCO) and the Captain Carl Rebl (the son of a soldier), who looked suspiciously older than his alleged 53 years.

Giuseppe Gorani was forced into the companionship of men of this kind when he reached the regiment of Andlau as subaltern in 1757. He was welcomed warmly enough by the colonel commandant, but he encountered a rude reception from his captain, 'a self-made man who detested the nobility; he believed that it was impossible for a noble to have a grain of common sense. The first lieutenant of the company was also a soldier of fortune, and extremely coarse, while the second lieutenant was the son of a blacksmith and every bit as brutal'.[20] The contrast with the Prussian officer corps was striking, for its members were linked by a caste cohesion which resulted from their real or presumed nobility.

The Protestants

Religious toleration was a matter of necessity in the Austrian army, at least among the officers, for an outright ban on Lutherans (if not Calvinists) would have depleted the leadership of a number of the Hungarian regiments, and broken a link with some of the best military families of the *Reich*.[21]

Protestantism was nevertheless a hindrance rather than a help to promotion, and the careers of prominent officers like *FM*. Joseph Friedrich Prince Sachsen-Hildburghausen, and the soldier-diplomat Johann Friedrich Brettlach were undoubtedly advanced by their well-known conversions from heresy. Jacob Cogniazzo (who may have been a covert Protestant) claims that men who had indeed converted out of self-interest rather than conviction were known in the army as the *Neubekehrten* ('Newly-turned').[22] The command of Breslau in 1757 was a special case, for this was a Protestant city which had just been reclaimed from the Prussians, and where it was important to keep the goodwill of the townspeople. Maria Theresa therefore took good care to appoint the Calvinist *FML*. Sprecher as governor, and the Lutheran *GFWM*. Wolfersdorff as commandant of the troops.

The Foreigners

Most commentators saw the cosmopolitan nature of the Austrian officer corps as a positive advantage, for it enabled the monarchy to draw on military talent wherever it was to be found. Old *FM*. Khevenhüller had proclaimed that the army could show many living examples of foreign soldiers who had won their way to rank and influence, while 'others, even if not so fortunate, may spend their old age eating the Emperor's bread in peace'.[23] A number of the Germans were sufficiently wealthy and influential in their own right to raise regiments for the service largely at their own cost, while the rich and high-ranking foreigners as a whole brought much of their own money with them, and spent it in the provinces where they happened to be quartered'.[24] (For a favourable assessment of the foreigners as a group see p. 192).

The muster lists tell us nothing about the relative numbers of the foreign-born generals, but provide some perspectives on the foreign element among the 4,251 listed regimental officers up to and including the rank of colonel commandant (See Appendix VI: Regimental Officers by Nationality). The need to officer the regiments of hussars and Hungarian infantry accounts for the overall preponderance of the Hungarians, though officers from the *Reich* formed by far the largest single national group among the 'German' regiments. The representation of Bohemians was large in absolute terms, but proportionately only about one-third of the presence of Bohemians in the other ranks.

Attachés, Volunteers and Military Tourists

In the summer of 1757 the French major-general Antoine-Marie de Malvin, comte de Montazet, came to Vienna as an authorised attaché of Austria's ally. Montazet reported to his masters on 29 June that he had been fortunate enough to make his mark with Kaunitz, 'for I have been told that all grades of generals in both field armies are extremely jealous of volunteers, even those who have come here without any ambitions concerning appointment, rank or authority. From this you may imagine what kind of opinion and reception they would have had ready for me, if Kaunitz had not bound them to show a little more trust and warmth'.[25]

Daun himself was seldom less than affable in his everyday dealings with foreigners, but he resented the French attachés in particular for the critical reports they were known to write to Versailles, for the suspect 'volunteers' who clung to their coat-tails, and for the avenues they opened to the influence of Kaunitz.[26] In March 1759 a ridiculous incident gave Daun a useful advantage over the *Staatscanzler*.

A French captain of horse, the Chevalier de Verneville, was travelling to join Montazet with the army when he fell into an argument with a party of Austrian *Feldschere* in Raudnitz. Verneville claimed that the medical orderlies had called out *'du Französ!'* ('You Frenchman!'), and confronted him with drawn swords, but investigation showed that Verneville had yelled out 'fuck you, I'm an officer!' and without the slightest provocation had proceeded to beat these humble folk with fist, stick and sword.[27]

It further transpired that Verneville was a notorious trouble-maker, as Daun was pleased to inform Kaunitz on 16 April. He wrote to him further on 5 May to remind him that Maria Theresa had resolved that no foreign volunteers were to accompany the army without her express permission, and that he had been surprised to learn that yet another French officer, the comte de Boisgelin, had been authorised to come on campaign, 'and especially because volunteers of this kind are brimming over with presumption, request quite exceptional privileges, and demand to be admitted to full knowledge and understanding of all that concerns our operations and plans.' He therefore asked Kaunitz for some guidance, and especially as he had likewise discovered that Montazet was already on his way back to the army.[28]

Daun wrote directly to Maria Theresa in December to complain of another breed of volunteer, the great princes, 'who are an absolute pest on account of their servants, secretaries and all sorts of riffraff, among whom are a number of spies who attach themselves to their suites.' Worst of all was Dom Juan de Braganza, who was 'extremely arrogant, who is intoxicated by his very limited talents, and who pronounces judgements and criticisms at random… altogether a highly undesirable piece of furniture to have with the army'.[29]

These protests brought some alleviation, and on 13 June 1760 Kaunitz had to write to his protégé Loudon that he must banish the volunteers from his corps, since those people 'often keep up a damaging correspondence, and in any case consume much of the army's supplies'.[30] Some good men suffered under the prohibitions as well as the many bad ones. The Northumberland squire Horace St. Paul is certainly to be counted among the undeserving victims. He had killed a man in England in a duel which had been none of his own choosing, and he found his way to the Austrian army in time to accompany *FM.* Browne in the first campaigns of the war. He entered 1760 with experience as acting colonel of cavalry and a volunteer on the Staff, but he spent the campaigning season in Vienna along with the other volunteers, waiting in vain for a call to the theatre of war.

The Fledgling Officer

Direct Entry

The great majority of Maria Theresa's officers reached the army in the same state of unpreparedness as their counterparts in earlier centuries, that is to say, devoid of any formal training, and with the presumption that they would learn trade through their everyday work and the example of their superiors. One of the latter declared that

> the young officers, and especially the gentlemen… must be encouraged to pursue the reading of military books and military literature, and to apply themselves to the accurate prosecution of their duties in the field, and the serious and meticulous execution of orders. They must learn to do without comfort, too much gear and excessive eating and gambling, and here I have in mind the nobles, for they are destined for the highest ranks… In time of war it is important to have many young gentlemen (once they have mastered the necessary knowledge) attached to the generals as adjutants… so that may become accomplished in the higher levels of the service.[31]

Little vocational training of any kind was offered in the Church schools, if we except the regime enforced in the Jesuit establishments, where the harsh discipline made the military variety seem mild in comparison. However the intellectual content was still governed by Jesuit *Ratio Studiorum* of 1599, and, according to Guiseppe Gorani, the Barnabite brothers (another of the teaching orders) inculcated nothing of value during 10 out of the 11 years he studied at the Noble College in Milan. Only in his final months did two unusually gifted fathers take him in hand to inculcate the elements of geometry, fortification and tactics, and inspire his passion for literature. The young Gorani's favourite book became the Italian translation of Voltaire's *Histoire du Charles XII,* and 'this reading ignited my ardour for the profession of arms, so that I became beside myself at the very sight of a uniform'.[32]

Young Gorani was neglected by his parents as well as by most of his teachers, and he made a first blundering attempt to escape from the College. He was hauled back, but a few days later his spirits were revived by seeing the Austrian garrison of Milan at drill, and he spent all his available cash to buy wax, steel, wire, coloured papers and leaden buckshot, 'and I was able to make up a large number of miniature soldiers, all fitted out perfectly with uniforms and weapons. I made another army for the King of Prussia, and a number of drilled-out keys did service as cannon. The large table in the middle of our room was covered with soldiers, my artillery and all my other military equipment. I imagined myself to be a commander-in-chief already, and I issued the necessary orders to my comrades, who helped me out enthusiastically'.[33]

For the carnival season of 1757 Gorani and his fellow pupils performed theatricals to entertain the citizens and the officers of the garrison. Among the latter was Francesco chevalier de Perelli, colonel commandant of the infantry regiment of Andlau. The colonel had once been an aide-de-camp to Gorani's uncle Cesare, a commander of the older generation who had served with Browne in Italy, and he at once invited Giuseppe to join his regiment.

There are close parallels with the motivation of the young Charles-Joseph Prince de Ligne, who belonged to one of the leading families of the military aristocracy of Hainault. He spent his childhood among the veteran troopers of his uncle's regiment of dragoons, who carried him about on their shoulders, and told him about their battles. By the age of seven or eight he had lived in a town under attack, seen three further sieges from his window, and heard the pitched battle of Fontenoy. He was at one with Gorani in believing that the vocation to the military life must be a consuming passion: 'Do you dream of warlike things? Do you devour military books and plans? Do you revere the veteran soldiers, and do tears spring into your eyes when they relate their old battles? ... If not, you must cast off the uniform which you disgrace'.[34]

De Ligne's military education was, if possible, even less systematic than that of Gorani. Indeed a suitable senior schooling to fit a young man for any kind of public career was difficult to find and expensive to finance. The Habsburg monarchs and *Stände* met the need in part by setting up *Ritterakademien,* like the school at Liegnitz in Silesia, which had been founded by Joseph I in 1709, or by paying for places for the sons of poor nobles in comparable institutions, such as the *Theresianisch-Savoyische Ritterakademie,* which had been opened in 1749 by Marie-Therese, widow of Duke Emanuel of Savoy-Carignan, or the *Theresianum,* which was taken under official control between 1749 and 1751 as a free school where 100 sons of poor officers and nobles could be prepared for the state service. Franz Moritz Lacy had been a pupil of the Liegnitz school, which now lay in Prussian territory, and in 1751, on the advice of his regimental agent, he placed one of his nephews in the *Theresianum* as an acceptable substitute.[35]

The would-be officer (the young Prince Albert of Sachsen-Teschen).

The syllabus of such institutions concentrated on philosophy, law and history, which were then seen as vocational subjects. Until the 1750s there was only sketchy technical training available for would-be military engineers, and no provision at all for the future officers of the infantry and cavalry, or indeed any organised avenues of entry for these people into the army.

'Children of the State' – The Laimgrube Preparatory School and the Wienerneustadt Military Academy

According to Gorani, his uncle Cesare had drawn up 'various projects' for military education, and it was on the basis of these schemes that Maria Theresa founded not only the Military Academy at Wiener Neustadt (below), but the reformed *Theresianum* – which she entrusted to the Jesuits over the protests of the old general. 'We all know how much these institutions have benefited Austrian education, and it would have benefited still more if the Empress had not distorted the plans of my uncle'.[36]

However the verifiable and continuous history of military education in Austria dates from 28 November 1751, when *FZM*. Daun, Rudolph Chotek as head of the *Directorium, Kriegscommissar* Salburg and other specialists first met under the presidency of Haugwitz, who explained that Maria Theresa had decided to fund 'a military school or academy, motivated by her motherly care as sovereign for such noble youth of her kingdoms, principalities and other lands, who suffer from lack of education on account of the poverty of their parents, or for other reasons'.[37]

As a foundation for the Military Academy Maria Theresa desired to set up a preparatory school for 100 noble lads and sons of poor officers, who would be admitted at the age of seven, and fed into the senior academy at the age of 14. The Commission decided that the best location would be in the grounds of the *Chaosische Stiftung* in the Laimgrube suburb of Vienna. This establishment was as eccentric as its name suggests. It had been opened in 1666 by Johann Conrad Richthausen, who had been ennobled by Leopold I 'in consideration of the good order he brought to the [Hungarian] mines, after finding them in dire confusion or chaos when he entered on his office as manager'.[38]

In the 18th century the *Chaosische Stiftung* accommodated 250 pupils from all the nations of the monarchy (the *Theresianisch-Savoyische Ritterakademie* being founded as an offshoot), and as one of its peculiar traditions it emphasised the teaching of military history. However the *Chaosische Stiftung* had no direct links with the army, and the *Militär Pflanz-Schule* which now arose in its grounds was a completely new institution, designed as a preparatory school for the senior academy at Wiener-Neustadt.

Maria Theresa intervened directly to expand the number of pupils from the initial 100 to 150, and she drew them widely from the German Hereditary Lands. She contributed sums of her own, and sent word to the *Stände* that they must support her initiative, since the education of young nobles promoted the welfare both of the monarchy as a whole and the individual provinces.[39] As a further inducement the aristocrats were told that the pupils would be paid directly from Maria Theresa's purse, that the boys would be at liberty to leave at any time, and that they were under no obligation to enter the army, 'since the knowledge and noble exercises they learn will be of some use even outside the military service.'[40]

Nothing was to be expected from Hungary or Transylvania, but on 12 January 1754 the *Stände* of Lower Austria offered freely to contribute an annual 5,000 florins. The other *Stände* responded in proportion (another 5,000, for example, from Moravia, and 2,500 from Carniola), and the *Militär Pflanz-Schule* was able to provide teaching, accommodation, food, clothing and all other requisites free of charge. The number of pupils could now be expanded to 200, and the first course opened on 1 January 1755.

Pupils were admitted up to the age of 11, and this circumstance, together with the congestion at Wiener-Neustadt, resulted before long in many lads being detained at the preparatory school well beyond the official leaving age of 14. The task of controlling the frustrated adolescents proved to be beyond the capacity of the teachers, who as lay officers were unable to employ the same means of physical and spiritual coercion which came naturally to the monks and Jesuits in the other schools.

In contrast the senior academy is remembered as one of the glories of Maria Theresa's reign, and was regarded at the time as an example to the rest of Europe. An English visitor wrote that

> The Military Academy at Neustadt is on such a flourishing footing, that it would be singly sufficient to eternise the reign of the Empress Queen. Those who have seen it are filled with admiration... such good regulations have been made, that this Military School cannot fail, in good time, to produce excellent officers... had we the benefit of such an Academy in these kingdoms, how much better would our army be supplied with officers than it is at present?
>
> Men would be officers by their ability, not from distaste to other professions, or a want of proper qualifications for them.[41]

The Commission resolved to found the senior academy at its first meeting, on 28 November 1751, and determined that the initial cost of 95,095 florins could be raised by eliminating one soldier from the establishment of every company throughout the army. Maria Theresa gave her approval in a businesslike way, and insisted that 'nothing is to be undertaken without previous notification to me by written memorandum'.[42]

The charter (*Gründungs-Urkunde*) was dated 14 December 1751, and on 14 January 1752 the *Hofkriegsrath* authorised the printing of the necessary publicity. Through this document Maria Theresa required the provincial administrations, the provincial commanding generals and the *Invaliden Hof-Commission* to draw up lists of the children of deserving officers, together with details of the boys' age and attainments, and of the circumstances of their parents, 'so that the nobility and the military men will have the assurance that, if they put their lives and fortunes at risk for the common good, their descendants will be preserved from poverty, and maintained and educated under the protection of our most gracious monarch as children of the state for the service and good of the fatherland'.[43]

The Academy's home was the old Imperial castle (*Burg*) at Wiener-Neustadt, in a great plain 45 kilometres south of Vienna. The castle had long been unoccupied, and the architect Matthias Gerl, his assistant military engineer, and the Imperial *Hof-Quartier-Meister* Joachimsburg (who collected the materials) got

The Military Academy at Wiener-Neustadt.

down to work without delay. Maria Theresa and Daun as *Ober-Director* visited the site on 17 July 1752, and found that the conversion was already far advanced. With some ingenuity the interior spaces were being rearranged to provide the necessary *Cameradschaftszimmern,* and the whole was carried out in a way which emphasised the simplicity and dignity of the old building:

> The castle is very spacious, and well built; it is situated at one of the extremities of the town of Neustadt, in a dear and wholesome air; the gardens are large, and divided into several compartments; the apartments in the castle are laid out in such a manner, that besides those of the Counts Daun and Thürheim, the Lieutenant-Colonel, and the Major, there are two handsome dining-rooms, a very large hall for their exercises, and a particular hall for each school.[44]

The Thürheim mentioned here was the *GFWM*. Franz Ludwig, who was appointed as the first *Unter-Director* under the overall direction of Daun as *Ober-Director* of both the new Academy and the *Militär Pflanz-Schule* in Vienna. Thürheim left to take up a field command inl 756, and was replaced by *GFWM*. Franz Carl Count Cavriani.

The cadets were formed into two companies of 100 cadets each, one of the companies providing for the sons of the nobility of the Hereditary Lands, and the other for the sons of officers who had 'served for 10 years as senior regimental officers to the satisfaction of their superiors, the reason being that an officer who has served for that length of time may be regarded as ennobled'.[45]

Within each company the military instruction was directed by one captain, two first-lieutenants, two second-lieutenants, and 10 ensigns. In addition two *Feldwäbel,* 10 corporals and

20 *Gefreyten* were appointed from the best of the senior cadets as a cadet government. Within this hierarchy the lieutenants had an important intermediary role, for they were not only to keep the cadets in good order, but ensure that they were not maltreated by their cadet government.[46] In addition the Academy supported an establishment of six officers who taught fortification and mathematics, together with riding instructors, masters of fencing and dancing, and teachers of Bohemian, Italian and French (important qualifications for command in this multinational army).

The Academy opened, as planned, on 1 November 1752. On weekdays the cadets were roused by the beating of *Tag Wacht* at five in the morning, whereupon they muttered their prayers, and threw themselves into the business of washing and making themselves presentable. After a hurried breakfast the cadets assembled in the open courtyard or in one of the large halls for inspection by their captain and lieutenants. At six a further drumbeat summoned the cadets to the magnificent old castle chapel, where the officers stationed themselves to keep the cadets in view and ensure that they all prayed in a dignified way. The service ended with the singing of the hymn *Freuet Euch ihr lieben Seelen,* whereupon the cadets progressed by their *Cameradschaften* to their halls of study to the ringing of the *Studir-Glöckl.*

The typical working day incorporated periods devoted to mathematics and its military applications, dancing, fencing and foreign languages, and one or two hours of drill. Provision was made for the religious education of the younger cadets, and riding instruction for the seniors, and for practical engineering, weapons training and drilling by larger units in the park on Sundays. In such a way a reasonably diligent cadet ultimately made an officer who was physically agile, and versed in a range of accomplishments and practical knowledge. A Swedish officer commented that 'in this establishment no expense is spared, whether concerning the maintenance of the young people, or their education in the subjects they must master. There is little doubt that in the course of time it will benefit both society in general, and the military in particular'.[47]

The cadets were issued with two free uniforms a year – one was probably of blue for everyday wear, and the other the parade uniform of white with light red facings. Servants were assigned to the *Cameradschaften* to clean the weapons, the brass and the leather-work daily, and 'as to their diet, each table consists of 10 Academicians and an officer, and is supplied with the best of everything; they have clean table linen every day; their eating is the only object belonging to the foundation which has been censured; many think, they ought to be accustomed early to the hardships which they must unavoidably suffer thereafter in the field'.[48]

The orders laid down that 'in general all the officers must bend their best efforts to bring the cadets to a good way of life, and never cease to inculcate courtesy, modesty, good manners, accord among themselves, but especially subordination, obedience and respect'.[49] Thürheim did what he could to establish a tradition of strict discipline, and he almost at once issued a stream of protests concerning the entrepreneur Raigerwarther, who provided drinking and music in the nearby public garden in ways which threatened the morals of the cadets. He himself entered this den of iniquity at the end of September 1753, and rooted out the Academy servants and laundrymen who were disporting themselves with bad women in the bushes.[50]

Maria Theresa received weekly reports on the affairs of Wiener-Neustadt, and she came to the Academy at least once a year. She and Francis Stephen visited the place in particular style on 7 May 1755. After hearing Mass in the chapel they repaired to the principal academic hall, where their likenesses were displayed in large portraits on the wall; Maria Theresa looked in vain for the bronze bust of the *Ober-Director* she had given to the Academy, and finding that Daun had veiled it in black cloth out of modesty, she ordered the covering to be removed. The Imperial couple heard the cadets undergo oral examinations in German, Bohemian, Italian and French, and after lunch they were invited to the park, where they viewed a mock siege and saw the cadets drilling by companies. Maria Theresa returned to Vienna delighted at what she had seen.[51]

Little documentary evidence survives concerning the interior life of the Academy during its formative years, for the records of the *Local-Direction* have not survived, and the papers for the period from 1757 to 1762 are missing from the records of the *Ober-Direction*. The correspondence between Daun and Maria Theresa indicates that a minor crisis of some sort had arrived by 1760, for a series of disorders in one of the companies compelled the *Linter-Director* to suspend the relevant captain, and hand over the command to the senior first-lieutenant. To the foreign visitor, however, the discipline of the Academy appeared admirable: 'It is impossible to see the military exercise performed with more order, justness, and exactness, than by theses youths: they mount guard every day, go the rounds, make the report, and perform all other parts of the service of a fortified town, with as great rigour and formality as the veterans do, who are garrisoned at Luxembourg'.[52]

As vacancies for ensigns or cornets happened to arise in the regiments, a certain number were held open on Imperial order for the products of Wiener-Neustadt. During the war the regiments of cuirassiers and dragoons were allowed to fill some of these vacancies by their own nominees.[53] However this exemption applied only to the cavalry, and among the infantry the compulsory intake from Wiener-Neustadt amounted to an important retrenchment of the old freedoms of the *Inhaber* (colonel proprietors). In 1761 we find *FZM*. Lacy writing to a friend that he was unable to find a place for one of that gentleman's protégés, 'since not even the *Inhaber* have it in their power to grant a single ensign's place in their own regiments'.[54]

The sovereign provided every graduate of the Academy with a full uniform, 200 florins, and horse in addition for the entrants to the cavalry. The new ensigns and cornets were allowed one year from the date of their passing out (*Ausmusterung*) to fit themselves out, and meanwhile the assigned regiments were obliged to keep their places open for them, with the exception of the cavalry mentioned above.

The first cadets passed out in 1755, and by the end of 1763 the total of officers commissioned from Wiener-Neustadt had reached 310, of whom the largest single body was formed by the sons of simple nobles, who made up 41.93 percent of the whole. Out of the young men who were commissioned by the end of active hostilities, at the end 1762, altogether some 242 may be identified by place of birth. They came respectively from:

Hungary:	18.59 percent
Bohemia:	14.04
Lower & Upper Austria & Vienna:	9.09
Netherlands & Luxembourg:	8.26
Styria:	7.43
Carinthia, the *Reich*:	6.19 each
Austrian Italy:	5.78
Silesia (undifferentiated):	5.36
Moravia:	4.95
Görz and Gradisca:	4.54
Carniola, Croatia with Slavonia, Italy (other):	2.89 each
Tyrol, Breisgau:	0.41 each

The nearest 'peer group' is that of the ensigns, cornets and second-lieutenants listed in Appendix VI, which inevitably included a number of the Wiener-Neustadt products. A drop of the cadets born in the *Reich* was to be expected, given the nature of the funding and the placing of the young men in question, but the most remarkable feature of the WienerNeustadt figures is the emergence of proportionately large numbers of cadets from the provinces of Inner Austria (Styria, Carinthia, Carniola, and Görz and Gradisca) none of which individually accounted for as much as 1 percent of the young officers appeared in the muster lists. The names of the Inner Austrians are almost entirely those of the smaller gentry, which reinforces the impression that Maria Theresa succeeded in at least part of her aims.

However the higher aristocracy held itself aloof, and as early as 1755 Maria Theresa noted that 'it is quite incredible that nobody desires to profit by my gracious concession'.[55] In the long term the Military Academy at Wiener-Neustadt emerged as one of the most significant institutions of the Austrian army, but its output in its first years was highly irregular, the total by the end of the Seven Years War amounting to probably less than 6 percent of the size of the officer corps, and it was 'still too few to provide for such a large army, and especially for the Hungarians and Croats, who stand in greater need of education than the others'.[56] The great majority of the Austrian officers had therefore not come to the army as 'children of the state,' in Maria Theresa's phrase, but with their local and class characteristics untouched by any formal military conditioning.

THE REGIMENTAL OFFICERS

The Establishment

How effectively a regiment was commanded depended not only on the quality of its officers, but also their quantity. According to the *Regulament* of 1749 the standard infantry regiment was supposed to be staffed by one colonel commandant, one lieutenant-colonel, one major, 14 captains, four acting captains (*Capitain-Lieutenants*), 18 first-lieutenants, 18 second-lieutenants and eight ensigns. Francis Stephen pointed out before the Seven Years War that the regulation number of officers and NCOs was insufficient to manage the number of files in a regiment'.[57] Complications came when the regiment was divided into two field battalions and one garrison battalion, and when, from 1757 and 1758 the fusiliers as well as the grenadiers were drawn up in three ranks instead of four, which extended the line still further across the landscape. As for the cavalry, a squadron might be left with just two or three officers after the rest had been sent away to command detachments.[58] Kaunitz was therefore right to complain that 'the shortfall in officers is one of the chief defects of the Imperial and Royal Army. All other powers, and Prussia in particular, who manage their affairs in a most economical way, nevertheless have a much larger number'.[59]

Volunteers, Ensigns and Cornets

Unless they were products of Wiener Neustadt (who were appointed directly to a *Fahne* or *Estandart* at the disposal of Maria Theresa), most intending officers entered the regiment as *Volonteirs* (to be distinguished from the foreign volunteers mentioned above). Such people did no regular service, for they were busy learning the fundamentals of their trade under the supervision of a good NCO or some other responsible senior. In the infantry regiment of Andlau Giuseppe Gorani was fortunate enough to be schooled by Johann Wümmer, who drilled the young Milanese with the troops, perfected his German, and weaned him away from the sodomitical practices he had learned at his College.[60]

According to the Prince de Ligne the junior officer was proud of his first command, prouder in fact than he would be if he ultimately commanded an army as Field Marshal. If the troops were well disciplined they would obey and respect him, and take him under their collective wing. 'He's a brave lad," they will say, "let's follow him. We won't leave him in the lurch"'.[61]

Meanwhile the infantry and dragoon *Fähndrich* and the cuirassier cornet were at the beck and call of the lieutenants for helping with the everyday business of the company or squadron, and in addition they had the special responsibility of attending to the welfare of the sick and wounded. In the early campaigns of the Seven Year War they might also have carried on the ancient practice of bearing a colour (two per battalion) or the squadron standard, which was a physically demanding and tactically dangerous task.

Officers of the 'German' infantry. (Ottenfeld, 1898)

In 1759 the dragoon *Fähndrichs* and the cuirassier cornets were converted to second-lieutenants, and yielded up their standards to a new grade of NCO, the *Estandart-Führer*. The infantry *Fähndrichs* were now at a relative disadvantage, and towards the end of the war they constituted the only officer grade of the which Austrians had a surplus, amounting to nearly 600 individuals by April 1762. Over the opposition of the *Hofkriegsrath* (which objected to the expense of fitting out) Maria Theresa insisted that these folk should be offered the chance of transferring to the cavalry.[62]

Lieutenants

In the properly-run company or squadron the *Unter-Lieutenant* and the *Ober-Lieutenant* were busy men, who inspected and drilled the troops daily, accompanied them on every parade, supervised the allocation of duties, and made sure that the uniforms, weapons and equipment were complete, and fit to survive scrutiny at the Saturday inspection. Most of the commissioned former NCOs could be trusted with this kind of work, which was normally the limit of their ambitions and abilities.

The Captains

The captain (*Haubtmann* in the infantry and dragoons, *Rittmeister* in the cuirassiers and hussars) was responsible for the leadership and good order of the company or squadron, which was the most important sub-unit of the regiment. His immediate instrument was his First-Lieutenant, from whom he received a daily report, and he in turn made a weekly report to the major, and conducted a close inspection of his company or squadron every Saturday. Three of the companies (squadrons) of the regiment were under the nominal command of the colonel, the lieutenant-colonel and the majorrespectively – in other words senior regimental ('staff') officers who had important responsibilities elsewhere – and so the acting command devolved upon officers who were termed '*Capitain Lieutenants*.'

Majors

The major (*Obrist-Wachtmeister*) was a hardworking, hard-driving executive officer, who maintained standards of drill, turnout and discipline throughout the regiment or battalion. He verified and signed the lists of officers and *Dienst-Tabella* (duty rosters), he kept a journal of all the documents received by the regiment or issued by himself, he designated the alarm stations, he placed the outposts, he made sure that the regimental lines were clean and orderly, and he licensed and supervised the sutlers and the butchers, to the point of determining the weights and measures. The good major was therefore 'indefatigable, diligent, exact, phlegmatic and vigilant, and with a serious turn of mind… he should certainly live on good terms with the other officers, but he must put aside all familiarity and friendship when it comes to matters of the service, and inspire great fear and respect when he appears with the regiment'.[63]

A second major was introduced in each regiment of infantry in the course of the Seven Years War, which emphasised the role of the major's role as a tactical commander, and made it possible to assign one to each of the two field battalions. At the same time the original title *Obrist-Wachtmeister* fell into disuse, being replaced by *Major* (pronounced 'Mayor,' with the stress on the second syllable).

Lieutenant Colonels

At first sight the role of the lieutenant-colonel (*Obrist-Lieutenant*) resembled that of the major. Every evening he issued the new *Parole* (password) and the orders for the coming day, and he was to be present in person whenever the regiment drilled or paraded as a body. He made daily and weekly reports to the colonel commandant, being answerable for the accounting, clothing and equipment of the regiment as a whole, but in addition he had a wider responsibility for the well-being of the officers and men. He interceded for delinquents, and normally showed a less savage face to the world than did the implacable major. When he reached his new regiment Giuseppe Gorani encountered one of the best of the kind in the person of Lieutenant-Colonel Ludovico Baron Terzi, 'a man of genuine merit and considerable knowledge'.[64]

Colonel Commandants

The colonel commandant (*Obrister Commendant* or *Titular Obrister*) exercised the everyday command of the regiment. He led it in action, he was responsible for its economy, he read and signed the daily reports, and he distributed the personnel among the companies. According to Armfeldt he possessed the devolved authority to consign the officers and all other personnel in the regiment to the provost's arrest; the death penalty also lay within the power of the colonel of infantry, but not that of the cavalry, 'a distinction... which proceeds from the fact that in the Austrian service the cavalryman is always regarded as more noble than the infantryman'.[65]

The colonel commandant's authority was inherently limited by the fact that the regiment was virtually 'owned' by another officer, the colonel proprietor (*Obrister Inhaber,* below), who was normally absent on business, and devolved only as much of his power as he saw fit. As an *Inhaber* of a regiment of hussars G.d.C. Hadik told his colonel commandant that 'marriages are forbidden without prior notification to me ... Likewise, without my order not the slightest change is to be made in the officers' uniforms as established in the regiment, or in the clothing of the NCOs or men.' The commandant was to take care to prevent any factions developing among the officers:

> and the best way to attain this salutary end is to treat the officers in an unfailingly courteous manner, as befits their condition and rank. At suitable moments you should single out for congratulation those officers who do the most for the service, and are of good conduct generally. When officers fall short you must bring home to them where their fault lies, and punish them as circumstances dictate, but ... never reproach them any further on account of mistakes for which they have already been disciplined, and still less make them the targets of any kind of vendetta.[66]

There was limitless potential for friction between the two kinds of colonel, especially when they were serving in the same field army, in which case the commandant might have to report to the *Inhaber* everything that was happening in the regiment, but in Armfeldt's experience 'they usually get on so well that, under the overall authority of the *Inhaber,* the regimental commandant has a free hand in everything'.[67]

Lacy states that 'they never appoint a colonel commandant contrary to the choice of the *Inhaber*'.[68] Loudon was not so confident, and he applied to his protector Kaunitz for help, after his regiment lost an excellent commandant in Marquis Botta, who was promoted to general. In the normal course of things the post would have gone to Baron Schroder, who was Botta's deputy. Schroder, however, was too sick to be able to exercise effective command, and Loudon wished to have the excellent Lieutenant-Colonel Wallis appointed in his place. He feared that the process would be obstructed by Schroder, 'who has many friends in Vienna, especially among the officials... I therefore humbly ask Your Excellency to recommend the said Lieutenant-Colonel Baron Wallis to her Majesty for promotion to colonel commandant as if on your own initiative; I will then take care to forward his name in my recommendation to the *Hofkriegsrath*'.[69] So much for the reputation of Loudon as the political innocent.

Colonel Proprietor

The colonel proprietor (*Obrister-Inhaber*) held one of the most influential positions in the army, in that he had it in his power to promote or obstruct the reform and good administration of the infantry and cavalry. The *Inhaber* perpetuated the traditions of the military entrepreneurs who had arisen in late feudal Europe, and in Austria their privileges were founded on the *Kriegsartikel* (1508) of Emperor Maximilian I, which granted them the right to appoint personnel within the regiment up to the rank of captain, full and independent judicial authority (the *jus gladii et aggratiandi*), power over the economy of the regiment, together with a number of minor privileges and perquisites. Many of the proprietors were generals in their own right, and they were therefore able to sustain the interests of military proprietorship in the highest counsels.

There were probably more good proprietors than bad, and some of them promoted reform actively, but their existence as a privileged class imposed distinct limits on the ability of Maria Theresa, Kaunitz and Daun to mould the army according to their will. Things were managed differently in Prussia, where the captains had greater administrative autonomy than in the Austrian service, and where the *Chefs* (the Prussian equivalent of the *Inhaber*) answered directly to a fierce and vigilant king.

The appointment of the proprietors lay in the power of the sovereign, who was swayed by a variety of considerations. Maria Theresa moved entirely on her own initiative when, after the death of *FM*. Browne, she gave his regiment (No. 36) to his second son Joseph, the colonel commandant. It was contrary to the custom of the Austrian army for a commandant to succeeded to the proprietorship of a regiment in which he was already serving, and a courtier claimed that this act of impulsive generosity was displeasing to 'men of firm principles and austere virtue'.[70]

A commander in the field could enter a powerful plea on behalf of an officer by sending him to Vienna to present the formal news of some victory. In such a way *FM*. Daun was able to secure the vacant dragoon regiment of de Ligne for his nephew *FML*. Benedict Daun after the battle of Kolin. Individuals who believed themselves qualified might apply through intermediaries, as when Adam Joseph Bethlen entered a bid for the vacant hussar regiment of Morocz in 1758.[71] Bethlen was successful, and in this case the decision must have been swayed by the knowledge that the Bethlens were great men in Transylvania, able to support a regiment by their authority and resources. Indeed it was not necessarily a good thing to give a regiment to an officer who owed everything to his military career, and regarded his regiment primarily as a source of income. A wealthy colonel had it in his power to help needy officers and their families, attract fine recruits by offering high bounties, and add panache and style to the life of the regiment.[72]

The *Obrister Inhaber* ruled his military kingdom virtually as he wished, checked only by the findings of the Commissaries at the periodic *Musterungen*. He could fill officer vacancies up the rank of captain, except for the posts reserved for the graduates of Wiener Neustadt. He had no direct power to appoint the senior regimental officers, though he made his preferences known. The system was open to appalling abuses, and there were cases when the colonel made officers out of his companions at the card table, the protégés of his servants or mistresses, or company clerks (*Fourier*) who could help him out with his accounts.[73]

Some of the proprietors were embarrassed by the power at their disposal in this respect. *FM*. Count Birkenfeld came to regret a promise he had made to *FM*. Prince Salm, to provide a company for his son, and he appealed to Daun to help him out of his dilemma. Daun had to reply that he could not interfere in a matter which lay within the discretion of the *Inhaber*. In the private letters of Lacy we can sense that the man actually welcomed the new regulations which allowed him to deny vacancies to his petitioners.[74]

Lacy had obtained his regiment in October 1758, and he wrote to one of his lady friends that he knew nothing of his new officers. That was nothing unusual, for the Austrian military tradition was hostile to the notion of a commandant in any way 'inheriting' a regiment, as we have seen, and this prohibition offered one of the few safeguards against corruption. There was a price to pay. A number of officers regretted the consequent instability, and the grenadier captain Baron de Vigneulle made a useful but vain suggestion that the name of some recruiting area should be added to that of the current *Inhaber,* forming a compound like Brünn-Colloredo' which would preserve an element of continuity. 'A regiment which has done well under a particular name, usually loses some of that reputation at a change of nomenclature, and loses also some of the morale which had sustained it. Conversely a regiment which has done badly believes that the stain on its honour disappears along with its old name, and has no incentive to repair the disgrace'.[75]

Regimental officers dreaded the coming of a fresh *Inhaber,* who might ordain a new design of uniform, or, worse still, make further arbitrary changes during the time he owned the regiment, which put the officers to huge expense.[76] The Prussian officers were safeguarded against this abuse by the specific and binding details which were laid down in the *Dessauer Stammbuch* (1729, expanded 1737), which held sway throughout Frederick's reign.

Frequent changes in an officer's garb might flatter an *Inhaber's* vanity and sense of power, and the same man might well force his soldiers to wear their uniforms for two or more years, to save him money. This was one of the charges laid by Johann Baron Freyenfels, commandant of the infantry regiment of Starhemberg, against his *Inhaber FZM.* Emanuel Michael Starhemberg and the reign of corruption in their regiment.

The *Hofkriegsrath* investigated the affair, and took the side of Starhemberg against the valiant and honest Freyenfels. It declared that Freyenfels had been at fault in two respects, by telling the officers to discard their partisans for muskets (which was happening in many regiments anyway), and by degrading a civilian whom Starhemberg (admittedly under false pretences) had appointed as an officer. Freyenfels was lucky enough to have *FZM.* Loudon and *FML.* Ellrichshausen to speak up for him, and on that account Maria Theresa resolved that no further proceedings were to be taken against him, though he was instructed to behave towards his *Inhaber* with all due respect.[77] This episode was hardly an incentive to principled officers to make a stand against the criminality of their superiors, though Freyenfels was able to vindicate himself indirectly when he gained the Military Order of Maria Theresa for his part in the defence of Schweidnitz in 1762.

General Officers

The ranks of the field officers ran in the following ascending order:

General Feldwachtmeister (*GFWM.*) = Major-General
Feldmarschall Lieutenant (*FML.*) = Lieutenant-General
Feldzeugmeister (*FZM.*) (infantry); *General der Cavallerie* (cavalry) = Full General
Feldmarschall (*FM.*) = Field Marshal

Whereas the number of *Inhaber* was determined by the quantity of regiments, there existed no fixed relationship between the numbers and grades of general officers on the one hand, and the numbers of troops, units and formations on the other. In the field:

Two or three regiments (or between two and five battalions) normally constituted a brigade under a *GFWM.*
Two or three brigades made up a division or *Departement* under a *FML.*
The full general (*FZM.* or *G.d.C.*) might command a whole line or a wing of infantry or cavalry.

In 1760 both Maria Theresa and Prince Liechtenstein maintained that the command of the army was top-heavy.[78] Daun had been of like persuasion early in the war, when far too many incompetents were to be found among the generals, but he now argued that there were actually too few generals for the needs of the service, 'for which reason I humbly represent that Your majesty might consider a larger promotion, for I believe that a single *GFWM.* is not nearly enough for every six battalions, or a *FML.* for 12 battalions; likewise for the cavalry we need more than one *GFWM.* for every three regiments, and one *FML.* for six.[79]

Our further investigations are hampered by the fact that no systematic official records exist in the period for the total numbers of field officers on the books. The only substitute is the occasional privately-published army list, such as the one printed by I.A. Steiflinger in Augsburg in 1761, from which it is possible to draw only some general deductions. On evidence like this it appears that the army supported about 330 field officers at any one time in the Seven Years War, of which the *GFWMs.* made up some 30 percent, the *FMLs.* 47 percent, the *FZMs.* 13 percent, and the *FMs.* 10 percent.

Unlike the muster lists, Steiflinger's *Schema* gives no places of birth, and the types of surname present only a very unsatisfactory substitute, giving, for example no indication of the degree of assimilation of the family in the Habsburg dominions:

Types of Names of Field Officers

	GFWM.	FML.	FZM/G.d.C.	FM.	Total
German:	47.05%	42.48	55.80	47.00	46.22
Hungarian:	11.76	12.41	9.30	11.76	11.78
French:	8.82	11.76	11.62	11.76	10.87
Italian:	8.82	20.09	11.62	8.80	14.80
Spanish:	4.90	3.92	4.65	5.80	4.53
Irish:	0.98	2.61	2.32	3.00	2.11
Bohemian:	0.98	1.30	2.32	nil	1.20
Other Slavonic:	7.84	3.26	nil	nil	3.92
Scots:	2.94	0.65	nil	nil	1.20
English:	0.98	0.65	nil	nil	0.30
Unidentifiable or illegible:	4.90	0.65	2.32	11.76	3.07

About half the names are those of 'backswoodsmen,' who were beyond any active campaigning by the time of the Seven Years War. This applies in particular to the Spanish and the Scots, whose days of glory lay in the past.

GFWM.
The duties of the major-general corresponded closely with those of the major within the regiment, albeit on a much larger scale, for he was in charge of a brigade consisting of two or more regiments. The conscientious *GFWM.* could never relax, for he was in immediate charge of positioning his brigade in camp, directing it on the march, and commanding it in battle.[80]

FML.
The lieutenant-general commanded a division or *Departement* of two or more brigades. Lacy defined the duties of this post after the Seven Years War, and emphasised that the *FML.* was responsible not only for directing the division as a whole, but making sure that the brigadiers were managing affairs properly at the regimental level.[81] The division made up a significant element in a line of battle. Moreover *FMLs.* were the most junior field officers normally entitled to command large mixed detachments, which gave them an opportunity to make a name for themselves.

FZM. (Infantry), *G.D.C.* (Cavalry)

These were full generals and men of considerable importance, who had the power to command a wing or line, or even lead a whole army in their own right, as was appreciated by Kaunitz in 1761, when he wished to give the operations in Silesia a decisive turn, 'and for that reason he [Loudon] was promoted over the heads of many other *FMLs.* to *FZM.* This rank not only made him an Imperial Privy Councillor, with a seat on the secret state and military conferences, but authorised him to direct considerable armies as commander-in-chief'.[82]

All the same in the Austrian service this rank was held to be less than satisfactory in a number of cases. As Armfeldt observed, it was strange to have commanders designated 'separate generals of infantry or cavalry, according to the branch in which they had served',[83] and this distinction inevitably derogated from their credibility if they were in charge of mixed commands. Moreover the infantry general's title of *Feldzeugmeister* was an antique anomaly which derived from *Zeug,* or ordnance, which led some foreign officers to assume that the bearers must be specialists in artillery. It is not surprising that Maria Theresa once considered dispensing with this rank altogether for command in the fields.[84]

FM.

Though cheapened by needless multiplication, the rank of Field Marshal stood at the summit of the Habsburg military authority in the Seven Years War. The serving Field Marshal (a much rarer bird than the Field Marshals in disgrace or effective retirement) commanded an entire army with disposition over the *Kriegs-Cassa,* and at least nominal powers to replace unsatisfactory generals. He corresponded directly with Vienna, from where he received political as well as military guidance.

The Officer's Career

Career Profile

Some General Characteristics

The evidence of the Austrian muster lists (see Appendix VII: Age and service of the Regimental officer) corresponds reasonably well with Houlding's study (1981, p. 109) of the service record of British infantry officers in 1759, which shows lieutenants with an average of five years of service, captains with 14, majors with 19, and lieutenant-colonels with 15. The impression in both the Austrian and British cases is that of a considerable depth of experience.

After every allowance has been made for corruption and favouritism, the Austrian army remained unique among the armies of the major European powers of the time, in that 'courage, experience in the service, and intelligence may enable the humblest private soldier to progress in such a way as to exchange his musket for the riband of the Theresian Order, and his place in the tent *Cameradschaft* for one in the *Hofkriegsrath*'.[85] Here Cogniazzo was writing about something which could happen, rather than something that did happen as a matter of routine, but the principle was recognised and admired, and Ravizza, Walther von Waldenau and Krammer von Obereck furnished living examples in his own time.

In outline the mechanism of officer promotion was very simple. While the regimental proprietors controlled the promotion to captain and lieutenant, and most of those to ensign and cornet, the *Hofkriegsrath* was responsible for appointing all the generals, and the senior regimental officers from major upwards. The *Hofkriegsrath* in addition took over all the promotions among the Croats, and within the regular regiments where the post of *Inhaber* was vacant and there was therefore nobody to commission the junior officers.

Seniority

Maria Theresa waived the rule that had obtained under Charles VI, that promotion of regimental officers must proceed by strict seniority, and the Prince de Ligne set himself against the principle of seniority *per se*.[86] However there was still understood to be a rough equation between seniority and fairness, and Lacy found it useful to refer to the idea when he told one of his correspondents that it would be unjust to give one of her protégés a company in the regiment 'at the expense of so many officers who have prior claims of seniority over him'.[87]

Lacy himself benefited from a rapid promotion out of turn, which advanced him from colonel to Field Marshal in nine years, by when he was still not quite 40. However he had rejected, or been deprived of the opportunity of supreme command after Daun had been wounded at Torgau in 1760, as he explained to another of his ladies. He thanked her for her congratulations:

> but you should have been able to foresee that I would never have been so rash as to take on such a responsibility, the burden of which must necessarily have surpassed the strength of a man of my years, and demanded an experience which I have so far been unable to acquire. *FM*. Daun was well aware of the embarrassment this would have caused me, and the inconveniences consequent upon such an upset in the army, and he took it on himself to suspend the publication of the Court's order... I therefore hope that O'Donnell will remain in command of the army, as corresponds with his services, and that all the generals will continue to serve under him as their ranks dictate.[88]

Lacy's friend the Prince de Ligne claims that if Lacy had taken up the command he would have been made Field Marshal.[89]

Loudon, the real or supposed rival of Lacy, was promoted from major to *FZM*. in only five years, and this too occasioned some resentment. *GFWM*. d'Ayasasa was one of those who had been left behind by rapid ascents such as these, and he pressed for promotion to *FML*, as due to 'my grey hairs and multiplicity of wounds, and out of regard to the few years remaining to me'.[90] The mention of scars was no literary conceit. Old Gottfried Baron Wollwarth describes the last episode of his career, which came towards the end of the battle of Kolin, when he encountered half a dozen squadrons of Prussian dragoons: 'I attacked this body with a number of our own squadrons... and on this occasion, and in the 71st year of my age, I received two cuts in the head, one of which slashed through the crown of my hat and cut my wig in two, occasioning a deep and painful wound'.[91] The jockeying for position among the generals presents further features of interest, which will be discussed shortly.

Great disparities obtained between the ages of officers within the regiment, and between one regiment and the next. The officer corps of the infantry regiment of de Ligne was virtually wiped out in the course of the campaign of 1757, and yet Giuseppe Gorani could enter the regiment of Andlau at the same time, and find

Old *FML*. Gottfried Baron Wollwarth, 1686–1770. (From the mss. of his memoirs, State Archives, Bratislava)

himself in a regiment 'where the only officers who died were those who expired from old age, for they all survived this year's [1757's] battles, and yet we lost a very large number of soldiers. Our colonel was 68, Lieutenant-Colonel Gillich 74, Major Baron Terzi 58, the second colonel – another Baron Terzi – 59, Second Major Metternich 71, and O'Brennan my captain was also in his 70s'.[92]

Merit and Favouritism

Merit as such was an excellent reason for promotion, but it was a principle which required further definition, as the Prince de Ligne recognised. In his experience 'merit' applied equally well to officers who were brilliant in the hurly-burly of war, but otherwise useless, and to those who excelled at drilling soldiers and in the technical side of tactics.[93]

The difficulty lay in determining paths and speed of promotion once the principle of seniority (which could at least be quantified) was set aside. Second-Lieutenant Csaktornaya of the Desswessfy Hussars burst out publicly 'if I'm passed over yet again, I'll go straight to the King of Prussia... I'll ask him if he behaves like that, and passes over the Catholics in his service in the same way as the Imperial service abuses and passes over the Lutherans and Calvinists – everyone except the Catholics.' The commandant Colonel Hintzmann rejoined that 'we pay regard not just to seniority, but to services and conduct'.[94]

The *Hofkriegsrath*, as the organ responsible for promoting officers from major upwards, was not immune from pressure from ministers. Kaunitz himself intervened on behalf of officers as junior as major and colonel-commandant.[95] We must presume he was invariably well-intentioned and well-informed, but the same did not necessarily hold true of others who exploited such avenues.

The author of the long protest called the *Patriotic Reflections* (*Patriotisch-... Reflexionen*) conceded that it was sometimes useful to advance young noblemen out of turn:

> but to promote the whole herd is to disgust many a brave officer, and is painful to one who is zealous for the service and sees it suffer thereby... The great families must be weaned from the habit of demanding rapid promotion for their children and relations. They will be affronted, it is true, but not offended so much as when in the course of time their protégés are shown to be incapable of living up the responsibilities of their high rank, or are passed over, or have to be banished from the army altogether.

Great damage (he continued) was done when such undeserving officers became generals:

> without knowing the meaning of unconditional obedience. They respect scarcely any orders which happen to conflict with their convenience, and they make a joke out of it. They treat the *Reglement* in the same way. They introduce new usages as the fancy takes them; their subordinates lose no time in following their example, knowing that their transgressions will be overlooked; their comrades see what is going on, and they draw the necessary conclusions and do the same – an example which is followed down the chain of command to the ordinary soldier. The consequences are shown in disorderly marches, camps and quarters, in unbridled plundering, in devotion to comfort, and in blunders in action. You may imagine how hard it is for the Field Marshal to pull together such indisciplined regiments and generals over the course of six months or even an entire year.[96]

The interests of favouritism and corruption were served by a number of procedures which were recognised, tolerated, or ultimately ineradicable. Among these *Aggregation* was a process whereby officers of one regiment could be taken onto the strength of another outside the establishment. The less scrupulous proprietors found this device to be a convenient means of accommodating family and friends, and for that reason it was decided in 1748 that *Aggregation* must be abolished. The prohibition had no lasting effect. Not only were the colonels soon up to their own tricks,[97] but we find Daun himself writing to Maria Theresa for permission to take on a nephew of Kaunitz as an *aggregirter* captain in his regiment of infantry. He hastened to claim that he was motivated purely out of regard for the talents of the young man in question, 'without his uncle having the slightest influence therein'.[98]

Purchase

The purchase of commissions – and most significantly the purchase of a company or squadron which came with the rank of captain – was a practice which combined undeniable advantages with an almost unlimited potential for corruption.

The defenders of purchase could point out that a commission, company or squadron represented an investment of time, effort and perhaps also of money on the part of the officer who held it, and that when that officer came to the end of a career of service it was inherently no more wrong for him to apply to realise his investment than it would be for a lawyer or physician to sell his practice. When the thing was managed properly, the proposals of the would-be seller and buyer were forwarded through the *Inhaber* to the *Hofkriegsrath,* and thence to Maria Theresa. The authorities might well be glad of the opportunity they were now given to get rid of a bad officer, or cushion a deserving man at his retirement. The service might well benefit if the newcomers were wealthy young men, 'who are always useful in a regiment'.[99]

The scandals came when commissions, companies and squadrons were traded like commodities at an exchange, and without proper application to the *Hofkriegsrath,* which regarded the leave to buy and sell as a concession and privilege.[100] The extent to which the commerce was reduced to a routine is revealed by the experiences of the English volunteer Horace St. Paul, who enquired of Colonel Joseph Count Ferraris what might be the costs of buying a squadron. Ferraris replied in a matter-of-fact way that he must think of laying out at least 2,886 ducats (at eight florins to the ducat), comprising the basic price of 2,500 ducats, another 250 due to the sovereign as 10 percent of the purchase price, 50 to the *Hofkriegsrath* for the patent as *Rittmeister,* a further 50 to the major, 24 to the governor of Vienna, and a final 24 as sweeteners to the Adjutant (regimental sergeant-major) and others on the first day of mounting guard. 'This is supposing everything at the cheapest, and I don't mention a dinner which is always given that day to the officers of the regiment.[101]

The authorities themselves might be open to manipulation, as is indicated by a letter addressed from Vienna to Captain Joseph Pesser of the Netherlands regiment of Los Rios. The correspondent explained that he was writing on behalf of 'an Italian gentleman,' who wished to purchase a company in the regiment, and 'as the gentleman in question enjoys protection here he will soon gain the permission of the Coure.[102] The author of the *Patriotic Reflections* explains that when a would-be purchaser was unable to get his way through the colonel, he would hide himself behind an agent or official in Vienna, who would manage the business for a bribe of 100 ducats.

All of this made for bad feeling. The Pálffy Hussars may be taken as an example. *GFWM.* Rudolph Pálffy was a dedicated officer who tried to run a tight regiment, and yet we find a large number of his officers at odds with their superiors. After an unauthorised sale of a commission had come to light, the *Hofkriegsrath* ruled that *Rittmeister* Count Auersperg (a member of a prominent family) was to be dismissed from the service with retention of honour, while Lieutenant Camely was cashiered with disgrace, and sentenced to three weeks' arrest in irons. Again we find that Second-Lieutenant Huszty spent only three months in his rank before he protested at being passed over, which, he asserted brazenly, was poor reward after he had spent several hundred florins to obtain his original cornetcy, and could claim connections with 'many Hungarian noble families.[103]

Officers remained free to bring their complaints before the *Hofkriegsrath,* though they were warned that they would draw unfailing punishment on themselves if their allegations proved to be unjustified.[104]

Retirement

There was no stipulated age for the retirement of an officer, but one who wished to retire for self-evident reasons, such as unfitness associated with years, sickness or wounds, was required to submit his petition in writing, and remain with his regiment until the answer arrived. It was to his advantage to observe the formalities, for a properly-sanctioned retirement gave entitlement to a pension, however small, and at least a moral claim to call on the goodwill of the *Hofkriegsrath*.

Maria Theresa disapproved strongly of officers who wished to retire for personal convenience (especially at the start of a campaign), or just to enjoy the benefits from the sale of their post. They lost all claims to protection, and they forfeited the caution money they had lodged with the regiment.[105]

Generals and Promotion

From the foregoing it will not be difficult to imagine the hopes and outraged vanity attending the promotions of the generals, which were seen as the immediate gifts of the sovereign. Hadik was affronted to learn that his official promotion to *G.d.C.* had been postponed for six months, even with post-credited seniority. He protested to Daun that the public would read the delay as some kind of punishment, and that he must remind him that 'the prospect of high and rapid advancement is the driving force of ambition, and of the urge to distinguish oneself by great deeds'.[106]

When Maria Theresa came to the throne in 1740 she found that she had inherited 40 Field Marshals, most of them entirely useless. For many years she nevertheless continued to advance senior officers for a variety of thoroughly bad reasons. Four additional Field Marshals and 43 other generals were promoted on 15 October 1745, merely to celebrate her name day and cheer up the army. The promotion of 17 Field Marshals in June 1754 was still less excusable, 'and especially because it was impossible to hide the true motive, which was to bring in as many fees as possible. Thus a horde of generals was promoted solely according to seniority, and quite regardless of individual merit'.[107] In the course of that year the various military and civil promotions brought the state a profit of 200,000 florins.

The most scandalous of these proceedings occurred in 1758, when the workings of seniority ought to have placed Paul Anton Prince Esterházy in command of the entire cavalry in the field. Maria Theresa was in some embarrassment, for the prince was plainly not up to the work, yet belonged to a family which had helped to rally the Hungarian magnates behind the throne in 1741. His wife was intelligent and popular at Court, which also had to be borne in mind. Maria Theresa's solution was to please Esterházy and his *gute Freunde* by promoting him to Field Marshal, 'and so, in order to avert further – and rather more justified uproar – shortly afterwards we had to publish the promotion of a whole batch of field marshals'.[108]

Austria had at least been spared from a needless disaster in the field, and the reason was that Maria Theresa was now looking to Daun, as the victor of Kolin, to recommend the best men for the active promotions and commands. Daun's character sketches now made up a significant part of his correspondence with the Empress-Queen. In a typical comment he predicted that when General Los Rios heard the command appointments 'he will cry out as he usually does, without any logic whatsoever… the truth is that he has no kind of career in front of him… and I must add that his short sight makes him virtually unemployable'.[109]

The appalling Serbelloni remained in command on the Elbe until almost the end of the war, probably on account of the political influence of his family in Lombardy, but many of the newer appointments were excellent, and they were being made without any regard for inherited influence. Historians make altogether too much of the alleged injustice done to Loudon as one of the 'upstarts,' or rather a member of the minor nobility of Livonia.[110] Loudon had no reason to complain of tardy promotion, for he had been advanced to *Obrister* on 17 March 1757, *GFWM.* on 25 August the same year, *FML.* on 2 July 1758, and *FZM.* on 20 November 1759. The complications arose in the summer of 1761, when the influence of Kaunitz placed him in charge of an independent army in Silesia. Several of the generals of the main army in Saxony thereupon proved unwilling to transfer to Loudon's command[111]. Kaunitz began to wonder if he had done the right thing, and he sent the respected Commissary Johann Georg Grechtler to find out whether Loudon should be supported by expert advisers, or possibly replaced altogether. Grechtler reported on 8 August that Loudon would not lack for suitable advice, but that it would be difficult to find willing subordinates: 'In my judgement O'Donnell, Maguire, Lacy, Wied and Beck will certainly do their duty here under an able commander, but none of them – even if the commander here [Loudon] were made a Field Marshal – would serve willingly. The reason is that a certain prestige, and high birth in particular, is required in one who would command great armies'.[112]

It would be wrong to conclude that Loudon was being singled out for any particular discrimination. In this case the social objections were not the only ones, for Loudon was more of the Muscovite than his admirers will allow: he was a poor disciplinarian, and his moments of activity and inspiration were interspersed with seemingly endless periods of lassitude and indecision. The fundamental trouble was that at that juncture it was proving very difficult to find generals who were at once reasonably competent, and prepared to serve under somebody else. Meyern was reported to be drunk from morning to night; Guasco was too slow-moving to command in the open field; Lanthieri and Stampa were sick and 'taking the cure'; 'Beck has declared that he is unable to serve under Loudon or Lacy, but would be happy to be used anywhere else'; Loudon himself had lost trust for a time in Campitelli, the commander of his cavalry, and Daun reported that Plunkett too was unacceptable to Loudon: 'Last year, with reference to Plunkett, he told me "the only conclusion I can reach is that they wish to send me all the Irishmen." In fact O'Kelly and Butler are at present with the corps at Zittau, and the former gets on badly with Plunkett'.[113] All of this was deplorable, but it had less to do with an exceptional animus against Loudon than with the climate of petulant self-indulgence which Maria Theresa had to tolerate in the high command.

Pay and Personal Conditions

As was common in armies of the time, the remuneration for officers in the Austrian service was reckoned as compound of basic pay and rations. The following rates were in force from November 1757:

Rank	Annual Pay	Bread Rations	Fodder Rations
FM.	10,000 fl.	45	50
FZM./G.d.C.	8,000	30	44
FML.	6,000	25	24
GFWM.	4,000	20	18
Inhaber	4,000		
Obrister-Commendant	1,908	12	10
Lieutenant-Colonel	1,410	9	2
Major	1,206	2	6
Captain	912	4	2
Capitain-Lieutenant	504	2	3
(in cavalry)	576		
First-Lieutenant	342	2	3
Second-Lieutenant	222	2	3
Cornet	360	2	2
Ensign	288	2	2

It was laid down at the same time that the rations of bread and fodder were to be made over in kind, and no longer in their cash equivalents. This put a considerable burden on the *Commissariat*, for the 'system' of Haugwitz had liberated the provinces from all obligation to provide free bread, meat, beer, wine and so on, and anything raised by the army had to be paid for by the military authorities in cash. In addition all officers received *Servis,* comprising allowances for bedding, firewood and candles, which were given in the actual commodities to ensigns, cornets and second-lieutenants, but in cash to all the senior officers.

In order to have his promotion validated in the first place, the officer had to pay a fee (*Tax*) on a sliding scale ordained by a *Tax Ordnung* of 2 April1745. The sums went towards the salaries of the officials of the *Hofkriegsrath*. A fee of 100 florins was demanded when permission was given to sell a company or squadron, and 200 was demanded of the purchaser, all in addition to the price of the unit concerned. From 1 March 1755, on a suggestion from Maria Theresa, part of the officers' pay was held back in the regimental chests until it reached the amounts necessary to equip them to take the field in the event of war. These deposits were fixed at 400 florins for each captain, 200 for a lieutenant, and 150 for the ensign or cornet. The other standard deductions from pay included those made for regimental expenses, and for the upkeep of the *Invaliden Haus* in Pest.

FM. Gideon Ernst Loudon, 1716–90 (Sigmund L'Allemand, Austrian Army Museum). Loudon was Austria's foremost fighting general of the 18th century. He was a major at the start of the Seven Years War, and full general (*FZM*) by the end, having made his name by his contribution to the Russo-Austrian victory at Kunersdorf (12 August 1759), and the coups de main against the fortresses of Glatz (23 June 1760) and Schweidnitz (1 October 1761). This celebrated painting represents Loudon at Kunersdorf. It is accurate as regards the characterisation, though on the actual day his face and uniform were so darkened by powder smoke that he was at one time mistaken for a Prussian and nearly killed by his own troops.

Conversely the income of a high-ranking general would be augmented in a very agreeable way if he received the full allowances due to him in wartime (which might bring the pay of a *FZM.* to 14,000 florins per annum), or if he were also a fortress governor, or an *Inhaber* – in which case he received all the normal income of a colonel proprietor, and that of the *Inhaber* of the *Leib-Compagnie*. However the government ran so short of money in the later stages of the Seven Years War that promotions to *FM., FZM.* and *G.d.C.* were being made without any increase in pay.[114]

The senior generals might complain about the hardships and unfairness of their condition, but they were shielded from true poverty by the multiplicity of their incomes. However Armfeldt reckoned that the lower-ranking generals were badly off, 'and this is because there are too many of them'.[115] The regimental officers lived in a state of some insecurity. An individual might find himself exposed, if, for example, a promotion was not confirmed, or if he had to meet essential expenses for his unit from his own purse, like the outlay of 3,203 florins by *Obrister-Commendant* Baron Freyenfels of the regiment of Starhemberg, after his predecessor had been captured by the Prussians, along with the regimental chest.[116]

In 1753 Maria Theresa had been confident that there was no good reason for her officers or men to fall into debt, for she was paying them regularly and well. However many officers fell deeply into the red anyway, on account of their improvident ways. In the Bohemian *Musterung* of October 1755 the Commissaries discovered that the captains Kruglin and Faber of the regiment of Alt-Wolfenbüttel were so incorrigible that their lieutenant-colonel had to take their pay out of their hands. 'Both men are married, and their wives and children suffer the pangs of hunger. Faber's wife has been unable to go to church for five weeks, since her clothes are in rags and she has nothing to wear'.[117]

The new war brought both individual and collective crisis. Armfeldt explains that at the outset of the war the Austrians observed 'not the slightest economy. Great sums were expended, in some cases without need, and the army was paid more than usual. This state of affairs lasted for a number of years until it was realised that the war could last a long time, and that funds for the pay were running short'.[118]

From 1759 the debased Prussian coinage and the payment in coupons wreaked successive havoc. The Carabinier *Rittmeister* Frédéric de Bryas complained in March 1760 that his pay was arriving irregularly, and that the officers were having to subsist their horses on daily rations of five pounds of hay or seven of straw, 'from which you can imagine what my poor Ardennes horses would like to say, after having done me such good service on the little they have had to eat over the last campaign … Please God, the end cannot come quickly enough! Otherwise I cannot imagine how man and horse will be able to hold out any longer. The winters bring not the slightest relief. Surely there has not been so much to put up with in any war over the last few centuries!'.[119] De Bryas was living like a beggar, after 13 years of service, and he was unable to find the money to travel to a spa to gain some relief for his arm, which he had broken in a fall.[120]

By the last year of the war any kind of misfortune was likely to prove catastrophic for the typical ensign, whose monthly pay was reduced by stoppages and the devalued coupons to 5 florins 39 creutzer.[121] Some officer widows were living in a state of destitution, to judge by the case of Mme. Pesser, the relict of Captain Joseph Pesser of the regiment of Los Rios, who had died after 30 years of service. As the most senior captain of the regiment Pesser had for many years done the work of the major, but he had been passed over twice for the substantive rank by better-connected officers – the Prince de Gavre and the comte d'Alsace. He was already badly off when he fell ill on campaign, and the expenses of the unavailing treatment during the last 22 months of his life had exhausted his finances'.[122]

Officers had to call heavily on their own resources to make themselves fit to take the field, and one of the reasons why the Pessers were reduced to such straits was that Captain Joseph had been forced to re-equip himself four times over in the course of the war. Dress and other gear made a heavy and unavoidable item of expenditure.

Specific designs of generals' uniforms were first laid down in 1751. The red breeches were common to all grades, but there were detailed variations in the design of the gold lace which was worked into the red waistcoats and the cuffs and fronts of the white coats. The most spectacular array was sported by the Field Marshal, who was distinguished chiefly by the broad undulating whorls which wound down his coat front and around his cuffs. In fine detail the gold lace of all field ranks was fashioned in a characteristic zig-zag pattern which endured until the end of the Habsburg monarchy.

On parade and (until some time into the war) the officers were normally obliged to carry partisans – six foot-long pikes, which were differentiated according to rank by the gilding of the grades and the size and material of the ornamental tassels. In some regiments the officers already carried muskets instead of partisans, though, as we have seen, *Obrister-Commendant* Freyenfels of the regiment of Starhemberg got into trouble for telling his officers to do the same. Another semi-optional piece of gear was the cane. There were gradations between the canes of the different ranks of officer and NCO, that of the ensign being little more than a flexible wand. In practice he, the lieutenants and the captains usually handed over their canes to be carried by the drummers.

No single pattern was laid down for the officers' swords, and a great deal of variety existed in the design of the sword knot – the strip of metallic fabric which was wound about the sword guard, and from which hung two tassels of the same material. The sash was worn about the waist above the waistcoat, and was folded over in such a way that the tassels of the two extremities hung down the left-hand side; sashes of golden thread were reserved for the generals, while those of the regimental officers were of golden or yellow cloth.

Except for the probably finer material, and the broad cut of the coat skirts, the basic dress of the officers of the infantry, artillery and German cavalry were essentially the same as those of the NCOs and private soldiers. This (commented Cogniazzo) proved useful when officers wished to take part in plundering. However the Austrian officers regarded excessive uniformity as the sign of a hireling, and the regulations railed in vain against the custom of appearing on duty with embroidered fronts, cloaks, night caps under their hats, or (in the case of the German cavalry) light and comfortable boots instead of the stiff and bucket-topped regulation pattern.[123]

The modern officer can take it for granted that the army will furnish him with nearly everything he needs to subsist, move and fight. This did not hold true in the 18th century, and in the Austrian army of that time the state provided the officer in the field only with pay, rations, possibly a tent, and certain allowances – two soldier-servants (*Fourierschützen*) from volunteers from the regiment's invalids (*Erlass* of 1 March 1755), and a modicum of shared transport for personal effects – two four-horse carts per regiment, and an additional two for each company or squadron.[124] The officer had to fit himself out with every other commodity at his personal expense. When Horace St. Paul asked Colonel Ferraris to detail the items needed for a squadron commander, he was told:

Full Generals of infantry and cavalry.
(Ottenfeld, 1898)

    Four carriage horses, two riding horses, one pack horse, and the necessary harness and saddles:
        374 ducats
    Tent: 24 ducats
    Second-hand carriage: 60 ducats
    Kitchen service: 14 ducats
    Bed and chairs: 35 ducats
    Total: 532 ducats, not including the cost of a great variety of personal effects, and the pay and
        upkeep for an extra servant, driver for the carriage and two grooms.

The authorities were scandalised by the way a number of the generals and senior regimental officers helped themselves out at the expense of the army and the theatre of war. People like that were determined to 'dine as finely as in Vienna or Prague, and take along a whole tribe of exotic servants',[125] and by 1759 they had requisitioned so many draught horses from the countryside that agriculture was being crippled, and the peasants were stripped of the provisions and fodder which should have been available to support the army as a whole. The cavalry horses were sometimes reduced to subsisting entirely on straw, which in turn was denied to the soldiers, who now had nothing to lay on the ground inside their tents or winter hutments.

Regardless of the *Bagage-Reglement* of 1758, which stated that the new units of Staff Infantry and Dragoons would safeguard the train of carts, unscrupulous officers were still detailing troops on a massive scale to escort their private effects and plunder to the rear; four or five men were being sent away with every vehicle, and another two or three with every one or two horses, and the result in some regiments was to reduce the effectives in men and service horses to scarcely one-third. In the Prussian army detachments of that kind were regulated carefully, 'but in the Imperial and Royal service you will find that on a day of battle men will be absent from each company, having been sent away with the baggage, and they are usually the best and must trustworthy of the lot'.[126]

Wealthy officers could in fact look after their own interests extremely well. Horace St. Paul had to abandon his first set of baggage in Breslau, after the battle of Leuthen, but by January 1758, a matter of a few weeks later, he had re-equipped himself with an open carriage, 12 horses, six servants, a kitchen canteen, a case of wine, and a tent and other gear to be carried on pack horses and mules.[127]

At the same time junior officers were living on the edge of subsistence, as we have seen, 'for we have to reckon on fitting ourselves out with a new set of baggage at the end of every campaign, for everything will have been reduced to tattered ruin'.[128] Lieutenant Giuseppe Gorani was in a bad way at the end of 1757, having lost his two horses, and seen his other effects reduced to three sorry shirts, two black neck stocks, two handkerchiefs, two pairs of stockings, and the coat he wore on his back. In the spring he had the extraordinary good luck to be quartered with the wealthy Bohemian Hussite miller Jan Guelich and his wife, and these good people fitted him out in a style which befitted a general (see p. 61).[129]

In the following autumn Gorani survived the battle of Hochkirch, and was one of the officers assigned to oversee the clearing of the field. He was a gambler by instinct, and he paid four ducats to an hussar for a locked chest which had been found among the Prussian effects. It was the kind of container used to store hats, but when it was forced open he found 'just one general's hat with its white plume. There were also three dirty shirts, three clean ones… four pairs of stockings, and 12 plates and six services of fine but very thin silver, as befits the miserliness of the Prussian character. But the most important items in my prize were two purses, one containing 50 Saxon crowns, and the other 50 [Bavarian] *Max d'or*'.

As Gorani explained, the season of winter quarters was the one which brought the Austrian officers and the local communities into the most intimate contact. At one extremity the Field Marshal was entitled to accommodation on the scale of eight rooms, two smaller chambers, and two kitchens; ensigns, cornets and second-lieutenants had an official allotment of two rooms and one kitchen, but in reality probably had to make do with very much less. Few officers of any kind knew what to expect. In the winter of 1758/9 we find that the Croatian general Sermage had to lodge at Nachod with an eccentric 80-year-old man, who kept his house alternately freezing cold or intolerably hot, 'but I must learn to be patient, for there is nothing I can do to change things'.[130] At the other end of Bohemia our informant Gorani was living much more comfortably at a castle of the Dietrichsteins at Pomeisel, where he was looked after extremely well by the steward. He dined off game and suckling pigs, washed down with the finest Hungarian wines, 'and so I had a marvellous time, and not least because the servant girls were pretty and easy-going'.[131]

In the later years of the war Dresden formed the focal point of the winter quarters of the army on the Saxon theatre, and many officers came to know that city well. The architecture was magnificent, but for a variety of reasons the experience was a miserable one. The nobles and the Court had decamped to Warsaw, taking with them the keys to the royal picture gallery and apartments, and leaving only the burghers and the artisans. 'In general we Austrians are little liked here, and though we are allied to the Saxons, they prefer the Prussians to us'.[132] Dresden nevertheless represented luxury, compared with the conditions of some of the officers who found themselves in Prussian captivity.

Prisoners of War

Guests of the Prussians

Daun suspected that a number of the Austrian generals had allowed themselves to be taken prisoner in circumstances that were not particularly creditable. However there is little that some of the junior officers could have done to avert their fate, to judge by the surviving evidence. Captain Hans Joseph Khevenhüller-Metsch, son of the senior Court official, had been in charge of 100 sick and wounded men, and therefore effectively immobilised, when he was captured during the campaign of Leuthen. Our unfailing source of information, Giuseppe Gorani, had just been given the brevet rank of first-lieutenant when, on 29 October 1759, he was dispatched with a party of 400 troops to stake out a camp at Hermsdorf in Saxony. Whether through malice or poor visibility, the Saxon guides led the force instead to Lungwitz, and when the fog lifted the Austrians found themselves in the midst of 3,000 Prussian cavalry:

> but our commander was a man of resolution. The first thing he did was to have our guides shot, and then he formed us up in battalion square. It was not at all difficult for the Prussians to overrun our battalion, and they killed or wounded 83 of our men in the process. We were able to get off only three volleys before we had to surrender, but even so the Prussians did not go unscathed. I received a sword cut in the head, and if I had not had three iron bands inside the hat my skull would have been split in two.[133]

Oddly enough, both Gorani and Khevenhüller-Metsch soon had the opportunity to encounter King Frederick in person. Old Fritz was passing through Grossenhayn when he was told that a wounded Austrian officer was eager to see him; he had Gorani brought before him, and consoled him with a few polite words.[134] Frederick showed a different face when he summoned Khevenhüller-Metsch to a peasant hut, and asked him how he had been captured. Hans Joseph explained that he had been taken prisoner along with his party of sick and wounded, and thus had not been present at the battle of Leuthen. The king spoke dismissively of the Austrian performance there, whereupon Hans-Joseph retorted that he had been present at four other actions which had proved very instructive, namely at Kolin, Moys, the cannonade at Liegnitz, and just recently at Breslau (all of them Austrian successes). Frederick now chose to change the subject.

On 15 March 1758 Khevenhüller-Metsch was exchanged for a Prussian captain at Jägerndorf. Hans Joseph travelled on to Vienna, where his parents found him 'so tanned by the sun that you would have taken him for a gypsy, but otherwise healthy and looking well. We chatted until late in the night'.[135]

A Prussian officer was congratulated by a friend on his easy relations with his captured Austrian counterparts: 'your quarrel with the enemy officers is confined to combat. Once that is over all hostility comes to an end'.[136] At this level the encounters were seldom less than cordial, and they helped to establish a rough equality of benefit – the Prussian officer prisoners enjoying the scenery, the beer and the wine in the Austrian lands, while the Austrians could expect to find intelligent conversation, fine libraries, attentive hostesses, well thought-out sermons (if they were so inclined), and the unaffected hospitality of the ordinary people.

In the first years of the war most of the Austrian prisoners were accommodated at Frankfurt-an-der-Oder, where 700 of them were living in excellent conditions early in 1758. The Prussian courtier Count Lehndorff was unimpressed by the first batch of these people to be forwarded to Berlin in February of that year, for 'the fundamental trait of their character is a coarse ignorance'.[137] However a better sort arrived shortly afterwards, and Lehndorff formed a good opinion of a number of the individuals he encountered later in the war. He describes *GFWM*. Philipp Levin Beck as 'a little man with fine features and a penetrating gaze. He is a person who rose through his own merit, and he makes use of his time in Berlin to gather information – intelligence that might make him dangerous to us when he is exchanged'.[138] In 1760 Lehndorff fell into a long conversation with the gifted Austrian staff officer James Nugent, who had been captured outside Dresden:

> He is a most likeable man. He is Irish by birth, thinks like an Englishman, and seems to judge the present state of affairs impartially. He has a personal admiration for our king, and admires his brilliant talents, but says that he regards Prince Henry as the most dangerous of our generals. He adds that in spite of their numerical superiority the Austrians could do nothing against him over the whole of the last campaign without him smoking out their plans in advance, however subtle those schemes might be… Out of all the enemy generals who have so far fallen into our hands, I reckon him to be the most considerable. Nugent was Daun's right-hand man, and privy to every detail.[139]

For a time Berlin was the scene of much coming and going, for the Austrian, French and Russian officer prisoners arrived in waves, and were thinned out again by the exchanges. In April 1759, however, Frederick banished all the foreign officers from Berlin to Spandau on the advice of the city commandant, von Rochow, who had drawn attention to the threat to security. The only Berliners to be pleased were the husbands, who were now relieved of their anxiety for the faithfulness of their wives.

The exchanges were becoming more slow and difficult, and the Austrians were faced with worsening conditions in their indefinite captivity. Their pay was being made over in the notoriously debased currency, and Gorani was left so badly off that every time he washed his single shirt he had to stay in bed until the garment dried.[140] In the autumn of 1761 a number of senior Austrian officers were caught up in a cycle of reprisal which had been initiated by the notoriously awkward Prussian lieutenant-general Fouqué, who had been captured at Landeshut, and whom the Austrians had banished to Carlstadt in Croatia. On 21 October *FML*. Gemmingen (captured at Pretzsch) was uprooted from his quarters in Magdeburg town and held in close confinement in the citadel. *FML*. Angern followed him there on the 25th, *GFWM*. Bülow on an unknown date, and *GFWM*. Thürheim arrived from Stettin on 20 November. Gemmingen protested that 'when we want a little fresh air we are not allowed to venture any further than the sentry who is posted outside the door. Moreover we are forbidden to establish any kind of communication with anyone whatsoever. For our quarters each of us has a little chamber which is damp and unhealthy, and which some of us have to share with our servants'.[141] To his credit Gemmingen was no less concerned about the conditions of the Austrian private soldiers, and he refused to be set free if this would put Vienna at a disadvantage in the bargaining process.

In support of Gemmingen and the others Maria Theresa had the unoffending Prussian corps commander Lieutenant-General Finck and the middle-ranking generals Bredow and Diericke locked up in the castle of Kufstein in the Tyrol (below). Both sides now relented, and their respective hostages were released from their cells and allowed to return to their quarters.

All of this was childish enough, but the Prussians were justified in keeping a close eye on at least some of their captives. Cogniazzo claims that when a number of young Austrian officers escaped from Prussian captivity after Leuthen, and returned to the regiments expecting to be treated like heroes; they were shunned by the rest of the officer corps, as the only suitable treatment for 'self-ransomed' people like these, and they were sent back to the Prussians on the strict order of the Vienna Court.[142] There is no documentary evidence for Cogniazzo's assertion, and in any case it is contradicted by the case of the cadet Thomas Vocaillovich, who was one of these escapees. He had served for some time in the 'German' regiment of Arenberg, but he now wished to rejoin his Warasdiner Croatian countrymen. The *Hofkriegsrath* supported his application, and Maria Theresa noted: *Placet,* and give him 30 ducats so that he can fit himself out'.[143]

Magdeburg was the strategic heart of Prussia, and the large numbers of Austrian prisoners who had been transported thither were probably more dangerous to Frederick's interests than they had been in Berlin. The Austrian prisoners were suspiciously well informed of the events of the war, and the Prussian *Generalpostmeister* Adolph Gotter began to open the correspondence they were conducting with various tradesmen. In a packet belonging to the merchant Stevesandt the Prussians discovered a seemingly innocuous letter from the Austrian lieutenant Huber to his wife; a slip of blank paper was enclosed, and when it was exposed to heat it was found that Huber had written a message in milk, according to which the approach of a friendly army would be the cue for the prisoners to send up rockets from the most weakly-guarded sections of the fortifications. Hüber's quarters were duly searched, and a stock of rockets and weapons came to light.[144].

In the late summer of 1762 Magdeburg was endangered by the progress of the *Reichsarmee* and the Württemberg corps, and Frederick decided that he could no longer tolerate the presence of so many Austrians in the place. On 5 September Gorani and a number of his companions were told to get ready to move, and shortly afterwards they were piled into peasant carts and sent off to the Baltic port of Stettin. This was the first stage in a mass deportation of Austrian prisoners to the remote province of East Prussia. Gorani and his comrades embarked at Stettin on 29 October, and reached Königsberg after a difficult voyage on 15 November. From there he was transported with 91 officers by sledge to Tilsit. Their party was fortunate, for many Austrian officers and men were drowned in a number of shipwrecks. The *Hofkriegsrath* was angry, and took the Prussians to task for having exposed the prisoners to unnecessary risk.[145]

From 1 January 1763 the Austrian prisoners at Tilsit went unpaid, and their plight worsened from day to day. They knew that the Austrian colonel Kreitz was planning to raise all the prisoners who were being held in the area of Königsberg, and Gorani and 16 of his fellow officers resolved to do something on their own account at Tilsit. Armed with swords and sharpened sticks, the Austrians overcame their guards and the tiny garrison on 11 February. They made for the town hall and forced the treasurer to hand over the monies due to them, and Gorani proposed that they should act in concert with Kreitz to seize the fortress-port of Memel, where they could expect help from the Austrian soldiers who had been enlisted by force in the garrison: 'if Kreitz succeeded, and we did our part as well, we could then have seized the whole of East Prussia and delivered it to our sovereign'.[146]

188 INSTRUMENT OF WAR

News now came that the Prussians had discovered the scheme of Kreitz and placed him under arrest. The grand enterprise had collapsed, but Gorani now urged that all the 300 Austrian officer and soldier prisoners in the neighbourhood of Tilsit should band together and make their way by side roads through Poland, across the Carpathians and so to Hungary. Three days were lost in debate, and nothing had been decided before 450 Prussian horse and foot arrived on the scene and overpowered the escapees.

The Austrians were taken to Königsberg under arrest, and Gorani as the ringleader was confined in the castle and threatened with execution – which would have made him effectively the last casualty of the Seven Years War, now that peace had been signed at Hubertusburg. He was reprieved through the intervention of the Princess of Holstein-Beck, née Dohna, who belonged to one of the great families of East Prussia. Gorani was removed to comfortable quarters, and released not long afterwards. He set out at last for Austria with a column of fellow ex-prisoners on 16 June 1763.

Prussian Guests

The Austrians enjoyed a run of successes which extended from the battle of Kolin to that of Breslau (18 June-22 November 1757), and this presented them with a pleasing novelty – that of accommodating significant numbers of Prussian prisoners of war. The lot of the Prussian junior officers is typified by Lieutenant Christian Wilhelm Prittwitz, who had been ridden down by the Austrian cavalry at Kolin and captured. He was accommodated on parole in a house at Krems, on a beautiful stretch of the Lower Austrian Danube. 'The town of Krems lay in a romantic situation, with the great river Danube on the right-hand side, and to the left the terraced hills, where the densely-packed vines extended to the summit. Fine avenues ran hard by the magnificent river to the monastery and town of Stein, and the village of Mautem. All of this gave the opportunity for agreeable walks, and we could enjoy them as we wished in complete security'.[147] The local people were friendly, and the beer at the inn of the *Weisse Ochs* at Stein was so strong that it left a number of the young officers poleaxed.

Krems retained its reputation for hospitality, and another of the Prussian subalterns, Lieutenant Carl Wilhelm Halsen, was fortunate enough to be conducted there after he had been taken prisoner at Maxen. He lodged with a craftsman, who was happy to talk about politics, 'and persisted in asking about our great king. Tears sprang into his eyes, when I related stories about that great man. *"Jesus Maria!"* he used to call out. "What a man he must be! If only I could see him just once! Why hasn't he married our Maria Theresa?"'[148]

Even at a late stage in the war the Prussian officer prisoners in the Tyrol were allowed to gather in the coffee houses and other places of public resort, and make the acquaintance of the local people. Ensign Busch took advantage of the liberty to make a local girl pregnant, whereupon a general order was issued to all the men-folk of the Tyrol to 'keep their wives and children in future under better control, and not allow them to mix so freely with the Prussian officers'.[149]

Lieutenant-General the Duke of Bevern was the first of the Prussian high commanders to be taken in the war, falling into the hands of the Austrians immediately after the battle of Breslau. Bevern was an agreeable individual, and he qualified on every account to be numbered among the privileged circle of Maria Theresa's 'house prisoners' (*Hausgefangenen*) at Schönbrunn, where he proved to be excellent company until he was released as a gesture of magnanimity in the spring of 1758.[150] Towards the end of the war a party of Austrian officer prisoners happened to encounter Bevern in his capacity as governor of Stettin. He had not forgotten his good treatment, and he did everything possible to make the captivity of the Austrians as agreeable as possible.

Officers of all ranks were being released on a more formal basis through the system of exchanges, as regulated by a *Cartel*, which provided not only for a direct trading of individuals of the same rank, but set out a table of equivalents which put, for example, the worth of a Field Marshal at 3,000 private soldiers or 15,000 florins. The details were managed by standing commissions, which had their seats on the borders of Austrian and Prussian territories. The system survived in a way that was little more than miraculous, because feelings on both sides were becoming inflamed.

When the Austrians released Bevern in 1758 they did so without demanding any equivalent in cash or kind. Frederick in turn released *FML*. Winulph Starhemberg and thereby avoided being under a moral obligation, though it was observed that Starhemberg was not of the same calibre as Bevern, and that the king was careful to hang onto his better prisoners.[151]

The Austrians began to look more carefully at the quality of the officers and men they were sending back to the Prussians, and the kind of people they were receiving in return, and Daun concluded that although the trade might be equal in terms of money and heads, the Austrians were plainly getting the worst of the deal. The issue could no longer be evaded when the number of Prussian prisoners continued to grow, and the Austrians grasped that they had a powerful weapon of attrition in their hands. By then the Austrians could cite a number of cases of their officer prisoners being held back in unjustified confinement, like the Captain Rovera and the Lieutenant Capponi who were punished for having been in charge of the escort of the Prussian prisoners after the battle of Breslau.[152]

The Austrians became more slow and obstructive about releasing their captives,[153] which enabled them to gain more benefit from the rich hauls of prisoners they proceeded to take at Maxen, Glatz, Landeshut and Meissen. The Prussians continued to provide the Austrians with moral justification, and particularly in November 1759, when their 'partisan' leader Friedrich Wilhelm 'Green' Kleist descended on the Bohemian spa of Teplitz, which had been declared neutral ground, and made off with the Austrian officers who had been taking the cure there. The Austrians were further affronted to discover a particularly offensive Lutheran tract which was in circulation among the Prussian officer prisoners, namely Conrad Mell's *Der eröffnete Gnaden-Thron, oder Communions Predigten* (Berlin, Stettin and Leipzig, 1760). The text was brought to the attention of the Austrian censor, the professor of theology Ferdinandus Kopf, who found the Catholic Church described therein as 'a wasteland, a dwelling-place of wild beasts and dragons, who spew forth fire and flames; a hideous Sodom, the Whore of Babylon'.[154]

Every possible source of friction was exploited by Lieutenant-General Heinrich de la Motte Fouqué, who had been taken prisoner at Landeshut after an Austrian officer had misguidedly prevented the cavalry from hacking him to pieces. The Austrians were mistaken if they expected any gratitude, for Fouqué was a *Saupreuss* of Huguenot descent, bitterly anti-Catholic, and a member of Frederick's small circle of intimates. This pestilential individual proceeded to harass the Austrian authorities so unmercifully that the *Hofkriegsrath* had to devote a not insignificant part of its time to dealing with him.

Fouqué discovered a particularly rewarding source of trouble-making in the question of pay. The Prussian officer prisoners had found it difficult or impossible to subsist without falling into debt, but until June 1761 the Austrians had at least made over the pay and allowances regularly and at the rates agreed by cartel. The Austrian prisoners in Prussian hands were much less advantageously placed, for Frederick was paying them in debased currency, whose purchasing power amounted to only half its face value.[155]

The Austrians retaliated by withholding the Prussian officers' pay for three months, and then making it over in Dutch ducats, worth only four florins and seven and one-half creutzer, as against the full eight florins of the Austrian ducat – a measure confirmed by Maria Theresa in a decree of 4 August 1761. Fouqué refused to accept his pay under such conditions, took up the cudgels on behalf of his fellow officers, and used expressions concerning Maria Theresa and Kaunitz 'of a kind which would go unpunished only in England'.[156]

Frederick instructed one of his field commanders, Markgraf Carl of Brandenburg-Schwedt, to enter a protest. Carl duly wrote to Loudon on 21 September 1761, and Loudon forwarded the letter to Kaunitz. The *Staatscanzler* formulated a strongly-worded reply, and explained to Maria Theresa that firm language was essential, 'for the arrogance of the enemy will only increase if they detect that we are being too compliant, which they will interpret as a failure of resolution on our part'.[157]

The rejoinder was sent to Margrave Carl in Loudon's name on 20 September. The Prussian was informed that his expressions were all the more extraordinary as coming from a party whose career of violence was a notorious as its violations of the conventions of war. Kaunitz cited the beatings and destruction in the *Reich*, and the uncivilised way Kleist had violated the sanctuary of the baths at Teplitz. Concerning the Prussian officers' pay, the Austrians were only retaliating in proportion to the injustices already done to the Austrian prisoners, and if the Prussian officers continued to complain, they could always be sent to locations were prices were cheaper – a hint that they could be dispatched to the wilds of Hungary or Croatia.[158]

By that time Fouqué had inaugurated a new round of reprisals which succeeded in bringing relations to their lowest point. Convenience and security had been the reasons why, in February 1760, the 800 Prussian officer prisoners being held in the town of Wiener-Neustadt had been sent to join their comrades along the Danube in Krems, Ybbs and Stein; the burghers were sorry to see them go, for the Prussians had brought them valuable trade.[159] In September 1761, however, the tiresome Fouqué was removed from Bruck-an-der-Leitha (his first place of detention), and consigned as a punishment to near prison-like confinement in Carlstadt in Croatia.

In the consequent retaliation and counter-retaliation the Prussian lieutenant-general Finck and a number of his fellows found themselves locked up in the rock-castle of Kufstein in the Tyrol. Finck (not to be confused with the truculent Fouqué) wrote on 19 December to Neipperg to beg

Kufstein Castle in the Tyrol.

him to intercede for the captives with Maria Theresa, 'who is known throughout the world as the most gracious of princesses.' He asked at least for the services of a cook, 'for there is absolutely nothing to be had to eat in the fortress, and the town does not have so much as a half-decent inn. The only food obtainable there is bad, and the distance is too far for our servant – the only one we have – to bring it from the town'.[160] Two days later Maria Theresa learned that her firmness had been rewarded, for news came that the Austrian generals had been released from the citadel of Magdeburg, and she ordered Finck and the rest to be let out of Kufstein forthwith.

Professional Conduct and Relationships

The private behaviour of Maria Theresa's officers is of some social interest, and will be described shortly, but their professional conduct had to stand immediate comparison with the ferociously high standards which obtained in the army of Frederick the Great.

Forms of address counted for a great deal in the Austrian army, and we find the correct modes laid down in the regulations and instructions. For the simple English word 'you' the German language had manifold gradations, each of which conveyed an understanding of the relative status of speaker and addressee. The use of the intimate and comradely *Du* was discouraged among the regimental officers,[161] and it was considered still more out of place when addressed to an ordinary soldier, 'for, instead of instilling proper pride and military spirit in the men, it will incline them towards base and unacceptable behaviour'.[162] The Prussians had no need to be reminded of such things, since their officer corps was a closed caste, in which the norms of behaviour were known and observed.

Among the senior generals the *FM.*, the *FZM.* and *G.d.C.*, and sometimes also the *FML.* were entitled to be addressed as *Excellenz*, and noble officers as *Wohl-Gebohrner Graf* or *Wohl-Gebohrner Freyerr*. The wretched Commissaries were instructed in the correct forms, and told to be extravagant rather than miserly in their use of compliments.[163]

As for the visual signs of respect, the Austrian officer was expected to raise his hat in reply after a soldier saluted by presenting arms. On encountering a senior, the officer not only doffed his hat, but stood still until the great man had passed.[164]

In November 1757 a Prussian rifleman cut short the career of one of the most promising officers of the army, the young Hungarian colonel Joseph Baron Kökenyesdy de Vettesz, and his grenadiers and their weeping wives could hardly bring themselves to leave his bloodstained body. Not long afterwards a brigade commander commented on the example set by Colonel Baron de Cöök of the regiment of Browne on the retreat from Silesia to Bohemia in December 1757. He was still suffering from a wound he had sustained at Lobositz, but he refused an opportunity to set out in comfort ahead of his men, and stumbled on through the snow with the help of his soldiers, saying that he would 'undergo any hardship and risk rather than abandon his regiment in circumstances like these'.[165]

Officers like these were recognised as true leaders, and they stood out all the more because the example set by some of their fellows was so poor. Pietro Verri states that he was appalled by the behaviour of his comrades:

> You must imagine the poor soldier marching in the heat of summer, which in this country can be crushing. He is dressed all in wool, complete with coat and waistcoat, and a belt of heavy leather passes over his shoulder; he has a knapsack and a copper kettle on his back, and he bears in addition his musket, his cap (if he is a grenadier), perhaps a tent pole as well, and sometimes also the partisan which his officer has the inhumanity to make him carry. Weighed down by all of that, the wretched soldier can hold out no longer. And do you know the remedy? They beat him![166]

Verri was no particular admirer of the Austrians, but in this case his strictures are confirmed by Lieutenant-Colonel Rebain, who had returned from Prussian captivity with new perspectives on officer-like behaviour. He contrasted the harsh and distant ways of the Austrian officer with that of his Prussian counterpart, who treated his soldiers like comrades.[167] The author of the *Patriotic Reflections* adds that 'as well as enduring the necessary hardships and discipline, the poor soldier is oppressed in mind and spirit by his officers and NCOs even when he is not on duty. Very few generals, senior regimental officers or other officers speak to him cheerfully on such occasions, or on the street, during the march, or when other opportunities might offer.' They could not bring themselves to do 'what many army commanders or even sovereigns have done – when the soldiers have to withstand heavy exertions or bad weather, or are lying in hospital – which is to find a friendly word for them, cheer them up, promise good times ahead, crack the occasional little joke, or just listen to what they have to say'.[168]

The *Militär Feld-Regulament* of 1759 had to lay on generals the obligation to display a friendly cheerful interest in the soldiers, and to give an example in this respect to the regimental officers, 'for many of them are almost ashamed to speak in a light-hearted way with the soldiers, and some are possibly under the… scandalous misapprehension that it is impossible to converse with the ordinary soldier other than blows with the stick, and threats or curses'.[169]

Such an attitude was unwise as well as reprehensible, for in action the officers came to depend on their soldiers for their reputation, and in more than one way also for their lives, for the musketeers' aim had a way of straying from the Prussians to the persons of unpopular superiors. Colonel Francesco Valentiniani was mortally wounded at the battle of Hochkirch, which was quite possibly connected with the fact that he had volunteered the regiment of Clerici for the first assault, displayed his sword to his men, and announced that he would 'skewer anyone who is cowardly enough to show his back to the enemy'.[170]

The author of the *Patriotic Reflections* was struck by the fact that the senior officers who set the most store by showy drill, and tight and fancy uniforms which left the soldiers gasping for breath, were also the ones who were most negligent on active service.[171] These comments were reinforced by Armfeldt, who noted that Daun had a sound grasp of what was genuinely useful in action, but:

> the more influential of the other generals, who could have used their influence to endow the infantry with more mobility, and school it better in things that matter… devoted most of their attention to the appearance of their troops, and the look of their uniforms, the design of which changes constantly – such is the object of the study and efforts of most of the generals and colonels.[172]

Armfeldt detected the influences of birth, wealth, favouritism, poor education, and also the national character of the native Austrians, Moravian and many of the Bohemians.

> I do not deny that is possible to come across a good number of intelligent men among them, but you do not find as many as elsewhere… if the House of Austria did not have so many foreigners in its service its military establishment would be in a worse way still. It is fair to say that foreigners make up two-thirds of the generals, senior regimental officers and other officers; they are of all sorts and nations, and most of them strive to surpass the natives [see also p. 158]. For that reason the foreigners have always succeeded in distinguishing themselves, and if you come across someone who has some notion of military affairs, you can be pretty sure that he is a foreigner.[173]

Pietro Verri's process of disillusionment may be traced to 14 July 1759, when he arrived at Daun's headquarters in Görlitzheim with a letter for the Field Marshal. He found that the generals and general-adjutants reading the *Wiener Diarium* to find out what was happening in the war [which was reasonable enough], but with more justification he was disturbed to find that none of the adjutants could tell him the name of the enemy commander, or give him any idea of the strength of the rival armies. He was able to obtain intelligent answers only from the Englishman Lloyd, and the able young *GFWM*. Joseph Prince Lobkowitz (1725–1802). His business at headquarters over, Verri went in search of the regiment of Clerici, his future home. Nobody had so much as heard of the regiment, and Verri finally blundered into its lines when he heard soldiers speaking Italian and was able to identify them by their uniform.[174]

The Prussian officer of the Seven Years War brought a sharp-eyed professional expertise to his work, and could, if necessary, make an acceptable soldier out of a recruit in four weeks. Six months or more were needed before an Austrian soldier was in a fit state to appear before the enemy. One reason was the unnecessary elaboration of drill and ceremonies, but another, 'as many believe, arises from the fact that a large number of officers are themselves not fully schooled, having passed through the junior ranks to the senior without having had to give any account of themselves, and thus having neglected that knowledge of the fundamentals of the art of war which is needful in an officer'.[175] Armfeldt comments that the slack discipline of the army would permit an officer to advance painlessly to colonel commandant, and even then concern himself only with the appearance of his regiment, and leave all the tedious detail to the major; 'but if the major too is of high birth, and thus of the same way of thinking, you may easily imagine what state of order will exist in such a regiment'.[176]

The Prussians were alive to the difference between the peacetime routine, where detail and ceremony had their place, and what was essential in war. Austrian officers at every level found it difficult to make the distinction, and if they were diligent but stupid they could arrive at high rank and still be preoccupied with minutiae, as Armfeldt commented. His observation is confirmed by one of his French counterparts, the attaché Champeaux, who reported that 'without some kind of miracle none of them is capable of shaping up into a great captain. Serbelloni and Stampa are the most senior generals of the army, but all they have to recommend them is their courage and their knowledge of the routine of their trade. Field Marshal Daun is incontestably the best of their commanders'.[177]

Statements like these indicate the scale of the problems with which Maria Theresa and Daun had to contend. We have already touched on the failings among the junior officers, where even a number of the willing souls were unable to master the new drills (see p.134). The *Conduits-Lista* of the regiment of Erzherzog Carl of 10 March 1757 grades the competence of its officers as follows:

	Good	Poor
Captains:	10	3
Capitain-Lieutenants:	4	nil
First-Lieutenants:	12	6
Second-Lieutenants:	13	4
Ensigns:	5	2

This assessment is probably typical of the army as a whole, and the high proportion (50 percent) of unsatisfactory first lieutenants is probably explained by the fact that this rank was normally the highest which could be obtained by an indifferent officer who had no useful connections.

It is important, however, to emphasise that a number of officers (like the captains in the above *Lista*) strove to give of their best, and that Austrian officers could be numbered among the most trenchant critics of the prevailing culture of the army and society. The Prince de Ligne was at the same time a child of privilege and one of the new professionals – an excellent and by no means unique combination which was not always given its due credit by Armfeldt and the Frenchmen, whose own armies were performing somewhat less than brilliantly in the war. De Ligne took issue with the old generals who delighted in telling impressionable ensigns how good things had been in the old times: "We didn't bother with drill, our soldiers had stained uniforms, the officers danced all night with serving girls, or got back to their tents from headquarters drunk or ruined... in our day we were happy, we were dirty, and...," "and," I would interject, "you got beaten!".[178]

Lieutenant-Colonel Hans Joseph Count Khevenhüller-Metsch, the son of the leading courtier, refused the life of ease which was open to him in Vienna, and early in 1759 he caused something of a sensation in society because he was so determined to get back to his regiment. Maria Theresa called him to her presence so that she could say her farewell to him in person. This was designed as a snub to the young officer's prospective mother-in-law, the formidable Countess Hohenems, who had declared that she would refuse her daughter to him if he left for the army.[179]

Albert Prince of Sachsen-Teschen was a man of the same stamp, and he found a telling contrast between the conditions of the army in the field, and the extravagance displayed by the nobility during the marriage celebrations of Archduke Joseph in Vienna in October 1760 (see p. 23). No doubt these people were in the capital on urgent business, but at the official close of every campaign the stream of officers to Vienna became a flood: 'anybody who has a horse hastens thither, in the justifiable fear that others will get there before him and that... he will see himself passed over. The great fear is that of being forgotten'.[180]

On 15 December 1760, a matter of weeks after Joseph's marriage, Maria Theresa had to write to her commanders in the field to convey her great displeasure at having learned that during the last campaign a number of officers had not only absented themselves from their regiments (sometimes helping themselves to official funds in the process), but even gone over to the enemy, and afterwards used their high social standing to exact retrospective written authorisation from their colonel commandants. Such officers were now to be punished according to the full rigour of martial law 'without any consideration whatsoever for their birth or family'.[181.]

Maria Theresa's letter touched on offences a good deal more objectionable than absenteeism. The opportunities for fraud have been explored already. As for treason and suspicious dealings with the enemy, the most notorious case was that of *GFWM.* Brunyan (see p. 99), but it was far from being the only one. The two Banal Croatian captains Tapp and Wulacowich told a hearing about the remarkable circumstances which attended the capture of Lieutenant-Colonel Baron Brandt on 16 September 1758. The captains had warned Brandt not to approach a wood which they believed to be occupied by the Prussians, but the lieutenant-colonel rode on regardless, and repeatedly shouted out *'Ho! Ho! Ho!'* in the direction of the trees. The troops of a Prussian free battalion duly sallied from the wood, and Tapp noticed that 'when the lieutenant-colonel was surrounded by the enemy they did not take his horse or rob him, which was contrary to their

Full general of infantry (*FZM.*, Austrian Army Museum). One of a series of modern figurines by Captain Krauhse; the craftmanship is remarkable.

usual practice.' They concluded that Brandt was a deserter, and their testimony was supported by a Second-Lieutenant Hochauer, who encountered Brandt as an apparently free man on the next day. He was unaware of what had happened, but his suspicions were aroused when Brandt questioned him about the locations of various bodies of Croats'.[182]

Brandt returned from his supposed Prussian captivity on 10 December 1758, and claimed that on the fateful 16 September he had been on a mission to deliver a letter to Loudon. This was found to be untrue. Against the weight of circumstantial evidence a court martial acquitted Brandt on the charge of treason, and was content to order him to be cashiered (without loss of honour) for his reckless conduct and for having told a lie. The unfortunate Lieutenant Hochauer was sentenced to two months' arrest in irons for having given allegedly false testimony.

It was in fact both difficult and dangerous to try to bring a bad officer to book, as was further exemplified by the case of the lieutenant-colonel of the regiment of Joseph Esterházy, Gottlieb Weiss, who had abandoned his regiment at Hochkirch, claiming that he had been trodden underfoot by a mob of fugitives. The charge was proved beyond doubt, and the main body of the *Hofkriegsrath* was rightly outraged to learn that *the Justiz-Collegium* had not only acquitted Weiss on the grounds that his accusers, two captains and two lieutenants, had failed to observed the proper formalities, but dismissed those officers from the service as mutineers.[183] In this respect the contrast with the Prussian army was striking, for there the officers and even the private soldiers had the right to band together to bring accusations against their immediate superiors.

It is likely that Brandt and Weiss, like many others, had been sheltered by powerful patrons. It did not necessarily end there, for 'the worst thing of all is that those individuals who are actually cashiered, or dismissed from their regiments with disgrace, are sometimes able to gain protection, and are reassigned by the *Hofkriegsrath* to other regiments or to the Croats'.[184]

The Senior Officers in Particular

The customs and ways of the field officers bore directly on the prosperity of the army as a whole, and so the behaviour of these people calls for closer attention.

The officers who were in the most frequent everyday contact with the generals were their adjutants and aides-de-camp. Most of the time Daun had at his command three or four colonels to serve as general adjutants, and four majors as *Flügel-Adjutanten,* whose duty (as their title suggests) was to represent him on the wings of the army. A full general (*FZM., G.d.C.*) was entitled to three adjutants, and the *FML.* and *GFWM.* one each. According to Armfeldt the general adjutants wore the uniform of the regiment of Kaiser, the *Flügel-Adjutanten* a special uniform of blue or red, with red cuffs and facings, and yellow buttonholes and epaulettes; the other adjutants carried their ordinary regimental uniforms.[185]

The regulations were interpreted as loosely as we might have expected, and it was normal for generals even of the lower grades to have two or three adjutants with them, one or two of whom saw the routine paperwork, collected the password at the *Parole* and so on, while the other acted as little more than a domestic steward, and dealt with the baggage drivers, cooks, tradesmen and so on.[186]

Daun judged his adjutants solely on their professional merits, and he gave a highly qualified character reference on behalf of one of the tribe, the Flügel-Adjutant Major Emanuel-Alexandre Baron Franquet, a member of the Hainault aristocracy. Franquet had gained the *Kleinkreuz* of the Theresian Order for a desperate deed at Kolin, but Daun knew that he was addicted to intrigue, and had been promoted too fast for his own good. 'I must also add that he got himself taken prisoner like an idiot (which he isn't), in spite of all the precautions I told him to take... he claims that he will be able to make a grand marriage; I cannot answer for the truth of that, but in any case the lady in question ought to prefer the man for himself and not for his rank'.[187]

Aides-de-camp, unlike the adjutants, had no official standing, being essentially personal messengers who stood at the immediate disposal of a general as part of his military family. Generals who had an eye to their personal advantage were glad to accommodate the sons of wealthy or influential houses, and the author of the *Patriotic Reflections* explains that there was much potential for corruption, since unscrupulous members of the generals' staffs could make rewarding deals with contractors.[188]

Volunteers (see p. 161–162) offered a further source of recruits for the personal staffs. The Prince de Ligne describes them as pestilential exhibitionists, who galloped flat-out on mostly imaginary missions, throwing dust in the troops' faces, and who hung back from the firing line on a day of battle, but reappeared towards the end of the combat in a state of high excitement to thank the troops and congratulate the officers, so conveying the impression that they had been in the thick of the fight.[189]

Many of the messengers were simply junior officers who were assigned to a senior commander on a day-to-day basis. Some of their viewpoints are conveyed by Giuseppe Gorani, who found himself attached to *GFWM*. Ferdinand Friedrich Bülow during the retreat to Bohemia after the battle of Leuthen. The Hessian Bülow, one of the finest generals of his rank in the army, sent Gorani to find the Croatian colonel Franz Friedrich Vela. Deserted by his guide, Gorani got lost in the hills and collapsed in the snow; he came to his senses the next morning, and was lucky enough to find a peasant who pointed him in the right direction. Velha accepted the message, gave him a good meal, and made sure he had a restorative sleep.[190] In June the next year Gorani was attached to Daun as a brigade orderly officer, and the Field Marshal sent him on another long journey to deliver a letter to *GFWM*. Reinhard Baron Gemmingen, who was a notoriously haughty and ill-mannered individual. Gemmingen put his reply in writing, and sent Gorani away like a dog. In August 1759 Gorani happened to be assigned as an orderly officer to Loudon. 'Usually one stays on duty for just 48 hours, but this hero kept me with him for 17 days. I had already done service with him the previous year, and he had been very good to me … Without my knowledge he had already made soundings as to my character, and my superiors told him of my services at Zittau, Liegnitz, Domstadtl and Hochkirch.' Loudon promised to call him back and give him a permanent place, but Gorani was taken prisoner before the end of the campaign, and so was unable to take up the invitation.[191]

Gorani's early encounter with Gemmingen was revealing. In the Prussian army the officers of all the branches, except the artillery and hussars, were linked by their presumed nobility, which indicated that officers of every rank were entitled to a comradely respect. While a Prussian subaltern would have held it beneath his dignity to wait on a senior officer at table, or hold a stirrup while the great man hoisted himself into the saddle, the author of the *Patriotic Reflections* found it necessary to urge that 'the generals ought to be forbidden to address regimental officers as *Er!* [a demeaning form of 'you!'], as if they were servants, and still less to employ them on domestic or other duties which are incompatible with their standing as officers'.[192]

The conscientious Daun believed that generals were under a positive obligation to entertain their junior officers at headquarters. The young officers stood to gain a good deal in the process, and most immediately because they were probably enjoying their first good meal for some time. It was also to their advantage in the longer term, for the generals might remember them when the time came to recommend appointments and promotions.[193]

Lieutenant-Colonel Navarro maintained the tradition of hospitality under some difficult circumstances at the Austrian siege of Dresden in 1758, when he commanded a detachment of 600 men at the Grosser Garten. Although a Spaniard by origin, he acquired a taste for the table and good wine like the Germans, 'in the same way as you end up howling by keeping company with wolves'.[194] After a number of hours spent repelling Prussian sorties he invited his officers to dine with him at three in the morning, and plied them with wine and liqueurs until they were in a state of frenzy and stupefaction.

The less dedicated leaders were physically as well as mentally remote from their commands. The regulations laid down repeatedly that the *FMLs.* and *GFWMs.* were to encamp with their divisions and brigades, and not find comfortable quarters elsewhere under a roof. Daun enforced this prohibition in his own army, 'but in all the other armies and corps the generals believed that it was unfair to make them live in camp; orders were indeed issued to this effect, but they were poorly observed'.[195] Hours could therefore be lost in trying to convey an important message to a general in his quarters, and that was one of the reasons why Frederick held his generals under an absolute prohibition to lodge anywhere but in a tent with their troops (this practice saved the Prussian from being wiped out when they were taken by surprise at Hochkirch). The Austrian generals' habit of living in houses had the further effect of multiplying their train of servants and cooks; the generals took it as their right to lay hands on the peasants' fodder and horses, and to send officers, NCOs and soldiers in advance to seek out good quarters at their next destination.[196]

Cogniazzo and the Prince de Ligne indicated how the enlightened thinking of the time defined a good general when it came to combat. He must have a technical mastery of his trade, together with the faculty of sizing up a situation and taking a rapid and appropriate course of action (*coup d'oeil*). A certain robustness was needed to put that decision into effect, and de Ligne was inclined to believe that it was 'better to make a whole-hearted blunder, and follow it through, than to do the right thing without conviction'.[197] However good leadership was more than a product of confidence and the inspiration of the moment. It was also the expression of a carefully-cultivated relationship with one's army:

> I would advise a Field Marshal to be in the habit of riding along the front of the camp with a brilliant suite, and stopping every now and then to talk to some brave officer, or question a few soldiers. It is good to see how all the other troops will come up to hear what is being said, and display their esteem for the Field Marshal; it does not take much to win them over – a few little compliments and a scattering of ducats. If he is willing to share their misfortunes, when things are going badly with them, they will be willing to face anybody.[198]

The foreign attachés tried to assess how far the Austrian generals lived up to such requirements. Armfeldt was unimpressed, as we have seen, while Montazet reported on 11 September 1759 that Daun was unable to find anybody better to command the detached corps than the generals Harsch and de Ville. 'You may judge from this what the others must be like,' commented the Frenchman, 'doesn't it make you shudder ?' Daun had the highest regard for Lacy and Loudon, but neither happened to be available at this time, for Lacy was serving as chief of staff, and Loudon was with the Russians.[199]

It was true that some excellent middle-ranking officers were being brought on by the experience of leading light troops, but almost by definition colonels and generals of this kind stood low in rank and seniority, and it had required a special effort on the part of Kaunitz to advance Loudon to the command of an army. This magnificent generation was in one sense too young for the Seven Years War, just as it was to be too old to beat down the French at the time of the Revolution.

The Austrian monarchy was in fact still fundamentally weak, and it still depended too much on the consent of class and regional interest-groups to have permitted even an autocratically-minded male sovereign to enforce his will on the army at that time. The consequences are fundamental to our understanding of the Austrian art of war.

Affairs were managed differently in Frederick's army. There was a distinct style to the Prussian generals. They had a basic knowledge of their craft, they had an unreserved commitment to the military life, and they showed themselves to be alert and active, while observing an unquestioning obedience to their chiefs and their king. By way of contrast the lack of consistency among the Austrian generals is striking, and it derived less from their obvious national diversity than the prevailing culture of favouritism and obligation. 'One commander will impose tight discipline, but the next none at all, or at least very little… All of this makes for bad blood in the army, in the same way that two good cooks can end up by spoiling a meal, unless you make them prepare their dishes in the same way'.[200]

The spirit of partisanship flourished among the generals to a degree that invited comparison with an infection of the blood.[201] Envy and *Schadenfreude* had been identified among the Austrians in the last Turkish war.[202] They now made it possible for the Lorraine party to rejoice in the downfall of Browne in 1757, and they presented Lacy and Loudon as rivals even when there had been no ill will between the two. Prince Liechtenstein drew attention to the evils of division when he proposed a plan of campaign for 1760, and took the liberty of telling Maria Theresa that 'the factions in the army are supported from here [Vienna], and they do endless damage; this corrupt element in the service must be excised without regard for individuals.' He asked her to consider what would happen if Daun fell ill or were rendered hors de combat, and Buccow or somebody like him took over the command of an army 'on which depends the survival of Your Majesty's House, Your Majesty's people, and the whole of Europe'.[203]

In the high summer of that year the debacle at Liegnitz exacerbated the ill-feeling between the champions of Loudon on the one side, and Daun and Lacy on the other. On 8 September Daun denied to Maria Theresa the existence of any such divisions among his generals in the field, 'but what you will find is that each individual speaks out as the caprice takes him, being plunged into gloom in the morning but full of optimism in the evening'.[204.]

In the Prussian army the absolute authority of Frederick kept within bounds the enmities that might otherwise have developed between the hard-nosed Dessau tradition, and the more humane and politically-moderate group of officers headed by his brother Prince Henry. Neither Maria Theresa nor Daun had this kind of power at their disposal. The Field Marshal read and admired the *General-Principia vom Kriege* of Old Fritz, and 'concerning the discipline of our troops, I believe that it is an object deserving of great attention, and I only wish our officers and generals displayed more energy on that point'.[205]

The dismissive comment of an arrogant young lieutenant, when he was called to task for poaching (see, p. 205) gives support to the contention of a critic that the officers as a whole were in the habit of obeying the orders of their commander-in-chief with something less than complete accuracy and devotion, a trait which was never more dangerous than on a day of battle, when so much depended on precision. The Austrian generals were good at explaining themselves away, but in the Prussian service no excuse was accepted if a general failed to see the signal which had been concerted for an attack.[206]

The detached Austrian corps were usually run on a looser rein than the main army, but Dawn's correspondence shows that his writ was far from absolute even among his own generals. He told Maria Theresa in September 1759 that he could not prevent Pálffy and Esterházy falling back before the slightest Prussian advance, 'and we have to hold councils of war every day, when you will hear no end of excuses. But to set all the generals aside would cause a widespread alienation and only make things worse… [also] large detached commands call for generals of a certain rank, which therefore deprives me of freedom of choice'.[207]

The Pálffy in question was the *GFWM*. Rudolph, who was by no means a rebel by nature, and had in fact been trying to enforce subordination in his own brigade of hussars. His officers were in the habit of interpreting and executing orders as they saw fit, 'whereby whole expeditions have been delayed and brought to nothing; we have to make force marches to repair those mistakes, which makes the troopers disgruntled and ruins the horses'.[208] Pálffy's efforts incurred the hostility of a number of his officers, but he was supported in his continuing endeavours by *FZM*. Lacy, who wrote to Daun that the other generals believed that they could shut their eyes to what they considered minor infractions, but Pálffy was right to insist on the letter of the law.[209]

On the eve of the battle of Kolin the French attaché Champeaux noted that Daun stood isolated in a crowd of mediocre generals,[210] and this perception was confirmed repeatedly in the course of the war. The Field Marshal appeared to have been at fault for having failed to do anything decisive to exploit the great victory which had been won by Saltykov and Loudon at Kunersdorf in 1759, but in his defence an Austrian claimed that 'we know from experience that the enemy move with speed and resolution, which has the effect of throwing our forces at once into a state of indecision and agonised anxiety. The main reason is that *FM*. Daun lacks the kind of subordinate generals who can lead a corps effectively, maintain discipline and morale, and, in the case of a reverse, not only take well-considered and courageous decision, but put them into effect as well'.[211]

The failure at Liegnitz in 1760 offered further evidence to the effect that Daun was an isolated figure, who had little confidence in his generals and still less in himself.[212] Nothing had changed by 1762: 'It is true that a number of the generals are well-motivated and make an effort, but there are not enough of them to provide the necessary commanders for so large an army... the Cabinet might devise excellent plans of campaign, just as the commanding officer might work out fine dispositions for an operation – and by every reasonable calculation everything promises well – but we are still faced with the lack of men who can execute those schemes with vigour and precision'.[213]

Accountability

It is probably no exaggeration to say that by 1759 the Austrian officer corps was in a state of disciplinary crisis. There was good reason to doubt the competence of the *Justiz-Collegium* in the matter, as we have seen, and on 27 March Maria Theresa made it known through Daun that existing disciplinary measures had proved of no avail against officers who continued in their bad ways, regardless of the warnings of their superiors. It would have been too drastic a procedure to haul them up before courts martial, and she instead required the colonels and brigade commanders to detail the offences of the incorrigible officers in writing, so that they could be dismissed without a formal hearing. She told Daun to begin the process with Major Baron Königsegg of the regiment of Königsegg.[214] Daun confirmed that he had received and published the order, and would take immediate action against the officer in question.[215]

By 8 March 1760 the purge had claimed only 16 officers, though they were headed by Maria Theresa's initial target, Major Königsegg, 'on account of the monies he had received on behalf of the regiment, and diverted to his own use'.[216] Maria Theresa was wholeheartedly committed to this summary form of justice,[217] and by the end of the year the total bloodletting amounted to 96 offenders, of whom 36 had been forced to resign, 24 consigned to the reduction, 17 cashiered, and 19 had escaped by running away. The infantry regiment of Neipperg produced some interesting cases, which must have embarrassed the Vice-President of the *Hofkriegsrath*. Second-Lieutenant Baron Donschütz was struck from the list on account of excessive gambling, getting into debt, and fraudulent money changing, and because he spent more time in provost's arrest than out of it; he finally deserted from his regiment in Silesia. The regiment was also well rid of a so-called 'Ensign Arioldy,' who deserted to the Prussians after it was discovered that he had been no more than a servant to the genuine Count Arioldy, and had enlisted as a cadet under his master's name. However the infantry regiment of Kollowrat had the distinction of producing the largest crop of culprits, and lost no less than nine of its establishment of officers; eight of the lieutenants and ensigns had resigned or been cashiered on account of various kinds of dishonesty, while First-Lieutenant Adelsbrecht had deserted to the enemy.[218]

It was still too easy for a well-connected offender to evade the full consequence of his misdeeds. Officers who had been cashiered or dismissed, or had resigned for their own convenience, could be re-assigned elsewhere through the help of friends, or got into the way of wearing the uniforms of their old regiments, as if they were still serving officers of good repute.

There is documentary proof that three at least of Maria Theresa's foremost advisers exerted a degree of influence, amounting to favouritism, on behalf of some thoroughly unworthy characters. Daun himself circumvented Maria Theresa's disciplinary decree of 1759, which would otherwise have visited automatic dismissal on Second-Lieutenant Pacher of the Stampach Cuirassiers – a drunk and a gambler who had already undergone three months' provost's arrest in irons. His commandant, Colonel Waldstein, opposed this punishment 'out of regard for the memory of his father, who died as lieutenant-colonel after many years devoted to the... service,'[219] and Daun duly reinforced this plea.

It was on the express recommendation of the *Reichs Vize-Canzler* Colloredo that Hadik took into his regiment the staff quartermaster Wollin, who can only be the deplorable creature of the same name who was entered in the Conduits-Lista of the regiment of Erzherzog Carl (below, see p. 206) in 1757. Hadik discovered the man's true nature for himself, whereupon he complained to Colloredo that his misdeeds had culminated in an episode in the German town of Cronach, where, for no reason at all, Wollin had lashed out at the Bürgermeister and his wife with a coachman's whip. Hadik clapped Wollin in irons, which effected no improvement in the man's language and behaviour, whereupon the case came to the notice of Maria Theresa, who decided that Wollin must be brought to Vienna under secure guard, and transported from there to a fortress in Hungary.[220]

Colonel Zorn von Plobsheim tells of another attempt to interfere with the course of justice, in this case in favour of First-Lieutenant Baron Formentini. Proceedings had been taken against him the grounds of fraud and unauthorised absence, but they were dropped at the instance of Prince Liechtenstein 'out of particular favour, and in the hope that he will behave in future, and mends his ways'.[221] Formentini behaved as badly as ever, whereupon Zorn placed him under open arrest and made him march on foot with the troops; Formentini finally exclaimed in exasperation that he wished to leave the regiment, which gave the colonel the excuse he needed to throw him out.

Maria Theresa was meanwhile searching for ways that would keep Vienna informed about the behaviour and capacity of the officers as a whole. The regiment of Erzherzog Carl was probably not the only unit which was in the habit of assessing its officers in confidential reports. The author of the *Patriotic Reflections* applauded the practice, and Maria Theresa decreed in February 1762 that regimental commanders must now send a return of this kind to the *Hofkriegsrath* every year.[222]

Daun had in any case kept Maria Theresa up to date with the performance of the generals under his command, and he turned his particular attention to the regiments and their senior officers after Hochkirch. The Austrians had won the battle, but in a way which fell short of Daun's expectations, and he and Lacy took careful stock of the strengths and weaknesses which had been revealed. The Schmerzing and Portugal Cuirassiers were unlikely to improve under their respective lieutenant-colonels Gabelkoffen and Kolb, but something could be done for at least the first of these regiments by transferring two excellent men from the Erzherzog Ferdinand Cuirassiers, namely Lieutenant-Colonel Bosfort, 'who is one of our most able officers' in the capacity of colonel commandant, and *Rittmeister* Steffen, 'who did particularly well in the last battle, and is a good brave officer.' Lieutenant-Colonel Angonys was too weak to command the Bethlen Hussars, and Lieutenant-Colonel Khevenhüller too young, 'especially as this regiment needs a very able man in charge'.[223]

In the Thirty Years War the Austrian discipline had been savage, and a terrible punishment had been visited on the first of the regiments of cuirassiers to break before the Swedes at Breitenfeld. The standards of the offending regiment were ripped up, the swords broken, the majors beheaded, every cornet and NCO hanged, and one in 10 of the troopers strung up along the wayside.[224] While measures of this sort were no longer acceptable, the *Militär Feld-Regulament* of 1759 now enjoined on the generals the formal duty to keep a narrow eye on the regiments and officers in battle, and note who was behaving well and who was behaving badly. The generals were to send their reports to the commander in chief, who would in turn forward his account to Maria Theresa, 'so that those of the first category may receive signal reward, and those of the second punished in a way that befits their dishonour and unworthiness'.[225] This requirement formalised what Daun was doing already, and it was plainly part of the process by which Maria Theresa was now seeking to hold the army to stricter account.

Encouragement and Reward

The same procedures which identified inadequate, corrupt or disloyal officers also revealed a large number of good men. Senior commands continued to send informal recommendations of *bons sujets* who had come to their special attention,[226] while the new annual confidential reports set out the qualities of the officers in a more systematic way. In the pioneering *Conduits-Lista* of the regiment of Erzherzog Carl we read of the particular virtues of Captain Samuel Horosoky, an unmarried man of Lutheran religion, and an excellent individual who was the best officer of the regiment at staff work, and who had raised nearly 1,700 recruits through his own efforts. Horosoky did not survive the battle of Kolin, where the regiment did magnificently, but his comrade Second-Lieutenant Jakob Cogniazzo (the future commentator) was mentioned in favourable terms, and Cogniazzo's friend the grenadier captain Procopius Hennebrith was singled out as 'one of the most able officers of the regiment, who performs all his duties with good humour and boundless energy. His conduct and his whole style of life are admirable'.[227]

Maria Theresa had determined on positive measures to bring on people like these, and encourage more like them. Her achievement must be measured against the deplorable state of the morale of her army at the outset of her reign, when the prolonged crisis of 1740–1 had provoked a mass of desertions from the officer corps. After the Second Silesian war the Prussian ambassador noted how she defied her high nobility to show her regard for her officers, without concern for their birth (see p. 159). That was at the beginning of 1747, when the work of military reform had scarcely begun.[228] In 1751 Maria Theresa decreed that every officer was entitled to appear at Court wearing his uniform, without the need to seek special permission, or purchase the frilly golden official Court dress (the *Mantel-Kleid*). In 1757, the second year of the great war, she ordained that irrespective of social rank all officers were qualified to appear in uniform at the solemn celebration of victories, and at the regular *Seelenandacht* which was offered for the souls of the dead soldiers. Thus the Emperor Francis Stephen, the three elder archdukes, and the officers present in Vienna occupied a pew in St. Stephen's Cathedral in a white-coated phalanx on 20 November to mark the capture of Schweidnitz. Maria Theresa herself used to wear the white and red uniform when reviewing her troops, to show her regard for the military condition, and Cogniazzio states that after the defeat at Leuthen she received whole parties of escaped soldiers at Court, without any obligation on their part to tidy themselves up, 'for you know in what state an escaped prisoner can appear'.[229]

On 12 January 1757 Maria Theresa decreed that all officers who had given 30 years of unblemished service were entitled to be raised to the nobility. Some objections were made to elevations to all but the lowest grade, on the grounds that few officers would have the means of living in an appropriately fine style (see p. 159). She replied that she would make sensible choices, 'and just think how many poor counts we already see about! A few more will make no difference'.[230] There was, however, no presumption that the new nobles would be entitled to lands or a place in the provincial *Stände*, which were the stronghold of the traditional aristocracy. The titles were granted free, though the new nobles had to defray the immediate costs – parchments, scribe, artist and heraldic authentication – of the actual patents.[231]

For a long time Maria Theresa and her advisers had been asking themselves whether the monarchy should found an order of military chivalry, something roughly comparable with the Prussian *Pour le Merite,* the French *Saint-Louis* or the Russian *St. Andrew,* which might spur the ambitions of military men, and attract able civilians to the officer corps. Daun made a first proposal in 1749, and he returned to the charge two years later, but Maria Theresa feared that a new order might detract from the lustre of the Golden Fleece, which was the highest gift in the hands of the Habsburgs. Moreover the qualifications suggested by Daun – a quarter of a century of military service, of which 10 were to have been active – were not such as to fire the imagination.

The project lapsed until the early spring of 1757, when a major new campaign was imminent. Francis Stephen broached the subject to Kaunitz, who replied on 12 April that no time was to be lost. The *Staatscanzler's* sense of urgency impressed the Imperial pair, and work on the statutes (in which Kaunitz had the decisive role) went ahead. News of the victory at Kolin reached Vienna on 20 June. Maria Theresa delayed no further, and because the groundwork had already been laid the new order could be proclaimed with seemingly miraculous speed, and its foundation back-dated to the glorious 18 June. On the 22nd Maria Theresa wrote to Daun that she had had the order in mind for a considerable time, 'but what was needed before we could put this aim into effect was some suitable opportunity. This has now been furnished by the masterly victory which has been attained by you and the army under your command. I shall therefore proceed without delay, and pay the honour which is due to you by proclaiming to posterity that the new order is the child of that victory'.[232]

The new order was styled the *Militärischer-Maria Theresien-Orden,* a name suggested by Daun, who believed that to call the order after a saint, as was usual in Catholic monarchies, would be less acceptable to the many Protestant officers in the army. The M.M.T.O. was awarded initially in two classes. The bearer of the *Grosskreuz,* the higher class, wore a large cross on a red-white-red riband of silk, a hand's breadth wide, which ran over the right shoulder and down to the left hip. This grade was reserved by statute for generals who had made significant contributions to winning battles or campaigns. The self-explanatory *Kleinkreuz* of the lower class (that of *Ritter*) was suspended from a red-white-red silk ribbon, two fingers broad, which hung from a button hole of the coat or waistcoat. Altogether nine of the *Grosskreuze* and 164 of the *Kleinkreuze* were awarded in the first nine promotions (1758–63 of the Order).

The crosses of the two grades were of a common design, enamelled in white, and bearing a red circular shield which was crossed by a white bar, and set inside a golden circle that carried the motto: FORTITUDINI (For Valour). A third class, that of *Commandeur,* was instituted in 1765, whereupon the *Grosskreuz* was worn as an embroidered star on the left-hand side of the coat chest. Pensions were established for each grade, along with privileges and civil titles. The M.M.T.O. brought automatic elevation to the Ritterstand (which was the second grade of nobility, above the 'simple nobility'), and it was up to individuals to apply to be made up to something grander like baron (*Freiherr*) or count (*Graf*).

The M.M.T.O. was distinguished from foreign orders in that it was not granted at the whim of the sovereign, but only through the recommendation of a Chapter, and officers who considered themselves worthy of consideration were to make a written application on their own behalf, detailing the relevant action or actions, and attaching affidavits from one's commander and five or six other officers, or, if no officers were available, 12 NCOs or private soldiers. The petitions were assessed, the judgements collated, and the final decisions taken at a meeting of the order's Chapter.

After the Grand Master had pronounced his approval, the names of the new knights were made known to the field army at the next *Parole.* 'The relation of the deed, together with the approval of the Grand Master, are to be read out at this gathering, whereupon the commanding general or his deputy hangs the insignia from a button hole of the recipient to the accompaniment of trumpets and drums; he embraces and kisses him, and all the other bearers of the *Grosskreuz* and *Ritterkreuz* follow in succession' (Statute No. 10).

Emperor Francis Stephen was proclaimed as the first of the Grand Masters, but the greater influence was probably exercised by the Chancellor, or administrator, an office which was held by Kaunitz from 1757 until he died in 1794, and by his grandson-in-law Prince Metternich from 1813 to 1859, which extended the influence of Kaunitz in a curious way for more than a century.

The thinking of Kaunitz had shaped the peculiar character of the Order from the start. It was in the first place not a recognition of accumulated service (as Daun had intended), but a reward for specific deeds regardless of birth, rank or age. Such deeds embraced not only physical courage (*Herzhaftigkeit*), which had a particular appeal to Maria Theresa, but also cunning schemes and bold personal initiatives. Kaunitz hoped thereby to raise the level of independent thinking in the officer corps, and in the long term he succeeded so well that by the 1870s some officers had taken to believing that the Order could be awarded for actions that had been taken in deliberate defiance of commands. Finally, and most remarkably, it was up to a deserving officer to apply on his own behalf – a provision which was supposed to circumvent the normal workings of seniority and favouritism.

The public life of the M.M.T.O. opened with the first *Ordenspromotion* on 7 March 1758. The last campaign had ended so badly that some people doubted whether it ought to go ahead, but so much publicity had been given to the new Order that greater embarrassment still would have been created by abandoning it, and Maria Theresa had in any case committed herself unreservedly to her creation. The promotion was held in the *Ceremoniensaal* of the Hofburg, where Francis Stephen as Grand Master instituted the first four of the grand crosses, namely Prince Charles of Lorraine (for the battle of Breslau), *FM*. Daun and *G.d.C.* Nádasdy (for Kolin), and *FML*. Hadik (for his raid on Berlin). The choices were disappointingly conventional, and the promotion of Nádasdy was inevitably seen as a sop to him for having been removed from active command. Charles of Lorraine was generally held to be the true author of the disaster at Leuthen, which posed an awkward problem for Kaunitz when he rose to eulogise the prince, but he was able to acquit himself with admirable tact (see p. 28). Kaunitz also announced the award of a further 10 *Grosskreuze* and four *Kleinkreuze* for officers who were serving at that time in the field. Daun was designated the plenipotentiary of the Grand Master, and he invested the knights at the camp of Skalitz on 23 April.

Few men had entertained an aspiration to the remote and grand Golden Fleece. Now the officers were presented with an honour which was in principle within the grasp of all, and they responded in ways we might have expected. Holders of the *Kleinkreuz* did not hesitate to canvass Francis Stephen directly, if they had aspirations to the *Grosskreuz*.[233] Again, the proceedings of the Chapters were the subject of much gossip within the officer corps, and not least because they had no predictable membership, date or location. Many of the conclaves were inevitably held in Vienna, but Daun was plagued with the responsibility of presiding over the Chapters when they were held in the field, 'where it is difficult to put aside the time just now. The enemy are so close that I have to spend the whole morning in camp and riding about, constantly ready for action and always on the alert'.[234]

In such circumstances the confidentiality of the debates was still more difficult to observe in the army than it was in Vienna, and early in 1760 Philipp Beck learned that Daun and the gunner general Walther von Waldenau had recommended him for the *Grosskreuz*, but 14 other assessors only for that of the *Kleinkreuz*. Beck therefore entered a protest to Kaunitz as *Ordenscanzler*, and he was duly promoted to the *Grosskreuz* a few days later.[235]

On 24 August 1761 Daun forwarded to Maria Theresa two letters of protest which had been occasioned by the last Chapter, but he told her that he could not have voted otherwise: 'I have to say that with things as they are, and the statutes as they exist, the success in obtaining the *Kleinkreuz* or the *Grosskreuz* depends much more on the mentality, inclinations and caprice of the Chapter members than on the true merit and rights of the candidate. You just have to read the minutes of every Chapter held up to now to find the proof. I fear that the Order will be debased, which is very painful to me'.[236]

Armfeldt noted that 'the Austrian officers themselves wish the Order to be distributed more sparingly',[237] and Cogniazzo claims that it was all too easy for officers to get together to devise attestations for their mutual benefit.[238] Cogniazzo himself was caught up in the disgrace attending one of the knights, *GFWM*. Conrad Emanuel Count Brunyan, who in April 1763 was court-martialled, dismissed from the service and imprisoned for unauthorised correspondence with the enemy.

Cogniazzo (as Brunyan's messenger) was sentenced to 14 days' detention. Brunyan himself was lucky to escape with his life. He forfeited his *Kleinkreuz* along with his pension, but the episode was kept from public knowledge (Brunyan still stands alongside his more honourable fellow in the official history of the Order by Jaromir Hirtenfeld [1857]), and he was shameless enough to ask Maria Theresa for at least part of his pension to be paid to his wife as if she were a widow. 'The reason why I am so very badly off is that, the day after my sentence was pronounced, all my effects were confiscated under the pretext of paying the cost of my commission of enquiry in Dresden. All that I have left are an old, torn Slavonian hussar uniform, seven shirts, six handkerchiefs, one hat with his fittings, and one old cloak. I am thus left naked after 30 years of loyal, zealous and distinguished service'.[239]

By far the greater number of promotions went to officers who came to terms with the formalities and emerging conventions, and exploited the wording of the Order's statutes. *FML*. Draskovich supported the successful candidature of *G.d.C.* de Ville by citing his 'intelligent' retreat from Troppau to Olmütz on 27 April 1758, and retrograde march on 1 May 1759.[240] Conversely, if you wished to link your name to a successful attack, the best course was to show that you had planted the original inspiration in the mind of the commander, and intervened at the decisive moment when the affair was in progress. When good connections counted for so much, it is not surprising to find that in the first nine promotions the generals gained a relatively high percentage (18.90) even of the *Kleinkreuz*, which was the same proportion as the the captains, who were far more numerous in the army as a whole.

However the most important promotion in the lifetime of Maria Theresa was the one which lay closest to the Order's purpose, namely the award of the *Kleinkreuz* to the 16-year-old Second-Lieutenant Anton Ulrich Baron Mylius for his part in the storm of Glatz in 1760. The officers who were aware of the Order's shortcomings were still alive to its peculiar prestige, as being for military men 'the finest in the world'.[241]

The places of birth of the Knights are not recorded with any consistency, but when we also call on the evidence of the surnames it is possible to establish a very approximate order of origin for the two grades, which would the leading representations as coming from the *Reich* (22.00 percent), the Netherlands (11.00), Ireland (9.50), and non-Austrian Italy (up to 6 percent).

It is likewise impossible to define the identity of each Knight by his arm of service, because so many of the officers transferred from one branch to another in the course of the war. We take as our yardstick the service for which the individual was best known at the time, which establishes the rough order of the leading categories as being the infantry (54 percent), cuirassiers and dragoons (20 percent together), and the Croats (10.5).

The M.M.T.O. actually outlived the monarchy. The Chapter was convened for the 50th and last time on 3 October 1931, when it appointed the last of the 1,241 Knights, and declared that it was the last assembly competent to pronounce on the record of the war of 1914–18.

Private Conduct and Relationships

Away from the immediate presence of the enemy, the Austrian officer would try to complete his routine duties in the morning, and so have the rest of the day at his free disposal. As a wealthy

Netherlandish nobleman the Prince de Ligne could write of the gathering of the officers at coffee as a time for amusing or improving conversation.[242] The same did not apply to the company at the sutlers' tents, or the gambling hells where young officers like Ensign Anton Kunig were apt to fall into all sorts of trouble. He became 'so friendly with a hat-maker of Stein that he did not shrink from engaging in a game of skittles with him. Afterwards this caused them to fall out so badly that they lost their tempers and resorted to fisticuffs, so that the whole thing degenerated into an all-out brawl'.[243]

Bohemia and Moravia were renowned throughout Europe for the quality of their game, and no amount of prohibitions could deter lovers of fresh air or the steaming pot from expending their gunpowder on targets less stringy than the Prussians. *FM.* Browne (himself a Bohemian landowner) complained to *FML.* Hadik that the poaching by the people under his command was becoming intolerable, citing the experience of a gamekeeper on the Clary estates who had told three of the officers that shooting on the lordly reserves was forbidden: 'Upon this, Second-Lieutenant Nostitz replied that he should not take it on himself to forbid anything of the kind to officers, who were answerable only to the Emperor and Empress; the general could issue as many orders as he liked, he himself would do whatever he liked'.[244] By 1759 poaching had attained such dimensions that the *Militär Feld-Regulament* decreed that all officers found in the act would be sent to headquarters under arrest, their huntsmen or servants consigned to the regiments as recruits, and their dogs banished from the army or shot.

Practical jokes and noisy romps could also be counted as healthy sports for junior officers. The cult of sensibility and a dedication to professional reading had already begun to affect the subalterns of Frederick's army; the young Austrian officers were as yet immune to such influences, and long afterwards the Prince de Ligne remembered with affection the uncomplicated joys of his rococo youth. He found himself in command of a regiment at the age of 22, 'and I have to admit that we caused some mighty commotion… I recall how in winter quarters we walked around in chains pretending to be ghosts, changed the shop signs around, seized the sedan chairs from porters who were carrying people to some great supper and performed country dances with them, or cried out *Fire!* And serenaded the citizens who duly appeared at the windows, or collapsed tents onto their occupants'.[245]

Dinner fulfilled a variety of social and practical functions, and Rudolph Pálffy emphasised that 'the best place to cultivate manners is at headquarters'.[246] Here was the setting where good junior officers could make their mark with their seniors, and commanders in their turn could get to know their subordinates, feed them up if they looked hungry, or simply take the opportunity to relax. The censorious Pietro Verri noted that 'Field Marshal Daun never talked about war at his table… where matters proceeded as if we were in some distant city; there was no mention of the Prussians, and the conversation never touched on the campaign'.[247] In the harsh winter of 1759/60 the French attaché de Marainville betook himself with his company of musicians to Daun's headquarters at Pirna, which needed some cheering up. 'As I am something of a musician myself, I acted as conductor on my violin. The Duke of Braganza, who was an extremely accomplished musician, joined us and sang very well. The generals O'Donnell and Pellegrini also wished to take part, and they played the flute'.[248]

Drunkenness is listed as a failing of a large number of personnel in the confidential reports, and it figures again in the accusations against the officers who were listed as 'incorrigible' in the later years of the war. There was stupidity as well as self-indulgence in the cases of the two lieutenants Bremser and Godar. They 'betook themselves to the headquarters at Alt-Jauernick at a time when action was expected any moment, and drank themselves into unconsciousness. They came to themselves the next day, and found that the army had marched away the previous night. Their conduct was particularly badly-timed, and they have been arrested, court-martialled and cashiered'.[249]

GFWM. Gemmingen was among the senior officers who detested gambling and its truly destructive potential, and he and his kind could invoke an order of the *Hofkriegsrath* whereby all ranks were forbidden to engage in any game of chance.[250] Count Corti experienced the risks incurred by young officers when he stopped in Vienna on his way to join his regiment early in the Seven Years War. He accepted an invitation to play, and proceeded to win 1,428 ducats from one of the counts Colloredo. His embarrassment turned to horror when a servant duly delivered the golden coins in a weighty sack, and conveyed Colloredo's request to be allowed an opportunity for revenge. Corti took advice and departed at once for the field, on the pretext that he must obey an urgent order.[251]

Gambling continued to draw in even such officers as the Prince de Ligne, who disliked cards and did not know how to play them, and our Lieutenant Gorani, who made repeated and vain attempts to break his addiction. He tells us of a game at Marklissa on 8 July 1759, when he staked all that was left from his pay and won 18,000 florins. The next day he bought a horse from his colonel, and fitted himself out with a repeating watch, several pieces of silver, along with boots, cloak and overcoat, and material for uniforms and 24 fine shirts.[252] He promised his colonel never to gamble again – and three days later he lost all the money in his purse at another game. He lapsed once more when he was a prisoner in East Prussia, and he learned that a large number of the army's seemingly bona fide players were in fact semi-professional card sharps who went by the collective name of the *Grecs*.

After the Seven Years War the authority of Maria Theresa had considerable success in banning play from the army. Until then it had been probably the most important single reason why so many of her officers had fallen into debt. In the regiment of Erzherzog Carl, directly linked with the Imperial family, Second-Lieutenant Georg Wollin was just the worst placed of the several officers who are listed as having been in default: 'he is a man of considerable ability, which he unfortunately never devotes to his duties. He is dedicated to gambling and running up debts, and he owes so much money outside the regiment that for many years now he has had to live on half pay'.[253] Later in the war Second-Lieutenant Thaddeus Stieber of the regiment of Kollowrat was reduced to such straits that he stole sums from his colonel, sold the sash and the coat from his own back, and still found himself 900 florins in arrears.

The gentry of mid 18th-century Europe seem to have lived in a perpetual state of affronted dignity, which had the effect of putting even the most calm and unoffending officer at the mercy of a malcontent who demanded satisfaction in a duel. This was a challenge which could never be refused, if he were to retain his personal honour – an honour which in this case could take him to an early grave: 'It is bad enough to be bored by some stupid individual, without getting yourself killed by him'.[254]

The *Duell- and Ausforderungs-Poenal-Mandat* of 20 June 1752 ordained death by beheading for all persons who took part in a duel whether as principals or seconds, and even if the encounter just ended in a wounding. If the officers escaped arrest by flight, they were to suffer the confiscation of all their property, which was to be held in trust by the state until their deaths, whereupon it reverted to their heirs. Further details are brought to light through the case of the First-Lieutenant Grandmenge of the regiment of Wenzel Wallis, who had engaged Second-Lieutenant Kraith in a game of chance in a coffee house; they fell out during the play, and a few days later Grandmenge killed Kraith in a formal duel with swords. According to military custom Grandmenge was three times summoned by drum beat to show himself; he failed to appear, whereupon his name was nailed to a gallows, and the order given to confiscate enough of his money and effects to support the wife and children of the man he had killed.[255]

The full letter of the ferocious *Poenal-Mandat* was virtually unenforceable, because the senior officers were setting such a bad example to the whole army. Thus Maria Theresa was vexed to learn that the generals O'Donnell and Angern, both men of repute, had fought a duel after failing to agree about the promotion of another officer.[256]

In practice the authorities went to some trouble to discover the rights and wrongs of the individual cases. In 1761 a bloody encounter among the officers of his own regiment came to the notice of *G.d.C.* Hadik, who expressed a 'genuine regret' that the blameless *Rittmeister* Mohr had to undergo a formal investigation. He emphasised that after a first clash his troublemaking opponent, Second-Lieutenant Liebling, had gone back to fetch his sword, and attacked Mohr anew and wounded him. Hadik interpreted Liebling's act as an 'aggravating circumstance' under the *Poenal-Mandat,* and told his colonel commandant to place him under arrest'.[257]

Fisticuffs were a less lethal, but also less dignified manifestation of the officers' readiness to resort to violence. In the regiment of Alt-Colloredo the ensigns Speck and Heinrich Count Orlich were at such odds that the provost placed them under arrest until such time as their parents arrived to haul them away. They had excelled even the subalterns' reputation for mindlessness when they staged their last exchange of curses and blows in front of the provost's tent, and in full view of a crowd of soldiers, servants and wives. *G.d.C.* de Ville asked for leniency, 'out of regard for the family of Count Orlich,' but Anton Colloredo as *Inhaber* replied that the two young officers fully deserved their fate, that he would replace them by better men, and that he would answer for it personally to the *Hofkriegsrath*.[258]

Bad women reduced many a good officer to an impoverished, disease-ridden wreck. Gorani had already lost his virtue, and felt very much the adult when Colonel Perelli took him as one of his new ensigns to the theatre in Milan, 'where in spite of my blundering-about I tried to pass myself off as a man of consequence. This caused considerable and well-justified amusement'.[259] One of the ladies seduced him in her coach on the return journey – the kind of liaison which, according to the Prince de Ligne, could be a young man's best introduction to the world and fine manners.[260]

There was held to be a difference in kind between relationships with women of taste, and those which officers established with the whores who hung about the sutlers' tents, or who worked for the officers under the guise of cooks, cleaners, washerwomen and the like. However Gorani confesses that he was already at grips with servant girls on his way from Milan to Bohemia, and he testifies that by the end of the campaign of 1759 venereal disease had taken a heavy toll of the Austrian officer corps, and that it had a way of turning otherwise survivable wounds gangrenous and lethal.[261]

Daun believed that immoral ladies made for trouble, regardless of their social pretensions, and he wrote to Maria Theresa early the next year from Dresden: 'The Berlichingen woman has come here as well, which should not be allowed. It makes a bad impression – it is shameful for the husbands, and does little honour to the ladies'.[262] Frederick noted a few weeks later that 'the Empress-Queen has taken delivery of 400 prostitutes whom Daun has consigned to Hungary. The story goes that he had two of them drowned in the Elbe. Now I wonder what the Pompadour would say to that?'[263]

The military chaplains were supposed to enforce moral standards at the regimental level. This was an impossible task which only lessened the already low regard for religion among men of style. The author of the *Patriotic Reflections* maintained that officers of that kind typically owed their rise to favouritism, and now wished to acquire a reputation for worldly wisdom. When such a man became colonel he would deploy a few well-chosen terms to give the impression that he had an understanding of the wider reaches of the military art, and in the same way he would read great monographs to 'turn himself into an *esprit fort* on matters of philosophy and religion; few of them have religious beliefs, and they scorn those who harbour them... These then are the sort of gentlemen who bend military discipline to their convenience, and who do incalculable damage by manipulating everything to the advantage of themselves and their favourites'.[264]

It was a different matter when physical extinction stared a soldier in the face, and on the murky morning of the battle of Hochkirch the Prince de Ligne, that man of fashion par excellence, was taken off guard when two officers of his regiment came up to him in succession to ask whether he believed in God. 'I made an unconvincing profession of my faith… bullets were falling around me like hail, and a moment afterwards, and to my great surprise, I found myself making the sign of the cross like a true believer'.[265]

Freemasonry was spreading rapidly through the army in the Seven Years War, and an officer who had a taste for mystery and ceremony could, without incurring ridicule, have himself initiated into the craft. Although Maria Theresa set herself against freemasonry, as inimical to genuine religion, her husband Francis Stephen had been a mason since he was a young man, which gave the craft sanction in the highest quarters, and Gorani records that he himself was inducted into a military lodge by the Prince de Ligne and the dukes of Arenberg and Urselthe leaders of Netherlands military society. Gorani went on to discover four fellow spirits among the 97 Austrian officers being held prisoner in Tilsit in 1762. Within a few days they had formed a new lodge, into which they admitted further officers, along with a number of merchants of Tilsit town, who made sure that they were never short of good food and wine.[266]

In January the next year Gorani took up the proposal of a Hungarian captain at Königsberg, and opened a further lodge, that of *la Felicité*. Gatherings like these, sociable and ephemeral, were harmless enough, but authority as a whole could only have been subverted by the better-connected lodges, which established secret parallel hierarchies extending through all levels of command.

GFWM. (GM.) Charles-Joseph Prince de Ligne, 1735–1814, wearing a look of surely feigned innocence in this portrait by Andre Jäger (Military Academy, Wiener Neustadt). By the end of the Seven Years War Charles-Joseph had risen to colonel commandant of his father's regiment of Netherlands infantry, and thereafter had a successful and varied military and diplomatic career. He was remembered chiefly for the wit of his writings and entertainments, and his diary and chaotic memoirs remain our most important single source on the life of the Austrian army in the Seven Years War.

The cult of domestic affection visited Austria only later in the century, and here, as in Europe generally in the 1750s, the married state was held to be incompatible with a genuine commitment to the military life. While Maria Theresa (unlike Frederick) can scarcely be held to be hostile to the institution of marriage as such, she had to recognise that few of her officers were in a condition to support wife and family. This fact was brought home to her repeatedly.

When the army was mobilised in 1756, and the officers were therefore called to active service, it was found that many of the military families were living on the edge of subsistence, and were now incapable of surviving on the regulation deductions from their husbands' pay. Maria Theresa made additional monthly grants of eight florins to the wives of lieutenants, and of six florins to the wives of ensigns and cornets, and she re-located officer families from the Hungarian countryside, where they had been living like gypsies, to marginally better conditions in the towns. Again in 1758 she intervened to extend her protection to the orphaned daughter of First-Lieutenant d'Andrade, who had been killed at Leuthen; the 10-year-old girl had been found begging in the streets of Troppau, and since the *Hofkriegsrath* refused to accept any responsibility, Maria Theresa arranged to have her brought up in the Ursuline Convent in Olmütz.[267]

Marriage in the Austrian officer corps had to contend with some formidable obstacles. An officer wishing to marry had to apply in the first place for permission to his *Inhaber,* who then, if he gave the match his provisional consent, forwarded the request to Vienna, where the *Hofkriegsrath* was under instruction from Maria Theresa to make sure that the officers committed themselves to no 'unsuitable matches'.[268]

The would-be husband was then required to lodge a deposit in cash or promissory notes with his regiment, to ensure that his widow and children would receive some support in the event of his death. The deposits were determined by rank (a mighty 1,200 florins, for example, for a second-lieutenant, and 2,000 for a captain), and these sums were carried around in the regimental chests until March 1759, when they were transferred for better safekeeping to a *Universal Depositen Amt* in Vienna.[269]

The wonder is that so many regimental officers were willing to brave all these deterrents, as we may see from the following:

Percentage of Married officers by Type of Regiment	
German infantry:	4.21
Hungarian infantry:	22.10
Simbschen regiment:	25.00
Italian infantry:	22.95
Netherlands infantry:	22.36
Cuirassiers:	16.58
Dragoons:	19.42
Hussars:	30.36

The senior officers were more advantageously placed to provide for wife and family. The besotted Hadik took his wife around with him on campaign, ignoring the amusement he provoked, and French military attachés went to some length to obtain little luxuries which he could pass on to his beloved. Daun was better advised. Comparatively late in life he made a politically advantageous marriage to the widowed Maria Josepha Countess Nostitz, née Fuchs, and this ally remained throughout the war in Vienna, where she could safeguard his interests when he was absent with the army.

While the Austrian officers as a whole were not renowned for particular bookishness, almost every reading of the contemporary memoirs brings to light men of the calibre of Lieutenant-Colonel Lestwitz and Lieutenant Elvenich (the patrons of Joseph von Sonnenfels), or Gorani's Lieutenant-Colonel Terzi: 'He was a straight man, who had a great fund of knowledge at his command; he was the only officer in our regiment [Andlau] who had a love of study, and he devoted all his time to that occupation, rather than wasting it on gambling, at the inn or with girls, like the rest of the officers.'[270]

A working knowledge of at least one foreign language was an essential though unofficial requirement for every officer in this cosmopolitan army, and a great deal more was demanded of the officers of the Hungarian regiments. The enlightening *Conduits-Lista* of the regiment of Erzherzog Carl specifies the linguistic attainments of 42 of its officers, from which it is possible to deduce the following:

Command of Languages by Number of Languages	
Two languages:	16.66
Three:	50.00
Four:	33.33

Command of Language by Individual Language
German:	92.23 of officers
Hungarian:	90.47
Latin:	83.33
French:	23.80
Bohemian:	9.57
Ratzisch:	9.52
Illyrian (in this context Serbo-Croat):	4.76
Italian:	2.38

Second-Lieutenant Nicolas-Joseph Cugnot (1735–1804) of the engineers was consumed by the conviction that it was possible for man to travel by mechanical means. In 1760 the *Hofkriegsrath* asked Jean-Baptiste de Gribeauval (a highly-accomplished French artilleryman, then serving with the Austrians as a general) to look into this strange young man's request to leave the army. Gribeauval replied from Dresden:

> I know Cugnot from the time he worked with me for two or three months on the fortifications. He has an understanding of mechanics and theory, he is extremely diligent, and he is exact when it comes to the detail of the service, but he is absolutely devoid of the kind of activity and application that are required to put things into practice. He is otherwise an honourable officer and one who is of unimpeachable behaviour. In 1752 he passed over all the ensigns by gaining admittance to the Engineering Corps as first-lieutenant. When he was in Brussels he proposed to apply fire to impart movement to vehicles. He worked in 1753 and 1754 to try to put his project into effect, but he failed... He began service in the fortresses in 1755, and came to the *Reichsarmee* in 1758; several of the officers whom he had passed over have now regained superior rank, and nearly all of them have considerably more practical skill than is at his command.[271]

Prince Charles was of the same mind, and declared that if Cugnot wished to resign, nothing should stand in his way.

This episode is of some interest, for Cugnot was the inventor of the first working steam locomotive – in fact of all mechanically-propelled vehicles – and Gribeauval's comment shows that he had begun work on steam propulsion as an Austrian officer, and well before the date of 1765 which appears in the literature.[272] Gribeauval changed his tune after the war, by when Cugnot

Illustration to Johann Gottlieb Stephanie's comedy 'Die abgedankten Officiers'. (The Redundant Officers)

Cugnot's Artillery Transporter – The full-scale version of 1771
Developed from the small-scale prototype of 1770, this machine was completed in June 1771, but lost its funding before it could show its paces in field trials. The oval-shaped boiler had a capacity of about 500 litres, and was contained in the pot-shaped firebox which projected from the front of the vehicle. The initial heating was provided by a fire lit on the ground below the firebox. Thereafter the driver would have stopped periodically to feed the flames from logs taken from the wicker basket suspended beneath the seat. The boiler would have to be replenished with water at further stops at every 10 kilometres or so. The two high-pressure bronze cylinders each drove a ratchet drive one-quarter of a rotation, and worked alternately to give continuous motion. Adjustments to the ratchet at the halt enabled the machine to go into reverse. On a firm, level road the vehicle would have proceeded at walking pace and carried a load of 4–5 tons of artillery, evidently lashed to the loading platform. The cross-country mobility would have been limited drastically by, among other things, the immense weight which bore on the single driving wheel, and the very great stresses carried by the pivot. Cugnot's designs were nevertheless the first essays in steam locomotion, and rested on principles which he explored in the 1750s when he was still in the Austrian service.

had indeed quit the Austrian army, and with Gribeauval's support and that of the French War Ministry Cugnot made such progress that by March 1770 he was able to demonstrate his first working machine, a reduced model of an artillery tractor which travelled at a slow walking pace for 12 or 15 minutes before it literally ran out of steam. The device as it existed was plainly unsuitable for its stated purpose, but Cugnot had devised one means of translating linear movement of steam pistons into continuous rotation, and he was sufficiently encouraged to begin work on a full-scale version. The new machine was ready in June 1771, but the duc de Choiseul, the patron of the Gribeauval and therefore indirectly of Cugnot, had by now resigned, and there was no money to support the demonstration. The project therefore lapsed.

Gribeauval's role in all of this awaits elucidation. The opinion of Cugnot, although a junior officer, had been sufficiently regarded in Vienna that his complaint of being passed over had precipitated an elaborate investigation into the Austrian engineering corps (see p. 31). It is not beyond the bounds of possibility that Gribeauval recognised the potential of Cugnot's experiments from the start, and was ready to seize on anything that might extract him from the Austrian service.

Meanwhile a number of senior Austrian officers had become not insignificant figures in European culture. Leopold-Philippe duc d'Arenberg (1690–1756) is known outside the military context as a promoter of polite literature. Although he is now forgotten, the engineering general Philipp Harsch earned a reputation in his time as a skilful flautist and a supporter of musicians. The musical talents of the composer Carl Ditters von Dittersdorf were uncovered by *FM*. Joseph

Friedrich Prince Sachsen-Hildburghausen, who proved to be a generous master, just as the name of Nicolaus Esterházy survives not as a general or an *Inhaber* of a regiment, but as the patron of Haydn.

Much of the behaviour of the Austrian officers differed only in degree from that of the officers in other armies, and it could hardly have been otherwise, when the 'Austrians' were drawn from so many different regions of Europe. What marked out these 'Austrians' from everybody else except the English was their chauvinism, which seems at first sight to be a contradiction in terms, but makes sense if we consider it as the product of a need to reinforce a corporate identity when it had no single national foundation. When it was impossible to give a precise definition of the word 'Austrian,' a brotherhood of sorts could still be built up by a common animosity to the population of wherever the army happened to be. 'Our people are… coarse-grained, especially in their behaviour towards foreigners. They scorn them and they scorn their religion, which engenders hatred in return'.[273]

8

Adam Bauer— The Austrian Private Soldier

> Adam Bauer, born in Prague, 20 years of age, Catholic by religion and baker by trade, unmarried, no previous service, has in return for a bounty of eight florins enlisted voluntarily in the infantry regiment of … at Baden in Lower Austria on 1 January 1749, and has been fitted out with complete new uniform, musket and side arms.
>
> (Specimen enlistment form, *Instruction fur die Kriegs-Commissariatische Beamten*, 1749, 9)

Recruitment

Systems of Recruitment

Possible Alternatives

In the autumn of 1758 Vienna resolved to capture the Prussian fortress of Neisse, and the authorities succeeded in putting together a sizeable corps for this purpose with no apparent difficulty. A French observer was prompted to write to his minister of war that he had been 'very surprised when this army appeared on the scene… it proves that this power has limitless sources of manpower'.[1] Three years later the Austrians were able to maintain their strength in the field only with the greatest difficulty. The Prussians, however, were in a still worse state, and Maria Theresa would probably have brought the war to a triumphal conclusion if her Russian allies had stood by her.

In these terms the manning of the Austrian army must be accounted a success – a success that was all the more unlikely because Maria Theresa and her ministers were unable to devise any coherent and uniform system of recruiting. Every foreign model was ultimately found to be inappropriate. A patent of 4 August 1753 had proclaimed the setting-up of a permanent *Complettirungs-Mannschaft* of 24,000 men, to which each of the provinces was to contribute according to the size of its population. These part-time soldiers were supposed to be drilled for four months of every year by officers and NCOs from the regular regiments stationed nearby, and they would serve as a pool of manpower for the army in wartime. The scheme was the inspiration of Wenzel Kasimir Baron Netolitzky, as President of the Bohemian administration (*Repräsentation und Cammer*), who probably wished to combine features of the well-established French Milice, and the still more effective Prussian system of cantonal recruiting (to the extent of stipulating neck stocks of Prussian-style red for the recruits). Neither the central government nor the *Stände* did anything to put the scheme into effect, and the *Complettirungs-Mannschaft* fell into abeyance without a single drill having taken place.

In the autumn of 1761 Heinrich Cajetan Count Blümegen (President of the Moravian administration) proposed that the Austrians should adopt the Prussian system of cantonal recruiting outright. The project was superficially attractive, but it was rejected by Kaunitz in a magnificent memorandum which showed a deep understanding of the nature of the Austrian and Prussian armies and societies. Cantonal recruitment certainly provided every Prussian regiment with a reliable core of locally recruited conscripts, but at the price of giving the Prussian captains near-tyrannical power over the communities. Such 'slavery,' argued Kaunitz, would be unacceptable in the Habsburg domains, and incompatible with two elements of the Austrian military tradition, namely those of the multi-national regiments, and of the constantly-changing garrison locations.[2]

The principle of general conscription as such, repeatedly recommended by Prince Liechtenstein during the Seven Years War, was adopted only in 1780. Having rejected standing militia or reserves, and the obligation of universal military service, the state was therefore thrown back on its historic means of recruiting for the army. These were:

> The enlistment (by force if necessary) of marginal elements of society, as devolved to the provincial *Stände*
> Voluntary enlistment by regimental recruiting officers.

Recruiting by the Local Estates (Landständische Werbung)

The provincial assemblies raised altogether 215,546 units of manpower for service during the Seven Years War, whether *in natura* (actual men under arms), or by cash equivalents under the arrangement called *Reluition*. There was nothing novel about the principle of *Stände* recruiting in itself, for it had been instituted towards the end of the Thirty Years War, and became an important support of the army from 1690 (after Belgrade had been lost again to the Turks), but Maria Theresa and her counsellors hoped to put the thing on a new and more rational basis with the help of the great census of 1754, the first its kind in the Habsburg lands. This survey established the number of households in Hereditary Lands, and divided the population into male and female, married and unmarried, and into five age groups, of which the first to be listed was that of the men between 20 and 40 – in other words the population of military age. Maria Theresa wisely did not emphasise the military priority in the relevant decree, which stated cryptically that the census was being instituted 'for various reasons tending to the good of the Imperial service as also that of the public.'

The results of the census were available in 1755, and a first *Postulatum* (demand) for 6,000 recruits was made to be German Hereditary lands on the basis of one body from every 150 households. After a process of haggling the individual *Stände* promised to deliver the men by the end of the year, but the start of the war found the infantry still short by 10,455 men, or about 8 percent of its establishment of 130,690.

Further demands arrived at a rate of two, three or more for each of the war years, and non-compliance was met by a doubling of the quantity of recruits from the recalcitrant (*morosus*) province. Separate and heavy demands were made on the estates of the Austrian Netherlands (see p. 85). Although the Tyrol was exempt from the *StandischeWerbung*, the German and Hungarian Hereditary Lands bore a roughly equal share of the burden of this obligation.

For every recruit delivered, the central government reduced the *Contribution* (tax) due from the relevant *Stände* by 20 florins, on the supposition that the landowners would raise the men from the more expendable of their serfs or by rounding up vagabonds. Until the records of the *Stände* have been investigated it will be impossible to establish in detail how the unfortunates were enlisted, but a body of evidence suggests that the *Postulata* presented the provincial assemblies with intractable problems. Although Maria Theresa was willing to make due allowance which derived from 'manifest impossibility',[3] she was otherwise unrelenting, as the example of Styria will show.

On 13 May 1757 Maria Theresa demanded 1,100 men from the *Stände* of Styria, in addition to a first *Postulatum* of 1,538 recruits; a further 1,300 recruits were required on 19 December, by when the repeated calls were over-stretching the capacity of the province. By the end of the war Styria had furnished a total of 23,806 recruits *in natura,* which amounted to nearly half of the unmarried male population aged between 20 and 40, and left the wartime generation heavily depleted. Indeed the census of 1771 revealed only eight 35 year-olds in the entire Circle of Bruck.[4] In economic terms Upper Styria was hit disproportionately hard, on account of the effects on the salt- and ironworks – activities which likewise suffered in nearby Carinthia.

Hungary proper, if not Transylvania, seems to have answered the initial demands reasonably well, and the *Hofkriegsrath* noted that between 1 January and 15 April 1758 the Counties were able to raise 9,193 volunteer recruits.[5] By November 1759, however, recruiting in both Hungary and Transylvania was in a state of crisis. A commission under the presidency of Leopold Count Pálffy reported that the regiments of Hungarian infantry were 4,881 men under-strength, a deficiency which was likely to amount to 7,000 by the end of the campaign. The normally popular hussars were deficient by 1,219 men, or by 7,219 if Maria Theresa carried through her intention to increase the establishment of the individual regiments from 1,000 men to 1,500. The commission stated that these new demands were likely to worsen the already greatly depleted manpower of the kingdom of Hungary, 'which is thinly populated in proportion to its extent'.[6]

In Transylvania, the newly appointed Commanding General *FML.* Immanuel Voghtern was alarmed to learn early in 1758 how the officials of the various Counties and Districts had so terrorised the Wallachians by their brutal ways of recruiting that the young men had fled to the woods *en masse* and were now living as outlaws. The officials persisted in 'binding the forcibly-enlisted recruits hand and foot, and dragging them here [to Hermannstadt] in chains to be enrolled. Bishop Baron de Sala himself was responsible for having more than 40 of them… brought here in fetters under heavy escort… the uprooting of the Wallachians will surely bring further recruiting to an end, for not a single Hungarian or Saxon is being taken. Moreover the fields will be left uncultivated, which will lead to a general falling-away of the contributions.'

Voghtern appointed a commission to investigate the problem. This body decided to put an immediate end to the forcible conscription, and publish proclamations in the German, Latin, Hungarian and Wallachian languages to make it known to all the peoples of Transylvania, 'but especially, through discreet means, to the runaway Wallachians, that the only men to be enlisted will be the ones who wish to become soldiers, and voluntarily and without coercion choose to contract for service for two or three years, or the duration of the present war'.[7]

Young men were already fleeing from the Inner Austrian provinces to seek refuge in the depths of the woods or the wilds of Hungary and Croatia, and on 13 May 1758 the *Hofkriegsrath* asked *FM.* d'Aspremont-Lynden to issue a comparable amnesty.[8]

Mass evasion of another kind was being practised by the young folk who suddenly discovered a vocation for the dishonourable trade of slaughterman, and thereby rendered themselves ineligible for military service. The Moravian *Reprdsentation and Cammer* asked the *Hofkriegsrath* for a ruling on the matter, and was told that the slaughtermen by family trade were still inadmissible, but the others were to be taken on after they had been made 'honourable' by due military ceremonies.[9]

In such circumstances, any men who could be inveigled or forced into filling the quotas of the *Stände* recruits became valuable commodities. In 1760 the cavalry regiments complained that most of their recruits were being taken back by their feudal lords, who then put them forward again as *Stände* levies for the infantry (a much less popular branch of the service). The *Directorium* ordered the practice to be halted.[10] The desperation of the *Stände* is revealed still more clearly by their desire to enlist Prussian deserters by holding out huge bounties, an issue which will be examined shortly.

It is clear that bodies were still more difficult for the *Stände* to obtain than cash. The practice of *Relution* (money substitution) therefore brought some relief to the localities, at the same time as it provided Vienna with money which could be devoted to more productive ways of generating recruits. In May 1758 Maria Theresa, against her immediate inclinations, admitted this principle for Transylvania, where it was being urged by *FML.* Voghtern, 'bearing in mind that the forcible enlistment of recruits has turned the subjects against the military life.'[11] In August 1759 the Lower Austrian *Stände* and the Upper Styrian mining authorities asked for urgent relief from the demands on their manpower, which were now having serious economic consequences. Maria Theresa was persuaded, and she granted *Reluition* on an altogether unprecedented scale (see p. 44–45), namely to Lower Austria for 1,000 of its obligation in recruits, to Upper Styria for two-thirds of its obligation, to Carinthia and Carniola for one-third, and total exemption to designated mining towns of Bohemia and manufacturing towns of Upper Austria. The *Reluition* was set at an initial 40 florins per recruit, which was much less than the *Stände* were now willing to pay for Prussian deserters and other cannon fodder.

Voluntary Enlistment

Immediately after the War of the Austrian Succession Maria Theresa flattered herself that she could recruit her army entirely from volunteers. Indeed the vision of being freed from the obligation of providing recruits was one of the inducements which persuaded the *Stände* to make over their taxation revenues to her for spreads of years at a time. A decree of 21 December 1748 therefore authorised the regiments to set up recruiting centres in the districts where they were garrisoned, and the *Commissariat* Instructions of 1749 described voluntary enlistment as the basic and most desirable means of completing the army.[12]

Maria Theresa ought to have known that the prospect of lifelong service as an infantryman would deter all but the most feckless and stupid folk from joining the army as foot soldiers. The shrewd *General-Kriegscommissar* Franz Ludwig Salburg warned that voluntary enlistment would not answer the needs of a new war, and in fact the scheme collapsed even more quickly than he had prophesied, for three-quarters of the 20,000 new recruits deserted in the summer of 1749. In the following year Maria Theresa had to appeal to the Bohemian *Stände* to gather up 3,000 recruits as a gesture of goodwill, and in 1752 she made a new and heavy demand on both Bohemia and Austria. By then there was little more talk of benevolent intentions.

Unpredictable and uncontrollable though it was, voluntary enlistment remained an essential component of recruiting, and its relative importance increased in the course of the Seven Years War, when the provinces proved unequal to sustaining the *Stände* enlistment. For most of the war the regiments recruited on their own account, though in the middle of 1761 Maria Theresa substituted a *General-Werbung,* whereby recruits were thrown into a pool for the whole army.[13] The regimental recruiting parties were thereby deprived of any particular incentive, and Daun protested that the effect would be to 'send many fine men back to the enemy'.[14] The *General-Werbung* was abandoned in its turn, and on 14 October 1762 the *Hofkriegsrath* ordered the regimental recruiting to be resumed with all urgency, and made the sum of 50 florins available for every man enlisted by the 'German' regiments.

The recruiting of the regiments of Luzan and Clerici was financed by the revenues of Austrian Italy, just as the Netherlands national recruiting was supported by the funds of the Netherlands.[15] The recruiting for the Tyroler *Land- and Feld-Regiment* was administered directly from Vienna, since the Tyrol was free from the obligation of *Stände* recruiting, and did little or nothing to support the regimental effort.

The voluntary recruiting was prosecuted throughout the monarchy (with the exception of the Military Borders), and also in Germany, where it was thought to yield particular advantages, for it not only spared the thin population of the Hereditary Lands, but deprived potential recruits to the Prussians. In the early years of the Seven Years War a number of princes, knights, clerics, cities and towns of Germany showed their solidarity with the Emperor by putting useful quantities of recruits and money at his disposal, quite apart their contributions to the *Reichsarmee,* and the regiments signed over to the Austrian service by Würzburg and Mainz. By March 1759, when the practice came to an end, the well-affected Germans had delivered about 4,000 recruits *in natura,* and 175,791 florins by way of *Reluition*. The largest single contingents of men had been given by the ecclesiastical electorates of Trier (2,000) and Mainz (800), the territory of Eichstadt (400) and the bishopric of Salzburg (200). Fifty-four princes, knights, ecclesiastical communities or municipalities had made cash grants, led by the Prince zu Mury (10,833 florins) and the Bishop of Fulda (10,000). Smaller sums had been advanced by Cologne, Aachen, Regensburg, Nuremberg, Rothenburg-ob-der-Tauber, Augsburg and Heilbronn, a large number of the little towns of Swabia, and by 15 abbeys or convents.[16]

Meanwhile the recruiting parties of the individual Austrian regiments had been competing with each other, with the recruiters from allies, enemies and neutrals, and from the increasingly-desperate *Stände* of the Hereditary Lands which were ultimately offering gigantic bounties.[17]

The Austrian *Feld-Kriegs Commissar* Weiss had meanwhile been collecting the men and money donated directly by the *Reich* in the way just described, but he had no power to coordinate the activities of the Austrians. On 1 November 1758 he therefore urged the need to create a unified system, and he cited the varying experiences of the Austrian recruiting parties.[18]

These representations proved effective. Early in 1759 *GFWM*. Würzburg was commissioned to direct a new *Reichs-Werbung*, which would recruit in Germany for the army as a whole. Würzburg was an energetic individual, and he got the scheme off to a promising start, aided by the balance of 68,951 florins remaining from the *Reluition* advanced by the Germans (above), and by substantial grants from Colloredo's *Reichs-Canzley* and the *Staats-Canzley*. By August, however, Würzburg had become weary of the paper-work and wished to see active service with the *Reichsarmee*, while the recruiting chest was running out of money. The *Directorium* reported the impending crisis to Maria Theresa on 13 August, and suggested a number of remedies. It was important to stop the *Stände* of the Habsburg lands from competing for recruits in Germany; as for the missing funds, they could be replaced by partial *Reluition* for the manpower obligations from Lower Austria and a number of the provinces of Inner Austria, and by commuting in their entirety the obligations of the Austrian and Bohemian mining and manufacturing centres. These proposals were adopted (above).

Not even a direct order from the *Hofkriegsrath* could prevent Würzburg leaving for the *Reichsarmee in* the spring of 1760, but *GFWM*. Burmann proved to be an acceptable successor,[19] and he gave the *Reichs-Werbung* a new lease on life. There was intermittent competition for recruits by the individual Austrian regiments, but the central authorities continued to pursue an aggressive and co-ordinated recruiting policy in the *Reich*. Colloredo had to reprove the *Hofkriegsrath* for proposing to steal a large number of Germans who were on their way to the army of Piedmont-Sardinia, while the *Hofkriegsrath in* turn reproved Burmann for having detained a party of would-be Dutch soldiers in Cologne.[20]

How the Recruits were Raised

The *Stände* tried to meet Maria Theresa's demands by rounding up vagabonds and the more useless of their serfs, and making up the shortfall by cash *Reluition* or recruiting among Prussian deserters and in the *Reich* (above). However most of the volunteers were enlisted by parties detached from the individual regiments, or by professional recruiters like the Swiss Major Gottram, or the semi-criminal Colonel Tottleben who we discover recruiting for the Austrians in 1757.

The central or provincial funds allowed a certain sum for every man who could be persuaded to enter the service, from which money the recruiters had to offer their target an enticing bounty, and still have enough remaining to fit him up with a uniform. The allowance could rise to 40 or 50 florins for recruits in the *Reich*, where there was a good deal of competition, and where the more humbly-born Austrian officers made a poor impression alongside their stylish Prussian counterparts.[21]

Much smaller sums were set aside for recruiting in Hungary, and Maria Theresa was displeased to learn that so little benefit had been derived from the 10 florins per man which had been assigned to the recruiters of the regiment of Adam Batthyány in 1761. Seven or eight florins of this paltry sum were somehow diverted along the way, and the numerous recruiting parties had failed to enlist a single man over the course of four weeks.[22]

The authorities wisely left the recruiters a free reign when it came to the tactics of their trade. A typical party consisted of an officer, a senior NCO, a clerk (*Fourier*), a medical orderly (*Feldscher*), and selected musicians, corporals and soldiers – 'and the last three categories should be chosen from the best and the tallest men in the regiment'.[23] It was a good idea to dress the party in exotic uniforms, to give the impression that it was recruiting for a new regiment. Some days should be spent in getting the feel of a locality, and two or three days more in hanging about the village fair – and then, when the peasants ran short of money and began to fight – it would be easy to prevail on the trouble-makers to enlist, as an alternative to judicial punishment.[24]

From his experiences in the Empire *GFWM*. Burmann owned frankly that 'when we go recruiting in the inns our efforts must be reinforced by a glass of wine, beer or spirits, for rarely or never will a recruit enlist in the open air, or betake himself to a recruiting house to be signed up'.[25] Cogniazzo adds that the recruit finally came to his senses when he awakened on the hard floor of a guard house, but by then it would be too late for him to do anything about it.[26] It is scarcely surprising to find distraught mothers appealing to the authorities for the return of sons who had been snatched from them 'through fraud and force'.[27]

Most of what has just been presented applies only to enlistment in the infantry, where the service was hard, dangerous and to a large degree mechanical. It was a different story among most of the mounted troops, for 'there is not a country in the world where men would not much prefer to serve in the cavalry'.[28] The cavalry were better paid than the foot soldiers, they prided themselves on their sense of honour, and they drew most of their recruits from men who genuinely volunteered their services. Carl Paul Pálffy represented in December 1758 that 'the heavy cavalry… in particular deserves different and better horses, and taller, stronger and finer recruits than have so far been supplied to the regiments by the *Stände*'.[29]

Maria Theresa had in fact already resolved that the cuirassiers and dragoons would no longer tap the *Stände* conscription, but instead prosecute their recruiting in designated areas (*Rayons*) (See Appendix VIII: Designated Recruiting *Rayons* for the Cavalry). However the regiments were unable to raise enough men from the *Rayons* to supply their needs, because the recruits were being reclaimed by the *Stände* for the infantry, and Maria Theresa had to allow the cavalry to gain its revenge by drawing volunteers from the *Stände* recruits, with the cuirassiers having the first choice. She nevertheless stipulated that the taller men must always go into the infantry (below), and that nobody must be forced to serve in the cavalry if he preferred to serve in the infantry[30] – which must have been a rare happening.

The recruiting of the gunners passes virtually without comment in the official documents. The artillerymen formed a distinct class, and they replenished themselves through family and local connections, and by drawing on students and other individuals who were fit to contribute to a 'learned' arm.

Qualifications, Disqualifications and Conditions

Height
The heights of the soldiers were not entered in the Austrian muster lists at the time of the Seven Years War. It is therefore impossible to present the height of the men in a systematic way, and the evidence regarding stature, although copious, is therefore largely indirect.

According to calculations made in France in 1778 only one Frenchman in 30 stood five foot or more tall, while a stipulated height of five feet three inches would have required a population base of 79,000 souls to produce 400 men.[31] Five foot three was the official minimum demanded for recruits for the Austrian infantry and cavalry, and that requirement was formidable, even if we accept that the men coming to military age in the Seven Years War were taller than those of the 1770s,[32] and that most Hungarians, Moravians, Bohemians and Austrians were taller than most Frenchmen.

While the taller soldiers could load and wield the long, heavy muskets with greater ease, Cogniazzo maintains that 'it is no longer a question of dispute among military men of experience that the troops of middling height are the best fitted to withstand marching and fatigue.' This fact was borne home to him when the Austrian army went to war in 1756, and again during the forced marches in the later campaigns.[33]

The pressure for some kind of relaxation became irresistible, and on 13 December 1758 the *Hofkriegsrath* made a first concession, which was in favour of the *Stände* recruits from Styria, and it informed Daun that he could take on men 'in a discreet way' (*dissimulando*) if they did not meet the letter of the regulations, but were otherwise strong and healthy.[34]

More and more exceptions were made in the course of the war. Lower Austrian peasants were already being accepted under the minimum height, and assigned first to the *Staabs-Infanterie-Regiment,* and then to the artillery as unskilled *Stück-Knechte,* while five feet two inches was taken as an acceptable minimum for the *Stände* recruits from Hungary.[35] Finally in June 1761 Maria Theresa decided that although the requirement of five feet three inches must stand for official purposes, she was willing to take men under that height if they were otherwise 'suitable for service'.[36]

While height could be measured against marks on a wall or a stick, the ultimate decision (*Superarbitrium*) as to the acceptability of a recruit hung on this 'suitability for service' as well as the stature. As the *Stände,* the Commissaries, the medical personnel and the officers all had a hand in processing the recruits, the question of acceptability occasioned delays and confusions until the end of the war.[37]

The rules were applied more rigorously and consistently to recruits from the Germany. In November 1759 the *Reichscanzley* complained that the official minimum of five feet three inches had reduced recruiting in the lordships of Austrian Swabia to virtually nil, and that a modest reduction of one inch would bring in many hundreds of men who were now being lost to foreign armies.[38] Maria Theresa had nevertheless given a positive order that nobody under the regulation height was acceptable, and we find that in March 1760 the ruling applied to Germany as a whole.[39]

There was a long and never entirely resolved conflict concerning the acceptability for the cuirassiers and dragoons. The officers of the German cavalry were glad to accept volunteers from among the *Stände* recruits, but they were alarmed to discover that all of the taller men were being creamed off for service with the infantry (above). Five of the colonels represented that the smaller men were unable to meet either the physical or psychological demands of the service, and *G.d.C.* Carl O'Donnell forwarded their protest to Daun, with a covering letter which indicated his support (see p. 283).[40]

The *Hofkriegsrath* tried to persuade the colonels in question that they had no cause for alarm, for the cavalry was still being allowed to recruit men up to a height of five feet four inches. However the infantry were still greedy for tall men for their grenadiers, and the *Hofkriegsrath* became less and less insistent on a minimum height for the German cavalry, considering that stature was less important for that service than strength and general aptitude.[41]

Admissible Age

Recruits were generally accepted between the ages of 18 and 45. This was a remarkably wide span, and it must have been wider still when we consider the potential for misrepresentation that was open to both the recruit and his recruiter. Daun wrote to Maria Theresa in October 1761:

today I saw 20 recruits, and it makes me want to cry. It's true that the officials declared them acceptable, but they are just babies. I am not given to exaggerate, but I have to say that they are worse than the ones I had reason to send away from the camp at Königgrätz, and yet recruits of this kind are being received by most of the regiments… It seems very poor economy to take on recruits of this description, for we still have to provide for their upkeep, and the cost is increased by that of the hospitals, which are full of boys like this.[42]

Stipulated Length of Service

Until the end of the Seven Years War, most of Maria Theresa's regular troops left the colours only through death, desertion or physical collapse. The first exceptions seem to have been among the Netherlands national regiments, where recruits were being taken on by *Capitulation* (contract) for a six-year term of service, on the expiry of which the payment of *Ersatz-Geld* for the recruiting of a substitute entitled them to their release. The regiment of Claude de Ligne was a special case, for the captains had raised the companies at their own cost in 1742, and demanded no *Ersatz-Geld* from the recruits. They therefore believed themselves entitled to retain the men indefinitely, and the *Musterung* of 1755 discovered men who had served for 12 years, which amounted to double the normal term. The Commissaries supported the soldiers' petition to be released, for they would otherwise regard their service as slavery, which would have 'a most deleterious effect on the recruiting in the Netherlands, which is already going badly'.[43]

On 27 December 1757 the *Hofkriegsrath* authorised the Italian national regiments of Luzan and Clerici to offer *Capitulations* for six years or the duration of the war[44] and on 4 January 1758, a matter of days later, a Military Conference discussed the practicability of offering *Capitulations* throughout the infantry and cavalry. Some of the members argued for a term of two years, which would have been extremely short, but Maria Theresa and the majority settled on the 'Clerici' terms.[45] The final decree of 3 April 1758 authorised the *Stände* of the German Hereditary Lands to offer *Capitulations* to all potential-recruits when the time came to meet the next *Postulata*.[46] It soon transpired that regiments recruiting in the *Reich* were at an advantage if they could offer flexible terms of this kind,[47] and from October 1758 attractive three-year *Capitulations* were made available to Prussian deserters. It is safe to say that by the end of the war nearly all Austrian private soldiers were listed as serving on contract.

From the outset the authorities held out the prospect of advancement to NCO to all such Austrian, Bohemian and Moravian recruits who could write German as well as speak it, and in April 1762 these men were told that they would not be retained beyond the end of their agreed term of service, 'so that promotion will in no way act to their disadvantage'.[48] This assurance was very needful, for the actual date of release still hung upon the decision of the troops' superiors.

By November 1761 several regiments asked for guidance concerning those time-expired Capitulants who had taken the matter into their own hands and deserted, whereupon Maria Theresa ruled that all Capitulants who made off without permission would be punished like other deserters, with a concession being made for those who would otherwise have been executed on account of 'aggravating' circumstances, such as deserting a sentry post; these people would still be sentenced to death, but would undergo forced labour instead of being sent to the scaffold.[49]

In February 1762 O'Donnell, as acting commander of the field army, ordered several time-expired Capitulants of the regiment of Salm to be punished with 'measured severity' for 'having failed to show due respect' at a mustering.[50] However the *Hofkriegsrath* gave a sympathetic reception to Capitulants who had the patience to go through the proper channels. On 27 November 1762 it asked Maria Theresa for the free release, amongst others, of the soldier Rochus Pfeiffer of the infantry regiment of Kollowrat, who had been wounded five times over, and had twice escaped from Prussian captivity; another deserving double escapee, Johann Nagy of the infantry regiment of Alt-Colloredo, had likewise served beyond his allotted term, and had made the reasonable request to be allowed to return to civilian life to support his wife and children.

On balance the recruiting by *Capitulation* was a flexible system which helped the state to meet the demands of manning during the wartime emergency, yet relieved it of the burden of a permanently-enlarged establishment; at the same time it attracted to the army men who would otherwise have rejected the notion of life-long military service. Several years after the war *FM*. Philipp Ludwig Moltike stated that he was glad to have 642 Capitulants in his regiment, and that these people provided some of his best NCOs.[51] The advantages were summarised by Cogniazzo, who observed that the celebrated loyalty of the Croats in fact owed a great deal to the fixed duration of their service, as well as to their national spirit and family connections. He also pointed out the single danger – a justified one, as we have seen – that the state would not live up to its side of the bargain, and would fail to release the men at the end of their agreed term of service.[52]

Bounty

Bounty money was the sum that was spread before the prospective recruits by the recruiting officer, in the hope that in their desperate or drink-befuddled state the inducement of cash would impel them to embrace the military life. The cost of the bounty was met from the *Werbegeld* (recruiting money), which was the sum set aside to meet all the expenses of recruiting, including (from the *Intercalar* system of 1758) the fitting-out of the man with his uniform. The size of the bounty varied according to the source of the recruiting funds (the Italian and Netherlands revenues, and the *Directorium* as well as the *Hofkriegsrath*), the location of the recruiting and the competition which might be encountered there, and the good management of the regiment.[53]

In October 1761 Daun urged Maria Theresa that it would be useful for the regiments to have considerable reserves of cash in hand, so that they could snap up Prussian deserters when opportunity offered.[54] These representations seem to have had their effect, for early the next year Maria Theresa resolved to allow the regiments *Werbegeld* at a rate of 50 florins per head, with the uniforms on top, and to meet the cost from the *Reluition* which had been promised by the *Stände* – raising the money by 'executive action' if necessary.[55]

Towards the end of the war recruits were unlikely to be generated by any bounty less than this stipulated 50 florins per head. By this time also the needs of the belligerents were being exploited by a mass of rootless German mercenaries: 'The Germans from the Rhine, the Main and the upper Danube go along with the winners. If the Emperor is prospering they desert to him from the King of Prussia, and they go back again if fortune favours the king'.[56] Already by 1758 the *Stände* were offering to pay up to 80 florins' bounty to every Prussian deserter, and those men had scarcely reached their regiments before they deserted again. They spent the winter hiding among the peasants, and emerged the next spring to re-engage for another magnificent bounty. 'That is the cause of the constant gaps among the regiments once the army is on campaign. Even when the men are recognised as deserters, the commander cannot return them to their original regiments, but has to turn a blind eye and leave them in whatever regiment they are now encountered'.[57]

The experienced *GFWM*. Burmann warned the authorities that they must also be on their guard against misrepresentation on the part of the recruiters. He recommended that two NCOs should be on hand to make sure that every recruit signified his enlistment by signature or mark, so that the recruiting officer accounted properly for his bounty money. The NCOs would also keep an eye on the examining medical orderlies, 'for on occasions of this kind the orderlies can become very timorous, and, fearing physical violence, they reject recruits on account of the slightest physical defect; these men are then enlisted by the *Stände* for huge bounties'.[58]

The Background of the Recruit

Undesirables
Earlier in the 18th century deep-rooted political and cultural traditions had prohibited the recruiting of Jews, gypsies, French and Italians: 'there is not much to be done with people like that, for they do not fit in well with our style of *Cameradschaft* [the body of tent companions], and they are great deserters and loudmouths who go from one service to another, and lead astray and corrupt good men'.[59] Again in 1749 the officials of the *Commissariat* were told to exclude householding townsmen and peasants and their only sons, and servants who had been dismissed for dishonesty, as well as the prohibited races according to the old tradition.[60] By the time of the Seven Years War the prohibition on the Italians had been relaxed, to judge by the quantities of such people to be found in the regiments, though Frenchmen from within the historic borders were still rarities.

From the time of their victory at Kolin on 18 June 1757, until the middle of November of that year the Austrians reaped a first crop of 21,000 Prussian prisoners, even before their further success at Breslau (22 November). An officer noted that the number of Prussian deserters probably amounted to 40,000, but that the Austrians had not been able to derive proportional benefit, for the men who came to the army had been recruited by the *Stände* in the usual unsystematic way and had deserted again – either out of distaste for the white Austrian uniform, or to enlist again for a fresh bounty. The deserters must instead be entrusted to good officers and designated 'grenadiers'.[61]

Loudon was possibly the author of the paper in question. In any event he returned to this principle in 1759, when he proposed bringing suitable deserters together in two battalions of grenadiers. He based his thinking on considerations which might appear trivial to an observer, but which bulked large in the mentality of the Prussians,

> who by nature have a greater love of freedom than you find among our natives… There are a number of prerequisites:
> 1. These battalions must always be deployed on outpost duty with the Croats, and will therefore not be constrained in the same way as a regiment which camps in a line with the rest of the army,
> 2. They must be regarded as genuine 'grenadiers,' a name which awakens a certain pride among the ordinary soldiers – and pride matters a great deal to the Prussians,
> 3. They must have green coats instead of white, which will save them the labour of keeping them clean,
> 4. They must be recruited by *Capitulation,* and therefore not bound to life-long service.

Loudon had his way, and he was able to set up a highly successful regiment of 'Green Grenadiers' on his plan. This was however just one unit, and therefore only a partial solution to the problems posed by the masses of the Prussian prisoners and deserters. Some of Maria Theresa's advisers recognised that nothing positive could be done with the genuine Prussian patriots, who must be segregated from the other troops, 'whom they lead astray by their arguments, and the high opinion they impart concerning their king'.[63]

By the middle of the war the turn of fortune once more favoured the Austrians, and great numbers of Prussian deserters were roaming the countryside. In April 1760 Maria Theresa therefore ruled that the feudal lords must turn over all such people to be processed by five mixed civil and military commissions, sitting respectively in Prague, Brann, Linz, Troppau and Vienna. She hoped that it would now be possible to categorise the deserters in a useful way. Genuine volunteers for the Austrian army were to be taken on at a bounty of 30 florins, raised by *Reluition* from the *Stände.* Men who did not wish to enlist were to be given passes to travel to regions of the *Reich* or elsewhere which were remote from Prussian authority, and forbidden to return to the Habsburg lands. The Prussian deserters as a whole were to undergo careful examination, and suspicious characters detained as prisoners of war.[64]

Nothing more is heard of the commissions, and in October 1760 we find the *Hofkriegsrath* arranging for intelligent officers to tour the localities where the Prussian prisoners were being held to offer *Capitulations* for the duration of the war; the immediate bounty amounted to only 16 florins, but 30 florins in addition would be given to the men when they came to the end of their engagements. Vienna was confident that the men would flood in from this source, and the *Stände* were told that they could redeem up to one-quarter of their obligation in recruits for cash *Reluition* at a rate of 50 florins per head.[65]

By February 1761 Maria Theresa was forced to recognise that centralised recruiting was failing to meet the desperate need for manpower, and 'in order to fill the gaps which are now being seen in the army, I have resolved that from now onwards the regiments will be allowed to recruit on their own behalf, and take on men of all descriptions where and how they might be found: natives, vagabonds, deserters and discreetly – Prussian prisoners of war… even if they are born Prussians and Brandenburgers'.[66]

Thus an old and wise precaution was cast aside. In the same month a court martial passed sentence of death by hanging on the Lutheran Brunswicker Johann Heinrich Bittner – an ex-Prussian soldier who had spent nine months in an Austrian regiment of infantry, then a similar time in the *Sappeurs-Corps* before he deserted. He admitted that he had long intended to return to the Prussians, and 'on 22 October last year, when the Corps marched from Reinerz, he remained there with this object in mind. After travelling by side paths he reached Gabersdorf near Wartha; there he pretended that he had been sent to an officer of his Corps who was sick in bed, and asked the nearest way to Reichenbach.' At this an Austrian officer became suspicious and placed him under arrest, and further proof of the man's perfidy came to light when he was found to be in possession of a knapsack he had stolen from a comrade.[67] Loudon intervened to commute the sentence to one of 10 years' fortress labour. The case was not untypical, and it revealed a hankering after the Prussian service on the part of one who was neither a born Brandenburger nor a born Pomeranian.

The figures for desertion from the Austrian army in the summer of 1762 (p. 235) show that nearly twice the numbers of enlisted prisoners of war had made themselves scarce as the ex-Prussian deserters, who could still have a useful role. In the experience of the Prince de Ligne, the Prussian deserters were 'nimble, brave and determined individuals. We ought to take them on'.[68] As for the ex-prisoners of war, the *Hofkriegsrath* and Daun concluded that the best thing to be done with them was to consign them to remote garrisons in Italy, Hungary or Transylvania, where they could do the least damage if they decided to make trouble.[69]

Nationality

An earlier chapter of the present book touched on the singularity of the many nations which were represented in the army, and we shall turn shortly to the character of the 'Austrian soldiers as a whole. A total of 107,083 other ranks (excluding the Croatian infantry and the *Grenz-Husaren*) may be identified by place of birth from our muster lists:

Other Ranks by Place of Birth	
Bohemia:	28.14%
Hungary:	15.20
(17.40 with Transylvania)	
The *Reich:*	11.95
Moravia:	11.06

Upper and Lower Austria, with Vienna:	9.71
Prussian Silesia:	5.18
Netherlands and Luxembourg:	5.41
Styria:	2.27
Transylvania:	2.20
Carniola:	1.13
Poland:	0.90
Carinthia:	0.80
Prussia (other than Silesia):	0.69
Tyrol:	0.58
Austrian Silesia:	0.57
Croatia, Austrian Italy, Alsace:	0.41 each
Italy (not Austrian governed):	0.38
Switzerland:	0.37
Görz and Gradisca, Lorraine:	0.36 each
Vorder Osterreich:	0.27
France (other than Alsace and Lorraine):	0.24
Holland:	0.14
Slavonia:	0.09
England with Scotland, Liège, Russia:	0.07 each
Spain:	0.05
Denmark:	0.04
Sweden, Swedish Pomerania:	0.03 each
Ireland:	0.008
Dalmatia:	0.007

Religion
The covert Protestants of Bohemia, Moravia, the Austrian lands, and probably also some regions of Hungary and the *Reich* would have been unwilling to declare their confessional allegiance openly, which makes the evidence of the muster lists particularly unreliable in this respect, apart from showing the clear predominance of Catholics in the cavalry:

Religion of Private Soldiers in the Regular Infantry and Cavalry

	Infantry	Cuirassiers	Dragoons
Catholics:	93.92%	97.76	99.17
Lutherans:	5.31	2.19	0.80
Calvinists:	0.75*	0.03	0.01

* Almost entirely in the Hungarian infantry.

Civilian Trades
Men who were accustomed to hard and continuous skilled or semi-skilled labour, like blacksmiths, butchers, masons and ploughmen, were considered particularly suitable for the military life, while students could make good NCOs or gunners. It is not easy to assess how damaging was the withdrawal of this labour from civilian life, or how representative were the soldiers of the economy in their native lands. Here it is perhaps worth quoting the Duke of Wellington in relation to the British army of the Napoleonic Wars: 'The man who enlists in the British Army is, in general, the

most drunken and probably the worst man of the trade in which he belongs, in the town or village in which he lives.'

A recruit might declare such and such a trade to a Commissary when he enlisted, but we have no means of telling whether it was a full-or part-time employment, or what degree of skill he attained in it. Except for natives of Vienna and Prague the townsmen are virtually absent from the Austrian muster lists, which shows that the Austrian army, unlike the French army of the time[70] had an overwhelmingly rural character, and yet, apart from a few tenders of vineyards, there is no mention of the agricultural labour which must have been the daily work of most of the recruits. A memorandum of 1758 claimed that the effect of recruiting on rural life had been exaggerated:

> As proof… we just have to look at the situation of the genuine peasant, and we will find that he has the means of employing a number of workers to cultivate his land, and that women will meet the call for work of other kinds. Thus, if we take away one of his sons, the only damage to his economy will be the loss of one pair of hands, which, as a peasant, he ought to be able to replace by taking on more labour.[71]

The peasants in question can only have been the free or nearly-free small landowners of Upper and Lower Austria. All the other evidence suggests that the *Stände* of the German Hereditary Lands were unwilling in the extreme to see their productive serfs taken as soldiers, and that they were prepared to pay very heavily for substitutes of one kind or another.

The occupations of the time defy scientific categorisation, and not least when it is necessary to match standard German terminology with local variations and (for the Netherlands regiments) with French trade descriptions. For the sake of convenience the former civilian trades of the soldiers are here grouped into 11 broad categories, related less by speciality and skills than by the way they fitted into economic life (See Appendix IX: Civilian Trades by Category). More than one-quarter of the soldiers declared a civilian trade upon being recruited, and out of a total of 30,700 about two-thirds (20,863) of these men came from Habsburg territories.

	Habsburg Territories Only	Overall
Former Civilian Trades of All Military Personnel by Categories		
Textile:	13.87%	13.00
Manufacture & upkeep of clothing & footware:	27.51	27.77
Building and furnishing:	12.90	13.46
Food Processing:	17.46	17.28
Mining and metal working:	5.64	5.91
Manufacturing & processing: 8.22	8.19	
Transport-related trades:	1.98	2.16
Medical:	1.84	2.34
Students:	2.67	2.43
Service trades:	7.47	7.05
Unidentifiable:	0.14	0.15
Leading Former Trades (first 20 only)		
Tailor:	12.67	13.26
Butcher:	6.86	6.54
Weaver (wool/cotton):	6.24	5.26

Carpenter/cabinet maker:	6.28	6.61
Cobbler:	6.11	6.31
Miller:	5.70	5.61
Shoemaker:	5.63	4.95
Mason:	5.31	5.25
Smith:	3.88	3.83
Gamekeeper:	3.13	3.24
Clothmaker:	2.67	2.53
Student:	2.66	2.41
Baker:	2.27	2.64
Linen weaver:	2.15	1.92
Cooper:	2.01	1.88
Brewer:	1.77	1.62
Locksmith:	1.54	1.61
Barber surgeon:	1.42	1.65
Gardener:	1.36	1.30
Stocking knitter:	1.27	1.50

The Soldier's Life

The New Soldier

Once a potential recruit had given passable signs of assent, the recruiting officer lost no time in pressing the bounty into his hand, and fitting him up with items of uniform as a sign that he was now *obligat*. In cases of emergency a cartridge pouch might be considered adequate, but in April 1758 Maria Theresa ordered that at the first opportunity the recruits were to be given uniforms complete with facings in the regimental colour.[72] Requirements of this kind could prove a considerable burden for the recruiting parties, for by November 1758 the 'extraordinary rise in the price of Iglau cloth' amounted to 84 percent since the beginning of the war, which brought the price of a full uniform with bayonet to 23 florins.[73] When the recruits happened to be rounded up by the *Stände,* the regiments were supposed to send parties to collect them – a process which was attended with considerable confusion, as Kaunitz complained.[74]

The recruits were led to the place of their *Assentirung,* the final stage of their induction, when a *Kriegs-Commissar* and a surgeon or medical orderly were supposed to verify that the men met all the specifications laid down for age and height, and did not fall into one of the forbidden categories. In time of peace it was normal for the recruits to be given some rudimentary training at the assembly point, and a little more on their way to the regiment. The chief recruiting officer designated an officer or NCO to travel ahead to deliver a detailed report on the new men, and 'when the officer arrives with his convoy he must see that the men are in full uniform, and clean and smart with curled hair, and marching in the regimental style to the sound of music, and in proper rank and file with muskets shouldered upright.' On arrival, the finest looking-men were likely to be chosen for the grenadiers, and the rest divided among the companies by having their names drawn from a hat.[75] This custom represented in miniature the policy of general recruiting as it applied to all except the 'national' regiments,

> and thus the recruits furnished by Bohemia and Moravia were distributed proportionately among all the German regiments. It was the same with the recruits from Austria, Styria, Carniola and Carinthia, so that each regiment included men from all the Hereditary Lands,

and, together with the recruits from the *Reich,* formed a compound in which one nation was indeed mixed with another, but not so closely connected as to ever give rise to undesirable consequences.[76]

Within the companies the NCOs proceeded to divide the recruits among the *Corporalschaften,* which were the basic social units of the army.

All of these procedures were subject to changes under the pressures of war. We find Neipperg talking in a Military Conference of 4 January 1758 of a great convoy of 4,000 recruits that was due to set out for the army in three columns, regardless of severe weather and the lack of shelter along the way. The men were clearly being sent directly to their future regiments, though in considerably greater batches than before. More often, however, the recruits were now being dispatched to intermediate regimental depots (*Depositories*), which were located near the theatre or war, or to the newly-established third or garrison battalions, which might well be stationed in a distant province.

The better-disposed soldiers were spurred on by their encounter with the novelties of military life, and, being unacquainted with danger, they went into action like heroes.[77] This precious resource was in fact threatened less by enemy bullets than by the infections which were liable to overwhelm the recruits who were thrown together in crowded conditions before age and acquired immunity could give them a degree of protection against disease.

By now a veteran soldier would have taken the recruit under his wing, and told him how to care for his person, clothing and equipment, and laid the foundation for the basic skills of his branch of the service. The foot soldier was to learn 'how to stand straight, with his head held high, and how to keep looking to the right in an easy and unforced way, as also how to make his turns with snap, and to march ahead with stiff knee'.[78] In the cavalry he must:

> sit on horseback with his foot extended straight through the stirrups and planted firmly in them; his legs must not stick out, but at the same time they must not press against the side of the horse. He holds his reins in his left hand; they run on either side of his little finger, and are retained by the thumb across their width, while the ends are thrown over the hand… The two elbows must be held in a natural way close to the body above the hip, with the hand holding the reins kept at a height of about three fingers above the pommel of the saddle. Every rider must be able to guide his horse effectively by reins and heels.

Special attention was to be given to adjusting the height of the stirrups, 'so that the cuirassier or dragoon rides neither too long nor too short, but in such a way that he can raise himself a fair height from the saddle'.[79]

The official and private regulations emphasised, with minor variations, that the new soldier must be spared from kicks, blows and foul language, 'so that his first experiences do not leave him timorous or cowed, but make him well-inclined and enthusiastic in the service'.[80] The military physicians were well acquainted with the depression which might afflict the young soldier, and which went by the name of 'nostalgia.' The official textbook of military medicine emphasised that 'a newly-recruited soldier will have been snatched away abruptly from his parents and place of birth, and he is commonly downcast and dejected. Agricultural labour is demanding enough, but it scarcely compares with the hardships and exertions of a soldier's life. He will adapt much better if he is accustomed to his new condition gradually. If you can devise any way to cheer the recruits up, you will find the effort very worth while'.[81]

The more enlightened officers believed that sessions of drill should be staged at the most once a day, and should be extended for no more than three hours, accompanied by frequent spells of rest, since the unfamiliarity of the thing soon exhausted the recruits. In the summer it was best to terminate the drill by eight or nine in the morning, though an officer should be free to depart from the norm for genuinely useful purposes. The Prince de Ligne claims that he never found it difficult to convince his soldiers why it was important to know what it was like to drill in the noonday sun, or to march through ice and snow and across rugged terrain. Afterwards a few words by way of compliment, a cash bounty or free drink would make the soldiers ready to face anything. In the same interests of realism he used to stage a variety of mock combats; the soldiers enjoyed the variety, especially when the 'dead' and 'wounded' fell to the ground, but they also learned such important lessons as how to range themselves in rank and file without being directed by their officers or NCOs.[82]

The Prussians at the time of the Seven Years War could make a useful infantryman out of a raw recruit in three or four weeks, 'and that is one of the main reasons why the King of Prussia has awakened universal astonishment by surviving so long against the multitude of armies ranged against him; and he will continue to hold on in the same way, unless superiority of numbers eventually decides the outcome of the war'.[83] Cogniazzo knew of Austrian regiments which had gone through the motions of drilling their recruits all through the summer of 1758, but still had two or 300 men each who were incapable of facing the enemy by the time of the battle of Hochkirch in the middle of October.[84] The underlying reason was that Prussian discipline brought together professionalism, ferocity, common sense and humanity in a way that was beyond the reach of the Austrians.

Except in the direst emergency, the Prussian recruit was spared the tribulations of formation drill until the attentions of his immediate officers and NCOs had given him confidence and proficiency in everything he needed to know; in the Austrian army young officers and veterans alike were all too often subjected to exhausting and demoralising sessions of drill which were staged twice a day, and prolonged for hours on end under the threat of the stick.[85]

The Prussians moreover reserved displays of parade ground virtuosity for peacetime, but reduced their evolutions and drills to the bare minimum in time of war. The Austrians, on the other hand, were unable to win free of the baroque accretions that encrusted all their proceedings. The cuirassier and dragoon regulations of 1749–51 devoted 14½ pages to the ceremonies which attended the presentation of a new standard – which was the same span as the section on the regiment in battle (see p. 148). The companion infantry regulations of 1749 were replete with all the various twirlings and reversals of weapons, the salutes and genuflexions that were engendered by the appropriate dignitary or occasion.

Lastly the Prussians were masters of their trade, which was certainly not the case among many of their Austrian counterparts, as we have frequent occasion to note. Well into the war many of the officers were still unable to adapt themselves to the 'new' provisions of the infantry regulations of 1749.

Pay, Rations and Accommodation

The soldiers' pay varied according to circumstances of service, and whether the remuneration was made over in cash or kind. The standard daily rates ran as follows, and were measured in creutzer (abbreviated to 'xr.') at 60 to the florin:

Infantry grenadier:	6 xr.
Infantry fusilier:	5 xr.
Cuirassier carabinier & dragoon grenadier:	6 and one-half xr.
Cuirassier & dragoon trooper:	
(mounted service)	6 xr.
(dismounted service)	5 and one-half xr.

The cost of the bread rations was deducted from these sums, though the infantry soldier no longer had to pay for the cost of his uniform, and the obligation of the cavalry was supposed to be confined to the smaller items. The daily ration was made over either in bread at a weight of two Viennese pounds, or in biscuit at one and three-quarter pounds.[86]

The evidence as to the soldiers' standard of living is contradictory, though the positive testimony outweighs the negative. It has been established, for example, that most of the troops of the Netherlands regiments were as well off as the best-paid textile workers in civilian employment, though the married men (a minority) were in a bad way,[87] probably because the payment for the bread ration reduced their cash in hand. The periodic *Musterungen* give an insight into conditions in the army as a whole until the outbreak of the Seven Years War, and the reports of the Commissaries and inspecting officers indicate that by the end of 1755 most of the old abuses had been eliminated. They testified that in the Bohemian *Musterung* of October 1755 they had:

> looked most carefully into the treatment of the soldiers in all the regiments, and we found that everywhere the pay and uniforms had been made over without deduction, and that the men are not required to pay for the smaller items of clothing out of their own pockets – except in the cavalry where it continues according to custom, though without the use of force. Here the only regiment to overstep the mark was that of the Hohenems [later Erzherzog Ferdinand] Cuirassiers, which made the troopers buy far too many of such items... The men are perfectly willing to pay for their third shirts and other bits and pieces, for they give two or at the most three creutzer for their rations, which are so sustaining that the soldiers are unable to eat all their bread, and are in the habit of selling half of it.

Meat (not included in the rations) cost three creutzer a pound in Prague, but two-and-a-half or very much less in the country. The soldiers' single complaint related to the beer, which they considered too expensive, especially in places where a contractor had a monopoly.[88]

Wartime brought the private soldier a winter supplement of one creutzer in daily pay, and an extra creutzer at all seasons when he was serving beyond the Habsburg borders, and on 15 October 1758 Maria Theresa ordered free rations of meat and rice to be given in future to all troops who had done particularly well, or who were serving under arduous conditions.[89]

By that time the soldiers' pay was being made over in copper coins, and in April 1759 Kaunitz complained to Maria Theresa that the daily pay had lost much of its value now that the troops were being fleeced by the money changers on the theatre of war:

> We see the consequences in the rate of desertion, which last year was much heavier in Your Majesty's army than among the enemy. Although the true state of affairs has been concealed by those who have a private interest in the money changing, I believe I am right to suspect that the cause of the desertion is that which I have just mentioned. The situation is aggravated by the fact that the King of Prussia gives his soldiers two or three pounds of meat a week, in addition to their daily six creutzer. When the Austrian troops are in foreign territory they too receive six creutzer, but without any meat, which makes a striking contrast which can only augment the desertion from our army, while deterring men from deserting from that of the enemy.[90]

Oddly enough, two of the two most normally biting critics of the Austrian service insist that the Austrian soldier was being supported extremely well. Cogniazzo served almost to the end of the Seven Years War, and in very diverse conditions, and he emphases that the pay (doled out every five days in the captain's tent) was distributed with absolute regularity, that the backing of the Bohemian *Stände* gave paper coupons the full worth of cash, and that the intrinsic value of the metal in the heavy copper creutzer amounted to the same value as the silver original.[91]

Armfeldt goes further. He testifies that everything that concerned the troops' cleanliness, feeding and welfare was provided to the highest standard: 'you never see a sloppy or badly-dressed soldier; no day passes, whether on the march or in camp, without the whole army cooking as a body. As regards the food, every colonel makes a deal with a contractor to have cattle brought from Hungary, so that there is never any lack of fresh meat'.[92] When a contractor provided for several regiments at a time he maintained a butcher in each of them, from which the companies obtained their meat at fixed prices. Armfeldt concluded that 'the troops never go short of pay, meat or bread. In the Austrian army both officers and soldiers find everything they need'.[93]

In wartime the greater part of the army was sheltered in tents during the campaigning season, and in whatever civilian accommodation could be found for the winter cantonments. The locations of such camps and cantonments were inevitably determined by operational needs. In peacetime, and in provinces remote from the scene of war, the stated policy of 'extraterritoriality' (see p. 150) dictated that the regiments must be in continuous movement from one garrison location to another:

> so as to avert the notorious dangers which might arise from too close contact between the soldiers and the townspeople and peasants of the localities where they are quartered, as would be the case if they had permanent garrison locations like the provincial regiments in France or the Prussians with their local cantons. No regiment may stay more than three years in any one garrison, and upon the elapse of this time it must move on – from Bohemia to Austria, for example, then from there to Styria, then on to Hungary or Transylvania, and finally back to the Austrian Hereditary Lands. No regiment is exempt from this three-yearly rotation.[94]

Charles VI had begun to build barracks in a systematic way in the 1730s, but the progress had been confined largely to the borders with Turkey. The burden of accommodating the troops in peacetime rested with the *Stände* until 1749, when an important provisions of the reforms of Haugwitz shifted the responsibility to the state. The troops were housed either in civilian billets, or in 'semi-barracks' (*Quasi Casarmen*) which were adapted from buildings like disused monasteries.

The accommodation was supposed to be in pleasant and healthy locations, complete with windows, stoves, privies, spacious kitchens, stabling as necessary, and fitted out in such a way as to suit the officers as well as the men.[95] The author of the *Patriotic Reflections* paints a different picture, and refers to the troops barely surviving in dark, damp, and chilly hall-like chambers. The generals and the senior officers tried to do better for themselves, but the civilian authorities had 'such a predominance over the military' that they were able to spin out the arguments until the commander gave up the struggle out of exhaustion, or the time came for the garrison to leave.[96]

Marriage

Conditions of the kind just outlined were scarcely conducive to married life. Permission to marry in the first place was granted (if granted at all) by the colonel commandant on the recommendation of the regimental chaplain and the soldier's captain-a system which enabled the peacetime army to regulate the suitability and number of marriages.

Percentages of Married Personnel

	NCOs	Non-combatants	Other Ranks
German Infantry (excluding 'new corps') 17.06	15.50	10.81	
Hungarian Infantry:	14.75	14.65	18.33
Italian Infantry;	8.70	18.49	5.72
Netherlands Infantry:	15.33	15.48	2.92
Simbschen Regiment:	10.60	8.10	9.43
Cuirassiers:	9.68	28.65	5.03
Dragoons:	12.73	24.23	5.51
Hussars:	13.88	31.37	7.81
Sappeurs:	14.28	nil	6.13
Pioniere:	25.00	25.66	12.05

In 1780, in one of the last acts of her reign, Maria Theresa overcame the opposition of the *Hofkriegsrath* to establish a system of schooling for the children of her soldiers. In the meantime the brats were devoid of all education save that in the fundamentals of Christianity, and perhaps also those of reading and writing, which were provided by the regimental chaplain. The Prince de Ligne was tempted to believe that the state should assume the responsibility for arranging marriages with healthy and respectable girls, and providing for the women and children: 'If attention were given to this matter we would no longer witness the spectacle of those sickly children who are scarcely able to drag themselves up the narrow and squalid stairs of the barracks'.[97]

As was usual in armies of the time, a number of the wives accompanied their men-folk on campaign. They sought to justify their existence by seeing to the soldiers' laundry, but there was scarcely a regiment which did not drag along with it a train of wives who were on no kind of ration strength, and who survived by plunder.[98]

In 1758 Daun decreed that the only wives of the infantry to be allowed to march along with the regiments were childless women who could serve the soldiers with spirits. All the rest were to march under close escort at the tail of the column, and a detachment of the new *Staabs-Dragoner-Regiment* would root out any who tried to linger in the villages along the way.[99]

The more ferocious of these wives helped to make up the camp followers – the jackal-like train of sutlers, hucksters and thieves which shadowed the regiments, ransacked the peasant houses, and plundered the dead and wounded on the battlefield. Daun therefore ordered all unauthorised tradespeople to be placed under arrest, and insisted that even the licensed sutlers and regimental wives must obtain their provisions and goods well away from the immediate area of the army, for otherwise they inflated the local prices, and their threats and violent ways deterred the peasants from bringing their produce for sale.[100]

Much greater numbers still of the soldiers' wives had already been left behind when the regiments departed for the field, and the problem was augmented when the numbers of the married *Stände* recruits soon exceeded the desired limit of one in ten. A Military Conference of 28 November 1756 sought to throw the responsibility for their care on the feudal lords. 'It cannot be denied that this order was harsh, as well as being difficult to put into effect. But we could not think of any other means of averting the evils and dangers of having so many married men and their children with the army'.[101] This solution proved inadequate, and a further sitting on 13 June 1757 decided that there was no alternative but to allow five creutzer per day to each of the women, and to provide for them *en masse* at Enzersdorf, and at another location yet to be determined in Hungary.

Age and Service

The muster lists shows that the typical Austrian infantryman and cavalryman of the period of the Seven Years War was a man in his middle twenties, which was noticeably older than the average of conscript cannon fodder in the World Wars of the 20th century. The figures relating to the Austrian artillery are misleading, for they have survived only for the year 1762, by when the veteran gunners had been depleted and replaced by much younger men. From the tactical point of view age is of less relevance than service. Here the figures indicate a predominance among the infantry of soldiers with less than two years of servicemen, in other words, whose training was still in progress or barely complete. The cavalrymen of all branches were men of greater experience (See Appendix X: Age and Service of Private Soldiers).

Leave

The Prince de Ligne regarded the granting of leave to reliable soldiers as a kind of compensation for the trickery or force which had brought them into the service, and so deprived them of their liberty. 'We ought to issue the so-called "recruiting passes" to trustworthy men of this kind. They are truly attached to their colours, and when they return from their native villages they would bring back recruits with them'.[102]

Some of the regiments were so trusting or negligent that they let their men go without demanding any kind of security, and in 1762 the *Hofkriegsrath* had to remind the commanders that all soldiers released on leave must lodge a monetary caution, and that the colonels would be held responsible for any men who failed to come back.[103]

Discipline

The state of discipline in the Austrian army had a mixed record. Whole regiments had once been literally decimated for having failed in battle, as we have noted (see p. 200), and Cogniazzo suspected that severity of this degree had served to make up for indifferent tactics.[104] Collective

Standard drill movements of the Austrian infantry. (*Regulament* of 1749)

punishments had since fallen out of use in the Austrian service, though not in the Prussian.[105] The weight of Austrian discipline now fell on the individual.

The Articles of War were printed in three languages – German, Bohemian and Hungarian – and in some companies it was the custom to read them out to the men every month, with every offence matched with its appropriate punishment: 'For such and such an infraction the dungeon, chains, beatings with the hazel stick, running the gauntlet under a lashing from the stirrup leathers, or facing the musket – that instrument of military death – or the sword, the gallows or the wheel'.[106]

Summary punishments, at least in the cavalry, were supposed to be limited to three or four blows on the spot. The troopers were not to be addressed by the demeaning *Du,* and 'should any officer or NCO kick any of his subordinates or subject them to other degrading punishment, or strike them with a stick on the head, in the face or in the feet – such an officer or NCO will be held to severe account'.[107]

The scale of allotted military punishments began with inconveniences like extra spells of guard duty, or discomforts like being forced to stand for prolonged periods carrying a cuirass or some other weighty item of equipment. Periods of detention could be aggravated, if necessary, but reducing the rations to bread and water, confinement in fetters, or binding the limbs tightly together. A common form of physical punishment was being forced to run the gauntlet between two ranks of troops wielding sticks or (in the cavalry) stirrup leathers. It was a less serious affair than in the Prussian army, where the experience could cripple or kill. Among the Austrians 'all that running the gauntlet does is to get the blood circulating. It doesn't do much harm.'[108]

The beatings did little to deter certain individuals. In 1754 the *Justiz-Collegium* addressed the problem of those soldiers who had set themselves up as part-time dog-killers, and so occasioned their automatic dismissal from the army, 'Manifold experience shows that bad characters like that are so hardened by their evil ways that they shrug off physical punishment as long as they gain their objective, which is to be released from military service'.[109] They were therefore to be relegated to menial labour with the regiment, and hanged without question of mercy if they tried to desert. The ultimate form of non-capital punishment was a prolonged period of fortress labour, typically for eight or 10 years at Esseg, Peterwardein or another of the eastern strongholds.

Although it is difficult to draw direct comparisons, physical punishment of a nonlethal kind was probably more severe in the Prussian army than in the Austrian. However capital punishment was undoubtedly much rarer in the Prussian service, and it was virtually unknown in the armies which stood under the direct command of the squeamish Frederick, who reserved ultimate judicial powers to himself, and almost invariably commuted any sentences of death. In the Austrian army, on the other hand, the *Jus Gladii et Aggratiandi* was devolved to the *Inhaber,* or effectively to the *Obrist-Commendant* acting under his authority. Cogniazzo knew of hearings where the regimental lawyer (*Auditeur*) arrived bearing the death sentence drawn up according to the colonel's wish, and before the man's guilt had even been established.[110]

Conventional misdemeanours with women were rarely punished, but bestiality was answered by the burning alive of the offender and the animal in question. Cogniazzo witnessed the fiery execution of a soldier and an artillery horse at Trautenau in 1758, and it was an horrific occasion.[111]

As for hanging, 'our armies employ a tree or post 10 or 12 feet tall, and a nail is hammered in at an appropriate height. The unfortunate soldier is made to climb onto a bench; this is then pulled away, and the executioner seizes him by the hair and tugs until he believes he is dead'.[112] On 7 June 1758, during the Austrian retreat in Moravia, ensign Gorani noted how the regiment of Andlau found time to hang the soldier Nepomuk Starck for desertion. Shortly afterwards the Prussians arrived on the scene, and the Austrians left Starck hanging apparently lifeless. He was revived by a Prussian surgeon, and within a matter of hours he had been enlisted in the Prussian regiment of Knobloch, escaped back to the Austrians – and been duly hanged for a second and final time.[113]

Shootings were performed in a way that left the outcome in no doubt. Six soldiers were told off for the purpose. The first three took up position, one aiming at the head and another two at the chest, and they opened fire. If the offender still showed signs of life, the process was repeated by the remaining three men.[114]

Sensible officers exercised the terrible powers at their disposal with some discretion, and took proper account of the circumstances of the case, and the character of the individual concerned. Thus the Prince de Ligne was careful to establish a distinction between the *raisonnable* – the thinking soldier who gave of his best when he saw the purpose of an order – and the *raisonneur* who was out to make trouble, and deserved the stick or something more drastic still.[115] The *Justiz-Collegium* itself believed that case-hardened soldiers were impervious to beatings (above), while the hussar general Rudolph Pálffy observed that, for minor offences at least, 'we should start by assuming that the men are beyond redemption, for it often happens that lenient means of correction have the power to make "incorrigible" soldiers mend their ways and live a better kind of life'.[116] Opinions of this kind nevertheless seem to have been in the minority.

As regards the state of discipline in the Austrian army in general, Armfeldt and the native critics speak unanimously and with such a strong voice that their views deserve respect. The Austrian discipline was at first sight savage and unrelenting. Armfeldt saw well over 100 men hanging from the gallows in a camp where the army had spent only 11 days, and he records that nearly 1,000 men were hanged in the winter of 1759/60. 'Hardly a day goes by without executions for a variety of offences, and the regimental commanders make a kind of game out of signing death warrants. There are certainly cases of soldiers being spared, but these are usually the taller lads'.[117] This matches Cogniazzo's observation that it was all too easy to deliver soldiers to the hangman if a commander wished to gain a reputation as a tough disciplinarian.[118]

These severities co-existed with a seemingly ineradicable disorder, and Armfeldt investigated the reasons. The army's pay and provisioning had improved beyond measure, but forces were still at work to undermine genuine discipline. The hussars and Croats bore comparison with the wildest Tartars, Kalmyks and Cossacks,[119] and they ravaged the theatre of war alongside the artillery drivers and camp followers. The discipline suffered accordingly in the army as a whole, and in the detached corps in particular, where the commanders often sought to win over their men by giving them leave to plunder at will in enemy land. Several thousand men at a time were always absent from the army on such activities, and many of them never returned, having fallen victim to the peasants or been cut off by the enemy.[120]

> Moreover it contributes to the disorders in the Austrian army that the young men of the great families are promoted rapidly to regimental officers and the command of corps without the necessary experience, or having the slightest concept of subordination... The senior officers and the generals who command corps tolerate a variety of disorders, and it is consequently difficult for the commander-inchief [Daun] to maintain the requisite discipline in such a large army, and especially since his policy is not to act to the disadvantage of his subordinates. This is not to say no disorders ever come to the Field Marshal's attention, or that infractions go unpunished, but the kinds of misdemeanours which are brought before him are of a minor nature, and all complaints are conveyed through so many hands that the offender has the time to win over the superior who is supposed to report the matter... If an officer has been guilty of various offences, but the colonel or somebody else with influence speaks up for him, the matter is usually forgotten.[121]

The critics pointed out that, amid all the show of ferocity, discipline was neglected when it ought to have counted the most, which was on active service, for 'when the men are undergoing a more than usually strenuous march, a spell of duty like digging fortifications, or going into action, or having to endure a cannonade longer than is to their liking, they will give vent to loud grumbling even in the presence of their officers. Far from punishing this insubordination, the regimental staff officers and other senior officers start complaining against the order on their own account'.[122] On this point Armfeldt adds that the consequent breakdown in order could affect an entire army on a day of battle.[123]

The Deserters

Desertion fastened on the armies of old Europe like a pestilence, and in the Seven Years War this malady deprived the Austrians of 62,220 of their military personnel., or 20.49 percent of their losses as a whole'.[124] (See Appendix XI: Losses through Desertion, by Arm and Regiment)

Maria Theresa regarded desertion as one of the several signs of the indiscipline that she was determined to eradicate in the later years of the war. Just as she tried to subject her individual officers to a stricter reckoning, so in the summer of 1762 she took steps to single out the regiments of the regular infantry and cavalry which were losing the most men from this cause. The results were presented in *Tabelle* for the months of May, June, July and August, which revealed a total of 4,495 deserters, namely:

Natives:	46.31% of the whole
Foreigners:	36.64
Enlisted Prussian deserters:	6.62
Enlisted Prussian POWs:	10.61

Desertion was shown to be largely a disease of the infantry (at 90.45 percent of the whole), and Maria Theresa singled out for special investigation the German regiments of Angern, Carl Colloredo, Kayser, Pallavicini, Platz, Maguire, Salm and Starhemberg, the Hungarian regiments of Adam Batthyány, Forgách, Haller and Preysach, and the Italian regiments of Clerici and Luzan.

At this time Maria Theresa assumed that the reasons for desertion were readily identifiable as three – the shortage of provisions, an irresponsible lack of attention on the part of the officers, and the excessive exertions which were being demanded of the troops. The remedies appeared to her to be just as obvious. Ample supplies had now been assembled to feed the army through the rest of the campaign. Desertion in a particular unit would now work to the disadvantage of its officer when it came to promotion, and with this in view she asked to be furnished with the names of the captains whose companies were afflicted with particularly high rates. Finally the officers were told that if they demanded extra efforts from the men, they must explain to them why the exertion was necessary, and promise them some relief.[125]

The returns from the regiments showed that the problem was more complicated than Maria Theresa had supposed, and also tell us a great deal about the relations between the men and their senior regimental officers. Lieutenant-Colonel Carl Perneda of the regiment of Platz reported that he and his officers had asked the soldiers if there was any cause for complaint, and had been assured that there was none. He could only suppose that the reason was that the regiment had contained many Prussians and other unreliable foreigners, who had taken advantage of an opportunity to escape to the corps of the Prussian general Werner, which happened to be nearby.[126] The commandants of Adam Batthyány, Carl Colloredo, Luzan and Clerici confirmed that the enlisted enemy prisoners formed a restless and dangerous element.

The defections of natives from the Hungarian national regiments were striking, and were traced to the forcible and patently unjust ways in which the Counties of Hungary and Transylvania raised their recruits. The regiment of Haller lost the high number of 22 men from desertion in

August alone, but the commandant asked the *Hofkriegsrath* to consider that nearly all of them had been 'living in Wallachia with their wives and children, and been taken from the land by force to be enlisted in the Imperial service'.[127] Thirty-two men deserted from the regiment of Forgách in the same month, and the commandant pointed out that 'all the men supplied by the Hungarian *Stände* are either foreign vagabonds and deserters, who have been taken up from the road, or natives who have been made into soldiers by force, leaving behind a wife and two or three children – love now impels them to return home.' No less reprehensibly the authorities had broken their word by refusing to release any capitulants after their agreed term of service had expired, and the men concluded that they were being bound to the army for life.[128]

Long and arduous spells of outpost duty were also seen as conducive to desertion, for they gave the men both the motive and the opportunity to make themselves scarce. The regiment of Angern had been under continuous alarm for weeks on end before it had to face the full brunt of one of the Prussian attacks at Burkersdorf on 21 July, and it was pushed back in some disorder through the woods, where many of the ragged men seized the chance to desert.[129]

The regiment of Salm was afflicted with all of these maladies, and some others which we have not yet considered. 117 of its complement deserted in the course of June, July and August, and its commandant Colonel Zorn von Plobsheim (a brave and conscientious officer) described the succession of misfortunes which had overtaken his command. At the *Musterung* in March the Commissary, the brigadier and the then commandant had refused to release the time-expired capitulants, citing an order of Maria Theresa that all were to remain until the end of the war, 'and the result was that most of the men mutinied, and we had no alternative but to arrest the ringleaders and such as refused to accept their pay or bread, take up arms or do any further service; after a due hearing according to military law they were made to run the gauntlet.' As a concession to the less hard-boiled mutineers one or two men at a time from each company were allowed to return to their homes in Bohemia on 14-day leaves; two of these men had failed to return, and were entered as deserters. Almost all the deserters were either time-expired capitulants or Prussian deserters or prisoners of war.

Discipline had been further eroded in the Salm regiment through contact with bad women in the cantonments, and many men had already abandoned the colours before the regiment was hounded by the enemy in the course of a retreat from Altenburg. This harrowing experience was succeeded by six hard weeks on duty at an abatis. Zorn von Plobsheim had asked in vain for some relief, and a further desertion set in as a result.[130]

After reviewing the submissions of the commanders, the *Hofkriegsrath* informed Maria Theresa in November that 'for our part we find that the colonel commandants and their officers are in no way to blame'.[131]

Most officers would have concurred with these expressions of defeat. The most dreadful punishments were unavailing, for 'a world full of gallows would not deter men of that kind; their lives no longer matter to them, and they regard death, which would bring all their miseries to an end, as preferable to their present condition'.[132] Heavy-handed measures of security, like telling off sentries to observe one another, were self-defeating, for they were a sign of general distrust, and offered no guarantee that the two men would not escape together. It was better to be on the alert for the secret language of the intending deserters. 'They will drop a phrase like: "It's fine weather for a walk!" which indicates that they are about to make off, and inviting others to do the same. They also have a certain way of examining the weather, the country and the state of their shoes'.[133] The Infantry Regulations of 1769 added that the mens' background would tell the officer those who were the most likely to desert, and that he should cultivate crafty informants among the private soldiers.[134]

The penalties for desertion were applied in ways that were seemingly inconsistent, but which corresponded with the realities of this near-intractable problem. Hanging was the ultimate price of desertion, and the Austrians undoubtedly exacted the death penalty for this crime far more freely than did the Prussians, who applied it only in severely aggravating circumstances like a desertion plot. When the Austrians could not apprehend the deserters in person, the authorities could still deprive them of all their property and rights of inheritance.[135]

A useful differentiation was nevertheless made between a simple deserter, and the *Überlaufer* who went over to the enemy.[136] 'Internal' deserters were treated leniently, to judge by the case of Johann Peter, a native of Denmark, who served for 18 months with the Loudon Green Grenadiers, but was then transferred against his will to the Sappers. After he was captured 'he admitted freely that when the corps was at the siege of Glatz he escaped, wearing his old Loudon uniform, and made his way through the woods to Gross-Hennersdorf, where sheer necessity compelled him to sell his old coat to a peasant for two groschen, but all the time intending to return to his former regiment... he never had it in mind to desert, let alone go over to the enemy.' The court martial declared unanimously that Peter was to be released at once, in consideration of his good intentions and the long and hard imprisonment he had already undergone.[137]

Deserters who returned of their own free will were in practice welcomed with open arms; their excuses could be accepted without question, however feeble they might have been,[138] and they were even allowed to go to another regiment of their own choice, if their original unit was uncongenial to them.[139] The measured leniency of the Austrians became known to the population at large, who would never have betrayed the runaways to a certain death. The Commissaries had reported in June 1756 that nearly two-thirds of the deserters were being hunted down and returned by the peasants, which helped to dissuade some of the men who were thinking of making off.[140]

The periodic General Pardons amounted to an open invitation to Austrian deserters to return to the colours and resume their military careers with a clean slate. Daun at least believed that these amnesties should be used with discretion, for by August 1762 the fact of desertion was meaning so little that men were going over to the Prussians and returning as the whim took them.[141]

All the time the authorities offered a wholehearted welcome to deserters from the Prussians, and Daun told Hadik that more of these useful people would be inclined to come over if they were not likely to be beaten up and robbed by the Croats.[142] The Prussian deserters could provide immediately useful tactical intelligence, such as that furnished by the infantryman Pierre Mandalieu, who in 1761 gave Loudon precise information concerning the fortifications and garrison of Schweidnitz.[143] Three years earlier the Prussian *Ober-Feuerwerker* Friedrich Christian Gessler had deserted to the Austrians in Saxony. He passed on considerable technical detail concerning the Prussian artillery, and maintained that all the gunners currently with the Prussian army had been trained by him. These were big claims, but he invited questioning by the Austrian artillerymen, who would be able to vouch for his credentials.[144] At the most basic level, it was better to have characters like these for a time at least at the disposal of the Austrians than back with Old Fritz. Loudon set up his regiment of Green Grenadiers as a receptacle for the Prussian renegades, and for that reason both this unit and the comparable free battalion of Beck escaped the reduction of the army in 1761/2.

The ex-Prussian deserters (unlike the Prussian prisoners) ran from the Austrian army at a comparatively modest rate, making up only 6.62 percent of the desertions recorded between May and August 1762, as we have seen, and the Prince de Ligne goes so far as to describe them as a great asset to the army (see p. 222). This bold statement does not correspond entirely with his own experience:

> One day Lacy wished to obtain intelligence of the enemy, and called out to a Prussian hussar on outpost duty: 'There's 10 ducats for you if you desert!' He had no real hope of succeeding, but the man came up at a gallop, braving a carbine shot from his comrade. He said what he knew, and Lacy duly paid him, even if his information was not worth the money. We now had to decide what to do with him, and Lacy suggested I should take him on as a servant.

He went about stealing and lashing at people with his sabre, and in fact he was so dangerous that whenever I returned to the camp at night I kept my hand on a pistol and made him walk in front of me. It is one of my weaknesses that I have never been able to get rid of anybody. Luckily he killed a sutler and deserted, and so I was rid of him.[145]

A rare perspective from a Prussian deserter is provided by the Swiss writer Ulrich Bräker, who had been enlisted by fraud in the ferocious regiment of Itzenplitz. He took advantage of the confused fighting towards the end of the battle of Lobositz (1756) to steal away from the scene of the heroic corpse-making, and was fortunate enough to fall in with a party of more-than usually benevolent Croats, who gave him tobacco and spirits instead of robbing him. There was no obligation on the deserters to enter the Austrian service, and Bräker and others like him were provided with passes and travel money to enable them to return home. Thus equipped, Bräker and his companions set off from Prague on the first stage of their journey:

We were an amazing mixture of Swiss, Swabians, Saxons, Bavarians, Tyrolean, Italians, French, Polacks and Turks. It was already evening when we marched out of Prague. We were soon climbing a hill, and when we looked back we had an incomparable view over the whole of the city, which presented an entrancing sight when the genial sun touched the countless copper-clad towers with his golden hand. We stood motionless for a little while to enjoy this magnificent spectacle, while we chatted among ourselves and a multitude of emotions coursed through our hearts. I could hardly have enough of it, but then my thoughts turned to home, my own folk, and my Anneli.[146]

It would be entirely wrong to group Maria Theresa's Saxon auxiliaries along with the generality of the Prussian deserters. In October 1756 Frederick had captured the main force of the Saxon army intact at Pirna, and at once compelled the rank and file to enter his service. The procedure was as stupid as it was brutal, for he swore in the Saxons by entire units, instead of distributing the soldiers among his reliable Brandenburgers and Pomeranians. The result was that the Saxons took the first opportunity to overpower their Prussian officers and come over to the Austrians in bulk. On 10 April 1757 an Austrian colonel reported that the regiment of Rutowski had arrived in its entirety, together with its weapons and horses, and 'you may imagine, judging by this example, just how little reliance the king can place on the Saxons'.[147] By September most of the Saxons had been sent to Hungary to set free the Austrian battalions which had been garrisoned there. There were 20,000 of them, dressed and paid by the Austrians, and they had been rejoined by their own officers, who had been released by the Prussians and had been living without employment in Saxony.

On 11 March 1758 the representatives of Saxony, Austria and France signed an convention whereby 10,000 of the Saxons were to be attached as a corps to the French army, half the cost being defrayed by Austria and half by France. The command of the corps was to be assumed by Prince Xaver August of Saxony (fourth son of Augustus II) who had no military education, but was burning with the ambition to make a name for himself independently of the Austrians. These instincts were shared by the Saxon infantrymen, who had been well provided-for in Hungary in the physical sense, but found life in the remote garrisons only marginally preferable to that in the Prussian army.

The chosen troops were at first glad to serve once more under their own colours, but disillusionment set in when the Saxon contingent marched west across Germany, where they found that their fellow-Lutherans sympathised with Frederick. Finally the experience of living with the French convinced most of the Saxons that they were fighting on the wrong side.[148] Maria Theresa derived much better value from the six regiments of Saxon horse which remained with the Austrian army, and which continued to perform excellent service. The Saxon cavalry carried on a blood feud with the Prussians which dated from 1745, and the example of this fast-moving force persuaded the Austrians to convert some of their dragoons to *chevaulegers* in imitation.

Prisoners of War

The Prussians

In the first years of the war the Austrian authorities looked on the enemy prisoners as an expensive and possibly dangerous liability, and they expressed especial concern at the large numbers of men being held in the Spielberg citadel at Brünn, as the one place of security in Moravia.[149] The solution was to get rid of them as soon as practicable by exchanges through the standing Austro-Prussian commission at Jägerndorf, 'as long as it is head for head, rank for rank, and a healthy man for another who is just as healthy'.[150]

By the end of 1759 the Austrians had come to see the prisoners in another light, as a human resource which was to be denied to the enemy, and turned to one's positive advantage. The policies had taken a new direction on the urging of Daun, when he surveyed the rich haul of prisoners he had made at Maxen on 21 November:

> now we have another crop of people to exchange, but I suspect that the enemy would gain more advantage thereby. Your Majesty has already replaced most of her missing officers, whereas the enemy will experience a marked shortage in that department. Moreover generals like Finck and Wunsch have always commanded independent corps and are some of the best they have, while the generals in their hands are ones we could easily do without. Those captured regiments of theirs are likewise among their finest, and made up mostly of veterans, and they would dearly like to have them back.

Daun therefore recommended that the Austrians should not be over-hasty in pushing the exchanges.[151] He wrote with still more emphasis on 6 December that the Austrians should devise difficulties that would provoke the Prussians into delaying the exchanges, and he advised that the Prussian prisoners should be removed from Bohemia to provinces more distant from the theatre of war.[152]

By January 1760 the Austrians held 19,400 Prussian rank and file, distributed among 18 small towns in groups of 600 to 1,200 men each. The number of prisoners taken had been greater still, but many of them had failed to survive the march to the remoter places of confinement which had been chosen on Daun's advice. Hundreds if not thousands of the 'Maxen' prisoners were overtaken by the bloody flux on the way through Lower Styria to Croatia, and they were buried half an hour from Rann at the Rannerhof Farm on the road to Agram.[153] Austrian invalids were given the responsibility of guarding prisoners of war on the march and in hospital,[154] and it is probable that they were in little better state of health than the men who had died at Rann and other places.

The dead Prussians would never have the chance of serving Frederick again, which was some kind of negative advantage. Most of the living Brandenburgers and Pomeranians would have been only too eager to return to the Prussian colours and standards, as a number of authorities warned, but by the high summer of 1761 the military and economic needs of her monarchy persuaded Maria Theresa to offer comprehensive terms of employment and settlement to every Prussian prisoner and deserter, regardless of his place of origin. All suitable men were to be given the chance to enlist in the Austrian infantry, and those who wished to remain in the Austrian dominions after the war 'will not only be accorded their release, but each of them granted places and plots of land in Hungary, the Bánát or Transylvania – wherever they wish – so that they can take immediate possession, build a house and make a livelihood.' They were guaranteed religious freedom, and to give them a good start they would continue to receive their military pay for six months after the end of their service with the army, and enjoy five years' freedom from taxes and dues of every kind.[155] Similar terms were offered to prisoners of war who did not wish to enter the Austrian service, but who were practitioners of peacetime trades.

The notion of resettling the Prussians in the east originated with Kaunitz and one of the leading lights of his *Staatsrath,* Egyd Baron Borié, who believed that Hungary was a backward land which had not been making a proper contribution to the war. At the end of July 1761 Maria Theresa accordingly told the Hungarian *Hofcanzley* of the new initiative, and expressed the hope that private colonisers would follow the lead that was being set by the state. There seems to have been no lack of volunteers from among the ranks of the Prussian prisoners, but the Hungarian landowners proved to be unexpectedly hostile to the colonisation. Only 600 plots were made available, and they were confined to three widely-scattered locations – the *Comitat* of Bars in central Hungary, the estates of Imre Count Sztaray in the *Comitat* of Zemplen in the north-east, and the *Comitat* of Szerem across the southernborder in Slavonia.[156]

The Austrians

F.E. Boysen was a preacher in St. Johann, the principal church of Magdeburg. By his account this great Prussian fortress-town on the Elbe held 18,000 allied prisoners. 'Among these captives… the Austrians, Russians and Swedes showed themselves markedly superior to the French and the troops of the Empire in their discipline, cleanliness and standards of conduct… among the Austrians the best-behaved men were the Croats, who are so often accused of primitive savagery.' The *Grenzer* committed no vandalism in the High School, where they were quartered, and they greeted Boysen on his visits with dignified courtesy; he learned from Dr. Damisch, their assigned physician, that the Croats were men of property, and that they paid him handsomely for his services.[157]

The prisoners in Magdeburg were fortunate. Young Prussian officers were appalled by the conditions in which the Austrians were confined in the companion fortress of Cüstrin on the Oder. One of them remembers that 'as we were passing through the fortifications we were greeted by a further ghastly sight, namely a whole cartload of stiffened corpses of the Austrians confined there, who after their inhuman sufferings were being carried to their place of eternal rest'.[158] The prisoners included 800 Croats who had been captured at Prague, and who were heaped together in casemates with not so much as straw to lie upon.[159]

The plight of the Croats in Cüstrin came to the notice of *GFWM.* Philipp Lewin Beck, who was held captive in Berlin. He contrived to pass a message to the *Hofkriegsrath* explaining that the men were of the Carlstadt, Slavonian and Warasdin borders, and that by 23 May 1758 551 out of the original 3,302 had died, largely through having to spend the last winter cooped up in the damp casemates. Thirty of the Croats had been hauled off to Stettin to be enlisted into the Prussian army by force, whereupon Beck had made it known to the Prussians that 'they may be assured that when we have in our hands an equivalent number of native Prussians, Pomeranians or Brandenburgers, we will send them to Slavonia and Croatia to work on the household plots of the men who have been forced into their military service.' Fortunately the governor of Stettin was Lieutenant-General the Duke of Bevern, a decent man who had just been released from comfortable detention in Austria. Whether motivated by a sense of honour, or Beck's threats, he asked the Croats whether they genuinely wished to enter the Prussian service. They gave a firm 'no,' whereupon he sent them back to Cüstrin.[160]

Beck feared that more of the Croats would die in Cüstrin unless something were done for them. His concern was not shared in Vienna, which began to make difficulties about the exchanges (above), and Daun argued that the returned Croats represented particularly poor value under the head-for-head rate which obtained.[161]

In such circumstances the behaviour of the Austrian prisoners was all the more admirable, for many of them considered themselves to be still at war with the Prussians, and wished to contribute to the Austrian effort as far as lay within their power. The military playwright Stephanie the Younger created a recognisable type in his fictional *Feldwäbel* Fleckmann, who decided to while away the time in his fortress prison by sketching the defences. His first thought was to work them up into engravings for sale to the public, and he looked forward to seeing his name commemorated at the bottom of the prints: *Fleckmann delineavit*:

> But I hankered after greater glory still, by making my mark with our army and thereby gaining promotion. I therefore hatched a scheme concerning the fortifications. One night I ventured onto the main rampart, and was lucky enough to slip past the sentries. Without being detected I measured the works against lengths of twine, converted the result into the equivalent paces, and so made sense of the layout. I calculated the dimensions of the outworks by counting the number of bricks. From all of this I was able to work up a sketch.[162]

The mass breakout was the most spectacular and most risky of the acts of defiance, for success depended entirely on timing and co-ordination. At Schweidnitz on the night of 30 September/1 October 1761 the 150 Austrian prisoners in the Wasser-Fort held their hand until Loudon's storm was well under way; they then broke open the doors of their casemates, seized the gorge (rearward) wall and its drawbridge, and called out to the Croats who were approaching from outside that their way was clear. This coup completed the capture of the whole fortress complex.

On 1 August 1762 sheer desperation persuaded the 800–1,200 Croats in Cüstrin to make the bold attempt to seize the fortress and link up with an Austrian detachment which was reported to be at Cottbus nearby. The time seemed opportune, for the recent peace between Prussia and Russia had lured the townspeople into a state of happy complacency, while most of the garrison was lodged outside the fortress in the Lange Vorstadt and the Neustadt. At 4.45 a.m. the Croats overpowered the sentry at the barrier of one of the gates, then surged into the guardroom and overcame the main body of the watch, which had been sheltering from the heavy rain. The commotion attracted the Prussian captain Arnim, who locked the gate, but the Croats spread out along the ramparts, opened a heavy fire of artillery against the suburbs, and repelled every attempt on the part of the garrison to break in. However the Croats had failed to prepare the ground with the other prisoners, the 2,900 or so Austrian regulars, and these men now refused to join in.

At this critical moment the preacher Benicke prevailed on the Croats' two chaplains – a Catholic priest and an Orthodox pope – to go to their flock and ask the mutineers to desist. At nine in the morning the firing ceased, and the Croats returned to the casemates of their own accord. The Prussians had lost 13 killed and another 20 or so wounded. The Croatian casualties amounted to 58 killed in action, and 100 wounded, many of whom later died. Once the place was secure, the Prussians exacted a due revenge. The five ringleaders were executed, and on Frederick's orders one in 10 of the others was beaten with sticks.[163]

Now that Frederick was at peace with Russia, he organised the mass transportation of Austrian prisoners to Pomerania and thence by sea to East Prussia. The outcome of the Cüstrin mutiny did not deter Colonel Kreitz from plotting an altogether more ambitious uprising of the prisoners who were now being held in the region of Königsberg. Officers and troops of all kinds were involved, and with more secrecy on the part of the Austrians in Königsberg, and more resolution shown by the smaller party at Tilsit, the possession of the whole of East Prussia might have been at stake (see p. 187). Your best chance of escaping came before you reached a secure place of confinement. The pattern was set after the battle of Prague (6 May 1757), when escapees by the hundred found their way to the new army which Daun was forming in eastern Bohemia. The behaviour of men like these might be the only consolation which the Austrians could draw from a defeat. In January

1758 Maria Theresa arranged for escapees to be rewarded with one ducat each,[164] and men who had been lost at Leuthen and elsewhere were still returning in significant numbers in the early summer of 1758. A French attaché counted 300 of them in the regiment of Wied alone: 'Many of the prisoners enlisted in the King of Prussia's free companies so as to have the opportunity to escape back here. They are returning every day, and to all the regiments'.[165] It was the same story after the defeat at Torgau in 1760, when a *Jäger* made his way back to the army, and reported that 600 fellow prisoners had been able to escape simultaneously.[166]

Maria Theresa maintained her interest in the deeds of these excellent men until the end of the war. Her imagination was caught by an event on 18 June 1762, when a convoy of 394 prisoners was being shipped down the Oder from Breslau to Cüstrin, probably as part of the general re-location of prisoners which was taking place at this time. Daun reported that

> these men, driven by patriotic zeal and a love of Her Majesty's service, made the bold resolution to break out of enemy captivity to freedom. To this end *Feldwäbel* Ladislau Halassy and Corporal Jacob MacElligot of the Kaiser Hussars, and Corporal Michael Szegedy of the Kálnoky Hussars got together with the most reliable of the rank and file. In consequence, when the convoy of seven boats had reached Ratzdorf above Cüstrin they seized it by surprise, forced the boatmen to land, and thus freed themselves and the rest of the Austrian prisoners. Taking the enemy guards with them as captives, they made off in two columns, the first of which reached Dresden, and the second Zittau.[167]

Maria Theresa commissioned Halassy as first-lieutenant, and MacElligot and Szegedy as second-lieutenants. She gave them 150 florins each to fit themselves out, and one ducat to each of the other escapees.[168]

Motivation and Honour

Criminals or Heroes?

> 'The ordinary soldiers are either scum who have been assigned to a regiment rather than the galleys, or idlers who have sworn their oath of loyalty just for one more chance of getting drunk'.[169]

It is easy to see why Pietro Verri should have carried away such a negative impression of the Austrian soldiery. In the experience of the Prince de Ligne the mens' killer instincts, drunkenness, brutality and readiness to take offence were likely to trigger off 300 fights a year in a typical regiment.[170] We have touched already on the forcible enlistment practised by the *Stände,* and few officers set much store by the element of free will even among the 'volunteers' who were rounded up by the regimental recruiting parties:

> There are a number of attractive tricks which work almost irresistibly on the minds of the mob – a ringing hand-bell, the persuasive patter of a recruiting officer who is up to all the tricks of the charlatan's trade, seductive music, and a beaker which is kept full of sparkling wine... We should not permit ourselves to be blinded by delusions about 'love of country' or 'inclination towards military service.' If we take the trouble to investigate the most important impulses which bring the lads to the recruiting table, we will find that they are things like drunkenness, a frenzy of passions, love of idleness, a horror of any useful trade, a wish to be free of parental discipline, an urge towards debauchery, an imaginary hope of untrammelled

freedom, sheer desperation, the fear of punishment after some sordid crime, or however else you care to define the motives of worthless people like these.[171]

Appeals towards patriotism could have little force in a multi-national army, while sentiments of nationalism in the narrower sense were discouraged, as dangerous to the cohesion of the monarchy. There was, however, still room for the indulgence of criminal instincts. On 1 August 1759 a *Rittmeister* and a troop of 12 hussars forced their way into the Prussian town of Halle, and split up in search of loot:

> They spared nobody, whether lad, girl, or the humblest labourer. They pointed their carbines at the chests of whoever they encountered on the streets, and forced them to yield up whatever they had. We do not know whether they had been sent expressly to plunder, or whether they were acting on their own initiative, but in any event they came well prepared, carrying such necessary implements as axes, hatchets and crowbars. If the householder did not open his door in the instant they would smash it open, present their sabres to his throat, and threaten to cut him in pieces if he did not at once unlock all the chests where he kept his cash and valuables.[172]

Rudolph Pálffy, Andreas Hadik and other hussar leaders tried to restrain the robber impulse when it led to their men disappearing in the course of an action, 'since disorders of that kind often encourage the fleeing enemy to turn about, and beat the troops when they are engaged in plundering'.[173] However the commanders respected the right to plunder as such, and they laid down that 'once an action is over the booty is to be brought together, sold off to the highest bidder, and the proceeds conscientiously divided up and distributed'.[174]

Plundering was associated with the hussars and Croats in particular only because those folk had more opportunity to engage in that pastime than anyone else. The prospect of making booty in fact held an immense appeal to troops of all kinds. There was no town which the men would not storm enthusiastically when they had this prospect before them. At Landeshut in 1760 Loudon's troops swarmed down from the hilltops they had just captured and gave themselves up to the sack of the little town below. Loudon hoped to avoid a repetition of these scenes at Schweidnitz in 1761, by promising his men compensation in cash instead. After the forts had been stormed the Russian contingent indeed re-formed in rank and file in perfect order, but the Austrians ransacked the town anyway.

The army came to see Loudon's army as a symbol of the freedom to plunder, a liberty which extended to despoiling the townspeople and peasants as well as the enemy camp. Officers too were known to take part, for in the Austrian army there was nothing to distinguish them from the private soldiers except the sash and the sword knot. 'The regiments therefore longed to come under Loudon's command as part of his corps, for that promised them greater liberty as

Veteran trooper (Ottenfeld, 1898). Men of this description were the most reliable single element in the army.

well more action. To the same degree they were unwilling to be assigned to the corps of Beck, where the discipline was unappetisingly strict'.[175]

Cogniazzo, the author of these words, nevertheless insisted that the soldier's trade was inherently noble, and that (like the Duke of Wellington after him) something useful and fine could be fashioned from distinctly unpromising material. 'There are a thousand like me, who are not content to perform the service in a mechanical way, and who have been convinced by experience that the least desertion is to be found in those regiments and corps where the commanders have the skill and patience to bring even their lowliest soldiers to an exact performance of their duties not by the severity of the punishments, but by inculcating principles of honour'.[176]

The chief obstacle emerged not as ill-will on the part of the soldiers, but the position of the army in Austrian society. The military authorities sought, with varying success, to defend their estate against insult. The custom of the army denied entry to men who followed the ignoble trade of slaughterman, and commanders insisted on a proper burial even for the meanest soldier to die in garrison. Senior officers did not hesitate to take bishops to task when the clergy failed to accompany the man's coffin to the graveside, and for Colonel Aeneas Count Caprara at Innsbruck the offence was compounded whenhe discovered that the sacred ground of the cemetery of the *Tyroler Land- and Feld-Regiment* had been violated by the burial of a criminal who had died under judicial interrogation. Caprara complained that it was all of a piece with the behaviour of the civilians in 'putting the regiment under my command at one disadvantage after another. They act with impunity, and they do everything they can to render us contemptible in the eyes of the enemy, for our province accommodates many captured Prussian generals and troops... who never stop talking about the extraordinary prestige which the military condition enjoys in their own land'.[177]

Some officers strove to give military honour expression of a more positive kind. It was undeniably easier to cultivate among the regular cavalrymen than the other troops, for they regarded themselves, albeit at many removes, as the modern representatives of the knights of old. One of their commanders writes that when the cavalry was about to close with the enemy what mattered most was 'a few short words to the men about honour, and to remind them of their duty. Love and loyalty towards one's sovereign are instincts that must be imprinted on the heart'.[178]

In the summer of 1762 the colonel commandant of the Erzherzog Leopold Cuirassiers took the trouble to inform the *Hofkriegsrath* of the names of 27 of his troopers who had just distinguished themselves in action, and suggested that they should be rewarded by double pay. The *Hofkriegsrath* believed that a cash reward of three or four ducats would be enough, but when Maria Theresa came to hear of it she ordered five ducats to be made over to every man without more ado, and that if these heroes became invalids they were to enjoy their full active pay until the end of their days.[179]

We are still left with the problem of awakening the finer instincts of the infantryman. The Austrian soldier could not be impelled by religious fanaticism, as among the Turks, or by the nationalistic hero-worship which moved the Prussians. There remained the foundation of trust and goodwill.[180] Firm but fair, the effective officer was alive to the collective mentality of his soldiers, which did not differ in kind from that of schoolchildren or old folk. They showed the same thoughtless mischief, the same irrational changes of mind, the same attraction towards whatever would do them harm, and the same penchant for lying. They were at the same time sly and observant, and would gain- the upper hand over any officer who failed to check them on the instant.[181]

How were men like these to be managed? The Prince de Ligne believed that two things were necessary. The first was to lay down firm rules. The second was never to lose sight of the essentially childish nature of these people, hence 'it just comes down to re-arranging their toys, and the playthings of the soldiers are not expensive. A trifle will bring them to life and get them on the move'.[182]

The author of the *Patriotic Reflections* leads us through a more elaborate argument. One of the ways to instil pride in a soldier was to make sure that he dressed cleanly and smartly – 'it is or means, I will allow, but just as all men are not the same, so a single means will not be uniformly good and effective.' The soldier lived a hard life, and even that life might be forfeit in battle:

> What can we give him in return? Certainly not enough in terms of cash or land, for armies nowadays are huge, and no monarchy in the world is wealthy enough to offer sufficient money to persuade men to embrace a trade which goes so much against their natures. Very few will consequently risk their lives for money alone, and so, in addition to the modicum necessary for a bare subsistence, all that we can hold out are the abstractions of honour and distinction.... In what do these consist? They consist in a privileged position in relation to civil society. The Austrian soldier, however, is insufficiently distinguished from the peasant and the ordinary townsman – indeed they despise him, and they hold the advantage over him in almost every situation. That is why few men enter military service of their free will. And yet the townsman, the peasant and the bureaucrat have not the same need of honour and privilege… they strive not out of pride, like the soldier, but just to make money.

All that was left to the officer, therefore, was to draw out feelings of honour through his patient attentions over a long period of time. He must treat his soldiers like human beings, not be afraid to encourage them by the kind word and the little joke, and maintain a discipline that was recognised as reasonable.[183]

On the last point the Prince de Ligne was careful to establish a distinction between 'firmness' (*sévérité*), which did not need to be reinforced by the apparatus of repression, and what he called 'meanness of spirit' (*austerité*), which only made for misery and trouble.[184] The author of the *Patriotic Reflections* was of the same mind, and supplies specific detail. He noted that there was less desertion when an army was marching against the enemy than when it was immobilised in standing camps, where the regiments might find themselves at the mercy of newly-arrived colonel-commandants who made their mark by putting the troops through useless drills, and yelling at officers and soldiers alike:

> The ordinary soldiers know what is, and what is not necessary in their duties and in their drill, and especially the ones who have served in a number of armies – and they put their comrades wise. Contrary to the will of our most gracious sovereign, and the provisions as set out in the regulations, the uniforms in some of the regiments are cut so unmercifully tight that the men turn blue with the constriction… and can scarcely move. The consequence is that the blood stagnates, and the drill – when the men should be as free as birds – becomes a torture.

Young colonels (he continued) were in the habit of requiring the white uniforms to be kept as spotless on campaign as in garrison, and so the soldier had to buy several pounds of chalk and carry it around with him in his knapsack. 'It should therefore occasion no surprise to find that our troops are almost more prone to desert than those of the enemy, who have been kidnapped or taken prisoner from the population of half the world.' The contrary might have been true at the beginning of the war, but it no longer held good in the campaign of 1761, when the Prussian army was hemmed in at Bunzelwitz for a month, yet suffered little from desertion. 'When we did manage to recruit a number of his deserters and prisoners, they mostly made off back to the Prussians after a short time, even though the troops were better off in our camp. There must have been some reason for that.' He found it in a distorted notion of discipline, which plagued the Austrian soldier with stupid trifles, but turned a blind eye to genuinely harmful irregularities on active service.[185]

The Austrian army was certainly burdened with many bad officers like the ones just described, but there were many others who would have agreed with the Prince de Ligne that 'nobody could be more free than a soldier who is known to be a good man. His officers trust him, his comrades respect him, and the young look up to him'.[186] When, in addition, the higher leadership was expert and could lead the army to victory, the outcome was a growing confidence and a feeling of corporate pride. Cogniazzo recalled that there had been a time when 'the very sight of a blue Prussian coat, or the sinister glitter of their fusilier and grenadier caps had been enough to induce panic among our troops. But at Kolin they did not exercise the same effect, or at Breslau, while in the dawn at Hochkirch they were less potent still'.[187]

Foreign observers agreed that the human raw material was potentially excellent, for the Austrians represented 'an unquestionably better stock of soldiers than the Prussians',[188] and the Bavarians and Württembergers could not begin to compare with the fine Austrian grenadiers.[189] According to Henry Lloyd, who served for a time with the Austrian army, the troops were

> composed chiefly out of the class of labourers, vassals of great lords; they are obedient and patient, and bear without murmur the greatest hardships; and though their religion does not rise to any degree of enthusiasm [i.e. fanatical frenzy], probably for want of being excited by an able leader, yet it keeps them sober, and free from vice; objects must strike hard to make any sensible impression, which once received lasts long, because not easily effaced. By education and temper, little disposed to reason about causes and events; and therefore very proper to form a good soldier, and superior to any others, who are not raised by some species of enthusiasin.[190]

They were, at the least, worthy opponents of the finest army in the world.

The Literary Evidence

It has long been recognised that the greatest single frustration encountered by historians of the armies of *ancien régime* Europe is the near-total silence of the private soldier. Almost everything that we know about him comes from the observations of his superiors, or the arid records which survive in the official papers. Two ex-soldiers of the Austrian army nevertheless became celebrated authors in their own right, and their testimony is valuable because it is so rare, but we should be surprised that when they set pen to paper they were guided as much by intellectual fashion as the reality of their military lives.

The man we know as 'Joseph von Sonnenfels' was born in Vienna late in 1732 or early in 1733, at least according to the details entered in the muster list of the regiment of Deutschmeister. The family home was in Nikolsburg just across the Moravian border from Lower Austria, where Joseph's father, Lipman Perlin, was a traditional Hebrew teacher. Perlin was ruined by some kind of financial crisis in the 1740s, and for a time he was unable to give his son any further support, apart from an investment he had made in his family's future by converting to Christianity.

Joseph wandered through Austria without any schooling or direction, and it was therefore without any sense of a military calling that he enlisted as a private soldier in the Deutschmeister infantry regiment at Klagenfurt at the turn of 1750 and 1751. This regiment provided Joseph with the framework of discipline and purpose which had hitherto been lacking in his life. Already on 25 May 1752 he was promoted to corporal, and he soon acquired the reputation of being very successful at drumming up recruits.

In 1754, however, an improvement in his father's financial condition, together with the intervention of Count Dietrichstein, a family friend, enabled Joseph to buy his release from the military service. He returned to Vienna to read law in the Philosophical Faculty of the reformed University, and he excelled in his studies as much as he had done in his soldierly duties. In 1763 he became Reader in Public Administration and Economics (*Lektor in Polizey und Kameralwissenschaft*), and acting from this position of authority he became an intellectual ally of Maria Theresa in her programme of 'Enlightened' reform. Sonnenfels' interests and influence therefore extended well beyond that of a trainer of bureaucrats. He promoted the reform of the German language and theatre, he became Austrian provincial of the elite Masonic lodge *Zur wahren Eintracht* ('True Unity'), and he defended the Viennese way of life against censorious visitors from north Germany. He died on 25 April 1817, laden with honours and distinctions.

For our purposes we turn to the formative episode of that remarkable life, the career of Sonnenfels as a private soldier, and ask what those four years signified for him, how far they reflected the common Austrian military experience of his time, and what influence they had on the views which he developed concerning the military condition and patriotism.

This 'patriotism' was not the nationalism of the early 19th century, but one of its literary precursors, a cult which emerged in intellectual Europe in the third quarter of the 18th century. In the case of Sonnenfels the relevant offerings are to be found in his *Gesammelte Schriften* (10 vols., 1783–7), and more particularly in the essay *Über die Liebe des Vaterlandes,* which was written in 1771.

One strand in the thought of Sonnenfels connects the notion of individual contract and personal advantage – an essentially feudal concept – with the impulse to Enlightened reform. In terms that will probably strike us as cool and distant he advocated a patriotism founded on an awareness of the good fortune that was enjoyed from living in a particular country, with its laws, form of government, and society of fellow-citizens. There is a comparable statement by Carl Abraham Zedlitz that was delivered (in French) to the Berlin Academy in 1776, under the title *Le Patriotisme considéré comme objet d'éducation dans les états monarchiques.*

For Sonnenfels the reformer this notion of objectively beneficial laws and arrangements was a dynamic force, for it laid on Austrian monarchs the obligation to ensure that their subjects enjoyed conditions that were indeed advantageous. Why, for example, should the serf-ploughman be a patriot when he had no ownership or security in the land he ploughed?

Another aspect of Sonnenfels' patriotic' thought relates more closely to his career as a private soldier, and this was the concept of shared glory. Again there are a number of Prussian parallels. For Gotthold Ephraim Lessing, the flag of national honour covered everyone in the service of the Prussian monarchy. He could therefore pose the rhetorical question: 'And was Field Marshal Keith any less the Prussian because he was born in Scotland?' Two influential statements of a similar kind are to be found in the second edition (1760) of Johann Georg Zimmermann's *Von dem Nationalstolze* (*On National Pride*), and in Thomas Abbt's celebrated *Vom Tode fürs Vaterland* (*On Death for the Fatherland*) (1761), where Abbt denied the common contention that patriotism was the peculiar property of republics, and declared that subjects could participate in the glory of a monarchy, at least when it was embodied in a hero-king like Frederick of Prussia. In Sonnenfels, however, we encounter a significant variation, which turns the idea upside down, by elevating the honourable status of the components of the monarchy, in the form of its private soldiers:

> How contemptible those people… have always seemed who make it a reproach to me in their letters that I have carried a musket, and spent my time in a guardroom. Since the soldierly condition as a whole is worthy of esteem, those little men have forgotten that every element has a share in that esteem, and THAT WHICH FORMS THE HONOUR OF THE ENTITY IS THE HONOUR OF ITS INDIVIDUAL PARTS.[191]

Sonnenfels never threw away his uniform of Austrian white, and he was glad to show it to his friends.

It is time to turn to the experience of Sonnenfels as one of those private soldiers. From the muster list of the regiment of Deutschmeister of late May 1752 it is possible to confirm the statement in his memoirs that he served in the lieutenant-colonel's company. Among the private soldiers and NCOs of the company we encounter 44 Germans (reflecting heavy recruitment in the German lands of the Teutonic Order), 15 Bohemians, nine of Sonnenfels' fellow Moravians, and just five Austrians. The three largest trades of civilian employment were represented by the occupations of:

   Cobbler: 5 soldiers
   Carpenter: 4
   Butcher: 3

The soldiers of the company were evidently simple men, for there is no trace of the *Apotheker, Jurist* or *Studiosus* who sometimes leaven the mixture in other units.

Sonnenfels remembered the names of his senior company officers with great affection. Lieutenant-Colonel Carl Ludwig Baron Lestwitz was 63 at the time the muster was taken, and he had served for 44 years. He was a single man, a Protestant, and born in Schlauber in Silesia. The acting company commander, *Capitain-Lieutenant* Paul Silvester Elvenich, was 37 years of age, and had served for 24 years. He was an officer's son, a Catholic, and unmarried – like the great majority of the officers and men. By themselves these details suggest that both officers, Lestwitz and Elvenich, were dedicated, long-serving professional military men, and not amateurish aristocrats. It was probably in keeping with their type that they recognised the potential of Joseph, the almost uneducated Jewish lad, and that they did everything in their power to develop it. Sonnenfels writes that he was 'very far from having any cause for dissatisfaction with the condition state – on the contrary, I have every reason to prize it... in that estate I laid the foundation of that knowledge to which I owe my advancement... I should be neglecting an essential duty if I failed to avow my esteem for a way of life to which I owe so much'.[192]

Such a concern on the part of regimental officers was by no means an exception. Twenty years after Sonnenfels' service many elements in the army responded enthusiastically to the initiatives of Maria Theresa and Bishop Ignaz Felbiger in primary education, which they believed would not only provide a source of literate NCOs, but benefit the private soldiers as individuals and society at large.

Again, we find that Sonnenfels conforms with the identifiable Austrian military ethos of the time, which rested on the mixing of the nations and the movement of the regiments through the lands of the monarchy. He served in Styria, Carinthia, in Bohemia (where he took part in the important manoeuvre camps of 1752 and 1753), and in Hungary (where he participated in the manoeuvres of 1754). He acquired the French and Italian languages from the foreign soldiers in his regiment, and Bohemian under intimate circumstances from the girls at Sobotka and Jung-Bunzlau.

And yet, in fundamental ways, Sonnenfels was not a typical private soldier or a professional military man. Most obviously, not many private soldiers could become Professor of Public Administration and Economics. Then again, Sonnenfels writes as a man of letters of his time, and not as a soldier, when he remembers his association with the army as no more than an interesting phase in his career. There are resemblances to the career of Stephanie 'the Younger', another of Maria Theresa's temporary soldiers.

Johann Gottlob Stephanie was born in Breslau in 1741, conscripted into the Prussian army, and captured at Landeshut on 23 June 1760. The duchy of Silesia, although it was now Prussian territory, was still an important source of soldiers and NCOs for the Austrian army, and it was not remarkable that Stephanie should have changed sides and risen to the rank of *Feldwäbel* in the Austrian service.

Stephanie left the army after the war, but he continued to look back on his military past as a fund of inspiration, and the result was a famous sequence of plays – *Die Werber (The Recruiting*

Officers) (1763), *Die abgedankten Officiers* (*The Redundant Officers*) (1770) and *Die Kriegsgefangenen* (*The Prisoners of War*) (1771). The first of these pieces, *Die Werber,* was based on *The Recruiting Officer* by the British playwright George Farquhar, but Stephanie adapted it to accord with his own experience of the Austrian army. In the Introduction Stephanie writes that Farquhar was first an actor, and then became a recruiting officer. 'But with me I think it was the other way around. I was a recruiting officer, and afterwards an actor – and they flatter me by saying that I was a successful one. I had plenty of opportunity to learn about life from more than one side, and notably the military aspect, which offers such rewarding material for the theatre'.[193]

Similar ideas were put into the mouth of Major von Tellheim, in the celebrated *Minna von Barnhelm* by Gotthold Ephraim Lessing (written in 1763, published 1767). Lessing, although he had never been a soldier, had served as secretary to the fierce old Prussian general Tauentzien, who had defended Breslau successfully against Loudon in 1760, and he writes of himself at one remove in some of the passages he gives to Tellheim:

> I became a soldier out of attachment to a cause, though the politics thereof are something of a mystery to me, and from the notion that it was good for every honourable man to experience that condition of life, so as to know what danger means, and learn something of composure and resolution. But only dire necessity would have ever compelled me to turn this experiment into a vocation, and make a trade out of a temporary occupation.

In this respect Lessing, Stephanie and Sonnenfels were following an intellectual fashion, if not a soldierly one.

The Evidence of the Muster Lists

When the literary testimony turns out to be less than completely satisfying, it might seem altogether absurd to think of deducing the soldiers' motivation from sets of figures. All the same the muster lists offer striking comparisons between the feckless deserters, and the loyal soldiers who broke away from Prussian captivity and found their way back to their regiments (see below).

Many more soldiers made off than had their names actually entered as 'deserters' on the muster lists. On the basis of the existing record, however, it would appear that infantrymen of a few months' service were most likely to desert, and that loyalty and determination were most commonly to be found among the veteran dragoons.

	Captured or Returned Deserters (245 recorded)	Escaped Prisoners of War (955 recorded)
Arm of Service		
Infantry	95.51%	79.16
Cuirassierss	0.81	5.13
Dragoons	1.63	11.51
Hussars	2.04	4.18
Average Age	25.5	28.00
Married	19 = 7.75%	49 = 5.13
Owning Civilian Trade	39 =15.19%	145 = 15.18
Service	Marginally under 1	6
	(cases recorded 157)	(cases recorded 801)

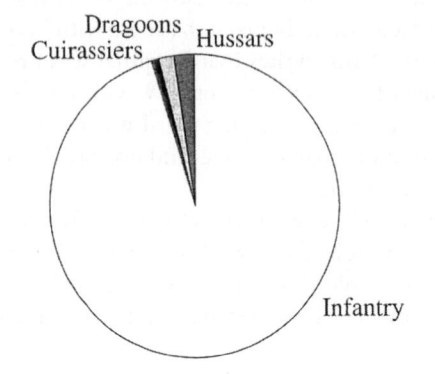

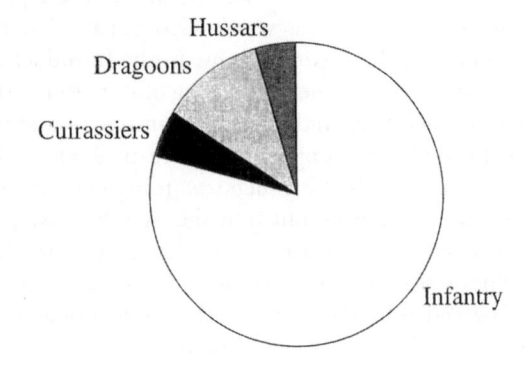

9

The NCOs and the Regimental Staffs

Under the eye of the colonel commandant and his officers, the greater part of the everyday business of the regiment was devolved to the non-commissioned officers, corporals, and a number of non-combatant specialists – the *Quartiermeister, Auditor (lawyer), Proviantmeister, Wagenmeister, Profos* (provost), *Regiments-Tambour* (drum major), and the chaplain and surgeon whose work will be considered in a later chapter.

At the level of the company, the company sergeant-major (*Feldweibel*) and the *Führer* and the *Fouriers* together made up the oddly-named *Kleine Prima Plana* ('little first page'), so called from the listing of their names after the officers on the first page of the company muster list. Further contributions to the life and running of the company were made by the *Corporalen* and the *Gefreyten*, and the officer servants (*Fourierschützen*), drummers and fifers (*Tambours*).

The Sergeants and Corporals

The NCOs were appointed by the colonel commandant under the overall authority of the Obrister-Inhaber. Thus Andreas Hadik as proprietor of a regiment of hussars told his new commandant, von Sprung, that he had the power to place all NCOs up to and including the *Wachtmeister* (regimental sergeant-major), though as a newcomer he must consult his officers as to the most suitable candidates, and Hadik reserved the right to appoint individuals as he wished.[1]

By general consent the Austrian NCOs nevertheless fell short of their Prussian counterparts both in their exercise of command, and their standing in the army and society. It was partly a question of numbers, but the quality of the intake was another consideration. Lieutenant-Colonel Rebain had seen the Prussian army at work, and emphasised that 'we should take care to appoint as NCOs such men as have already been in battle, and take them as far as possible from the ranks of the private soldiers, so as to awaken a spirit of ambitious improvement among the ordinary men'.[2] In Frederick's army it was unthinkable that it could have been otherwise.

Seeking to widen the intake, the authorities hoped that good NCO material might be found among the German-speaking Bohemian and Moravian capitulants, while the grenadier captain baron de Vigneul believed that the appeal should be extended to educated and intelligent sons of the bourgeoisie, if those lads could be convinced that the Austrian NCO had an honoured status, and the prospect of good civilian employment when he retired.[3] In this respect, as in many others, Austria still suffered from the consequences of the loss of the greater part of Silesia, which until 1741 had provided the army with its most productive recruiting ground in terms of quality. After this elapse of time the Silesian constituted a valuable if fast-diminishing asset, those from Prussian Silesia still making up 6.81 percent of the body of *Gefreyten*, corporals and full NCOs at the time our musters were compiled, and Kaunitz reckoned them still to be among the best. The *Reich* supplied the army with nearly one-quarter of such personnel, and Bohemia with more than one-fifth – which was large, but nevertheless well below the representation of the Bohemians among the private soldiers.

252 INSTRUMENT OF WAR

The author of the *Patriotic Reflections* argued towards the end of the Seven Years War that the typical Austrian NCO was still lacking in ambition and intelligence. The regiments had complained of the shortage of NCOs in peacetime, and in wartime the state of affairs was even worse, for the most able men were being whisked away to become officers. 'It is easy to see why it is hard for us to find good NCOs, and the first reason is that in many of the Hereditary Lands the peasant is unable to read or write – a primitive person generally – while the townsman is too soft... and disinclined to see his son become a soldier.' The second and related reason was the low regard for the Austrian NCOs in civil society. He did not wish to see the civilians being beaten up or oppressed in any way, but only that they should give the NCO the respect that was his due.[4]

It is curious to reflect that the authority of Maria Theresa and her generals rested ultimately on the *Gefreyter* (lance-corporal; private first class), a reliable soldier who had to kick a *Cameradschaft* of six or seven men into wakefulness every morning in their chamber or tent, and make sure that they were in a presentable state to

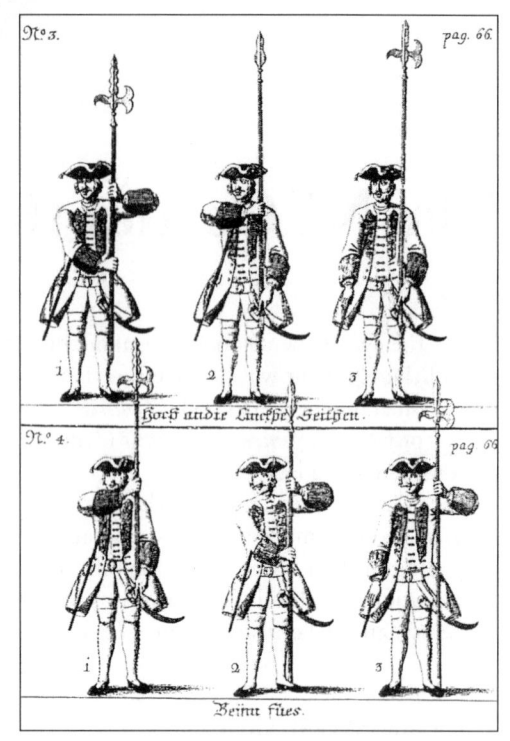

NCO drills with the *Kurzgewehr*. (*Regulament* of 1749)

go on parade or guard, take to the road, or face the enemy in action. Mundane chores continued to occupy the *Gefreyter's* days, even though he was literally 'freed' from strenuous duties.

The *Cameradschaften* were in turn grouped into *Corporalschaften,* numbering between three and six in every company. The full Corporal, as head of this fundamental administrative unit, held one of the most onerous posts in the company, 'for he has no rest day or night; he must be the first to know what is going on, and he must report everything to the *Feldwäbel*. On that account we must appoint men who are good, healthy and not too old; they must be discreet, know how to read and write German, and not given to gambling or drinking'.[5]

This corporal saw to the execution of orders, the maintenance of discipline, the upkeep of the uniforms, equipment, weapons and any horses, and he commanded guards and other small detachments. A small writing table was part of his own gear, for he was responsible for keeping up a number of simple records. Drawn for the most part from the ranks of the soldiers, he nevertheless had to keep his distance from them, and address them with the impersonal and peremptory *Ihr!* instead of the comradely *Du!* They in their turn had to receive their orders from him hat in hand, and call him their *Herr Corporal*.

Men who were steady, brave and physically strong were good material for promotion to *Führer*. They might on occasion act as deputy to the *Feldwäbel,* but their fundamental task was to carry a company colour or squadron standard. Theirs was arduous as well as dangerous work, which had proved to be beyond the capacity of the young *Fähndrichs* and comets – fledgling officers who in any case had responsibilities elsewhere. The *Fähndrichs* of the infantry had handed over their colours (now two per battalion) to *Führers* in 1748, and the mounted regiments followed their example with their standards in 1759.

The company sergeant-major (*Feldwäbel* in the infantry, *Wachtmeister* in the cavalry) was supposed to be a formidable individual, 'since the responsibility of keeping the men up to the mark lies mostly with him; his position therefore calls for exactitude, experience, and knowledge of the relevant procedures'.[6] The *Feldwäbel/Wachtmeister* executed the orders of the captain and lieutenants, oversaw the distribution of rations to the *Gefreyten,* inspected quarters and camp lines, and maintained the alignment and order of the company or squadron on the march. He was a full non-commissioned officer, and 'for this appointment we usually select men who can be made into officers in the course of time'.[7] This principle was admirable, but it leached the corps of Austrian NCOs of their best men. In the Prussian army promotion from NCO to officer was extremely rare, though the Prussian NCOs occupied a prestigious position in their own right, and when they retired to civilian life it was common for them to become such figures of local authority as tax collectors or schoolmasters.

In 1759 the company NCOs of the infantry exchanged their *Kurzgewehre* (miniature pikes, seven feet six inches long) for muskets, but they were still distinguished from the ordinary soldier by their sticks, and by whatever signs might be decreed by regimental custom, such as wearing yellow gloves on parade. 'As far as the punishments of the NCOs go, they include arrest in irons, the carrying of the *Kurzgewehr* for long periods of time, and degradation in rank – all according to the judgement of the regimental commander'.[8]

The NCOs as a body stood under the authority of the regimental sergeant-major (*Wachtmeister-Lieutenant* in the infantry; *Adjutant* in the cavalry), who occupied a key position in the regiment. He inspected the guard, issued and saw to the execution of regimental orders, received the morning and evening reports, collated the company muster lists, and kept records of all guards, detachments and working parties. He helped with the commandant's official correspondence (which added to the piles of paperwork associated with the Austrian NCOs) and was inevitably the man to whom the commandant first turned when he wished to know what was going on inside the regiment. In battle the RSM's position was alongside the major (*Wachtmeister*), which accounts for his title (*Wachtmeister-Lieutenant*) in the infantry. While the RSM observed a guarded politeness towards the officers proper, he might provide his own horse (a sign of independent status), and he was free of all corporal punishment.

The Distribution of *Gefreyten,* Corporals and NCOs in the Army
Our muster lists show a total of 15,352 lance-corporals, corporals and full NCOs (excluding those of the Croatian infantry), distributed as follows:

German infantry (incl. the 'new corps'):	9,528
Hungarian infantry:	2,080
Simbschen regiment:	47
Italian infantry:	401
Netherlands infantry:	907
Cuirassiers:	737
Dragoons:	637
Hussars:	750
Artillery:	330
Pioneers, Miners, Sappers:	40
National Origins of the Above	
Reich:	22.93%
Bohemia:	21.42
Hungary:	14.57
(*with Transylvania*	*16.91*)
Lower and Upper Austria, Vienna:	9.02

Moravia:	7.07
Prussian Silesia:	6.81
Netherlands and Luxembourg:	4.60
Transylvania:	2.34
Styria:	1.52
Prussia (other):	1.03
Austrian Italy:	0.91
Slavonia:	0.64
Tyrol, Lorraine:	0.52 each
Alsace:	0.48
Carinthia:	0.43
Spain:	0.41
Austrian Silesia:	0.38
Carniola:	0.37
France (other):	0.24
Görz and Gradisca:	0.14

Average Age of the Above

Infantry:	32 years
Cuirassiers:	34
Dragoons:	34
Hussars:	35
Artillery:	34
Pioneers, Miners, Sappers:	32

Average Service of the Above

Infantry:	10.5 years
Cuirassiers:	14.5
Dragoons:	14.5
Hussars:	14.0
Artillery:	13.5
Pioneers, Miners, Sappers:	not recorded
Average Age of RSMs alone:	32 years
Average Service of RSMs alone:	14 years

Percentage of Married *Gefreyten*, Corporals and NCOs

German infantry (excl. 'new units'):	17.06%
Hungarian infantry:	14.75
Simbschen regiment:	10.60
Italian infantry:	8.70
Netherlands infantry:	15.33
Cuirassiers:	9.68
Dragoons:	12.73
Hussars:	13.88
Pioneers:	25.00
Sappers:	14.28

DRUMMERS, TRUMPETERS AND FIFERS

The makers of military music occupied a central place in the life of the company, squadron or regiment, for they signalled the routine of the day (the posts, reveille, call to prayer, tattoo etc.), transmitted commands in action, and celebrated the military life in march and fanfare, or through the splendour of embroidered and painted heraldry, silver instruments, hangings and tassels of precious metal, and the pyramids of drums that were assembled by the *Regiments-Tambour* at the *Feldwache*. The drummers and fifers of the infantry were distinguished by the characteristic swallow's nest (*Schwalbennest*) epaulettes, while the kettle-drummers and trumpeters of the cavalry sported garishly-coloured coats richly adorned with stripes.

Every company of infantry owned two *Tambours* (drummers) and two fifers, making a *Spiel* of one drummer and one fifer for each of the company colours. Their counterparts in the cavalry were the kettle-drummers and trumpeters. A special order of 24 January 1748 exempted the latter from the physical punishment of carrying the cuirass, 'for punishment of that kind can cause damage to the chest'.[9]

Musicians could turn their spare time to good use by acting as servants, like the company *Tambour* assigned to Gorani in the Seven Years War. 'He was an exceptionally fine-looking young man, but very much the libertine. He had been servant to one of the regiment's officers, who had seduced and corrupted him. The morals of this regiment [Andlau] were kept under strict supervision, but the conduct of this drummer had escaped detection entirely'.[10]

The hierarchy of the musicians was headed by the *Regiments-Tambour* or *Regiments-Paucker*, who recruited, trained and led the *Spielleute* as a whole. 'It often happens that the *Regiments-Tambour* is sent to the enemy under cover of truce; it is therefore highly desirable that he should speak several languages, and he must be in addition a cool-headed, intelligent and discreet kind of man'.[11]

In the cavalry the trumpeters liked to think they had the status of independent contractors, as was brought to light by the case of the two *Feld-Trompeter* Franz Jesenzky and Franz Leininger, who in February 1759 abandoned the Kalckreuth Cuirassiers to take service with the Kaiser Hussars. A few days later Colonel Commandant Osterberg of the Kalckreuth regiment denounced the pair as deserters and thieves, whereupon the whole guild of official trumpeters (*Ober Hof Hatschier Landschaft- and Feld Trompeter*) brought the affair to the notice of the *Hofkriegsrath*. Osterberg had to admit that he had reduced the trumpeters' pay by five florins a month, 'and this was because a number of the trumpeters had already appeared in uniforms of different colours than their usual ones, and gone about in torn and extremely scruffy clothes, and turned up for duty with unsuitable horses, and sometimes with no horses at all'.[12] Trumpeter Jesenzky had in addition got himself deeply into debt, while Leininger had stolen a valuable watch from an officer. Jesenzky was beyond recall, and the *Hofkriegsrath* advised Osterberg just to let his companion Leininger go, and replace him by someone more suitable.

Drummers. (*Regulament* of 1749)

The members of the civilian 'music' were not entered on the muster lists, and were employed at the private expense of the colonel commandant or proprietor. The Infantry Regulations of 1749 speak of a regimental establishment of eight *Hautboisten,* comprising two *Faquotisten,* two *Waldhornisten,* and four *Hautboisten* proper, but in practice some of the colonels probably employed considerably more, as a manifestation of their wealth and taste. The music was of a high standard, for the Bohemian woodwind players were the finest in Europe, and thus in 1756 a group of citizens petitioned for the *Hautboisten-Banda* of the regiment of Daun to remain in Vienna when the army marched off to war. The band's days were in any event probably numbered, because the bands had already been abolished by official order, and the Commissaries and inspecting officers found that none survived in the regiments that underwent the *Musterung* in Bohemia in October 1755.

Tradesmen, Specialists and Professionals

Every company of infantry had on its establishment two *Zimmerleuthe* (singular *Zimmermann*) or pioneers – soldiers who were expert with the axe, and were put to work clearing paths of brushwood and other obstructions, repairing wheels and the like, and making gabions, fascines and ladders in fortified camps and during sieges.

Further craftsmen answered the special needs of the cavalry. The *Ober-Schmied* not only supervised the endless process of shoeing the horses, but also acted as the chief veterinarian of the regiment, inspected the remounts, and weeded out the unserviceable horses. He worked in close association with the *Sattler* or *Riemer,* who kept the saddles and harnesses in good order.

The state granted every company of infantry three florins a month for the repair of its weapons. In some regiments the sums were left at the disposal of the companies so that they could make their own arrangements, but in others the moneys were used to employ a qualified gunsmith (*Büchsenmacher*) on a six-yearly contract. 'This provision is one of the best in our army, and it proved its worth fully over the course of the campaigns'.[13]

A serving or retired NCO made a good *Wagenmeister,* the functionary who directed the transport train of the regiment in wartime, and attended the *Parole* in order to make the necessary arrangements for moving the vehicles on the next day. He claimed in addition the privilege of acting as sutler to the regimental staff, and he was free of the taxes which were levied on the other *Marquetender.* The *Wagenmeister* was in everyday contact with the *Proviantmeister,* the holder of another wartime appointment. He had the status of an NCO, and was responsible for drawing the regimental provisions and fodder from the army's *Proviant-Amt.*

Much of the routine business of the company devolved on the civilian *Fourier* (company clerk), who answered immediately to the captain, but also took directions as necessary from the *Proviantmeister* and the *Regiments-Quartier-meister* (below). The *Fourier* maintained the company correspondence, accounts and muster lists, oversaw the issue of uniforms, bread and fodder, and, strikingly, played the part of a staff officer when it came to staking out the lines of the company tents in camp. For this purpose the *Fourier* called on the help of his assistants, the *Fourierschützen,* who were soldiers also assigned to act as officer servants.

The *Fourier* was more intelligent and better-educated than most of the people he encountered, which rendered him, like most civilians working in a military environment, both indispensable and an object of contempt. A Prussian subaltern writes that 'the notions, principles and dealings of the [Austrian] *Fouriers,* as civilians, often ran directly counter to the way of thinking and interests of the soldiers. Discipline meant little to them. The effect was felt in disputes and muddles of a kind which were unknown in the Prussian camps, where everyone was a soldier, and therefore worked in harmony towards a common end'.[14]

The *Fouriers,* along with the surgeons, medical orderlies and tradesmen, in fact occupied an unsettled and not particularly enviable station. Some regiments entered them on their lists in a haphazard way, and the colonel commandant might, according to his whim, deal with them variously as commissioned officers, ordinary soldiers or hired help. Their 'pretensions' received short shrift from men like the author of the *Patriotic Reflections,* who maintained that the status of the genuine officers was:

> challenged in an unacceptable way by every last servant, functionary of the supply train (who is usually just a workman), apothecary's assistants, the commissaries and their clerks... It is wrong to have the physicians and the surgeons arrogating to themselves the distinctions and signs of the officer, and especially the sword knot.

These people had often been the servants of great lords, and their presumptions were reinforced by continuing 'protection' from above.[15]

Company *Zimmerleuthe.* (*Regulament* of 1749)

The *Fouriers* forwarded their muster rolls and accounts to the *Regiments-Quartiermeister,* a military officer who kept up the regimental books. He was simultaneously muster master, chief accountant and regimental staff officer, and in these various capacities he assembled the regimental muster lists, received and disbursed moneys, recruited and trained the *Fouriers* and went out with them to assign billets and stake out the regimental camps.

The regimental *Auditor* was a civilian, but one who was too valuable, and privy to too many secrets to be treated other than with respect. He was the chief secretary of the regiment, who kept records of all the orders from the *Hofkriegsrath* and generals, maintained the lists of the officers, and carried on the more confidential correspondence of the regiment and often the private correspondence of the commandant as well. The *Auditor* was also, and more significantly, the chief legal officer of the regiment, who acted as executor of the military officers' wills, and managed *Standrecht* (military justice) in concert with the commandant.

Individuals convicted under *Standrecht* and other proceedings were delivered to the care of the regimental provost (*Profos*), who supervised the administration of the punishment and the detention of prisoners, not excluding the erring officers. He was authorised to collect taxes from the captives, and was in a position to render their confinement more or less agreeable. Further opportunities for power and profit came with his other responsibilities, for he kept up the cleanliness and order of billets and camps, checked the weight and quality of the provisions that were supplied by the sutlers and butchers, and collected the taxes that were due from them on behalf of the major. His staff of brutish *Scharfrichter* and *Steckenknechte* kept him at one remove from the physical administration of discipline, and this office held great appeal for veterans NCOs, as is shown by the many applications for vacancies to the *Hofkriegsrath*. 'While the Prussian provost ... is a dismal creature, his Austrian counterpart is a person of standing, whom the soldiers and officers address as *Herr Vater!* He is well paid and he is smartly dressed'.[16]

Analysis of Non-combatant Supporting Personnel (including chaplains, surgeons and medical orderlies)

Total from Muster Lists   7,354
Nationality (1 percent and over only)
Bohemia: 25.16
- Reich: 24.12
Lower and Upper Austria, Vienna: 12.75
Moravia: 8.58
Hungary: 7.19
Netherlands and Luxembourg: 5.80
Prussian Silesia: 5.64
Styria: 1.26
Average Age: 27 years (including *Profos* at 52)
Average Service: 3.5 (including *Profos* at 30)

The figures entered above include 1,718 *Fouriers,* whose origins are of some interest, on account of the high degree of literacy and numeracy demanded by their post (leading seven locations only)

Reich: 17.69%
Bohemia;   14.72
Lower and Upper Austria, Vienna: 9.25
(incl. 5.52 from Vienna)
Moravia: 6.63
Prussian Silesia: 5.87
Hungary: 3.78
Prussia (other):   1.33

10

The Infantry

ORGANISATION

The Austrian infantry of the period of the Seven Years War constituted nearly three-quarters of the personnel of the army as a whole, and was made up of some 65 regiments or units (excluding the Croatian infantry):

> Thirty-nine regiments of 'German' infantry'
> Ten regiments of Hungarian 'national' infantry, or 11 with the regiment of Simbschen
> Two regiments of Italian national infantry
> Four regiments of Netherlands national infantry
> 'New corps' – the Anhalt-Zerbst battalion, the specialised *Feld-Jäger-Corps, Staabs-Infanterie-Regiment* and *Artillerie-Füsiliere-Regiment,* and a number of free battalions and units
> Four units of auxiliary infantry, namely the regiment of Toscana, the regiment of Mainz (Lamberg), and the regiments of Blau- and Roth-Würzburg (amalgamated into one in the course of the war). In addition subsidised contingents of Württembergers and Bavarians made a brief appearance on the 'Austrian theatre of war in 1757, while a hired Modena contingent garrisoned fortresses in northern Italy

In 1748 the Military Reform Commission resolved on a strong regimental peace establishment of four battalions (2,408 officers and men) as a solid base from which to progress to war, rather than a cadre system (skeleton regiments, to be recruited up to strength as necessary) as favoured by Daun. This was a sound principle, which averted a crisis in recruiting when war approached. The establishment underwent two modifications:

> Revised Peace Establishment, spring 1756
> Regiment of three field battalions, two grenadier companies, one garrison battalion (2,408 officers and men), re-defined as:
> War Establishment, 1756–7
> Effective field regiment of two field battalions, each of six companies of fusiliers (some 140 officers and men apiece); also two grenadier companies per regiment (below)
> Garrison battalion of six fusilier companies, reduced to four late in 1761.

Wartime or actual combat brought about various complications. Most obviously, the garrison battalion of the regiment remained behind when the two field battalions marched off to join the army. On the theatre of war the two grenadier companies left the parent regiment, and joined the grenadiers from the other regiments to form combined battalions of elite troops. When, finally, the moment arrived to face the enemy, the battalion was divided into:

Sixteen tactical platoons (*Züge*), which were in turn grouped into
Eight half divisions (of two platoons each)
Four full divisions

The Grenadiers

The first Austrian grenadiers came into being in 1700, at the height of the European vogue for grenade-throwing heavyweight infantry. The fashion passed soon enough, for the grenades were cumbersome, tricky to ignite, and (in so far as they were dangerous at all) only marginally less perilous to the thrower than to the target. However the grenadiers themselves survived in virtue of being elite troops in their own right, and they were marked out by their stature, their swarthy complexions, their bristling moustaches, their arrogant demeanour, their grenadier marches (characterised by alternate passages on the rim and the skin of the drum), and their grenadier caps, which in the Austrian service were brass-fronted bearskins. The colonel proprietor lavished care and money on his grenadiers, for these folk to a great extent represented the public face of the regiment, and:

> a captain of grenadiers should be… an officer experienced in war, of reputation and imposing appearance, and capable of withstanding whatever exertions he is called upon to make in the field. He should also be a man of polished manners, for in garrison service and on general watches he will be more in the view of the generals than are the other officers – a circumstance which he can turn to great advantage.[1]

In the course of the Seven Years War the Austrian grenadiers acquired a new significance as a corps of elite troops, who could be employed to spearhead assaults, or meet emergencies on the battlefield. The way was shown by *FM*. Browne, who brought together 22 companies at Prague on 6 May 1757, and very nearly turned the battle in favour of the Austrians. Grenadiers were again used *en masse* at the storm of Gabel on 15 July 1757, and thereafter they were frequently combined in massed battalions which represented up to 10 companies at a time. The next step was to separate the grenadiers from their parent regiments for the duration of the campaigning season, and place them at the direct disposal of *FML*. Lacy as head of the new General Staff. This measure was taken when the army marched from the camp of Skalitz on 29 April 1758.

A few officers continued to oppose the elite status accorded to the grenadiers. The Prince de Ligne disliked specialised categories of infantry

Grenadier officer of the regiment of Deutschmeister (figurine by Krauhse, Austrian Army Museum). Grenadier officers (unlike those of the fusiliers), carried muskets and belt cartridge pouches. At once deferential and full of guile, the expression of this gentleman suggests that (like many of his kind) he had high military and social ambitions.

on principle, and he noted how at the battle of Prague the departure of the grenadiers left the rest of the army with gaps in its line.² This objection lost much of its force once the grenadiers were brought under combined command in 1758, in the way we have just seen. *FM*. Anton Mercy discovered the strength of feeling in favour of the grenadiers when he proposed abolishing just two companies of these people from the establishment of the Slavonian Croats. He put the question to the military members of the *Hofkriegsrath* in February 1762, and was told by one of the Colloredos that it would be entirely wrong to incorporate the grenadiers among the fusiliers:

> for such a demotion would undermine the morale of those men, who are far more highly-motivated than the other troops, as is shown by their record in action, when they strive to give of their best and distinguish themselves. And so, in my humble opinion, we should retain the grenadiers with both the Croats and the regulars, and all the more because by cultivating them we shall inspire the other men to perfect themselves in the service, so that they too may become grenadiers.³

The same language was heard from the other members of the *Hofkriegsrath,* and the project fell through. The Prussians and the foreign military attachés continued to regard the Austrian grenadiers as fine troops, and probably the best in the army.

GARRISON BATTALIONS AND OTHER RESERVES

The third, or 'garrison' battalions were separated from the field battalions early in the war, 'so as to make good the shortfalls among the field battalions and grenadier companies from time to time, and to be of assistance to the regiment in the event of disaster'.⁴

The garrison battalions could not compete in glamour with the grenadiers, but in their modest way they made a useful contribution to the Austrian effort in the war. Neipperg spoke on the subject to a Military Conference of 30 January 1757, explaining that he had set up these battalions with two main objects in mind, namely to keep the field battalions fully up to strength with ready-trained men over the course of several months at a time, and to save the field army the nuisance of having to make detachments to guard magazines, convoys and so forth in the rear areas.⁵

If the garrison battalions had not been in existence, the officers and men who were invalided out of the field battalions would probably have been lost to the service altogether. Together with the smaller regimental *Depositorien,* which were established on the actual theatres of war, the garrison battalions also acted as receptacles for the otherwise uncontrollable masses of untrained recruits who were being raised by the *Stände.*

In the later years of the war Maria Theresa was persuaded that the regiments were employing the garrison battalions and the *Depositorien* as safe havens for their personnel, to the extent that individual regiments had salted away as many as four of their captains and six of their lieutenants. In July 1761 the *Hofkriegsrath* transmitted her instructions to purge the *Depositorien,* and in the winter of 1761/2, as part of the notorious reduction of the army, two companies were struck from the six-company establishment of every garrison battalion. Even now Maria Theresa was not convinced that the process had gone far enough, and in September 1762 she ordered a further weeding out of the troops in the already-depleted garrison battalions.⁶

Without some kind of permanent institutional base, the *Depositorien* and the garrison battalions were inevitably vulnerable to raids of this kind. However it was still necessary to provide 'garrisons' in -the literal sense to guard fortresses, and an *Invaliden-Corps* was set up for this purpose in 1756 and 1757, and provided 16 companies for the fortresses of the Hereditary Lands, and another seven for the Netherlands. A full *Österreichisches Garnison-Regiment* was established in 1760, and was kept on foot for the rest of the war.

The German Infantry

The army rested on the firm foundation of Maria Theresa's 39 regiments of German infantry. Most of the units were 'German' only in a figurative sense, for the troops hailed from all over Central Europe, with by far the biggest single contingent being provided by Bohemia.

German Infantry Regiments (designations as of 1759)
Andlau
Angern (Kheul -1758)
Arenberg
Baden-Baden
Baden-Durlach
Bayreuth
Botta
Colloredo-Alt (Anton)
Colloredo-Jung (Carl)
Daun-Alt (Heinrich) (O'Kelly 1761–)
Daun-Jung (Leopold)
Deutschmeister
Gaisruck
Harrach
Harsch
Hildburghausen
Kayser
Kollowrat
Königsegg
Lacy (Hagenbach -1756; Sprecher 1757–)
Lothringen
Maguire (*Tyroler Land- and Feld-Regiment*)
Marschall
Mercy
Moltke
Neipperg
Pallavicini
Platz
Puebla
Salm
Sincere
Starhemberg
Thürheim (Piccolomini -1757)
Tillier (Browne -1759; Kinsky 1761–)
Waldeck
Wallis
Wied
Wolfenbüttel-Alt (Carl) (Loudon 1760–)
Wolfenbüttel-Jung (Ernst Ludwig)

The Hungarian National Infantry (see p. 73)

Whereas the Italian and Netherlands infantrymen could be considered as exotic additions to an already diverse army, the 10 Hungarian regiments formed nearly one-sixth of the infantry as a whole. The Hungarians counted as one of the 'hot' nations of Europe, along with the emotional English and Italians, and it was in accordance with the national character that the Pressburg *Landtag* of September 1741 voted to raise a mighty 21,600 men or 13 regiments of foot, in addition to the three regiments (Batthyány, Gyulai, Leopold Pálffy) inherited by Maria Theresa. However the recruiting could sustain only five new regiments (Bethlen, Erzherzog Carl, Joseph Esterházy, Nicolaus Esterházy, Haller). A sixth new regiment was raised in 1756 (Pálffy, Johann, from 1758 Preysach). The regiment of Simbschen stood out as an anomaly. It was dressed in the Hungarian style, but was a lineal descendent of the notorious *Panduren-Corps von der Trenck,* and was recruited in the areas of Slavonia lying outside the Military Borders.

The Hungarian infantrymen were at their best when they were in the immediate presence of the enemy, which encouraged Armfeldt to describe them as among the best of Maria Theresa's foot soldiers.[7] The difficulty was not to get them to fight, but to enlist in the first place. Armfeldt noted that 'it was only out of necessity that the Empress-Queen used Hungarians as infantry, and at a time when recruits could not be raised from Bohemia. None of her ancestors had employed Hungarians for that purpose, for they were convinced that they were unsuitable for dismounted service'.[8]

The military reforms certainly established the Hungarian national regiments in full parity with the rest of the infantry, as Khevenhüller-Metsch discovered when he sounded Maria Theresa as to the wisdom of his son Hans Joseph leaving a German regiment to enter that of Bethlen as a first-lieutenant, for 'she was gracious enough to give me the direct assurance that now that these regiments have equality with the German regiments, the officers have the same standing in rank and every other respect. This banished all my reservations'.[9]

All the regulations in the world nevertheless failed to shake the conviction among the Hungarians that to be 'stuck among the infantry' was the worst fate that could befall them. *GFWM.* Joseph Draskovich was entrusted with the task of supervising the Hungarian recruiting early in the war. He was replaced on 14 September 1757 by Colonel Franz Anton Count Károly of the regiment of Joseph Esterházy,[10] but the appeal of the Hungarian infantry service was not strengthened by an order of 3 January 1758, which authorised the regiments to recruit deserters and foreigners regardless of their nationality.

The case of the regiment of Forgách is instructive. Its recruiting was given a short-lived impetus by the wealthy Hungarian *Hofcammer Präsident* Anton Count Grassalkovich, who in

Hungarian infantryman (Krauhse, Austrian Army Museum). He is of the regiment of Erzherzog Carl. White coat with yellow cuffs and turn-backs; blue dolman and *Gatti-Hosen*.

addition enjoyed local authority in the *Comitat* of Neograd in his capacity of *Obergespan,* and who succeeded in raising 1,000 recruits for his pet regiment, 'since from time immemorial the nobility have held this family in uncommonly high regard'.[11] The *Hofkriegsrath* nevertheless ruled that such an accession of fresh blood would have made the Forgách regiment as strong as any three other Hungarian regiments together, and diverted the recruits to the regiments of Erzherzog Carl and Haller, which had suffered heavily in the field. By the autumn of 1761 the local enthusiasm for the Forgách regiment had abated altogether, and the commandant was forced to offer explanations for his uncommonly high rate of desertion.

Already by November 1759 the Hungarian infantry as a whole and the regiment of Simbschen were short by 4,881 of their establishment of 29,920 troops, and the authorities never succeeded in finding means of attracting new men to the colours, or stanching the outflow through desertion.[12]

The dashing style dress had not proved to be a sufficient incentive. In 1749 the authorities had settled on an interesting ensemble which combined elements of Western and Magyar fashion. The hat was a felt tricorn on the normal pattern, but it sat on locks of plaited hair which hung down over the sides and back to the head to give the wearer a ferocious appearance. The white coat was distinguished by rows of tasselled buttonholes, and pointed cuffs of the regimental colour. The waistcoat was replaced by a Hungarian dolman (usually blue, and bound about the middle by a barrel sash), and this garment was so substantial that in action the outer coat was often laid aside to enable to men to wield their muskets more readily. Towards the end of the battle of Kohn an enemy officer approached a regiment which was seemingly clad in blue coats in the Prussian style, and he was greeted by an outburst of fire which disabused him of his error.[13]

In place of the conventional breeches and gaiters the Hungarians sported long breeches (*Gatti-Hosen*) and half-boots. The legwear in question were decorated down the front of the thighs with Hungarian knots, and in some regiments they were cut so tightly that the men had to wear hussar-type sabretaches to store their little effects. A curved sabre reinforced the visual connection with the Magyar mounted troops. Only the regiment of Leopold Pálffy seems to have dressed in the 'German' style.

> Hungarian National Regiments (designations as of 1759)
> Batthyány
> Bethlen
> Carl, Erzherzog (Ferdinand, Erzherzog 1762–)
> Esterházy, Joseph
> Esterházy, Nicolaus
> Forgách
> Gyulai
> Haller
> Pálffy, Leopold
> Preysach, (Pálffy, Johann -1758)
> Simbschen

The Italian National Infantry (see p. 81)

The Italian National Infantry comprised some 4,000 troops. Luzan, the senior regiment, was joined in 1744 by the 2,300 ruffianly recruits who made up the new regiment of Giorgio Marquis Clerici. In the Seven Years War the two regiments figured relatively high in the army's rates of desertion and sickness, though a number of German regiments did worse. All the same they appear to have performed respectably enough in the field. Luzan was distinguished at the storm of Schweidnitz in 1757; in the following year the brutal Colonel Francesco Valentiniani gained for Clerici the 'privilege' of leading the assault on the churchyard at Hochkirch, and the regiment lost several hundred dead and wounded over the next few minutes. Valentiniani was numbered among the casualties, and eventually died of his wounds.

> Italian National Infantry (designations as of 1759)
> Luzan Clerici

THE NETHERLANDS NATIONAL INFANTRY (SEE P. 86)

Four regiments (d'Arberg, de Ligne [Claude], Los Rios and Sachsen-Gotha) made up the Netherlands national infantry in the Seven Years War. The generic name of the time, the 'Walloon infantry,' referred both to the prestige which the Walloons had long enjoyed in the service of European monarchies, and to the leading role played by the French-speaking aristocracy of Hainault.

In 1756 the first of the Netherlands troops set out from their homeland for the theatre of war. They comprised the dragoon regiment of Ferdinand de Ligne, and the infantry regiments of d'Arberg and Los Rios – each made up of two battalions of 600 fusiliers apiece, and two augmented grenadier companies. The contingent had been organised by Prince Charles of Lorraine, in his capacity as Netherlands *Statthalter*, and he explained that 'the corps which will be set in march will be made up of picked men. It will also be highly mobile, for I have taken care to select the men who are the best suited to withstand the hardships of the field, leaving behind all those who are sick, feeble and invalid, as also… all the officer's ladies, and all the soldiers' wives who are superfluous to requirement'.[14]

This leading contingent was engaged very heavily at the battle of Prague, on 6 May 1757, when the Austrians, after early successes, were defeated and split apart. Such troops as managed to escape found their way to Daun's camp at Czaslau on 11 June, when it was noted that 'they [the Netherlanders] had taken the heaviest punishment of all. Out of 1,500 men who made up the two battalions of Los Rios, there are only 600 left.' The whole of the second battalion of d'Arberg was missing, while 'the first is in a deplorable state, and only its grenadiers survive – they complain loudly that they were left in the lurch by the Austrian cavalry of the right wing'.[15] Seven days later the de Ligne Dragoons accomplished the most celebrated Austrian unit action of the entire war, when they headed the charge which precipitated the defeat of the Prussians at Kolin.

GFWM. Charles-François comte de Dombasle (a Lorrainer) was meanwhile putting together a second contingent, consisting of one battalion each of the regiments of Claude de Ligne and Sachsen-Gotha, and additional battalions of d'Arberg and Los Rios. Dombasle's men were diverted to the French army of the Marshal d'Estrées, and at first assigned nothing more arduous than the work of occupying towns in Prussian Westphalia. On 26 July 1757, however, the de Ligne and Sachsen-Gotha battalions were in the thick of the fighting in the early stages of the battle of Hastenbeck, where they beat off two Hanoverian attacks, and gave time for the French to put themselves in order and advance to final victory. Dombasle heard that the Austrians were giving bounties to troops who had served well in Bohemia, and he asked for the same favour for the equally deserving men of de Ligne and Sachsen-Gotha.[16]

By the end of July, therefore, nobody could doubt the fighting qualities of the Netherlanders. However the losses among the infantry were probably never completely repaired. When 500 recruits, most of them Prussian deserters, reached the main Austrian army on 11 September, it was decided to admit:

those who speak French, or are French deserters, so as to complete the badly under-strength Walloon regiments, in virtue of the convention which has been signed between the King [of France] and the Empress-Queen. The battalion of the regiment of Prince [Claude] de Ligne is with the army, but incapable of doing further service: the son [Charles-Joseph] of the prince is the only remaining captain; its two companies of grenadiers have been reduced to one, and they remain on that establishment; three weak companies of its fusiliers are down to 150 men.[17]

The battalion of de Ligne had still not recovered before it was in action again at Leuthen, and suffered further heavy casualties.

In the early summer of 1758 Dombasle's brigade was assigned by agreement to the Austrian army.[18] On 8 June Dombasle reported that his force was gathering at Würzburg. He had six battalions under his command (one battalion each of d'Arberg, de Ligne, Los Rios, Sachsen-Gotha, and the 'German' regiments of Lothringen and Platz), but the whole made up scarcely 3,500 men, 'among whom there are many recruits who have never wielded arms'.[19]

It was becoming clear that the greatest shortcoming of the Netherlands forces was not their notorious love of argument and plunder, but their dependence on recruiting from their remote homeland. The losses at Leuthen had precipitated a drive to raise 5,200 men, and the efforts of the military recruits were seconded by those of the civil police and the magistrates, who were authorised to enlist men on their own initiative. This measure supplied more than half the stipulated contingent, among which there must have been many men who were saved from prison or the gallows. Vienna was insatiable in its demands, and in the later years of the war it required hefty annual instalments of 4,000 recruits. All the shortcomings were reported to Maria Theresa, who learned in July 1762 that the Netherlands were still 836 men short on the latest *Postulatum*.[20]

Netherlands National Regiments (designations as of 1759)
d'Arberg
de Ligne (Claude)
Los Rios
Sachsen-Gotha

JÄGER AND OTHER LIGHT INFANTRY

The rise of light infantry formed one of the most significant developments in European warfare in the second half of the 18th century. The Prince de Ligne recalls an action at Zehren, where he commanded a respectable force of hussars and Croats, 'but before I could dislodge a Prussian free battalion from a wood I had two of my officers killed. They had been standing in front of my horse, and I had been assigning them to various positions… The enemy killed a fair number of my soldiers as well. I lost patience, fired a general salvo in their direction, and advanced my command through the brushwood. They all made off. I went forward to see whom I had killed – there was nobody'.[21]

Thus the availability of light troops of their own would give the Austrians the means to answer the Prussian free battalions in kind, and help to bolster the flagging efforts of the Croats. In a wider context, the existence of light or irregular forces enabled the Austrians to attract Prussian deserters who would otherwise have wandered off or gone back to the enemy. That was why in the autumn of 1761 Kaunitz exempted Loudon's Green Grenadiers and the Beck *Volontiers Silesiens* from the general reduction of the 'new corps.' Looking further ahead, Daun wrote to Maria Theresa at the same time that free troops would be indispensable in the event of a new Turkish war, for the Croats would be largely tied down in local defence. He believed that the battalion was the ideal size for a unit of these men, for companies were too small to be kept going for any length of time, while full regiments were needlessly expensive.[22]

Deutsches Feld-Jäger Corps

> You should not tell a recruit: 'I will make you into a *Jäger*!' You must instead take them from the forests. They know how to perch on a rock, how to conceal themselves in one of those fissures which open in the ground after a great drought, or hide behind a mighty oak. They make their way slowly and softly, so as not to make any sound, and in such a way they can creep up on a post and take it by surprise, or shoot down the enemy generals. (de Ligne)[23]

The *Jäger* were the professional huntsmen and gamekeepers of Central Europe, employed on the great estates to preserve the shooting and hunting in good order, and provide game for their masters' tables. Their classic weapon was the rifle, which was slow and difficult to load, but offered marked advantages in accuracy and effective range over the smooth-bore muskets which were carried by the rest of the infantry.

Such skills were of immediate use in war, and the Austrians raised a first batch of 50 *Jäger* in Bohemia in 1756. In the early summer of 1758 a battalion of Tyrolean sharpshooters did much execution during the Prussian retreat through the tangled hills on the borders of Moravia and Bohemia,[24] and this unit probably furnished the recruiting base for the *Deutsches Feld-Jäger* Corps which came under the direction of the chief of staff, *FML*. Lacy in the course of the same year. The Jäger now acted under the immediate direction of the Staff, and provided cover for the work of the *Pioniere*. Early in 1760 Lacy urged Vienna to augment the *Jäger-Corps* by 400 men, and procure the necessary rifles. The *Directorium* objected to the great expense that would be incurred, but Maria Theresa ruled that 'the *Jäger* must be brought up to a strength of 1,000'.[25] The augmentation went ahead, and the 1,000 men were organised into an impressive establishment of 10 companies.

The *Jäger* won full independence of the *Pionier-Corps* in 1761, and they continued to perform excellent service until the end of the war, when they were disbanded. They had meanwhile tapped the military instincts of the Tyrolese, which could find no other expression at the time. Their duchy was exempt from the *Stände* conscription, while the *Tyroler Land- and Feld-Regiment* represented an unhappy compromise between a field and a garrison regiment, and existed primarily to give employment to young Tyrolean noblemen as officers.

The *Jäger* sported low caps of black leather, and were clad in coats, waistcoats and breeches of bluish-grey (*Hechtgrau*, or pike grey), with green collar, cuffs and turn-backs.

Jäger Corps Otto

The *Deutsches Feld-Jäger Corps* was an eminently respectable unit, and stood under the eyes of the Chief of Staff. *The Jäger Corps Otto* expressed another contemporary phenomenon, that of the free battalion or free company, which was recruited by an individual entrepreneur, and fought or ravaged on the fringes of the regular armies. The corps immediately in question was raised in 1759 by the Saxon-born Captain Otto, and consisted of a company of sharpshooters, with attached *chevaulegers* and hussars.

The corps operated in loose association with the *Reichsarmee,* and therefore in Saxony and in adjacent states (where Otto was familiar with the ground). It was engaged in a series of lively little actions, and experienced a scarcely less turbulent internal life, to judge by a petition which was forwarded to *G.d.C.* Hadik, allegedly on behalf of the whole corps, on 9 April 1761:

> for six months now the service has been neglected totally… namely since the time control was assumed by a certain immoral woman, who whores about with all and sundry, and now and then helps herself to what she likes by way of theft. She passes herself off as an honourable and virtuous cousin of the commandant, but lodges with him in chamber and bed. There was a time when she had not a pair of shoes to her name, let alone a complete dress, but now she holds state in satin and silk, gold and silver, like the wife of a great general. Your Excellency ordered the commandant to get rid of this woman, but all he did was to move her to another house, where his visits lasted from evening to morning, and now she is back again in his quarters. When any of us comes up to ask to be released, because his time has expired, or to be better provided for, he is answered with beatings, and all at the behest of this 'cousin,' who is the one giving the orders.[26]

Enough men stayed with Otto to form a force of 145 infantry and 120 horse which descended in 1762 on the little Bayreuth town of Bayersdorf, and exacted recruits, remounts, fodder and bread under the threat of force (see p. 93).

Other Free Corps and Battalions

A number of free units have scarcely a trace beyond their names. These were:

> Netherlands *Freicorps Béthune* (renamed *Freicorps Drais* on 1760): The original three companies were raised in 1757; increased in 1762 to eight companies of infantry (about 950 men) and seven companies of horse (about 450). Netherlands *Freicorps Le Bon*: Raised in 1762 as three companies of foot (about 560), and one squadron each of hussars and mounted *Jäger* (together about 230)
> *Freicorps Kuhwein:* Raised in 1762 as seven companies of infantry (about 1,000) and two squadrons of hussars (together about 230).

These units were intended for the local defence of the Netherlands, and possibly shared the same manpower base as the units of *Gardes-Côtes* which were raised in 1758 to meet the threat of British invasion (see p. 413). In contrast two further units were linked with some of the most active commanders of the Austrian service:

> *Volontiers Silesiens Beck*
> This was a force of six green-clad companies constituted under the command of *GFWM.* Philipp Levin Beck in March 1760. Beck recruited heavily from Prussian deserters among the native Silesians, and this was one of the reasons why it was spared in the reduction of 1761/2, along with the Green Loudon Grenadiers (below).

> *Grenadier-Bataillon (Regiment) Grun Loudon*
> Loudon was ascending rapidly in the service when in 1758 he recruited a free battalion of six companies. He had intended to raise a second battalion at the same time, but his proposal was rejected on the grounds that it would draw men away from the German regiments. He returned to the charge in 1759, and explained his thinking in some detail. As a full regiment his troops would be able to lend solid support to the Croats, who had a way of dispersing after

a successful attack, while their uniforms and designation as 'grenadiers' would attract and keep Prussian deserters.[27]

Loudon was now given leave to go ahead, and he succeeded as promised in raising the second battalion, aided no doubt by the rumours that men under his command had plenty of opportunities for plunder. This regiment is to be distinguished from the regular German infantry regiment of Loudon, and it derived its name from its coats of green.

Auxiliary Troops

Toscana

Although Tuscany did not belong to the Habsburg body politic proper, Emperor Francis Stephen had exercised personal sovereignty over the duchy since 1737 in his capacity as Grand Duke. He had long striven, with mixed success, to build up a small but efficient Tuscan army of German and local troops, and in 1758 he consolidated his forces into the regiment of 'Toscana,' which was taken into the Austrian pay. On 17 March 1758 the first contingent was inspected by Francis Stephen and Maria Theresa outside the Imperial *Stallburg* (Stables) in Vienna, after which the troops continued on their way to Bohemia. Reinforcements to the number of 1,500 arrived in 1759, and the regiment was ultimately assigned to Loudon's command in Silesia in1760. The German officers had obeyed the initial summons readily enough, but the Italians, who made up most of the rank and file, were much less enthusiastic, and about 4,000 young Tuscans escaped from the duchy to avoid conscription.[28]

The Tuscans went into battle under very unfavourable circumstances at Liegnitz on 15 August 1760, when Loudon's unsupported corps attacked the main Prussian army and was beaten back. Loudon was nevertheless able to report that 'the Tuscan troops of His Majesty the Emperor… distinguished themselves in this action, and have proved that they lack neither courage nor firmness'.[29]

The Modena Contingent

Duke Francesco III d'Este, an independent sovereign, hired out three regiments of infantry and one of the cavalry in 1757. The Modena troops were never intended for combat against the Prussians, but were placed in garrison in the Austrian fortresses in northern Italy, and thereby released the regiments of Pallavicini and Mercy for active service.

The German Auxiliaries

The Anhalt-Zerbst Battalion (see p. 412)
This small and under-recruited unit was raised on the initiative of Friedrich August of Anhalt-Zerbst in 1760. Its military worth was low, but its political value ensured that it was spared from the reduction of the army in the winter of 1761/2. The battalion was counted technically as one of the 'new corps.'

The Mainz Regiment
The Mainz regiment of Lamberg was taken into Austrian service in virtue of a treaty of 1 November 1756, in the form of two field battalions, two grenadier companies and one garrison battalion. The field troops were badly mauled on the right wing of the Austrian army at Prague (6 May 1757), and thereafter they performed useful if not outstanding service

The Würzburg Regiments (see p. 412)

The ecclesiastic Electors counted as Austria's firmest supporters in the *Reich,* which facilitated a convention of 16 September 1756 with the Bishop of Würzburg, whereby the Austrians took into their pay two excellent regiments of infantry, those of Blau-Würzburg and Roth-Würzburg, so called after the facings of their white uniforms. The Würzburgers repeatedly earned their keep in action, and the Red regiment's heroic defence of the churchyard at Leuthen on 5 December 1757 was remembered as one of the few redeeming features of that dismal day. The depleted troops were united in a single regiment later in the war, and did service in this form in Saxony in 1761 and 1762.

The Hired Bavarians and Württembergers

Through the help of France the Austrians gained the services of 4,000 Bavarians and 6,000 Württembergers in 1757. These were hired troops, which were not assigned permanently to Austrian command, and not taken onto the Austrian establishment like those of Anhalt-Zerbst, Mainz or Würzburg.

Bavaria was sinking down the ranks of third-rate powers, and was in military decline. The Württemberg troops were of greater inherent value, and their duke, Carl Eugen, was said to be 'a prince of vast genius, high-minded, diligent, active and resourceful... He directs in person all the military, civil and judicial affairs of his states, and the finances as well'.[30] However Carl Eugen and his subjects were divided by religion, the duke being Catholic, while the Württembergers were for the most part Protestants and enthusiasts for the Prussian cause. The Landgraf of Fürstenberg warned the Austrians that the Württemberg troops ought to be consigned to garrison service and kept under close surveillance,[31] but his advice went unheeded, and these people along with the Bavarians accompanied the Austrians in the campaign in Silesia in 1757.

The Württemberg contingent did well at Nádasdy's siege of Schweidnitz, while at the battle of Breslau their grenadier companies served without reproach alongside their Austrian counterparts. On 5 December, however, the Württembergers faced the full impact of the first Prussian assault at Leuthen, and collapsed under the ordeal, whereupon the Bavarians took to their heels. In fairness to the Württembergers it must be said that even the most devoted troops could scarcely have held out any longer, but the Austrians had 'particular reasons for attributing the unfortunate outcome of that disastrous day solely to them. So much contempt was heaped on the Württembergers in consequence that it would have been too risky to see them with an Austrian army ever again'.[32] This was the end of all direct association between the main Austrian forces and the troops of Bavaria and Württemberg.

UNIFORMS, WEAPONS AND EQUIPMENT

The outfit of the Austrian infantryman comprised a black felt tricorn hat (or bearskin for the grenadiers), a forage cap, a neck stock, white coat, waistcoat and breeches (but coloured waistcoat and *Gatti-Hosen* for the Hungarians), one pair each of white and black gaiters, a pair of shoes, two pairs of stockings, two or three shirts, a cartridge pouch, an oil flask, a water flask, a priming needle, brushes and other cleaning materials, a knapsack of ticking of calfskin, a musket and bayonet, and (if he were Hungarian or a grenadier) also a curved sabre.

The regiments were distinguished by the devices on the coat buttons and the metal shields of the cartridge pouches, the design of the clasps at the coat turn-backs and the strap (*Dragoner*) on the left shoulder, and most obviously by the colour of the 'facings' (the coat lapels and cuffs; the turn-backs in the Austrian service were of the same white as the rest of the coat). Poppy red (*Ponceaurot*) was the historic colour of the facings in most units, though three regiments had facings of green

(Los Rios, Arenberg, Luzan), others a variety of shades of blue (Deutschmeister and Botta a dark blue; Baden-Durlach and Browne/Tillier/Kinsky probably a light blue), Salm black, and de Ligne an equally distinctive rose red. The showy regiment of Harsch was unique in having Prussian-style embroidered button holes (*Litzen*).

In practice the colonel proprietors carried individuality further still, and the failure of Maria Theresa's attempts to enforce some kind of uniformity tells us a great deal about the location of power in her army in the middle of the century. After a series of earlier orders had been disregarded, Maria Theresa and the *Hofkriegsrath* tried to impose uniformity once and for all by a decree of 16 March 1754. The coat was to be of such a length that the bottom edge stood two fingers (about four cm.) clear of the ground when the man was kneeling, and the garment was to be cut generously enough to allow the lapels to be buttoned across the chest in cold weather with no tugging or stretching; likewise the round 'Austrian' cuffs were to be readily pulled down to protect the fingers against cold and the musket lock against damp.

The *Musterungsberichte* of 1755 nevertheless revealed a large degree of licence among the regiments in Bohemia and Moravia, where the proprietors were caught up in a spirit of competition. All of the cloth was furnished from the Bohemian *Hauptmagazin,* which ought to have put the regiments on an equal footing, but two of the regiments had their uniforms made up expensively by Prague Jews instead of their own soldier-tailors, and the desire to put on a good show actually led to the muskets being lacquered.

Scandals of this kind resulted most immediately in an *Ordnung* of 1755, which set out a scale of stipulated peacetime prices and the duration of the individual items of uniform and equipment. Attempts were made to keep up the controls throughout the war, and thus Armfeldt could report that an infantry coat, for example, was priced at 6 florins 1 xr., and was supposed to last for two years, a waistcoat at 3 florins 5 xr. and last two years also, and a musket sling at 12 xr. and last for nine years.[33]

On 28 June 1757 Maria Theresa decided to resolve the issue of dress throughout the army by settling on uniforms of white faced with red throughout the infantry and cuirassiers, and of dark blue with red facings for the dragoons. Neipperg as Vice-President of the *Hofkriegsrath* was responsible for putting the decision into effect, and difficulties and complications arose at once.

Neipperg believed that he must first sound *FM*. Daun as to the means by which the individual regiments could still be distinguished, and he admitted to Maria Theresa that he had forgotten to make any provision for the Hungarian infantry and the Croats. In the event the colonel proprietors were asked to put forward their own suggestions (orders of 16 and 17 August) and the replies duly arrived over the course of September, suggesting minor variations in the colours of the shoulder straps, or in the design and grouping of the buttons. Neipperg himself doubted whether anything of the kind would prove sufficiently distinctive, and Prince Charles of Lorraine wrote in his support.[34]

Maria Theresa insisted that she must be obeyed, but she was defeated by the impossibly short deadline, namely 1 November, which had been set for the issue of the new uniforms, and by the cumulative force of the protests which came to her ears. On 27 October the *Hofkriegsrath* was able to tell the regiments that they were to wear their existing designs of uniforms for the duration of the war.

Maria Theresa still hoped at least to be able to improve the lot of the soldiers, who were the powerless victims of the proprietors' sartorial fancies, and on 17 December 1761 she instructed the *Hofkriegsrath* to find means of enforcing an acceptable standard of fit for the infantrymen' uniforms. The *Hofkriegsrath* reported that in a number of the regiments the coats were cut so short that they gave no protection against the weather, and so tightly that the troops 'must virtually force themselves into them, which means that they will be slow to get themselves dressed and ready in the event of a sudden alarm.' The *Hofkriegsrath* therefore urged that the fit must be comfortable enough to allow the lapels to be fastened across the chest, as was the original purpose, and the turn-backs undone and closed across the front with buttons. The same rule of commodity must be applied to the waistcoat, the breeches (at present cut as tightly as the coat) and the neck stock, and that finally 'the hat must not be excessively large, but calculated to protect the men against bad weather and the sun, and capable of being seated well down on the head.' Maria Theresa noted that 'all extremes are harmful and unseemly, but so that the uniforms may be kept under accurate control, a special military commission must be set up to propose suitable patterns for the army. These will then be presented to me for my judgement, and a firm and undeviating norm will be laid down for future observance in all the regiments'.[35]

It is doubtful whether the proprietors took any more notice of these good intentions than they had of the earlier decrees.

We shall now fit out the Austrian infantryman from top to toe. The fusilier hat was the characteristic European felt tricorn of the 1750s, with the forepeak rising at an angle of about 45 degrees (it tended increasingly towards the vertical as the century wore on). The edges were trimmed with plain braid, and the hat was further decorated with coloured woollen bobs at the two rearward corners, and a cockade on the left side.

The cap of the grenadiers was a low bearskin, decorated in front by a brass plate, and down the back by a long tasselled cloth in the regimental colour. In everyday service and in bad weather the grenadier normally packed the bearskin in a bag of waxed linen, and substituted the tricorn which was otherwise tied above his knapsack or cartridge pouch. If by any chance the bearskin became wet, it had to be brushed assiduously to prevent the fur becoming matted. Off-duty both the grenadier and the fusilier wore a forage cap made up from old coats.

The hair was dressed at the side in double locks, according to an order of 16 March 1754, and it extended down the back in the characteristic military pigtail, which reached as far as the waist. Moustaches were worn by some of the soldiers, and the men appear thus adorned in the illustrations to the infantry *Regulament* of 1749, though not in the *Bautzen* or *Albertina* manuscripts of 1762.

A military bearing was assisted by a stock (neck-cloth) of stiff red or black fabric, which in some regiments was drawn so tight as to become a virtual instrument of torture, and, together with the woollen coat and the sleeved waistcoat (*Camisol*) it undoubtedly contributed to many deaths from heat exhaustion on the march. The circulation of the blood was further constricted by the tightly-cut breeches, and the close-fitting gaiters (*Gamaschen*) with their multiple fastenings; an order of 1754 allowed Prussian-style black gaiters to be worn in field conditions, and the white gaiters reserved for formal parades. The Hungarian infantry sported *Gatti-Hosen* leggings, and half-boots instead of shoes.

The best shoes for the German infantry were held to be durable objects of thick black leather, stitched with good waxed thread, and coated regularly with wax. As was normal at this period, no differentiation was made between the left and right feet, though in the regiment of Joseph Esterházy it was the practice to identify one of the pair with a spot of red paint, and change the shoes around daily.

Spare shirt, gaiters, cleaning materials and other small items were packed into the reasonably capacious knapsack, which hung in the small of the back, and was suspended from a strap passing over the right shoulder. Well-off regiments took advantage of the order of 5 June 1755, which allowed knapsacks of unshaven calfskin to be substituted for those of ticking. The soldiers' ration of bread might be carried in a separate linen bag, and the man could slake his thirst from the characteristic round Austrian water flask of wood.

The cartridge pouch was a box of stout leather, protected from the elements by a long leather flap which passed over the top and hung down the outer side. It was worn behind the right hip, and hung from a substantial strap of whitened leather which passed through a fabric strap positioned just behind the left shoulder. The powder and ball were encased in paper cartridges (36 or more), which stood upright in holes drilled in the wooden block which filled the bottom of the pouch. The *Regulament* of 1749 still prescribed a powder horn for filling the priming pan of the musket, though it is likely that in the Seven Years War the soldiers primed their pans directly with powder from the cartridges.

An order of 16 March 1754 notified the regiments that they must procure drums, *Kurzgewehre* and swords on the pattern of models that were to be sent to them shortly. The swords, or rather sabres, were inscribed along the blades with the motto *Vivat Maria Theresia,* and were on issue to the grenadiers and the Hungarian infantry generally. The German, Italian and Netherlands fusilier had to be content with his musket, which left him in an embarrassing situation if (as often happened) this weapon became unserviceable[36] (see p. 449).

The muskets were procured by the central government, and bought by the individual regiments from the Imperial Arsenal in Vienna. Three models are relevant to our story:

M 1722: 18.3 mm. calibre; ball one and a half ounces; weight 11 kg; curved lock plate; barrel secured by pins; wooden ramrod. This was patterned on the French M 1717, and was a generally adequate weapon, though its fragile wooden ramrod placed the Austrians at a disadvantage in the two Silesian Wars, when they had to face Prussians equipped with the iron ramrod. Since the regiments purchased their muskets from the Arsenal according to need, it is probable that most *Inhaber* were content to fit the M 1722s with iron ramrods, and keep them in service long after a new pattern of musket was introduced in 1745 (below). The bayonet was in the form of an obtuse-pointed knife.

M 1745: 18.3 mm. calibre; ball one and a half ounces; weight 4.86 kg.; curved lock plate, replaced by flat plate 1748; overall length without bayonet about 157 mm.; barrel secured by two steel bands; cost 4 florins 3 xr.; iron ramrod; in 1748 the knife bayonet was replaced by a triangular-sectioned bayonet which had greater penetrating power, and inflicted a wound which was impossible to close by stitching.

M 1754 *Commissflinte:* 18.3 mm. calibre; overall length without bayonet 151 cm.; barrel length 112 cm.; flat lock plate of wrought steel; barrel secured by four steel bands (including the sleeve towards the muzzle; stock of beech-wood stained brown or black (for fusiliers), or of polished walnut (for grenadiers); iron ramrod; triangular-sectioned bayonet; contract price 4 florins 45xr., rising to 5 florins 50 xr.

The M 1754 *Commissflinte* was devised by a committee of generals and technical experts sitting under the presidency of the *General Artillerie-Director* Prince Liechtenstein. The weapon incorporated features from four designs which came to its attention – a musket proposed some years before by the military clerk Johann Schmied, and three designs submitted by the leading arms manufacturer Penzeneter. The new musket could be recognised most immediately by the four bands which secured the barrel to the stock, but its main advance was represented inconspicuously enough by the barrel itself, which was manufactured from high-grade iron, and bored out in a single carefully-controlled operation. The trigger guard and butt plate were of good solid iron, as opposed

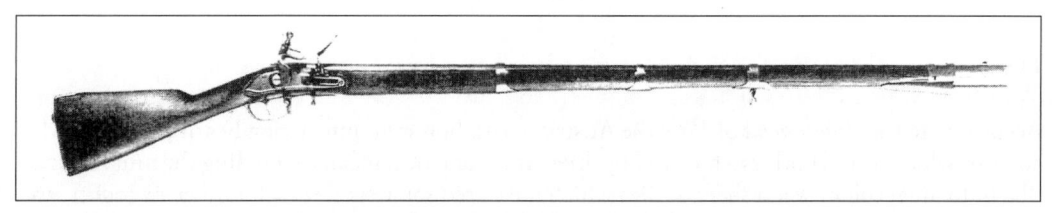

The *Commissflinte* of 1754. (Austrian Army Museum)

to the brass of the Prussian weapon. The sling was made of whitened leather, and equipped with a little hollow flap (*Kolbenfutteral*) which could be slipped over the frizzen of the lock to keep it dry.

In October 1755 the Commissaries and the inspecting officers found that in Bohemia in 1755 'all the infantry regiments quartered here are now equipped with new muskets of uniform calibre, the only exceptionbeing the regiment of Kaiser, which still carries captured French muskets, and its own kind of bayonet'.[37]

The Austrian gun was of marginally smaller calibre than the Prussian M 1740 (18.3 mm. as opposed to 18.5 mm.), which was no disadvantage in itself, but it was prevented from realising its full potential on account of the coarse-grained gunpowder, which was 'slow to take fire and often does not ignite at all, and spurts in the mens' faces and eyes. Both the quality and the quantity of the powder in the Prussian cartridges are superior; they say that in the battle of Leuthen, or Lissa, the Austrian musketry inflicted many contusions but few wounds'.[38] The musket itself continued to command the respect of the Austrian infantry: 'Our musket is serviceable, and ever since the wooden ramrod was replaced by one of iron, and the single-edged knife by a well-designed version of triangular section, we have the finest weapon in the world – or at least we think so... we have to take them as they are delivered from the factories, and to the credit of the manufacturers it must be said that they are mostly of good quality'.[39]

The first Austrian *Jäger* were armed with the same sporting rifles they carried on their masters' estates. From 1759, however, the fast-expanding *Deutsches Feld-Jäger Corps* was equipped with a new Penzeneter rifle of 15 mm. calibre, whose 79-mm. long barrel was furnished with exterior facets, and six polygonal interior rifling grooves. The general conformation was that of the classic Germanic *Stützen,* a short weapon of relatively heavy calibre, which was suitable for bringing down a deer or a charging boar in close country.

The soldier had to attend assiduously to the proper upkeep of his person, clothing, equipment and weapons. The most detailed description of what was involved is to be found in the private Joseph Esterházy regimental code of 1747, and the basic procedures held good in most regiments during the Seven Years War. The men were told to:

> cultivate cleanliness, and keep themselves free of vermin in the head and clothes. They are to wash and comb themselves frequently. Twice a week they must have themselves shaved and put on a cleanly-laundered shirt. Hats are always to be kept clean and neatly turned up. Likewise the grenadiers must cultivate the habit of hanging their bearskin caps in the sun and air, and beating them out so as to prevent the fur from becoming matted; they keep their tricorns tied behind them to the strap of their cartridge pouch. The hair is to be kept neatly combed and curled, so that it does not hang in the eyes, and the pigtail is to be carefully braided and it is to reach down to the waist. The stock is to be wound tightly around the neck above shirt... Shoes are to be changed around daily, and the soldier must turn out in a white shirt and cleanly dressed on parade and on every Sunday and feast day. He is to obtain whatever brushes are necessary to keep the uniform and shoes clean. He must also furnish himself with a handkerchief, so that he does not have to wipe his nose on his cuff, or blow through his fingers.[40]

Flags

According to the *Regulament* of 1749 the Austrian battalion went into action bearing two unfurled colours, which served both as a focus of loyalties, and a practical means of holding the unit together. The individual colour was a sheet of silk, which measured some six feet by four feet six inches, and was decorated with devices in applied silk and embroidery. They were all worked up by Theresia

Sybald of Vienna and her son-in-law Andreas Wessmayer, which ensured a uniformity of style. The *Leibfahne* was distinguished by a white field, and (taking the staff as being to the left) bore on the left side a representation of the Virgin Mary), and on the right side a double eagle. The matching *Regimentsfahne* had a yellow field, and carried the double eagle on both sides.

All the sets of colours were given a lively appearance by edgings of triangles or flames on the three open sides; these tongues were of alternating white, red, black and yellow, with considerable variations in the actual order between the regiments. Long after the Habsburg Empire ceased to exist the tradition of the jagged border was perpetuated in Central and Eastern European armies such as the Czech and the Rumanian.

Regimental Transport

A complement of animals and vehicles helped to provide for the more mundane needs of the regiment. At the outset of the war the regimental transport consisted of six four-horse provision carts, three four-horse tent carts, and one four-horse field smithy. In 1759 the three tent carts were replaced by 30 pack mules, for, as Armfeldt explains, the regiments had often had to spend whole nights under the open sky before the vehicles could catch up with them. The mules were hired from Italian contractors, and assigned three at a time to the individual companies – an arrangement which proved to be cheap and efficient. The regiments had purchased their six provision wagons at the beginning of the war from an allowance amounting to 60 florins for each cart, 50 florins for each horse, and 40 florins for the harness. The vehicles were maintained from an allowance of two-and-a-half florins per month, and the civilian drivers were paid from Vienna.[41]

The Austrian Infantry – an Assessment

The infantry *Regulament* of 1749 was central to Maria Theresa's ambitions to form a proficient and responsive body of foot soldiers. Nobody had taken much notice of the first official code of the kind, a *Regulament und Ordnung,* which had been published in 1737, when Austria's military reputation was sinking to its nadir. Various private regimental codes were cumulatively more influential, and the most notable of these were those of the regiments of Wallis (1705), George Browne (1717), Regal (published posthumously in 1728), Ludwig Andreas Khevenhüller (1744) and Joseph Esterházy (1747), No particular regulations were associated with the regiment of Harsch, but the authorities held its dress and procedures to be the smartest in the army.

Khevenhüller is said to have entrusted all his manuscripts to Daun, and commended him to Maria Theresa on his deathbed as the best man to carry on his work.[42] Daun was in any case one of the prime movers of military reform, and he had put together instructions for his own regiment. He was now commissioned to compile an authorised code for the entire infantry, and he published the fruit of his labours in 1749 as the *Regulament und Ordnung des gesammten Kaiserlich-Königlichen Fuss-Volcks*. On the first page the introduction by Maria Theresa drew minatory attention to 'the fact that We have learned that Our Imperial infantry observes neither a uniform drill nor uniform military practices. These two deficiencies have given rise not only to various shortcomings, but to dangerous, detrimental and damaging consequences for military activities whether in field or garrison'.[43]

Part I of the new *Regulament* explained the organisation of the regiment, the arrangement of the ranks and files, the recommended treatment of recruits, the qualities of the good officer, and the details of drill and tactics. Part II laid down the order of parades, the composition of detachments, the issuing of the *Parole,* and the routines of the day – down to such detail as the behaviour to be adopted by NCOs and private soldiers when making their reports:

> If, having rendered his report, the man is presented with a glass of wine, he must lower his musket from the 'present arms' to a position just in front of his left foot… he takes off his hat in the prescribed way, but instead of raising his fingers in salute [Boy Scout style, by the side of the head] he takes hold of the glass; having drunk, he replaces his hat and presents arms.[44]

The tempo of the drums and fifes was to be 'according to the present usage of the regiment of Harsch'.[45]

Probably the greatest strength of the *Regulament* resided in its many and eminently clear illustrative engravings, which had been worked up from some endearingly naïve sketches, possibly by the hand of Daun himself, to judge by the line. The pictures, together with the exercise camps which were held in the early 1750s, helped to give the regiments a common base of reference. However the work as a whole was far too long and over-elaborate, and whole sections (the drill with the *Schweinsfeder* spears, for example) were irrelevant outside the Turkish theatre, or (like the passages on the secular and religious ceremonials) were of no utility in any kind of combat. The new war with Prussia overtook the army at a time when many officers had still not mastered the new drills (see p. 134), which in any case had to be adapted to the three-rank line of battle which replaced the four ranks in 1757 and 1758.

The work of tactical and administrative reform in fact had a long way to go, and Daun was the only man to drive it forward. Armfeldt describes Daun in this respect – as in many others – as an isolated and unsupported individual (see p. 135), and the picture is confirmed from Austrian sources. In the matter of the infantry code Cogniazzo states that it was entirely predictable that objections would arise 'from the people who imagined that they could devise something better and more useful than could Daun. When it came to drilling the troops those officers, by which I mean the colonel commandants, mostly acted as their own notions and whims took them'.[46]

Enemies and foreign observers were unanimous in their judgements on the performance of the Austrian infantry in the Seven Years War. The Prussian hussar Warnery maintained that the whitecoats fought consistently well, and undoubtedly better than in the two Silesian Wars, but that the Austrians still could not match the Prussians when it came to moving with speed and precision in large formations.[47] On the question of the improvements, Armfeldt entered a number of illuminating comparisons. The Austrians' infantry was now as superior to their cavalry, as the cavalry had been to their infantry in earlier times; when rated against foreign infantry, the mobility of the Austrian foot soldiers now ranked between that of the Prussians and that of the Russians.[48] The Austrians were good at ranging themselves in order, but that order fell to pieces once the Austrians were pursuing the enemy, or were being pushed back by them, 'and they rally in such an indolent style that they need twice the time to do it than the Prussians… I have often seen how one or two enemy squadrons, by putting in an attack at the right time, have broken whole regiments.' This failing could give an unexpected turn to events late in an action, 'and it is especially dangerous for them to go rushing on in pursuit of the enemy if the terrain is such that their own cavalry is unable to come up quickly enough, and the enemy have horse still available to act against them. Several thousand Austrians were captured for that reason at Torgau, and if Finck at Maxen had taken the slightest heed of the disorder among the Austrian grenadiers when they were pursuing him, he could have counterattacked with a few squadrons… and restored the whole affair'.[49]

Note

For tactics of the infantry, cavalry, artillery and Croats see the chapter 'Operational and Tactical Dimensions' in Part III 'Waging War.'

For particulars of uniforms of all arms see two important studies of contemporary illustrated manuscripts:

Kornauth, F. (ed.) *Das Heer Maria Theresias. Facsimile-Ausgabe der Albertina-Handschrift 'Desseins des Uniformes des Troupes I.I. et R.R. de l'année 1762,* Vienna 1973

Thtimmler, L.-H. (ed.) *Die Österreichische Armee im Siebenjährigen Krieg. Die Bautzener Handschrift aus dem Jahre 1762,* Berlin 1993.

Information in a highly-accessible form, compiled by Philip Haythornthwaite, with excellent illustrations by Bill Younghusband, is to be found in three volumes of the 'Osprey' *Men-at-Arms* series:

No. 271: *The Austrian Army 1740–1780: 1 Cavalry,* London 1994
No. 276: *The Austrian Army 1740–1780: 2 Infantry,* London 1994
No. 280: *The Austrian Army 1740–1780: 3 Specialist Troops,* London 1995.

Grenadiers, in toy array. (Austrian Army Museum)

11

The Cavalry

The distinctive feature of the mounted arm was its mobility, which could be exploited in a number of contexts. The cuirassiers inherited the role of the medieval knights as the dealers of hammer blows on the battlefield, where they clashed with the enemy cavalry, and exploited favourable opportunities to crush the enemy infantry. According to *FM*. Carl Paul Pálffy 'a cuirassier must be rooted as immovably as a wall, and withstand an enemy onslaught with resolution. When he is ordered to attack, he and his comrades must break into the enemy ranks with undaunted courage, united forces, and concert and order'.[1]

The cuirassiers were seconded in their work by the dragoons, who were more lightly mounted and equipped, being descended from mounted infantry. Finally the hussars counted as light horse, and were supposed to excel in the 'little war' of outposts, raids, ambush and reconnaissances, though (in the Austrian service at least) they were unwilling to intervene on the battlefield.

THE CUIRASSIERS AND DRAGOONS

The Austrian heavy and medium cavalry in the Seven Years War comprised 18 regiments of cuirassiers, and 14 of dragoons (including the *Staabs-Dragoner* from 1758, and the Jung-Löwenstein *chevaulegers* from 1759). In addition six regiments of Saxon horse were maintained in the Austrian service.

    Cuirassier Regiments (designations as of 1759)
    Anhalt-Zerbst
    Anspach
    Birkenfeld (Stampa 1761–)
    Bretlach (or Pretlack)
    Buccow (Lucchesi-1758)
    Daun (Benedict) (Radicati-1756; Löwenstein-1758)
    Ferdinand, Erzherzog (Max, Erzherzog 1761–)
    Kalckreuth (Albert, Prince of Sachsen-Teschen, 1760–)
    Leopold, Erzherzog
    Modena-Alt
    O'Donnell
    Pálffy
    Portugal
    Schmerzing (d'Aysasa 1762–)
    Serbelloni
    Stampach
    Trautmannsdorf
    de Ville (Gelhay-1759)

Dragoon Regiments (designations as of 1759)
Althann (Koháry-1756)
Batthyány, Carl
Darmstadt, Hessen-
Joseph, Erzherzog
Kollowrat
Liechtenstein
Modena, Jung-
Sachsen-Gotha
St. Ignon *chevaulegers* (de Ligne, Ferdinand-1758; Daun, Benedict-1759)
Savoyen
Württemberg
Zweibrücken
Staabs-Dragoner (disbanded 1762)

Maintained Regiments of Saxon cavalry (designations as of 1761)
Cuirassiers: Carabinier-Garde
                 Gardes du Corps
Chevaulegers: Graf Brühl
                 Herzog Carl von Curland
                 Prinz Albrecht
                 Rutowsky

Organisation

The regiments of cuirassiers and dragoons were structured almost identically throughout our period:

Wartime Establishment 1756
Six *ordinari* squadrons of two companies each; one squadron of elite horse (carabiniers in the cuirassiers, mounted grenadiers in the dragoons). *Ordinari* squadrons of 80 troopers, three officers (*Rittmeister* [cuirassiers] or *Haubtmann* [dragoons], Lieutenant, Cornet or *Unter-Lieutenant*, and three corporals. Élite company of three officers (as above) and 97 men. Total 1,015, including small staff

1758
One of the squadrons in each regiment now designated *Reserve Escadron*; one of its component companies became a *Depot Compagnie*, while the other was assigned to detached duties, such as convoy escort.
  The new NCO rank of *Standartenführer* took over the carrying of the company standard from the cornets, who now became *Unter-Lieutenants*; the former Lieutenants were re-named *Ober-Lieutenants*

Winter 1761/2
As part of the general reduction of the army, two companies were struck from the establishment of regiment of cuirassiers, reducing the regiment to 850 officers and men, while the regiments of hussars (below) were reduced to 1,000 each. In the course of 1762 the regiment of *Staabs-Dragoner* was run down and finally disbanded, and its remaining personnel re-assigned to their original regiments.

Daun protested that the reduced establishments made no allowance for wastage, and so 'it would make a good deal of sense to restore the cuirassiers to an establishment of 1,000 horses and men for otherwise they will be unable to survive. As it is, they usually number five or at the most 600 men by the end of every campaign, which makes them unable to do anything against the enemy cavalry'.[2]

The question emerged again late in 1762, for Kaunitz took fright at some apparently threatening movements on the Ottoman side of the border, but Maria Theresa decided to hold her hand until the situation became clearer. Meanwhile she decided to recruit the cuirassier regiments up to their full reduced establishment, which would facilitate any further augmentation if that proved to be necessary.[3]

The Emergence and Temporary Eclipse of the Austrian *Chevaulegers*

In the middle years of the Seven Years War the cuirassiers and dragoons had to confront a demand for a general lightening of the cavalry; it was occasioned partly by the cost of procuring and feeding the heavier animals, but also by the need to match the Prussian cavalry, which was gaining a clear predominance in the 'little war.'

In November 1759 Daun set himself against a first proposal to convert two regiments of cuirassiers to dragoons outright: 'I cannot advise changing regiments of cuirassiers to dragoons. The distinction between the two, such as it is, amounts just to the wearing of the cuirass, but that makes a great impression on the Turks, against whom we will be fighting sooner or later. In any event we have enough dragoons already, and the two regiments in question would be mightily displeased and perform poor service. In the war against our present enemy the most useful force of cavalry is presented by the *chevaulegers*'.[4]

In January 1760 we find Maria Theresa returning to the subject, when a proposal was made to do away with four of the cuirassier regiments altogether (see p. 141). In the event the reduction of 1761/2 maintained all the regiments of cuirassiers, though on a reduced establishment.

The *chevaulegers* mentioned by Daun were a kind of cavalry which was new to the Austrians, being light dragoons who could serve alongside the cuirassiers and the conventional dragoons on the battlefield. They were also capable of executing raids and other fast-moving enterprises, and doing outpost duty in difficult country at least as effectively as the hussars, and certainly better than the dragoons, who had by now ceased to count as light horse. Lieutenant-Colonel Rebain pointed out that in older times the dragoons had been a versatile arm, sufficiently lightly mounted to manoeuvre with speed on the flanks of the cuirassiers, and still capable of doing service as mounted infantry, ready to fight on foot with their long carbines, but 'now in the Austrian army the dragoons' uniforms and equipment weigh them down as heavily as the cuirassiers, if we except the breastplate. We have completely abandoned the practice of using the dragoons for reconnaissances and raids, or employing them to circle around the enemy and hit them in flank, or make diversion'.[5]

Something of the old dragoon character was rediscovered in the *chevaulegers*. The regiments of refugee Saxon light horse had shown the Austrians how useful such folk could be, and on 14 January 1758 a new and rich *Inhaber* of dragoons, *FML*. Christian Wilhelm Prince Löwenstein-Wertheim augmented his regiment to a mighty 12 squadrons – the six additional squadrons being lightly mounted and designated 'Jung-Löwenstein,' On 17 June the new squadrons surprised and defeated the finest of the Prussian dragoons, the super-large regiment of Bayreuth, and captured their silver drums. It would be difficult to imagine a more spectacular demonstration of the value of the light dragoons, and the squadrons of Jung-Löwenstein were allowed the privilege of retaining their prize drums and playing the *Reitermarsch*.

Both 'Alt-' and 'Jung-Löwenstein did well at Hochkirch, but the combined regiment was proving unwieldy, and in March 1759 Jung-Löwenstein was raised to the status of an independent regiment under the designation of the *Chevaulegers-Regiment Löwenstein*,[6] while 'Alt-Löwenstein' passed to a new *Inhaber*, GFWM. St. Ignon. The St. Ignon Dragoons themselves converted to *chevaulegers* on 6 February 1760. Both regiments retained the historic Löwenstein coat of green, with red collar and cuffs, which ultimately became the uniform of all the *chevaulegers* in the Austrian service, and the favourite garb of the future Emperor Joseph II.

The dragoon regiments of Württemberg, Zweibrücken, Sachsen-Gotha and Jung-Modena were ordered to transmogrify into *chevaulegers* simultaneously with St. Ignon, in 1760, though Württemberg and Sachsen-Gotha reverted to heavy dragoons the same year, and Zweibrücken and Jung-Modena followed their example in 1763. In all probability the costs of conversion had proved excessive, for all ranks would have had to be remounted on light Polish horses, and fitted out with lighter saddles and bar-bits.[7]

Free corps of infantry came into increasing prominence in the course of the war. However the authorities were unwilling to encourage comparable units among the dragoons, and in 1758 they turned down proposals to this effect from two Netherlands noblemen, the comte de Mastaing and the enterprising Peter Franz de Piza.[8]

Uniforms, Equipment and Weapons

Cavalrymen of all kinds spent most of their duty time on mundane chores like grooming their horses, mucking out stables, cleaning their equipment and weapons, and gathering forage, and for these purposes they wore a simple forage cap and smock. On parade, on guard and in the presence of the enemy they appeared in full fig, which in the case of the cuirassiers and the dragoons was surmounted by a tricorn of black felt. The hat was on the same general pattern as that of the infantry, but considerably larger, and it was lined with a circlet and crisscross crown of iron strips. This ironmongery gave good protection against sword cuts, but it was burdensome to wear, and, together with the massive boots, it rendered the cuirassier in particular very vulnerable once he was unseated. Maria Theresa asked the *Hofkriegsrath* to look into the matter in the autumn of 1762, when the original regulation stocks of the hat crowns were exhausted. As a result she approved a new and lighter design, and ordered contracts to be placed for 12,000 of the hat items at a cost of 28 xr. each.[9]

As for the hair, the cuirassiers and dragoons were told that it must be kept 'well combed, but never curled up with papers or powdered. Still less is it permissible to blacken the moustaches'.[10] Contemporary illustrations show that the moustaches were worn by the other ranks of both the cuirassiers and dragoons, but that the officers were clean-shaven.

Maria Theresa set up the uniform of the Radicati regiment as the standard for the cuirassiers, just as the regiment of Harsch served as the model for the infantry. The white coat of the cuirassiers had no lapels, but was offset by collar, cuffs and turn-backs of an almost universal poppy red. However the facings of the Alt-Modena Cuirassiers were of blue, while the regiments of Anhalt-Zerbst and Anspach were dressed in the Prussian style with a leather jerkin and a short under-coat (*Leibel*, *Kollet*) or kersey. After the war FM. d'Aspremont-Lynden was asked to investigate whether the combination of jerkin and *Leibel* might be practicable wear for all the cuirassiers. He reported that they gave such poor protection against cold and damp that in the campaign of 1762 the regiments of Anhalt-Zerbst and Anspach had been unable to mount guard as early as October, and that the Austrian gunners would probably open fire against any cavalry which had a Prussian appearance. The conventional coat was priced at seven florins and seven-and-a-half xr., and was supposed to last for six years, which seems very optimistic.

The cuirassier breeches were of red or straw colour, and the massive bucket-topped boots were equally distinctive objects, being fashioned of thick leather, and furnished with *Faschinen* – stiff leather linings which reached down to the soles. The stout boots were considered necessary to protect the legs when the files of cavalry were pressed together, and they figure in the particular instructions for the officers, which condemned embroidered coats, the wearing of plumes on top of the hats or night-caps below, and light and comfortable boots in the Hungarian style.[11]

The riding cloak (*Radmantel*, lit. 'wheel-cloak') was a wide garment which proved valuable in calm weather, but flapped about so violently in high winds that it slapped the rider in his face and sometimes dislodged his hat. Again, when the cavalryman tried to push the cloak back to free his arms, the weight was taken around his neck and threatened to strangle him.

The items of spare uniform, the cleaning equipment, horseshoes, bread, the bag of oats and the horseman's share of the tent were carried either in a saddlebag (*Reittasch*) which hung from the front of the saddle, or rolled up with the cloak in a sausage-like *Mantel Sack* which was fastened to the rear. There was much dispute as to which was the better arrangement: some regiments adopted one, some the other, and in a number of further regiments both styles could be seen. The *Mantel Sack* was apt to get in the way of the trooper's right leg when he swung himself into the saddle, while the bulging *Reittasch* prevented the files from being closed up as tightly as might have been desired, especially in combat against the Turks.

The whole business of gear and packing was undoubtedly more complicated for a cavalryman than for a foot soldier. The vastly-experienced FM. Carl Paul Pálffy commented that neatness and uniformity should be disregarded in case of emergency, and that men who were in close contact with the enemy would seldom unpack anyway.[12]

Some officers believed that the weight of the regulation saddle was cruel,[13] and that it could be usefully shortened to 16 inches. Pálffy however maintained that the short saddles did more harm than good, for the *Reittasch* or the *Mantel Sack* would take up so much space that the rider could hardly find room to seat himself in the saddle.[14]

The horse was relieved to some extent by the *Schabraque*, or saddle cloth, which was of identical form for the cuirassiers and dragoons. The saddle cloths formed the most immediately recognisable guide to an officer's rank, at least according to an order of 6 September 1755, which stipulated two broad decorative edgings for the colonel, lieutenant-colonel and major, one broad and one narrow for the captains, and a single broad edging for all the other officers.

The pistol holsters (*Schabrunken*) were fastened on either side of the front of the saddle, and were made of the same fabric as the *Schabraque*.

The identity of the heavy cavalryman was linked indissolubly with his wrought iron breastplate or cuirass. At about 32 pounds it weighed far more than its medieval ancestor, and before it could be accepted into the service it had to withstand proof against a musket shot, which produced the characteristic circular indentation which may be seen on all surviving cuirasses at the present day. It was padded on the inside with ticking (leather for the officers), edged with a rim of chamois leather (with a cloth frill in addition for the officers), and fastened across the black with leather straps. The exterior surface was painted or lacquered in black.

The cuirass was notoriously burdensome to wear, and demanded a strong man and a well-built horse. The official manual of military medicine (1758) remarked that in summer it could become unbearably hot, which might cause dehydration and heat exhaustion.[15] In the same year an anonymous officer repeated these objections, and maintained that a rider who was unencumbered by a cuirass could sit more easily in the saddle, and charge home with greater speed; for the officer in particular the cuirass was so inconvenient that he had to hire a special servant just to carry it about for him when it was not being worn. Carl Paul Pálffy, who was both a Field Marshal and a colonel of cuirassiers, rejoined that the French, Prussians and Saxons also wore the cuirass, which proved its utility in Western warfare, while the Austrians in addition had the demonstrable need for this piece of armour in combat against the Turks. The armour could not simply be left in store to be taken up when it was needed, for a man could not wear the cuirass without long conditioning:

> We just have to remind ourselves of what happened when the former [dragoon] regiment of Preysing was disbanded [in 1750], and many of its grenadiers were reassigned to the [cuirassier] regiment of Erzherzog Leopold. On their very first marches these men became so exhausted and enfeebled that they begged and prayed to be returned to the dragoons. An old trooper, however, who has served for many years in a cuirassier regiment, will be so accustomed to the breastplate that he will find it very odd to be told to lay it aside permanently. The officer and the veteran trooper know very well why they carry the cuirass, whereas a young man will be thinking of his comfort rather than utility and purpose.[16]

The status of the cuirassiers was simultaneously coming under indirect attack from the military authorities. Men of good build (a very rare commodity) among the *Stände* recruits were volunteering for service among the cuirassiers, but all such as measured five feet or three inches or taller were being assigned to the infantry. Five of the cuirassier colonels protested that men of lesser height would be unable to swing themselves into the saddle over the pack, but they were fobbed off with the curious reply that they would have to choose recruits with unusually long legs. They pointed out that strangely-proportioned men were generally weak, and that a little man would be unable to so much as lift his left boot into the stirrup of the mighty cuirassier horse, and that he would be incapable of wearing the standard cuirass.[17] As the colonels' immediate superior *G.d.C.* Carl O'Donnell gave the remonstrance his blessing, and forwarded it to Vienna through Daun. The regiments could gain no satisfaction on the question of stature, but they were at least able to retain their armour and designation.

The dragoons were dressed very much in the style of the foot soldiers, and their long carbine (which was capable of mounting a bayonet) harked back to their origin as mounted infantry. There were very considerable variations in the colours between the regiments, and late in 1757 Maria Theresa sought to introduce an all-blue uniform to the whole of the dragoons. This attempt proved as unavailing as her ambition to enforce uniformity among the infantry. The dragoon outfit was completed by a pair of boots, of lighter build than those of the cuirassiers, and by the gauntlets which were common to the cavalry. An order of 6 September 1755 named a certain Heuldorff as the authorised glove-maker for the cavalry, just as Jauner, Kayser and Kueller were specified as the haberdashers.

Cuirassier of the regiment of de Ville (Gelhay until 1759) (Krauhse, Austrian Army Museum). White coat and waistcoat; red cuffs, turn-backs and breeches.

The *Inhaber* of the cuirassiers and dragoons procured the blades for their own regiments direct from the manufacturers, in general conformity with a norm which had been laid down in 1722. The blade (excluding the hilt) was about 36 inches long, one-and-a-half inches (3.5 cm.) wide at the hilt, ground on both sides with a broad and shallow blood channel, and pointed along the central axis. The length was supposed to be sufficient to enable the rider to cut down to the navel of an infantryman. One of the officers noted, however, that 'the sword of the Austrian cavalry is about six inches shorter than that of the Prussians, and therefore does not have the same reach. It is objected that the Prussian swords are too long, but all we would have to do is to drill the men in cutting with this weapon, and they would be able to wield the long sword just as well as do the Prussians; after all the type of man is very much the same in both armies, and since the Austrian cavalryman rides with shorter stirrups… he will have the advantage of a greater reach with the long sword.' He added that the blades must be ground sharply, and the edge retained by forbidding the troopers to use their swords to cut or split wood.[18]

The design of the hilts had always been left to the *Inhaber*, but Carl Paul Pálffy and the well-informed Lieutenant-Colonel Rebain were strongly of the opinion that the swords of both the cuirassiers and dragoons must be furnished with a full basket hilt. 'Our present wars with the Prussians and French are fought out mainly with cold steel,' commented Pálffy, 'and our men frequently fall into disputes and duelling among themselves. It is important to give proper protection to the hand, for a single nasty cut will make a man unfit for any kind of service'[19]

Every horseman was equipped with a pair of pistols, jammed muzzle-downwards in holsters secured to the front of the saddle, and with a carbine, *Musqueton* or *Gewehrhaubitz*, which was carried in a shoe down the right hand side of the horse, or suspended from the bandolier of the cartridge pouch. The pistol in question (M 1744) was common to the whole of the Austrian cavalry. It was a substantial weapon, with a calibre of 17 mm., and overall length of 48.5 cm., and it weighed 3.5 kg. The carbines came in three models – the virtual musket of the dragoons, the stubby weapon of the hussars (overall length 90 cm.), and the carbine of the cuirassiers (125 cm.). The carbines were of the same 17 mm. calibre as the pistols. Rebain observed that 'the Prussian cavalry carbines are two-and-a-half Viennese feet long in the barrel, and those of their hussars only one-and-a-half feet. The Prussian cavalry set no store by carbine fire from the saddle, and it seems to me that the Austrian cavalry carbines are too long and cumbersome. Our carbine belts are likewise too wide, and it would be better if we had the carbines hanging from the end in the Prussian style, instead of being fastened inconveniently far up according to our practice'.[20]

The original Austrian carbine otherwise differed in no essentials from that of other armies, but from 1759 12 cuirassier troopers were told off from the flanks of every squadron, and armed with the *Musqueton* or *Trombon* – a long-barrelled blunderbuss with a muzzle flattened out to 4.6 cm.,

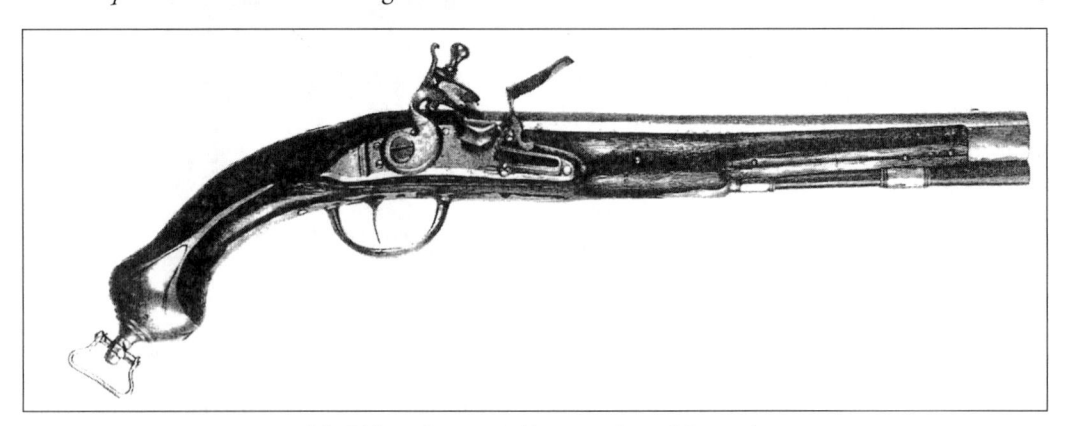

M 1744 cavalry pistol. (Austrian Army Museum)

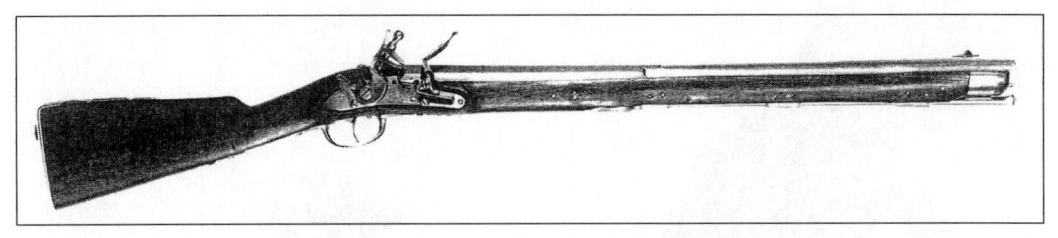

Trombon scatter gun. (Austrian Army Museum)

which was designed to discharge 12 buckshot in an horizontal swathe. Already in 1758 a number of grenade-throwing *Gewehrhaubitzen* were carried experimentally in action, and evidently with some success, and in 1761 several dragoons in every squadron of mounted grenadiers were equipped with this stocked-up miniature mortar.

The standards of the cuirassiers, dragoons and hussars were small flags, heavily embroidered with metal thread, and carried originally by the cornets (*Fähndrichs* in the dragoons), and then from 1759 by the holders of the new NCO rank of *Standartenführer*. The music of the cavalry combined the brilliance of the trumpets with the thunder of the kettle-drums. The drums of the dragoon/*chevaulegers* regiments of Jung-Löwenstein and Kollowrat were objects of considerable pride, for they had been taken from the Prussians in combat (Jung-Löwenstein on 17 June 1758, and Kollowrat on 23 June 1760). The Austrians secreted their drums in safety during battle, lest the Prussians should take it into their heads to capture or reclaim any of the instruments.[21]

Two dozen tents were provided for every squadron of cuirassiers or dragoons, and the four or five men of each tent *Cameradschaft* were accustomed to carrying them and other gear by rotation on their riding horses – the little tent itself being borne on one of the horses, the cooking pot and water flask on another, and the tent pegs and ropes on the other three.[22] Carl Paul Pálffy pointed out in December 1758 that the rotation worked fairly, and that the modest weight was a small penalty as against the facility of having shelter always at hand, 'for as soon as they enter camp the troopers can get down to pitching their tents and bringing their uniforms, saddles, harness, gear – and most importantly their weapons – into the dry.' He recalled a recent case where tents had been supposed to have been forwarded to some fast-moving detachments by independent transport, but were found to have been rendered heavy, stiff and immovable by rain and frost. Pálffy attacked a proposal to introduce tent-carrying mules to the cavalry on the same basis as among the infantry. He was overruled, but the tent mules enjoyed only a short existence among the cavalry before they were abolished early in 1760.

Every regiment of cavalry was furnished in addition with four provision carts, and Pálffy maintained that they were essential, for they transported not only the bread, but fodder as well, and the sick and wounded, the uniforms and equipment retrieved from dead troopers, and the quartermaster's correspondence and books – 'for under the present arrangements the regiments are involved in more paper-work than ever before'.[23]

Horses (Cavalry as a whole)

Remounts
Much of the bureaucracy mentioned above had to do with the business of obtaining and keeping up the horses, which bulked particularly large in the affairs of the 'German' cavalry. The cuirassier trooper was a big man, who carried the dead weight of his breastplate, and was mounted on a great, greedy beast which stood 15, 16 or more hands high. The dragoon horse was only marginally smaller. Mounts of this kind were rarely to be found in the Hereditary Lands.

Officer of cuirassiers. (Ottenfeld)

The Allgauer horses of the Tyrol were not without their virtues, but they entered into consideration for the artillery rather than the cavalry, and therefore came under the purview of Prince Liechtenstein as the chief gunner. On 9 January 1757 the *Directorium* entered into cavalry remount contracts with the town fathers of Klagenfurt and the Carinthian horse dealer Nägerle, and a year later Haugwitz was able to report that had bought up 1,000 draught horses in Carinthia and another 700 in Carniola. All of this suggests that a modest horse-breeding capacity existed in Inner Austria. However the privately-owned studs of Austria as a whole were too expensive and too small to answer more than a tiny proportion of the army's needs for cavalry horses, and *GFWM*. Ludwig Adam Starhemberg explained that as a result of war and calamities it was no longer possible to obtain good peasant-bred horses for the cuirassiers and dragoons in Silesia (now mostly lost to the Prussians), Bohemia and Moravia, or for the hussars in Hungary. Great numbers of foals were born in Upper Austria and Bohemia, but the peasants were too ignorant and lazy to raise them, and most of the animals were being sold off and sent abroad; the peasants worked the remaining horses to death in a couple of years, and they made up any deficiencies by purchasing the cheapest nags they could find at the local fairs.[24]

The authorities were left with no alternative but to obtain most of the horses from abroad through the agency of dealers. The contractor Johann Heinrich Altvatter signed a typical document whereby he agreed to supply healthy and well-proportioned cuirassier and dragoon horses for the campaign of 1757. They were to be aged between four and seven years, measure at least 15 hands 2 or 3 inches for the cuirassiers, and 14 hands 2 or 3 inches for the dragoons. They were to be black horses (*Rappen*) or at least dark brown, and all fox-coloured animals or greys were excluded, as well all those with excessively large white patches. For every acceptable cuirassier horse Altvatter was to receive 97 florins 30 xr., and for every acceptable dragoon horse 82 florins 30 xr.[25]

Altvatter had already made a lucrative deal in July 1756, and he went on to sign a further contract on 9 January 1757. The documents also refer to considerable agreements with:

Nathan Moyses Goldschmid of Cologne (7 August 1757, 26 July 1759, and (in association with Thomas Petz of Regensburg) 10 May 1762
Norbert Kolinsky of Moravia (9 January 1757)
Johann Georg Nägerle of Carinthia (9 January 1757, above)
Pazelt of Prague (9 January 1757)
Pinzker (July 1756, early January 1757)
Michael Czecky (light dragoon horses from Moldavia and Transylvania, for delivery 1761/2)
Tiltsch and Harmloscher (November 1762, for dragoon and hussar horses from Transylvania)

In general the best cuirassier horses were to be had from the fat lands of Hanover, Westphalia and Holstein. At the other extreme the horses from Hungary, Wallachia, Poland and the Ukraine were of lighter breeds, more suitable for the dragoons and hussars and the officers as a whole, and some of the fastest of all were to be obtained from the Tartars and Moldavia. Early in the Seven Years War Maria Theresa was concerned to find that her hussars were mounted on horses as small as 13 hands, which was plainly inadequate, but Haugwitz assured her that for the campaign of 1758 the contractors were being obliged to supply animals of between 14½ and 15 hands.

The horses were delivered by the contractors for approval to a number of collection points, usually at Prague, Pilsen or Commotau in Bohemia, Iglau in Moravia, or Linz in Upper Austria, where they were inspected by *GFWM*. Henri Baron de la Reintrie du Pin or other connoisseurs of equine quality. Unfortunately nobody in particular was responsible for the welfare of the horses when they were on the way to the army, and, since the horses were mostly delivered from the contractors only in the February or March of each year, there was usually not enough time to train the remounts and bring them back to condition before the campaign opened.[26]

De la Reintrie assumed the overall direction of procurement in 1760. He had to maintain the existing system for the duration of hostilities, and only after the war did he have the opportunity to put the business of remounts on a new foundation, by encouraging the breeding of good cavalry horses within the Hereditary Lands.

The waste among the horses in service was also unnecessarily high, for Austria had yet to establish veterinary schools to compare with those of Sweden or France. The regimental *Depositorien* were established too far from the field squadrons, and too little care was taken to select good regimental farriers (*Fahnenschmiede*).[27] In January 1758 Kaunitz (himself a considerable horseman) advocated setting up proper hospitals for sick or wounded horses close behind the army, a proposal which occasioned much debate but no decision.[28]

All of this posed great problems for mounting the cavalry, and particularly at the outset of the Seven Years War, when great quantities of animals had to be bought up in haste. The regiments of hussars had been kept on a low peacetime establishment of horses, for their little beasts were comparatively cheap and plentiful in Eastern Europe, but the authorities were now embarrassed by the sheer quantity of the remounts which had to be purchased at short notice. The peacetime establishment of the cuirassiers and dragoons was proportionately higher, but additional animals still had to be procured from Holstein and other locations in northern Germany, in other words from a part of the world which was politically sensitive. On 3 January 1757 the Hanoverians prohibited the export of horses from the electorate, and Kaunitz was surprised that they had not taken this measure earlier. A few weeks later the Prussians invaded Bohemia in great force, which awakened fears that the enemy would make off with whatever horses were still to be found in that part of the world.[29]

The contractors found ways of re-routing the convoys of remounts around territory under hostile control, but in retrospect the costs and the risks were recognised as having been unacceptable. Millions of florins were expended in foreign states to buy remounts, and lost for ever to the Hereditary Lands, and the supply was the most precarious just when it ought to have been the most secure.

Losses of Army Horses in the Seven Years War (killed, died, disabled, sold out of service as unfit)

Total:	47,169
Artillery Horses:	14.60%
Cavalry Horses:	85.40% of which:
cuirassier horses:	39.59
dragoon horses:	33.00
regular hussar horses:	28.84
Grenz-Husaren horses:	1.55

Feed

In peacetime the prime season of growing grass (25 May–15 July) allowed the cavalrymen to supplement the feed of their horses by turning them out to graze. The pasture could best be conserved by fastening the animals to posts, but there was nothing to compare with the sight of a horse being allowed to run free over a meadow.[30] On campaign the cavalry engaged in foraging expeditions, whereby the troopers took hay or grain from the peasant stacks or barns, or mowed the grass in the fields and gathered it into bundles to be carried on their horses. This was an expensive business for the Austrians, for they were supposed to pay due compensation in Bohemia, Moravia, Austrian Silesia and allied territory in the *Reich*, and they were inhibited from ravaging at will even in Prussian Silesia, which they were trying to reclaim as Austrian sovereign territory. The costs were increased by corrupt Commissaries, who were able to divert consignments of hay, mix it with manure, and sell it on for their own profit.[31]

This left the greater part of the army's fodder to be obtained from private contractors, and the consequent cost probably amounted to the greatest single item of wartime military expenditure. Löbl Hönig, the dealer for Bohemia, was forced to withdraw from his contract in April 1762, having been unpaid for a long time, and left the army in the lurch in the leanest season of the year (see p. 358).

The ingredients of the feed, and the proportions between them, varied greatly in the course of the war, however the main constituents were hay (German *Heu*, French *foin*) at 11–12 lb. daily, straw (*Streu, paille*) at approx. 10 lb., and oats (*Hafer, avoine*) about 6 lbs., and sometimes a quantity of wheat. Some critics considered that the Austrian rations were lacking in nourishment,[32] and Maria Theresa summarised a debate which was held on the subject in January 1760. Most of those present argued for retaining hay at its present weight (currently 10 lb.), and reducing the expensive wheat – though leaving it at the discretion of the commander-in-chief to increase the ration when the horses were having to put in extra effort.[33]

The Cuirassiers and Dragoons – an Assessment

In the early 1700s the Austrian cavalry had been known as 'the chief support of the throne'.[34] The Austrian horsemen were still decisively superior to those of the Prussians at Mollwitz (11 April 1741), and yet by the closing campaigns of the Seven Years War the ascendancy of the Prussian cavalry was nearly absolute. What had been happening?

In the Turkish War of 1737–9 the Austrian cavalry had still fought in a disciplined way, for the troopers knew that they would be massacred by the swarming enemy if they allowed themselves to fall out of formation. The Austrians proceeded to break the Prussian cavalry at Mollwitz and again at Chotusitz in 1742, but on the latter occasion hardly a squadron held together, for the men split up in search of plunder. At Hohenfriedberg and Soor in 1745 it was the Prussians who manoeuvred and attacked in well closed-up formations.[35]

After the end of hostilities of 1748 a praiseworthy attempt was made to reform the tactics and service of the cavalry, by introducing sensible innovations while retaining the best of the old practice. It was obstructed within the regiments by elements which were opposed to change of any kind. At the same time officers as senior as Ferdinand Carl d'Aspremont-Lynden and Carl Paul Pálffy pointed out that the complicated drills were impossible for a recruit to master even after a year of instruction, while many valuable veterans of all ranks were lost because they were unable to adapt to the innovations.[36]

The main evidence as to the German cavalry's state of morale between the wars comes from the reports of the Commissaries at the periodic *Musterungen*. On 31 January 1755 the Commissaries reported the outcome of the main concentration of cuirassiers, amounting to 15 regiments stationed in Hungary, Transylvania and the Bánát of Temesvár. They had come across 'men of 50, 60 years or even older, who will be unable to hold out if they ever have to go on campaign.' They were also struck by the high rate of desertion from the regiments of Radicati, Stampach and Schmerzing. No immediately obvious reasons came to light, but that 'should not lead us to suppose that the routine *Musterungen* are capable of revealing the actual state and interior life of a regiment; on the contrary, the very recent episode in the regiment of Stampach shows that a man who, in all confidentiality, discloses his genuine plight to the *Commissariat* at a mustering or similar occasion, has no guarantee that he will not be betrayed, and then find himself exposed to exemplary punishment for the slightest offence.'

The Commissaries looked into the matter more closely, and discovered that the troopers of Schmerzing were being forced to pay an altogether extortionate 29 florins 27 xr. for items of clothing and equipment, in addition to meeting the expense of shoeing their horses. The Commissaries suspected that investigation would bring to light similar abuses in other regiments, 'although it is difficult to extract specific instances of oppression from the men, when they are inhibited by reticence and fear.' It was good in principle to make the men pay something towards the cost of their outfits, for they would not take good care of them otherwise, but anything more than small charges would make unacceptable inroads into the cuirassiers' pay, which at the time amounted to only four xr. per day, or 25 florins over the year.[37]

The Commissaries who inspected the cuirassiers in Bohemia in the following October were happier with what they saw, or perhaps they were less observant (see p. 349). The evidence for the morale of the cavalry in the war years is indirect or statistical (see p. 249), but suggests that, whatever the maltreatment might have been in peacetime, the troopers went on campaign with high motivation and corporate pride.

The Prussian cavalry had meanwhile been in a state of continuous improvement, as became evident in the first encounters of the Seven Years War: 'they form up like the wind, and are eager to manoeuvre against the enemy flanks.' This was a deadly enemy to the Austrian cavalry in its fallen state; the defeats at Prague and elsewhere should have taught the Austrians to mend their ways, 'but it takes less effort to stand immobile, and so the enemy get there before us, find our flanks and strike them, and in such a way accomplish our defeat'.[38]

The Austrian cavalry's lack of speed was both physical and mental. In normal circumstances the cuirassiers were forbidden to gallop, and, on the few occasions that they did so, the riders hung on grimly to the reins with both hands until their horses ran out of breath. They could do little harm to the Prussians when they attacked in this way, and when they tried to make off they were easily overhauled and likely to lose a great number of men.[39]

One of the reasons for this sorry performance was that most of the Austrian cavalry had been scattered before the war in penny packets over the little villages of Hungary, where the horses could be fed cheaply, whereas the Prussian cavalry was concentrated in the rich plains of Silesia, and was put through its paces en masse in alarmingly realistic exercises. It was not easy for the Austrians to repose any trust in their riding instructors when those gentlemen were not masters of their own mounts: 'most of them could do little more than hack around on old broken-down English horses'.[40] If the Austrians became acquainted with anything, it was with the many ways of falling off a horse: 'the higher a cart is loaded, the more likely it is to topple over. It is the same with the saddles of our cavalry horses... In every action I have noticed how... whenever our men strike out, or parry a cut, the saddle is likely to revolve under the horse and deposit them on the ground'.[41]

In the judgement of the author of the *Patriotic Reflections* the lack of leadership and professionalism also accounted for a great deal. 'There is a damaging abuse among the cavalry, namely that so many of the companies are offered for purchase, and come to be commanded by very young men. Most of the higher regimental officers therefore lack the necessary experience.' Their seniors were unacquainted with the Prussian principle of progressive training, whereby the enemy cavalry learned to manoeuvre with speed, and drive home attacks with the sword. The Austrian commanders preferred to keep their squadrons intact and well turned-out:

> and you often hear them saying in the presence of the NCOs and men that our cavalry is being kept under cannon fire for too long, or that it is being committed to action on the wrong kind of terrain. Nothing satisfies them except perfectly level fields or heath-land where the enemy have deployed no cannon; they regard the most insignificant ditch or group of bushes as major obstacles, and use them as an excuse to grumble against the commander-in-chief.[42]

THE HUSSARS

The Insurrection

Vitam nostram et sanguinem consecramus! ('We dedicate our lives and blood!'). The call which ran through the castle hall at Pressburg on 11 September 1741 was the summons for the Hungarian Noble Insurrection, an historic and primitive form of military service, whereby nobles by the thousand were supposed to rally to the support of their king (who in this case happened to be female). Some units of exclusively noble horse indeed saw action against the French and the Bavarians, but a more useful contribution was in fact made by the 7,400 *Portalisten* (sons of townsmen and peasants), who were mostly incorporated into the existing regiments of the regular hussars.

The Insurrection was well-nigh forgotten until it re-emerged in discussions towards the end of the Seven Years War. In October 1761 the thought crossed Daun's mind that Nádasdy might usefully lead a new Insurrection into Prussian territory.[43] Maria Theresa in turn wrote to Daun on 6 June the next year to commend a proposal which he had made to raise a local Insurrection of the *Comitat* of Trentschin.[44] Nothing came of either proposal.

The Regular Hussars

The word 'hussar' probably derives prosaically enough from the Hungarian 'husz,' or the number 20, but it is easy to see the attraction of the supposed derivation from the Latin 'cursarius' (runner, or raider) as evoking the fast-moving and ferocious ways of the original hussars, the Jazygier and Kumanen peoples of the region of the river Theiss. The oldest surviving regiment of regular hussars was that of Nádasdy, originally raised in 1688. Maria Theresa inherited altogether seven regiments, and the addition of three in 1741–2, and another two in 1756 brought the total to 12.

> Hussar Regiments (designations as of 1759)
> Baranyáy
> Bethlen (–1759 Morocz)
> Dessweffy
> Esterházy (Paul Anton) (1762– Luzinsky)
> Hadik
> Kayser
> Kálnoky
> Palatinal (or Török)
> Nádasdy
> Pálffy (Rudolph) (Kálnoky –1759)
> Splényi (Esterházy, Emerich 1762–)
> Széchenyi (Festetics –1757)

Establishments

> Peace Establishment
> Nominal 600–610 officers and men; 365–400 horses; five squadrons
>
> First Augmentation, winter 1756/7
> 800 officers and men, 800 horses; six squadrons of two companies each
>
> Second Augmentation, early 1757
> 1,300 officers and men, 1,300 horses; six

Baranyay Hussar (Krauhse, Austrian Army Museum). Light green pelisse (trimmed with black) and dolman; light blue leggings; red barrel sash with yellow knots; black (or yellow) Hungarian boots; fur kalpak.

squadrons. By the middle of May the regiments were still well short of the new targets, and the regiments and *Comitate* were ordered to report how many men and horses had been recruited

Reduced Establishment, 1758
1,000 officers and men, 1,000 horses; any surplus to be carried on the establishment as supernumeraries

New Augmentation, late 1758
1,500 officers and men, 1,500 horses, though without any increase in the number of companies, which were now on a nominal strength of 125 officers and men each. Leopold Pálffy reported on 10 November that the necessary recruiting would go ahead, in spite of the difficulties which he foresaw (below); the latest available figures showed that the regiments still fell short even of the reduced establishment of 1758. The total came to 10,781 officers and men and 9,679 horses, whereas the 12 regiments should have numbered 12,000 officers and men and as many horses.[45]

Reduction 1761
The monarchy was now direly short of money, and in November 1761 Vienna struck two companies from the establishment of every hussar regiment, which brought the number of companies down to ten, each of 100 officers and men and 100 horses, and thus a total of personnel and horses of 1,000 apiece. This might seem a sensible way of reconciling the establishment with the already under-strength numbers, but the example of the 'German' cavalry showed that the numbers had a way of dropping in proportion with any reduction in the paper strength, and thus leaving the regiments with no buffer against wastage.

The Grenz-Husaren

These folk formed the mounted representation of the Military Borders. The original four regiments were founded between 1746 and 1750, and corresponded with the reorganisation of the Borders into four *Generalten*. At the outset of the Seven Years War their establishment stood as follows:

Slavonian:	6 squadrons
Warasdiner:	1 squadron
Banal:	4 squadrons
Carlstädter:	4 squadrons

The terms of engagement were similar to those of the Croatian light infantry, and so the men usually turned homewards of their own accord when their tours of duty came to an end. Neipperg, although Vice-President of the *Hofkriegsrath*, could not always be certain where these people might be.[46]

In 1762 two ethnically-based regiments of light horse were raised in Transylvania, namely a Szekler *Grenz-Husaren* regiment and a Wallachian *Grenz-Dragoner* Regiment. They did not see service with the field army, but were put on guard to defend their principality against possible invasion by the Tartars and Turks.

The Men

The Commissaries' *Musterings-Berichte* of 1754 and 1755 were every bit as damning of the conditions among the hussars as they were of those obtaining among other regiments of the army. Maria Theresa noted that 'things are even worse with them than among the German cavalry. Nádasdy is here in Vienna, and so he must be made to render an explanation point by point; the others must be called to account in the same way'.[47]

National myth would have it that every Hungarian was a born light horseman, but it was not easy to attract and retain good men for service in the hussars as they existed in the middle of the 18th century. During the years of peace the regiments of hussars had existed without being replenished with recruits or remounts, and the outbreak of the Seven Years War found them reduced to an average of about 400 men each, only 100 of so of whom could be mounted on respectable horses. The call now came to augment the establishment to 1,300 men and horses, and Nicolaus Pálffy as Hungarian *Hof-Canzler* explained that the loyal Hungarian nation was thereby compelled to raise 'agricultural labourers instead of trained hussars, and plough and draught horses or even completely unbroken horses instead of cavalry mounts'.[48] Andreas Hadik protested against the large numbers of unformed youths who were also being recruited to fill the void, while Rudolph Pálffy, who would have liked to have seen the age limits relaxed in a sensible way, remarked that 'we should not be taking on those babies who lack the necessary physical strength, but older men who are capable of withstanding two or three campaigns.'

As for the geographical origins of the recruits, Rudolph Pálffy observed that some useful hussars had been drawn from the *Comitate* adjoining Moravia, Lower Austria and Styria,[49] Hadik nevertheless rejected the recruitment from the Austrian borderlands entirely, for it merely brought in still more of the feeble juveniles, whereas 'if we went recruiting deeper into Hungary we would find no lack of suitable men, and so bring the hussar regiments up to establishment in a short time, supposing always that uniforms and horses are available'.[50]

Here we touch on the issue of competition with the Hungarian infantry. A life with the hussars even now held more appeal for the Hungarians than service with the foot soldiers, but potential recruits had become wary, because recruiters on behalf of the infantry had tricked men into believing that they were being admitted to the hussars.[51] The best remedy was to have the recruit's uniform, weapons and horse immediately at hand, so that there could be no deception. However a commission on hussar recruiting put the cost of fitting out a recruit at a formidable 140 florins, and Leopold Pálffy, as president, reported to Maria Theresa on 10 November 1760 that for this reason the lead ought to be taken by regiments which enjoyed particular advantages – Kaiser with its wealth and prestige as the regiment of the Emperor, the Palatinal regiment through its connection with the traditional recruiting areas of the Jazygier and Kumanen peoples and the Hajdúa towns, and the regiments of Károly and Bethlen through the influence of their *Inhaber* in Transylvania.[52]

The Officers
In society and on campaign the hussar officers represented their high-spirited nation in its most public face. They acquired a reputation of men who were much given to bragging, and they owned a lively sense of honour, or at least of injured vanity. The Prince de Ligne noted that it was for that reason that the Hungarian regiments made up the only element in the Habsburg army which it was inadvisable to put under the command of foreigners[53] (see p. 69). In June 1757 Daun and Nádasdy agreed that the command of the hussars destined for service alongside the French could be entrusted safely to either *FML*. Kálnoky or *GFWM*. Széchény, 'for both are fluent in French, whereas Colonel Baron Mittrowsky, who was originally assigned, is a foreigner who would awaken jealousy rather than trust among the Hungarians'.[54]

It is to the hussars' credit, rather than otherwise, that the harshest critics of their leadership came from their own kind. *GFWM*. Rudolph Pálffy was an intelligent disciplinarian who took his officers to task for being on the one hand too familiar with the men, but on the other too ready to invoke drastic punishments when leniency and encouragement would have proved more productive. His officers were also insufficiently aware of their dignity, which was compromised by habits like delivering letters for payment, as if they had been postmen.[55]

Uniforms, Weapons and Equipment

The hussar fashion was in some respects absurd and impractical, but it came to exercise a potent appeal throughout Europe to military men who imagined themselves to be as dashing as the original sons of the Puszta. Oddly enough the style originated in the higher ground of the Slovakian hills, from where it was transmitted to a couple of semi-Asiatic peoples who had settled on the plain of the Theiss – the Scythian-Sarmatian Jazygien from the Black Sea, and the Turkic Kumanen. From these remote beginnings the dress was taken up by the Hungarian magnates, and gained an altogether wider currency.

The hussar's hair was tied up at the side into plaits, like those of the Hungarian infantryman, and was crowned by a cylindrical fur cap (*Kalpak*), 10 or 11 inches high; the *Kalpak* was topped with a cloth flap (red in most of the regiments), which hung down one side or other of the head, and was secured to the brim so that it did not get into the man's face. The Szaklhaube (shako or *mirliton*) was an alternative headgear which was more suitable for everyday use. It was a tall cap of black felt, sitting on the head like an inverted flowerpot, and was considerably cheaper than the *Kalpak* with its appurtenances. The officers were in addition free to wear the ordinary tricorn of Western Europe.

The characteristic dolman came by way of the tight-fitting shell jacket of the Jazygier and Kumanen peoples, and was fastened across the front by toggles and loops. The cords were worked into fanciful shapes, and featured again as Hungarian 'carpetbeater' knots as ornamentation on many other items of the dress. The hussar regulations of 1751 respected the spirit of the dolman and ordained that it must be 'tight rather than loosely-fitting, and of such an length that an inch shows below the belt'.[56] The belt in question was a multi-coloured sash of skeins of coarse wool, kept in position by set or tubes or 'barrels.'

The pelisse was a fur-lined outer jacket, which was to be 'cut carefully and in such a way that when the man sits in the saddle, there should be one-and-a-half inches of clear space between the edge and the seat; the arms should not be too heavy, and are therefore to be lined only with good ticking'.[57] In cold weather the pelisse could be worn like a conventional jacket. It was otherwise so hot and encumbering that in normal circumstances only the left arm was inserted through a sleeve, and the rest hung loose down the back, suspended from a cord which passed over the right shoulder; in this manifestation the pelisse looked as if it had been flung back in a moment of abandon, and did much to augment the reputation of the hussars.

In company the hussar leggings exercised a powerful appeal to women, even if, according to the regulations, they were to be cut sufficiently generously to allow the man to sit, fall to the ground and mount horse with ease. On service the leggings were in any case protected by loose-fitting overalls, or outer trousers. The whole outfit could be covered by a broad cloak, with a collar which was wide enough to give some additional protection to the shoulders.

There was little room in the hussar's clothing for pockets, and so his papers and other small personal effects were carried in his sabretache, a flat-sided cloth pack which hung down his left-hand side. Bread and feed for up to two days could be held in a capacious *Haabersack*, and everything else was packed into the roll of the *Mantel Sack*. The sabretache, the saddle cloth and the pistol holster colours appeared in the distinctive colours of the regiment. In 1757 Maria Theresa sought to impose a universal dark 'French' or 'Berlin' blue but the hussar *Inhaber* held out as successfully against the innovations as did the colonels of the infantry and dragoons.

The Hungarian hussars rode with short stirrups by the standards of the German cavalry. The light boot therefore rested on the iron just in front of the heel, instead of by the toe, which exposed the hussar to the danger of being dragged along the ground if he fell off his horse. The hussar spurs, which were unusually long, likewise lay alongside the broadest part of the horse's chest, which 'prevented the hussars from being closed up in their squadrons, which for that reason can be seen to be in a state of constant movement'.[58]

In place of the straight sword (*Pallasch*) of the German cavalry, the hussars were armed with a curved sabre. The blade was of a form prescribed in 1748, and was about 32 inches (70–84 cm.) long, sharpened along the whole of the outer edge and along the inner edge towards the point, and inscribed with the encouraging slogans *Vivat Maria Theresia* or *Vivat Husar*. The design of the knuckle guard (brass or iron) was left to the *Inhaber*. Some officers used for preference the traditional mace (*buzogány*) or axe (*fokos*). The armament was completed by a bandolier and cartridge pouch (for 22 rounds), a pair of pistols and a carbine. From his observation of the Prussian hussars Lieutenant-Colonel Rebain maintained that the Austrian hussars should be equipped with a longer and heavier sabre, but with a carbine short enough to fire single-handed.[59]

The Hussars – an Assessment

In the early years of Maria Theresa's reign the Hungarian hussars represented probably the most effective light cavalry in civilised Europe, and an accession of physical and moral force which was associated with the survival of the monarchy and the prestige of Austrian arms as a whole. It was a different story in the Seven Years War, after which Armfeldt reported to his king that 'the Austrian hussars were once the best, but daily experience in the last war shows that they are no longer what they were'.[60]

The first indication that something was wrong came in the brief autumn campaign of 1756, when FM. Browne reported that the Austrian hussars were finding it difficult to get to grips with those of the enemy. The happenings of the late spring of 1757 were more alarming still, for when the Prussians irrupted into Bohemia their hussars swept the Hungarians from the countryside, and roamed around as they pleased to make off with fodder, cash, horses and forcibly-enlisted recruits. The main armies clashed at Prague on 6 May, and the hussars did little to avert the disaster which overtook Austrian arms. Later encounters confirmed that the hussars liked to hang back until the issue had been decided one way or another, and 'they can be employed only if the action of battle turns out well, and then only to pursue the scattered enemy. If you need proof, you will find it in the modest losses they suffer on a day of battle, compared with those of the regular troops'.[61]

In Saxony in 1761 FZM. Lacy saw the hussars of his corps disintegrate before his eyes. He ordered Colonel Hohenzollern to investigate the heavy desertion which had set in among the Dessweffy Hussars in May, 'and tell the troopers that it comes as an unpleasant shock to find that a regiment which consists of men of a nation which is otherwise so much praised for its zeal and devotion towards its sovereign, is now excelled in loyalty by a force [i.e. the Prussian hussars] which has been brought together from the four quarters of the world'.[62] The wastage continued unabated, and a few days later Lacy had to report to Daun that the Dessewffy regiment was now incapable of independent action.

The regiment of Paul Anton Esterházy was scarcely more reliable. In September one of its hussars was heard in a shouted conversation with a Prussian officer across the Elbe, telling him everything he knew about the destinations of the various Austrian detachments. Lacy wrote to the colonel commandant that 'this man, if he is still on outpost duty, is to be relieved immediately, made fast and brought to the regimental prison, so that he can undergo a formal enquiry. You are to bring it home to the regiment in the most urgent terms that if any NCO or trooper allows himself to be drawn into a conversation with the enemy, regardless of the excuse, he will be unfailingly shot through the head'.[63]

On the night of 16/17 August a patrol of the Esterházy Hussars had been ambushed at Wendisch-Borschütz and scattered to the winds, displaying the same lack of tactical sense which had allowed a post of the Dessewffy regiment to be wiped out at Senftenberg in June. These developments were particularly disturbing, for they presented incontrovertible proof that the Hungarian hussars were not only virtually unemployable in pitched battle, but had lost their historic ascendancy in 'little war,' and were disinclined to push home their attacks even in actions on the smallest scale'.[64]

GFWM. Wartensleben argued that a disadvantage of that kind was exceptionally damaging, for 'if we look for the force… which offers us the heaviest opposition… and does us the most damage in the kind of theatre in which the war is being waged, I don't think anyone will argue with me that it is the light cavalry'.[65]

As we have seen, Maria Theresa identified the manifold failings of her hussars with poor leadership and discipline, while Leopold Pálffy drew attention to the difficulty of expanding the hussars from their small peacetime base (see p. 292). In justice to the hussars it must be said that not all of their difficulties were of their own making. As some excuse for their battle-shyness Hadik explained that:

> in general the hussars have not been employed as they should have been employed, for it is quite wrong to send them to attack artillery head-on, and the ordinary trooper is quick to note when he is being misused. I could cite many examples, for I have been called upon to execute a number of attacks of this kind with my regiments, and seen 50 or 100 men struck down in an instant by roundshot and canister. Such experiences have made the young men wary, and afterwards, when opportunities arise for putting them to truly effective use, they have failed in their duty, as in the action on 18 June [i.e. Kolin].[66]

Unlike the cuirassiers and dragoons, the hussars received no proper rations from central sources, and yet their regiments, which were already under-strength, were weakened still further when the Commissaries snatched away men to gather in forage or peasant transport for the benefit of the rest of the army. These troopers were lost to their parent units indefinitely, so that their commanders had very little idea of where they were, and a force of a nominal two regiments of hussars might well be 600 strong at the most.

The authorities showed the same lack of regard for cohesion when it came to deploying the hussars on outpost duty. The high command typically told them off in small detachments, which were assumed to be self-supporting in matters of supply, and so the parties would set off laden with three days' rations of bread, oats and hay, and were thereafter supposed to provide for themselves. No particular limit was set to such assignments, and little thought was given to any relief. 'The commander-in-chief has many more important things on his mind, and cannot always give consideration to such trifles, and so the detachments are not only left for two or three months on end, but are often split up still further without need or necessity, and often again without knowledge of the commander.' Uniforms were reduced to tatters, and the wear on discipline could be greater still.[67]

When, finally, the hussars encountered the enemy, if was usually on fatally disadvantageous terms, remote from any possible support, and facing odds of up to 10 to one. Such episodes often showed that the Hungarian officers could be as lacking in tactical sense as the 'Germans,' and after the post at Senftenberg was lost in 1761 Lacy remarked that its commander should never have allowed his detachment to stay immobile for more than 48 hours on end.[68]

In objective terms the decline in the Hungarian hussars' proficiency since the 1740s was probably not very great. What mattered in the Seven Years War, however, was that they now had to measure themselves against the Prussian hussars, who had meanwhile been transformed by Lieutenant-General Winterfeldt, and were now directed by the charismatic General Zieten. Every informed commentator agreed on the advantages which now lay with the enemy. In terms of numbers alone the Prussians enjoyed a clear superiority. Late in 1762 the Austrian major-general Wartensleben calculated that the Prussians had built up their light horse from 80 squadrons at the beginning of the war to their current strength of 135, and he knew from a list found on the Prussian colonel Dingelstadt on 31 May that the number of personnel had reached 22,275. 'We confront them with 12 regiments of hussars on an establishment of 1,000 men each, making 12,000 men; we have to add some Slavonian and Banal [Grenz] hussars, and two or three regiments of *chevaulegers*, and although the quality of our hussars and *chevaulegers* counts for a great deal, it cannot make up for the superiority of nearly 8,000 which is owned by the enemy'.[69]

By the time of the Seven Years War the training of the Prussian hussars had made them familiar with the principle of mutual support, which remained a stranger to the Austrians. Just as the Prussian hussars manoeuvred in close order on the flanks of the Prussian army in battle, so they enjoyed the close support of artillery and parties of infantry and dragoons when they roamed over the countryside, forming an entity which almost invariably gained the upper hand over the outnumbered, isolated and increasingly demoralised Hungarians.[70]

To Lacy and Hadik it seemed contrary to the natural order of things, and matter of reproach to the Hungarians, that authentic Magyars should have been beaten in light cavalry work by the international rabble which made up the Prussian hussars. The Prussians in fact foreshadowed the future of European light forces in general, which were to be drawn no longer exclusively from hunters, backwoodsmen or frontiersmen of various sorts, but also from the ordinary stock of humankind which could be endowed with the proper skills by training.

A former officer of the Prussian hussars, Charles-Emanuel Warnery, made a valid point when he suggested that, in attempting to put their hussars on a more respectable basis before the Seven Years War, the Austrians had merely created amphibians, who had lost the cut-throat proficiency of olden times, without acquiring the more solid virtues of regular cavalry.[71] It is significant that the first official code for the hussar service (*Regulament and Ordnung, fur gesammte Kaiserl. Konigl. Husaren-Regimenter*, 1751) largely corresponded with that of the German cavalry, together with all its complicated orders and drills, and referred to the peculiar needs of the hussars only in a few passages on tactics and the distinctive items of hussar uniform.

The author of the *Patriotic Reflections* was for bringing the traditional skills of the Hungarians up to date, so that their officers would be able to render militarily useful reports, and:

> to that end it would be a good idea to translate a couple of texts on 'little war' for the benefit of that nation, and better still to put together a compilation from various authorities, adapted to the nation's character and way of war. As things are, the hussar officers are unable either to read maps or speak the local languages, and, being incapable of questioning the peasants properly about routes, rivers, passes and so on, they lose their temper and beat and rough up the local people, and treat them in a generally bad way. What they should be doing is to enter into conversation with them, and elucidate the

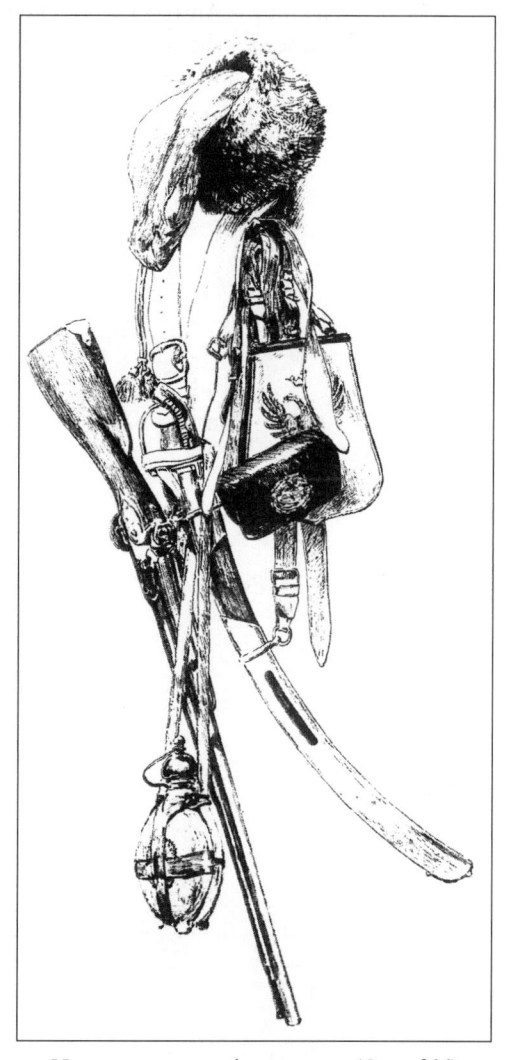

Hussar weapons and equipment. (Ottenfeld)

information politely. Hardly any of the hussar officers could put a name to the village where their own detachment is located, let alone the village next door. How then is it possible for them to make a proper report concerning a piece of ground, the destination of the enemy, or where they enemy have located their outposts? And yet the generals are supposed to take their guidance from wretched reports of this kind.[72]

In reality any attempt to educate the hussars in those respects would have been rejected as a 'German' plot, and that is probably why in the Habsburg army the hussars remained a speciality of the Hungarians. In the short span of time available to them in the Seven Years War the Austrians would have done better to commit the hussars to local defence on the Turkish borders, and put more effort into building up their versatile *chevaulegers*. The Habsburg horse as a whole might in any case have sustained its former reputation throughout the war if Maria Theresa's German cavalry had been schooled or motivated by an 'Austrian' Seydlitz, and her hussars by a Winterfeldt or Zieten. As it was, she had lost her most inspirational mounted leaders by the end of the second campaign, for Radicati and Lucchese had been killed, and Nádasdy was in undeserved disgrace.

It was fortunate for the Austrian service as a whole that the gunners owned just such a figure in Joseph Wenzel Prince Liechtenstein, who not only gave Maria Theresa's artillery the ascendancy on the battlefield, but endowed European artillery as a whole with a significance which was to reach its apogee in the massed batteries of Napoleon Bonaparte.

12

The Artillery

Prince Liechtenstein

Probably never has the death of a patriot been so unanimously and universally regretted as that of this genuinely great and unforgettable man, who was the benefactor of his Fatherland, and who extended a paternal care to so many thousands of its subjects. As a reward for his active dedication to that Fatherland he was honoured by a decree of the Court with the distinguished title of "Highness." After he died our great Theresa wished to immortalise his memory, and to this end she minted gold and silver medallions with the inscription: THE EMPRESS MARIA THERESA TO THE REFORMER OF THE ARTILLERY. TO A MAN WHO EXCELLED IN WAR AND PEACE ALIKE. TO HER FRIEND AND THE FRIEND OF THE FATHERLAND.[1]

Infantry won its engagements by *Contenance-Halten* and the slow moral and physical attrition that was caused by its musketry. The cavalry manoeuvred, threatened, attacked with cold steel when it felt particularly bold, or stood off and skirmished feebly with its carbines and pistols. Nothing could compare with the concentrated destructive power that was inherent in the cannon and howitzers, and especially in a period when it became possible to say that 'the fate of an army often depends on how well or badly its artillery is served'.[2]

There is little in the earlier history of Joseph Wenzel Prince Liechtenstein (1696–1772) to suggest that he would devote his wealth and the most productive years of his life to perfecting one of the technical services. He rose as an officer of dragoons, and indeed he remained the *Inhaber* of a dragoon regiment until he died. His family were grandees of the grandees, and typically of their class they owed their rise to a Carl Liechtenstein, their first prince (1659–1627), who converted to Catholicism, and made himself useful to a succession of Emperors. Carl's descendants married into important landed families, which expanded their holdings still further, and by 1700 the Liechtensteins and the Dietrichsteins together owned one-quarter of Moravia. The territory of Vaduz (the present Principality of Liechtenstein) was purchased by the family as an afterthought early in the 18th century; it was a poor and remote place, tucked up against Switzerland, but it gave the house the standing of independent sovereigns within the *Reich*.

The defining experience of the life of Joseph Wenzel was the battle of Chotusitz (17 May 1742) when he was cut down by enemy cavalry, but, as a disinterested patriot, was still more pained to see that the Austrian artillery was being outgunned decisively by the mobile and powerful Prussian ordnance. Liechtenstein designed and cast a light 3-pounder cannon at his own cost, and a number of the new pieces saw service on the Rhine campaign of 1744. They did not work very well, as we shall see later, but Maria Theresa was so impressed by the man's enthusiasm that in the same year she snatched the *Feld-Artillerie* from the control of the *Hofkriegsrath* and united it with the *Haus-Artillerie* under the command of Liechtenstein as *Feld-und Haus-Artillerie General-Director*.

As commander of a field army Liechtenstein won the battle of Piacenza (16 June 1746) which turned the military balance in northern Italy decisively in favour of the Austrians and their Piedmont-Sardinian allies. Two years later he became head of his house after the unexpected death of Johann Carl Prince Liechtenstein, and inherited the very considerable fortune which enabled him to give the Austrian artillery an impetus which would have been completely beyond the power of the state at this time of financial stringency. It became possible not only to augment the establishment of the personnel, but to fund costly experiments, improve professional standards, and support the widows and orphans of the corps.

Liechtenstein's wealth and manners fitted him to move at ease in the highest circles, and he sustained his reputation for lavish and ingenious hospitality through the entertainments he offered at his two palaces in Vienna, the cannon works nearby at Ebergassing, at Pressburg in his capacity as Commanding General of Hungary from 1753, and inevitably also at the artillery training and experimental grounds at Moldauthein in Bohemia.

Liechtenstein's devotion to his invalid wife Maria Anna was perhaps less characteristic of a man of his class, at least after he had left the free ways of his youth behind him. He betook himself to the Netherlands late in 1751 to join her at Spa, and their parties in Brussels became the talk of the winter season which followed. She died on 20 January 1753, leaving the memory of a pious and intelligent woman, and one who was loved greatly by her husband.

Here we have some indication of the qualities which made Liechtenstein so successful as the builder of a team. The old gunners were inevitably set in their ways, and he knew that repeated practical experiments were the best means to convince them that improvement was possible:

> His next step was to assemble commissions to determine what was best and most useful for the Imperial service. The General Director wisely avoided anything that might have smacked of the arbitrary or dictatorial. He waited until the tried and tested men of the commission resolved that such and such a thing was worthwhile, and he confirmed their decisions by his approval. Every gunner was allowed to approach him with ideas for innovations, and all received encouragement and reward.[3]

Liechtenstein observed the same principles with the foreign technicians who came to Bohemia at his invitation, and he was unfailingly generous to them, even if a particular line of research proved to be unproductive. His professional family embraced talents as diverse as the Berliner Schroder, the Swiss carpenter and mechanic Jacquet, *Ober-Stückhauptmann* (Major) Adolph Nicolaus Alfson (arrived from Norway 1754), Joseph Theodor Rouvroy who came from Luxembourg by way of the Saxon service, and a trio of native Austrians – Ignaz Walther von Waldenau (1713–60), and two representatives of an ancient line of Habsburg gunners, namely Andreas Franz Feuerstein (1697–1774), and the Anton Feuerstein who was ennobled with the suffix of 'von Feuersteinsberg' in 1757. In due course Alfson, Rouvroy, Walther von Waldenau and the two Feuersteins distinguished themselves in active artillery commands in the Seven Years War (Walther von Waldenau paying with his life at Torgau), and they were joined by the French gunner and engineer Jean-Baptiste Gribeauval, who was to form the living continuity between the artillery reforms of Liechtenstein and those of the last decades of the *ancien régime* in France.

FML. Andreas Feuerstein von Feuersteinsberg, 1700–73. (Military Academy, Wiener Neustadt)

Organisation in Overview

The **Feldartillerie** *consisting of:*
    Feld-Artillerie Staab (below)

    Feld-Artillerie Corps (below), including a *Haupt-Corps* and a Netherlands national artillery corps

    Artillerie-Füsilier-Regiment (below)

    Feldzeugamt
Namely the ordnance branch, which saw to the storage, repair and forwarding of the pieces, ammunition and other material, and organised the siege park. Its extremely diverse personnel comprised clerks, locksmiths, cartwrights, saddlers and the blacksmiths' assistants (Schmiedgesellen) who formed the largest single category, and whose numbers rose from 95 in 1759 to 148 in 1762. The personnel of the *Feldzeugamt* as a whole climbed from 351 to 416 over the same period.

    Rosspartei (below)

    Minier Compagnie (see following chapter)

Professional *Büchsenmeister* and Artillery Fusilier. (Ottenfeld, 1898)

Hausartillerie
This was a formation of 800 or so gunner invalids, who manned and maintained the artillery which was scattered in the fortresses over the monarchy.

So much for the outline. Some of the branches call for further explanation:

Feld-Artillerie Staab
The Staff formed the nerve centre of the corps, and consisted of 101 personnel in 1759, declining slightly to 98 in 1762. In structure it resembled an infantry regimental staff writ large. In addition to normal staff functions the artillery staff had an important educational role, and its establishment included a professor of mathematics.

Feld-Artillerie Haupt-Corps
The *Haupt-Corps* consisted of three brigades, each of an original eight companies, but augmented to 10 in 1758, which made a total of 30 for the remainder of the war. Armfeldt states that each company numbered 110 personnel, which probably refers to the serviceable average, since the nominal company establishment rose from 96 to a final 140 in 1759. He continues: 'A major-general is usually commander of the first brigade, and colonels of the other two. Each brigade has a lieutenant-colonel and a major, and there are four officers in each company. The brigades as a whole stand under the authority of the major-general, who is in turn answerable to Prince Liechtenstein. There is in addition a lieutenant-general who directs the corps in the field'.[4]

Niederländische National-Artillerie

The Netherlands artillery corps was a semi-autonomous organisation, which came under the command of Lieutenant-Colonel Walther von Waldenau before the Seven Years War, and possessed its own *Feldzeugamt* and *Rosspartei*. Its original eight companies gave it a nominal establishment of 768 personnel. The companies rose to the number of 12 in the Seven Years War, though the number of gunners who saw active service never exceeded 300. The Netherlands gunners arrived on the theatre of operations in 1757, and for the rest of the war their contribution in terms of pieces amounted to between 30 and 35 3-pounders, four and seven 6-pounders, and one or two 12-pounders.

The Personnel

The establishment of the field gunners rose from 800 in 1746 to 1,000 in 1749, and to more than 2,000 in 1755. The numbers in subsequent wartime service amounted to:

	Artillerie Haupt-Corps	2 Niederländische National-Artillerie
1756:	1,620	nil
1757:	2,054	253
1758:	2,428	98
1759:	2,834	166
1760:	3,126	162
1761:	2,952	300
1762:	3,009	243[5]

The gunners retained their ancient structure of ranks, namely:

Ober-Stückhauptmann = *Obristwachtmeister* or *Major*
    He commanded a half-brigade of four or five pieces
Stückhauptmann = *Hauptmann* (captain)
Stückjunker = *Ober-Lieutenant*
    Commanded between four and six pieces
Alt-Feuerwerker = no exact equivalent Especially responsible for the preparation of materials and the technical training of the company
Jung-Feuerwerker = full NCO
    In charge of a single piece
Büchsenmeister = *Gemeiner*
    The professional private gunner.
The *Handlanger* and the Regiment of *Artillerie-Füsiliere*

The ordinary *Büchsenmeister* were expensively-trained specialists, and by the practice of the time much of the hard manual labour involved in serving and moving the pieces was carried out by *Handlanger* – soldiers borrowed from the infantry. The Austrian 3-pounder cannon required the help of six such *Handlanger*, the 6-pounder eight, the 12-pounder 12, the 24-pounder 16, and the 7-pounder howitzer eight. In addition the regiment of infantry had to detach two of its *Zimmerleuthe* to each of its assigned 3-pounders, so as to hold the horses after they had been unhitched, together with a corporal who had to prevent the civilian artillery drivers from running off.

The *Handlanger* came to the artillery totally untrained, and were likely to be exhausted and demoralised by the unfamiliar work with the guns. The artillerymen were just as unhappy, for the infantrymen were sent and reclaimed by their regiments by relays, 'and so scarcely had the time to become familiar with their tasks. They were in any case usually the worst men of their regiments, who either made off or hid themselves when they were most needed, thus abandoning the pieces, or if they got to work, they did so in a clumsy, recalcitrant and negligent way'.[6]

There was no realistic prospect of raising enough qualified gunners to take the place of the *Handlanger*, and so in 1757 and 1758 Liechtenstein raised a specialised regiment of *Artillerie-Füsiliere* on an establishment of 2,784 personnel. The three component battalions corresponded with the three brigades of the *Artillerie Haupt-Corps*, and each battalion comprised eight companies of 116 officers and men. At first the artillery fusiliers were recruited directly from the *Stände* conscripts. When this supply failed in the spring of 1760 the *Hofkriegsrath* was only too glad to fall in with Liechtenstein's proposal to set about his own recruiting, and the necessary stations were duly set in Vienna, Prague, Olmatz and Troppau.[7]

Thinking officers of the other arms acclaimed the artillery fusiliers as an excellent institution.[8] This enthusiasm was not shared unreservedly in Vienna. On 21 November 1761 the *Hofkriegsrath* ordered Liechtenstein to strike six companies from the establishment of the regiment, as part of the notorious programme of reductions which was being instituted during the winter. In his reply Liechtenstein could demonstrate that even at full strength the fusiliers fell short by 1,128 men of the total of 3,912 assistants needed by the gunners. If he proceeded with the reduction the artillery would have to revert to the bad old practice of taken men from the infantry. The structural damage would be just as great, for the fusiliers did not work as a whole, like the other regiments of the army, but in greater or smaller detachments, each of which demanded a full establishment of officers and NCOs. Liechtenstein pointed out that in the present year the personnel assigned to Loudon's army alone amounted to 25 officers, 10 NCOs, 70 corporals, 17 non-combatants, 36 *Zimmerleuthe* and 1,333 private fusiliers.[9]

The *Hofkriegsrath* conceded the strength of these arguments, but told Liechtenstein that the decision was irrevocable, and could only suggest that he should turn to the expedient of engaging the infantry *Handlanger* on a semi-permanent basis for a whole campaign at a time.

Joseph Wenzel Prince von Liechtenstein, 1696–1772. His work for the artillery made it the most potent single arm of the Austrians in the Seven Years War, and founded a tradition of excellence which endured into the 20th century.

The Inner Life of the Corps

Liechtenstein assumed command of the Austrian artillery at a time when it still bore something of the character of a trade guild, as befitted its bourgeois origins. If the Austrian cavalry still invoked the patronage of St. Christopher (the help of wanderers), the gunners honoured 4 December as the feast of St. Barbara (who called down lightning on her heathen father) with the excellent food, beer and music of Bohemia, and they celebrated with scarcely less style on May Day and on the occasion of promotions. The idiosyncratic names of their ranks recalled the earliest days of gunpowder artillery, and they still called their types of guns by the names of snakes or birds of prey. A standing feud with the engineers was another important part of the gunner inheritance'.[10]

Liechtenstein's task was to 'militarise' the artillery and bring it closer to the work of the rest of the army, while building on the best of the old traditions. His appointment as overall *General-Director* in 1744 was a crucial step in itself, for it brought the artillery for the first time under central control, and from this position of authority he was able to place the corps on a solid institutional base, with a recognisable hierarchy of ranks and appropriate scales of pay. The artillery still lacked a code of service to compare with those of the infantry and cavalry, but the gap was finally filled in 1757 by a *Reglement fur das Kaiserliche Königliche gesammte Feld-Artilleriecorps*. In somewhat daunting terms Maria Theresa declared in the introduction that she had sanctioned the code 'so that all abuses may be terminated once and for all.[11] However the main body of the Reglement amounted to a comprehensive guide to all the business of the corps, ranging from the treatment of ordinary gunners to the status of married men, the responsibilities of the ranks, the scientific work and training of the corps, gun drill and the repartition of personnel to the pieces, and the contribution of specialised branches like the *Rosspartei*.

The entrants to the artillery corps were of generally high quality, for this well-paid, meritocratic and 'learned' arm attracted students, volunteers from the other arms, and sons of tradesmen and townsmen as well as the children of the corps. A new source of recruits came into being during the war, for Liechtenstein was able to describe his regiment of *Artillerie-Füsiliere* as an invaluable training school for the artillery, since it formed handy and experienced men who could pass into the main corps as Bfichsenmeister.[12]

The artillery recruit was to be well-built, stand at least five feet five inches (171 cm.) tall, and, more importantly still, to be literate in German. Foreigners and married men were generally discouraged, though 'it is not a bad idea to have four or five married men in each company, so that their wives may provide the men with laundered shirts and other necessities, and so keep them clean'.[13]

The preponderance of Bohemians in the corps was absolute, and amounted to well over half the personnel in all grades – the officers and the NCOs as well as the ordinary *Büchsenmeister*. The birthplaces of the Bohemians in question were clustered in the north-western and south-central Circles, and German surnames outnumbered those of Slavonic origin, all of which points to the influence of local and family traditions (see Appendix XII: The Background of the Personnel of the Field Artillery).

The recruit was assigned to a *Corporalschaft* for his basic training, ' and here the main thing is not to assail the new man with brutality, curses and yelling, otherwise he will become timorous and sad, and lose his enthusiasm for the service.' The men were to be treated with the same consideration throughout their lives in the corps, 'and those officers who behave otherwise will not only incur severe reprimand, but suffer in their careers and promotion'.[14]

The disciplinary powers of the senior officers were more restricted than in the other arms, and many further details of the service reinforced the professional status of the ordinary gunners. Thus a party of NCOs and *Büchsenmeister* must always be present whenever a contract was signed for the purchase of uniforms – something which would have been unthinkable in the regiments of infantry and cavalry. In extreme cases offenders were put to fortress labour. Confinement (if necessary on bread and water) could be imposed on lesser malefactors, but a greater deterrent still was the threat of being dismissed from the corps or consigned to the infantry. Former gunners were rarely readmitted, and then only after they had three times pleaded for the restoration of their honour in a circle of their former comrades. Expulsion from the corps was therefore tantamount to being rejected by a family, and it was also painful in the material sense, for the pay of the officers and men was one-third higher than for the equivalent ranks in the infantry. Married men had still more to lose, for the corps had a tradition of generosity towards orphans and widows.

Favouritism had no place in a corps where promotion depended on demonstrable and tested accomplishment. Every brigade headquarters had a school for the theoretical instruction of NCOs; the best pupils progressed to the Corps school at Budweis, with good prospects for further advancement; the officers in their turn trained under the supervision of an *Ober-Feuerwerkmeister* and a *Professor*.[15] It was possible for an officer to resume a course of studies if he failed an examination, but only on paying five florins *Lehrgeld* to the *Ober-Feuerwerkmeister*, who thus had an incentive to be rigorous in his marking.

The new artillery was central to the Austrian military reforms, and the high regard of the monarchy was shown in the award of the Military Order of Maria Theresa to seven of its members for service in the Seven Years War: the *GFWMs*. Jean-Baptiste Gribeauval and Franz Ulrich Kinsky, the colonels Wenzel Barnkopp and Walther von Waldenau, the lieutenant-colonels Adolph Alfson and Theodor Rouvroy, and Major Joseph Frierenberger.

Old social prejudices still had to be overcome, and they were actually reinforced by the high standards now prevailing in the artillery:

> There are few nobles to be found in the corps [commented Armfeldt]. The young men of the great families prefer to make their way through the favouritism they enjoy by right of birth, rather than seeking their fortune in a corps where promotion to high rank depends on courage and effort. The officers of the artillery are therefore regarded as tradesmen, who are employed for as long as they are needed... Prince Liechtenstein has so far been unable to overcome the unwillingness of the high nobles to serve in the artillery.[16]

The artillerymen worked in an environment of flying sparks and enveloping smoke, entirely unsuited to the white uniforms of the infantry and cuirassiers. The gunners and the artillery fusiliers therefore wore coat and waistcoat of a sensible greyish brown, known variously as Rehbraun (deer brown), *Wolfsbraun* or *Wolfsgrau*. The coats of the *Haupt-Corps* were plain affairs, carrying a single row of buttons, and ornamented only with 'Saxon' cuffs of red; the Netherlands gunners were distinguished by red 'round' cuffs on the same pattern as the infantry, and by red lapels. Both corps wore boots instead of the infantry shoes and gaiters, and carried their small items of equipment in a box of black leather positioned at the front of the waist belt. The artillery fusiliers were equipped with a similar box of white leather, which served as their cartridge pouch. The traditional long hunting knife (*Hirschfänger*) of the artillerymen was replaced in 1758 by a curved sabre, which was common to the German and Netherlands gunners and the fusiliers. The officers of the artillery wore their hair in two distinctive styles: the one a short club-like pigtail called the *Kanone*, and the other the long, stringy *Rattenschwanze* or 'rat-tail.' The artillery drivers were hired civilians, but dressed in a military style in a *Wolfsgrau* uniform with yellow collar and cuffs.

The surviving muster lists of the *Haupt-Corps* and the Netherlands artillery date from 1762, and thus near the end of the war, by when, according to Armfeldt, 'after so many bloody battles and other actions the entire old stock must have been lost, and extremely young men taken on instead'.[17] The following figures indicate that the Netherlands corps survived better than the main branch, but that both corps had been recruiting heavily in 1759 and 1760:

Age and Service Structure of the *Büchsenmeister*, 1762

Age

Haupt-Corps (2,497 cases)
Average: 24. Largest single age: 22 at 16.09 percent
Groupings

16–20	21–25	26–30	31–35	36–40	41–45	46–50	51–55
10.37	49.57	31.11	7.24	1.12	0.48	0.04	0.04

Netherlands Corps (308 cases)
Average: 27. Largest single age: 23 at 9.34
Groupings

16–20	21–25	26–30	31–35	36–40	41–45	46–50	51–55
8.44	33.11	31.16	18.50	6.49	11.29	0.64	0.32

Service

Haupt-Corps (2,617 cases)
Average: 3.5. Largest single year: 2 at 18.34
Groupings

up to 5	6–10	11–15	16–20	21–25
75.41	22.22	1.47	0.78	0.03

Netherlands Corps (310 cases)
Average: 5. Largest single year: 3 at 15.80
Groupings

up to 5	6–10	11–15	16–20	21–25
46.42	50.63	2.24	0.32	0.32

Artillerie-Füsiliere
Average age 1760, 1,998 private soldiers: 23 Average service 1760, 1,866 private soldiers: 1

THE SERVICE OF THE PIECES

In peacetime the regiments of the Austrian infantry and cavalry marched across the length and breadth of the monarchy from one garrison station to another. The gunners were unique, for they returned every year to the headquarters of the Staab at Budweis in southern Bohemia, and the experimental grounds and ranges nearby on a hill outside Moldautein. Here the *Büchsenmeister* could train on full-sized pieces instead of the miniature practice guns that were held in their garrisons. In the process they learned the duties of every number of the detachment on the pieces, and they acquired the skills required to judge ranges and build batteries.[18] The officers were expected to become proficient in the use of the quadrant, and they learned ballistic theory from the editions of Belidor and Deidier which Liechtenstein printed at his own expense.

Liechtenstein paid out 50,000 florins every year in peacetime to ensure that these annual camps were as useful as possible. 'At Moldautein the shot and shell were aimed against targets, and all the exercises carried out there were an accurate and realistic representation of what went on in combat and sieges. Everything was executed with a seriousness which allowed no place for pedantry or triviality'.[19] Maria Theresa and Francis Stephen honoured one such occasion with their presence between 12 and 15 July 1753.

The artillerymen were assigned to individual pieces for the duration of each campaign, 'and so the officers and men had an interest in looking after their equipment and ammunition, for their honour was at stake'.[20] A well-trained gun detachment went about its work in an easy and unforced way, devoid of any unnecessary drill or ceremonial.[21] The numbers and duties of the individual gunners were identical for the 3-, band 12-pounder cannon, except that an extra gunner helped to bring up the ammunition for the heavier pieces. By tradition:

> No. 1 stood to the left of the piece, and inserted the cartridge and the shot or charge of canister into the muzzle
> No. 2 stood to the right, and wielded the combined mop and rammer
> No. 3, the *Vormeister*, held the rank of *Jung-Feuerwerker* and commanded the whole detachment; in addition he aimed the piece and inserted the priming tube into the vent
> No. 4 touched off the priming tube with his linstock at the command of No. 3
> No. 5 was responsible for traversing the piece under the direction of No. 3
> No. 6 and (if any) No. 7 brought up the ammunition

A set of contemporary illustrations for the employment of the pieces nevertheless show a much larger detachment which included soldiers of the *Artillerie-Füsiliere*. There were consequent variations in the numbering, Thus in the drill for the 3-pounder:

> Nos. 1 and 2 remained as above
> Nos. 3 and 4 stood to the left and right of the piece respectively, ready to push on the *Avancirstangen* (below)
> No. 5 saw to the elevation No. 6 had the linstock
> No. 7 was mounted on the single horse which helped to move the piece once the cannon was unlimbered
> No. 8 was assigned to the traversing spike No. 9 was the *Vormeister*
> No. 10 was assigned to the limber
> No. 11 was assigned to the ammunition cart

The service of the 7-pounder howitzer demanded somewhat more expertise than that of the cannon, and in this case the detachment was commanded by an *Alt-Feuerwerker*, who determined the range, chose the type of ammunition and charge, aimed the piece, and inserted the priming tube. Two *Jungen-Feuerwerker* stood beside the muzzle, the one on the left inserting the charge, and the one on the right the shell or the load of grape. The four common *Büchsenmeister* were assigned respectively to the linstock, the traversing spike, the limber and the ammunition cart.

The *Handlanger* (and later the artillery fusiliers) provided the less technical labour. Six of them were assigned to the 3-pounder cannon, eight to the 6-pounder, 12 to the 12-pounder, 16 to the 24-pounder, and or eight or 10 to the 7-pounder howitzer.

Elaborate provisions were made to ensure that the ammunition flowed to the pieces smoothly. At any given time ammunition was to be found in:

> The army depot, established in the nearest convenient town or other location on the theatre of war
> The army mobile reserve, located to the rear of the army in battle
> The ammunition carts (*Karren*) assigned to the pieces in the second line of battle
> The ammunition carts assigned to the pieces in the first line of battle
> The detachable box (*Laffettentrüchel*) carried normally between the cheeks of the trail of the piece, but removed in action
> The box (*Magazin*) carried on the axle of the piece beside the barrel
> The rounds and charges carried in satchels by the *Handlanger* (later the artillery fusiliers) and available for immediate use.

The piece, the limber and the ammunition cart together formed a triangle, the limber being positioned 20 paces to the left rear of the piece, and the ammunition cart 20 paces to the right rear, the limber and the ammunition cart standing 10 paces apart.

The practice was to draw the ammunition first from the ammunition cart, which was sent back to the army mobile reserve for replenishment as soon as it was exhausted. Its place was taken initially by a second ammunition cart which had been brought up from the unengaged artillery of the second line, and any hiatus in the supply filled by the emergency ammunition held in the *Laffettentrüchel* and the axle Magazin. The first ammunition cart would meanwhile have taken on fresh stocks at the reserve, and be on its way back to its parent piece.

Ordnance Stores

The greatest single depository of the monarchy's ordnance was to be found in the Vienna Arsenal (*Zeughaus*), a large plainbuilding (since demolished, not to be confused with the municipal *Zeughaus* still standing in the Am Hof square) in the western part of the Inner City. Huge Turkish cannon stood guard at the entrance, and great quantities of cannon, howitzer and mortar barrels were ranged in the courtyard. Gun carriages, ammunition carts and other items of equipment were kept under cover, and muskets, pistols, swords and other weapons by the thousand were formed into columns and arches in the spacious and lofty halls.

There was probably no alternative to Vienna as the site for a depot that might have to support campaigns as far distant as the Black Forest, northern Italy, Silesia or Transylvania. The Austrians still had to address the problem of moving the ordnance to the locations where it was actually needed, and Liechtenstein chaired a meeting which was called to address the subject on 24 January 1757. Here it was decided to take advantage of the present hard-frozen state of the roads to move half of the field artillery reserve to Prague without delay; the park of siege artillery would also be transported nearer the present theatre of war – some to Olmütz, but most to Prague – where they were good facilities for fitting it out.[22]

Presuming that the scale of ammunition for the Netherlands pieces were identical with those given for the *Haupt-Corps*, the allowance of rounds for the field artillery rose from 111,588 in 1759 to 131,624 in 1762. In detail:

Allowance of Rounds for the Field Artillery

	1759	1762
Cannon shot	64.3%	70.7%
Canister	26.3	19.6
Grape	6.1	5.7
Shells	3.2	3.8

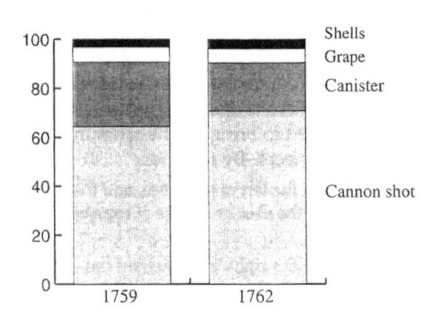

On the same basis, the allowance per calibre of piece may be estimated as follows:

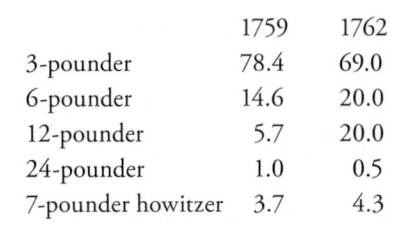

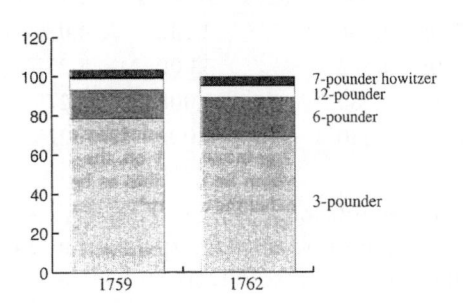

	1759	1762
3-pounder	78.4	69.0
6-pounder	14.6	20.0
12-pounder	5.7	20.0
24-pounder	1.0	0.5
7-pounder howitzer	3.7	4.3

There was evidently a significant shift in favour of the medium-calibre 6-pounder.

In addition to meeting its own considerable needs, the artillery produced and delivered the small arms ammunition and entrenching tools for the rest of the army in the field. Over the years 1759–62 the calculations were made on the basis of the requirements for 124–127,000 regular infantry and Croats and 20–25,000 cavalry, who were allotted ammunition on the scale of 36 ball and 12 buckshot cartridges for each infantryman, and 12 ball cartridges for each cavalryman. In 1759 alone the requirement for flints alone came to 372,000 stones for the muskets, 40,000 for the carbines and 80,000 for the pistols.[23] Thirty-six rounds per man were carried in each caisson of the regimental artillery, along with 1,000 flints, 48 horseshoes, 360 horseshoe nails, and the artillery ammunition.

The musket cartridges were made up in packets of a dozen, 'which means that they can be distributed to the men in a much more convenient and orderly way'.[24] By 1753 the powder for the small arms was reaching a consistent '51' on the scale of the testing device, instead of between 40 and 50 as recorded in earlier times, and Liechtenstein therefore diminished the quantity in each cartridge by one-third; this was carrying economy too far, for it put the Austrian infantry at a needless disadvantage against the Prussians, who were armed with muskets of almost identical calibre, but were firing with heavier charges.

Transport

The artillery owned no permanent transport organisation of any kind, and instead conjured up a *Rosspartei* (lit. 'horse party') of drivers and horses to draw the pieces and ammunition carts, together with the further drivers, horses and vehicles needed to transport the reserves of ammunition and stores, and the baggage of the corps.

In the emergency of 1756 the contractor Dietrich was paid four florins per day for every four-horse cart he supplied to move the ammunition and artillery from Vienna to the theatre of war, and he worked so effectively that he was able to transport the two consignments with remarkable speed – one to Pardubitz in six days, and the other to Prague in seven.[25]

The *Rosspartei* proper was commanded by an *Oberwagenmeister* and his assistant the *Obergeschirrmeister*, and it was divided into 60 Truppen, each consisting of an *Wagenmeister*, two *Geschirrmeister*, 100 horses at full establishment (80 from 1759), and two *Stück-Knechte* to every horse. A total of 1,868 horses were on the strength of the *Rosspartei* in 1756, and 3,663 in 1757, and detailed figures are available for 1759 onwards (see chart).

	Horses for drawing pieces	Horses for vehicles	Total, with allowance for wastage	Stück-Knechte	Number of carts
1759:	1,306	2,242	4,080	2,444	1,177
1760:	1,572	3,000	5,257	2,912	1,177
1761:	1,580	3,008	5,275	n.a.	1,177
1762:	1,580	3,008	5,275	2,915	1,177[26]

In addition 166 four-horse peasant carts with 644 horses and peasant drivers were hired for the duration of hostilities. After the battle of Torgau (3 November 1760) the acting army commander G.d.C. Carl O'Donnell had to signal a desperate need for 2,500 additional artillery horses, which indicates that on this occasion the losses far exceeded the normal 15 percent allowed for wastage.[27]

The absence of a permanent militarised artillery transport organisation made some sense on purely economic terms, for a large proportion of the *Rosspartei* could be stood down during the winter, and the organisation could be dissolved almost altogether in time of peace. This arrangement was typical of 18th-century armies, which had to live with the necessary penalties. Most of the *Stück-Knechte* were hired peasant hands, 'and you have to station a guard behind them if they are not to make off with the horses at the first opportunity. This they do if the action seems to be taking a bad turn, and often also when it seems to be going well'.[28]

Armfeldt nevertheless found a much to admire in the system of Austrian artillery transport, for 'in general the horses are good and strong,' and the efficient administration enabled the artillery officers to devolve all the responsibility for movement on the Ober*Wagenmeister*, whom he describes as being a lieutenant-colonel of the cavalry.[29]

The Austrian and Prussian Artillery – A Quantitative Comparison

On 24 January 1757 Liechtenstein was delighted to be able to report that in addition to a sum of 8,000 florins assigned to the artillery, it had been decided to allot a further and impressive 72,764 florins to enable the artillery to keep pace with the augmentation of the army.[30] The effect may be seen in the figures of the pieces that the Austrians put into service in the course of the Seven Years War (the numbers after the obliques show the additional pieces furnished by the Netherlands artillery)

	3-pdrs.	6-pdrs.	12-pdrs.	24-pdrs.	7-pdr. Howitzers	Total
1756:	154	24	12	nil	12	202
1757:	245 /35	54 /8	30 /2	nil	16	390
1758:	256 /30	60/7	30 /1	nil	20	404
1759:	330 /30	70 /7	40 /1	6	30	514
1760:	336 /30	84 /7	54 /1	8	36	556
1761:	352 /33	90 /4	58 /1	6	36	580
1762:	352 /33	90 /4	58 /1	6	36	580

Quantity and Proportions of Austrian Pieces in the Later Stages of the Seven Years War

1759
Total: 514 pieces
Throw-weight in shot: 2,178 pounds
Throw weight in howitzer shell: 210 pounds (stone weight)

	Quantity of Pieces	Proportion of Whole	Proportion of Weight of Shot
3-pdr.:	360	70.03%	49.58
6-pdr.:	77	14.98	21.21
12-pdr.:	41	7.97	22.58
24-pdr.:	6	1.16	6.61
7-pdr. Howitzer:	30	5.58	

1760
Total: 586 pieces
Throw-weight in shot: 2,586 pounds
Throw weight in howitzer shell: 252 pounds (stone weight)

3-pdr.:	396	67.57%	45.93
6-pdr.:	91	15.52	21.11
12-pdr.:	55	9.38	25.52
24-pdr.:	8	1.36	7.42
7-pdr. Howitzer:	36	6.14	

1761/2
Total: 580 pieces
Throw-weight in shot: 2,571 pounds
Throw weight in howitzer shell: 252 pounds (stone weight)

3-pdr.:	385	6.37%	44.92
6-pdr.:	94	16.20	21.23
12-pdr.:	59	10.17	27.53
24-pdr.:	6	1.03	5.60
7-pdr. Howitzer:	36	6.20	

Verifiable Quantities of Pieces in Field Actions

	Austrian	Prussian
Lobositz 1756:	94	102
Prague 1757:	200	192
Breslau 1757:	220	138
Hochkirch 1758:	340	200
Liegnitz 1760:	130	120
Torgau 1760:	360	320
Reichenbach 1762:	100	60

Total Throw-Weights of Field Artillery Austrian

	Total of Shot		3-pdrs.	6-pdrs.	12pdrs.	24-pdrs.	Howitzer Stone Weight
1756:	759 lb.	=	61.6%	19.2	19.2	nil	83 lb.
1757:	1,596	=	52.6	23.2	24.0	nil	112
1758:	1,632	=	52.5	24.6	22.7	nil	140
1759:	2,178	=	49.5	21.2	22.5	6.6	210
1760:	2,496	=	43.9	21.8	26.4	7.6	252
1761:	2,571	=	44.9	21.9	27.5	5.6	252
1762:	2,571	=	44.9	21.9	27.5	5.6	252

Prussian

1756:	2,250	=	23.7	16.5	32.0	27.7
1758:	2,871	=	19.5	8.5	56.8	15.0
1760:	3,312	=	14.4	21.7	63.0	0.7
1761:	3,498	=	11.8	25.0	63.1	

(The Prussian numbers for the years 1757, 1759 and 1762 are not available; howitzers are excluded from the Prussian lists, since they make no differentiation between the 7- and 10-pounders, which makes it impossible to establish the total throw-weight of shell)

Totals of Prussian Cannon and Howitzers
1756:   360
1758:   424
1759:   536
1760:   513
1761:   626

Relative Austrian Quantitative Superiorities and Inferiorities

	Totals of Pieces	Throw-weight of Shot
1756:	-28.1	-50.0
1758:	- 2.5	-27.5
1759:	- 2.0	n.a.
1760:	+ 5.1	-32.6
1761:	+ 4.9	-36.0

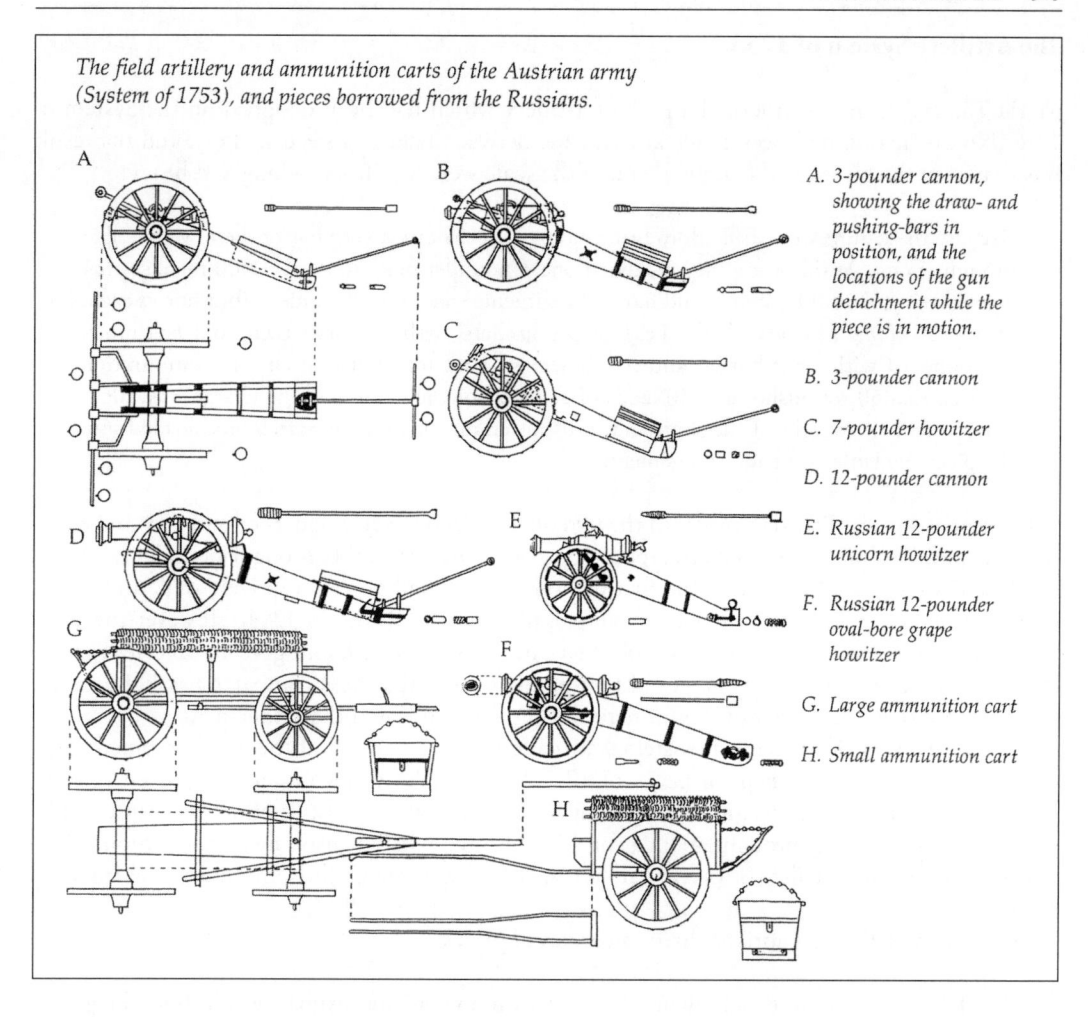

The field artillery and ammunition carts of the Austrian army (System of 1753), and pieces borrowed from the Russians.

A. 3-pounder cannon, showing the draw- and pushing-bars in position, and the locations of the gun detachment while the piece is in motion.

B. 3-pounder cannon

C. 7-pounder howitzer

D. 12-pounder cannon

E. Russian 12-pounder unicorn howitzer

F. Russian 12-pounder oval-bore grape howitzer

G. Large ammunition cart

H. Small ammunition cart

These figures amount to a long-winded way of saying that artillery became of greater importance as the Seven Years War progressed. In the final years of the war the Austrians accepted a ratio of five pieces per 1,000 troops as the norm, which corresponds to the 580 pieces available for the campaigns of 1761 and 1762. Daun was urging greater efforts still:

> I agree that the artillery must be increased, and Liechtenstein is the man best qualified to tell us how to augment the personnel and the teams of horses – which must be built up as well'.[31]

As far as comparisons are possible, they show that the Austrians had gained an advantage in the number of pieces available by 1761, though not in the weight of shot, for the Prussian artillery maintained a marked preponderance in the higher calibres. The numbers take no account of the effort the enemy had to divert against the Russians, the Swedes and the *Reichsarmee*. All the same the superiority of the Austrian artillery, which was undoubted, must have lain in dimensions other than weight of quantifiable firepower. Morale and training have been considered already. The technology must claim our attention next.

The Artillery System of 1753

Maria Theresa's gunners inherited a park of artillery which had been designed on the System of 1716. No distinction had been made at that time between field and siege artillery, and the result was that even the pieces at the 'lighter' end of the scale were inordinately long and heavy:

> Because these guns were difficult to bring along with the army, very few of them were in fact brought along. At that time they reckoned one 3-pounder piece to every 1,000 men, so that a given army of 24,000 men would have 20 regimental pieces with teams of four horses each, four *Feldschlangen* ['fieldsnakes' – i.e. long 3-pounders] with six horses each, four Falcaunen [6-pounders] with eight horses, and two howitzers with four horses each. The ammunition carts carried 50 roundshot and 10 loads of canister for each cannon. The charge was calculated at half the weight of the shot, and transported on the carts in barrels, and loaded into the pieces by ladles – a bad arrangement.[32]

In comparison the Prussian pieces in the two Silesian Wars were wonders of mobility and effectiveness, and Liechtenstein's first attempt to compete – the 13½ calibre-long 3-pounder he developed in 1743 – proved a failure. The first demonstrations had gone deceptively well, and it was decided to take a number of the pieces campaigning on the Rhine in 1744. However the swell at the muzzle (by which the gunners took their aim) was too small, and gave an excessively high elevation; moreover the heavy charges of that period overheated these comparatively light pieces, and soon put them out of action.[33] Gunnery was more complicated than it seemed.

In the same year of 1744 Liechtenstein was made *General-Director* of the new combined corps of artillery, and after the general peace of 1748 he was able to devote most of his energies to building up teams of experts and testing designs. The outcome of all this effort was expressed in findings 'which not only brought about a considerable saving in expensive metal and ammunition, but made for greater facility of movement and speed of operations, thus promoting the Imperial service.[34]

The System of 1753 comprised three categories of pieces:

1. Field artillery: 3-, 6- and light 12-pounder cannon, all approximately 16 calibres long, and land 1-pounder howitzers
2. Battery pieces: 12-, 18- and 24-pounder cannon in long and short versions
3. Mortars: 10-, 30-, 60- and 100-pounder mortars, and 100-pounder stone-throwing *pierriers*.

The years of experimentation had enabled Liechtenstein and his team to lighten both the barrels and the carriages without any sacrifice of robustness or performance, and thus reduce the overall weight of the pieces by up to half. Considerable margins of safety were provided by the comparatively light propelling charges, and the loose fit of the shot and shell (the generous windage gave ratios of shot to bore of 8: 9 for the cannon, and of shell to bore of 7: 8 for the howitzers.

It should be noted that the Viennese system of weight was based on the Nuremberg pound of 0.45 kg., or between one-fifth and one-sixth less than the French pound utilised in the Gribeauval system (evolved between 1765 and 1774). Antique custom dictated that the poundage of the howitzer shells and mortar bombs referred to the weight of a stone ball of the same diameter. The 7-pounder howitzer actually fired a gunpowder-filled cast iron shell weighing a considerable 7.5 k. (14–15 lbs.), while the 10-pounder howitzer rarely if ever appeared with the field artillery to which it was supposed to belong. The 'pace' measured 2 feet of 12 inches each.

Specifications of Individual Field Pieces:
  1-pounder *Tschaiken* Cannon
  Ball: 0.45 kg.
  Diameter of ball: 49.2 mm.
  Diameter of bore: 53 mm.
  Barrel length: 84.8 cm.
  Team: 2 horses

This ultra-light piece did not form part of the System of 1753, but seems to have been inherited from the armament of the Danube gunboats. It was assigned to the Croats, and proved very useful at Kolin, but it was out of service by 1758.

  3-pounder Cannon
  Ball: 1.37 kg.; diameter 71.7 mm.; charge 14–16 oz.
  Barrel: diameter of bore 75.5 mm.; length 114.7 cm; weight 240 kg.
  Detachment: 6 gunners, 8 *Handlanger* or *Füsiliere*
  Range: point blank 500 paces; maximum effective with roundshot 1,600 paces, with canister 400 paces
  Penetration: 1.5 m. of well-rammed earth; 19 men at 400 paces

3-pounder Cannon.

Although some 3-pounders were held in the artillery reserve, most pieces were assigned directly to the battalions to augment the firepower of the infantry. The 3-pounder could be manhandled with relative ease over short distances, otherwise its mobility was impaired badly if just one of the two horses were disabled. At the camp of Kolin in 1754 Neipperg told a French visitor, the comte de Gisors, that he and many other generals opposed the introduction of the piece. Gisors reported the news to Frederick, who commented: 'I am not surprised they told you that, my dear friend, because they do not wish you Frenchmen to have anything of the sort. You ought to tell your father [Marshal Belle-Isle, the minister of war] to assign some of those pieces to your infantry, otherwise they will be at a great disadvantage if they have to fight the Austrians'.[35]

  6-pounder Cannon
  Ball: 2.75 kg.; diameter 90.5 mm.; charge one-and three-quarter pounds for solid shot, one-and-one quarter pounds for canister
  Barrel: diameter of bore 95.7 mm., length 151.5 cm.; weight 414 kg.
  Detachment: 7 gunners, 8 *Handlanger* or *Füsiliere*
  Team: 4 horses
  Range: point blank 600 paces; maximum effective with roundshot 2,000 paces, with canister 500 paces
  Penetration: 2.2 m. of well-rammed earth; 28 men at 800 paces

  12-pounder Cannon (field piece)
  Ball: 5.5 kg.; diameter 113.5 mm.; charge two-anda-half pounds for all ammunition, though Gribeauval (1762) quotes three pounds for solid shot
  Barrel: diameter of bore 119.5 mm.; length 191.2 cm.; weight 812 kg.
  Detachment: 7 gunners, 8 *Handlanger* or *Füsiliere*
  Team: 6 horses
  Range: point blank 800 paces; maximum effective with roundshot 2,300 paces, with canister 700 paces
  Penetration: 2.4 m. of well-rammed earth; 36 men at 800 paces

7-pounder Howitzer
Shell: 7.5 kg.; diameter 144.5 mm; charges of 16, 24, 30 and 43 oz.
Barrel: diameter of bore 153 mm.; length 94.4 cm.; weight 280 kg.
Detachment: 7 gunners/bombardiers, 10 *Handlanger* or *Füsiliere*
Team: 2–3 horses
Range: maximum effective with shell 1,800–2,000 paces, with canister 6–700 paces.

'From now onwards the calibre of all the field howitzers will be of seven pounds stone weight, for this gives a longer range than all the other calibres, as well as being easy to move, and having lighter ammunition'.[36] In modern technical parlance the piece was a gun/howitzer, for it was capable of firing at both low (i.e. below 45 degrees) and high elevations, though Liechtenstein preferred the latter for shell fire, because it gave the fuze more chance to catch properly alight. At low elevation the canister could reach to 5–600 paces. As well as being a versatile piece in field actions, the 7-pounder howitzer was employed in sieges for 'ricochet fire,' whereby its missiles were sent bounding at low trajectory down the length of covered ways and ramparts.

In the final years of the war ammunition was allocated for a number of 24-pounder cannon in the capacity of field pieces, namely six in 1759, eight in 1760, and six again in 1761 and 1762. These were probably not the fully bored-up Austrian 24-pounders, but the light and conical-chambered captured Prussian versions, which the Austrian gunners were forced to take with them 'though the outcry of the admirers of the Prussian products.' Gribeauval describes them as a 'species of howitzer devoid of solidity, range and accuracy'.[37]

Features of the System of 1753

Barrels
Bronze was the almost universal material of gun casting in continental Europe, and the standard Austrian mix comprised 100 parts of copper to 10 of tin (though the use of scrap metal would have altered the proportions). The chief foundries were located in Vienna and at Malines (Mecheln) in the Netherlands, and pieces were also cast in Prague, Graz in Styria and Hermannstadt in Transylvania.

Moving the 3-pounder.

Nothing was known at that time about the importance of the behaviour of the pour during the casting process, when the molten metal was beginning to form its crystalline structure, and any pronounced irregularity in the exterior surface of the mould was projected inwards as a plane of 'notch weakness.' The Austrian technicians, like those of the rest of Europe, believed that to cast the piece with 'reinforcing rings' would give added strength at critical locations (though it was found in the middle of the 19th century that the contrary was the case). It was fortunate that every Austrian barrel was proved with successive increments of charges, those for the 12-pounder field piece, for example, weighing two, four and 66 pounds.

The bore of the Austrian barrel seems to have been cast in the rough around a spike in the mould, then drilled out by the conventional boring machine of the time, as improved by the Swiss technician Jacquet, rather than drilled out of the solid metal by a novel method which had been perfected in Holland. The vent was bored with a slight forward slant, so that the priming tube (below) would be thrown clear of the gun detachment when the main charge took fire.

Gun Carriages

Jean-Baptiste Gribeauval came to admire the rationality which formed the many features which combined to make the new Austrian gun carriages at once light, strong and serviceable, and in March 1762 he sent a report to his masters which may be taken as the beginning of the decisive pre-Napoleonic artillery reform in France.

In the old days the barrel of the piece had been depressed by hammering in a wedge beneath the breech of the barrel, and elevated by pulling it out again – a hit-and-miss affair. The wedges of the new design were driven by screws, which made aiming much more a matter of precision.

Care was given to as simple a matter as the balance of the piece. In the older 'systems' the relationship between the positions of the trunnion channels and the axles represented a bad compromise between the requirements of combat and transportation, which resulted in pieces that were too trail-heavy to be trained or manhandled with ease, yet still threw too much weight on the gun axle when the trail was lifted onto the limber for road transport. Now the cheeks of the 6- and 12-pounder carriages were furnished with an additional rearward set of trunnion channels, onto which the barrel was lifted by tackle when the pieces had to be moved for any distance. The load was thus spread more evenly between the wheels of the limber and those of

From a mss. in the Austrian Army Museum.

the gun carriage. The axle of all pieces was set further to the rear than before – which diminished the weight thrown onto the trail, and made for a gun that was more evenly balanced when it was unlimbered.

The cheeks of the gun carriages were reduced to the thickness of one calibre (i.e. about 75 mm. for the 3-pounder, 95 mm. for the 6-pounder and so on), but solidly built and reinforced with iron in a way that brought together lightness and durability.[38] Uniformity of manufacture was taken as far as was practicable in this preindustrial age, and instruments were used as necessary to ensure the exact positioning of every cut that was sawed and every hole that was drilled. The interchangeability of parts was a central feature of the System of 1753, and it depended on considerations like these. The limber (*Protze*) was little more than an axle on two wheels, furnished with an upward-projecting central spike which received the hole at the end of the trail when the piece was in motion.

In the immediate presence of the enemy the field piece was released from its limber, and an entirely new procedure was adopted to move it around the scene of action. One of the horses was freed from the limber, and it hauled on a rope which was hooked to the trail or the front of the gun carriage, according to whether the piece was to be moved backwards or forwards. Additional traction was applied by the *Handlanger* or *Füsiliere*, who were assigned partly to the wheels, and partly to the *Avancirstangen* a pair of wooden poles which passed through tubes fixed at the end of two sets of iron bars which projected from the front of the carriage. All the time one of the gunners or assistants held the trail clear of the ground with the traversing spike.

Liechtenstein settled on a standard artillery wheel, 50 inches in diameter, with rims two and-a-quarter inches broad. It was fitted to all the field cannon and the 7-pounder howitzer, and also served as the rearward wheels of the ammunition carts. The wheel was disproportionately heavy for the 3-pounder, but that was a small price to pay for the asset of interchangeability, 'which means that if a wheel happens to break, another can be fitted without difficulty or loss of time, and in case of necessity the wheel of a peasant cart can do service instead'.[39] By the same token a standard wheel of 36 inches diameter was fitted to the limbers of all calibres and to the front axle of the ammunition cart.

The axles of all the field pieces were of wood, and were fixed at a diameter of four-and a-quarter inches. The ends which passed through the wheel hubs were shod in brass, which was found to be kinder to the wood than had been the original iron.

A small quantity of ammunition was stored in a detachable box (*Laffettentrüchel*) which was carried between the cheeks of the trail – one of a number of features of the System which was to be copied widely over Europe. The main reserve of ammunition was however to be found in carts which were positioned behind the pieces in action. The old ammunition cart or caisson (*Karre*) was a two-wheeled vehicle, drawn by two horses which were harnessed in 'line-ahead' inside a double fork; it was small and unstable, cruel on the horses, and in the event of an upset the driver and the horses were cast to the ground as well. The cart of the System of 1753 was four-wheeled, stable and capacious; the horses were harnessed on either side of a central pole, and were spared the alternating upwards and downwards tugging of the old fork, which had disabled most of the animals after a couple of campaigns. The forward tractional effort was increased only marginally, for the new carts were of light construction, with wickerwork sides, and a covering of canvas over a horizontal wooden pole stretchers.

The gun carriage, the ammunition cart and the limber were all protected by oil paint – the woodwork in dark yellow, and the ironwork in black, 'which is eminently practicable for the service, for the cost is repaid amply by the greater resistance of the wood against the damp and bad weather of all kinds.' All items were branded with the same number as the piece, 'so that everybody knows whom they belong to, and can he held responsible for looking after them'.[40]

The System of 1753 increased the rate of fire of the mortars (used exclusively for siegework) by about the same degree as that of the field pieces. All the work of elevating and depressing the massive barrels was now done by a simple and sturdy screw device, which could be operated by a single *Büchsenmeister*. Likewise the quadrant (for establishing the degree of elevation) was replaced by a graduated scale on the elevating mechanism, which was another time-saver.

Ammunition

The most common round of all pieces except the howitzers and mortars was the solid round-shot of cast iron, which in the Austrian service was re-heated after casting and forged over to diminish any brittleness. The System of 1753 provided in addition full-bore hollow-shot for the 3- and 6-pounders, though these missiles seem to have fallen out of use in the Seven Years War. A 'shotgun' effect was provided by the multiple balls of canister (*Kartütschen*) and the larger grape (*Schrottbüchsen*).

The container of the canister was a cylinder of sheet copper, sealed at the top with an iron lid, and at the bottom by a wooden sabot which sat on the cartridge (below). The intervals between the balls were filled with sawdust, to prevent the missiles dumping together. Canister with iron balls was preferred when the intention was to spray the landscape, and canister with leaden balls against more concentrated targets. Two canisters could be loaded on top of one another when the enemy were very near.

For the field pieces, howitzers and battery cannon Liechtenstein did away with the slow, wasteful and dangerous business of loading the loose powder down the muzzles from open-topped ladles, which were replenished from open powder kegs. The charges were now contained in linen cartridges, which were inserted into the muzzle intact, rammed down solidly against the bottom of the barrel, and the missile in turn seated firmly on top. Some uncertainty attaches to the protection that was given to the fabric of the cartridge. The explanatory text to the System of 1753 merely speaks of good linen of the same quality as the regulation shirts, which was coated with oil paint and was proof against water, if not fire, for 'the piece must be washed out after every discharge.'[41]

Firing the 3-pounder. From a mss. in the Austrian Army Museum.

This must correspond with the 'varnish' which Armfeldt describes as protecting the cartridges at the start of the Seven Years War, and which, among, its other virtues, diminished somewhat the risk of the ammunition carts exploding in action. Dolleczek in his reliable history of the Austrian artillery nevertheless mentions charges contained in pigs' bladders, and Hirtenfeld's history of the Theresian Order attributes this invention to Adolph Alfson, who entered the Austrian service in 1754. All sources agree that the new cartridges, whether of pigs' bladders, or protected by paint or varnish, failed under the test of sustained and heavy firing at Kolin in 1757, when the build-up of a gummy deposit ultimately made it impossible to ram the cartridges home. Armfeldt explains that the Austrians turned to a new type of varnish which left the barrel clear of deposit and embers. A piece could now be fired up to 100 times without the necessity of washing out with the mop, and the cartridge was so water-tight that it could be left in water for 24 hours without coming to harm, and even (for the sake of demonstration) fired from a gun barrel which had been fully submerged.[42]

The conventional way of priming the vent of a piece was to fill it with fine powder from a flask, which took a number of precious seconds, and left the exposed powder in danger of being soaked by rain or blown away by wind; moreover a cartridge of any sort, let alone the water- and fire-proof Austrian version, would have to be pierced beforehand by a long pricker inserted down the vent. The Austrians replaced these procedures by an expendable priming tube, which Gribeauval describes as a thin tube of copper or tin, which came ready-filled with fine powder; at the end was 'a little copper cone, turned on the lathe and very sharp, which was driven by the charge of the fuze and pierces the cartridge, however sharp it might be'.[43]

The gunpowder was divided into categories according to the proportions of the ingredients (musket powder demanding a higher proportion of saltpetre) and the relative fineness of the grinding (the more coarsely-corned stuff being designed for the artillery). So as to ensure that quality was consistent within each grade, the powder was tested in a little device which drove weights up a graduated scale. Liechtenstein stipulated that the artillery powder was to reach between 35 to 40 degrees on the scale, musket powder a uniform 51, and blasting powder 70. Armfeldt describes the Austrian powder as being of good quality, which he ascribes in turn to the quality of the saltpetre,[44] which was the most expensive of the ingredients. However the musket powder was probably too coarse for its purpose, and Liechtenstein over-compensated for the increased strength of the new powder by cutting the amount in each cartridge (above).

The cumulative effect of this multitude of improvements was to enable the lighter field pieces to fire up to four times a minute, or as fast as any musket. A high rate of fire could not be sustained indefinitely without causing the bore and the vent to erode, and the barrel to droop. Liechtenstein

The large ammunition cart. (System of 1753; from a mss. in the Austrian Army Museum)

put the upper limit over a period of 24 hours at 100 rounds for the heavy battery pieces, and 120 for the light battery pieces, though in 1777 an experiment showed that a rate of fire of 1,070 rounds over 17 consecutive days caused an increase in bore among the battery pieces of only 2 mm.; the 6-pounder field pieces fared less well, for a rate of fire of between 4–7,000 rounds caused the bores to erode by between 1.5 and 6.5 mm.

The Artillery – An Assessment

The Austrian artillery was not only incomparably the most improved arm of the Austrian service, but the one which operated to the most consistent and deadly effect throughout the Seven Years War. Frederick as a man of taste knew of Liechtenstein's finely-cultivated interest in the arts, and he had corresponded with him on the subject, but he had no conception that the same wealth and intelligence was being devoted to re-making the Austrian artillery before the war. In 1756 Karl Christoph Schmettau returned from of spying tour of Bohemia to report that Austrian officers had told him that they would be able to bring together 300 cannon and howitzers in a future battle, and that they now had 12 men available to serve each piece. 'The king believed that this account was so exaggerated that he laughed, and asked himself how an old officer of Schmettau's experience to permit himself to give credence to fairy tales of that kind. He ought to know what a great quantity of ammunition and horses would be required for such a mass of ordnance'.[45]

The first encounters of the Seven Years War compelled Frederick to revise his opinion. After Kolin he remarked to the British envoy that 'it was not the enemy's soldiers, but their artillery, upwards of 250 cannon well posted, that made his men retire'.[46] Frederick manufactured a new 'Austrian' 12-pounder in direct imitation of Liechtenstein's original, and he conceived a lasting respect for the corps of Austrian artillery, which he described as being 'as fine as it possibly can be'.[47]

13

The Engineers and Other Technical Support

THE ENGINEERS

Public History

The fundamental business of military engineers in the 18th century was to build and attack fortresses. Nobody was better at this work than the French, who under the inspired direction of Sébastien Le Prestre de Vauban (1633–1707), the chief engineer of Louis XIV, had fortified the frontiers of France with multiple lines of strongholds, developed techniques of scientific precision to capture the fortresses of the enemy, and established a corps of engineers on a professional footing, complete with an exhaustive training, and a military structure of ranks and pay. The Austrian engineers, by way of contrast, were scarcely more than hired architects and draughtsmen, like their predecessors of two centuries before.

The first signs of awakening may be traced to 1732, when two 'brigades' of engineers were set up in the Austrian Netherlands, based respectively in Brussels and Malines. The Netherlands engineers maintained only the most tenuous communication with Vienna, and their complement of 30 or so officers preserved its independence even after the rest of the engineers were combined into a unitary corps in 1760, one of the reasons being that the Netherlands engineers would have been out of their element in the Hereditary Lands, where the language, the methods of construction, and the local economy and prices of materials would all have been unfamiliar to them.[1] The author of the *Patriotic Reflections* declared two years later that 'the best of them [the engineers] are still the Netherlanders, or the ones who have come over from the French service'.[2]

On 6 February 1747 Maria Theresa had approved a proposal from the *Hofkriegsrath* to establish an engineering corps of four brigades, namely the existing Netherlands brigade, and new German, Hungarian and Italian brigades to set alongside it. She appointed her brother-in-law Prince Charles of Lorraine as *General-Genie-Director,* with his seat in Brussels (from where he ruled simultaneously as Governor-General of the Netherlands), with Colonel Paul Ferdinand Bohn as his deputy, or *Pro-Director,* working from Vienna. In this context 'brigade' signified no more than a colonel and a handful of engineers, and the first and very basic task of Charles and Bohn was to establish the whereabouts and identity of their own scattered personnel.

Maria Theresa approved a *Regulament über das Kaisl. Königl. Ingenieurs-Corp* on 20 July 1747. The officers of the corps were to enjoy the same ranks and privileges as the officers of the field army, and Bohn was authorised to admit suitable newcomers upon examination. He was to visit the fortresses and borders every spring, and not only to review the defences but find out whether anything could be done to make the provinces more productive and healthy. In the winter (and again in accordance with the French practice) he was to examine the plans and projects which were sent to him by the brigade commanders.

The corps comprised 98 officers at the time of its foundation, but 11 years later a *Specification* of 1758 listed only 30 available for service in the field.³ The one individual of note was Lieutenant-Colonel Rebain of the German Brigade, who had been an associate of the late Field Marshal Browne, and who (during a brief period of Prussian captivity) came to know how far short many of the standards of the Austrian army fell of those among the enemy.

The old and sickly Bohn finally died in November 1759. Daun recommended *GFWM*. Ferdinand Philipp Harsch as 'the best and only man' to succeed as *Pro-Director,* and Maria Theresa followed his advice in January.⁴ It was probably no coincidence that the engineers emerged as a unified corps a few months later (above), and the initiative almost certainly came from Harsch. On 21 May 1760 Maria Theresa wrote to inform Prince Charles that he was to remain as the corps *Director,* but that she had decided to bring the German, Italian and Hungarian brigades together under a single organisation, allow the officers to transfer between the three brigades as necessary, and to fund the corps from a joint treasury.⁵

FML. Christoph Baron Engelhardt, 1685–1768 (Military Academy, Wiener Neustadt). This genial old soul was a survivor of the earlier generation of engineers, having been the first Director of the Vienna engineering academy (1717), and thereafter active chiefly on the border with Turkey.

By the end of the Seven Years War the 'Austrian' engineers consisted of the 30 independent Netherlanders, and about 120 members of the combined corps. The original uniform of the engineers was common with that of most of the infantry, namely of white with red facings. In March 1761, however, Maria Theresa decreed to the altogether more practical garb of 'pike-grey' with carmine red facings.⁶

Interior Life and the Case of Nicolas-Jospeh Cugnot

The outbreak of the Seven Years War found the scanty human resources of the Austrian engineers devoted mainly to the upkeep of the fortresses on the old theatres of operations in the Netherlands, Italy and Hungary. The single exception was that of the construction of the new ten-bastioned fortress of Olmütz in Moravia, which guarded the northern access to Vienna. These various works left the field army with almost nobody who was available or competent to direct a siege or a defence in the new war against the Prussians.

The main Austrian army was defeated outside Prague on 6 May 1757, and for the next six weeks it was shut up in the city under blockade and bombardment. Prince Charles, whom we now see in the capacity of a field commander, found that in this emergency he had to turn to the counsel of the Saxon/French volunteer Major-General Ludwig Johann d'Hallot. Daun and the army of relief beat the Prussians so convincingly at Kolin (18 June) that he was able to break the siege of Prague, and the united Austrian forces proceeded to carry the war into the Prussian territory of Silesia, which was stiff with fortresses. In September the Austrians made ready to besiege Schweidnitz, and Charles and his co-commander Daun thought of employing the *Pro-Director* Bohn, and the old *FZM*. Ernst Dietrich Marschall who had defended Maastricht with some distinction in 1748, and counted as 'the only man of that rank who has the slightest notion of this branch of warfare'.[7] However the ultimate decision lay with Maria Theresa, who decided in favour of yet another Frenchman. She explained to Prince Charles that 'reasons of state, as well as my implicit confidence in the ability of Brigadier Riverson, have induced me to entrust the direction of the siege of Schweidnitz to him… I am only too delighted to be able to oblige His Most Christian Majesty by giving such a prestigious task to the man he has sent to me'.[8]

This episode could not fail to be humiliating for the Austrians and their new corps of engineers.[9] Daun would have been only too glad to be able to dispense with Riverson and his presumptuous countryman, the attaché Montazet, but he was forced to admit that they were indispensable for siegework, 'where those gentlemen are still more capable than our own engineers'.[10]

In a longer perspective, however, the interchange of military technology proved to be one of the more productive outcomes of the Diplomatic Revolution, once the Austrians had brought themselves to overcome their very natural resentments. In 1758 King Louis sent one of his colonels of artillery and engineering, Jean-Baptiste Gribeauval de Vaquette (1715–89) to lend further help to Maria Theresa, and on 10 March 1759 the *Hofkriegsrath* admitted him to the Austrian service with the rank of *GFWM*.[11] Gribeauval put on an impressive demonstration of the newest siege techniques at the camp of Neustadt in Moravia, and it was some sop to the Austrians' pride that a man of such obvious ability could now be counted as one of their own officers.

We have encountered Gribeauval already as a commentator on Liechtenstein's ordnance, which was to provide the inspiration for the celebrated 'system' of artillery which he introduced in his homeland after the war. He repaid his hosts when he initiated a thoroughgoing investigation and reform of engineering in Austria. The process was begun unwittingly by the eccentric engineer (and inventor of the steam locomotive, see p. 210) Nicolas-Joseph Cugnot (1725–1804), a native of Lorraine, who wrote to the *Hofkriegsrath* for permission to resign, claiming that the Austrian engineering corps was ridden with favouritism. The *Hofkriegsrath* was alive to the sunken state of the engineers, and on 20 January 1760 it asked Gribeauval and Prince Charles of Lorraine to look into the state of the corps under a number of headings, namely to establish whether favouritism rather than merit determined promotions, whether Cugnot had any reason to complain on that account, and to find the reasons why morale among the engineers was so low.

Gribeauval replied first, and informed the *Hofkriegsrath* on 2 February that the malaise had many causes. Merit had indeed been neglected in the promotions, the rest of the army held the engineers in low regard, their officers were riven by factions, and they lacked any progressive training. As remedies he proposed purging the engineers of aged or infirm officers, and that the Austrians should set up a number of supporting services which had proved useful in France – a corps of sappers to help the engineers directly with their work, together with draughtsmen and cartographers who would take over some of their more specialised tasks.

The *Hofkriegsrath* passed on Gribeauval's paper to *GFWM*. Harsch, and asked him to comment in his capacity as the new *General Pro-Director*. Harsch replied that he was unable to answer for the merits of individuals, as he had been in office for only a matter of days. He nevertheless supported Gribeauval's notions, and suggested in addition that the business of educating and selecting the engineers should be taken properly in hand. As a praiseworthy example he held up the French academies and schools of artillery and engineering, which were renowned for their high standards of theory and practice, and he proposed that for a start the Austrians should fund between 15 and 20 cadets in their own corps, to ensure a constant supply of qualified young officers.[11]

All of this amounted to an indictment of the state of the corps under the regime of Prince Charles and the late *Pro-Director* Bohn. Charles forwarded his statement on 7 March. It was a lengthy and guarded submission, which supported the positive recommendations of the other two reports, but met Gribeauval's more trenchant criticisms by asking him to specify individuals who had been at fault. He was otherwise satisfied that the corps as a whole was 'good and solid,' and all that mattered was to observe the *Regulament* of 1747 to the letter.[12]

The great men had only a few words to spare for Second-Lieutenant Cugnot, the occasion of all these cogitations. Gribeauval (later to take Cugnot under his wing) observed that he was a competent officer and theoretician, but completely lacking in the skills necessary to put his knowledge to practical use (see p. 210). Harsch as a newcomer deferred to Gribeauval's opinion, but Prince Charles stated that Cugnot had been seeking for some time to be allowed to retire, and 'if he asks again we should not stand in his way, for he would lose nobody of any value'.[13] We are nevertheless indebted to Cugnot, not only as the begetter of all mechanical transport, but for what he helped to reveal of the earliest days of the Austrian engineering corps, which we can now trace in some detail, beginning with the fundamentally important work of technical training.

In his paper Prince Charles shared the enthusiasm of Harsch for the way the French were managing their engineering education, for by now the relevant Austrian technical schools existed in little more than name. Prince Eugene had founded an academy on the Leimgrube in Vienna in 1717, and another in Brussels in 1718. By the middle 1750s, however, the Brussels academy had lost focus and become an institute of general education, while the Leimgrube school had supplied hardly nobody to the corps for many years, and the instructor of engineering had never seen a siege in his life.[14]

The reformers saw more promise in the private academy in Gumpendorf, another suburb of Vienna, which had begun life as an orphanage established by Johann Conrad Richthofen, Baron von Chaos, in 1663 (see p. 164). It had been reorganised as a specialised *Ingenieurschule* from 1715, and enlarged in the 1730s, and its alumni included the new *Pro-Director* Harsch, and the *GFWM*. Rochepine and the Colonel Giannini (below) who distinguished themselves in the defence of Olmütz in 1758. All the same the best of the more recent graduates (like Giannini himself) had been lost to the infantry, where promotion was relatively fast, 'and virtually nothing but the rubbish remains for the engineer corps, which nevertheless has to accommodate them, for it has no other intake'.[15]

Harsch therefore proposed that all the would-be young engineers should be concentrated at Gumpendorf, and accepted into the corps after a convincing performance in examination and in the field.[16] Maria Theresa acted almost at once on his recommendation. On 27 February 1760 she decided that the Gumpendorf school must come under the complete control of Harsch as *Pro-Director* of the corps, and that the authority must be transferred from the beginning of April.[17]

Meanwhile the generally feeble efforts of the existing engineers continued to be supported by enthusiasts who stood outside the corps. Thus the *Conduits Lista* of the regiment of Erzherzog Carl made special mention of the First-Lieutenant Ignatius Müller, who had risen from the rank of *Fourier* over 11 years, and done excellent service as engineering assistant to *FM*. Browne in the campaign of 1756.[18] In May 1758 Ernst Friedrich Giannini offered to try to get into the beleaguered fortress of Olmütz on foot, and 'although I was not of the engineering corps, being a colonel of infantry, the high command endorsed my proposals wholeheartedly… then [once inside Olmütz] *FZM*. Baron Marschall… gave my proposals for the last-ditch defence of the fortress his full and gracious approval, and commanded my scheme to be put into effect without any loss of time'.[19]

The memoranda of Gribeauval and Prince Charles had addressed themselves to the issues of career structure and further promotion, which had also to be taken in hand. Gribeauval did not spare his language:

> I do not know what system has been followed… but I can assert that a number of officers, even among those who have reached high rank, are devoid of the aptitudes needed for their profession, and have never been equal to meeting their responsibilities. In contrast there are several

well-educated junior officers who have ideas and abilities which fit them for a successful career in the higher reaches of their profession, but they nearly all complain of having been passed over repeatedly in promotion, and a number of them – including some of the best – up to 12 or 15 times. They say it is because they did not enjoy the benefit of favouritism.[20]

These comments put Prince Charles on the defensive. He assured Maria Theresa that he had been in constant correspondence with the late *Pro-Director* Bohn ever since the corps had been established in 1747, and he was certain that nobody had been admitted to the corps other than on the basis of qualifications and merit, and, even if some of them had been promoted beyond their deserts, 'a *Pro-Director* is not like a regimental commander, who has the opportunity to become acquainted with every officer in detail. He must instead rely on reports.' Gribeauval himself had intervened to make a couple of promotions out of turn, 'and all advancements of this kind engender resentment even among senior officers, for it is part of human nature to have an inflated and unrealistic opinion of oneself'.[21]

Concerning the morale of the corps in general, Gribeauval could find 'factions, intrigues and cabals without end, but little evidence of enthusiasm, and not at all of ambition. Most of them have shunned effort on the excuse that their goodwill has been abused – and here they are not entirely wrong. However by dint of making promises (which we are admittedly not sure we can keep), and by pricking their vanity, we have begun to bring them to a better way of thinking'.[22] On this subject Charles observed that the feuds could best be countered by disciplinary action. He agreed with Gribeauval that much of the frustration of the engineers could be relieved by setting up units of sappers, and passing over some of the routine work to draughtsmen and cartographers (below), and he made the valid point that the military engineer was faced with the prospect of a lifetime's labour with no further reward than promotion to colonel in extreme old age.

The ignorance, the divisions and the demoralisation were at once the cause and the result of the low standing of the engineers in the eyes of the rest of the army. To the author of the *Patriotic Reflections* it seemed that instead of being the least regarded branch of the army, the engineers, along with the artillerymen, ought to be the most honoured, for their work called for zeal and intelligence as well as courage. The contrary was the case, and the reason was that the engineers were 'men of exceedingly low birth, and who consequently lack the necessary education, manners and style. They hide themselves away, they keep company mostly with common folk, and they rarely come under the eyes of the generals except when duty calls... you hardly ever see them at the gatherings of the nobility'.[23] This judgement is confirmed by Gribeauval, who adds that the engineers were

treated in a way which is harsh and even indecent. A number of generals know only how to convey their orders in terms of threats, holding out the prospect of confinement in chains as if

Officer of engineers and Sapper private. (Ottenfeld, 1898)

they were criminals. When an officer, no matter how junior, is dispatched on some mission, he invariably takes a couple of engineers with him to see to the hard and uncongenial parts of his task; they load the blame on them if anything goes wrong, but take the credit if it turns out well. Just look at the state of the engineers towards the middle of any campaign – you will see that most of them have lost their horses and money, and that they are worn out by exhaustion and maltreatment.[24]

When all the authority of Prince Liechtenstein had been unable to win over the nobles to the artillery, there was precious little prospect of gaining them for the engineers, for 'an aristocrat with an income of 30–40,000 florins a year will be unwilling to consign his son to a corps where courage and hard work are the only way to mark yourself out'.[25] This comment of Armfeldt's was reinforced by the author of the *Patriotic Reflections,* who commented that not a single engineering preparatory school existed in the whole of Hungary, and that in Bohemia there was only one – or rather a single professor who was received with derision when he asked the *Stände* for a little money to enable him to take on more pupils and conduct practical demonstrations. 'The most ludicrous episode of all was when two young gentlemen of style came to ask him to teach them a little engineering – as long as he was quick about it. They could then go back to their papa and tell him that they were now acquainted with the subject, after which he would send them to a regiment without further ado.' Having warmed to his theme, the author gathered himself for an attack on the aristocracy as a whole:

> How can they... complain that we have so few good officers and generals? After all, they do nothing to fit themselves for command, and they fail to pay them [the serving officers] the regard which is their due, or provide them with the means of waging war beyond our borders – which does not prevent them from urging that the enemy must be pushed back a comfortable distance from their estates. They complain loudly when they have to deliver a little fodder to our troops in Silesia, and they would rather run the risk of the authorities exacting their obligations by force than respond to the call of a suffering army which has conquered whole provinces on their behalf, and secured them in their privileges... such are their inclinations and such is their mentality. They wish everything to be turned to their advantage, without any application on the part of themselves or their children, without tormenting themselves with study, without enduring harsh discipline or bad weather – and they still demand privileged and speedy promotion... One thing we can say for certain, that if the nobles devoted more effort to acquiring useful knowledge than indulging their taste for luxurious living, then not only the engineering corps, but the army and the whole state would prosper.[26]

The *Sappeurs-Corps*

The engineers and the field armies would have been in a position to do one another a great deal of good, if only they had been able to bring themselves to work together more closely. Lieutenant-Colonel Wenzel Pawlowsky von Rosenfeld cited his reconnaissances at Kolin, Breslau and Maxen to support his application for the Theresian Military Order, claiming that he was the only officer of the engineering corps who had gained a mastery of what he called 'the practical detail as to how to reconnoitre terrain, stake out camps, and – if the ground is not particularly favourable – supply what is lacking by artificial means'.[27] Pawlowsky gained his Order, but the wording of his statement makes it clear that he was acting as an isolated individual.

The army was otherwise left with totally inadequate technical support, as the Prince de Ligne discovered when he saw the field works which had been cast up outside Dresden in the winter of

1759/60. The regimental officers had little idea of what ought to have been done, and they had committed faults as basic as having the earth from the parapets excavated from inside the works instead of just outside, which would have made for a respectable ditch obstacle as well as a good high parapet.[28]

The same blunders made a powerful impression on Gribeauval, who pointed out in his paper of 2 February 1760 that nobody seemed to have the slightest interest in doing anything better. 'The soldiers and even their officers… just wish to exist until they are overtaken by nightfall or the end of their spell of duty. New troops arrive, and with them a new crop of difficulties.' The remedy must be to raise 'companies of sappers which will be distributed along the works to second the efforts of the soldiers. Such companies will in any case be indispensable if we wish to equip ourselves to conduct sieges, and they can carry out demonstrations for the benefit of the officers of the engineering corps, which at the moment has neither the structure nor the training for this kind of warfare'.[29]

Gribeauval forwarded specific proposals to the *Hofkriegsrath* on 16 February 1760. The officials wrote in turn to Maria Theresa on 20 March that such units would certainly prove expensive, but that the cost would be more than repaid by the relief that would be given to the infantry, and the impetus imparted to the works themselves. A single scribbled *Placet* in the margin shows that Maria Theresa gave her immediate consent, and on 23 March the *Hofkriegsrath* was able to write to the commandants of the infantry regiments that the Empress-Queen had resolved to setup a *Sappeurs Corps* of three companies, and that every regiment was required to furnish it with up to four men – healthy, strong and well-built fellows measuring at least five feet six inches tall, one of whom must be literate and suitable for promotion to NC0.[30]

A number of genuine volunteers had addressed themselves to Gribeauval in 1759, when he had first thought of setting up his sappers. He was canny enough to know that the regiments would be unlikely to offer up their best and most willing men for his new corps (indeed the authorities looked kindly on a Loudon Green Grenadier who deserted back to his unit, see p. 328). By 20 April 1760 altogether 186 men had arrived from the army, and 60 more were on their way, but Gribeauval held their pay down to an initial daily 8 xr., until he had an opportunity to know them better.[31] He had already returned a number of men *de très mauvaise conduite* to their regiments, and he would issue new uniforms only to soldiers of proven worth.

Gribeauval specified his material needs as one field kettle to every six men, one water flask to every two, along with a total of 50 pairs of picks and shovels, six palisade axes, four large saws, and an allowance of 45 cartridges per man. There was no immediate need for tents, since the battalion would be quartered in Dresden while it trained and worked on the fortifications under the direction of Major Johann Bechardt. He determined on a uniform of the same bluish-grey cloth as that of the *Jäger*. The coat was to be short but of generous cut, capable of being buttoned all down its length, and with sleeves sufficiently wide to enable the man 'to put on his coat unaided' (a telling comment on the usual fit of the infantry coats). The cuffs and the narrow collar were to be of carmine red. Since the Sappers would be working in all weathers they were to be furnished with a cloak in the Croatian style, and with long breeches of stout leather. The black gaiters were to reach up inside the breeches, 'but, to avoid giving offence on parade, a little artificial knee covering will be fixed to the gaiter by a buckle or button.' The Sappers were to wear the same design of cap as the *Jäger*, and for the armament Gribeauval recommended a carbine, a long bayonet, and a short but substantial sword.[32] Cuirasses and helmets were added to the list a little later.[33]

The new corps was in action sooner than Gribeauval had expected. The Sappers were assigned to Loudon's corps for the new campaign in Silesia, and on 25 July 1760 they established their reputation beyond all doubt when they played an important part in the storm of Glatz. The Sapper captain Jakob Eghels gained the Military Order of Maria Theresa for his contribution, while Loudon granted Major Bechardt the signal honour of carrying the 33 captured colours to Vienna, where he was shortly afterwards promoted to lieutenantcolonel.[34]

Sappers in action. (Ottenfeld, 1898)

In 1761 the establishment of the Sappers was reduced from three companies to two, though the corps managed to support three companies' worth of officers until Maria Theresa noticed the discrepancy on 21 November. Thus the Sappers were not spared the ignorant and harmful purging of the 'new corps.' The combat losses in the final campaigns of the war were heavy, and they culminated in those sustained by a party of 24 in the epic defence of Schweidnitz in 1762. Ten of the number were killed and 11 wounded, and three of the officers were awarded the M.M.T.O.

Bechardt at once set about repairing the damage. He wrote to Daun on 20 October that it was important not only to replace the men who had been lost, but to compensate for the unreliable Prussian deserters and fugitives who had been drafted in to make up the numbers. He argued that it would be dangerous to employ suspect men on projects that would give them a knowledge of the Austrian fortifications and countermine galleries. 'Another reason why we need more reliable men with our corps than with the infantry is that they often find themselves under the command of officers who are unfamiliar to them, and detached entirely by themselves to work on fortifications or in woodlands for months on end.' He asked for permission to officer a bounty to Capitulants who were willing to serve on for an extra term, to enlist volunteers from the infantry, and to send recruiting parties to the principal cities of the monarchy to enlist lads with trades like mason or carpenter, who would be an enduring asset.[35]

The *Hofkriegsrath* gave its general approval, but balked at the notion of the bounty, for the authorities had broken faith with Capitulants of every kind, and were keeping them on for the duration of the war whether their service had expired or not, and without any compensation. 'If we therefore allowed a fresh bounty in the Corps of Sappers, it would open the way to unfortunate consequences'.[36] The *Hofkriegsrath* nevertheless gave way to its new President, *FM*. Daun, who had read Berhardt's memorandum and was convinced its arguments.[37]

The Corps of Sappers stood as Gribeauval's most important contribution to the Austrian engineering service. He would have liked to have done still more. In his original paper of 2 February 1760 he had proposed taking four or five auxiliary draughtsmen into the employ of the engineers. A further body of six civilian cartographers could be attached to the General Staff to produce maps of the terrain and camp sites, and:

> as this will be their sole occupation, they will soon acquire the necessary accuracy and facility – something impossible for an officer who can attend to such work for only a little while before he has to pass on. They will not be coming under fire, and will therefore have no right to military honours, which will put a limit to the cost and to any inconvenient pretensions on their part. They will be given rank equivalent to a junior officer, just so that they can wear a uniform, and be respected in their work by the soldiers and the local peasants. We have 80 of such people in France [the *Ingenieurs Geographes*] divided into first and second classes.[38]

These proposals were supported by Prince Charles and more strongly still by Harsch, but they were set aside in the financial crisis of the last stages of the war.

THE *PIONIER-CORPS*

If the corps of Sappers was the child of Gribeauval and the engineers, the Austrian pioneers were the creation of the infantry, and they met the immediate need of specialised labour to work ahead of the marching columns of the army, clearing obstacles, repairing, marking and widening the roads, and throwing light wooden trestle bridges (*Laufbrücken*) across streams and bridges.

The first proposal to this end was made by *GFWM*. Lacy, who argued in 1757 that the Austrians ought to mobilise enough 'pioneers' of this kind to enable detachments to be assigned to every force of 20,000 or so troops. Daun was not entirely won over, and on his advice Maria Theresa in January 1758 sanctioned the creation of just one battalion of four companies, each company consisting of 111 officers and men, together with a covering party of *Jäger* who would throw out a screen to cover the pioneers when they were at work. The pioneers and the *Jäger* wore the common uniform of *Hechtgrau* with a black cap, and they were typically recruited from 'men of their hands' – the *Jäger* from professional huntsmen and gamekeepers, and the pioneers in addition from miners, fishermen and boatmen. The light bridging train consisted of three sets per company of six-horse carts, carrying 10 foot long timber uprights, and 32 foot long beams to lay across the top.

The *Pioniere* were ready for service in March 1758, and they were placed at the immediate disposal of their founding father Lacy, in his capacity as Austria's first Chief of Staff. The new body at once proved its worth in the tangled hill country of southern Saxony, and in 1759 Lacy was able to build up the establishment of each company to 266 officers and men, and to assign the companies to support individual armies or corps in the way he had originally intended. The *Jäger* were simultaneously grouped into two companies of their own (see p. 267).

The pioneers ought to have been secure in their reputation as some of the most useful troops of the army,[39] but they were singled out by Kaunitz as a target for the radical economies which were enforced towards the end of the war, for it seemed to him that their functions could be taken over readily enough by the *Staabs-Infanterie-Regiment* and the *Pontoniers* (below). Daun represented that any savings would be illusory, for the pioneer functions could be carried out efficiently only by dedicated troops who were working under their own officers. He was overruled, and on 25 December 1761 the corps was disbanded, 200 of the personnel passing to the Staff Infantry, and the trestle bridges to the *Pontoniers*. Kaunitz showed himself here as very much the civilian, for he identified himself by way of compensation with the 'teeth' arms, and showed little understanding of their necessary support.

The *Pontoniers*

Rivers and the larger streams could be crossed only by means of pontoon bridges, and this was the responsibility of the Corps of *Pontoniers*. They wore a military uniform of light blue, with carmine red facings and waistcoat, but they formed a branch of the semi-civilian *Obrist-Schiffsamt*, whose chief peacetime duties were concerned with affairs as various as the bridges and navigation of the lower Danube, the transportation of cargoes of salt along the Hungarian rivers, and managing the visits of the Court to Pressburg.

At the outbreak of the Seven Years War the *Obrist-Schiffsamt* was ready to support the army with two *Pontons-Compagnien*, each consisting of 123 personnel (later augmented to about 170) and a train of 100 pontoons – rather more than half made of wood, and the rest of sheet copper. In 1757 the *Pontoniers* were in such heavy demand that, even though their efforts were seconded by a refugee Saxon detachment, the Austrians had to tell Hildburghausen that it was 'completely beyond their power' to send any bridging to the *Reichsarmee*.[40] The borrowed detachment was returned to the Saxon service in 1761, but the loss was made good to some extent by the *Pontoniers* taking over the light bridging material of the defunct pioneers.

The Miners

The *Mineurs* did not begin to register on the scale of Austrian social acceptability, and they spent their working lives literally out of sight of the rest of the army. They were nevertheless expected to engage in the most arduous forms of combat – emplacing undergoing charges that would destroy fortress ramparts, blow up siege trenches, or burst in the tunnels of the enemy miners.

Prince Eugene raised the first permanent company of Austrian miners in 1716. By the time of the Seven Years War the mining establishment seems to have consisted of two companies, each of 119 officers and men, standing under the authority of the artillery.[41] The individual company was commanded by a major, assisted by a captain, three or four *Feldwälbel*, and an idiosyncratic lower hierarchy of *Miniermeister, Miniermeister Corporals,* and *alte Mineurs* (equivalent to *Gefreyten)*; the 100 or so rank and file were termed *junge Mineurs*.

The *Feld-Artillerie Reglement* of 1757 laid down formidable qualifications for miners of all ranks. The men were to be of robust health, and recruited from mining and other appropriate civilian trades. The officer was to have a range of mathematical sciences at his command, and especially those relevant to mining and to fortification, 'of which he is to possess not just historical and general notions, but a sound and specific knowledge'.[42]

The Austrian miners had little to say for themselves (even the heroic Joseph Pabliczek seems to have gained the M.M.T.O. without a formal submission), but their deeds spoke for them eloquently enough. The defence of Schweidnitz in 1762, the greatest sustained Austrian feat of arms in the war, was prolonged for as long as it was largely through the efforts of Captain Pabliczek and his men, who displayed a clear superiority over the Prussians in the underground war.

Muster lists have survived for the *Sappeurs* and *Pioniere* for 1760, and the *Mineurs* for 1762, and they record a total of 971 other ranks and 40 NCOs.

The *Sappeurs, Pioniere* and *Mineurs*
Nationality
Other Ranks
Bohemia: 24.70%
Carniola: 24.40
Lower & Upper Austria with Vienna: 14.93

Reich: 9.98
Moravia: 4.94
Styria: 4.84
Prussian Silesia: 4.32
Hungary: 2.47
Netherlands: 1.23

NCOs
Bohemia: 25.00
Reich: 22.50
Hungary: 12.50
Moravia, Netherlands: 5.00 each
Lower and Upper Austria with Vienna,
    Styria, Carniola, Austrian Silesia,
    France, Switzerland: 2.50 each

Age (other ranks only)
Sappeurs
Average: 26
Largest single year: 24 at 10.14%
Pioniers
Average: 25
Largest single year: 22 at 7.36%
Mineurs
Average: 25
Largest single year: 26 at 9.92%

Service (other ranks only)
Sappeurs
Average: 2
Largest single term: 2 at 21.84%
Pioniere: Not entered in muster list
Mineurs
Average: 4.5
Largest single term: 4 at 16.78%

14

The Croats

– a hardy, brave people, faithful to their sovereign and indefatigable
(Major-General Joseph Yorke, 1758)

– it is safe to assert that they are the best troops of the Empress, whether in their capacity to withstand hardship, or from the fact that they never desert... The Croats bear comparison with the AncientRomans.
(Armfeldt, 1763)

Origins and Recent History

The principle of stabilising a long and threatened frontier by means of settlements of soldier-colonists had been put into practice by the Roman and Byzantine Empires, and by the Russian Tsars in early modern times. The Habsburg version dated from the 1530s, and it was precipitated by a powerful and sustained offensive by the Ottoman Turks, who destroyed the old Hungarian state on the field of Mohács on 26 August 1526, and laid siege to Vienna in 1529. The streams of south Slav refugees – both Catholic and Orthodox – now became a flood which washed up on the approaches to the Venetian territory on the Adriatic, and the long eastern borders of Inner Austria (Styria, Carinthia and Carniola).

As early as 1526 the orphaned *Stände* of Croatia proclaimed Archduke Ferdinand of Austria as their king. In the 1530s the Duchy of Inner Austria proceeded to grant privileges to refugees who were willing to lend a hand in defence, and in the 1550s the *Stände* of Styria were made specifically responsible for running the settlements of the Warasdiner Border, while the *Stände* of Carinthia and Carniola managed those of the Carlstädter border. Joint military affairs were directed by the Inner Austrian *Kriegsrath,* which operated in Graz quite independently of the *Hoflcriegsrath* in Vienna. The 'Croats' gained land and collective security under the Crown, while on their side the Habsburgs not only acquired a bulwark against the Turks, but a resource which might be deployed in war against European enemies, as was demonstrated by the deeds of Isolani's *'wilden Croatenhorden'* in the Thirty Years War.

In the 1690s a new and extended crisis brought Serbian refugees by the tens of thousands into the territories of Carlstadt, Slavonia, Batschka and Baranya, and reinforced the Orthodox element in the Borders (*Grenzen*) as a whole. All the time the Borders were managed, or rather mismanaged, by the Inner Austrian *Stände* and the Graz *Kriegsrath,* whose chief interest was now to place their own nobility in positions of authority in the eastern lands. The 'Croats' became increasingly restless, and in 1735 Charles VI commissioned *FZM.* Joseph Friedrich Prince of Sachsen-Hildburghausen to put down a rebellion in the district of Warasdin, in the heart of military Croatia. Hildburghausen acted firmly and effectively, and his experience convinced him of two things – that these were fundamentally good people who responded to discipline when it was applied consistently, and that Vienna must take them under direct control, independently of the Inner Austrian *Stände* and the Graz *Kriegsrath*. These were perhaps unlikely insights to find in a German grandee whose record of field command is one of almost unrelieved misfortune, beginning in the Bosnian campaign of 1737 (when the Austrian cavalrymen escaped across the river Vrbas by clinging to their horses' tails), and ending in the debacle at Rossbach 20 years later. Intelligent, creative and eccentric to an extreme degree, Hildburghausen was as big a man in his way as Prince Liechtenstein. Just as that great artilleryman found fellow spirits among mechanics and Bohemian gunners, so Hildburghausen was alive to the potential of the Borders, which he described as a treasure more precious than anything which could be measured out in gold.[1]

Everything that had been achieved so far was put in jeopardy by the new and ill-advised Turkish War of 1737–9, when a run of defeats was terminated only by the humiliating Peace of Belgrade. The Austrians retained the Bánát of Temesvár, which had been conquered by Eugene, but they lost Serbia again to the Turks, and a last influx of Orthodox refugees settled in Habsburg territory, and more particularly in the Bánát and along the Danube and the Sava.

Even in their contracted form the Borders were still of impressive extent, for they stretched for more than 1,000 kilometres from the Adriatic and military Croatia in the south-west, across the plains of the rivers Sava, Danube and Theiss north-east to the Carpathians and Transylvania. The inhabitants – Catholics and Orthodox alike, the Croats proper and the Serbs, Albanians and smaller communities – were known at that time under the generic name of the 'Croats,' and historians find it convenient to retain the usage in this context.

The work of reforming the Borders was interrupted by the Turkish War, and it had scarcely resumed before the monarchy was overtaken by the crisis of 1740–1, and the sequence of campaigns against the Prussians, the French and their allies. The value of what Hildburghausen had achieved so far was shown by the performance of the Warasdiners, who were the first of the Croats to arrive in the field, and who earned the praise of the Austrian commander FM. Neipperg. Maria Theresa's enemies had nothing of the kind to match them, and the Warasdiners and their fellow Croats carried to Silesia, Saxony, Bavaria, the Rhine, the Netherlands and Italy the image of a people uniquely adapted to the warrior life and the service of their sovereign.[2]

To their undeserved discredit, the Croats were sometimes confused in the popular imagination with the semi-criminal Pandours, a free corps raised by the Slavonian landowner Franz von der Trenck. Maria Theresa misguidedly agreed to expand the Pandours to a strength of 2,000 men in 1745, but the record of their atrocities finally became impossible to ignore, and Trenck was called to account two years later. He died in captivity in the Spielberg citadel at Brünn on 4 October 1749. The cadre of his corps survived to become the totally unimpeachable regiment of Carl Simbschen, which was put on a regular footing in October 1756.

In 1743 Maria Theresa's thoughts began to turn to the unfinished work in the Croats' homelands, and from then until 1770 she and her advisers reorganised the Borders into a near-uniform military and bureaucratic entity. There were a number of motives. Control by Vienna and its deputies would put the Borders at its immediate disposal, free alike from the interference of the Inner Austrian authorities, and of any acquisitive ambitions which might be harboured by the *Stände* of civil Croatia (which made up half of the Croatian territory) and Hungary. Vienna could turn (it was hoped) military Croatia into a economically self-sufficient territory, where improved agriculture would sustain the increasing population, and the soldier-landowners and the bourgeoisie of new towns could be called upon to pay taxes. Finally, and in spite of the Turkish advances in the war of 1737–9, many of the areas of the Borders were in fact still comfortably removed from the actual borders with Ottoman territory, which suggested that the military role of the Croats ought to be primarily that of war against European enemies. The Croats had done well against the Prussians, and it was to be supposed that they would do even better if they were clothed and armed on uniform lines, and given a firm military organisation in the way which had been pioneered by Hildburghausen among the Warasdiners.

The Inner Austrian authorities were showing themselves hostile to any extension of regimentation beyond the *Generalat* of Warasdin, and as an essential first step in the process of reform Maria Theresa abolished the Graz *Kriegsrath* in October 1743, and early the next year transferred its functions to Hildburghausen in his capacity as a new *Militär- Ober-Director und Commandirender General in denen Innerösterreichischen Landen, wie ouch beiden Warasdiner und Carlstädter Generalaten*. Hildburghausen was answerable only to Maria Theresa and the Vienna *Hofkriegsrath*, and he was commissioned to extend his reforms to the Carlstädter *Generalat*. In 1746 the Inner Austrian *Stände* lost the power to nominate officers, and thus the last vestiges of their authority in the Borders, and on 12 April 1747 Maria Theresa decreed that the Carlstädters were to be given the same status as the regiments of the rest of the army, apart from being termed 'Grenzer' and coming last in the order of seniority. They were rescued from this position in 1750, when the relative seniority of the new Croatian regiments were sorted out, with that of the Warasdiners being dated from 1745, the Carlstädters from 1746, the Slavonians from 1747, and the Banalisten from 1750.

Armed with his new powers, Hildburghausen imposed a land tax and a ferocious legal code in 1745, raised regiments of *Grenz-Husaren* in both Warasdin and Carlstadt, and began to think about re-forming the Carlstädter infantry into four regiments (the Szluiner, Liccaner, Oguliner and Ottocaner), an undertaking which was completed by the *FMLs* Petazzi and Serbelloni.[3] The Warasdiner Border nevertheless retained Hildburghausen's particular affection, and although it stood geographically back from the Ottoman frontier, he was careful to preserve its independence from 'civil' Croatia, where serfdom still held sway.

Hildburghausen resigned in 1749, considering his basic work as finished. His *Directorium* disappeared with him, and a second generation of reformers took on the task of reshaping the Croats into specific regiments on fixed establishments.

In December 1749 one of Austria's Irishmen, *FML*. Johann Sigismund Maguire von Inniskillen, became chief of the Warasdin *Generalat*. He found that regularisation had so far amounted to little more than a declaration of intent, and that the Warasdiners themselves were impatient to embrace Germanisation. Maguire hastened to form his charges into two units, namely the Creutzer and St. Georger regiments, and in answer to popular request he transferred 90 villages from the former to the latter, so as to alleviate the burden of military service. As well set-up little landowners the Warasdiners were glad to buy 'German' hats and uniforms of white, they washed their hair so as to be able to dress it into pigtails, and they became familiar with the German words of command as pronounced (probably with an Ulster accent) by Maguire. By the spring of 1750 the two regiments were ready to take to the field at 24 hours' notice, and Maria Theresa was so delighted at what Maguire had done that in May – to the Warasdiners' regret – she whisked him off to command at Klagenfurt in Carinthia.

FML. Engelshofen and (from 1753) *FML*. Serbelloni pursued the comparable work of regularising the communities along the narrow corridor of the new Slavonian Border. The Slavonian Croats were now to go to war in the shape of three regiments of infantry (Broder, Gradiscaner and Peterwardeiner) and one of the *Grenz-Husaren*.

The little pocket of land of the Banal Border produced two regiments of infantry (unimaginatively termed the 'First' and 'Second') and the inevitable regiment of *Grenz-Husaren*. This was the doing of *FM*. Carl Paul Batthyány as Banus – the historic chief (under the Crown) of Croatia.

In 1754 the *Hofkriegsrath* issued a new administrative and legal code, the *Militärrechte für das Carlstädter und Warasdiner Generalat*. First designed for the military districts of Carlstadt and Warasdiner, as its title indicated, its provisions were soon accepted as setting out the rights and obligations of the *Grenzer* as a whole, with due allowance being made for local variations (it was extended formally to the Slavonian and Banal Borders in 1769).

For the time being at least, the processes of centralisation and Germanisation had reached their natural limits, and the authorities would have been ill-advised to push them any further. When the Slavonian Border was being consolidated in 1752, Vienna had rejected the idea of imposing a *Militär-Disciplin-Regulament* which would have subjected the Croats to specific and close military discipline, and transmuted the historic connection of landholding and military service into direct conscription. Neipperg recalled this episode to Maria Theresa in 1761, when she thought of introducing a code of this kind in the Carlstädter and Banal borders. He found it necessary to point out that 'the Carlstädters are suspicious enough people anyway,' and that drawing up the necessary conscript rolls would be likely to provide an uproar. The project was in any case bureaucratically impossible, now that so many of the Croats were away from home in the field or in Prussian captivity. It would be better to wait until peace had arrived, then have the conscription carried out by officers in whom the men had some trust.[4] Maria Theresa gave way with an ill grace, and this thoroughly bad idea was postponed indefinitely.

Far from being passive conscript hordes, the *Grenzer* had a lively sense of their dignity and what was due to them, and in this respect they maybe compared with the yeoman archers of late medieval England. The Warasdiners the first, the best, and the most loyal of the regularised Croats – told the Austrians as much in 1755, when accumulated grievances were brought to a head by some gross mismanagement on the part of the authorities.

In December 1754 the Warasdiners had been ordered to purchase new uniforms and equipment to do honour to Maria Theresa, who was supposed to be passing through their lands in the course of a journey to Trieste (which in the event never took place). The regulations required the Warasdiners to fit themselves out only every six years, and the men thought they looked presentable enough in their existing uniforms, which had undergone only four years of peacetime wear. In January 1755 General Joseph Guicciardini attempted to enforce payment of the *Montirungsgelder,* and provoked a mutiny of the Creutzer regiment which forced him to flee for his life to Warasdin town, which lay outside military Croatia. The respected Colonel Wenzel Matthias Kleefeld was able to prevent the outbreak assuming the dimensions of a full rebellion, while *FML.* Benvenut Petazzi was able to contain a sympathetic movement among the Carlstädters. The Warasdiners were however determined to force a hearing for their grumbles, which extended beyond the immediate question of uniforms to embrace a chapter of complaints against their officers – beatings, enforced labour, the maltreatment of the Orthodox clergy, and the very fact that so many of their officers were foreigners, which did not prevent the mutineers (with the illogic so frequently encountered on such occasions) asking their old patron Maguire to return to them as a member of a commission of enquiry.

Vienna ordered *FM.* Neipperg to assemble 16,000 regulars and put down the unrest, and under the influence of this threat – and a sense that they had already gone too far – the malcontents asked Maria Theresa for permission to put their case to her. Maguire was about to set out from Klagenfurt to Warasdin when he was ordered to stay put, on the grounds that he had been in unauthorised correspondence with the mutineers. In his place Lieutenant-Colonel Philipp Beck, commander of the Slavonian Broder, persuaded the mutineers to lay down their arms and send a deputation to Vienna to put forward their complaints in writing. Maria Theresa found that most of the grievances were justified, and she dispatched Neipperg to Kanischa to work out a solution. Neipperg insisted that a number of the ringleaders must be handed over for trial, which resulted in the execution of a dozen mutineers and the imprisonment of 24 more, but now that the requirements of military discipline had been met he was able to begin a reconciliation. On 29 June 1755 an accord was reached on the question of uniforms and swords (to be purchased by the men at controlled prices) and that of firearms (to be provided gratis by the state); on 11 October a supplementary *Regulament* confirmed what had just been agreed, guaranteed freedom from both forced labour and arbitrary punishment, and reserved two-thirds of the officer vacancies for native Croats (an undertaking which proved impossible to fulfil).

The Warasdiner 'rebellion reminded both parties of what they had to lose by a divorce. The Warasdiners had answered with a resounding 'no,' when Neipperg posed the central question as to whether they wished to abandon their military constitution and be integrated into civilian Croatia, and in this way the ex-mutineers became indirect allies of Vienna in its dealings with non-military Croatia. Maria Theresa's cabinet secretary Ignaz Koch hinted to the old Banus of Croatia, *FM*. Carl Paul Batthyány, that it was time to resign, for there was reason to believe that the Warasdiners would not have mutinied at all, if he had been more attentive to his work.[5] After some ill feeling and delay, Batthyány himself suggested that the Hungarian cavalry general Franz Nádasdy would be a suitable successor. This ignored the right of the Croatian *Landtag* to propose candidates, and Maria Theresa set aside further precedents when she appointed Nádasdy as Banus on condition that he would place his post at her free disposal every three years, and that he would never raise the question of absorbing the Borders into civilian Croatia.

For their part, the Warasdiners had won the redress of their most pressing grievances, and gained the support of the most eloquent and influential of possible champions in the person of Kaunitz. The *Staatscanzler* had declared his position in a conference on 23 March 1755, just before Neipperg was about to leave on one of his missions to Kanischa. He emphasised that from the economic point of view alone military Croatia was a valuable resource, for, next to Bohemia and Hungary, it could sustain more troops from its own resources than any other part of the monarchy. The Croats' achievements in the last war were a matter of record, 'and as these people are by nature brave, well-grown, strongly-built and inured to hardship, as if born for war, and little inclined to desert, Your Majesty has in them a stock which could be made into the best and most formidable infantry in the world'.[6]

The Croats were as slow to forget a service as a grudge, and they looked to Kaunitz as their friend throughout the Seven Years War. The officers of the Slavonian Gradiscaner felt no inhibition about writing to him to recognise the part he had played in raising their commander, Colonel Hieronymus Liubibratich to baron with the suffix 'von Trebinya.' They tendered their humble thanks, with the assurance that 'we and our descendants will pray incessantly to Heaven for the continuing prosperity of the House of the Counts Kaunitz'.[7]

Conditions of Domestic Life

By the middle of the 18th century the accretion of the *Grenzer* peoples had been in progress for more than 200 years, and within the Military Borders proper they formed communities which amounted to some 350,000 souls, of whom about half were Croats proper, one-third Serbs, and the rest Magyars, Albanians and other small groups.

The French officer de Guibert (not to be confused with the gunner-engineer Gribeauval) toured the *Generalat* of Carlstadt in 1773, and recognised that the Borders were a great asset to the Austrian monarchy, but also 'one which cannot be imitated by any other government, for it demands a people with peculiar conditions of life, devoid of commerce, industry and education; it demands also great tracts of land which are at the free ownership of the state'.[8]

The territories in question were divided into homestead plots of very divergent size. Some of the smallest were to be found in Carlstadt, measuring, for example, about 2,200 paces by 500. The plots in Slavonia were the largest of all, where the allocation of fully arable land among the Gradiscaner amounted in 1751 to 9.5 *Joch* (at 0.57 of a *Joch* to the hectare), among the Broder to 7.9, and among the Peterwardeiner to 15.8.[9]

The people now lived under the authority of their captains, who kept up the registers of population and agricultural produce, determined the households which were to furnish soldiers for the coming campaign, and judged any disputes between families. To that extent the regularisation was a success. However the 'new' towns languished, and the economy of most of the Border remained at the level of subsistence, and failed even to progress to the exploitative market-orientated agriculture which was developing in Hungary and Poland. It was found too costly to link the rivers Drau and Sau by a canal, which would have brought produce to within an overland journey of just nine hours to Trieste.[10] Again the navigation up the Danube from the Bánát and Slavonia had to contend against the current and the overgrown banks, which made the work of the draught animals and their drivers doubly difficult.[11]

Guibert encountered wretched pastureland, meagre crops of maize, oats and barley, and villages of draughty cabins; inside the hovels any utensils and items of furniture were heaped up in a corner, and the centre of the floor was occupied by a fire, on which the women could bake an unleavened bread of millet and oats for as long as the grain lasted; for most of the year they fed on roots and grasses, and meat and wine were totally unknown.[12] In some areas the conditions were worse still during the Seven Years War. Even in time of peace the subsistence agriculture would have suffered from spells of bad weather like the severe and prolonged winter of 1757/8, and the hot summer which followed. In the Carlstadt Border, at least, the system of orderly call-up for military service collapsed in the middle of the war under the demands for manpower, which ceased to take regard of the number of able-bodied males in a household, leaving a grandfather or perhaps no male at all to cultivate fields which were 'so bad and stony that even long and hard work cannot provide enough to sustain us over a year'.[13] The unprotected women were forced into domestic industry or hauling wood at the bidding of the captains and (alleged the Carlstädter) some of the wives abandoned their children and fled into Turkish territory. Military service combined with adverse weather to cause the proportion of land under cultivation in the Borders to fall between 1756 and 1763, and there was a temporary check to the otherwise growing population of the Carlstadt Border, which amounted to 185,583 in 1746, and still only 185,365 in 1764, though it climbed to 190,355 in 1767.

However it would be wrong to equate life in the Borders with military servitude. The homestead plots were the property of the families by right, and the families were free to leave at any time they chose, as long as they sold their plot within a year; they were likewise at liberty to subdivide their plots, providing that the ground which remained to them was sufficient to provide their upkeep. They were now liable to pay tax, but (except in the cases of unauthorised abuse) they were free of labour services, which gave them a valued advantage over the feudal serfs elsewhere in the monarchy, until serfdom as such was abolished in 1848.

It is also helpful to bear in mind that wide differences in conditions of life existed along the Borders. Guibert himself admitted that he had never visited the Warasdin Border, and indeed some of the truisms about the Borders as a whole have been drawn from the poor but relatively accessible Carlstadt and Banal districts. Thus the image of the Croats as a highland folk, accepted by historians from Archenholtz[14] to Braudel, was a projection of the wretched existence of the Carlstädters in their hamlets and isolated in the denuded mountains towards the Adriatic. Their population had grown rapidly at the turn of the 17th and 18th centuries, without any corresponding increase in agricultural production, and poverty was rife on the far side of the Maritime Border (*Meergrenze, Kapela*) in the lands of the Ottocaner, the Liccaner and many of the Oguliner.

Regularisation had been introduced only recently among the Carlstädters, and although the state furnished them with free uniforms to alleviate their poverty, they remained a backward and recalcitrant people. They had to furnish guards for the Ottoman border, as well as provide four battalions for the field army, and a double burden of this kind weighed more heavily still on their neighbours in the little Banal Border (this territory is not to be confused with the Bánát of Temesvár down the Danube; it is also easy to mistake the Slavonian Borders along the Sau with the Slovenian lands in Carinthia).

By comparison the Warasdiner Croats were blessed many times over. They had taken to regulatisation early and enthusiastically, they lived in fertile lowlands, they possessed no common border with the Turks, and they had received sympathetic attention from Hildburghausen, Maguire, Kleefeld, Neipperg and Beck. Their burden of service was also comparatively light. The proportion of the able-bodied male population enrolled for military service had admittedly risen from 31.4 percent before the Seven Years War to 41.7 percent in 1763, but this was still much less than the 65.9 percent recorded among the Slavonians in 1753, or the approximately 70 percent among the Carlstädters in 1764.

The Slavonian Border had been formed by a complex evolution from the old Danubian, Sau and Syrmian Borders, and as a result its territories extended for some 340 kilometres of generally flat ground along the northern bank of the Sau, or Save. Towards the end of 1761 the commanding general *FML.* Anton Ignaz Mercy argued for a reduction of the Slavonians' military burden. He maintained that five years of war had carried the Slavonian Border beyond the limit of what its people could sustain. In addition to furnishing three regiments of infantry the Slavonians put forth a large regiment of *Grenz-Husaren,* who had to purchase their horses mostly from neighbouring provinces, and provide their own uniforms and equipment – a tall demand for a society in which barter took the place of cash, and where 'in many of the villages scarcely one or two households will be in possession of even a small sum of money.' It was scarcely surprising that in 1756 not a single one of the Slavonians had volunteered for service with the hussars. Mercy concluded that the Slavonian *Grenz-Husaren* should be abolished, and their complement of men, such as it was, distributed among the infantry.[15]

Nobody in Vienna was convinced, and in fact the fundamental problem in the Slavonian Border was that the landholdings were very large in proportion to the size of the population, which was the reverse of the situation obtaining in the Carlstadt Border. Perhaps Mercy had 'gone native,' or perhaps he had been deluded by the Slavonians' cunning – a commodity which was in plentiful supply. The Commissary Eichinger looked into the affairs of the Gradiscaner regiment in detail in 1760, and found that on returning from the field towards the end of 1759 the officers and men had shamelessly presented the equivalent of 3,667 florins in debased Prussian currency for exchange at the very favourable rate allowed by the government. This was far more than they could have put away as savings, or taken from the enemy as legitimate booty, for they had never been in action. They had in fact taken note of the good rate of exchange offered by the state, and traded good Austrian money for large quantities of the dismal Prussian coinage.

Eichinger found that the men of the Peterwardeiner regiment were up to equally sharp practices. They claimed to have been very badly used, for they had been away for 18 months, including the outward and return marches. This had been the accepted norm, and only the Peterwardeiners now claimed that the marching time should be deducted from their term of service. They accompanied this protest by the blatant threat of deserting unless they received satisfaction. The Peterwardeiners likewise put in a request for free uniforms, on the same basis as had been allowed to the Carlstädters, ignoring the fact the Carlstädters had small and unproductive plots of ground, whereas the Peterwardeiners were 'virtually noblemen'.[16]

Protestants were rare birds along the historic Borders, though they were to be found in some numbers in the four additional units of infantry which were raised in Transylvania towards the end of the war. Maria Theresa was shocked to learn of the case of the Second-Lieutenant Prumnitz of the First Wallachian Border Regiment (*Erstes Walachen-Grenz-Regiment*), who was born a Catholic, but now professed Lutheranism among his Protestant comrades. *FML.* Siskovics reported to Daun that Prumnitz was unapologetic, 'and since the Lutherans hereabouts are uncommonly impertinent, and becoming more assertive by the day, I believe that I must bring this case… to the attention of Your Excellency, for determination as Your Excellency sees fit'.[17] Daun noted the apostasy to Maria Theresa, as we have seen, and she in turn consigned Prumnitz to Wiener-Neustadt for a new course of instruction in the Catholic faith.

Catholics predominated in the Warasdin Border, and in the lands of the Slavonian Broder and Gradiscaner, but Greek Orthodoxy was the prevailing confession among the rest of the 'Croats,' and a symbol of the rights of the whole *Grenzer* body. There is remarkably little documentary evidence of any discord prevailing in this period between the *Grenzer* of different faiths. However the Archbishop and Metropolitan Paulus Nenadovich was fully aware of the strength of his position as a spiritual leader of his flock, and he used every opportunity to advance the interests of the Orthodox. He wrote to Maria Theresa in such a vein from Carlowitz in June 1758 to assure her of the unfailing zeal, courage and devotion of the 'Illyrian Nation' – devotion which was nevertheless being tested by the absence of chaplains of their own confession, and the way their Catholic officers were forcing them to break their Wednesday and Friday fasts.[18]

The *Hofkriegsrath* duly reminded Daun that 'as is well known, those people are much attached to the externals of their religion, and are not easily persuaded to break their accustomed fast days. We therefore leave it to you to inform the generals Zweibrücken and Serbelloni in an appropriate way that any use of compulsion against these people is to be forbidden on pain of punishment'.[19] Later in the same year we find Nenadovich writing to Daun to congratulate him on his victory at Hochkirch; the men of the 'Illyrian nation would gladly sacrifice their blood and persons in the war, and he therefore believed himself justified in asking for Croatian officers to be promoted to high rank 'so as to encourage their compatriots'.[20]

The Austrians were sensitive to representations like these, for the seeds of pan-Slavism were present in what was seen as the shared language and religion of the Orthodox *Grenzer* and the Russians. A standing invitation to emigrate to New Serbia and other Russian territories was on offer to such Croats who were dissatisfied with life under the Habsburgs, and some 10,000 Serbs had taken this course in 1753 after the lands of the old Theiss-Maros-Border had been incorporated in the southern counties of Hungary.

The *Grenzer* (unlike some of the Hungarians) were assumed to be proof against Prussian blandishments, but Vienna became aware of a peculiarly threatening influence in the summer of 1762, for the new and unstable Russian sovereign Peter III was making common cause with Frederick. Maria Theresa wrote with some urgency to Daun 'on a matter which concerns the welfare of the state.' The conduct of the Russian lieutenant-general Zakhar Chernyshev, who had once counted as one of the great enemies of the King of Prussia, now led her to suspect that:

> he has in mind an undertaking against Hungary, or to foment a revolt among my Croats and other Orthodox Christians in Croatian territory... Such projects could be extremely dangerous if they are not nipped in the bud, and so I believe it is not being overcautious for us to keep a close eye on my Croats and Orthodox subjects, and do what we can to encourage those who are loyally inclined. You could there not only maintain your customary vigilance, but call on *FZM.* Loudon, *GFWM.* Brentano and other reliable officers, who know the nation well and command its trust, and concert with them how to prevent the Croats being led astray, and how best to keep the Orthodox firm in their loyalty, and averse to desertion or rebellion.[21]

The Austrians were meanwhile monitoring the continuing emigration of the Orthodox *Grenzer* from Hungary, and the activities of Major Sholokov and other Russian officers and soldiers who were roaming that kingdom, some of them without permission. Maria Theresa decided to stay her hand until the Russians made an overtly hostile move in Silesia, and, on the advice of Kaunitz, she told the Hungarian authorities to do nothing until the time came to take appropriate measures, which she would notify them when the need arose.[22] The occasion did not come, for the murder of Emperor Peter removed the immediate threat from this source.

The Military Commitment

The fundamental military obligations of the Croats were expressed in two articles of the *Militärrechte* of 1754, of which the first related to the historic duty of local defence:

1. Upon the imminent danger of enemy invasion the alarm signal will cause the officers and men over 18 years of age to take up arms, hasten to their assigned assembly points, and carry out loyally the further orders of their commanders. To this they are bound by their oath…
2. All able-bodied male inhabitants have an obligation of service and are subject to military discipline, for they benefit from the enjoyment of Imperial privileges. The statutes bind them to periods of drill [usually four weeks a year in peacetime], and to a willing acceptance of the relevant directions which are given by their officers. Refusal to carry out these duties will incur the forfeiture of the privileges in question, and corporal or capital punishment as may be indicated.'

Altogether 46,000 Croatian infantry were available for active service, and organised into regiments within the four groupings of the Borders:

Carlstädter Infantry:
Liccaner regiment
Ottocaner regiment
Oguliner regiment
Szluiner regiment

Warasdiner Infantry:
Creutzer regiment
St. Georger regiment

Slavonian Infantry:
Broder regiment
Gradiscaner regiment
Peterwardeiner regiment

Banal Infantry:
First regiment
Second regiment

The Croatian regiment was divided into three 'divisions' (levies), which served in wartime by rotation, each division in turn taking to the field for one campaign at a time. The other two divisions of the regiment stayed at home, but all save the Warasdiners still had to meet the residual obligation to guard the borders against the Turks.

The Carlstädter Liccaner were organised on a super-large regiment of six battalions, or 5,760 troops in all. The establishment of all the others remained as it had been determined in 1750, namely four fusilier battalions of four companies each. Two grenadier companies were attached to each regiment, as well as the small complements of gunners who served the 1-pounder cannon in the first campaigns of the war.

The Croatian cavalry took the form of regiments of *Grenz-Husaren* which amounted to a total of 3,000 men, namely the:

Carlstädter
Warasdiner (one squadron only)
Slavonian
Banal.

The Officers

On campaign the more conscientious officers of the Croats underwent privations incomparably more severe than any endured by their counterparts among the regulars, not excluding the Hungarian hussars. In peacetime the life of many of them was dismal in the extreme. They dwelt in little houses which had been built by the state, cut off from one another and from society by distance and the snows of the prolonged winters. De Guibert describes promotion as being slow and the senior ranks routinely up for sale, so that a poor and a long-serving officer would see strangers routinely promoted over his head, depriving him of the rewards of his hard and solitary existence.[24]

Loudon and Kleefeld represented the best type of the foreign officers to be found among the Croats. Unfortunately there were precious few to compare with them. In the Seven Years War the Croatian officer corps became a dumping ground for suspect officers of the German regiments, and a field of ambition for rich adventurers who brought their way into senior rank to exploit the opportunities for plunder. 'The Croatian soldier is observant, and soon takes the measure of the officers who have been set above him. The fact that they are self-seeking and sly does not escape his attention, and it provokes him to mutiny, just as the sight of them cowering under fire does not motivate him to do well in combat'.[25]

The Croats were afflicted with too many creatures like these, when, as Lacy insisted, the authorities should have been choosing:

> officers who are brave, intelligent and experienced in the art of war, and such... as know the conditions of the Borders in general and how they might be turned to the best advantage. They must also be able to establish useful personal connections among the Croats, and speak the language in a way which commands loyalty. The language in Poland, Livonia and Curland is very similar to Croatian, and we should therefore attract officers from those parts to our service, or seek them out if they are already in the army.[26]

We therefore find the Croatian rank and file complaining constantly about the opportunities which were being denied to them, and the poor quality of the leadership. The grumblers received short shrift from *FML*. Petazzi, as commanding general of the Carlstadt Border: 'All that the *Grenzer* need to know is the single rule... which I have impressed on them constantly, which is that they are all nothing more than soldiers who live from the produce of plots of Imperial ground, and are consequently under an obligation to serve under whoever is put in charge of them'.[27]

In fact Maria Theresa and Kaunitz were doing everything in their power to bring on potential leaders from among the native Croats. In 1756 the Empress-Queen singled out 20 young Warasdiners for appointments in the German regiments, 'so that they may acquire a complete understanding of the German language in the course of their military duties, and then proceed to do useful service among the regiments of the Warasdin Border'.[28] One of their number, the cadet Thomas Vocaillovich, contrived to escaped from the Prussians after he had been captured in Breslau, and on returning to the army he asked to be allowed to join the Warasdiners straight away. The lieutenant colonel of the Creutzer regiment supported his application, and Maria Theresa at once agreed (see p. 187).

No glimmer of genuine merit was likely to be ignored. In the Szluiner regiment Colonel Kleefeld was struck by the outstanding performance of Second-Lieutenant Joviza Budinovaz in the campaign of 1757, and recommend him, although 'only a *Grenzer*,' for promotion.[29] In the same year the ethnic Serbian major Paul Dimich von Papilla of the Gradiscaner served on a mission to the Russians, and took several battalions of Russian grenadiers under his command in the battle of Gross-Jägersdorf, addressing them in their common 'Illyrian' language. Dimich von Papilla was made a knight of the M.M.T.O., and he shared this honour with Arsenius Szeczujac 'von

Heldensfeld' (another Gradiscaner), the ethnic Bosnian Martin Knesevich 'von St. Helena' of the Carlstädters, and Johann Friedrich Tkalcsevich of the Broders. For no particular reason the majority of the *Grenzer* knights happened to be Catholics, and when he applied (successfully) to Kaunitz for admission to the Order in 1762, Hieronymus Liubibratich declared himself deserving both on account of his services at Olmütz and Landeshut, and because not a single Orthodox officer had so far been included.[30]

Promotion for the general run of native officers was certainly slow,[31] but in most cases it was deservedly slow. Loudon, who had made his name as a commander of the Croats, had to report to Maria Theresa in 1761 that 'out of all the colonels of the Carlstädter military district serving in the field, there is not one to whom I could safely trust the command of these troops on outpost duty'.[32] Liubibratich could scarcely be accused of prejudice against his fellow *Grenzer,* yet when he reviewed the character of the 10 captains present with him in Slavonia, he could find only one of them – Luca Klaichat all suitable for promotion, and even he could scarcely read or write.

The business of promotion among the Croats was complicated by the need to conduct a triangular exchange of correspondence between the senior officers in the homelands (where two out of the three sets of divisions were located at any given time), the commanders of the Croats serving in the field, and the authorities in Vienna. The *Hofkriegsrath* was understandably reluctant to accept at face value a list of Carlstädter promotions put forward by *FML*. Petazzi on 24 April 1758, in which he had proposed a captaincy for his son Adelmus, who was a volunteer and innocent of all military rank. The matter was referred to Daun, who asked the opinion of Loudon and Kleefeld, who had considerable knowledge of conditions among the Croats. Loudon had only one alternative to suggest. Kleefeld had several, but he expressed surprise at Petazzi's recommendation for Adelmus, for the promotion of a lad so lacking in experience was undesirable on two accounts, for it would do an injustice to many veteran first-lieutenants, and 'because Croatia, or more specifically the *Generalat* of Carlstadt, is not the place or setting where young gentlemen of his kind have any real opportunity to learn the fundamentals of military service'.[33]

The underlying problem was that Croatian society was insufficiently advanced to meet the new and expanded commitments of the Borders. Unmistakable sons of the Balkans served alongside the products of Europeanised or recently-arrived officers families who might have been educated by the Jesuits or Pauliner, who wore Western fashions, and who were accustomed to cutting a dash in the world, like the Major Rasp who exploited the social opportunities open to him during his captivity in Berlin. Frau von Göhren was devastated when he left on exchange, and a Prussian courtier explains that 'he was a fine man, as strong as Hercules, and a credit to his Croatian nation. He was the best dancer I have ever seen, and ladies who understand such things praise him for a further accomplishment'.[34]

The Croatian nobles as a whole were too few and too fragmented to take up a politically significant front like the nobles of Hungary. In Croatia the interests of the individual family were paramount, as may be perceived from the scarcely-literate correspondence of Lieutenant-Colonel Peter Troyllus Count Sermage, the third generation of a *Kaiserlich* family of Franche-Comte long settled in 'civilian' Croatia. Sermage was avid for promotion to colonel, and he kept a close eye on the health of his commanders, writing after the battle of Hochkirch how he was hoping for promotion before the war ended, and how in this respect the only news of note was that Colonel Barkozy had been badly wounded 'and has had a piece cut out of his skull; if he survives he will have to have it replaced by a silver plate… it is a pity about his fine hair'.[35] Sermage was court-martialled and dismissed from the service in 1759, probably because he had carried his intrigues too far, but his hunger for advancement and recognition was shared by his seniors in ways that were scarcely less extreme. He duly noted that the promotion of his brother-in-law Joseph Draskovich had left his colonel Zedtwitz 'totally disgusted,' but still striving by underhand means to be promoted to general.[36]

Meanwhile the Croatian regiments were left without enough officers, whether good or bad. Serbelloni cited the case of a contingent of 889 Croats which was commanded by just one captain and three first lieutenants. This handful of officers would have been unable to direct an equivalent force of regular German infantry, 'and still less can we hope for anything good from an irregular regiment of Croats like the Carlstädters, who are split up into a multitude of detachments, most of them doing outpost duty in the proximity of the enemy'.[37]

The NCOs

Native Croats could scarcely begin to supply the demand for the posts of *Fouriers,* lance-corporals and NCOs, where literacy was a basic requirement. Commissary Eichinger reported that whenever a Slavonian battalion was about to take to the field, a host of so-called 'NCOs' would appear from nowhere; they were appointed without the knowledge of the Commissaries or their own colonels, and they complained mightily if they were detected and duly degraded to private soldier.[38]

The same phenomenon was noted among the Carlstädters, where the soldiers complained that their NCOs had been promoted through favouritism or bribery. When the time came to go on campaign, these people paid substitutes to take their place. The substitutes were in turn 'mostly men who had not done a single hour's service in their lives, and some of them are not even natives who are settled in the *Generalat.*' They were a law unto themselves, interested only in plunder, 'and consequently the innocent are grouped with the guilty, and we are all seen as robbers'.[39]

The Men

The ordinary Croats did not strive for rank or status, but were typically tall and strong folk who showed 'astonishing courage in the face of hunger and thirst, frost and heat, and the greatest physical suffering, even under the knife of the surgeon. Death holds no terrors for thern'.[40] In their homelands everything reminded the stranger that 'you are in a colony of soldiers… What marks out the menfolk of the Borders is their military bearing, their moustaches, the bits and pieces of military uniform which they invariably wear… and the fact that they almost invariably go about armed, whether with muskets, swords or pistols'.[41]

The reorganisation of the Borders on regimental lines was inevitably accompanied by a regularisation of the clothing. The process was unwelcome to the Croats, and not just because all of them (except the Carlstädters) originally had to meet the cost out of their own purses. Lieutenant-Colonel Rebain observed that traditional modes had been abandoned in favour of 'a uniform in the Hungarian fashion, which was disliked by the Croats, and the Warasdiners in particular… Indeed it has been maintained that, but for the new uniforms, many Christian Bosnians would have enlisted in their ranks'.[42]

In 1757 Maria Theresa made a misguided attempt to standardise uniforms throughout the army, and Neipperg, as Vice-President of the *Hofkriegsrath,* was made responsible for collating the opinions of the regiments. He knew that the feeling was generally hostile, and his knowledge of the prickly Croats told him that further unwelcome novelties could provoke fresh uproar along the Borders. Petazzi told him that his Carlstädters 'liked red and blue rather than any other colours.' Neipperg added that it was still more important to respect local preferences among the other Croats, 'for they have to pay for their uniforms themselves, and are much attached to their favourite colours.' The Slavonian Broder and Gradiscaner should therefore be allowed to retain the dark blue, while the two Warasdiner regiments should retain their green dolmans. Maria Theresa had to give way, and she ruled that 'we should proceed no further with the standardisation, at least for as long as the existing uniforms last out'.[43] In August 1760 she decreed that the Warasdiners and Slavonians would be issued with free clothing on the same basis as the Carlstädters. The motive was no longer uniformity, which had been abandoned, but simply 'to alleviate the lot of the ordinary soldiers'.[44]

The Croatian military dress of the period of the Seven Years War was influenced by unwelcome Hungarian fashions, as has just been mentioned. The hair was dressed in plaits or pigtail, and was surmounted by a tubular cap of felt or fur. It is not known what happened to the 'German' tricorns which Maguire had introduced among the Warasdiners. The original open-fronted jacket (*Jacke*) was already longer than the related Hungarian pelisse, and in the course of the war it was transmuted among the Warasdiners and Slavonians and some of the rest into a short coat (*Röckl*), which was adorned with narrow round cuffs, a single turn-back on either hem, and six sets of Hungarian-style button holes (*Litzen, Schleifen*) down the front. Hungarian influence appeared again in the dolman (which took the place of the waistcoat), and the tight-fitting leggings with elaborate decorations down the fronts of the thighs. The Warasdiners, as the most Westernised of the Croats, sometimes wore hard shoes of the same type as the regulars, but the rest of the *Grenzer* preferred their comfortable and weatherproof *Opanken*, which were done up with elaborate leather bindings.

Among the Slavonians the *Hausmontur*, a simple coat of brown homespun, often took the place of the prescribed uniform, and in any case the Croatian infantry of all kinds carried a red cloak which was the sign of the nation as a whole. When it was not being worn, the cloak was rolled up and tied above the knapsack, the version of the Banalists being a large garment like the cavalry *Mantel*, which was made up into a bandolier and sported Russian-style diagonally across the chest.

Regulation muskets and sabres replaced the diverse Balkan weapons of earlier times (below), and much of the remaining gear also conformed with that of the rest of the infantry. *FZM*. Mercy represented in 1762 that his Slavonians were encumbered needlessly by their Western-style cartridge pouches with their heavy belts, 'for when a man has spent one, two or three weeks in action, in garrison service, or on patrol, the first thing he must do when he gets back is to clean his leather gear and restore it to its original white.' Something more simple and useful would spare the Croats valuable time, and spare the state money, and the same held true of the caps of the Slavonian grenadiers, which were peculiarly unsuitable for troops who operated mostly in woodlands, and for that reason were usually 'lost,' or rather thrown away.[45]

As late as the summer of 1758 Frederick was still convinced that his free battalions were incapable of matching up to the *Grenzer*.[46] He did not know how difficult it was for the Austrians to maintain a useful force of these paragons of military virtue in the field. Croatian 'loyalty' was legendary, in that it was almost unknown for a *Grenzer* to desert to the enemy. And yet, if the Croats detected or imagined a breach of faith on the part of the authorities, they resorted to something potentially much more dangerous, namely defying their officers and making off homewards, by force if necessary, and regardless of the stage of the campaign or the presence of the enemy.[47]

The more notorious of many episodes have found their way into the records. In February 1759 *GFWM*. Ried had to report that discontent was rife among his Szluiner and Ottocaner Carlstädters in Saxony. He had tried to reason with a disaffected unit of the Ottocaner, which was bent on going home, 'but when I had brought the company together the men as a body laid one hand simultaneously on a long staff, raised two fingers of the other in the air, and promised one another that neither force nor threats would deter them from carrying through what they had determined'.[48] Ried bided his time until he know that the mutineers had returned to their quarters in Rebisch. He then brought up two companies of regulars, confined the Croats to the houses, removed the ammunition carts and cannon from their reach, and sent the Ottocaners' officers and NCOs from billet to billet to tell the men to identify their ringleaders. The eight prime plotters were yielded up by the men themselves and the mutiny was at an end.

In fact the officers of the Croats considered themselves lucky if their disgruntled troops simply marched away without making any kind of trouble.[49] *GFWM.* Kleefeld (an experienced and conscientious commander of the Croats) experienced an altogether more violent parting at Gera in Saxony in 1760, and had to report how on the night of 4/5 May a battalion of the Ottocaner had mutinied, hacked down the doors of one of the town gates, gathered in the streets amid much yelling and firing of shots, and made off into the darkness. Only the fact that Kleefeld had secured the cannon in a building prevented the malcontents from taking the artillery with them.[50]

A couple of days earlier another 220 Carlstädter mutineers had materialised unannounced at Stockerau, on the far side of the Danube from Vienna. The *Hofkriegsrath* decided to notify them of its displeasure, but now that they had got so far it could see no alternative but to arrange their passage of the Danube, and provide them with money for the rest of their journeys.[51] Disorders and mass-desertions were reported at intervals for the rest of the war.

The unrest was most commonly experienced among the Carlstädters, though it was by no means confined to those folk. The occasions were the perceived lack of promotion, the poor state or the cost of the uniforms, arrears of pay, payment that was made over in debased currency, but most commonly the notion that the Croats were being kept in the field longer than their stipulated term of service. *FML.* Petazzi warned Maria Theresa in June 1760 that the numerical balance between the men called to the field and those who stayed at home was upset as soon as 12,000 or more men were summoned to serve at any one time,[52] and yet we find the authorities settling in 1762 for a call-up of no less than 20,000 Croats.[53] Some of the family men were so desperate that they had paid up to three substitutes in succession, at a cost of 30 or 40 florins a time, and then, having fallen deeply into debt, they had to go to the war anyway.[54]

Any tampering with the routine of these profoundly conservative people was in fact undesirable. It was impossible to call on troops of a Croatian division at home to make up the numbers of a depleted companion division in the field, as Maria Theresa discovered in November 1757.[55] Likewise in 1762 Hadik was compelled to warn against combining the much-reduced Croats in Saxony into a single battalion, as military logic seemed to indicate, 'for when so many different kinds of men are brought together the conditions will be ripe for mutiny, because some of the men will incite the others thereto.' The damage might not stop there, for 'an uprising might occur all too easily among the Croats as a whole'.[56]

If mutiny threatened, or actually occurred, the authorities might make an example of such ringleaders as fell into their hands. However it was known that many of the Croats' complaints might turn out to be justified, and in any case forcible procedures could not only 'make a highly unfortunate impression on the men who are on their way to relieve them, but in the Borders themselves, with prejudicial consequences'.[57] When it was recognised that a Croatian unit was genuinely being asked to stay on in the field beyond its tour, Vienna preferred to hold out inducements like a cash advance towards the cost of uniforms, the promise of red leggings (from which much was expected),[58] the prospect of promotion, or simply the assurance that a gesture of goodwill on the part of the Croats would 'make an exceptionally favourable impression on the Empress'.[59]

The Croatian contribution to the Austrian effort fell away markedly in the final period of the Seven Years War. This was the cumulative effect of the institutional inflexibilities, the tactical misuse and shortcomings, and the wastage through disease, casualties and mutinies. The Croats were never more needed than towards the end of the campaigning seasons, when the time came to think of making a final effort, or establishing a secure cordon for the winter quarters. A reliable source[60] puts the *Dienstbarer Stand* of the Croats with the field armies in July 1762 at 13,296, of whom 3,121 were with the forces in Saxony. Hadik nevertheless writes to Daun at the beginning of October that he had so few Croats at his disposal that he had to employ up to 3,000 of the German infantry on outpost duty in their place. By November the same year Saxony had become the main theatre of operations, and Hadik's complement of Croats had been reduced to about 1,200.[61]

Inevitably the authorities began to ask themselves whether the Croats were more trouble than they were worth, at least for wars against the Prussians. The question was first posed by Daun, in an extremely frank letter which he wrote to Maria Theresa after his victory at Maxen on 20/21 November 1759. Here he suggested that the Austrians should be in no hurry to regain their prisoners in exchange for their haul of Prussian captives (see p. 240), and that any Croats retrieved would represent a very poor return, for they would have to go home to re-equip, whereas the liberated Prussians would be available for immediate service in the next campaign.[62]

By 1761 the Austrians had still more Prussian prisoners on their hands, and the notoriously tough-minded *GFWM*. Ernst Friedrich Giannini urged that an exchange would be more unequal than ever. The Austrians would regain quantities of second-rate and enfeebled regulars who would be incapable of active service, and 'the same applies to our poor loyal Croats. We truly regret their lot, for their families in their own country suffer greatly through their absence, but these men too are good for nothing to be sent home straight away, which is of no benefit to the service of Your Imperial Majesty. The Prussians in return would receive healthy, well-fed native veterans and effective combatants'.[63]

The need for light troops as such could not be denied, and October 1761 found Daun and Kaunitz in agreement (a rare happening in itself) as to where complements or replacements for the Croats might be found. Economy was as important a consideration as utility, for the finances were in a bad way, and with this in view Daun wrote to Maria Theresa on the 6th that although it would be more difficult than ever to deploy an adequate number of Croats, the recruitment of free battalions would offer a cheap alternative. They did not need to be organised into full regiments with an establishment of permanently-assigned officers, 'and they need bear no other designation than the Blue and Green Free Battalions, or so on in accordance with the colour of their uniforms'.[64]

More striking still was the memorandum which came from Kaunitz on 17 October, for the *Staatscanzler* was known as the staunchest champion of the Croats. Faced with the necessity of making reductions, Kaunitz argued for keeping the Beck free battalion and the Loudon Green Grenadiers (which absorbed Prussian deserters so usefully), and 'ordering proportionately fewer of the Croats into the field. I recognise how useful these troops can be, but we can expect at least as much from the battalions just mentioned. We should also bear in mind that the number of serviceable men in the Borders has diminished greatly, and we should be thinking of their conservation rather than that of the foreigners …'[65]

Carlstädter Szluiner Croat (Krauhse, Austrian Army Museum). Blue jacket with red cuffs; red dolman; red (or blue) leggings.

All of this indicates that Frederick was deriving a better return from his morally deplorable free battalions than were the Austrians from their Croats. Hadik owned a probably unsurpassed experience in 'little war,' and towards the end of the war he wrote to Maria Theresa to put the central issues in perspective. She had asked him for his opinion on the question of increasing the number of light forces, and he had to reply that Frederick had attained 'the superiority in light troops,' for he had succeeded in recruiting ordinary men and Austrian and French deserters through the enticing prospect of the freedom he allowed to his free battalions, hussars, dragoons, *Jäger*, 'Croats' and *Bosniaken*. In the campaign of 1761 this preponderance had enabled Frederick to secure a large tract of land for his winter quarters, and to launch damaging raids and threaten the Austrian flanks. Hadik urged the need not only to restore the regiments of hussars to 1,200 men each, and bring the greatest possible number of Croats into the field, but to raise free companies and battalions from the army and in Poland. In the latter enterprise the excellent Colonel Andreas Prince Poniatowsky would be of much assistance. A great deal was at stake, for the end of the war could not be far away, and the Austrian light forces must regain the upper hand if a tolerable peace was to be in prospect.[66]

15

Logistics

> The supply of the military establishment as a whole is beyond dispute the largest and the same time the most necessary outlay which Your Majesty is called upon to make
>
> Kaunitz to Maria Theresa, January 1762

'Logistics' is a word which entered general military currency only in the 20th century, but the reality of the business was familiar to soldiers and statesmen of 200 years before, as it concerned everything that had to do with feeding troops, and providing them with clothing and equipment, and keeping them in battleworthy health. The subject does not make for compelling reading, but it determines to a large extent what can and cannot be done in war.

THE DIRECTION

The body most directly concerned with the management of logistics was the *General-Kriegs-Commissariat*. The *Commissariat* had been established in 1650, and for most of its existence it had taken its military direction from the *Hofkriegsrath*, just as it was financially dependent on the *Hofcammer* (Treasury). On 28 December 1746, however, the *Commissariat* was elevated into a full department of state (*Hofstelle*) under the greatly experienced Franz Ludwig Count Salburg, who had a record of service dating from 1707, and was now appointed *General-Kriegs-Commissarius*. As such he was the master of more than 700 officials. All the grades were well paid (a necessary safeguard against corruption), 'and it is safe to say that as far as income is concerned there is not a colonel in the army who may be compared with an ordinary official of the *Commissariat* or Supply (Proviant) branches'.[1]

The responsibilities of the *Commissariat* in general were defined as being to supervise 'the establishment, economy and discipline of the military personnel for the common good'[2]. The *Commissariat* directed many activities that are immediately recognisable as logistic affairs proper – it established magazines, disbursed rations for man and horse, managed accommodation, helped to provide clothing and remounts, and (in association with Liechtenstein) arms and ammunition, and it organised the transport of supplies in wartime through its *Feld Proviant-Fuhrwesen*. Medical care also fell within the purview of the *Commissariat*, which in addition became one of the prime instruments of military reform through its responsibilities for the good estate of the troops: it had a share in examining and enrolling the recruits (the '*Assentirung*'), and at least once in most years it descended on individual regiments to draw up the muster list of all ranks (and the horses as well in the cavalry), to review the rolls, listen to the soldiers' complaints, eliminate broken-down men as invalids, and investigate the state of the regiment's clothing, equipment, health and morals. *Revisionen* were irregular, sudden and unannounced inspections of regiments which had undergone a period of turbulence.

Thanks to the *Commissariat* the Empress and her advisers were able to feel the pulse of the army as a living organism. Count Eichinger and many of its officials were undoubtedly astute and conscientious individuals who had a nose for sniffing out fraud and maltreatment, while observing all due discretion. Their authority was reinforced by the infantry regulations of 1749 and the cavalry regulations of 1749–51, which reminded the regiments of the honour and respect that was due to the Commissaries (*Commissäre*) on their visitations.

The military men had nevertheless been accustomed to treating all civilian functionaries with disdain, and they formed an image of the Commissaries and the local *Amts-Officiere* as jumped-up servants of great men, like the former Kaunitz lackey who emerged as Baron Koschinna 'von Freudenthal.' The author of the *Patriotic Reflections* complains that the Commissaries as a tribe were 'crudely demanding to a degree which goes beyond a proper attention to their duties.' They were in the habit of summoning junior officers to them from distant posts and in bad weather, and sending them away again because it was not convenient to see them, moreover:

> it is almost impossible to keep up with the constant changes in the formulae and systems of accounting, so that hardly anyone knows where he stands concerning the troops' clothing and pay. The colonel has more to do with the wretched pen than the sword, and the good estate of the regiment suffers accordingly. They are sworn enemies of the officers, and the few educated men among them are outnumbered greatly by individuals who are nothing but clerks, and because their mental horizons are so circumscribed they cling to the letter of the regulations… only just recently we captured a fortress [Glatz or Schweidnitz] which contained many items of enemy uniforms. Our poor wounded were in a bad way, for many of them had lost their knapsacks in the attack, and they were unable to obtain new shirts, for these had been left behind in the regimental depots. For a number of weeks these soldiers had to go about in a deplorable state in their torn and soiled shirts… until the Commissary, who stuck by his rule to issue nothing until he had listed every item in his inventory, at last consented to help the troops in their distress by giving out the shirts – the same shirts which those men had helped to capture.[3]

In wartime the senior functionaries of the *Commissariat* and the local civil administration emerged as powerful figures in their own right. Joseph Maria Wilczek was a hard man[4] who exercised near-despotic power in Saxony as the Emperor's special '*General-Commissar*' with the *Reichsarmee*, and who functioned as the head of the *Commissariat* after it was incorporated in the *Directorium* in 1757 (below). On the main theatre of war the march routes, the care of the sick and many other details had to be processed through the relevant president of the provincial *Repräsentation und Cammer*, of whom the most important was probably the head of the Bohemian administration, Wenzel Kasimir Netolitzky von Eisenberg. Netolitzky was one of the people *FZM.* Lacy was commissioned to see when he went to Vienna at Daun's request in the spring of 1759, but he had to report that the man was so swollen by dropsy that Daun could expect little help from him in the coming campaign.[5]

The influence of the *General-Kriegs-Commissarius*, as supreme head of the branch, extended far into the sphere of operations, in view of his responsibility for keeping the army commander informed of the state and location of the supplies.[6] Daun was moved to complain that in reality the roles were reversed, for the commanding general was effectively subordinate to the *Commissariat*, and 'military operations can proceed only as the *General-Kriegs-Commissarius* sees fit'.[7] The state of affairs was doubly unsatisfactory, for administrative changes in 1757 had prevented the *Commissariat* from giving of its best.

For a time affairs had been going well. The *Commissariat* won its independence at the end of 1746, and it had gained by the great administrative and economic reforms initiated by Haugwitz in 1748 and 1749. In return for making over tax revenues for long spans of time, the *Stände* were relieved of the obligations to feed and shelter the army in peacetime. These responsibilities now passed to the *Commissariat*, which fed the man and horses from the new state magazines, and accommodated the troops in 'semi-barracks' adapted from private houses (see p. 230).

Altogether the period from 1747 to 1756 may be regarded as the apogee of the old *Commissariat*. By 1757 Count Salburg was ill as well as old, and incapable of putting up a defence against the complaints that were being levelled against his department by the provinces, 'and so the *General-Kriegs-Commissarius*... who was universally agreed to have an incomparable knowledge of his work, was compelled to resign all of a sudden, and his department was made subordinate to the *Directorium*'.[8] In other words the work of military supply was being handed over to the main organ of civil administration. Maria Theresa explained that within the *Directorium* the military tasks would be handed over to a sub-commission, comparable with that for coinage and mining (*Münze und Bergwesen*), and that Wilczek would take over the presidency.[9] The arrangements were alarmingly vague, and the *Directorium* proved unable to cope with its new and immense burden of military logistics and supervision. The immediate effect was to keep the army immobilised outside Breslau after the Austrians had captured the city on 25 November, so that the vengeful Frederick was able to advance unopposed and virtually force the Austrians to give battle at Leuthen on 5 December.

The delays and confusions became so great that as a temporary expedient logistic responsibilities were transferred on 3 February 1761 to Johann Count Chotek as president of a new *Commissariat Hofcommission*, which nevertheless fell short of a proper department of state. On 23 December 1761 Johann Chotek was appointed *General-Kriegs-Commissarius*, which represented a further modest advance, and in 1762 both Daun and Kaunitz entered the lists. Daun represented that it was important to pin down the status of the *Commissariat*, which functioned separately from both the *Hofkriegsrath* and the *Hofkammer*, had failed when it was buried within the *Directorium*, yet could not be counted as a proper department of state.[10] Kaunitz also looked into the matter, and concluded that the *Commissariat* was trying to meet too many disparate responsibilities at once, including the discipline and condition of the regiments, which should properly be the business of 'military men who have a full understanding of the service, and can supervise affairs with the proper forcefulness'.[11]

Before the end of the Seven Years War a partial solution was found by making the *Commissariat* responsible to the *Hofkriegsrath* for military supply in the narrower sense, and to the three departments of civil finance (*General Cassadirection*, *Hofcammer* and *Hofrechnungs-cammer*) for its contracts and accounting. In 1766, long after the war, the *Commissariat* found a final home in the *Hofkriegsrath*.

Even in the Seven Years War the Viennese central bureaucracy remained small in relation to the burden of administration. Just as a great deal of the business of civil life was devolved to the *Stände*, so much of the responsibility for the procurement of materiel still lay with the individual regiments. The colonels were not helped by the administrative turmoil in high quarters, and much later the *Hofrath* Passelt tried to reconstruct what he been going on.

Passelt explains that the end of the war of the Austrian Succession had found many of the regiments with their reserves of cash badly run down or in actual deficit. On 1 November 1748 a new *Oeconomie-Systeme* was based on a set of rules which set out the increased rates of military pay, and the authorised deductions for uniforms, the cloth for which was obtained from state magazines. In every case the coat or its equivalent turns out to be the most expensive single item of uniform and equipment, amounting to 6 florins 23 xr. for an infantry coat of 'pearl-grey Iglau cloth,' 7 florins for the coats of the cuirassiers and dragoons, and 6 florins 30 xr. for the hussar pelisse.

Both the Commissaries and the regiments worked hard to keep their books in order (continues Passelt), but the funds set aside from the soldiers' pay proved inadequate to meet the cost of the uniforms. Nobody had any idea how long the items of clothing and equipment were supposed to last, and not every regiment was equal to the responsibility for making up the uniforms from the bolts of cloth. Passelt describes how 'many regiments were blamed for having failed to take sufficient care in the matter of upkeep, others for trying to embellish their uniforms and equipment, and yet others for having been too greedy in procurement'.[12] The regimental tailors could work cheaply if not particularly elegantly, but something made up in Vienna or Prague could augment the price outrageously. The Commissaries became increasingly suspicious of what was transpiring in the Hungarian regiment of Leopold Pálffy, where the colonel commandant Zigan repeatedly failed to produce the contracts he had made with the Viennese tailor Ruland, claiming that it was enough to know that the prices had remained unchanged since 1752. Maria Theresa finally intervened in person to suspend Zigan from duty and summon him to Vienna to render account.[13] A key role in placing contracts, whether crooked or otherwise, was played by the men of affairs called 'regimental agents,' each of whom represented the interests of one or more regiments in Vienna, and who handled a great variety of official and personal business for the officers. The most considerable of such houses were those of Caballini, Piringer, Preiss, Sagmüller and Költz.

In 1755 seven colonels were called to Vienna to investigate the problem, and the fruit of their debates was a printed *Oeconomie Ordnung*, which set out the permissible duration of every item of uniform and equipment in peacetime. This was at best a partial solution, and it did not attempt to estimate how frequently replacements might be needed in time of war. On 1 November 1757 a complicated *Intercalar Systeme* re-defined the authorised deductions from the soldiers' pay, and left the regiments completely free to buy the cloth for the uniforms as well as make them up. The intentions were good, but the system never recovered from the blow it so very soon received at Leuthen, where the main army lost most of its uniforms, weapons and equipment. Not only were the costs of replacement huge, but the senior regimental officers and quartermasters were overwhelmed by their responsibilities under the new scheme, and Passelt states that the total debt incurred in the army finally amounted to five million florins, and that on 1 November 1761 the army reverted to the system of 1748, in which the state played a larger role. The administrative labours were reduced, but many of the regimental chests were by now cleaned out.

Procurement

In January 1762 Kaunitz stated as a matter of principle that the needs of the military machine should promote native industry and commerce.[14] His arguments probably weighed with Maria Theresa a few months later, when the authorities had to place the contract for uniforms for the Warasdiner Croats. Arguing on purely financial grounds the *Rechnungs-Cammer* (chamber of accounts) spoke in favour of the Thury factory in Vienna, whose bid was cheaper by 9,940 florins than that of its competitors, the partners Ruard and Desselprunner who had just taken over the Weitenhiller factory in Laibach in Carniola. The *Hofkriegsrath* nevertheless argued that the bid from Laibach still deserved serious consideration, for it was 'a question of the collapse of an entire factory which has been brought to its present advanced state of development at much effort and cost, and a question also of the ruin of so many expert workers and the hundreds of people who depend on them.' The two departments submitted their joint report on 26 August. Maria Theresa congratulated the accountants on having done their duty well, but she expressed her preference for the Laibach factory, which in any case produced cloth of incomparably superior quality.[15] The Carlstädter contract was duly awarded to the Weitenhiller factory two days later.

The main centre of military textile production was otherwise to be found in Iglau and the other towns of the Bohemian-Moravian border. The Walloon regiments were at an initial disadvantage, for uniforms of Netherlands manufacture were more expensive by between one-quarter and one-third, though the greater durability made the outlay worth while in the longer term. The green Brussels cloth of the Netherlands dragoons was adopted in the course of the Seven Years War for the newly-designated regiments of *chevaulegers*, and was reproduced after the war in countless portraits of Archduke (later Emperor) Joseph.

The work of obtaining arms and ammunition was managed mainly by Joseph Wenzel Liechtenstein, whose responsibilities as General Artillerie-Director embraced the procurement of weapons, and who placed contracts for firearms, swords, armour and other ironmongery by thousands of units at a time.[16] Affairs further afield were concerted with Prince Charles of Lorraine (Governor-General of the Netherlands from 1758) and the ingenious Major Franz de Piza, who were geographically well placed to contact manufacturers and merchants in the Low Countries, western Germany and Lorraine.

The arrival of the Seven Years War found the Austrians with the stocks of many of their weapons very low, and procurement therefore became a topic of urgent debate in the Military Conferences which were held from October 1756 onwards. The widely scattered centres of firearms production in the German Hereditary Lands were located at Vienna, Wiener-Neustadt, Hainfeld and Steyr in Austria, and Carlsbad, Pressnitz and Weipert in Bohemia. On 12 May 1757 Maria Theresa and Francis Stephen therefore endorsed a proposal of the Military Conference to the effect that 'all the gunsmiths and swordsmiths of the Hereditary Lands should be given appropriate directions to undertake no work for the duration of the war other than for the Imperial army, and to deliver all completed weapons to the Vienna Arsenal in return for payment'.[17]

At the beginning of 1758 the Austrians had a reserve of 45,000 muskets, most of them in poor condition, and only a few carbines and pistols.[18] As if the demands of the war against Prussia were not enough, the Austrians were faced with another serious shortfall towards the end of 1762, when they were faced with the apparent threat of a Tartar or Turkish invasion, and Liechtenstein accordingly gained permission to build up the necessary reserve of 60,000 muskets for the infantry and 10–12,000 sets of carbines and pistols for the cavalry.[19]

How were demands like these to be met? Anton Penzeneter, the largest single native contractor, had factories in Vienna and at Steyr and Hainfeld, but had been unable to produce more than 20,000 muskets a year, which fell far short of what was needed, and throughout the war the Austrians were forced to call on supplies from Malines in the Austrian Netherlands, the Bishopric of Liège, and other sources in the relatively highly-industrialised north-west of Europe. From 1758 many of the deals passed through the hands of Major Franz de Piza of the regiment of Wied (above), who had been wounded at Moys in 1757, but arrived in Brussels on 10 January 1758 to carry out a number of confidential commissions. His first task was to arrange the delivery of 10,000 firearms, whereupon he went to buy billets of iron and 30,000 pounds of gunpowder for the artillery. 'In 1759 [*recte* 1760] an express courier reached me with an order from His Royal Highness [Prince Charles] to go to Holland without delay to arrange for the delivery of 40,000 pounds of cannon powder and 20,000 of musket powder. I made the necessary deal at Amsterdam, even though the powder had already been sold to the enemy. I had it transported by inland canals to prevent it being taken by the English, and in four days I delivered it to the magazines in Antwerp'.[20] Later in 1760 de Piza managed to have 79 pieces of heavy artillery transported by canal from Holland to France, and the French reciprocated by delivering into his custody two Prussian spies, one of whom was later executed in Brussels. At the beginning of 1761 de Piza assumed the guise of an Amsterdam merchant and made his way through the enemy cantonments to Solingen, where he placed a contract for 4,000 sets of bayonets and steel ramrods, and arranged for the transmission of 4,000 fully made-up muskets.

Little can be retrieved from the official papers concerning the procurement of gunpowder, but it is clear from de Piza's comments that the Austrians were buying large quantities abroad. The manufacture and sale of gunpowder in the Hereditary Lands was a state monopoly, run by the artillery, and the manufacturing base was so small that the Military Conference of 12 September 1756 was told that the stocks amounted to no more than 8,000 hundredweight (*Zentner* = 100

German pounds or about 50 kg.). All the mills were set to work, a first consignment of imports was ordered from Nuremberg, and in a measure of near-desperation kegs of gunpowder were dispatched on courier horses to the exposed Moravian fortress of Olmütz.

Again and again, when the discussions of Maria Theresa and her advisers turned on armament, the conclusion was in effect to 'leave it to Liechtenstein.' Until the Liechtenstein family papers are opened up and investigated the story of Austrian military procurement in the Seven Years War will be incomplete. It so happens that the most accessible documents in the public record are those relating to the cavalry, and for the moment these will have to illustrate the very considerable attention which the Austrians devoted to the subject of their armaments as a whole.

The cuirassiers had fallen into some discredit in the campaigns against the Prussians, and they suffered accordingly when the establishment of the army was reduced in the winter of 1761/2. In the autumn of 1762, however, Kaunitz came to believe that Hungary and Austria were under threat of Turkish invasion, and as an inevitable consequence more attention was paid to the cuirassiers, for these heavy horsemen were a prime weapon in combat against the Turks and Tartars. The cuirassiers in their turn needed every protection against clouds of arrows and swarms of enemy light horse. Maria Theresa therefore agreed to augment the cuirassiers, at least in principle, and to purchase the necessary breastplates and the protective iron crosses which were worn inside the cuirassiers' tricorn hats.

Liechtenstein placed the necessary contract with Anton Penzeneter on 26 October. Penzeneter undertook to set his factories in Lower and Upper Austria to work to manufacture 2,000 breastplates, 2,000 back plates, and 1,200 of the iron hat crosses. Delivery was to be by instalments at the contractor's cost to the Imperial Arsenal in Vienna, and completed by the end of April next. The breastplates were to be of good elastic iron, free of cracks, and Penzenter was obliged to replace any breastplates which failed to stand proof against musket shot, and these and any of the other items which did not conform with the designated patterns. Liechtenstein would supply the ammunition for the proofing shots free, and pay on satisfactory delivery 3 florins 15 xr. for every breastplate, 2 florins for every back plate, and 24 xr. for every iron hat cross.[21]

The supposedly suspicious movements continued on the Turkish side of the border, and in November and December 1762 Maria Theresa approved the purchase of further items of cavalry armour, including 3,858 '*Casquets*',[22] a word which might refer to the conventional hat crosses, but more probably to the antique-style 'Pappenheim' or 'Cromwellian' iron helmets which (like the back plates) were employed only on the Eastern theatre.

The manufacture of sword blades was well established in Vienna and in the Austrian provinces at Wiener-Neustadt, Steyr, Sollenau (not to be confused with Solingen in Germany), Pottenstein and Weiz (by Mossdorffer and others) and sword hilts in addition in Vienna (Hauser and Pruchberger) and at Krems (Materna). Here the crucial issues were less about quantity than design and quality, and the consequent debates, which reached no firm conclusion before the war came to an end, tell us a great deal about tactical realities, and the state of the arms industry in Austria.

At the outset of the Seven Years War Maria Theresa determined to establish a great stock of swords for the cuirassiers and dragoons and sabres for the grenadiers, the Hungarian infantry and the hussars. Hitherto the regiments had made their own purchases according to the vague existing norms, and so now the first logical step must be to determine standard patterns for each kind of weapon, 'for I wish to establish absolute uniformity.' The owner of the Sollenau factory, Christoph Metzberg, heard of what was afoot, and made bold to write to Maria Theresa to commend his products, which would be found to be better and cheaper than those manufactured elsewhere in the Austrian provinces, and incomparably better than the Vienna swords.[23]

Nothing more is heard of the matter until 4 January 1758, when Liechtenstein was commissioned to do his best to obtain good swords. The results must have been disappointing, for in 1761 or early in 1762 Maria Theresa asked him to investigate the quality of the work in all the native factories. Liechtenstein established that the greatest problem was to forge a blade that would be neither too ductile nor too brittle. The products of the Wiener-Neustadt factory were very poor; the Sollenau and Steyr blades were more consistent, but best of all were those manufactured by Mossdorffer at Weiz in Styria, which could be flexed hard, and still spring back without distortion. None of the Austrian swords could yet match the excellent steel and the beautiful grinding and polishing of the product of Solingen in Germany, 'but we could induce our factories to do the same if they were serious about putting more work into the weapons, and producing a quality of steel that would make for better and more durable blades.' However the manufacturers of the blades must be forbidden from providing the hilts as well, for they did not have the necessary expertise, they would neglect their own speciality, and they would at the same time take trade away from the makers of the hilts 'who are poor men, and whose craft consists solely in mounting swords'.[24]

The relative prices of the existing products were listed as follows, all the quotations being for unmounted blades:

	Steyr	Wiener-Neustadt	Sollenau	Weiz	Solingen
Infantry sabre:	27 xr.	27 xr.	30 xr.	30 xr.	28 xr.
Cuirassier & dragoon sword:	36 xr. 1 fl.	54 xr. 1 fl.	48 xr.		
Hussar sabre:	45 xr.	48 xr.	54 xr.	48 xr.	48 xr.

(There were 60 creutzer to the florin).

On 23 July 1762 Liechtenstein submitted a pattern for a cuirassier and dragoon blade which was to be designated 'Nr. 1,' and which was priced at 51 xr. He did not conceal his preference for the Solingen swords, but he passed over the qualities of these and other foreign blades in service 'for Your Majesty has graciously ordered me… to take sword blades in future only from native factories'.[25]

Maria Theresa commended the project to the *Hofkriegsrath*, and a few days later Liechtenstein was asked to deposit specimen blades from the various factories in the Arsenal.

On 17 August 1761 the officials of the *Hofkriegsrath* asked Daun to sound the opinions of the field army. Not all of the returns have been preserved, but on 20 August *G.d.C.* Carl O'Donnell replied on behalf of a commission which he had set up among the cuirassiers and dragoons. The officers preferred 'Nr. 1' over a rival pattern which was priced at only 36 xr., though they believed that the swords in existing service were better than either, and there was universal admiration for the Solingen swords of the Erzherzog Leopold Cuirassiers, which handled well and were of first-class steel. The cheap 36-xr. blade would represent poor value, and it was so badly balanced that although it was thinner than the model presently in service, it actually seemed heavier.

O'Donnell's officers also looked into the mounting of the swords in various regiments, and were the most impressed by those of the Erzherzog Leopold and O'Donnell Cuirassiers, which combined a basket hilt with a leather-bound grip, and a wooden scabbard which was bound with good leather and equipped with furniture of brass or wrought iron. Whatever pattern of blade was approved, the officers believed that the regiments ought to obtain their blades directly from the specified factories, rather than take what was issued from the Imperial Arsenal, so that they could see what they were getting; likewise the regiments should order their hilts and scabbards under their own arrangements, and not least because the metal work was traditionally of brass in some regiments, but of iron in others.[26]

Daun passed on O'Donnell's recommendation to the body of the *Hofkriegsrath*, which decided in its turn to ask Liechtenstein to find out whether Mossdorffer in Weiz could produce blades of the same 'quality, breadth and lightness' as the highly-prized Solingen sword.[27] Another round of local consultations was set in train in December, but nothing more was determined before hostilities came to an end.

Supply in the Field

The resources that were expended on clothing and weapons were dwarfed in terms of both cost and tonnage by the effort which went into feeding the army's troops and horses. Here a leading role was taken by the *Feld Proviant-Amt*, which was bureaucratically part of the Treasury (*Hofcammer*), but which worked in close association with the *Commissariat*. It was headed by a civilian *Obrist-Proviant-Amts-Lieutenant*, whose staff expanded into the hundreds at the coming of war, and was drawn from the educated near-proletariat which was to be found throughout the more advanced countries of 18th-century Europe. The author of the *Patriotic Reflections* was predictably affronted by the social pretensions of the Proviant officials. Their pay (like that of the officials of the *Commissariat*) was good, but it could not support their spectacular style of life, for 'you just have to wait six or 10 months or a year before you see them decked out in gold and silver; a couple of years on they will appear fitted out most magnificently, living high off the hog, and making various other outlays. If it were the case of a single official you might conclude that he had a private fortune, but it applies to all of them who have ever been responsible for taking on a supply depot or passing it on'.[28]

Any fraud was virtually impossible to detect, for the quantities of foodstuffs were so great, and the consumption was subject to a great number of variables. At the beginning of 1757 Friedrich Haugwitz and Rudolph Chotek had to calculate the ration strengths of the army for the coming campaign, and in the absence of any detailed figures they worked on estimates of 200,00 daily rations of bread, and 80,000 daily rations of fodder.[29] They were not very far wide of the mark, as was confirmed much later by some investigations (1792) of the NostitzRieneck reform commission, which brought to light two relevant sets of figures. They differ marginally in detail:

Rations over War as a Whole

Total of all Combatant and Non-combatant Personnel in Field according to Establishment

Daily Bread Rations, incl. attached Non-combatants, and allowing usual Deduction of 15 percent for Wastage

		Infantry	Cavalry	Total	
1757:	164,070	126,713	31,582	158,385	
1758:	232,634	161,612	52,399	214,011	
1759:	227,974	158,016	51,733	209,749	
1760:	228,570	158,150	56,450	214, 600	
1761:	218,053	149,683	51,496	201,179	
1762:	186,630	(?)	140,053	46,030	186,083

Daily Fodder Rations for Cavalry and Transport Horses, allowing 15 percent for Standard Reduction for Wastage of Horses

1757:	56,005
1758:	76,786
1759:	89,067
1760:	96,600
1761:	not available
1761:	78,575[30]

Daily Rations in 1758

Infantry: (probably incl. requirement for private baggage)	175,488 men; 190,131 bread rations	2,096 horses; 17,136 fodder rations
Cavalry:	51,166 men; 61,645 bread rations	51, 490 horses; 60,081 fodder rations
Transport, bakery etc.:	5,980 men; 8,891 bread rations	11,580 horses; 15,619 fodder rations
Grand Total:	232,634 men; 260,667 bread rations	65,160 horses; 92,836 fodder rations
Minus Standard Reduction of 15 percent for Wastage of Men and Horses	221,567 bread rations	78,911 fodder rations.[31]

Neither set of figures makes allowance for the requirements of the artillery, General Staff, headquarters, or the technical services.

The ration, or rather food allowance of the Austrian private soldier in wartime, comprised one pound of meat and one-and-three-quarter pounds of bread. Unlike his Prussian counterpart, the Austrian had to purchase his meat from his own funds. However the regiments were under an obligation to make it available at reasonable prices from the authorised regimental butchers. The rates of consumption were never calculated exactly, though it was reckoned in February 1760 that 300 oxen a week would suffice for the Austrian troops in Saxony, and 700 for the army as a whole. The butchers bought their animals from the *Commissariat*, which in turn purchased them from a private entrepreneur who obtained his oxen from Hungary and Poland. The *Ober-Landes-Kriegs-Commissarius* Count Clary took the contractor Postl to task because his oxen had lost between 10 and 20 percent of their weight in meat by the time they had reached Vienna on the way to the army. A commission was convened to look into the matter, and was told by the Vienna butchers, 'who are by no means well inclined towards Postl,' that such a loss was inevitable, given the distance the animals had to be driven, and the lack of pasture along the way.[32]

The bread ration was made up of rye mixed with a little wheat, which caused a dispute in 1757 when the question arose of feeding a French auxiliary corps from Austrian sources. The attaché Montazet complained that such a diet would not suit the French, whereupon the Austrians replied that the much-lauded French rations were made up of equal parts of wheat, rye and bran, and were less nutritious than the Austrian formula.[33]

Except in a few emergencies, as during the disorganised retreat into Bohemia after the battle of Leuthen, the troops rarely went short of this basic commodity. The soldiers carried up to four days' worth of bread with them, and the army was supported by baking companies whose light and efficient ovens were the envy of Europe. They were built up (probably with bricks) around iron hoops, and they could be put together, taken apart for transport, and reassembled with remarkable ease.

The composition of the horse rations was a matter of much calculation and debate (see p. 288). Six pounds of oats per day was regarded as the foundation of the feed, though Carl Paul Pálffy pointed out that 'we should not confine ourselves to oats to the exclusion of all other grains. It is admittedly the most palatable and the most useful, but it is not the only one which can keep the horses going and in serviceable condition, for barley, rye and so on can be used if no oats are available'.[34] Indeed before the battle of Kolin the cavalry's horses were found to be in a bad way because they had been fed for months on oats to the exclusion of almost everything else. The requirement for 'raw' fodder (hay and straw) stood at between 10 and 12 pounds pounds daily, though it was hard to judge the proportions to everyone's satisfaction.

The difficulties were compounded in the case of a force which had to cut loose from its magazines and lines of supply. In September 1760 the Prince of Zweibrücken was attracted by the idea of launching eight battalions and four squadrons of the *Reichsarmee* in a raid on Berlin. However the enemy capital was 10 marches distant, and experience showed that the peasants along the way would be likely to hide their stores of oats before the corps arrived on the scene. The cavalry must therefore be furnished with at least half-rations of oats beforehand, to supplement whatever raw fodder could be commandeered along the way.[35]

In matters logistic generally the authorities constantly balanced two sets of considerations, the one relating to the locations where the provisions were to be obtained, and the other to the work of transporting the provisions from one place to another. Supplies were raised over areas of extraordinary extent, and Armfeldt found that the feed for the horses was derived not only from the theatres of war in Silesia and Saxony, but from Bohemia, Moravia, Austria, and Hungary as far as the Ottoman border. Even the *Reichsarmee* was deriving its oxen from distant Poland.[36]

The Prussians enjoyed the facility of transport up the water avenues of the Elbe and the Oder, which were studded with their fortresses and depots. The Austrians never had enough of Silesia in their possession for sufficient time to avail themselves of the Oder. When they made use of the Elbe, they had to haul their provisions and other materiel overland to Melnik or Leipnik, which represented only a marginal saving. The Danube was useful for transporting foodstuffs from Hungary, though ice might render the river impassable in late winter, in which case the road haulage would add very heavily to the cost.

The Prussians were also at an advantage in political terms. Frederick was autocratic master of Silesia, with its fine plains and prosperous towns, while in Saxony he grabbed everything he needed by a systematic application of force. The Austrians enjoyed no such freedoms. In normal circumstances they drew their *Naturalien* by contracts with the *Stände* of the German Hereditary Lands, the Hungarian magnates and private entrepreneurs. By August 1761, however, the system was under severe strain. A compulsory levy of 100,000 *Zentner* (i.e. about 5,000 tons) of flour was being exacted in the German Hereditary Lands, but Maria Theresa set herself against any further levies of the kind, for they would plunge her subjects still deeper into debt to the money lenders. Truly competitive commercial contracts were believed to be more economical and efficient, and Maria Theresa hoped that they would sustain the army in Silesia through the winter. It was a different matter for the army in Saxony, which simply could not live at the cost of Bohemia, but must extend its control in Saxon territory and raise the necessary supplies there. There were also military reasons for keeping an army in Saxony, and not least because it would deny Saxon resources to the enemy. The Austrian demands in the Saxon territory of Lusatia would amount to 200,000 *Zentner* of flour, 250,000 *Zentner* of hay, and 500,000 Lower Austrian measures (*Metzen*) of oats (or about 30,750,000 litres, at 61.5 litres to the measure), and if the *Stände* proved recalcitrant, the supplies would be raised anyway by executive action. The Austrians would set the prices, and pay one-third in redeemable coupons upon delivery, and the rest by instalments.[37]

These (unfortunately for the Austrian finances) were not empty promises, for it was important to emphasise the status of Saxony as an ally and fellow-victim of Prussian aggression, and the Austrians were already paying very heavily for what they were taking in the electorate.[38]

The expedient of private contract, from which so much had been hoped, collapsed in the early summer of 1762, for the chief forage contractor Löbel Hönig declared on 30 April that he had been left for so long unpaid that he could no longer deliver any supplies. It could not have happened at a worse time, for Daun's army in Silesia was due to take to the field on 14 May, and the harvest could not be gathered in before the end of July. The Austrians were rescued by energetic action on the part of their *Obrist-Kriegs-Proviant-Commissarius* Johann Georg Baron Grechtler, who without further reference to Vienna ordered up the available rearward stocks to the theatres of war, made heavy requisitions in the Bohemian circles of Chrudim, Czaslau and Königgrätz, and hired the necessary transport from the peasants.[39]

In fact at no time in the war were the Austrians troops free of the need to go a-foraging. This was intended to be a disciplined procedure, and, when it was carried out on a large scale, mixed or whole-unit detachments were put together from every battalion or squadron of the relevant wing or line. Officers and Commissaries were supposed to ensure that the parties did not stray outside their designated areas, or into villages without special authorisation, that they mowed the growing grass in the fields before they turned to the stores of hay or grain, and that all other cereals and crops were to be held sacrosanct for the use of the peasants, and spared even from being trampled down. On the return to camp a senior regimental officer was to examine the bundles of fodder and make sure that no stolen valuables had been secreted inside.[40]

In reality the prescriptions were widely ignored. According to Armfeldt 'the foraging was never carried out in an orderly way, at least during the time [1759–62] I spent with the Austrian army... An Austrian force is incapable of subsisting from a given area for as long as a force of Prussians'.[41] Lieutenant Giuseppe Gorani supplies some deplorable details. On September 1757 he descended on a village near Moys with 40 troops and a train of carts, under orders to commandeer a large quantity of oats and hay. The leader of the local community told him that his demands were impossible to meet:

> but my orders were so strict that I had no latitude. I had my men bring up a bench, and I had the village chief stretched across it to be beaten on his behind until he revealed where the requisite rations could be found. After three or four wallops the unfortunate man promised to meet my demand. He kept his word, for the slightest delay would have drawn down a hail of blows.

A few days later Gorani and his men were in confrontation with a party of the regiment of Hildburghausen, which had been assigned to forage on the same patch of ground; he arrayed his troops to receive an attack, but before battle could begin a senior staff officer arrived, and pronounced in Gorani's favour.[42]

There was scarcely a pretence of restraint in areas of Germany such as Saxony outside the political electorate. Thus for year after year the Austrians and the *Reichsarmee* had forced the little Sachsen-Gotha principality of Altenburg to yield up great quantities of grain and raw fodder, and in November 1761 the Austrians tested Duke Friedrich's tolerance beyond endurance, when their *Executions-Commandi* roamed at will over the country, and even broke into the stores of the ducal Schloss in Altenburg town (see p. 93).[43] This was poor reward for a family which had provided *Inhaber* for two regiments in the Austrian service.

At any given time a large proportion of the available provisions and fodder was stored in magazines, whether the large semi-permanent depots, or the '*filial*' or 'flying' magazines which followed the army and had no fixed location, as Daun explained to Maria Theresa in 1761.[44] There was seldom any lack of storage space in the cities of Prague and Dresden, towns like Königgrätz, Olmütz and Zittau, or in the multitude of smaller places scattered over both sides of the borders with Saxony and Silesia. Ready-milled flour, being particularly vulnerable to damp, was kept in barrels, and was stored in barns, monastery corridors and any other reliably dry locations.[45]

A review of the field magazines as they existed on 28 August 1757 showed that depots had been established in:

> *Bohemia*: Budweis, Czaslau, Eger, Gabel, Jung-Bunzlau, Königgrätz, Kolin, Kuttenberg, Moldautein, Nimburg, Neuhaus, Niemes, Pardubitz, Prague, Politschka, Deutsch-Brod, Wartenberg

Moravia: Brünn, Gross-Meseritsch, Hradisch, Iglau, Olmütz, Znaim
Lusatia: Zittau
Silesia: Landeshut, Trautenau

The commodities in store amounted to:

Rice:	1,554.32 *Zentner* (at 100 lb. to the *Zentner*)
Flour:	192,801.97 *Zentner*
Bread:	406,912 rations
Biscuit:	100,516 rations
Oats:	170,399 *Zentner*
Barley:	151,996.5 *Zentner*
Hay:	448,642 rations at 11 lb. each
Fodder straw:	30,144 rations at 14 lb. each
Camp straw:	17,930 bales at 12 lb. each
Full barrels:	26,166
Empty barrels:	21,453
Full sacks:	14,771
Empty sacks:	64,209[46]

The stores were removed and re-established many times in the course of the war, and Leitmeritz and Lobositz in northern Bohemia assumed increasing importance, for they were situated near the head of the navigation of the Elbe, and helped to support campaigns well into Saxony, at least once they had been stocked up by means of overland transport.

It was one thing to build a magazine conveniently near a theatre of active operations, but something altogether different to be able to secure it against the enemy. If we discount Prague and Olmütz (which were situated comparatively deep inside Bohemia and Moravia respectively) and Dresden (which was not always in Austrian possession), the Austrians had nothing to compare with the constellation of forward fortress-depots which were available to Frederick at Cosel, Brieg, Schweidnitz, Neisse and Glatz, which had strong defences, and were replenished by water transport or short overland haulage. To all intents and purposes Wittenberg and Torgau in Saxony could also be counted as Prussian depots, for they were in Prussian hands for almost the entire war, and were fed constantly by the channel of the Elbe from the great magazines at Magdeburg.

In the Military Conference of 9 January 1757 Neipperg mentioned that the element of security should not be neglected when it came to placing the magazines for the next campaign.[47] Maria Theresa instead followed the advice of the forceful FM. Browne, who argued that the magazines must be sited where they would be closest at hand to support Austria's coming offensive. He did not reckon on the enemy getting in their blow first. In April the Prussians launched an all-out invasion of Bohemia, overran the outlying magazines, and used the captured stores (especially the fodder at Jung-Bunzlau) to sustain their advance into the heart of Bohemia. The ensuing crisis lasted until it was resolved in favour of the Austrians when Daun beat Frederick at Kolin.

The Austrians never experienced misfortunes on this scale again. However the *Directorium* and the *Stände* were in the habit of planting magazines as happened to be convenient for the landowners, to save them the cost of transport, and Prince Henry of Prussia found that the exposed depots in northern Bohemia made productive targets before the main campaigning season began. After one such raid in 1759 Maria Theresa finally lost patience and ordered Netolitzky in Bohemia and Blümegen in Moravia to render reports on the state of their supplies to Daun every 14 days, and do nothing without his approval. If something went wrong, not only would those responsible be singled out for blame, but the *Stände* would have to replace the supplies that had been lost.[48]

Transport

The typical freight vehicle in the Austrian service was a four-horse cart which was capable of carrying a load of 17 *Zentner*, or the best part of a ton, and was almost invariably hired from civilian sources. The Prince de Ligne reckoned that 1,200 such vehicles in single file took up 18,000 paces of road.[49] The carts were assigned variously to the artillery's *Rosspartei*, to the regimental, private and sutlers' baggage, and in the greatest quantities to the official *Feld Proviant-Fuhrwesen* which transported provisions for man and horse. The Bautzen Manuscript of 1762 indicates that the *Proviant* carts had been 'militarised' to some extent by having an individual number painted on the front, and the load protected by what seems to be a red tarpaulin, held down by crosswise canvas bands, one bearing the number of the parent transport column, and the other the proprietorial sign '*Proviant Wagen*'.

In peacetime the *Feld Proviant-Furhwesen* existed only in the form of a handful of experienced civilian *Verwalter*, or overseers. These people sprang into action when the army was mobilised, and they hired carts, teams and drivers by the thousand for shorter or longer periods of service. The drivers remained civilians, although uniformed smartly in grey or greyish-blue coats with yellow collars, cuffs and turn-backs, and a yellow armband bearing the black eagle. 'From supervisor to driver they were all professional waggoneers and knew about horses. There was no costly corps staff, and no military officers' salaries to remain a burden to the state after the war had ended'.[50] The trains were brigaded into *Verwalterschaften*, of which there were two in 1756 and 1757; in 1760 a reorganisation increased the number to four, each consisting of six *Officiersschaften* of about 56 vehicles each.

The whole of the recent history of military transport was investigated by the NostitzRieneck reform commission in the early 1790s, and Lieutenant-Colonel Gomez supplies some details relating to the Seven Years War. The divergence between the two sets of figures are probably explained by short-term hirings:

Transport in Service

	Carts	Horses	Personnel
1757:	400	1,600	653
1758:	1,000	3,421	1,345
1759:	2,000	8,080	3,341
1760:	1,340	5,360	3,990
1761:	”	”	”
1762:	”	”	”[51]

Transport Requirements

	Number of Carts required	How far met
1757:	1,331	-475
1758:	1,816	+204
1759:	1,965	+105
1760:	2,072	+231
1761:	1,829	+382
1762:	1,744	+546

Gomez explains that the surplus from 1758 to 1762 proved useful for transporting the iron baking ovens, and especially in 1760, when the armies were very scattered; in 1761 part of the surplus was used to help the Russian army.[52]

On this evidence the *Feld Proviant-Furhwesen* in itself was an efficient organisation which more than met the needs of the army in bulk transport, and was flexible enough to respond to unforeseen circumstances.

The quantity of vehicles and draught animals in total was augmented literally beyond counting by the regimental transport, and the authorised (and still greater unauthorised) baggage of the officers, and by the transport of the camp followers, not to mention the trains of ox carts bringing up fodder to the magazines under arrangements made by the *Stände* or contractors. Armfeldt was struck by the bulk attained in the Austrian army by everything that was associated with the name 'provisioning.' This was in part the inevitable result of the distances over which supplies had to be hauled from Bohemia, Moravia, Austria and Hungary, but it was less easy to justify the eight or 10 carts which some generals found necessary for their personal service: 'altogether the baggage train of the Austrians is larger and heavier than in any other army in the world'.[53] Perhaps he would have modified his judgement if he had seen the Russian transport train at close quarters.

The question of the regimental baggage had escaped the attention of the military reformers, but on 19 June 1757 Maria Theresa enquired after the allowance of the relevant horses and vehicles. Neipperg replied that matters were still governed by a *Marche-Regulament* of 28 December 1747, which authorised two carts for the senior regimental officers, two for every company of infantry, one for every company of cavalry, and a 'proportionate' number of provision and tent carts.

The need for a strict and enforceable code was brought home by the chaotic retreat after the battle of Leuthen late in 1757. 'The blame certainly rests to some extent with the *Furhwesen*, for the convoys of carts are often so long that you cannot see from one end to the other, but the chief causes are the want of discipline among the convoys, and the lack of strong escorts. The baggage carts set off too early or too late, and, because no proper order is observed, each driver strives to race the others to their destination.' The officers cared only for the vehicles under their immediate command, 'and it is hardly surprising that 50 enemy hussars were able to reduce everything to a state of consternation and panic-stricken flight'.[54]

The regimental baggage proper was probably contained within reasonable bounds, but nobody was keeping a check on the personal baggage of the generals and officers, who were indifferent to the blockages they caused on the roads, and the inordinate demands they made on manpower and local resources. In the *Militär Feld-Regulament* of 1759 Maria Theresa had to remind the generals and officers that she had provided them with an allowance of free transport (as designated by the fodder rations), and that everything above that must be regarded as 'a superfluous luxury and indeed as selfish obstinacy'.[55]

The transport trains were lengthened still further by the carts of the butchers, regimental sutlers and camp followers – those mercenary men and still tougher women who retailed meat, coffee, vegetables, fruit, butter, plundered goods, and liquors of doubtful origin. 'Don't let the soldiers buy any wine,' warned the Prince de Ligne. 'The liquid on sale is a concoction of various red fruits laced with spirits, which gives the men frightful stomach cramps'.[56] The presence of this 'licentious and idle scum was tolerated by the army, for it was impossible for the soldiers to subsist on their rations of bread alone, and the regiments sought to impose a modicum of control by demanding licences and taxes, limiting prices, and subjecting the rabble to the authority of the *Profos*. The sutlers were supposed to gather in their stores well away from the camp, so that the local peasants could bring in their produce for sale without fear of intimidation. Likewise 'the regiments must send some really trustworthy men to frequent the tents of the coffee vendors, Jews and butchers, and the retailers at the headquarters, and keep their eyes and ears open to discover if there are any people there who are encouraging the soldiers to desert'.[57]

The sutlers' stalls nevertheless remained the haunts of soldiers' wives, thieves, cut-throats, prostitutes and spies. They kept themselves out of harm's way on the day of battle, and then, when the smoke was still clearing from the field, they sallied forth to strip the dead and wounded of their clothing and effects, leaving the soldiers lying bloody and naked scarcely minutes after they had fallen in the service of their sovereign.

16

Body and Soul

MEDICAL AND SURGICAL PROVISION

In no other branch of the Austrian service do we encounter such contrasts and contradictions between skill and ignorance, dedication and corruption, than in its health care. One of the reasons is that we catch Austrian medicine and surgery in the early stages of its rapid ascent from Hogarthian squalor to a status which, by the 1780s, was ranked among the finest of the continent. It was more than a question of reaching defined standards, because there was no agreement as to what good medical provision for an army should be. Bureaucratic muddle also played its part, for responsibility for the care of the soldiers was divided between the civilian *Directorium* on the one hand, and the military commanders and the *Hofkriegsrath* on the other.

The absence of clear authority was compounded by the fact that in Europe generally there was still no unified medical profession as such. The *medici*, or physicians, claimed superiority over the *Chyrurgi* and their assistants the *Feldschere* (orderlies), who at the lower end of the scale were represented by the creatures who let veins in barbers' shops – in other words people far removed from the image of mystical, masked and begowned authority represented by the word 'surgeon' in later times. The distinction was emphasised repeatedly by Van Swieten: 'How can you think of subjecting a physician to the judgement of surgeons when it comes to the treatment of diseases?'.[1]

The Pioneers – Brady, Van Swieten, Wabst and Graffenhuber

Any advance in medical care for the army would have to depend on two processes that went hand in hand – namely winning a degree of independence and status for the practitioners as a whole, and lifting the surgeons from their bloody mire through selection and training. The authorities in Vienna were unaware how bad things were until the middle 1740s, when some telling protests were entered by the *Proto-Medicus* (chief army physician) Dr. Brady, and by the Dr. Engel who succeeded him in September 1746. Unqualified and corrupt regimental and company *Feldschere* were being taken into the service without discrimination, and it was not uncommon for them to practice frauds to the tune of 8,000 florins per year. Likewise the disorders in the *Apotheken* (dispensaries) and hospitals went unchecked until the *Proto-Medicus* was finally allowed access and authority in 1746.

The work of the reformers was given new impetus by one of the leading figures of the 'Austrian Enlightenment, the large and genial Catholic Dutchman Gerhard Van Swieten (1700–72), a pupil of the celebrated Herman Boerhaave (1668–1702). Maria Theresa summoned Van Swieten from Leyden in 1745, and three years later she commissioned him to convert the medical faculty of the re-founded University of Vienna into a state-controlled school which would pioneer standards in the healing arts. In the period relevant to us the graduates of the new faculty were comparatively few, at a total of 91 between 1751 and 1762, and fewer still would have had anything to do with military medicine. However it is important for our story that Van Swieten now sought to control the admission of the regimental *Feldschere* (re-named '*Regiments Chyrurgi*' in 1752) and the company *Unter-Feldschere*, and also of the army's physicians. We find characteristic notes reaching the *Directorium* and the *Hofkriegsrath*: 'Michael Sebastianus Schober has undergone examination here [Vienna]. He is found to be most able, and has consequently been admitted as a physician. More physicians are needed urgently for Her Imperial Majesty's service. I propose Schober for inclusion in their ranks, and would ask for him to be sent without delay to take up his duties, for there will be much for him to do'.[2] On 7 April 1758 Maria Theresa reserved all appointments to the posts of headquarters *Staabs-Chyrurgi* and the regimental surgeons to herself, or effectively to Van Swieten, and she told the regiments that in future no *Feldschere* would be admitted without permission.[3]

Looking back from the end of the 1770s Cogniazzo pronounced that Van Swieten had rid the army of empirical quacks, and replaced them by regimental surgeons who combined high professional knowledge with the ability to impart that knowledge to the *Feldschere*.[4] At the time of the Seven Years War that process had scarcely begun, for many unqualified practitioners were still reaching the army uncontrolled, in defiance of the orders. Moreover Van Swieten was rooted for most of the time in Vienna, and he could exercise only a distant and indirect influence on standards in the field. Here the responsibility for building a respectable corps of physicians and surgeons fell largely on Christian Xaver Wabst (author of *De Hydrago Tentament Physio-Chemico-Medicum*, Vienna 1754), who held the post of *Feld Proto-Medicus* for most of the war.

Wabst first made his mark on 3 February 1757 when as *Feld Medicus Promorius* he attended a meeting under the presidency of Van Swieten. He told the *General-Kriegs-Commissarius* Salburg that the existing *Feld-Spittals-Ordnung* (1 May 1738) was a dead letter, for the sick and wounded soldiers were being left without proper attention, and their food was being ruined by ignorant and idle cooks. He had protested strongly against these abuses, but had been told not to meddle in affairs that were variously the concern of the military commanders, the *Commissariat* or the *Proviant-Amt*. 'He therefore pressed most urgently for Her Imperial Majesty to be gracious enough to issue a decree endowing him with absolute power over the hospital system... thus enabling him to manage every detail according to his judgement and instructions, without any need for further reference...' The other members supported Wabst's recommendations, and Maria Theresa gave her immediate and unreserved approval.[5] Armed with this authority the new *General Director gesamter K.K. Militär-Spitäller* was proof even against the protests of Brady, who complained that Wabst owed his power to the favour of Haugwitz, and was using it in an arrogant way.[6]

In April 1758 Wabst advised Maria Theresa on the distinction that must be made between the ailing soldiers who could be treated adequately in the regimental depots, and the more serious cases who were to be forwarded to the regular hospitals.[7] On 12 June 1759 he elaborated and expanded this and other notions in a lengthy draft *Instruktion für die Kaiserl. Königlichen Regiments-Chyrurgos*. The regimental surgeon was to be a qualified, skilful and diligent man who kept his instruments and medicaments complete and in good order (Articles 1, 2, 3) and procured his drugs, bandages and compresses from the *Feld-Apotheke* under strictly-controlled procedures (Articles 4, 5, 6), thus eliminating a major source of fraud. He was to admit only such *Feldschere* as had been examined in Vienna, issue them with copies of the new treatise of field medicine (*Tractat and Heilungsart*, 1758) and hold them under narrow supervision. 'Moreover, should he find that any *Feldscher* is so negligent, debauched or clumsy as to be incapable of learning or understanding, or of applying himself to his duties, he is to notify his name to the *Proto-Medicus* so that appropriate measures may be taken.'

Further articles defined the treatment of officers (13), the frequency of the rounds (15), the surgeons' and orderlies' responsibilities on the battlefield (16, 17), and the need to keep a full and up-to-date record of the comings and goings of patients among the three new categories of hospitals – the regimental depots, the *Interim-Spitäller*, and the *Haubt-Spitäller* (18). Wabst provided samples of forms where the necessary details could be entered, along with forms relating to the procurement and dispensing of medicines.[8] Maria Theresa and the *Directorium* approved this substantial document, whichmay be seen as the foundation of Austrian military medicine, and in October or November the printed copies were distributed by the *Hofkriegsrath*.

Wabst himself was probably mortally ill when Maria Theresa ennobled him on 7 August 1760 with the suffix 'von Leidensfeld' (Field of Suffering). He died shortly afterwards, and was succeeded by the former *Feld Medicus* Wolfgang Graffenhuber.

The reformers had to defend their hard-won gains against colonels who were given to clapping their surgeons in irons, and subjecting their *Feldschere* to demeaning corporal punishments. On such occasions the *Hofkriegsrath* almost always ruled against the military men, and in May 1758 Maria Theresa resolved a still more important issue, after Van Swieten claimed that General Baron Bretton had taken it on himself to question the professional competence of *Staabs-Medicus* Lackner and other senior medical staff in Moravia.

It was true that 2,000 men had died when Lackner was working in Olmütz, but Van Swieten explained that was only because half-dead men had been dumped there in enormous quantities. Lackner had graduated in Vienna and was duly furnished with his Diploma, 'which is a public confirmation of his ability, and one which I believe carries some weight.' He had nevertheless been summoned to answer before a kangaroo court composed of Colonel Leopold Utmann, a local surgeon, a number of *Feldschere*, and a single physician – *Creys-Medicus* (district medical officer) Christian Wandel. Van Swieten maintained that even Wanders competence was in doubt, 'for the stories about vampires in Moravia are still recent, and too much in need of rebuttal, for me to have a favourable opinion of the local physicians, who would never have allowed themselves to be taken in by these fables if they had been good doctors.' The *Creys-Medici* in Bohemia and Moravia in general were of dismal quality, and Van Swieten had just received a letter from Professor MacNeven of Prague University complaining about the ignorance and idleness of the Bohemian variety: 'I know seven of them," writes Mac-Neven, "who are so stupid that they give the impression of being unaware of even the first rudiments of medicine. You may judge for yourself from the report I enclose, which has been drawn up by one of the best of the bunch." I have this paper in my hands, and it is so contrary to the rules of the science, so badly written and so confused that I have never seen such a mess in my life'.[9]

Maria Theresa was convinced, 'and not just because he writes so entertainingly, but because every word rings true – which is rare nowadays!' She ordered the *Hofkriegsrath* to convey a verbal rebuke to Bretton, and order him and all the other local commanders to forward any complaints to Vienna, and not indulge in any further unauthorised proceedings.[10]

Much of what had been achieved so far was still being undermined by the failings of the overstretched *Directorium*, which had the general welfare of the troops among its many responsibilities. In the last years of the peace the Commissaries had still been vigilant in this respect. On mustering the 11 regiments in Moravia in 1755 they discovered that 'the soldiers are unhealthy… which is attributed in large part to the dampness of the barracks, which are built mostly from porous stone, though there is sickness also in the new barracks which are of brick construction. An important contributory factor is probably the way the troops are crammed together in winter time to spare firewood.' On reviewing the stocks of medicines held by the regiments they found that the regiment of Erzherzog Carl had drugs to the value of 637 florins 37 xr. in store, 'which is considerably more than in the other regiments, though this regiment has admittedly the most sick, which is blamed largely on the noxious air of Olmütz'.[11]

By 1760 the *Directorium* was clearly unequal to the burden of supervision, and it was probably for that reason that Daun proposed that the senior medical personnel of the headquarters and regiments should meet every month as a '*General Sanitäts Commission*.' On 3 December 1760 the new Feld *Proto-Medicus* Graffenhuber assembled the first such gathering, to confer about 'the endemic diseases and how they might be remedied'.[12] Records have been preserved of further commissions in 1761 at Dresden on 25 January, and at Cosmanos on 5–6 February, Neuhaus on 7 March, and at Cosmanos again on 25 April, and it is likely that they continued on a monthly basis until the end of the war. The measures decided related mostly to examining the surgeons and orderlies, inspecting the holdings of the *Feld-Apotheken*, and (in great detail) the state of care in the hospitals.

The Personnel

The *Staabs-Medici* were lordly and remote personages, who dwelt mostly at the headquarters of the respective field armies, while claiming institutional and intellectual authority over their immediate counterparts – the *Staabs-Chyrurgi*, and over the regimental *Chyrurgi* and *Feldschere* at the unit level.

The domain of the *Chyrurgi* and the *Feldschere* was historically that of external medicine – letting blood, pulling teeth, setting fractures, trussing ruptures, lancing boils, dressing wounds, burns and ulcers, excising superficial tumours and the more accessible bullets, and performing amputations. The *Chyrurgi* in military service also assumed responsibility for the internal medicine and the health of their charges in general – matters from which they would have been excluded in civil life. The Commissaries had a number of rough and ready criteria for judging the competence of these people at the periodic *Musterungen*. How diligent had they been at visiting the sick? Had they been too liberal in dispensing costly drugs from their medicine chests? No informed judgement was passed on surgical proceedings, though in 1755 the surgeon of the regiment of Alt-Colloredo was criticised for having made a bad job of setting the broken arm of one of the Commissaries. Rates of mortality from sickness were expected to be high, and thus the surgeon of the regiment of Kaiser could be praised for having brought the number of deaths down to 15 over a period of six months.[13]

More exacting standards were demanded by the new *Sanitäts Commission*en. At the first sitting, in Dresden on 3 December 1760, Graffenhuber and the *Staabs-Medici* and *Chyrurgi* reported that:

> sad experience confirms that up to the present date a number of the *Feldschere* possess little or nothing of even a superficial knowledge of human anatomy, and are therefore of not the slightest help to the wounded soldiers. We have accordingly concluded that we must hold a College of Anatomy here through the winter; we have already settled on the location, and all that remains is to obtain the consent of Baron Van Swieten.

The commission levelled the blame for this 'appalling ignorance' on the regimental surgeons, who had failed to live up to the obligation of instructing their orderlies.[14]

It is difficult at first sight to reconcile these failures with the work which Van Swieten and the rest had put into improving the state of military medicine, but the author of the *Patriotic Reflections* identified the reason as the constant wastage of personnel. Many of the intending *Feldschere* consisted of students, primitive barber surgeons and other young folk. 'They go on campaign for two or three years, and try their hand at the cost of the deaths of many thousands of poor soldiers, and perhaps they pick up a little knowledge in the process.' They were then in a position to leave the army, set up practice in civil life, and marry on their lucrative incomes.[15]

Our muster lists show up to 92 regimental *Chyrurgi* and 983 *Feldschere* listed under one or more of the headings which relate to nationality, age and service:

Chyrurgi
Place of Birth

Reich:	29.11%
Vienna:	8.86
Vorder-Österreich (a remarkably high figure):	6.84
Bohemia:	5.76
(incl. Prague at 1.26) Moravia, Hungary with Transylvania, Prussian Silesia:	5.06 each
Prussia (other), Italy (other), France (other):	3.79 each
Carinthia, Austrian Italy, Netherlands with Luxembourg:	2.53 each
Austrian Silesia, Slavonia, Alsace, Lorraine, Holland, Poland, Norway:	1.26 each
Lower and Upper Austria (excl. Vienna):	1.1
Other:	2.53
Average Age:	41 years
Average Service:	16.5 years

Feldschere
Place of Birth

Reich:	34.9 %
Bohemia:	16.39
(incl. Prague at	1.95)
Lower & Upper Austria (excl. Vienna):	7.85
Vienna:	7.65
Hungary with Transylvania:	7.43
Prussian Silesia:	5.46
Moravia:	5.13
Other:	16.42
Average Age:	28 years
Average Service:	2 years

Life and Death in Field and Hospital

On campaign the *Regiments-Chyrurgus* was supposed never to allow himself to be separated from his precious medicine chest, which accompanied him on a cart or packhorse, or to let the *Feldschere* escape from his supervision. This, however, was an area where it was proper for the military men to exercise their authority, and immediately before a battle the commanderin-chief was entitled to detach an experienced lieutenant (probably a promoted NCO) to help to bring the surgical personnel to order, for on such occasions they had a way of disappearing from view. They were now positioned in groups 600 or 700 paces to the rear of their respective divisions, where they kept up great smoky fires of wood or hay as a guide to the soldiers who were told off to carry the casualties to the dressing stations. All the other troops were forbidden to leave their rank and file on pain of death. The less seriously wounded men were patched up and sent back to the firing line, while the rest were given what attention was possible on the spot, and held ready for transportation.

The particular duties of the surgeon were spelled out in Wabst's *Instruction* of 1759. He was to make certain that all his *Feldschere* were equipped beforehand with the necessary bandages, compresses, lint, and hemp packing, and with spirits, vinegar or salted water to cleanse wounds.

Once in action the surgeon and his men were under a 'strict duty not to disappear in search or plunder, or otherwise absent themselves, for experience shows that when a *Feldscher* notices that a wounded officer has plenty of money, he will devote himself to his service out of self-interest, and go off with him.' Regardless of their parent regiments, all *Feldschere*, including those of unengaged units, were to lend a hand when wounded men were collected in any quantity.[16]

After the battle of Prague (6 May 1757) an officer of the Prussian hussars came across 150 wounded Austrian and Prussian cavalrymen who had been lodged in a barn, and found that 'nearly all of them had been injured in the right arm between the hand and the elbow'.[17] This was the effect of sword cuts, which were disabling rather than lethal. Conversely a soldier was unlikely to survive a hit by a cannon shot, and almost certain to die from any kind of penetrating chest wound (which occasioned a mortality of about one-third even in World War II). Only archaeological investigation of grave sites (an ethically dubious activity) would establish the nature of mortal wounds in the Seven Years War. However there is copious documentary evidence as to the character of the survivable injuries.

The researches of Andre Corvisier brought to light the records of admissions to the Paris Invalides from 1762, which show the wounds inflicted by the following categories of weapons:

Small arms:	68.8%
Swords:	14.7
Artillery:	13.4
Bayonets:	2.4[18]

If we knew the proportions of the mortal wounds, artillery would almost certainly figure more prominently, and the swords very much less so.

The most relevant Austrian details are those entered by the Commissaries when they weeded out disabled soldiers at the periodic *Musterungen*. The cause of the wound is rarely given, but the anatomical detail is usually specific, which makes it possible to arrange the evidence relating to the Seven Years War as follows:

Location of Wounds
By Individual Parts of Body

Left foot:	18.0%
Left hand:	9.8
Right foot:	8.1
Left arm:	6.5
Head, right arm, right hand:	5.7 each
Foot unspecified:	4.9
Left shoulder, hand unspecified:	4.0 each
'Couse' (thigh?):	3.2
Arm unspecified, left side, right leg:	2.4 each
Right shoulder, chest, left knee, both feet:	1.6 each
Other:	6.4

By Vertical Body Zone
Left:	45.26
Central:	12.63
Right:	22.10
Unspecified or unidentifiable:	20.00

By Horizontal Body Zone
Arms and hands:	35.2
Feet:	32.7
Trunk:	13.1
Head and neck:	9.0
Legs:	8.1
Unspecified:	1.6

These figures support Corvisier's conjecture that the predominance of wounds down the left body zone of the French invalids corresponded with the combat posture of the infantryman, who presented his left side to the enemy when he was ready to fire. The evidence also supports the observations made at the time that the Prussians shot very low.

What happened to the severely wounded after a battle is a matter of some dispute. In words that still have the capacity to chill, the French attaché Champeaux wrote to his minister of war on 30 June 1757:

> The men who were wounded in the battle of the 18th [Kolin] are beginning to die off... Monseigneur, I really must tell you about the way the wounded are treated here, whether they are Austrian or Prussian. It still makes my heart bleed to think about it.

Having been left untended on the battlefield, the wretches were simply dumped in the neighbouring villages,

> where they lay for another two days without surgeons, without food or the money to buy it; they had no visitors whatsoever, and they lacked the strength to ask for help from the passers-by. Forty-eight of these unfortunate men were left in the stables of the house where I lodged, and 28 of them died on the first night without any kind of medical or spiritual assistance; I did everything that lay within my power to relieve their condition, while I besieged the generals in the hope of moving their compassion and commanding their attention. You would have had to see them to be able to imagine how totally indifferent they were.[19]

Another commentator, Lieutenant Gorani of the regiment of Andlau, sprang to the defence of his Austrian colleagues after the next victory at Hochkirch. He did not spare his criticisms of Daun when he believed they were deserved, but 'we must always render justice when it is due. On this occasion Field Marshal Daun gave further proof of his humanity, for he devoted the greatest possible care to the treatment of the Prussian wounded, just as if they had been our own. All the officers of the army at once yielded up their horses and carriages to transport the wounded to the hospitals.[20]

Military surgery in Europe as a whole was still much indebted to the surgeons of two centuries before – men like Hans von Gersdorf (*Feldbuch der Wundarzney*, 1513) and Ambroise de Paré (1510–90) who had been among the first to address themselves to the new phenomenon of gunshot wounds in a serious way. They devised new instruments which enabled them to extract deeply buried bullets, along with dead flesh, and pieces of foreign matter and splintered bone.[21] If amputation were inevitable, Paré pioneered the method of cutting boldly through healthy tissue, sealing the multiple veins and arteries by ligatures (instead of the application of a red-hot iron), and removing enough of the bone to enable the soft tissue and its intact skin to be folded over to make a usable stump. By the 1750s the more advanced surgeons were using the screw tourniquet of Jean-Louis Petit (1674–1750), which greatly facilitated the tying of the Paré ligatures.

Little is known from official sources about any specifically Austrian surgical practices in the Seven Years War, apart from Wabst's warning to his people to keep their instruments shiny and free from rust. However the strictures of the Austrians on the general incompetence of their surgical personnel are relieved by the testimony of the Prussian subaltern Barsewisch, who had been shot in the neck at Leuthen. He and his suffering comrades were entrusted to the care of the captured regimental *Chyrurgus* of the Alt-Modena Cuirassiers:

> a Netherlander from the French borders who could not speak a word of German. He had nevertheless studied surgery at the school of anatomy in Lyon, and gave us excellent service, being extraordinarily skilful in his art … He examined my wound carefully, and found it severely inflamed from my journey and badly congested with blood. He pronounced that he must extract the bullet this very evening, while he could still feel it. He had lost his watch and the sum of 100 ducats to the hussar who had captured him, but he regretted much more that of his fine silver instruments he employed for cutting and closing wounds. He was unable to find any other instruments, in spite of every effort, and so our host – a cobbler – finally had to yield up a pen knife, crude and blunt though it was. Luckily the regimental surgeon knew what he was about, and in spite of the inadequacy of his instrument he was able to extract the bullet at the tenth or twelfth attempt. I still have it with me, and you can see the many cuts in its surface.[22]

For a time there was a more general shortage of material for bandages, which persuaded Maria Theresa and the ladies of the Court to set an example to Vienna by making up appropriate strips of linen. 'Thus a fashion was set, and ultimately a fad which spread through the city. Workmens' wives too played their part in the war by emptying their old linen chests and sacrificing their husbands' shirts. This gave an immense impetus to the linen trade in Austria, and so many cart loads of bandages were being sent to the field that the army finally had to ask the ladies to desist in their good work'.[23]

All the time many more men were being carried away by sickness and disability than by enemy action. Disease was to a great extent the product of the season – the season of a soldier's life as well as the time of year. Recruits were peculiarly vulnerable, as has been noted on many occasions already. Some were in a bad way when they arrived at the army, like the goitre-afflicted mountain lads from Inner Austria, or the recruits who had reached the regiments in 1755, and were expected to remain sickly 'until they have become used to military food, and until their poor state of health – the result of their primitive life and the inadequate sustenance of the peasant – wastes out of their systems'.[24] Recruits from the remoter regions were still more liable than the rest to fall prey to unfamiliar infections, and to *Nostalgie* – the depression resulting from homesickness and disorientation.

'What do we have to lose after the age of 45,' asked the Prince de Ligne, 'but a few uncertain years which end up in a fair state of misery?'.[25] There was no fixed upper age limit in the Austrian service, and the Commissaries determined the issue of how old was meant by 'old' by looking at the condition of the individual soldier. Out of the 327 cases of disability entered in our muster lists, the first onset of disqualifying age as such is recorded at 33 years, with a first heavy culling on this account between 39 and 41, and the survivors eliminated from 'extreme old age' from 42. The relationship between age and causes of disability emerges as follows:

Average Age of Disqualifying Disability
Epilepsy:	22
Apoplexy:	23.5
Old wounds:	32
Fistula, cancer:	33
'Strupirt' ('disabled,' in most cases probably hernia):	35
'Always ill':	38
Poor hearing:	38
Eye trouble:	39
Poor sight:	39
'Stiffness of the limbs':	39
'Tightness of the chest':	40.5
Age as such:	43
Insanity:	46

Another cycle of disease was the expression of the passing year. According to the official manual of military medicine (below) springtime brought rheumatism and the 'intermittent spring fever' (*Frühlings-Wechselfieber*), which was not particularly serious, but had a way of re-visiting the patient every three days. This was in fact the form of malaria transmitted by the mosquito parasite *Plasmodium vivax*, which left the patient anaemic and somewhat jaundiced, but which rarely killed. The height of the summer campaigning season could be cruel to men who were left on guard in the sun, to the cuirassiers in their iron breast plates, and most of all to the marching infantry, with their multi-layered woollen uniforms, and the arrangement of belts and straps which constricted the chest and transmitted all the weight of the soldier's load vertically onto the spine. The occasional death through vagal spasm persuaded officers and military physicians of that time (and long afterwards) that 'when soldiers are heated by exhaustion nothing could be more harmful to them than to allow them to lay aside clothing to give access to the fresh air, or gulp down a cool drink when they are still hot'.[26] The high incidence of epilepsy (below) was probably associated both with the consequent dehydration and the rhythm of the march and drill.

Dysentery made its appearance in the late summer and early autumn, and was linked with the eating of unripe fruit and drinking bad water. It was now that the noxious vapours (or rather the *Plasmodium falciparum* parasite of the seething mosquitoes) arising from the ponds and marshes engendered the autumn intermittent fevers, which were far more dangerous than their springtime cousins, and especially 'after a very hot and dry summer'.[27]

'Angina,' coughs and pleurisy were companions of the soldiers throughout the year, and for these and other ills the authorities indicated the necessary procedures, medicines and diets in the *Kurze Beschreibung der Krankheiten welche am öftersten in dem Feldlager beobachet werden* (*Brief Description of the Illnesses most often Observed in Field Camps*), published in German, French and Latin editions in 1758 in Vienna, Prague and Trieste. The guide is usually attributed to Van Swieten, though the authorship cannot be established for certain.

The physicians set great store by their medicines,[28] and a number of the contemporary remedies were demonstrably effective. Ipacecuana and opium, along with thin soup, were prescribed for dysentery, chinchona for the malarial alternating fevers, and mercury for syphilis – although in the latter case the cure could be as deadly as the illness. The manual emphasised that 'the eating of cabbage, green vegetables and fruit is not only a preventative against scurvy, but restores those who already suffer from it'.[29] This prescription was taken seriously, and the regimental surgeons were authorised to keep fresh stocks of a mysterious but particularly useful anti-scorbutic ' Krenn Bier' in their medicine chests.[30]

We have now reached the practical limits of the medical arts of the day. As pupils of Boerhaave, the leading physicians Van Swieten and Wabst attributed bodily ills to an imbalance of internal fluid pressures. This concept was not as distant as they imagined from that of the 'humours' which medicine had inherited from Hippocrates (c. 460–377BC) and Galen (AD129-c.126), for in each case harmony was to be restored by purges, emetics, expectorants and blood-letting. In this persuasion the new Austrian military doctors bled their patients just as enthusiastically as the old-timers, maintaining that this procedure relieved a great variety of ills, from 'angina' to the spring-time rheumatisms and alternating fevers. In the case of pneumonia 'we must let a great quantity of blood from the arm, and if there is no alleviation of the distress, and the breathing is no easier, we must repeat the operation time and time again... if the emitted blood is thin, remains fluid and does not clot in a cup, this is a bad sign'[31] – this was a very bad sign indeed, for it signified that the poor man was being bled to death.

From the Prince de Ligne we know something of the common-sense 'managerial' approach of a colonel of infantry, which probably did more good than the science or pseudo-science of the physicians. For de Ligne the essence of the thing was prevention: *sublatu causa, tollitur effectus*. He knew that damp could be a real killer, unless the soldiers were given the opportunity to dry themselves off, and forbidden to lay their clothes on the ground. He sought to provide his men with uniforms of comfortable cut, a varied and wholesome diet, new straw and airy quarters. Fresh latrines were to be dug repeatedly, and the old ones filled in; in the interest of purity of water, new wells were to be surrounded by pebbles, and further gravel deposited at the bottom.[32]

Ambiguities of vocabulary, the nature of the records, and changes in the character of diseases themselves render it difficult to arrive at an overview of the maladies and disabilities which afflicted the Austrian soldier in the middle of the 18th century. Dr. Giovanni Gabavlio investigated the mortality in some notoriously unhealthy Austrian garrisons in north Italy between February and June 1751, and identified the main causes as:

Fever:	28%
Scurvy:	18
Wounds and infections	15
Veneral disease	11
Other:	28[33]

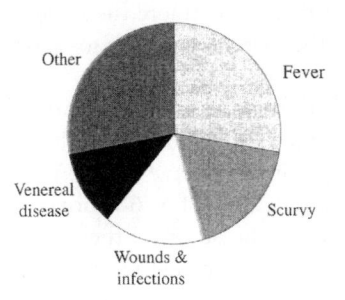

The Commissaries provide some evidence of wartime conditions in their rough and ready categorisation of the soldiers they declared unfit for further active service. They had no particular interest in the underlying illness or disability (ignoring, for example, the many possible causes of 'tightness of the chest' , and their diagnostic skills were somewhat limited ('his feet are no good'), but their testimony is of some value in the absence of any better-informed survey:

Causes of Disability	
Old wounds:	28.1%
'Tightness of the chest' (*Engbrustigkeit*):	20.7
Age:	11.9

'Always ill' ('*bestandig krona*'): 7.9
Eye Trouble: 7.3
'*Strupirt*': 6.7
'Stiffness of the limbs' ('*Steiffheit der Glieder*'): 5.1
Poor sight: 3.3
Epilepsy: 3.3
Poor hearing: 1.8
Insanity (overall, but 5.5 in the cavalry): 1.5
Fistula, cancer: 1.2
Apoplexy: 0.6

The medical men, the officers, the Commissaries and Maria Theresa agreed that the hospitals themselves were becoming engines of disease: 'a battlefield where more men die than on the scene of combat'.[34] In fact the foul air of those places was believed to cause a specific 'hospital disease' or 'continual putrid fever' ('*Lazaret Fieber*,') which was expressed in individual cases variously as dysentery, yellow fever ('*die gelbe Sucht*') or scurvy.[35]

This was a most disappointing outcome, because Maria Theresa took a personal interest in the well-being of the patients,[36] and she and her advisers had expected much from the system of triage which they announced in April 1758:

> The less seriously sick and wounded were to be accommodated in the depots of the individual regiments on the theatre of war, where they would be tended by their own surgeons and *Feldschere*
>
> More serious cases were taken from regimental care, and referred to the so called or '*Interim-Spitaller*'

The intractable cases were forwarded to the larger and more elaborately-equipped '*Haupt-Spitaller*,' where it would be possible to 'supervise the men properly, which cannot be done when the patients are scattered... furthermore the *Haupt-Spitaller* have an adequate supply of bedding and bedsteads, and so the men do not have to lie on straw on the bare earth, which is the case in the Interim-Spitaller'.[37]

Officers were detached from the army to administer the hospitals and keep them under military discipline, and as part of the reforms of April 1758 Maria Theresa instituted *Invaliden-Compagnien* of half-invalids to help with mundane tasks. A further elaboration emerges in 1761, when the report of the *Sanitäts-Commission* of 5–6 February mentions that the sick were being grouped in separate wards according to the nature of their diseases.

For a variety of reasons the patients received all too little benefit from the attention and the great sums which the authorities were devoting to their welfare. Some of the blame must be laid at the door of individuals. Maria Theresa was reluctant to sign over monies to the regiments for them to disburse as the whim took them, 'for the sad experience of earlier times shows that the officers gamble the money away until nothing is left, and engage in a multiplicity of frauds. This is because the regiments do not detach the best and most reliable officers for such work, but send only doubtful characters and young men who are not up to their responsibilities'.[38] The meeting of the *Sanitäts-Commission* of 25 January 1761 nevertheless reported that most of the colonels commandant had been conscientious at supporting their regimental hospitals, for they were providing coats for the patients when these were lacking, together with extra food, and free allowances of beer and wine to build up the strength of the convalescents.[39]

The main problems were in fact located in the larger establishments, where men were separated from their parent regiments and 'lost in hospital,' in the telling phrase of the muster lists. The provisions and the staffing fell short of what was needed even at the full regulation allowances. Maria Theresa's *Leib Chyrurgus* du Creux discovered as much when he had the opportunity of seeing the superior Prussian arrangements at first hand after the battle of Torgau in 1760. He learned that the Prussians provided every wounded soldier with half a pound of meat per day gratis, furnished every sick and wounded man with full bedding, and hired countrywomen and poor townsfolk at high rates of pay to tend the patients.[40] The last point was significant, for Wabst had turned down a sensible proposal from Daun to hire local labour to supplement the efforts of the *Feldschere* in the *Haupt-Spitaller*.[41]

The Austrian rations (such as they were) all too often reached the patients poorly cooked, in short or unbalanced measure, or in conditions which revolted even the strong stomachs of the time: 'it has been noted that wounds are often dressed on the eating tables, which deprives the sick men of all appetite for their food'.[42]

Some of the shortcomings were endemic in the system. Purpose-built military hospitals were as yet almost unknown in Europe, and there was something to be said for a wounded or sick man crawling away to die in privacy in a ditch, rather than die in any case after an elapse of time in the collective squalor of whatever building had been commandeered as a hospital. In Prague the *Haupt-Spital* was established in the *Invaliden-Haus*. It was supposed to be the showpiece of the new hospital system, but Wabst had to report early in 1760 that the place was crowded well beyond capacity. During this very cold winter it was impossible to open the windows and doors to allow the air to circulate, 'and so the exhalations of all these sick men turn the trapped air into a deadly fug. The most closely-packed rooms resemble a bath-house, where the walls, windows and ceilings are so... sodden that all the iron fittings become rusty, the water runs down in streams, and the beds are damp and mouldy.' Bedding was so short that' it sometimes happens that new patients are being laid in the same beds where other men have died only a short time before'.[43]

This was part of the testimony given on 22 January, when *GFWM*. Partini von Neuhaus debated the crisis in Prague with Wabst, his available colleagues, and Lieutenant-Colonel Rantzow as the administrative director of the *Invaliden-Haus*. The overcrowding was now so gross that 400 patients had to be distributed about the city with no care whatsoever. Out of the men still in the hospital, nearly 40 were dying every day, and up to 90 were suffering relapses, while 30 of the overworked *Feldschere* and attendants had fallen sick. The *Invaliden-Haus* was incapable of accommodating more than 1,800 patients in winter time, and only after making repeated representations to the *Commissariat* had Rantzow gained permission on 11 January to send the surplus to hospitals elsewhere (with fatal results detailed below). By then the number of patients had reached 2,600, a number augmented by a further transport which arrived on the 16th. Wabst supported everything that Rantzow had to say, and he assigned the blame to Baron Netolitzky, the head of the Bohemian civil administration, who had refused to believe that there was a great difference in the space available in winter from that in summer – when patients could be set out in the arcades. Commissaries had certainly arrived to investigate, but their reports were thoroughly unreliable, 'for they are normally afraid to enter a room where there are sick men, and they make up their minds as fancy and their preconceived ideas dictate'.[44]

At the opposite extreme Wabst noted that by September 1760 the sick and wounded had been scattered altogether too widely. There were ailing Croats spread over Moravia and the County of Glatz, and between 3,400 and 3,500 of the sickly regular troops had been distributed in hundreds of separate houses in northern-eastern Bohemia, where it was impossible for the medical personnel to reach them'.[45]

These and other investigations confirmed that the lack of order in transportation was the fundamental cause of the arbitrary distribution of the patients, and of many evils besides. The Austrians were not to blame for piling the sick and wounded onto peasant wagons or empty supply carts, for that was the common practice of the time, but the men suffered needlessly when, as so often happened, the authorities failed to provide covering and straw for the journeys in winter time. Lieutenant-Colonel Rantzow discovered that 78 of his former patients had frozen to death on the first day of their evacuation from the overcrowded *Invaliden-Haus* in Prague; there was no other reason for them to die, for they were suffering from nothing worse than mild chronic ailments and slight venereal infections.[46]

Many deaths were caused by the policy of evacuating poorly patients from hospitals that were in danger of being captured by the enemy, as if the Prussians were savages who would have massacred these helpless men.[47] All that mattered was to dump the sick and wounded out of reach of the enemy. Thus Joseph Count Waldstein complained to Daun in June 1758 that the sick hussars and Croats had been delivered in such quantities at Trebitsch in Moravia that the houses were jammed with 30 or more men apiece, and the whole little town was bursting. There was no provision for medical care, feeding or discipline, and the more able-bodied men had betaken themselves to the woods, from where they emerged to rob travellers on the road.[48]

Such conditions were unacceptable to the *Feld Artillerie-Corps*, which prided itself on its sense of welfare, and at the beginning of 1759 Daun gave the artillerymen leave to set up their own hospital, where standards of care, cleanliness and nourishment would be guaranteed. Wabst's deputy, Wolfang Graffenhuber, had no wish to disturb this arrangement, but pointed out that the artillery hospital should be located physically close to one of the *Haupt-Spitäller*, so that qualified help would be on hand in case of emergency.[49]

The officers claimed special provision by right, and Wabst recognised their privileges in 1759, when he enjoined his staff to behave towards the sick and wounded officers 'with all due respect,' tend them with 'all possible zeal and diligence,' and accept rewards only if they were offered freely.[50] Wabst was aware that officers were in the habit of making off with the medical personnel for their own service, and he warned his people against allowing themselves to be detached for this purpose, unless if were to accompany a wounded officer to somewhere where he could receive the attention of a senior surgeon. Many generals likewise commandeered the best houses in a village, which could otherwise have sheltered wounded soldiers. The Prince de Ligne would have been quite happy to see the commanders living in the countryside in pavilions of Asiatic splendour, 'as long as they leave the villages to men who are often of much more use'.[51]

Episodes in a Morbid History of the Seven Years War

The Austrian troops were in an excellent state of health in the last full year of peace, at least to judge by the Commissaries' reports on the infantry regiments quartered in Bohemia in 1755. The army was reaping the benefit of the policy of weeding out unfit men, and replacing them with young regimental and *Stände* recruits:

> and, with the exception of a number of individuals who are getting on in years, or have some minor ailments, all the regiments are recruited with men who are fully fit for service. The first and fourth ranks are made up entirely of tall and fine-looking soldiers, and, while it is true that most of the men in the second and third ranks are of middling stature, and some of the third are under the minimum height of five feet three inches, they are all well built and sturdy.[52]

There were nevertheless the portents of a decline in standards when, in October 1755, the Commissaries noted an order to release from service only such men who are 'totally blind, had lost a hand or foot, or were so disabled as to be incapable of doing any further duty with the regiment or in a garrison'.[53]

The fast-moving campaigns of autumn 1756 and the spring and early summer of 1757 gave little opportunity for epidemic diseases to take hold. The camp fevers finally made their presence known when the army was immobilised in a highly-concentrated mass in the position of Zittau from 20 July to 2 September 1757, when more than 24,000 troops fell sick. No kind of hospital was established, and 'you would have had to write whole sheets of paper to describe the miseries which the men had to undergo. It is hard to believe, but the soldiers were lying in hovels and barns not only without bed and cover, but even without straw; if their illness did not kill them off, they were eaten alive by the insects'.[54] This year's campaigning was prolonged well into the winter, and at the time of the siege of Schweidnitz in November it was noted that all branches of the army were being depleted by a large number of the chronically sick.[55]

In both the medical and metaphorical sense the problem took on acute proportions after the dreadful defeat at Leuthen (5 December 1757). Thus at every halt on the retreat to Austrian territory the officers of the regiment of Andlau had to rub the frozen arms, ears and noses of their soldiers with snow to restore the circulation before they allowed the men to enter the heated huts of the peasants. Without this precaution the affected parts were almost invariably lost to frostbite.[56] When the army reached Bohemia and Moravia there were whole carts full of nothing but men who were dying or already dead.[57]

The enfeebled survivors were overtaken by an 'Hungarian spotted fever,' which seems to have originated among the troops captured by the Prussians in Breslau, and which spread among friend and foe alike in its two-month course. The victims 'fell into a delirium at the first onset of the disease, and swellings appeared in the neck and armpits. It made no difference whether the physicians let blood or not, for everyone who fell sick invariably died. The infection was so virulent and speedy that it carried a man to the grave in three days.' The soldiers were tipped into the pits as soon as they were dead, or appeared to be dead, and it is likely that a large number of unconscious men were buried alive.[58]

Frederick invaded Moravia in the early summer of 1758, which jammed the fortress-town of Olmütz once more with human and material wreckage. Many of the men were still lying there weeks later, and the fathers of the Jesuit College (full of Christian spirit) complained to Maria Theresa that over 400 sick soldiers were crammed into the seminary, along with their wives; the Jesuit school was also still doing service as a hospital, and ammunition was stored in its cellars.[59] The offending objects were removed forthwith.

In comparison the Austrian army seems to have been touched only lightly by infectious disease in the main campaigning season of 1759, though men by the hundred succumbed to heat exhaustion on the forced marches during that year's notoriously hot summer. These numbers were eclipsed by the deaths among the corps of the Prussian general Finck, which was captured almost intact at Maxen on 21 November. The casualties were light, but the Prussians' route to confinement in Croatia lay through Styria, which experienced an average of 10 epidemics a year through the 1750s. One-third of onsets were caused by the bloody flux, and an outbreak of this kind overtook the Prussians on the march, consigning them by the hundreds or thousands to a mass grave outside Rann (see p. 239).

Disease was a familiar companion in winter quarters, and the Austrians were not spared when they finally sought shelter from the cold early in 1760. Daun observed that the troops quartered in Dresden remained much more healthy than those scattered over the countryside.[60] The reason, we may surmise, was that the troops in the city were accommodated in relatively spacious bourgeois houses, whereas the men in the villages were heaped together in stifling peasant cabins.

An unspecified epidemic coursed through the army later in 1760, and was reflected in the heavy mortality recorded for that year (below). It did not persist into the winter, and the regimental surgeons (who took the credit) assured a *Sanitäts Commission* 'with happy unanimity' that not a trace remained.[61]

378 INSTRUMENT OF WAR

In the last period of the war the army nevertheless experienced an irreversible decline in the state of its health. The veterans had largely disappeared from the muster lists, and were succeeded by intakes of juvenile recruits who had built up no resistance to hardship or infections. The war of manoeuvre had largely given way to positional campaigning in the hills of Silesia and Saxony, where fresh vegetables were hard to come by, and the troops subsisted on bread and a little meat.

In 1761, after weeks spent in camp in wet weather, the troops were concentrated for the winter in dense cantonments. The villages were reeking with the waste of old Austrian and Prussian hospitals, the water was contaminated, and the air in the crowded peasant huts was foul. The weakened troops were in a poor state to endure the new stalemate which supervened in 1762. An Austrian officer reported from the Silesian foothills that 'scurvy has taken such a firm hold on the army that in some of the regiments the number of the sick has reached three or 400. This malady… is well-night incurable. The mens' bodies and feet swell up, and most of them are destined to die. We can only hope to God for some improvement!'.[62]

The number of men of all ranks who died in hospital in the war from sickness or wounds reached 93,408, or 30.76 percent of the total loss of 303,595. The distribution of the hospital deaths over the years reveals a 'norm' of rather more than 11 percent, as attained in 1756, 1761 and 1762, but there were some marked variations in other years. The very high mortality in 1758 was almost certainly due not to that year's campaigning, but to the prolonged consequences of the battle of Leuthen in 1757.

Annual deaths in hospital from disease and wounds (as percentage of total of 93,408)

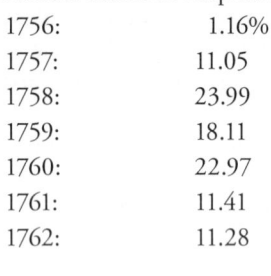

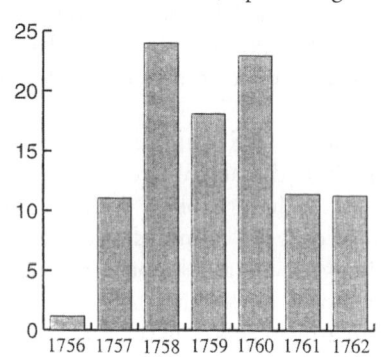

Year	Percentage
1756:	1.16%
1757:	11.05
1758:	23.99
1759:	18.11
1760:	22.97
1761:	11.41
1762:	11.28

The Invalids

The men who were discharged from active service were called 'invalids,' and the total lost to the army by this means during the Seven Years War amounted to 17,388, or 5.72 percent of the army's total loss of 303,595.[63] Their fate was of some concern to Maria Theresa, for they had a moral claim on her goodwill, and they were to be encountered every day on the roads and streets, as living testimony to the standing of the army in her realm. Armfeldt noted that such men as were capable of light service (the '*Halb-Invaliden*') were kept on the same scales of pay and rations as the rest of the troops, and employed on garrison duty or looking after the sick. Those full invalids who wished to return to their native provinces were supported by the *Stände* on a monthly pension of 1 florin 30 xr., 'which is paid to them meticulously and without any deduction.' The homeless natives and the foreigners were entitled to be lodged at the governmental invalid houses, which were maintained from deductions from the pay of the serving personnel – at 1 xr. per month from the private soldiers, and so upwards according to rank. Armfeldt was unable to ascertain the total number of invalids, 'though it must be very considerable, especially after such a bloody War.[64]

It seemed to Maria Theresa that many old soldiers were unaware of what was available to them. In 1757 she reminded the army that a house (for 2,000 men and 80 or more officers) was available in Pest in Hungary, and 'devoted to the welfare of those soldiers who have sacrificed their limbs and their health to upholding Her Lands and Her Service'.[65] A great *Invaliden-Haus* was being completed for 2,000 veterans in Prague, and accommodation had been provided for another 1,000 in Moravia, and a further 1,000 in an extension of the *Armen-Haus* (Poor House) in Vienna. Any surplus could be sheltered in a converted provision warehouse in Petau which had been donated by the Styrian *Stände*. In these establishments the invalids received a pension, free uniforms and bread, and accommodation for themselves and their families, and they were at liberty to leave at any time, if they applied through the proper channels.

Ten years after the war Vienna found it necessary to renew the invitation, for many men had conceived an 'unfounded prejudice and prejudice' against the invalid houses. The unnecessarily straitened last days of long-serving old soldiers was a awakening 'an ineradicable aversion to military service among the other subjects,' while their poverty-stricken superiors were driven to 'conduct of a kind which was demeaning to their status as officers'.[66]

The Chaplains

The regimental chaplain (*Caplan, Pater*) had to be a man confident in his mission if he was to be fortified rather than embarrassed by the authority invested in him by the Austrian army. He celebrated the obligatory Sunday Mass and intoned the victorious *Te Deum* before a congregation which almost invariably held unbelievers and both avowed and hidden Protestants. He spent much of his time with the regiment's children, instructing them in the rudiments of literacy and the Faith, and yet he was expected to enforce moral standards among hardened military men of all ranks. He was the harbinger of death who brought the Last Sacraments to the sick and wounded, and he pronounced the general absolution of sins over the bowed heads of the soldiers just before they went into battle – the moments when they least liked to be reminded of their mortality.

At the time of writing nothing has come to light which presents the experience of the chaplains in their own words, and so we are thrown entirely on the evidence of observers. It would probably be misleading to give any great weight to the disparaging comments of Jakob Cogniazzo, who was probably one of the covert Protestants, or of Prince Charles-Joseph de Ligne, a grandee of intellectual pretensions, for whom any expression of religious enthusiasm would not have been *bon ton*.

The most balanced available evidence happens to be furnished by the Commissaries, in their report on the *Musterung* of the regiments in Bohemia in October 1755. The one *Pater* they condemned without reservation was the chaplain of the regiment of Alt-Wolfenbüttel, who was to be sent straight back to his monastery as being negligent in every respect, and setting the worst possible example in a regiment which was heavily Lutheran. Conversely the Commissaries singled out a number of individuals for their commitment to preaching and the celebration of the sacraments, instructing the children, or, as in the regiment of Harsch, supporting the sick from his own pocket.

The chaplain of the Batthyány Dragoons was a bold man who 'often descends on the quarters of the regiment unannounced, to give Christian instruction, and investigate whether the officers as well as the men are behaving themselves.' The chaplain of the regiment of Nicolaus Esterházy was a man of the same stamp, and there was another fellow spirit in the Jesuit *Pater* of the infantry regiment of Kaiser, whose efforts were frustrated by the loose-living colonel commandant Leopold Baron Lagelberg, who was carrying on an affair with his major's wife. For moralists like these 'the only reward has been persecution,' and if the other chaplains had been brave enough to follow their example 'it would have been impossible for immorality to be displayed as publicly and shamelessly as it is.'

The chaplains seem to have found the most favourable environment in regiments that were not only well run in themselves, but of Germanic Protestant character, as in that of Hildburghausen, where the colonel commandant was a Lutheran and the major was a Calvinist. However it was one thing for Vienna to accept Protestants as fighting officers, but another as regimental surgeons who might be in a position to challenge the moral authority of the chaplain. The Commissaries thought it worthy of note that the surgeon of the regiment of Harsch 'is indeed a Lutheran, but one who keeps clear of religious matters, and looks after the sick who have returned to Catholicism just as conscientiously as he tends the others.' There is more than a hint of regret in the report on the surgeon who happened to be the only Lutheran in the Hohenems Cuirassiers: 'it is true that Her Imperial Majesty had agreed to keep him on for a further period, but he chose to resign immediately after the muster was taken. Everyone agrees that the regiment has thereby lost an excellent man'.[67]

The chaplain was a person who was aged on average 39 years, and had served for five. The muster lists also give some indication as to his origins:[68]

Origins of Chaplains by Religious Order (87 cases)
Jesuit:	29.88%
Franciscan:	22.98
Petriner:	5.74
Secular priest:	5.49
Maltheser, Pauliner:	3.44 each
Cistercian, Dominican, Piaristen:	2.99 each
Benedictine:	1.14
Other or not recorded:	21.83

Origins of Chaplains by Place of Birth (83 cases)
Bohemia:	31.32
Hungary and Transylvania:	21.68
Moravia:	13.25
Reich:	10.84
Lower and Upper Austria, with Vienna; Netherlands and Luxembourg:	6.02 each
Austrian Silesia, Croatia:	2.40 each
Styria, Tyrol, Görz and Gradisca, Austrian Italy, France:	1.20 each

Part III

Waging War

17

Strategic Dimenions

WHAT KIND OF WAR?

> The first, the supreme, the most far-reaching act of judgement that the statesman and commander have to make is to establish... the kind of war on which they are embarking; neither mistaking it for, nor trying to turn it into, something that is alien to its nature. This is the first of all strategic questions, and the most comprehensive.
>
> Carl von Clausewitz, *On War,* 1832

The Contest for Territory and Power

> What is at stake in this war is not some kind of middling or passing interest, not a couple of fortresses or small provinces more or less, but the existence or extinction of the new Prussian monarchy... This war broke out to decide whether this new monarchy will survive; it is an assemblage of different elements, lacking still in consistency and extent, but organised on totally military lines, and having all the hunger of a youthful and lean body'
>
> The Danish envoy Johann Hartwig Ernst Bernstorff to the duc de Choiseul[1]

Along with the colonial rivalry between the British and French, the ambition of the Austrians to recover Silesia was one of the most powerful engines of the Seven Years War. The antagonism between Austria and Prussia was undoubtedly expressed in its most tangible form in relation to that province. With the loss of Silesia the Habsburg state lost a territory of 35,000 square kilometres, a population of up to 1,200,000 souls, and the trade, the agriculture, the linen manufactures and the mining which helped to produce an annual Silesian tax revenue of some 3,900,000 florins per annum – which represented about 21 percent of the revenues of the German Hereditary Lands, and 10 percent of the funds available for the army from all the Habsburg dominions. Thereafter much of the additional burden fell on Bohemia. The Silesian recruits had been second in quantity only to those from Bohemia, and in terms of quality they were probably unsurpassed.

Lusatia had already been ceded to Saxony by treaty in the last century, and now by losing Silesia the Habsburgs ceased to be a power in northern Europe. According to the Anglo-Irishman Sir James Caldwell, who had once represented Austria on diplomatic missions:

> she [Maria Theresa] had always regarded the cession of Silesia to the King of Prussia not only as the greatest disgrace the House of Austria ever suffered, but as a very important diminution both of the strength and riches of her state. In her commercial views she was greatly disappointed by the Treaty of Breslau [13 June 1742], for just as the war broke out a project was upon the point of being carried into execution for establishing a very advantageous trade between Hungary, Bohemia and Silesia, and this commerce was to extend by the Oder to the Baltic, with a view to its further extension to Great Britain. Mr. Porter was sent from that

Court to Vienna in the year 1739, where he remained in order to negotiate that trade, until the year 1745.²

The Crown of Bohemia moreover lost feudal links with principalities in Silesia, while the judicial reforms of Frederick's lawyer Cocceji were going to separate Silesia from the legal system of the *Reich* as a whole.

Geographical continuities enabled Frederick to join Silesia to Brandenburg as the expanded core area of the Prussian state, and, as Kaunitz pointed out to Maria Theresa, 'the loss of Silesia and Glatz signifies that Hungary, Bohemia and Moravia have lost also their outer rampart, and acquired a close and dangerous neighbour who, through his recent gains of territory, can maintain an army of 140–150,000 troops in peacetime, and thus present a standing threat to Your Majesty's Hereditary Lands'.³

Austrian statesmen noted with chagrin that the Prussians actually gained more than the Austrians had lost. Through rational administration, and by promoting industry the Prussians had by 1743 almost doubled the tax revenues from Silesia to the equivalent of more than 7 million florins, without increasing the burden on the population.⁴ It was no coincidence that Friedrich Wilhelm Haugwitz was able to spur the Austrians into their programme of domestic reform by drawing attention to what the Prussians had been able to make of that province. Loudon, who reconquered the adjacent County of Glatz in 1760, likewise praised the 'many good and useful usages' which had been introduced there under the tyrannical rule of the Prussian commander Fouqué, 'for experience shows that the country people in these parts are much more inclined to follow military than civil direction, having become used to it'.⁵

At various times Maria Theresa and Kaunitz identified the rise of Prussian power as such as being more dangerous to the monarchy than the Swedish invasions at the time of the Thirty Years War, or the loss of Belgrade to the Turks. This was no ordinary neighbour, for Frederick had made lack of faith a principle of statecraft, and the Prussian sovereigns had established a military form of government which, through the enforced service of foreigners, had set on foot an army far larger than was warranted in a state with peaceful intentions. At the beginning of the 18th century Brandenburg-Prussia had been able to maintain scarcely 40,000 troops; Frederick William I had expanded this number to 80,000, while Frederick as master of Silesia and Glatz could support the peacetime establishment of 140–150,000 troops as mentioned by Kaunitz, and inevitably far more in the event of hostilities.

An Austro-Prussian contest for domination had also arisen in the *Reich*. Maria Theresa counted herself as German, and as the protector of the religious equilibrium between the Protestants and her beloved Catholics, now threatened by secularisation and militant Protestantism (below). Kaunitz associated himself fully with Maria Theresa's mission, and reminded her that she must also be on her guard against long-term geopolitical developments in that part of the world, among which he numbered the danger of the Houses of Ansbach and Bayreuth dying out and their lands falling to Prussia – an eventuality which would hem in Austria to the north-west, restrict Austrian communications with the Netherlands and the rest of the *Reich*, enable

Frederick of Prussia (engraving by the author after an original painting).

Frederick to raise 30,000 further troops and give him a base from which to annex Franconia. Kaunitz also mentioned that the days of the Wittelsbach dynasty of Bavaria might also be numbered, though in this case he did not spell out the consequences.[6]

In the thinking of Kaunitz, Austria therefore stood as 'the only obstacle to the king playing the dictator in the whole of Germany, and making his House the most considerable power in Europe'.[7] Kaunitz, Maria Theresa and the *Stände* of Bohemia and Moravia assumed that Frederick's voracity would not be satisfied with the conquest of Silesia and Glatz, and on balance they were probably right. We shall never know Frederick's innermost ambitions, or evaluate the full influence of his shadowy confidant Lieutenant-General Hans Karl Winterfeldt, but Frederick's brother Prince Henry, his foreign minister Podewils and a circle of liberal-minded officers believed that Frederick's reckless conduct had been responsible for precipitating Prussia into the Seven Years War,[8] while some of them maintained that Frederick and Winterfeldt aimed to overthrow the Habsburg state altogether and establish a universal Prussian monarchy – a dream that was dissipated in 1757, when the Austrians defeated Frederick at Kolin on 18 June 1757, and killed Winterfeldt in the action at Moys on 7 September.[9]

The Contest of Values, Ideology and Instincts

> Never talk about the 'policy' of Prussia, England, France, Spain, Holland and so forth. Private gain, the desire for revenge, the mood and the more or less rational thought-processes of the men and women of influence – these are the things which are dressed up in the shadowy guise of deep diplomatic calculation. So it is that wars have almost always been sparked off by personality.
>
> The Prince de Ligne[10]

In the making and waging of the Seven Years War intellect and statesmanlike gifts were demonstrably subordinate on occasion to passion and beliefs. Maria Theresa, the daughter of the Habsburgs, both despised Frederick as an upstart '*Theaterkönig*' and hated him as the author of the loss of Silesia. This episode was associated with the outset of her reign, and it engendered in her a commitment to 'her' Silesians, just as Charles VI had linked himself emotionally with his lost Spanish empire. She was convinced that nothing worse could befall her subjects than to fall under Prussian rule, and so she viewed her Silesians as singularly unfortunate souls who deserved liberation by her armies, and who were welcome as refugees at her Court.[11]

As one or another army gained the upper hand in Silesia during the war, so the province became a stage on which the rival sovereigns revealed themselves to *das Publicum*. Frederick gloried in his show of toleration, but after he recovered Silesia at the end of 1757 he ruled that no Catholic worth more 300 taler's salary must be permitted to hold an office in the province, and he allowed his crony Lieutenant-General Henri-Auguste de la Motte Fouqué, a fanatical Huguenot, to institute a religious persecution in the County of Glatz, culminating in the execution of the Catholic priest Faulhaber.

More offensive in its way was Frederick's appointment of another old friend, the disreputable Catholic cleric Philipp Gotthard Schaffgotsch, as Bishop of Breslau in 1747 over the objections of the Chapter and people. During the brief period of restored Austrian rule late in 1757 this arch-cynic, libertine and freemason tried to ingratiate himself by holding a solemn service of thanksgiving in honour of Prince Charles of Lorraine and his generals. It did him no good at all. Maria Theresa banished him to Johannisberg in a remote quarter of his diocese, there to wait until she made her pleasure known at the end of the war. Schaffgotsch the turncoat was now in equal disfavour with Frederick, who confiscated the bishop's property in Breslau. A loyal servant managed to spirit away a magnificent dinner service from the Schaffgotsch Schloss of Ottmachau, but before the crates could reach another of the bishop's castles, in Austrian territory, they were opened by the Austrian general de Ville, who requisitioned the pieces for his own use.[12]

Long after the end of Austrian rule in Silesia, John Quincy Adams (future sixth President of the United States) observed concerning the religions divisions that 'there is perhaps no part of Europe where the roots of bitterness between the two parties is yet so deep, and cleaves with such stubbornness to the ground, as here'.[13] Meanwhile the profound dynastic attachment of the Habsburgs to the Catholic religion was tempered by the need to maintain their authority among people of all Christian faiths. Vienna had been embarrassed both by the anti-Protestant zeal of the Bishop of Salzburg, and the fashion for converting to Catholicism among German princelings (see p. 93), and now in Silesia the Austrians showed meticulous regard for heretical sensibilities. When he held Breslau for a short time in 1757 Prince Charles of Lorraine therefore installed the Calvinist *FML*. Sprecher as governor, and the Lutheran *GFWM*. Wolffersdorf as commandant. It was a clumsy if well-meant demonstration of religious evenhandedness, for neither man had a particularly high military reputation. The Austrians were in possession of Glatz for much longer, from 26 July 1760 until the end of the war. They removed the mummified body of Faulhaber from its gibbet and gave it honourable burial, but expelled no more than 34 Prussian supporters from the town and county, and all on grounds of proven espionage or manifestly offensive behaviour. Many Protestants chose to stay behind, because religion had played no part in the purge, in spite of what was alleged in the Berlin press.[14]

The divisive potential of religion extended well beyond Silesia, which was why Maria Theresa and her advisers were greatly concerned to prevent the rough alignment of Catholic against Protestant, as expressed in the outcome of the Diplomatic Revolution, precipitating a sectarian war. Shortly before hostilities broke out the veteran statesman Ulfeld warned that if Britain and Prussia succeeded in representing the conflict as one of religion, 'Your Majesty would run the risk of losing a considerable number of generals and officers from Your army, or least be unable to rely on their loyalty'.[15]

In 1757 Austria's disastrous lack of attention to Hanoverian interests (below) allowed the electorate to slip into the enemy camp, which was assuming more and more of a Protestant character, and two years later the French diplomat Choiseul expressed the fear that the ostensible desire of Frederick and the British for peace was a device for promoting fundamental changes in the constitution of the *Reich*. Choiseul feared that German secular princes might be attracted to their camp by the prospect of annexing the lands of the ecclesiastical states, and such ambitions were likely to be supported by Sweden, Denmark, Holland, Saxony and the Protestant cantons of Switzerland.[16] Kaunitz or one of his associates added that Frederick was already being 'idolised' by the British people, most of the German Protestant princes and many of the Catholic as well, 'and so, favoured by fanaticism, the tempting prospect of the secularisations, and the strong solidarity which exists among Protestants… the kings of England and Prussian could become effectively the masters of the whole of Europe'.[17]

Pope Benedict XIV had died on 3 May 1758, leaving the reputation of a statesman and a scholar: 'he was particularly devoted to our Court, and had a personal love and regard for the Empress, of which he gave many important and sincere proofs'.[18] His successor Clement XIII Rezzonico was widely believed to lack Benedict's judgement, and Frederick used the opportunity to spread the story that the new pope had sent Dann a blessed hat and sword after the battle of Hochkirch.

In such circumstances the support of Sweden, and of Württemberg and other Protestant states of Germany had a value for Austria far exceeding the military worth, and Austrian statesmen, while sympathising with the sufferings of the Germans, could only rejoice as politicians in the depredations which were carried out in Frederick's name in Saxony, Mecklenburg, Anhalt-Zerbst and the towns and principalities of central Germany.

After the war the Prince de Ligne and Joseph von Sonnenfels, each in his way an old soldier of Maria Theresa, essayed intellectual definitions of Patriotism, the cult of which was then coming into vogue (see p. 244). In their way of thinking the state or Fatherland was an entity which was formed from the ties which attached the individual to the common good – attachments that were engendered by a permanent abode, and the benefit of laws and the forms of government. The soldier had a higher motivation still, for he was called by a special kind of Patriotism when the interests of his sovereign or Fatherland were threatened.[19]

It is doubtful whether many other of Austria's military men or subjects would have expressed their instincts in such clinical terms. Genuine national antagonisms came into being among the common folk of both the Prussian and Austrian states, but they were particularly prominent among the Austrians, 'for according to their political notions Frederick's war was a mutiny against the Emperor and Empire, which must incur punishment on that account, while their religious delusions led them to believe that they were fighting heretics, who deserved to be exterminated'.[20]

Cultural differences between Austria and Prussia ran deep even in the higher circles. De Guibert was struck by the 'difference which exists between the dress and manners of the Austrian and Prussian officers. The Austrian officers are entirely French in their style, what with their coloured waistcoats and the pronounced lack of regularity in the way they wear their uniforms... from officer to private soldier the Austrians are distinguished from the Prussians by their bearing, by their dress, and, if I may say so, by their cast of features'.[21]

The elite were beginning to discover unsuspected affinities between the two allied nations. Just as French neo-classical styles of architectural decoration (much favoured by Kaunitz) were shouldering aside the 'illogical' asymmetry of the rococo, so Kaunitz, the Zinzendorf half-brothers Ludwig and Carl, and Johann Carl Philipp Cobenzl and their circle came under the influence of French ideas which rejected the narrow protectionism of Mercantilist theory, and maintained that economic progress must be the product of a general advance of society and cultural conditions. 'In this respect, France occupied a prominent place in this transfer, for contemporaries perceived a striking resemblance between the two states, at least as far as sheer size of territories and population and form of government were concerned'.[22] We have already had frequent occasion to note the importance of the Franco-Austrian exchange in military technology, whereby the French contributions to Austrian military engineering were matched by the influence of Liechtenstein's reforms on the French artillery.

The Limited Contest

In 1758 Maria Theresa was shocked to learn that the Prussian garrison had burned down the suburbs of Dresden, and she wrote to the Electoral Princess Maria Antonia of Saxony that 'you may rest assured that I am enraged against this monster [Frederick], and that I will employ my every resource, and my very last troops to deliver you from this slavery. This man's atrocious deeds are the common talk of Vienna, and surely that good God will at last have pity on us and crush this monster'.[23] To what extent were the Austrians willing to assist this Divine work?

As regards the calls on manpower, it appears that by the final years of the war Austria had indeed reached the limit of what it was possible to mobilise, short of resorting to a centrally-directed system of conscription. The *Stände* had swept up all the physically-capable marginal elements of society, and were now competing among themselves and with the regimental recruiting parties to buy up Prussian deserters and low-grade soldiers of fortune.

When he looked back on the conflict in 1777 Kaunitz stated that to embark on a war was a most damaging enterprise, which could be justified, as in the last war with Prussia, only when survival was at stake. The huge cost of modern war was particularly relevant, for in addition to the internal damage to the state, the debts incurred could well exceed the revenues from a province which was recovered by force.[24] Here the evidence is slightly more ambiguous. The Austrian government, unlike its French or Swedish counterparts, was willing to address the provincial oligarchies head-on with demands for money, but Kaunitz refused outright to lay his hands on what seemed to be the intact wealth of the Church and nobility, and both Caldwell and Daun questioned whether the state had the will to mobilise all the economic resources within its grasp.

If these were misconceptions, they were encouraged by the fact that the Austrian sovereigns and officials were clearly reluctant to give overriding priority to the war against Prussia, or even on occasion to put the defence of their homeland at the forefront of their concerns. The daily record of the whereabouts and activities of Their Imperial Majesties shows that Maria Theresa, as well as the patently irresponsible Francis Stephen, was willing to absent herself on the Court's accustomed hunting excursions for days on end at the height of the campaigning season (see p. 23).

The bureaucrats too did not like to depart from established routine. A Conference of 2 September 1756 certainly resolved to send passports to allow cattle to be driven free of internal tolls to feed Brown's army in Bohemia, but Rudolph Chotek reported on 13 January the next year that the exemptions had cost 47,000 florins in revenue, and he persuaded the Conference to re-impose the dues. All the time the reinforcements on the way from the eastern frontiers to the theatre of were being processed with painful slowness through the plague quarantine (*Contumaz*) imposed by the *Sanitäts-Hof-Commission*. The standard quarantine of 40 days was prolonged if as much as a single soldier in a regiment died of the plague. This was a vital service which Austria performed for the public health of Europe as a whole, and which banished the plague from the civilised world,[25] but it is difficult to understand why the quarantine zone was not expanded beyond its narrow peacetime boundaries, which permitted the passage of only one regiment of cavalry at a time. Thus one of the badly-needed regiments of horse was ordered to march from Hungary in October 1756, but was expected to complete its quarantine only by the beginning of April the next year.[26]

Many needless advantages accrued to Frederick from the complaisance and lack of ruthlessness of the Austrians and the alliance in general. The allies were grouped on all sides of Prussia, yet they failed signally to exploit the advantages of their position. They could have made a much more thorough job of wrecking the important military-economic base of Berlin when it stood at their mercy in 1760;[27] they could (if Kaunitz had been willing to abate his distrust of the Russians) have been able to make use of Danzig as a staging-post on the way to Pomerania; they could have denied Frederick access to Polish recruits, remounts, cattle and grain; the French could have forbidden entry to their harbours to Prussian trading vessels, and Russia and Sweden could have held back from guaranteeing (on 20 March 1759) unrestricted trade for all ports on the Baltic, including those of Prussia.

The refugee authorities of Saxony – invaded, blackmailed and pillaged though the electorate was by the Prussians – insisted on being accorded full sovereign rights by Austria. They had considerable leverage, for regard for Saxony was vital for the credibility of the Austrian effort against Prussia. Prince Charles of Lorraine had benefited from the fact that Frederick's misdeeds in Saxony had brought him into wide discredit; conversely, the Austrians had to show that they were doing everything they could to liberate that oppressed land (see p. 97).[28]

From the tenor of the correspondence of the Saxon ministers we might suppose that Dresden stood in more danger from the Austrians than from the Saxons. The matter came to a head in the late autumn of 1759, when the Austrians wished to fortify the suburbs, and asked the Saxon authorities to supply 6,000 labourers and the necessary fascines and palisade stakes. The Saxon-Polish prime minister Brühl protested from Warsaw that the work would be useless as well as damaging, for Dresden could never be made into a tenable fortress. The Austrian demands would also complete the ruin of the neighbourhood, where three years of war had devastated the woods and left the country impoverished and depopulated; indeed the whole of Saxony, let alone the vicinity of Dresden, would be scarcely be able to furnish the able-bodied men for the work. Daun must therefore take his army down the Elbe and capture and hold Torgau and Wittenberg.[29]

Since the Saxons had taken the argument to the operational level, Kaunitz had to reply in kind. He explained on 17 November that the Austrian government would like nothing more than to expel the Prussians from Saxony and hold them at a distance. This however required energetic operations mounted from a secure base in Saxony, and the city of Dresden and its extensive suburbs offered the only possible facilities. In fact the inner city would gain security by having the enemy held at arm's length by the suburbs, once they had been suitably fortified.[30]

It was much the same story in the Saxon countryside. Prince Charles and Daun are much criticised for losing so much time once they had emerged north of the border hills into Lusatia after the victory at Kolin in 1757. A French officer provides the explanation, reporting on 10 July that 'the Empress-Queen has just ordered that the greatest possible care must be given to sparing the peasants and the country. The army has therefore been forbidden to go foraging, or take vegetables or anything else from the peasants. This prohibition has been enforced by penalties of great severity, and this, together with the way the Prussians have swept up the fodder, has multiplied the difficulty of supplying an army of this size'.[31]

In central Saxony the regard for sensibilities was taken to altogether absurd lengths. Thus the Austrians agreed without demur to the request of the Saxon *Kammercollegium* in Dresden to allow the Prussians to collect firewood from their depot on the eastern side of the Elbe; there was plenty of timber available to the Prussians closer to hand in the Hubertusberger Wald, but cutting there would have spoilt the favourite hunting of the King/Elector Augustus. Again, Serbelloni was bound by secret instructions from Vienna to allow the Prussians free passage of fodder and provisions from Torgau up the Elbe to their forward depot at Riesa. The reason was that Count Flemming, the Saxon representative in Vienna, had begged the Austrians to give way, for the Prussians would otherwise have confiscated all the peasant transport in Saxony.[32] The same niceties were observed in Silesia and again for political reasons, in this case to support the claim that Silesia was Austrian land in the process of being reclaimed from the Prussians. Thus the praiseworthy motto *Justitia et Clementia* inhibited the Austrians from exercising legitimate *raison de guerre*.[33]

A belated hardening of Austrian policies became evident from December 1759, when Maria Theresa authorised Daun to use a modicum of force if the Saxon authorities still refused to yield up the timber for the palisades at Dresden. As for the raising of supplies and other military requisites in Saxon territories, the people ought to be under an obligation to lend a helping hand to their liberators. The French were levying comprehensive requisitions elsewhere in the *Reich*, 'and so the Saxon subjects are in a position to judge what we can and must do if they fail to accede to our demands, which are reasonable and realistic.' In questions of doubt Daun was to give priority to maintaining his army, and 'not be led astray by the consequent outcry, protests and complaints'[34] Lacy pressed for similar forthright measures in Silesia. It is perhaps worth noting that the Austrians gave receipts for all their requisitions in Saxony, and honoured their debts after the war (see p. 358).

The limitation of war applies in its most recognisable form in the exercise of restraints and courtesies. It was still possible for individual commanders to maintain a jocular and easygoing friendship across the divide which separated the armies of Maria Theresa and Frederick. The Austrian Field Marshal Ulysses Maximilian Browne and the Prussian Field Marshal Keith were both products of the Jacobite emigration from the British Isles, and they corresponded by messages which passed under trumpets of truce; just as Keith felt himself entitled to ask Browne to return a valued cook who had deserted from the Prussian camp, so he was glad to send him a hamper containing four dozen bottles of English beer.[35] In the same way brotherly bonds induced Prince Louis of Württemberg to betake himself to the enemy outposts at Breslau to greet Prince Friedrich Eugen, a major-general in the Prussian service. The Prince de Ligne accompanied Louis to the encounter, and he used the opportunity to spy out what he could of the Prussian positions.

When a particular affinity was absent, officers could still pay scrupulous respect to the usages of war and polite society. *FZM.* Lacy wrote to Daun in 1762 to enquire whether he recalled the case of an NCO whom the Austrians believed to have been captured by the Prussians in violation of a truce. The man had since made it known that he had been taken prisoner fairly, and Lacy therefore now asked Daun to release a Prussian sergeant who had been seized in retaliation. Lacy had given his word of honour on the subject to the Prussians, 'and Your Excellency knows how much that matters to me'.[36] When in 1762 the post of the Austrian *FZM.* the duc d'Arenberg was captured by the Prussians, Prince Henry recognised the seal of the duchess on some of the letters, and forwarded them unopened to her husband with his compliments.

Nothing could have been more scrupulous than the behaviour of the Austrians in the case of one of their most bitter enemies, the turncoat and Prussian lieutenant-general Johann Paul Werner, whose baggage was captured by a party of the Liccaner Croats at Kauder in Silesia in June 1762. The effects which Werner had taken from the Austrians were to be returned to their rightful owners, but everything else was to be held in safekeeping, and Maria Theresa ordered this nicety to be given publicity in the newspapers.[37]

It is easy to imagine the embarrassment of Maria Theresa when she discovered that Count Emmerich Esterházy had helped himself to a great deal of personal plunder at Potsdam during the Austrian raid on Berlin in October 1760 – vases, figurines, table services of Chinese porcelain, books, 'a large painting of Diana,' and other precious objects. At the order of Maria Theresa the booty was confiscated at Prague, entered in a detailed inventory, and sent back to the Prussians without demur.[38]

Twice in the early months of 1758 the Austrians learned of deranged individuals who had harboured murderous intentions against Frederick. Kaunitz had to bring himself to write to the king on 17 January to communicate a report from Italy to the effect that 'a wine merchant of Bologna, on learning of the outcome of the battle of 5 December last [Leuthen], cried out: "Is there a knife to be found that will rid the world of the King of Prussia?" He then made his will and disappeared.' Kaunitz forwarded the news to Frederick, admitting that it was difficulty to know what weight to attach to it, 'but as the man is an obvious fanatic, and the consequences could be grave in the extreme, as touching on the sacred person of a great prince, Their Imperial Majesties desire Your Majesty to be informed as soon as possible'.[39]

Frederick's reply barely met the requirements of common courtesy, for he wished to be under no kind of obligation to the Austrians, which put Kaunitz in a still more difficult position when the Prince-Bishop of Würzburg forwarded a letter from the hosier Rose, who declared that he and his three brothers had been instructed by angels to do away with the King of Prussia, and that they would disperse among the various theatres of war to carry out their mission. The matter was laid before Kaunitz, who informed the bishop of Frederick's curt reply to the earlier warning, and advised him to clap Rose in prison and do nothing more.[40]

It is highly probable, though not entirely certain, that Vienna knew nothing in advance of the plot hatched in 1761 between the Lutheran Silesian landowner Gottfried Baron Warkotsch and the Catholic priest Franz Schmidt to kidnap Frederick from his badly-guarded quarters; the scheme was betrayed, and the two barely escaped with their lives to the Austrians. Cogniazzo claims that Maria Theresa had been totally ignorant of the conspiracy, and then, 'as I am assured by my old friend, the Treasury accountant von Meyer, she did not wish to see the wretched man [Warkotsch]. After urgent pleadings he received a small gift from her private purse, with the express order to take himself off'.[41]

Cogniazzo however adds that the Austrian generals must have known what was afoot, for elaborate arrangements for military support had been concerted with one Captain Wallis. Cogniazzo found it amusing that the great Austro-Irish family of Wallis disowned all relationship with the officer in question, for he was certain that they would have claimed him soon enough if the enterprise had succeeded.[42] After the event at least the Austrian authorities did not disown the luckless Warkotsch, and we find the *Hofkriegsrath* writing to Kaunitz that he had been furnished with a pass of indefinite duration made out in the name of a 'Count von Lobenstein'.[43] In itself the capture of Frederick was undoubtedly considered *de bonne guerre,* as Cogniazzo suggested, and for this purpose parties of Austrian hussars lay concealed in promising locations until late in the war.

It is usually accepted that warfare in pre-Revolutionary Europe was an affair of kings, cabinets and professional armies, it was innocent of atrocities, and it involved civil society scarcely at all. To what extent do these generalisations apply to the experience of the Seven Years War in the central theatre?

It is indeed remarkable that there appears to have been not a single recorded instance of a regular officer, in full command of a situation, ordering the murder of civilians in cold blood. The notion was so unthinkable that it never entered the minds of contemporaries, who lived through a war that seemed to many of them to be replete with lethal blunders, vandalisms, vicious reprisals and rancour.

Civil society and war on the larger scale were inevitably brought into immediate contact when fortified towns or cities came under attack. The Prussian general Karl Christoph Schmettau had seen service with the Austrians, and was one of the more humane of Frederick's officers, but he incurred much odium when, as the defender of Dresden in August 1759, he invoked military necessity to cause still more damage to the suburbs. Maria Theresa was predictably indignant, and the Prince of Zweibrücken as commander of the *Reichsarmee* declared that if Schmettau persisted he would act in kind against the Prussian towns of Halle and Halberstadt, and get the Russians to use reprisals throughout Brandenburg.[44]

In July 1760 it was the turn of the Prussians to attack Dresden, which was now being held by the Austrians, and a notorious bombardment (14–21 July) brought down the tower of the Kreuzkirche, and laid waste whole streets in the Altstadt. In 18th-century terms it was an atrocity, but milder in proportion than the Prussian bombardment of Prague in May and June 1757, and no worse than the destruction of Zittau by the Austrians on 23 July of that year. In none of these cases did the attackers use the population as such as a target, and they resorted to the crude weapon of bombardment only because they were too ignorant to be able to conduct a 'scientific' siege in the French manner.

There were certainly cases where near-defenceless combatants were cut down in battle, but (with the exceptions detailed below) they were produced by the heat of the moment, or the working-out of deadly rituals which are handed down through the generations. Almost every war in history shows examples of the 'no quarter' order, which has no sanction from the higher command, and yet spreads with lightning speed through an army and is given total credence. On the strength of such a rumour the Prussian troopers at Hohenfriedberg (Striegau) on 4 June 1745 cut down two battalions of Saxon grenadiers. In turn the cry of *'Dies Striegau!'* drove on the Saxon *chevaulegers* at Kolin to massacre such Prussian troops as were at their mercy.

The scene at Kolin was therefore the product of a cycle of revenge, deplorable no doubt, but understandable. However there was no absolutely compelling reason why *FZM.* Loudon should have done what he did at Landeshut (23 June 1760), which was to order his corps not to hold itself up by taking prisoners, but to cut down all who came before it. This was naturally translated by the troops into the straightforward command: *'alle die Kerls niederzuhauen!'* In these circumstances it was singularly unwise of the Prussian infantry regiment of Below to have inflicted all the damage it could on the Austrian troops, then all of a sudden throw down its muskets and cried *'Pardon!'*. It was too late, for it ignored the principle of reciprocity. It was the equivalent of the case of a machine gunner who might cut down his enemies by the score, and shout *'Kamerad!'* when he ran out of ammunition.

Otherwise nearly all of the truly unprovoked atrocities and breaches of *bonne guerre* were associated with the light troops of the respective belligerents. From the early years of the war the Bohemian spas were open to Prussian as well as Austrian military men who wished to take the 'cure,' an extraordinary complaisance which lasted until November 1759, when Friedrich Wilhelm 'Green' Kleist descended on Teplitz with his free corps and made off with a collection of Austrian generals, officers and soldiers. Vienna refused to recognise the captives as prisoners taken in the legitimate way of war, and this episode became one of the charges levelled against the Prussians by Kaunitz and Loudon in the acrimonious exchange of correspondence with Markgraf Carl of Brandenburg-Schwedt.[45]

The Russian regular troops were incomparably the best disciplined on the theatre of war in Central Europe, and yet the depredations of the Cossacks attached a reputation for barbarity to the Russian participation as a whole. Among the Austrians and Prussians, the rival *Jäger* had been given no quarter in the Silesian Wars,[46] and in the new conflict such Croats as fell alive into the hands of the Prussians were subsequently confined under appalling conditions. In May 1759 Loudon captured a Prussian redoubt which had been situated annoyingly near his camp; the work had been defended by 300 troops, but only two officers and 20 or so men were brought back alive, and it took Loudon in person considerable efforts to save these prisoners from the furious Croats, who were determined to give no quarter. 'This bloody-mindedness was not evident last year, but it has been inflamed in the present by those few Croats who were liberated by exchange from their dreadful imprisonment by the Prussians over the last winter. Their reports have embittered the fresh levies of Croats who have arrived for the new campaign'.[47]

On 13 April 1762 Frederick instructed Lieutenant-General Werner to take his mobile corps to join the Crimean Tartars at Kaschau, and accompany them on a raid through Hungary and into Lower Austria. 'So as to compel the Austrians to cover Vienna, you can allow the Tartars to carry out many more atrocities in Austria than elsewhere. It would be a good idea to set fire to a number of villages near Vienna – the ones which belong to the greatest magnates – so that the flames may be seen from the city. They will set up a mighty howl and reduce everything to confusion'.[48]

It was not from any lack of will on Frederick's part that the scheme collapsed, and the king in person was responsible for introducing an element of petty malice which would otherwise have been absent from the war. The evidence ranges from the despoliation of the Grosser Garten in Dresden, to the systematic wrecking of the properties of the King/Elector Augusts of Saxony-Poland and his prime minister Count Brühl, and the kidnapping of noblemen from Saxon and Austrian territories. In July 1760 Maria Theresa resolved that 'just as the enemy have made off with noblemen of the neighbourhood of Teschen, so we must snatch an equivalent number from their part of Silesia and send them to Olmütz as hostages'.[49]

The War of the People

In that supposedly autocratic age Maria Theresa and her circle believed to a remarkable degree that they were under an obligation to present their cause in a favourable light to '*das Publicum*,' an entity that was probably compounded of providers of financial credit (who must be convinced that they had made a sound investment), the bureaucrats and wielders of local power through whose goodwill alone the state could function, the Viennese crowds (who lived cheek-by-jowl with their Imperial masters) and the bewigged and bepowdered civilian strategists who uttered their considered judgements at assemblies, at the opera and in the coffee houses. In such a way Daun was taken to task for having done so little to exploit his victory at Hochkirch (14 October 1758). Lacy tried to cheer him by saying that he could safely ignore such ignorant chatter, for all that mattered was 'the sane element among the public, what is called the "intelligent public"'.[50] The carping continued, and in September 1761 another of Daun's confidants, Joseph d'Ayasasa, wrote from Vienna that Francis Stephen had assured him that he and Maria Theresa were influenced in no way by the talk in the capital; however the Emperor's further comments gave d'Ayasasa reason to believe that the contrary was the case.[51]

In the contest for international opinion Frederick delivered a considerable advantage to the Austrians when he broke the peace by invading Saxony at the end of August 1756. Kaunitz recognised the opportunity, and he lost no time in sending a printed circular to all the Austrian envoys in foreign courts, so that they would be able to declare the Prussian misdeeds with full chapter and verse.[52]

Kaunitz was also the author of the official relations of the battles and campaigns, which were inserted in the *Wiener Diarium* and dispatched abroad. His style was first shown in the way he edited Browne's account of the battle of Lobositz (1 October 1756). A couple of his adjustments were intended just to make the narrative clearer, but through others Kaunitz emphasised the role of units which had done well, and excised what Brown had written concerning the comparatively small Prussian numbers, and the loss by the Austrians of two standards and three cannon.

Atrocities were believed to be scarcely less dangerous to one's cause than misfortunes in combat.[53] The Prussians found, or invented, cause for complaint against the corps of Loudon, when it coursed through Brandenburg during the Kunersdorf campaign in the summer of 1759. The Austrians had long been collecting evidence of Prussian misdeeds in Habsburg territory, and, in response to the accusations against Loudon, Vienna now published an official *Circular-Rescript* which detailed the Prussian brutalities in the full-scale invasions of 1757 and 1758, and in the subsequent raids by the flying corps. In one of many comparable incidents Colonel 'Green' Kleist had descended on the monastery of Ossegg in Bohemia in 1759, and translated his threats into violent deeds when the monks managed to collect only 1,000 florins out of the 100,000 which had been demanded from them. Kleist dragged off the prior and 11 of his monks as hostages, while

> his rampaging soldiers ran into the chapel with drawn sabres, knocked over the two great candlesticks which were standing in front of the altar, broke open the tabernacle and threw the Sacred Host from the ciborium onto the altar steps, vandalised the picture of the Mother of God and cast it down the altar steps, despoiled the linen of all the altars, smashed the candlesticks and crucifixes, wrecked the great organ to the extent that it became completely unusable, and even broke a number of the altar stones.

The Prussians continued the devastation through the sacristy, the main abbey building and the library and set about beating the monks with swords and sticks.[54]

In this context the name of Kaunitz once more came into prominence in 1761, when an exchange of protests with the Prussian lieutenant-general Markgraf Carl of Brandenburg-Schwedt widened from its original subject, the maltreatment of prisoners, to a whole chapter of alleged atrocities by the two sides. The Prussians published a version of the correspondence in 1761, and it went unanswered until Kaunitz asked the *Hofkriegsrath* in the following May to look into the facts so that he could issue an informed refutation.[55]

With little or no official prompting, a comprehensive partisan literature sprang into being – accounts of battles and bombardments, letters from the theatre of war, verse dialogues, and the successive editions of *Poetische Bilder der meisten Kriegerischen Vorgänge in Europa seit dem Jahre 1756* by the Jesuit Michael Denis (1760), and Johann Rautenstrauch's *Österreichischen Kriegslieder* (in the style of Gleim's Prussian grenadier songs). The Austrian efforts were supported by the popular press of Frankfurt-am-Main and Augsburg, and inevitably opposed by the Berlin papers. The entertainment value of some of the exchanges was high, and the *Limping Messenger or the Abortive Siege of Neisse* (*Der hinkende Bote oder die aufgehobene Belagerung von Neiss*, 1760) mocked the Austrian pronunciation of words like '*Brief*' ('*Prief*', letter), '*ganz gewiss*' ('*kanz kwiss*,' most assuredly), '*nicht*' '*nit*'), 'Daun' ('*Taun*'), and 'Neisse' ('*Naiss*').

All of this argues for a substantial popular base for the causes of the belligerents in Central Europe. The supporters of the Austrian effort were moved by sympathy for the wronged sovereign, and outrage at the presumption of the parvenu and heretical Prussian monarchy. Cogniazzo commented that 'everyone who has served a Catholic power will be aware that an element of religious fanaticism will always creep into their wars with Protestant states'.[56] The 'war literature' continued long after hostilities ended, and Sir John Burgoyne noted in 1766 that 'the recovery of Silesia is at the heart of every individual in the Austrian dominions, and they will be ready at all times to sacrifice blood, or fortune in that cause'.[57] War with Revolutionary France broke out in 1792, and in the following year the Jacobins beheaded one of the daughters of Maria Theresa, and yet the feeling persisted that the Prussians were still Austria's 'real' enemy, and the revulsion became evident in something like its old force when Prussia abandoned the First Coalition in 1795.[58]

Good-hearted people of no great sophistication believed that it would be possible to raise bands of idealistic volunteers who would fight for Maria Theresa for the duration of hostilities, and independently of the conventional military structure. Kaunitz had to advise Maria Theresa against accepting the well-meaning offer of Greek civilians to raise a force of Epirot volunteers on her behalf (see p. 414). Two ladies – an Italian and a German – who described themselves as daughters of soldiers, wrote in the same vein to Vienna to solicit the support of some important minister to present their case, 'which might otherwise be dismissed as a flight of female fancy.' It was well known

> how a quite extraordinary love and respect for the person of Her Most Gracious Majesty fills the hearts of her German, Hungarian, Italian and Netherlands subjects, and how She in turn feels towards them as a mother. In the present critical circumstances this sentiment could be turned to advantage by enlisting a large number of fine men, quite apart from the designated contingents of recruits, and without any burden on the provinces.[59]

No record is preserved of the reply.

Daun welcomed in general terms the support of the people in a theatre of war. He read the relevant section of Frederick's *General Principia,* and noted how the king had found it impossible to bribe anyone in Bohemia or Moravia[60] (see p. 63). Likewise in the early summer of 1758, when Frederick was besieging Olmütz in Moravia, Loudon could write to a friend that the peasants had fled to the hills, and would now be able to disrupt the Prussian convoys on the long line of communication from Silesia. He could not

> say enough in praise of the zeal and loyalty of the entire province. All the peasants are ready to to take up arms and fall on the enemy – they only wish to be led. This could well occasion a peasant war, which is not something to be advised, but we most do all we can to maintain these folk in their enthusiasm, and I guarantee that in the event of the king retreating these outraged locals could perform excellent service.[61]

However few other men in authority would have been willing to accept the assistance of armed peasants even with the qualifications entered by Loudon. Not only was the soldierly etiquette of the time hostile to notions of civilians intervening in the affairs of military professionals,[62] but the conventional monarchies and the feudal order could not have made a place for active popular support without weakening the basis of their own authority.

Among the much fought-over Silesians the instinct for survival seems to have been paramount. During their siege of Schweidnitz in 1757 we encounter the complaint that 'apart from a few Catholics, the Silesians cannot conceal their antipathy towards the Austrians. It is possible that many of them are too afraid to make up their minds and declare for us, but it remains true that the non-Catholics appear to have a deep-rooted antagonism against the Austrians. This way of thinking must have been influenced by the pastors under the Prussian administration, and it can be eradicated only through the effect of time and through good behaviour on our part'.[63] Yet Lieutenant-General Winterfeldt, the arch-Prussian, had only criticised the minister Schlabrendorf to Frederick for his harsh administration of the province, and explained to the king that this was why 'the Silesians have become such good Austrians that it is impossible to recruit any spies among them, or even to rely on them telling us of the arrival of enemy detachments'.[64]

The dilemma of the Silesian landowners was observed by Cogniazzo during the campaign of Bunzelwitz in 1761, when they were under orders from Frederick to supply labour to build his entrenched camp, and simultaneously prohibited by the Austrian generals from doing anything of the kind. If they chose to obey the Prussians they put themselves at the mercy of the first deserter or disgruntled peasant to go over to the enemy, who in that case would haul them off to Austrian territory.[65]

The Price

The final index of the totality of a war must relate to its consequences and cost. The political and strategic results must await evaluation elsewhere. The financial price for Austria is readily quantifiable, as the extra costs of 262 million florins incurred by the war, and the total state debt of 284,963,042 florins. The census provides indirect evidence of a flight of population from Bohemia to the western provinces of the monarchy in the course of the war, and the devastation of Bohemia and Moravia was of an order which in the eyes of Kaunitz diminished their value relative to the intact 'peripheral' lands Austrian Italy and the Netherlands.

Thanks to the meticulous book-keeping of the *Hofkriegsrath* we know that the cost for the Austrian army reached 303,585 men of all ranks, of whom 126,030, or well over one-third, lost their lives.[66] However these were military men who knowingly put themselves in harm's way, or who were marginal to society. *FM.* Daun, who was by no means a callous man, could write to Maria Theresa that losing 3,000 to 5,000 troops at a time was of no great consequence (see p. 436). Was this therefore the last of the great conflicts in which it was possible to believe that war was not inherently evil?

The Prussian hussar major Warnery could see nothing good that had come of a contest which resulted in 'so much treasure expended, so many towns burnt, so many villages destroyed, so many innocent souls ruined, and the more than 400,000 men who had died or were killed'.[67] A contrary view was taken by a fellow-Walloon, the Austrian colonel the Prince de Ligne. In his experience he had seen 'too many displays of humanity, so much goodness to repair a little evil, that I cannot regard war as an abomination and nothing else, as long as we do not pillage or burn, and the damage is confined to the men who are killed – they are destined to die anyway in the course of time, and in less glorious circumstances.' Images sprang to his mind – his grenadiers giving their bread and pay to a poor family which had lost its home in a fire, the hussars who returned the purses of captured enemy soldiers, and shared the contents of their own with those unfortunate men. 'The greater the courage, the greater the humanity'.[68]

The Alliance

The Elusive Victory

As the war progressed, an extraordinary paradox impressed itself on allied statesmen and commanders. By all rational calculations, Frederick of Prussia should have been borne down by the odds which weighed against him. In terms of population Prussia owned about 3,500,000 souls as against the 70,000,000 of Austria, Russia and France, leaving out of account the peoples of Sweden and the well-affected parts of Germany. The balance was slightly more even when it came to putting effective troops into the field, but even here Frederick stood at a pronounced disadvantage: by early 1758 the belligerent forces were being massed in their full strength, and Frederick could deploy no more than 135,000 men as against the 150,000 troops of Austria and the *Reichsarmee* and some 98,000 Russians and Swedes, or a total allied force of 248,000.

Again and again triumph seemed to lie within the allies' grasp. Henrich Count Callenberg wrote in November 1757 that it seemed that only some kind of malignant fate had so far prevented the allies from surrounding and crushing the King of Prussia, whose eel-like twistings and turnings had reduced his force to such a state that he had not even been able to protect Berlin against the raid by Hadik's handful of men.[69]

Things once more promised well for the alliance after the Russians and Austrians had beaten Frederick at Kunersdorf in August 1759. The duc de Choiseul urged the Austrians that no more favourable opportunity had presented itself to accomplish the objectives of the alliance, 'but while these great advantages are still in our hands we must exploit them against this exceptionally vigilant enemy, before he can recover his wits and repair his damage'.[70] By the end of 1761 the Austrians and Russians had driven in Frederick's south-eastern and eastern flanks, and were in a position to open the next campaign within lethal distance of the Prussian heartland.

Peace came in 1763, but in a form which left Frederick in full possession both of his historic territories, and what he had seized from Maria Theresa in Silesia. When he looked back long afterwards Kaunitz commented on the astonishing nature of that war 'in which we and our allies, by the King of Prussia's own admission, brought him eight times to the brink of disaster, but in which were finally only too glad to hang onto what we had without further loss'.[71] As early as November 1757, in the letter already quoted, Count Callenberg found it intolerable that, in the midst of the mighty forces of the alliance, Frederick continued to parade his broken-down army up the length and breadth of Central Europe 'with that air of ease and presumption which he always maintains when things are at their worst for him, evidently being persuaded that he only has to show himself in person to be able to check and confound his enemies'.[72] He was penning these words when he was told that some disaster had overtaken the combined armies of Soubise and Hildburghausen in Thuringia. This turned out to be the battle of Rossbach. What had been going wrong? Part of the explanation lies in the nature of the alliance.

Kaunitz occupied a central political position within the league, comparable in its way with the central operational position of Frederick in the theatre of war. Just as Frederick exploited his interior lines to strike at each of his enemies in turn, so Kaunitz was at pains to keep the political initiative in his hands by separating the Franco-British conflict from the war on the European continent, by negotiating as far as possible separate treaties with individual allies, and by seeking to channel communications between them through himself – rather as he managed his diplomats when he reorganized the *Staatscanzley*. There were two obstacles in the way. The first was that it was inherently difficult for Kaunitz to be the driver of a coalition when he was not also the paymaster. The other was his temperament, which verged on meglomania. The Swedish envoy Nils Bark had detected prime ministerial ambitions in Kaunitz as early as April 1757. One year later he had to inform his masters in Stockholm that:

communication with this minister is becoming more difficult and infrequent all the time: he is over-loaded with business, being, as he is, at the head of all the departments, and yet seems inclined to allow himself a generous amount of free time. Formerly the foreign representatives used to have one day a week for their audience, but ever since the beginning of the war he has denied them access, claiming that he has too much to do.

The real reason (continued the Swede) was probably because Kaunitz was annoyed that passages from his confidential conversations with Count Flemming, the Saxon minister in Vienna, had been printed by the Prussians.

You are therefore reduced to asking for an appointment, but even then you must have specific orders from your court to communicate. He is much disinclined to talk about the matter in hand, whereas before we had an established right to put questions to him. He is scarcely to be seen in his usual social circle in the evening, and is very much disinclined to discuss business, to judge by the way he cuts short any conversation of the kind.[73]

The allied representatives in Vienna learned to exchange information among themselves, and consult the *Reichs*-Vizecanzler Rudolph Joseph Colloredo, who was good company, and well informed about the affairs of Germany in general.

As it concerned Central Europe, the basic strategy of the allies was to present Frederick with a multitude of threats. The idea was simple and the execution seemed practicable, yet Frederick was able to ask a friend in a rhetorical way in 1758: 'These people with their overwhelmingly superior forces, who throw themselves against us from the four quarters of the globe, what have they managed to do? How is it possible that with their depth of resources, forces and troops they have been able to accomplish so little?' He knew that a single well concerted plan would have finished him off, and he concluded that the very strength of the alliance was its undoing, for each partner wished only to shift the responsibility for action onto the others.[74] Was it possible that Kaunitz promoted Austria's narrower interests so well that he denied his allies of legitimate advantages, to the detriment of their will to combine against Frederick? This question has particular relevance to Austria's relations with the French.

France

I have never seen anyone more pleased with anything he had done than the Abbé Bernis appeared on this occasion. When he forwarded his paper to me he seemed to be saying: 'Now, you must agree that I am the greatest statesman in history!' Marshal Belle-Isle applauded by thumping with his stick and patting his stomach at every item in the abbé's catalogue of self-congratulation, while Madam de Pompadour indicated to me how fortunate I was to have been the instrument which such great minds had chosen to employ. As for me, I made myself humble and stupid and replied: 'I will tell you what I think when I have read it'... It became evident that this treaty – a huge document with all the agreements which had been entered into – was aimed basically at sacrificing nearly the whole of Europe to the aggrandisement of the House of Austria,
           the comte de Stainville learning of the Second Treaty of Versailles.[75]

The Seven Years War turned out very badly for the French – they forfeited the greater part of their possessions in North America, they saw their navy destroyed, they expanded their army to 270,000 troops for no lasting gain in continental Europe, their historic influence in Sweden,

Poland and Turkey was diminished, and they were precipitated into a financial crisis which hastened the coming of the Revolution.

In the passage reproduced above Étienne-François comte de Stainville (later duc de Choiseul) anticipates powerful tradition in historiography which attributes these undoubted disasters to the new connection with Austria, and thus with a needless land war in Europe which was none of France's seeking. The French historian Richard Waddingon concluded that at the Second Treaty of Versailles the Austrians had obtained the military and financial aid of the greatest power in Europe at a very cheap price. France in consequence threw the living force of the nation into a war in continental Europe in which her interests were only marginally engaged: 'It was in Germany, in a struggle in which the French battalions were effectively only the auxiliaries of the Austrian armies, it was on the fields of Rossbach, Krefeld and Minden that we lost our colonies in Canada and along the Gulf of the St. Lawrence'.[76] A later study goes further:

> French nationalists, by the 1760s, hated the Church because they associated it with defeat in war. In the Seven Years War… France, allied with Catholic Austria, had been decisively defeated by Protestant Prussia, allied with Protestant England. The Catholic monarchy and its Catholic ally had allowed the French nation to be humiliated. The detested alliance and the associated humiliation were incarnated in the person of the foreign queen: the hated Austrian, Marie Antoinette. Well before the French Revolution, French nationalists promoted the expulsion of the Jesuits from France as an act of liberation from Catholic internationalism.[77]

The matter calls for closer examination. Before any kind of agreement had been made, France had already gained immensely from the desire of Kaunitz and Maria Theresa to form a connection, and their decision (in October 1755) to stand aside from the coming Franco-British hostilities. If Austria had clung to the Old System, the French would have at the very least have had to maintain large forces on their Netherlands, Rhenish and Italian borders, and probably also engage in expensive campaigns beyond them.

As for the engagements at the Second Treaty of Versailles (1 May 1757), Starhemberg had certainly concluded an excellent deal from the Austrian point of view, and Kaunitz hailed his negotiation as a masterpiece, and yet the facts show that Austria had a genuine and lasting commitment to the alliance as such, and that France was far from being a passive victim of the Diplomatic Revolution as a whole.

Kaunitz recognised that interests could be joint, as well as relating to the advantage of particular states, and it became evident that Austria's share in the joint interest was of a kind to survive the war and Maria Theresa's final renunciation of Silesia in 1763. Kaunitz had not concealed the internal shortcomings of France from Maria Theresa, 'but one thing we can say for certain, that for as long as Your Majesty's connection and good understanding with France endures, we have no reason to fear hostile activity in the Netherlands, Italy or the Empire, or harbour any major concerns relating to the Turks. Thus the whole attention and resources of the Most Gracious House may be turned exclusively against the King of Prussia'.[78] Maria Theresa needed no prompting, for she was convinced that Austria and France were tied by enduring bonds of both interest and religion, and she upheld her commitment to the end of her days. Cultural and intellectual links were also being established, and (if we except the bumptious ways of the French attachés) the military men of the two nations also gained greatly by the connection.

The French did not necessarily compromise their narrower interests by their engagement to Austria and the land war. The historic strength of France lay in her armies, not her navy, which raises the issue of what might be termed 'convertibility,' namely the question of how far it would have been possible for the French to divert resources in a useful way into the war against the British. It was not simply a matter of cash, but of long-term investments in port facilities and skilled manpower of many different kinds. Moreover, as the American War of Independence was to show, the French could mount a realistic challenge on the seas only when the Spanish were at hand to divide the attention of the British, and in this conflict Spain intervened only in 1762, by when the French naval power had been effectively destroyed.

The duc de Choiseul himself, the promoter of the French colonial and maritime effort, warned against the wider dangers that were presented by the likely British and Prussian ambitions to unite the Protestant states of Germany, to strengthen them by secularising the ecclesiastical states (some of them clients of France), and to make fundamental changes to the constitution of the *Reich*. Moreover France had a lively interest in the welfare of Saxony, and the clamour of the French attachés and diplomats caused the Austrians and the *Reichsarmee* to waste time and men in conquering untenable ground in the direction of Torgau and Wittenberg (below).

Although the French territorial gains in the Netherlands had been made conditional on the defeat of Prussia, and were limited in geographical extent, they would nevertheless been of very great value, for they would have taken in some of the most highly developed lands of Europe, and advanced the outermost strategic barrier of the Ile de France a significant distance to the northeast. Meanwhile the French garrisons installed in Nieuport and Ostend formed a useful extension of France's strategic shoreline.

Otherwise the only deployment of French forces of even indirect help to Austria was the march of the corps of Soubise across Germany in 1757, and that was prompted less by the French engagements at the Second Treaty of Versailles than by a personal pledge on the part of Louis XV, who wished to do something to help Maria Theresa in her desperate straits in the early summer of 1757; these troops, together with those of the *Reichsarmee* and the reinforcements under Broglie, progressed no further than Thuringia, where they were routed by Frederick at Rossbach on 5 November.

The French never again showed their noses so far to the east. Soubise was on the march in the summer of 1758 with a force of 25–30,000 French when Maria Theresa learned that the main French army under Marshal Clermont had been thrown onto the defensive by the Prussian general Prince Ferdinand of Brunswick and his army of Hanoverians and smaller north German contingents. This unlikely force had been generated by English gold, and represented a new element in the war. Maria Theresa waived her right to the French auxiliaries (a deed hailed by Bemis as an act of self-sacrifice) and the Austrians did not revive their claim. Perhaps we should ask why the French had become embroiled with the Hanoverians in the first place, and what this might tell us about French objectives and interests in the continental land war.

The War of the Austrian Succession had ended in a run of French triumphs in the Austrian Netherlands and Holland. It was therefore natural to assume that in any new conflict the French could put their perceived superiority in land warfare to no better use than to conquer Hanover. The electorate was central to British dynastic, commercial and strategic interest, as we have seen (see p. 123), and, once it was in possession of the French, Hanover would have been a potent bargaining counter at any congress of peace. In November 1756 Kaunitz took alarm at the prospect, for he knew that George II had the money at his command to assemble an army in northwestern Germany at short notice, and he urged the French to send their forces to the help of the Austrians by way of Swabia, the Upper Palatinate and the Vogtland of Saxony – a roundabout route which would have passed safely to the south of Hanover. The French however pressed for access to Hanoverian territory, and on 4 January 1757 Kaunitz wrote to the Hanoverians to ask them to allow the French to pass through, but otherwise to stand aside from the war. George II made a disconcertingly bellicose speech to the British Parliament on 18 February, but even now he was not averse to some kind of arrangement, and he resisted an invitation from the old Markgraf of Hessen-Cassel to join him in forming a Protestant league.

It now became clear that the French demands on Hanover went well beyond those required by an army that was just on transit to help the Austrians, for the French called not only beyond free passage, and for bridges and other facilities to be put at their disposal, but for the Hanoverian troops to retire to their garrisons and not leave them without French consent. Lest there should be any doubt as to the will of the French to conquer Hanover, it must be pointed out that the French demands, strong though they were, represented a 'moderate' position on the part of the foreign minister Bernis, who had been resisting the arguments of the war party of Marshal Belle-Isle (appointed to the *Conseil* in May 1756) to invade Hanover without any kind of formality.

Kaunitz gave way to the French pressure, and on 27 April his ambassador in London, Carl Colloredo, delivered a near-ultimatum which corresponded to the French summons. Frederick's stock was now rising rapidly in Britain, and Colloredo's demand was couched in such peremptory terms that it was certain to be rejected.

In the short term the French leaders had the sort of war they desired. Marshal d'Estrées and his Army of the Lower Rhine invaded Hanover, defeated the Hanoverian army at Hastenbeck on 26 July (aided by an Austrian contingent from the Netherlands), pushed it back towards the North Sea, and forced it to capitulate at Kloster-Zeven on 8 September. The French proceeded to treat occupied north-west Germany as conquered territory, and they made no serious attempt to implement the stated objective of the joint French and Austrian operations, which was to lay siege to the great Prussian fortress-depot of Magdeburg.

The French left entirely out of account Kaunitz's warning of November 1756, relating to the generative power of finance at the disposal of George II. The Hanoverians repudiated the Treaty of Kloster-Zeven, and on 15 February 1758 Prince Ferdinand of Brunswick opened the offensive which drove the French from their winter quarters and back across the Rhine. The Prime Minister William Pitt was now able to commit the British Parliament to helping Prussia by subsidies, and to pledge both cash and a contingent of British troops to support the operations of Ferdinand of Brunswick.

Thereafter the French strove for peace with Prussia, while confining their efforts in Germany to the war against Hanover and its auxiliaries. The French finances were not equal to sustaining a land war over the long term, for the treasury had become over-dependent on loans, while the army had fallen too deeply into a slough of indiscipline and irresponsibility to be able to recover to an effective degree before hostilities ended. Kaunitz commented that 'the confusion would never have progressed so far if the French had followed our well-intentioned advice, instead of their desire to go in search of vast treasures in Hanover.'

Kaunitz recognised that it was impossible to hold the French to the letter of the treaties of Versailles in the face of the new realities. Their implementation depended on speed and military victory, but by now the French leadership had been demoralised by 'the fatal way they rushed into war with Hanover, the poor conduct of the French generals, the battle of Rossbach and other reverses which followed… and the fact that England now plays the complete master at sea and in America.' The French moreover feared that Holland would join the enemy ranks, if France dared to enter into possession of parts of the Netherlands in virtue of the second Versailles treaty.

France (so Kaunitz continued) would be driven into a separate peace if Austria insisted on fulfilling the old treaties, whereas a new arrangement would hold out the prospect of continuing the war on promising terms, especially since it seemed that Frederick's army and economy were severely weakened. Kaunitz knew that Louis XV had resolved to dismiss the defeatist Abbe Bernis, and replace him as foreign minister by Étienne-François comte de Stainville (soon to become duc de Choiseul). As a native Lorrainer Stainville had strong family connections with the house of Habsburg-Lorraine (he had a younger brother in the Austrian army) and he was at present serving as the French ambassador to Vienna.[79]

As Stainville/Choiseul qualified as a friend in so many respects, nobody could have been better placed to persuade the Austrians to make the necessary adjustments in the alliance. He had come to the conclusion that France must now put her main effort into the maritime and colonial war against the British, and before he left Vienna on 3 December 1758 he seems to have agreed with Kaunitz on reducing France's already vestigial commitment to the war against Prussia. The Third Treaty of Versailles (negotiated at the end of 1758, but signed and dated the 30 March following) distanced the French formally from the war on the eastern theatre by freeing Louis from the obligation to continue hostilities until Maria Theresa had recovered Silesia and Glatz, by commuting for cash (288,000 florins per annum) the old French duty to support the Austrians by 24,000 auxiliaries, and by reducing the French subsidy to about one-quarter of the level agreed at the Second Treaty of Versailles. The provisions relating to Don Philip were abandoned; Maria Theresa renounced her claims to the reversion of the Italian duchies, while she retained all the parts of the Netherlands which were to have been ceded to him in return. The French were now to hold their garrisons in Nieuport and Ostend only on a temporary basis.

French influence on the Austro-Prussian war was not entirely at an end. Louis XV was bound by close family connections with the ruling house of Saxony and Poland, and Versailles therefore had dynastic as well as political interests in the affairs of the electorate. Although the Austrians would have derived more direct profit from campaigning in Silesia, they had to pay due regard to the French envoys and military attachés, who were pressing all the time for the liberation of the whole of Saxony.[80] This was irksome in the extreme for Daun, who knew that it was easy enough to reconquer Saxony all the way down to Leipzig and Wittenberg when Frederick's back was turned, but impossible to sustain those gains in the face of any serious Prussian counter-offensive.

The French attachés gave further causes for annoyance. The Austrian commanders could not realistically have dispensed with the services of Gribeauval, Riverson and other French technicians, for this enabled them to attack and defend fortresses in ways that would otherwise have been impossible. It was an altogether different matter with two officers of the French cavalry – Brigadier Montazet and Captain Rutant de Marainville – who arrived as attachés in virtue of an agreement on military liaison. The Austrians could not deny them a certain flair and boldness, as they showed at Kolin and elsewhere,[81] but these virtues were attended by irresponsibility and an overweening presumption. The Austrians warned the French against wearing their blue officers' uniforms, which looked so much like the Prussian garb.[82] Montazet took no notice, and was duly hacked about by the Austrian cavalry at Hochkirch. He nevertheless recovered so well that 'he is not only in no way disfigured, but looks almost better than before, for his nose, which was previously rather crooked, has healed absolutely straight'.[83]

The irrepressible Montazet claimed to have established special relationships with Kaunitz in the management of strategy, and with *FZM*. Lacy in the field,[84] and French officers of all kinds had a way of presenting themselves at headquarters as if with special authorisation from Francis Stephen or Kaunitz (see p. 161). In their dispatches to Paris the Frenchmen attributed any success attained by Daun to their own sage counsels and brilliant execution, while assigning to him the exclusive blame for misfortunes and missed opportunities. The Austrians opened the reports surreptitiously (a famed Austrian skill) and so Daun was made fully aware of what was being reported about him, without being able to do anything about it.[85] Historians can judge the Frenchmens' credibility by the fact that Montazet could admit on 2 November 1760 that he had been four years now with the Austrians, and still did not understand German.

Russia

By the time of the Seven Years War the alliance with Russia was a generation old, and over the last decade the connection had gathered in purpose. Empress Elizabeth (who came to the throne in 1741) was a victim of extremes of temperament, which impelled her variously into bouts of energetic work, excesses of piety and spells of lassitude; her hatred of Frederick was never in doubt, and it was given focus and direction by her Grand Chancellor Aleksei Petrovich Bestuzhev, who in September 1745 had submitted a well thought-out memorandum on the nature of the Prussian threat. '*La destruction totale de la Prusse*,' as the Russians now put it to the Austrians on 20 April 1756, would be accomplished in an agreeable fashion by restoring Silesia and Glatz to Maria Theresa, by delivering Halle to Saxony and further lands in Pomerania to the Swedes, by Russian gains along the inland border with Poland, and by expanding Russia's frontage onto the Baltic by acquiring the Polish duchies of Curland and Semigallia. Poland was to be compensated by the Prussian duchy of East Prussia.

Bestuzhev was already losing ground to the Shuvalov brothers and the pro-French Vice-Chancellor Vorontsov. However the new men were dedicated just as strongly to the contest with Prussia, and in this respect the only alteration was that the name of Bestuzhev had been linked with the defunct connection with the British, whereas Vorontsov and the rest looked to France; the French reciprocated by taking over the payment of the 2 million florins per annum which had hitherto been due from Austria.

Kaunitz still had cause for concern. In his celebrated memorandum of 24 March 1749 he had pointed out that Elizabeth was a permanent invalid, and that upon her death Russia could well be subject to revolutionary changes of policy. Onsets of dropsy, asthma and convulsions threatened her life towards the end of 1756, and again in a particularly dramatic seizure on 8 September 1758; the Russian statesmen and commanders were aware that the designated heir Grand Duke (Prince) Peter of Holstein-Gottorp was a devotee of Frederick and all things Prussian, and that he would at the very least take Russia out of the war as soon as his aunt died.

For a man who prided himself on his logic, Kaunitz seems to have been unaware of the contradiction when he proclaimed in June 1756 that Austria and Russia were bound by immutable interests.[86] As they were understood in 1757, these interests appeared to coincide very closely, for the Russians had committed themselves gladly to helping Maria Theresa to recover Silesia and Glatz, while they were expected to conquer East Prussia only as a temporary measure, and hand it over to Poland at the triumphal peace.

Perceptions changed once the Russians had overrun East Prussia early in 1758, and found that the duchy (which they treated with sedulous care) was amenable to their rule. Kaunitz took fright, for such a marked expansion of Russian sovereign territory down the Baltic coast would bring the Russians within short marching or sailing distance of the *Reich*. He intrigued successfully to prevent the Russians gaining use of the Free City and port of Danzig, but the Russians regarded as a derogation of their status as a full '*puissance belligerante*' all the Austrian attempts to bind them to occupying East Prussia only as auxiliaries of Maria Theresa. In 1760, much against his will, Kaunitz had to agree to the Russians' annexing East Prussia outright, as the new price for recognising the return of Austrian rule to Silesia and Glatz.

Grand Duke Peter was still not to be moved from his commitment to Frederick, and Kaunitz stated at the end of 1760 that it was 'absolutely incompatible with the interest of the Most Gracious House to see the already considerable power of the Russian Empire extend still further and approach the borders of Germany. Future eventualities cannot be foreseen, and our apprehensions can only be increased by the knowledge of the great numbers of Orthodox believers who stretch from Moldavia to the Baltic. Thus there could be more to fear from Russia than from the King of Prussia, especially as Poland presents no kind of barrier. Curland is shut in completely by the Russians, and the finest harbours of the Baltic are in their hands.' It would be worse still if Peter retained his Holstein lands after he acceded to the throne of Russia, for then his ambitions would spread to Germany, and perhaps even lead him to becoming German Emperor himself.[87] The only constructive policy for the Austrians was therefore to derive what military advantage they could from the connection with Russia as long as Elizabeth lived. This time of grace expired when Elizabeth died on 5 January 1762, leaving Austria to fight on unsupported.

Over the course of the war the Russian army adapted itself in a cumulatively impressive way to the problems of fighting a formidable enemy so far from the homeland. The Russians' greatest asset was the quality of the private soldier. Disciplined, steadfast and ferocious, the Russian infantry gave an impressive account of itself from the beginning of the war, and the first encounter between the Russians and an army under Frederick's direct command (Zorndorf, 25 August 1758) left the Prussian survivors in a state of permanent trauma. The outbreak of the Seven Years War caught the Russian regular cavalry at a time when it was reorganising and expanding, and consequently at something of a disadvantage, but the Russian horse launched a number of effective counter-attacks at Zorndorf, and together with the Austrian cavalry it mounted the devastating charge which completed the overthrow of the Prussians at Kunersdorf (12 August 1759).

The Cossacks proved surprisingly poor at the business of scouting and screening, at which we might have expected them to excel, and their career of plunder, rape, massacre and incendiarism-helped Prussian publicists to attach an undeserved reputation of barbarity to the Russian troops as a whole. Seven thousand fine Don Cossacks were however in action from the second half of 1760, and by the end of the war they were acting in concert with the regular dragoons to get the better of the Prussian hussars in Pomerania.

The Russians owned some powerful and innovative types of artillery (below), thanks to the attentions if the Petr Ivanovich Shuvalov, while their gunners and bombardiers proved to be just as dogged as their infantry. The Austrian attaché *FZM.* Friedrich Daniel St. André reported that 'the artillery is an excellent state, indeed pretty near perfection. Its officers without exception are good, and it is also very well served by the ordinary artillerymen'.[88]

The reputation of the Russian regimental officers was generally poor, thus presenting a rare instance of an army whose undoubted strength lay in its soldiers rather than its leaders. Russian headquarters were stuffed with armies of clerks, but native Russian staff officers were almost non-existent, which was why the habits of campaigning on the steppes were perpetuated into the early campaigns of the war against the Prussians: the Russian army moved in a single mass, and at Zorndorf these herd-like instincts combined with the enemy pressure to reduce the Russians to fighting in a great oblong, as if they had been warding off swarming Turks or Tartars. Some remarkable improvements were nevertheless evident in the later campaigns. From 1759 the Russian armies marched by separate columns, according to the best modern practice, while the troops were deployed on the field of battle in ways specifically designed to counter the Prussian grand tactics.

Changes of a more fundamental nature were needed to reform the pattern and direction of the Russian operations. If we discount the overrunning of East Prussia in 1758, which was an uncontested occupation, the cycle of Russian campaigns in the early years of the war was ponderous in the extreme. The new Conference was supposed to co-ordinate all warlike activity, but in fact it failed to reach clear understandings with the Austrians before the campaigning seasons opened, and thereafter it tried to dictate the operations of the armies in the field through exchanges of correspondence between St. Petersburg and the theatre of war.

The supply base for the campaigns in Brandenburg and Silesia was the line of the Vistula, which ran through central Poland some 500 kilometres distant from the Oder. From the Vistula the Russians stocked their forward base at Posen on the Warthe, a right-bank tributary of the Oder, which thus became the assembly point of their main field army. From Posen the Russians debouched onto the scene of operations, dragging their vast supply train with them; the army manoeuvred, camped or fought for the few weeks available for such activities in the summer, then fell back towards the Vistula. Every campaign on the central axis therefore had to be begun anew. It was much the same story in the Baltic coastlands, where the Russians made no attempt to establish magazines at the East Prussian port of Memel after Fermor captured it in 1757, while Kaunitz for political reasons (above) obstructed all the Russian attempts to occupy Danzig, which would otherwise have offered an excellent depot near the mouth of the Vistula.

Of these two axes of operations, the one in the north against Prussian Pomerania and Brandenburg gave the Russians additional security for their prize of East Prussia, and at the same time aimed at the enemy heartland, thereby exercising a powerful diversionary action in favour of their allies. The main obstacle was the Prussian fortress-port of Stettin on the lower Oder, which interposed itself most awkwardly between the Russians and the Swedes. In 1759 the Russian Conference set its heart on a joint siege of the place, but it had to give up the idea when the Russians discovered what a great train of siege artillery would have been required for that undertaking.

From the map it seemed that the Russians and Austrians could work together much more directly by concentrating their forces on the southern axis, in Silesia, where they might be able to crush the Prussians by a pincer movement. Saltykov in 1759 and Buturlin in 1761 brought armies across the Oder for this purpose, but in each case the enterprise foundered – whether because the Russians were nervous about having their backs to the river, or because it was difficult to feed them in that part of the world, or because the Austrians were unwilling to commit their main forces wholeheartedly in that direction.

All of these seemingly intractable problems were surmounted to some degree by the end of 1761. The St. Petersburg Conference became quicker at making its mind up, and willing – indeed eager – for the commanders in the field to take the initiative for themselves. The Russians contrived to reduce their convoys of provision carts, and they began to make systematic requisitions in East Prussia, which had been spared hitherto out of regard for local sensibilities. Colberg in Pomerania finally succumbed to the Russian Baltic army on 16 December 1761, which now at last gave the Russians a forward base on the northern theatre for their sea-borne supplies. In Silesia it was as difficult as ever for the allied armies to act together *en masse,* but the Russians proved amenable to the notion of leaving an auxiliary corps of elite troops under Austrian command. Buturlin put such a corps at Loudon's disposal when the main Russian army abandoned the theatre in 1761, and on 1 October the joint force stormed the key Silesian fortress of Schweidnitz.

Week-by-week a great deal still remained to be negotiated with the individual Russian army commanders, and the fundamental task of the Austrian attachés was to puzzle out the relations of these people with their subordinates, with Elizabeth and the Conference, and the opposition 'Young Court' of Grand Duke Peter of Holstein-Gottorp, and to utilise this knowledge when it came to deploying arguments and bribes.

The Austrian ambassador Esterházy warned St. André to be on his guard against the flattering ways of the first of the series of commanders, Field Marshal Stephan Fedorovich Apraksin. St. André met Apraksin in person on 10 April 1757, when the Russian assured him of his lifelong devotion to Maria Theresa – a devotion reinforced by a present she had just given him. St. André reported that 'in general his cast of mind and temperament are such that with goodwill and the exercise of a little patience you can induce him to do a great deal, indeed almost anything, whereas threats and constant pressure accomplish nothing'.[89] Others were less convinced. Apraksin awakened suspicions in St. Petersburg on account of his slow advance into East Prussia, and the speed with which he retreated after his scrambled victory at Gross-Jägersdorf (30 August 1757).

Apraksin died of a heart attack before an investigation into his conduct was complete. His successor, *Generanshef* Villim Villimovich Fermor (1758 – June 1759) was a complicated individual of Baltic-German and Scots blood, who cared for the welfare of his soldiers, but was unwilling to commit himself to any determined course of action. Only rarely was St. André able to penetrate his defensive facade of prickly sensibilities. Fermor lost his command on account of the Austrian complaints to St. Petersburg, but he stayed in the army to act the part of a loyal subordinate to his successor Saltykov. A new Austrian attaché, *GFWM.* Finé, took pain to cultivate Fermor's good opinion as long as the man hovered about headquarters, but Fermor was probably unwilling to forgive the damage the Austrians had done to his career.

Field Marshal Petr Semenovich Saltykov (1759–60) was the most soldierly and alert of the senior Russian commanders in this war. Saltykov got on well with Loudon, and after their joint victory at Kunersdorf (12 August 1759) a couple of extra marches would have enabled the main Russian and Austrian armies to combine to overwhelm Frederick, but neither Saltykov nor Daun could find the trust in one another to take this step. Perhaps they resembled each other in too many particulars. 'Neither wished to put to stake the glory of his monarch's army, or simultaneously his own; neither dared to undertake anything without the absolute guarantee off success. In spite of their respective victories over the King of Prussia [Kolin and Kunersdorf], they still felt Frederick's ascendancy in their hearts'.[90]

Field Marshal Aleksandr Borisovich Buturlin (1761) was a notorious amateur, which lends credence to the story that at a council of war Lieutenant-General Zakhar Chernyshev handed him a map upside down to see if he would take any notice (the Field Marshal did not). Frederick nevertheless reckoned that Buturlin was the most dangerous of his opponents, for his actions were totally unpredictable, and the Russian forces which Buturlin left under Loudon's command played a signal part in the storm of Schweidnitz (above).

The episode of the borrowed Muscovite artillery adds a curious postscript to the Austro-Russian relations. The fertile imagination of Petr Ivanovich Shuvalov had engendered a new range of artillery, which, in addition to cannon of conventional design, included the 'unicorn' gun-howitzer, and an oval-bored 'secret' howitzer that was capable of discharging an oval shot, an oval shell, or a horizontal swathe of canister or grape. On 8 October 1758 a meeting of Maria Theresa's Conference learned that Prince Liechtenstein had long desired to see the actual pieces, and that Shuvalov had quite independently offered to send some specimens. The Russians had set great store by denying the knowledge of their discoveries from the King of Prussia, but they knew that the secrets could not be preserved from the enemy for ever, and their present démarches must undoubtedly have been made on the initiative of Empress Elizabeth, desiring 'not to leave the Austrian artillery at a disadvantage vis-à-vis the Prussian, and wishing to reveal these important discoveries as a gesture of esteem for Her Imperial Majesty and of her willingness to be of assistance'.[91]

A large and fully-equipped battery set off on 26 January 1759, and the quantity of ordnance, vehicles, horses and artillerymen was so great that Frederick concluded that some kind of corps must be on its way to reinforce the Austrians. The train reached Ebergassing on 21 July, and on 7 August the Russians staged a spectacular shoot to the satisfaction of Maria Theresa and Francis Stephen. Four of the secret howitzers and two of the unicorns were duly forwarded to Daun's army. Liechtenstein warned the army's chief of artillery, *FZM*. Feuerstein, that the Russians were suspicious and touchy, and that the Austrian gunners must be told to act with the greatest courtesy, 'as I am only too well aware how little regard our artillery has for foreigners. Our gunners invariably believe that the Austrians have the best of everything, and they treat all novel inventions with hostility and indeed with contempt'.[92]

Having seen the Russian pieces in service, the Austrians concluded that they were at once too heavy and too short-ranged to be able to compete with conventional artillery, and on 1 January 1760 Liechtenstein wrote to Daun that the objects should be returned, apart from a number which should be sent once more to the army for political reasons. Perhaps the Austrians should have persisted a little longer with the experiment. It was true that the Russians themselves very rapidly abandoned the eccentric secret howitzer, but they retained their unicorns as serviceable pieces for more than a century to come.

Sweden

On 21 March 1757 Sweden linked herself with the alliance which was forming against Prussia. In August the Senate (ruling council) committed Sweden to military intervention, hoping to regain the lands in East Pomerania (*Hinterpommern*) which had been lost to Prussia, and to re-assert Sweden's position in Germany as a co-guarantor with France of the Peace of Westphalia (1648).

The naval forces available to Sweden at that time consisted of eight serviceable ships of the line, and a close-support 'Army Fleet' of 57 galleys, four half-galleys, and four flat-bottomed gunboats (*Prähme*). The Swedes maintained a regular army of 13,682 troops, and a provincial-based militia (*Indelta*) of 34,367 men. Sweden's most gifted officer, Lieutenant-General Augustin Ehrensvard, complained that in the event Sweden contributed no more than an insignificant contingent of troops to the alliance, like some prince of Württemberg.[93]

A fundamental reason for Sweden's indifferent performance was that the war was projected from a limited domestic political base. The commitment was the work of the anti-Prussian party of the 'Hats,' but it was opposed by the 'Caps,' and the consequent divisions extended to the officer corps. Kaunitz warned the Austrian attaché, *GFWM*. Mednyansky, that he would therefore have to deal with two factions in the army. A significant party among the officers (supporters of the Caps) supported the intrigues of Queen Luise Ulrike (a sister of Frederick of Prussia), who wished to invest her husband King Adolf Friedrich with the near-despotic powers the monarchy had enjoyed until 1720, 'an ambition which is both unacceptable to the Russians, and incompatible with the interests of our House.' Mednyansky was therefore to throw his support behind the party of the 'Hats,' which still had the upper hand in the *Riksdag* (Parliament) and Senate, and was devoted both to restricting the royal power in Sweden, and pursuing the war against Prussia.[94]

The foundation of the Swedish campaigns was also constricted in the physical sense. Swedish Pomerania (western Pomerania, or *Vorpommern*) was a patch of low-lying ground, which covered only 4,400 square kilometres, and was seamed with swamps and meandering little rivers. It was isolated from Sweden by the Baltic, which froze over in winter and became totally impassable, 'and so the business of supplying the army across the sea is a slow, uncertain and very expensive business, and subject to unpredictable accidents'.[95]

The Swedish forces in Pomerania made a useful diversion in favour of the alliance early in 1758 (below), and they would have done so again if they had been furnished with strong and consistent support from the homeland, and if their commanders had been men of authority who were allowed freedom of action. None of these things were present.

Two Swedish generals had been executed during the recent war against Russia (1741–3), which did not bolster confidence among the higher ranks. Ehrensvard adds that commanders had to concert every detail of operations with the king and Senate in distant Stockholm, and work through subordinates who had not been of their own choosing: 'Scarcely two actions are followed through on the same principles; there is a lack of consistency in the debates, and there is uncertainty in the execution.' The successive commanders Field Marshal Mathias Alexander Ungern-Sternberg (1757), Lieutenant-General Fredrik Rosen (1757–8), Lieutenant-General Gustav David Hamilton (1758–9) and Lieutenant-General Jakob Albrecht Lantingshausen (1759–61) all took office unwillingly and resigned as soon as they could. Augustin Ehrensvard, himself the most intellectually able of them all, assumed command towards the end of the war (1761–2) and only after trying to excuse himself on grounds of ill-health.

The politicians chided the field commanders constantly for their lack of enterprise, yet failed to provide the support that was necessary to get the army on the move. The French attaché Caulincourt had to report in 1759 that 'there is nobody in the Senate here who has the least notion of military affairs'.[96] Like its French counterpart, the Swedish government was unwilling to take the risk of burdening its subjects with heavy taxes, and so resorted to the ignoble expedients of paper money, debasements and lotteries. The French subsidies amounted in all to 1,600,000 Swedish taler, but made scarcely any impression on the costs of the war.

It was the same story with military manpower. The Senate held back from a full-scale mobilisation of the historic *Indelta* militia levies, and so the field army comprised a mixture of regulars and militiamen which reached a campaign average of just over 15,000 troops, as opposed to the 20,000 which had been promised to the alliance. The contingent was not only small but unbalanced. The lack of a siege train and engineers made it unrealistic to think of directing a full-scale attack against the Prussian fortress-port of Stettin, which lay on the eastern flank of any Swedish advance into Brandenburg. As for operations in the open field, the Swedish cavalry was 'totally unaccustomed to war, and has scarcely two or three officers who have any understanding of this branch of the service'.[97] Until 1761, at least, the Prussians had a clear superiority in hussars and *Jäger*, and they were consequently able to act much more aggressively at the tactical level.[98] Caulincourt suggested that the Austrians should help the Swedes out by sending a corps which contained plenty of hussars and Croats.[99] The proposal does not seem to have reached the Austrians, and in any case nothing short of a transformation of values and culture could have reversed the decline in the Swedish military spirit.

Sweden was still living in the 'Age of Freedom' which was inaugurated by the constitution of 1720, and which lasted until the absolute monarchy was restored in 1772. Ehrensvard explored the implications: 'It is an incontrovertible truth that no one can stand under strict military discipline without losing some of his freedom. The nature of war is universal, and its laws observe identical principles – to ignore these laws is to conduct war in a manner which will be feeble and very soon disastrous.' The Swedes had come to make domestic comforts the object of their ambitions, and the changes in the nation had little by little made their way into the army,

> but war demands another kind of life entirely, and thus a completely different motivation; the soldier must endure all kinds of hardships, and face up to adversity and to death itself. We must take men as they are… they must have something which persuades them to withstand ill-fortune, to put at risk their lives, possessions and health, to enkindle their zeal, and to exert themselves tirelessly. This cannot be otherwise than through prompt punishment when they forget their duty, and prompt reward if they do more than their duty.[100]

If the operations of the Austrians, French and Russians often lacked concert, those of the Swedes seemed to exist in a strategic vacuum. This was the product both of lack of will and the constraints of geography. Swedish Pomerania was hemmed in to the east by Prussian Pomerania, and the effectively impregnable fortress of Stettin stood squarely in the path of physical co-operation with the Russians, as we have seen. Fermor in 1758 was willing to detach 10,000 troops to reach out to the Swedes, and the Russian Conference returned on several occasions to the project of a joint enterprise against Stettin, but all such schemes would have weakened the Russian operations along the Warthe logistic axis towards the middle Oder, and demanded more technical resources than either the Russians or the Swedes had at their disposal.

The alternative axis of Swedish operations lay to the south in the direction of Berlin. No great Prussian fortress was in the way (the little walled towns of Demin and Anklam on the Peene scarcely counted), and the Prussians could deploy only a militia and such troops as could be spared from the main theatre of war, but the Swedish forces had little offensive capacity, and a great extent of enemy-held territory obstructed the exchange of messages with the Austrians by courier. Thus on occasion the correspondence between the Austrian military attaché and Vienna had to be conducted by way of Danzig and Poland – such a roundabout route that a single letter could take four weeks to reach its destination.[101] Swedish operations therefore rarely extended further than minuscule campaigns which were designed to clear the Baltic islands of Usedom and Wollin, and gain the places of Demin and Anklam and a little ground on the far side of the border river Peene.

In 1757 the first 17,000 Swedish troops to operate in Prussian Pomerania held down only a negligible proportion of the enemy force, 'and they then melted away like snow, so that our army… was reduced to an insignificant detachment'.[102] The French attaché had been pressing for a thrust on Berlin, and Maria Theresa recognised the *Nützbarkeit* of such a move in her correspondence with Daun, but she declined to commit herself to any course of action.[103] Thus in October Hadik raided Berlin at a time when Ungern-Sternberg stood a full 100 kilometres distant on the Peene, without any concert between the two parties, after which the Swedes fell back into their own territory on 12 November.

The mere presence of the Swedes exercised a powerful if unintended diversionary effect, for it drew the whole of the corps of the Prussian Field Marshal Lehwaldt from East Prussia, and allowed the Russians under Fermor to overrun that duchy almost unopposed at the beginning of 1758. However direct co-operation between the allies proved as difficult as ever. Hamilton, as the new Swedish commander, genuinely desired to take the offensive, in the first place in concert with the Russians, but the battle of Zorndorf (25 August) and the subsequent Russian retreat supervened before the necessary instructions arrived from the Senate.

On 8 September Hamilton embarked on a new campaign into Brandenburg. He hoped to be able to co-operate with the Austrians, and therefore chose a route which lay south-west towards Neu-Ruppin rather than directly on Berlin. However there was no sign of any Austrian response, and the Swedes fell back to West Pomerania to avoid being cut off by a Prussian counter-offensive which opened on 26 September.

The Swedish land offensive in 1759 was a short-lived affair, made possible only because Prussian troops were called away to face the Russians in the Kunersdorf campaign. By the end of October the main Swedish force was back across the Peene, and in November the Swedes abandoned the islands of Usedom and Wollin. The one clear success of Swedish arms was on the waters of the Stettiner Haff (Stettin Lagoon), where an improvised Prussian flotilla was destroyed on 10 September; the alliance derived no lasting benefit, for the Swedes and the Russians had recently agreed to allow Prussian and neutral shipping free passage to and from the Prussian ports.

In the late summer of 1760 Lieutenant-General Lantingshausen with the main body of 11–12,000 Swedes established himself well inside Prussian territory at Pasewalk. He was still a formidable 100 kilometres from Berlin, but the episode is interesting because it persuaded the Austrians for the first and last time that it might be possible to carry out a joint operation. On 9 October Berlin capitulated to a Russian raiding corps. *FZM.* Lacy was standing just outside with a force of Austrians, and he wrote to *FML.* Mednyansky (as Austrian attaché with the Swedes) to explain that 'the Court of Vienna desired most urgently for his corps to unite with the Swedes and bring the Prussian field forces to battle.'

A lieutenant of Austrian hussars got through safely to Swedish headquarters with the message, but Mednyansky had to reply that the Swedish generals would find the scheme impossible to accept. Their army had not been very strong to begin with, and it was now depleted by disease, combat losses, and the need to garrison Stralsund and secure their left flank against Stettin. 'On top of this they are totally out of bread, since they have consumed all the small quantity of biscuit they brought from Stralsund, and they have brought no field bakery with them. The areas of Prussian territory into which their advance has taken them have been eaten up completely by the operations of the rival forces. They have therefore given up all hope of finding the necessary subsistence there'.[104]

With this, the prospect of significant and concerted operations came to an end. In the autumn of 1761 the Swedes formed a much-needed Light Division of 2,500 infantry and hussars, and they came under the leadership of Lieutenant-General Ehrensvärd (a man whose talents should have qualified him for a high command position in the alliance), but these improvements arrived too late to enable the Swedes to influence the course of the war. Hostilities on this theatre came to an end on 7 April 1762, and left the Swedes with no bargaining assets which they could bring to the conference table. The Peace of Hamburg (22 May) once more penned up the Swedes within the borders of 1720.

The *Reich*

The Reichsarmee

The *Reichsarmee* was the military expression of the *Reich*. The constitution of the *Reichsarmee* had last been reorganised in 1681–2, and remained fundamentally unchanged for more than a century. It was not a standing force, but was voted into being by the irregular meetings of the states of Germany to confront crises which were deemed to threaten the security of the *Reich* as a whole. The Emperor appointed the generals and staff, and he or his deputy directed the operations of the army, while the individual states, large and small, advanced the necessary funds, and either put forward their individual contingents, or (more commonly) incorporated their contingents with those of their neighbours into the joint contingents of the *Creise* (Franconia, Swabia and soon). *Reichstruppen* had performed respectably in the armies of Prince Eugene, and, as Armfeldt pointed out, there could be nothing wrong with German soldiers as such, if they were able to perform miracles when they came under Prussian command.[105]

The Seven Years War was the last contest in which the House of Habsburg was able to rally significant support for its cause within the *Reich*. Hessen-Cassel, Hanover and a number of smaller Protestant states ultimately entered the war as associates or de facto allies of the Prussians and British, while the cult of Frederick extended well beyond the Protestants of Germany. However Frederick had clearly broken the peace of the *Reich* when he invaded Saxony and Bohemia in the late summer of 1756, and on 17 January the next year the majority vote in the *Reichstag* sanctioned the creation of *Reichsexecutionsarmee* to carry out the appropriate '*Reichsexecution*' against the King of Prussia.

On 9 May 1757 Emperor Francis Stephen was given a free hand to appoint the army's generals, which he in fact used only to determine the successive supreme commanders:

> *Reichsgeneralfeldzeugmeister* Joseph Friedrich Prince Sachsen-Hildburghausen (1757– February 1758)
> *FM*. Friedrich Michael Prince Pfalz-Zweibrücken (February 1758 – March 1761)
> *FM*. Giambattista Serbelloni (March 1761 – August 1762)
> *Reichsgeneralfeldzeugmeister* Christian Carl Stolberg (August 1762 to the end of hostilities)

Grade for grade the other field ranks were divided equally among the Catholic and Protestant generals.

This sense of order did not extend to all of the components of the army. 'If we exclude the contingents from Bavaria, the Palatinate, Württemberg and a few other states of the *Reich*, the rest of the army was an assemblage of ill-trained hordes… there were many states of Swabia and Franconia which presented a single man. Many were responsible for furnishing an individual lieutenant or soldier, who was often a peasant who had been dragged away from the plough; others provided just a drummer, and gave him a drum from an old storeroom of arms'.[106]

Strict prohibitions were issued against any affront to religious sensibilities,[107] but the order was not strictly obeyed.[108] The individual failings were compounded by the the lack of joint arrangements concerning drill, weapons, tactics and supply. Few people were willing to listen to Hildburghausen's proposals for comprehensive reform, and his centralised supply system (*Generaladmodazion*) of 13 February 1758 fell apart later in that year when most of the contingents reverted to their original Jewish contractors. Shortages of kettles, tents and other basic equipment continued to delay the departure of the *Reichsarmee* for the field at the beginning of almost every campaigning season.[109]

Only with great reluctance did the Austrians put materiel at the disposal of such people. The *Hofkriegsrath* told Hildburghausen in July 1757 that it was impossible to supply him with either the pontoons or the artillerymen which he had requested, 'for we have already lost a large numbers of officers and gunners in the recent battle [Kolin], and we are going to be badly stretched to supply the artillery service in our own army; it would be no help to Your Highness to send you newly-enlisted men, and in any case artillery recruits can be raised at least as conveniently in Germany as here'.[110]

The *Hofkriegsrath* must have relented to a slight degree, for in 1759 and 1760 we discover an Austrian pontoon company assigned to the *Reichsarmee*, using copper pontoons from the depot in Prague.[111.] The artillery support remained niggardly. The *Reichs-Vizecanzler* Colloredo informed Zweibrücken in July 1759 that Liechtenstein had intervened to help him out with the artillery solely as a personal favour, for the *Hofkriegsrath* still opposed consigning Austrian gunners to the *Reichsarmee*, and even Liechtenstein's goodwill was being tested by the way the *Reichsarmee* was promoting Austrian artillerymen without reference to him.[112] Later the regiment of the Mainz Circle lost its four cannon in the first battle of Torgau, and this time it took the pleas of the Electoral Prince of Mainz and the intervention of Kaunitz to get Liechtenstein to replace them.[113]

Vienna probably considered that it was already doing more than enough, by committing formed bodies of Austrian troops to support the *Reichsarmee*. The Splényi and Széchenyi Hussars, the fine cuirassier regiments of Brettlach and Trautmannsdorf, and ultimately also the roving corps of Loudon appeared in Thuringia in 1757 to act with Hildburghausen's army and the French. The performance of the Austrians did something to mitigate the disaster at Rossbach (5 November), and afterwards Hildburghausen proposed that the only way to make any use of the troops of the *Reichsarmee* was to detach the best regiments, officers and generals and disperse them among the Austrian forces in the proportion of one of Germans to four of Austrians.[114] This would have amounted to a near-amalgamation, and it was probably too drastic to be accepted. In 1758 an Austrian corps or small army was constituted to act with the *Reichsarmee* in Saxony, and the Austrians maintained their commitment in this form for the rest of the war, though with the misgivings which will now be outlined.

As commander of the *Reichsarmee* in 1758 the Prince of Zweibrücken proposed that the first line of the order of battle should consist entirely of Serbelloni's Austrians, and the second line of *Reichstruppen;* this suggestion was rejected by the *Hofkriegsrath*, which determined that within each of the two lines the Germans must be placed in the centre, with the Austrian infantry and cavalry on the wings. Probably the *Hofkriegsrath* feared that under Zweibrücken's arrangement the all-German second line would have run away if it had seen that things were going badly with the Austrians in front of them.

Lacy reported to Daun from Vienna in March 1760 that not even the *Reichs-Vizecanzler* Colloredo was willing to see Austrian troops committed to the *Reichsarmee*, and that within the *Hofkriegsrath* only the official Franz Joseph Plockner was still fighting to continue the Austrian engagement.[115] The debates came to a new head in 1761. Neipperg, as acting head of the *Hofkriegsrath*, argued for reducing the Austrian presence to a number of Croats and hussars, for anything more would be a waste of good Austrian troops. *FM.* Carl Joseph Batthyány stood out for maintaining the policy of immediate support, for only the Austrian troops were capable of executing enterprises of any importance, and as long as they accompanied the *Reichsarmee* the less useful of the German troops could be told off for less demanding service in the rear, like garrisoning fortresses or escorting convoys.[116] *FM.* Serbelloni, as the new commander of the *Reichsarmee*, confirmed that his German troops were incapable of independent action, reporting on 14 June 1761 that since the beginning of April 2,318 of the German infantry and cavalry had deserted, along with 26 of the professional gunners and 56 of their *Handlanger,* 'and the reason is that the *Reichsarmee* is supposed to advance into Saxony, and more specifically in the direction of Dresden – a prospect which terrifies these men all the more as they are isolated, receiving no support from the Austrians in either infantry or cavalry, and because they will be marching into a part of the world where they nearly starved last year, and which is lacking in provisions of every kind'.[117]

In the event, the *Reichsarmee* and the Austrian contingent remained in a loose association until the end of hostilities. Prince Henry of Prussia was quick to detect any lack of co-ordination, and in the decisive battle of Freiberg (29 October 1762) his opening attack fell on the sector of the joint position which was held by the Germans, and at a time when the respective commanders of the *Reichsarmee* and the Austrian corps (Stolberg and Hadik) were out of contact.

When opinions of well-informed people during the Seven Years War were therefore so much at variance, it is not easy to assess the overall worth of the *Reichsarmee* and the Austrians to one another. Some kind of association was politically vital, so as to maintain the credibility of the Austrian dynasty as leader of the *Reich.* It was nevertheless embarrassing to find that the Austrians were incapable of preventing Prussian raiding corps from penetrating deep into Franconia in most years of the war, and unwilling to compensate the faithful Germans for their sufferings. Indeed the French seem to have been more alive than was Vienna to the damage that was being done.[118]

Daun and the other realists in the Austrian army were aware that the *Reichstruppen* were useful for filling gaps that would otherwise have been left uncovered, and for holding not-particularly exposed blocking positions (as at Maxen), but that any other gains that were won by the *Reichsarmee* at the expense of weak Prussian forces, as in Saxony in 1758 and 1759, would be forfeit as soon as any respectable opposition appeared on the theatre. Armfeldt put the diversionary value of the *Reichsarmee* at 6,000 Prussian troops at the most.[119] The evidence therefore supports the verdict of the Prussian cavalry general Seydlitz, who stated that 'we should not force these troops into combat, for they will certainly fight back; since, however, they are serving against their will, and with no interest in the war, we should content ourselves with manoeuvres which will induce them to retreat, but in a way which does not compromise their honour'.[120]

The Subsidised and Incorporated German Contingents (see p. 269)
Everything we have considered so far relates to the *Reichsarmee* as an entity. Under entirely different arrangements the Austrians and French made treaties with individual states of the *Reich* to take troops into their pay as auxiliaries as one kind or another. These units usually formed part or the whole of the military establishment of the states in question, and were quite separate from the contingents that were furnished under their obligation to the *Reichsarmee.* When war was imminent, Kaunitz explained that in normal circumstances it would not be worth spending money on foreign troops, but political considerations spoke for making subsidy agreements with, for example, Würzburg (an old associate) and Markgraf Carl Wilhelm of Anspach (who would otherwise have combined with Bayreuth to hold Würzburg in check). It was especially important to have a Protestant prince like this on Austria's side, 'and so ... emphasise the principle that we have no religious ambitions, but are concerned only with our security and upholding the Imperial authority in the *Reich*.[121]

As a rule of thumb the political leanings of the German auxiliaries were at direct variance with their competence, which is a pompous way of saying that the Catholic troops as a whole were militarily bad, and the Protestants militarily good. The contrast was most evident in the case of the Bavarians and Württembergers. Four thousand Bavarians were hired for the cause in 1757, and contributed little after they ran away at Rossbach. The original subsidy treaty between France and Württemberg dated from 1752, and thereafter underwent a number of revisions. On

20 March 1757 the Duke agreed to furnish 6,200 infantry, and later in the war the Württemberg troops still counted as 'the finest and best-drilled you could imagine'.[122] The uniforms and the military values of the Württembergers were linked closely with those of the Prussians, and Kaunitz suggested in April 1757 that these troops should be given four-inch wide white bands to wear on their left sleeves, thereby averting 'a disadvantageous confusion'.[123] The association with things Prussian was more than sartorial, for experience showed 'how very little desire they have to fight the King of Prussia'.[124] The Württembergers nevertheless did better at Leuthen than is generally admitted, and (after one unfortunate mutiny) they were held to their colours by their professionalism and their commitment to Duke Carl Eugen, who was a product of that last throe of the Counter-Reformation which was making so many converts to Catholicism in higher circles in the *Reich*. For a time the Austrians were able to exert indirect influence on Württemberg politics through the prime minister Samuel Count Montmorin, and the military administrator Franz Baron Werneck, but after the campaign of Leuthen the Württemberg troops never again came under direct Austrian command.

The young Friedrich August Prince of Anhalt-Zerbst (1734–91) remained a Protestant, but allied himself with the anti-Prussian party in the *Reich*. His hatred of Frederick turned into an obsession when the Prussians evicted him from his principality in January 1758. He was already *Inhaber* of a regiment of cuirassiers in the Austrian service, and in March 1760 he was given leave to raise an infantry battalion of four companies to the taken into the Austrian pay.[125] Many of the recruits were grotesquely undersized – virtual goblins – and as a newly-raised unit the battalion was naturally targeted for disbanding at the time of the reduction of the army in the winter of 1761–2. However Friedrich August was doubly valuable as a Protestant, and as the brother of Catherine (later 'the Great') who was the wife of Duke Peter of Holstein-Gottorp, the heir to the Russian throne. Maria Theresa ruled that 'the Anhalt-Zerbst battalion is not to be disbanded, and, if the men have already been dispersed, they are to be brought together again and the battalion restored to its original establishment'.[126]

There are exceptions to the rule concerning quality which was postulated a little while ago. The episcopal regiment of Mainz was taken into the Austrian service in 1756, and reorganised on the standard Austrian war establishment of two companies of grenadiers, and two field battalions of six fusilier companies each. Thereafter this reliable unit was incorporated into the order of battle on the same basis as the Austrian regiments proper. The friendship of Würzburg was worth having on several accounts. The bishopric spanned the crucially-important central German axis of the Main valley, and with the joint bishopric of Bamberg to the east it formed a bloc of 8,525 square kilometres on the western flank of Bohemia, separating hostile Hessen-Cassel from the decidedly untrustworthy states of Sachsen-Gotha, Ansbach and Bayreuth. Politically Würzburg was the most important state of the Franconian Circle, with the power to carry the smaller entities along with it. Lastly the Würzburg 'Blue' and 'Red' regiments were incomparably the best of Catholic Germany, and repaid their expense many times over.

The Saxon troops were a special case, having been taken over by the Austrians and France after they had escaped from enforced service with the Prussians. Early in 1757 the Austrians could think of no better use for a reassembled body of 2,500 Saxony infantrymen than to banish them to garrison service in Hungary. This was 'hardly calculated to appeal to the Saxons, besides, when those Saxons still in service with the King of Prussia hear that their comrades have been consigned to Hungary, this will deter them from deserting him'.[127] These unhappy men were ultimately made over to the French, and many of them deserted for a second time and were lost to the allies for good (see p. 239).

The Austrians retained six regiments of Saxon horse in their service, and by September 1759 the cost was put at an annual 500,000 florins in pay and equipment, and 800,000 in rations of bread and fodder. The Austrians tried to alleviate the cost by maintaining the Saxons from the resources of their native electorate,[128] but it was already being recouped in other directions by the political value of this association, and the excellent account the Saxon cavalry was giving of itself in the field.

The Threat of Wider Wars

War with Britain

The Austrians stood in a curious relationship with their former allies the British. The longstanding connection had been jeopardised by the breakdown of the Old System and by Austria's new relations with France, and it was broken finally in the spring of 1757 when Kaunitz effectively gave leave to the French to invade Hanover. Kaunitz had ensured that the wording of his engagements to France did not commit him to war with Britain, but he and his colleagues took the possibility of attack by the British seriously, and adopted due precautions. The Habsburg possessions were most vulnerable to overtly hostile action on their two littorals – along the North Sea and in the Adriatic – and measures of defence were taken in hand in the midsummer of 1757.

On 14 June a Conference decided to order expel all British naval and merchants ships from Ostend and Nieuport, and turn over these two ports to French garrisons. These precautions appeared amply justified in the summer of 1758, for the Hanoverian forces had taken the offensive over the Rhine, and the British were preparing a very large fleet which seemed to betoken an amphibious descent on the Netherlands (in fact the St. Malo expedition). The recently-retired *GFWM* de Baxeras offered his services to the overall commander of the Netherlands, *G.d.C.* de Bournonville. He was directed first to the citadel of Antwerp, to help to put the works in a state of defence, and then received a further order 'in virtue of which I went to Bruges on the 7th of the month in question [July] to take over the command, and oppose the English in case they attempted a landing between Ostend and the mouth of the port of Sluys. For the time being I had under my command a battalion of the regiment of Bayreuth, the [French] dragoon regiment of d'Aubignie, and three free companies, while awaiting the promised help from Dunkirk'.[129]

The alarm continued through 1759, when an exchange of correspondence between Prince Charles of Lorraine and Vienna shows that the basic Austrian strategy was to hold key points, and Antwerp in particular, long enough to allow help from the French to arrive in strength. By then Colonel Delaing had repaired and extended the defences of Antwerp citadel to general satisfaction, and a battalion of the Austrian regiment of Salm and a company of invalids furnished the immediate garrison. The three free companies mentioned by de Baxersas were still on foot, and in 1759 Prince Charles supplemented them by 600 men of a new force of *Cordes-Côtes,* which were recruited mainly from retired veterans, uniformed in white smocks and armed with reconditioned muskets. Four of the companies were concentrated in Bruges, and the men of the other two were deployed in the area of Ypres, Menin, Fumes and Dixmude. The coast watchers were engaged initially until October, after which the bad weather was expected to make British landings impossible, and (presumably to aid recruiting) the local authorities were told that the expected threat was merely from freebooters landed from Prussian privateers – which was far from being the case.[130]

In the summer of 1757 Kaunitz warned the *Directorium* that the British fleet in the Mediterranean posed a potential threat to the Austrian harbours of the Adriatic littoral – Zeng, Carlobago, Fiume, and more particularly the port-town of Trieste, 'for this trading centre is so important to us that we must devote all possible care to its security'.[131] In this case an amphibious landing was deemed unlikely, but reinforcements of troops (one regiment of regular infantry and 500 Croats) and consignments of heavy artillery from Styria were sent as a precaution against bombardment, and Colonel Schmidt was designated military commander of the Littoral, with the brief to establish the necessary batteries. Kaunitz recognised that Austria had no naval forces, and all that could be done for the merchantmen was to advise them to keep out of the way of the British. However 'in the event of actual hostilities being opened against us, I most obediently suggest that leave should be given to the people of Zeng and other places on the Littoral to cruise on English shipping. Moreover we should at once fit out a number of their vessels for war and employ them to defend the harbour of Trieste, compensating them as necessary for the cost of the material and crews'.[132]

As things turned out, the Royal Navy took no direct action against Austrian interests. However Kaunitz was right to be on his guard, for between September 1758 and the spring of 1760 Frederick of Prussia offered letters of marque to British privateers who were willing to attack allied shipping. At least four of the British privateers took up the offer, and proceeded to snap up French, Swedish and Austrian merchantmen. Kaunitz became so alarmed at the losses that he encouraged the Trieste entrepreneur Demetrio Voinovich to go on patrol with a converted merchant vessel, the *Maria Assunta,* which finally caught up with the notorious privateer *The Lancashire Witch* and battered her into submission in a ferocious battle. Voinovich hanged the captain, Charles Ratcliffe, from his own yardarm. 'A cruel fate,' observed Kaunitz, 'but nothing more than he deserved'.[133]

War with Turkey

Britain was an old friend, alienated under complicated circumstances. An old enemy, the Ottoman Empire, had succeeded in the late 1730s in wresting back some of the most important gains which had been made by Prince Eugene, and dictated the terms of the Peace of Belgrade (1739). The fortress-town of Belgrade passed to the Turks, and gave them the facility of advancing up the avenues of both the Sau (Sava) and the middle Danube.

Kaunitz believed that the peace was fragile in the extreme, and that the Turks would be well placed to re-open hostilities now that Austria was engaged so heavily with Prussia. In the spring of 1760 he was embarrassed to receive a petition from the people of the province of Cimarra in the Epirus of Ottoman-ruled Greece, asking leave to mobilise a battalion of their nation at Trieste, as a sign of support (see p. 394). Kaunitz could only advise Maria Theresa to tell these people that she must decline, while being grateful to them for their goodwill.[134]

Frederick awoke to the opportunities which now seemed open to him. Until the Diplomatic Revolution he had left it to the French and Swedes to represent his interests in Turkey, but now he had to negotiate with the Ottomans directly. His envoy was the Austrian renegade Gottfried Fabian Haude, alias 'Carl Adolph von Rexin,' who from 1760 was authorised to lay out massive bribes, and pledge Prussia's support for the return of the Bánát of Temesvár to the Turks if they declared war on Austria. The British ambassador Porter gave his support, and on 2 April 1761 Rexin was able to conclude a Prusso-Turkish treaty of trade and friendship. Frederick now redoubled his efforts. From the autumn of 1761 he opened immediate negotiations with the Khan of the Crimea (an independently-minded vassal of the Turks), with a view to unleashing a flood of Tartars on Hungary and Lower Austria in co-operation with Werner's raiding corps. In March 1762 Rexin once more urged Sultan Mustafa to open war against the Austrians and Russians, and this time he reinforced his offer by holding out an annual subsidy of one million taler.

In November 1762 Kaunitz warned Maria Theresa that her eastern dominions were open to imminent attack. He recalled the efforts which had been made to secure those frontiers after the loss of Belgrade and Serbia. Between 1750 and 1760 1,884,516 florins had been spent on the Danubian fortress of Peterwardein, and 1,009,318 on the fortress of Temesvár, 'but quite apart from the fact that these fortresses still lack most of their essentials, they are not nearly enough in themselves to be able to give a measure of security to the borders. We cannot regret the loss of Belgrade strongly enough.'

He conceded that the Sultan had drawn back from an offensive alliance with the Prussians (fearing the consequences of a war with Russia), and that he had ordered the Tartars back to the Crimea; however the Grand Vizier Mehmed Ragip Pasha remained a malevolent influence, and the Turks were still in a position to invade Hungary with 70–80,000 men at short notice.[135]

These concerns were being translated into measures of active security. Consideration was now being given to restoring the numbers of the cuirassiers, who had been a prime target in the reductions in 1761/2, but were of great value in combat against the Turks, and three regiments of Transylvanian militia were set on foot.

Kaunitz's judgement was badly astray, and the reason was that he could not bring himself to believe the assessments of the men on the spot. The Austrian envoy in Constantinople for most of the war was the orientalist Joseph Peter Schwachheim. He got on well with the Grand Vizier Ragip Pasha, who assured him in all sincerity that any response to Prussian overtures would not shake the commitment of the Ottomans to peace with Austria. The Prusso-Turkish treaty of 2 April 1761 amounted to no more than its declared character – an agreement relating to trade and good intentions – and Schwachheim reported that he had been unable to detect any physical signs of Turkish preparations for war.

Kaunitz was not convinced, and he replaced Schwachheim as *Internuntius* by Heinrich Christian Penkler, who had held this post until 1755. There was no sense of rivalry between the two men, and when they reviewed the evidence together Penkler concluded that Schwachheim's assessment was correct. On 16 October the good Ragip Pasha rebuffed Rexin's final offer in terms which ruled out any further dialogue with the Prussians.

18

Operational and Tactical Dimensions

The Austrian Style

Compared with the actions of the Prussian enemy, most of the operations of the Austrians in the Seven Years War appear distressingly ponderous: 'the key defect in the Empress's army is the lack of the wherewithal to move with speed' ...[1] 'the slow-moving ways of this nation'[2]... 'the tardiness and the lack of urgency in our enterprises'[3]... 'the slowness which is inherent in the system, which means that when anything turns out well it is invariably by chance and never by calculation'.[4]

Frederick of Prussia possessed the assets of single-mindedness, and the concentration of political and military authority. When those advantages were conceded, observers and participants were still surprised at how unresponsive the Austrian military apparatus actually was. In the first years of the war it was possible to find likely causes in the absence of a general staff,[5] or in the divided command. Neither of those arguments held any force from the spring of 1758, by when Austria had a new and good general staff, and Prince Charles of Lorraine had been banished from the field. The movements in the army were now undoubtedly faster in the physical sense, but the decision-making was still apparently ponderous, and chances were still going unexploited. Sir John Burgoyne concluded that the explanation was to be found in some intractable problems of the structure of state and society. The material of the private soldiers was excellent,

> it is the superstructure alone which has hitherto been defective. The military strength of the Court of Vienna has been kept depressed by deficiency of abilities in the department of finances, mismanaged pomp, a general spirit of profusion, and the want of a warlike prince... The military plans have been unwisely concerted in the Cabinet, and the commands injudiciously conferred in the field. Yet with all these disadvantages, such is the force of native zeal and goodwill, the Austrian troops in the late war were sometimes victorious, always respectable.[6]

Kaunitz was aware of the lack of liaison between the various departments of state, which he hoped to establish through the new coordinating body of the *Staatsrath,* which was established on 31 January 1761 (see p. 30); the *Staatsrath* proved its worth over the long term, but it came into existence too late to affect the course of the war, which was already entering its final stages.

Daun has been much blamed for holding the main Austrian forces for so long on the defensive – an accusation which ignores the risk of committing them to battle against the finest army of the century, and also leaves out of account the perspectives of the Prussians. The Prussian soldier-poet Ewald von Kleist expressed a general frustration when he wrote to a Swiss friend in October 1758: 'Both armies are now standing in the neighbourhood of Gorlitz, but Daun is up on the heights like an ibex. If those damned hills had not beaten us off so bravely every time we attacked them, we would have chased the Emperor from Vienna long ago'.[7] Two years later the Prussian courtier Lehndorff was in conversation with the Austrian staff officer Colonel James Nugent von Westmeath, who had been captured outside Dresden. Daun had placed some reliance on the Irishman,

> and now that he has to do without him it would be pleasant to think that the Field Marshal will allow himself to be enticed into some stupidity. But it seems to me that he is too prudent to leave himself open, and although we proclaim that he is over-cautious, I am convinced that he thereby holds us in check, and does us more damage than if he won battles. He follows the system which the Austrians have made their own since the end of the last war, namely he draws the conflict out at length and refuses to be lured into battle, with the intention of exhausting the king and his army. This has tempted us into a number of over-hasty attacks, in which we have lost our best troops.[8]

The Austrians' penchant for the defensive by no means excluded offensive action when a favourable opportunity offered. The battle-worthiness of their troops was never in doubt, and the commanders put it to use when they went over to the tactical attack at Breslau (1757), Hochkirch (1758), Maxen (1759), and Landeshut and (less happily) Liegnitz in 1760. The Prussians on their side were ready to dig themselves in and remain on the defensive for prolonged periods – Frederick at Schmottseiffen (1759) and Bunzelwitz (1761), and Prince Henry again and again in Saxony – though it has been the custom to praise them for their sagacity on such occasions.

The Brain of the Army

A copy of Frederick's *General Principia vom Kriege* (1753) was found in the papers of a 'captured Prussian general' on 23 June 1760, almost certainly at Landeshut and in the effects of Fouqué or one of his subordinates. Daun praised this work to Maria Theresa, and commented astutely on individual passages, but he despaired of raising the alertness and intellectual level of the Austrian generals to that of the Prussians.

Frederick reinforced his written memoranda with practices to which the Austrians could scarcely begin to aspire, like setting his generals unexpected tactical problems during momentary lulls in the campaign. The author of the *Patriotic Reflections* maintained that every now and then the Austrian generals and staff officers ought to be made to deploy the army on unfamiliar terrain: 'This would be the opportunity to correct their mistakes and bring home a whole series of useful principles. People will certainly object that these exercises would leave the troops exhausted, but an approach march and deployment carried out under such conditions would prove more productive than a whole week spent drilling on the regimental parade ground, which would tire out the troops still more and lower their morale – and all to no useful purpose'.[9]

For the Austrian officers, the management of affairs at the regimental level was determined by the printed infantry regulations of 1749 and the cavalry regulations of 1749–51. Daun compiled instructions of a wider scope when he was schooling his army before the battle of Kolin: the original *Lagerordnung, Ordre de Bataille* and *General-Schlachtordnung* were circulated in manuscript form in the camp of Czaslau on 24 May 1757, then worked up into a comprehensive printed *Militär Feld-Regulament* (12 March 1759), which set out the responsibilities of the field ranks, the daily routine of the army, the organisation of supply, the principles of humane man management, and the conduct of the march and battle. Within its limitations it was an excellent document, which on every page bore the imprint of hard-won experience.

Good professional reading was otherwise difficult to find, even for the officers who were willing to make the effort. Caesar's campaigns were more familiar to that generation than Austria's own, because there were so few military men who 'go to the trouble of reading useful accounts of campaigns, and entering their own observations thereon'.[10] The one 'Austrian' military theorist to attain European renown was Henry Lloyd, whom Archbishop Migazzi of Vienna commended to Daun in September 1758 as a young man who had spent two years in the Spanish artillery as a second lieutenant, and had lost his patronage through no fault of his own: 'I am unqualified to speak as to his military abilities, but to do him justice I have to say that he is universally esteemed and valued in Vienna. When he was here, I had a private conversation with him, which gave me the opportunity to recognise his outstanding talents to the full'.[11]

Having reached the field army, Lloyd fell in with a fellow spirit, Pietro Verri, who testifies that Lloyd made a name for himself by being so willing to speak his mind. 'At headquarters, in the anterooms – in fact everywhere – he was always at the centre of a circle of the most distinguished men of the army, who egged him on to say what we ought to be doing, and what was good or bad about our various manoeuvres.' He was once heard holding forth at Daun's very door.[12] This highly unstable individual (who was possibly a British spy) seems to have left the Austrian army not long afterwards to resume his roamings. Lloyd's major work (*The History of the Late War in Germany between the King of Prussia and the Empress of Germany and Her Allies*, 2 vols.) was published in London between 1781 and 1790, long after the war. It is impersonal in tone, geometrical in content, and tells us nothing about that conflict which could not have been derived from other sources, and can in no way be considered as representative of an Austrian body of thought on the conduct of warfare as a whole. We must look elsewhere to discover how the Austrians managed their campaigns. We turn first of all to some basic mechanics of communication.

Every army or independent corps owned a *Feld-Post-Amt* which was staffed with at least two officers, another two postal officials, and a number of couriers and who either travelled independently, or in conjunction with the civilian postal service. Armfeldt explains that Daun was responsible for the elaborate provision of the necessary post horses. These animals were assigned both to the headquarters of the main army and to those of the detached corps, and the total came to 400. 'If a *General-* or *Flügel-Adjutant* is sent on a mission, he invariably uses a post horse, and he is likewise forbidden to send any other officers on such errands on their own horses; when an army or corps commander is away from his headquarters he is followed by a number of spare post horses, so that he does not have to send back for them'.[13] Three or so times a week couriers sped to Vienna to enable Daun to render account to Maria Theresa of his most recent doings, and an Austrian officer complained that the Prussians gained greatly from the fact that:

FM. Franz Moritz Lacy,1725–1801 (Austrian Army Museum). Lacy was Austria's first chief of the General Staff (1758). He excelled alike in this function and then as an independent corps commander, and after the war he succeeded Daun as President of the *Hofkriegsrath* (1766).

Lacy never stood as high in public esteem as Loudon, but Maria Theresa and Joseph II prized his character and talents very highly indeed, and he gained an honoured place in Viennese society; his park in the Vienna Woods at Neuwaldegg introduced the Austrians to the 'natural' English style of landscape gardening.

In this portrait he wears the post-war uniform of a FM.; the Irish cast of features is unmistakable, and would not have looked out of place on an old-style New York policeman.

our Field Marshal Daun, great and brave though he is, loses so much time composing the official relations he sends to Vienna, and putting together his *Field Journal*. He gets up early, and his first occupation in the morning is to dictate from his bed, or review what he has written concerning the events of the previous day. We would much prefer him to follow the example of General Loudon. As a constantly active individual he is happier sitting in the saddle than at the writing desk; all sorts of schemes flash before his mind, and he puts them into effect with equal speed.[14]

Such indeed was Loudon's reputation, but the documentary evidence shows that his reports to Vienna were at least as frequent, and certainly longer than those of Daun.

Thus the closest associates of an army commander were not the members of his military suite, but the clerks of his *Feld-Kriegs Expedition,* which was made up of one or two *Hof Kriegs Secretäre* or a *Feld-Kriegs Concipist,* and their *Canzellisten* (copy clerks) and *Accessisten* (filing clerks). We know little about the life of the secretaries, though Hadik made a point of praising his *Feld-Kriegs Concipist* Hammerschmidt, who had to contend both with the laziness and ill-will of his junior clerks, and the need to keep in touch with the widely-scattered detachments of his corps.[15]

The commanders were in fact preoccupied with everyday business to a degree which made it difficult for them to work out routes and marches, or obtain and evaluate intelligence. In the campaign of 1757 the lack of order at the various headquarters had consequences which finally could not be ignored. An officer who served in that year saw the Austrian columns blundering about devoid of guidance, the only exception being a march to Liegnitz which was directed by Daun in person, when he should have been free to attend to more important things.[16]

Staff work was still being carried out by the few officers who had gravitated to that speciality out of personal inclination, and who functioned under the limited authority of Peter Franz Guasco, the nominal *Generalquartiermeister,* or Chief of Staff. Guasco protested about this unsatisfactory state of affairs on 27 July 1757 and again on 21 December, and he had a powerful ally in Daun, who regarded a proper staff as a necessity after the battle of Leuthen.[17] A paper from the French attaché Montazet seems to have been decisive. Daun wrote to Maria Theresa's cabinet secretary Ignaz Koch on 13 January 1758: 'I have the honour to put before you the memorandum of Monsieur Montazet, whose arguments are extremely sound. If Her Majesty will be so good as to leave the arrangements for setting up this department to me, I can guarantee that she will be well served'.[18] Daun foresaw opposition on the part of the Emperor and Neipperg, but Austria's new General Staff came into being in February, under the leadership of Daun's nominee *FML.* Lacy as *Generalquartiermeister.*

Armfeldt describes the new kind of *Generalquartiermeister* as a highly influential figure. He had all the light troops of the army at his ultimate disposal, and so he knew of the slightest movement of the enemy. 'He is informed of all his commander's intentions, all the plans of operations are communicated to him, and he is aware of the smallest detail of the everyday happenings, and the most confidential matters as well'.[19] His was the responsibility of determining march routes, the location of camps and quarters, the laying-out of field fortifications, and collection of intelligence and topographical knowledge. His normal post was at the right hand of the commander-in-chief at headquarters, but he was frequently exposed to personal risk when he rode out with his escort, the generals of the day and the *Fouriers* to select and mark out the camp sites. Lacy later prescribed that the *Generalquartiermeister* must have a thorough knowledge of both the infantry and cavalry service, be a good draughtsman – or at least able to orientate himself with facility from maps – be a good fast rider, and possess the gift of *coup d'oeil*.[20]

The *Generalquartiermeister* was assisted by a *GFWM.* in the capacity of a *Generalquartiermeisterlieutenant,* up to three colonels (important for transmitting orders), two or three lieutenant-colonels, eight majors, and eight first-lieutenants and another eight second-lieutenants

– replaced on 3 January 1759 by 14 captains, 'for personnel of that kind are very necessary, when we bear in mind the way the armies and detached corps are split up'.[21] The *Capitaine des Guides* had a specialised function concerning intelligence (below), the *Feld-Ingenieurcorps* of 14 officers and five *Conducteuren* saw to the building of field fortifications, and the four *Flügel-Adjutants* (two each for the infantry and cavalry) kept up the liaison with the body of the army.

The *Kleiner Generalstaab* comprised the Staff troops (below), the *Pioniere*, the *Staabs-Wagenmeister*, the legal officials of the *Auditoriat-Amt*, and that fearsome individual the *Generalgewaltiger*, who was the chief provost of the army.

Such a depth of resources made it possible to form independent staffs for separate armies, and for some at least of the detached corps. Thus Ernst Friedrich Alexander Giannini served as Loudon's chief of staff in 1760 and 1761, and (according to his own account) played a key part in the battle of Landeshut in the first of these campaigns: 'It is certainly true that the commanding general, with his wealth of experience, projected all of this in general terms, and that it fell to me, as *Generalquartiermeister* only to advance my opinions, which were duly approved and accepted. However in virtue of my office I was responsible for putting the scheme into detailed execution, with all the consequent toils and anxieties, and I was the one who would have had a great deal of explaining to do if it had turned out badly'.[22]

Letter heading, addressed to the 'All-Powerful and Invincible' Emperor. The official Austrian clerks were expert calligraphers, and their mastery of Baroque phraseology and titles made their work impossible to forge, as Frederick of Prussia found when he made the attempt.

In the main army Daun freely acknowledged what he owed to the contribution of gifted officers of comparatively low rank. Major Franz Kökényesdi de Vettesz was summoned to an informal council of war on the morning of Kolin, and Vettesz would probably have become a prominent member of the new General Staff if he had not been killed in a minor skirmish outside Breslau five months later. Major Tomiotti di Fabris found a way forward for the army when it hesitated on the way to Maxen, and almost immediately after the victory Daun recommended him for promotion to lieutenant-colonel.

One of the peculiarities of the Austrian General Staff was its complement of permanently-assigned staff troops – the units of infantry, dragoons, *Jäger* and *Pioniere*.

The *Staabs-Infanterie-Regiment* was raised in 1758 as four battalions on an establishment of 2,739 troops, and augmented in 1759 to 4,160, 'so that this regiment may in addition furnish what is needed for the separate armies and various detached corps'.[23] The work of the Staff infantrymen was mundane but useful, for they provided guards for headquarters, generals, magazines and the baggage, and thus limited the very large and often unauthorised drainage of manpower for these purposes from the main body of the army. The troops were recruited from undersized young men, and the officers were usually unsuitable for arduous service in the field. Lacy wrote to one of his lady friends in 1759 to explain that he had found a place as second-lieutenant in the regiment for one of her protégés, though he should not stay there overlong, for the post was 'hardly of a kind to enable him to show forth miracles of bravery'.[24]

The *Staabs-Dragoner-Regiment* helped to keep the baggage in order, but it had a more active police role than did the Staff infantrymen and also augmented the generals' escorts on reconnaissances. The regiment was founded in 1758 on the small establishment of 434 officers and men. In 1759 it was augmented to a strength of 1,000 like the other dragoon regiments, though Lacy insisted that its character must remain fundamentally different. He wrote to Daun in March 1760 that since the last year there had been talk of entrusting the regiment to a conventional *Inhaber,* and that GFWM. Caramelli was one of the people who had put himself forward for the post. Lacy could not advise such a proceeding, but if it went ahead the *Inhaber* must be reminded of his obligation to maintain the string of 400 post horses.[25] The idea of appointing an *Inhaber* was abandoned.

Both the infantry and dragoons wore uniforms of disconcertingly Prussian appearance, with dark blue coats, and in May 1758 Lacy duly arranged to have himself fitted out with a uniform of this description, in virtue of his new post.[26]

The corps of Staff *Jäger* was an elite force (see p. 266), recruited heavily from the Tyrol, and attached as close escort to the officers of the Staff when they were on reconnaissance or staking out camps. Those useful people the *Staabs-Pioniere* (see p. 329) were at hand to clear paths, make field fortifications, and throw light bridges across ditches and streams. The battalion was recruited from 'really healthy and strong men. Miners are the most suitable'.[27]

As 'new corps' the staff troops became prime targets for the reductions in the army from the winter of 1761/2 onwards. The infantry regiment was reduced from 16 companies to four, and the pioneers and dragoons disbanded. Daun protested vain that the economies were false, for 'we cannot exaggerate the usefulness of their services, which repay their cost most handsomely'.[28]

Topography and Intelligence

(See also the section 'The Reformed Austrian Army and Prussian Espionage' in Chapter 6.) Although the Austrians were institutionalising most of their staff functions, the collection of topographical knowledge remained largely the business of interested individuals. A few good maps were on general sale. Johann Georg Keyssler noted that 'the *Stände* of the Kingdom of Bohemia have spent 24,000 florins to have a good map of their land. It was compiled by Johann Christoph Müller, captain of the Austrian engineers, and was engraved by Michael Kauser at Augsburg in 1720, in the form of 24 sheets, which may be put together in a single-sheet general map which was engraved at the same time'.[29] Matthias Kurländer, as Lacy's regimental agent, was able to answer most of the calls on him to obtain maps of the theatre of war, though in May 1758 Lacy was still lacking coverage of parts of central Saxony and Lusatia.[30]

The most militarily useful maps remained the hand-drawn sheets which were compiled by the more conscientious generals and their draughtsmen, like the surveys which Hadik assembled of actual and potential camp sites, which helped him greatly to get his bearings.[31] Lacy's precious portfolio of maps was lost to the Prussian hussars at Goldberg just before the battle of Liegnitz; in his distress he applied to Frederick for their return, and the king obliged with truly royal courtesy – after his draughtsmen copied the contents. Lacy's old patron FM. Browne had sent an officer to survey some stretches of the northern borders in the winter of 1755/6, but most of the Austrian officers were incurious about their surroundings, and not long before hostilities broke out Browne expressed the fear that Frederick might catch the Austrians at a disadvantage even in Bohemia, where the Austrians still had only a sketchy knowledge of the theatre, whereas the Prussians were acquainted with every track and trail, and Frederick himself knew from his earlier campaigns how the ground could be turned to the best advantage.[32]

Accurate maps of enemy fortresses were a particularly precious commodity, and well-placed individuals could command high prices for supplying interested parties with details of defences like those of the Prussians at Magdeburg.³³ This was a sphere where professional curiosity merged with spying. The evidence of espionage is by its nature fragmentary, but enough evidence survives to show that the Prussians and Austrians attached great value to both political and military intelligence.

The sinister Lieutenant-General Hans Carl Winterfeldt founded the tradition of Frederician espionage, and he was busy planting agents, and suborning, corrupting or blackmailing suitable individuals until he was killed at Moys on 7 September 1757. In 1749 he had won over the retired Austrian lieutenant-colonel Count Gelhorn, and furnished him with a lists of questions of particular interest. Gelhorn responded with a report in 35 folio pages, which ranged widely over the issues of Austrian military and domestic policy. He was still supplying Winterfeldt with intelligence early in 1757, but then appears to have sought shelter in Prussian territory. The Austrians were aware that he was in Breslau in November 1757, and they sent a patrol to seek him out after they captured the city.

In 1750 Winterfeldt travelled to Bohemia in person, on the excuse of taking the waters at Carlsbad, and when he visited the garrison at Leitmeritz he succeeded in winning over Lieutenant-Colonel Rebentsich from the Austrian service. Winterfeldt was back in Bohemia in 1754, and this time he used the opportunity to reconnoitre invasion routes on the western side of the Elbe.

Rebentsich meanwhile returned to Austrian territory under an assumed name, and in 1753 he recruited the Austrian lieutenant Haude, who was able to furnish the Prussians with a plan of the new fortifications at Olmütz. On abandoning the Austrian service Haude was made a royal Prussian *Flügel-Adjutant* and appointed Prussian envoy to the Porte under the pseudonym 'Rexin.' In Constantinople, however the subtleties of Haude/Rexin were unequal to the guile of the pro-Austrian Grand Vizier Ragip Pasha, who deluded him with protestations of active support for his master (see p. 414).

Military rank seems to have endowed Austrian traitors with a remarkable degree of security. Mention has been already been made of the cases of Brand, and of Brunyan and of the officers who were implicated at least indirectly with him (see p. 98). *FML.* Wetzel, the commandant of Prague, was another man of dubious character, who was responsible for the mysterious release of the Prussian *Rittmeister* Tanner and his mistress Augusta Carolina Baroness von Leppert and Till. Tanner was a renegade, who had already aroused suspicion by corresponding with the Prussians when he was in the Austrian service with the infantry regiment of Kheul. He fell into Austrian hands in 1757, and Loudon sent him under close military arrest for safekeeping in Prague; the Baroness Till (who went about in male attire) was detained under civil jurisdiction in the same city. All of this notwithstanding, Tanner was set free in March 1758 to join a party of Prussian officers who were being released on exchange; he was joined by the Till woman over the protests of the *Platz-Lieutenant* Kestenach, who found that Wetzel could produce no authority from the *Hofkriegsrath* to set the pair free.³⁴ Wetzel had died from natural causes and the couple were long gone when the affair was investigated in 1759 by Ludwig Egon the Landgraf of Fürstenberg, who managed a shadowy Austrian *Sicherheits Commission*. We have encountered him already, when he expressed his doubts concerning the reliability of the Württemberg troops (See p. 270).

Commanders in the field had to exercise their own judgement concerning the many doubtful individuals who came to their knowledge. In May 1761 *FZM.* Lacy came to hear of a Pomeranian gentleman, giving his name as a 'Graf von Sack,' who had settled at Ratibor in Upper Silesia, and was dispatching men on unknown errands to Lower Silesia, and also to Saxony where a retired Prussian Captain Nostitz was living at Bautzen. This Nostitz was 'reported to be in close contact with the said Count von Sack, and is in the habit of disappearing from view completely for four or five days at a stretch, and re-appearing just as unexpectedly. When he has downed more wine than usual, he makes his Prussian sympathies clear, and tells everyone stories in praise of his king.³⁵

In the same year the collapse of the Prussian free battalion of Le Noble produced a fine crop of adventurers, among whom the grenadier captain Friedrich August von Fabri reported at the Austrian outposts along with his villainous servants. Lacy questioned him about the forces and the position of Prince Henry of Prussia, but Fabri replied that he refused to be a traitor to his fatherland. Lacy learned the next day that the Austrians had abandoned an outpost at Senftenberg on the strength of an unfounded report from Fabri that it was about to come under attack.[36]

It is almost a relief to turn to the subject of outright espionage. Count Podewils came to Vienna as Prussian ambassador after the Second Silesian War. He could feel the pulse of political and military affairs in general, but as a matter of principle Frederick kept him in ignorance of the handsome young men who were being sent to Vienna under a variety of guises: 'The main rule was for them to strike up an acquaintance with the chambermaids of a number of designated ladies. They were to pretend to fall in love with them, and do everything they could to win the girls' affections in turn... These Adonises made some quite incredible discoveries. There were cases where they kept up their liaisons with the Viennese chambermaids for two years on end, and sent letters which were more significant and weighty than all the dispatches of the whole tribe of ambassadors'.[37]

Information continued to flow to Frederick during the war years. He wrote to Field Marshal Schwerin in January 1757 that he was making use of two Catholic priests in Vienna, and 'on the subject of that man in Browne's office, you are to regard expense as being of no object; you must give him everything he wants, so that he keeps us supplied with good reliable information'.[38] On at least two occasions the tenor of meetings of the Vienna Conference came to Frederick's knowledge, which argues higher-placed contacts still.[39]

Frederick meanwhile flooded the theatre of war with more-or-less expendable individuals, like the thief Kosebier, who had been hauled out of prison in Stettin and promised his freedom if he would go a-spying. He twice made his way in and out of Prague when it was being besieged by the Prussians in 1757. He hesitated to go a third time, and was told by the king: 'If you continue to refuse to carry out my orders, I'll have you sent straight back to Stettin, and you'll spend the rest of your life in chains'.[40]

Kosebier deserted and was never seen again. He was wise, for the Austrians kept themselves well informed of suspicious characters, and circulated their particulars among their armies. Thus:

> This man is from Freyberg. He wears a grey coat and blue waistcoat. He is not particularly tall, and has dark brown hair, a broad face, eyes of brown-black, and a big mouth which shows his teeth when he speaks – and he speaks a great deal and boldly. He pretends to be a servant of the [Saxon] Prime Minister Count Brühl.[41]

During the campaign of Kolin the French attachés reported that Prussian spies were being arrested wholesale, including three who had been shot for trying to set fire to Daun's headquarters, and a fourth – who was no more than a lad – who had been caught on the same mission, and was likely to share their fate.[42]

The effort was still worth Frederick's while, for the Austrians were notoriously indiscreet, and news of any impending enterprise would be common knowledge for 24 hours or more in advance. Many Prussian deserters were in the habit of accepting the Austrian bounty, roaming around the Austrian camps at will, and returning to their masters. In 1757 they could scarcely fail to notice how staff officers were in the habit of sending their personal field kitchens in advance to the intended camp sites.[43] Much of value could also be gleaned from the official newspaper, the *Wiener Diarium*, which was accurate, detailed and surprisingly impartial.[44]

On the Austrian side we find Kaunitz evaluating the worth of potential agents. At least two of the kind came to his attention in 1758. One was a covert Jacobite, who accompanied the British major-general Joseph Yorke on a mission to Frederick in 1758, and offered to pass on information to the Austrians without acknowledgement or reward. Kaunitz wrote to Daun that he was not certain what services the Jacobite could render, being a foreigner and ignorant of the country, but the Austrians were in great need of reliable intelligence, and no possible source could be neglected.[45] A few weeks later Kaunitz notified Daun of a Herr Coppenzeller, currently a teacher of languages at Wetzlar, whose trustworthiness had been guaranteed by the diplomat and minister Johann Anton Count Pergen. Coppenzeller was the son and brother of Austrian officers, and had penetrated the Neapolitan camp at Velletri on behalf of the Austrians in 1744. 'At the present time,' wrote Kaunitz, 'he is particularly well placed, for his brother-in-law is in the King of Prussia's suite and enjoys the royal favour, and he has every hope that through this channel and the acquaintances he makes he will able to supply Your Excellency with reports that will be both weighty and useful. In effect he proposes to act as a spy in the immediate circle of the king.' Kaunitz assessed Coppenzeller as being committed, expert and intelligent, and he had persuaded Francis Stephen to receive him in audience, 'because men of this kind are hard to come by'.[46]

Every now and then the activity of allied agents threw Berlin society into a state of alarm. If Frederick had planted his handsome young men in Vienna, then a Russian spy-cum-hairdresser made himself popular with the ladies of the Prussian capital, and thus found his way into a number of the great houses.[47] Austrian and Russian officer prisoners on parole gained entry of a scarcely less compromising nature, and patriots were aware that the astute Austrian major-general Beck was seeing too much for their peace of mind. The Prussian Court was believed to be unsafe even in its refuge in Magdeburg, after the Austrians had opened a channel of communication with their prisoners there (see p. 187). This might have been the doing of Kaunitz, or even of the *Hofkriegsrath,* whose chief (effectively Neipperg for most of the war) had an important responsibility for gathering intelligence. He was to take a direct hand in recruiting spies and to be furnished with the necessary funds, 'and since it is inadvisable for such people to be made known to others and identified by name, the President of the *Hofkriegsrath* has a completely free hand in the disbursement of the money, without having to submit accounts, or answer for the expenditure in any way'.[48]

Individual Austrian commanders collected portfolios of spies and other confidential agents in much the same way as they assembled their portfolios of maps. Hadik's journal contains many references to their work (though he was careful never to commit their names to paper), and indeed one of his agents was arrested in Berlin at the same time as the Russian hairdresser mentioned above. Loudon's sensational storm of Schweidnitz in October 1761 probably owed a great deal to the Prussian deserter who furnished him with specific details of the fortifications, and of the size, character and routine of the garrison (see p. 237).

The greater part of the most immediately useful information was nevertheless obtained through the routine observations by outposts and patrols,[49] or the efforts of the *Captaine des Guides,* who was attached to the General Staff. He was to be 'an intelligent and alert kind of man, on the lookout for local guides, so that the various columns or even the entire army do not lose their way out of ignorance'.[50]

The Progress of the Campaign

The Organisation of the Army for the Campaign – The Missed Opportunity

Thanks to the work of Austria's new General Staff, the army in the field was able to move with speed and precision from the opening of the campaign of 1758 until the end of the war. The Austrians would have done better still if their army had not still been organised in the conventional style, whereby every grouping of forces above the regimental level – brigade, division (*Departement*) and corps – was a temporary affair, in which the components and the commanders were re-shuffled according to the relative seniorities of the regiments and generals at any given time.

Two men proposed an altogether more radical way of associating the commanders and the commanded. *FZM.* Lacy, writing in 1760, suggested defining a *GFWM.*'s responsibilities once and for all as a brigade of two regiments, that of a *FML.* of two such brigades, and that of the *FZM.* or *G.d.C.* as a mixed corps consisting of:

nine or 10 regiments of infantry
three regiments of cuirassiers
two or three regiments of dragoons
two regiments of hussars

Lacy argued that:

the repartition of the army in groupings of this kind would awaken in every formation the zeal to outstrip the others and excel in its movements, discipline and military standards. There would be an end to the practice which dictates that separate lieutenant-generals and major-generals must command the infantry, cavalry or hussars respectively. Instead it will be a question of striving to become a general *per sé,* and acquiring the necessary knowledge. Every commander of such a formation would get to know his generals, and these in turn would get to know their officers; thus all the members of the body would become acquainted with one another, and seek to win the others' friendship and trust. Each corps must stay together both in peace and war, and on the day of battle one of the corps should make up the first line, another the second line, and the rest the third line. Six corps of this kind would constitute an army. The divisions and brigades would also be permanent, in the same way as the corps just mentioned.[51]

A comparable proposal was advanced by *GFWM.* Wartensleben, who derived his inspiration from the legions of Ancient Rome. The system of legions had been praised by Vegetius, and more recently the chevalier de Saxe had suggested adapting the principle to form modern legions of 3,000 to 6,000 troops apiece. Wartensleben believed that de Saxe's proposal was unsuited for the Austrian service, for it would have involved splitting the individual regiments, and especially the hussars. He therefore advocated putting the field army on an establishment of 158,000 troops, who would be divided into 12 legions – each identified with a specific area of the monarchy to form, for example, a Legion of Hungary, or a Legion of Wallonia.[52]

These were radical thoughts. It is easy to see why Wartensleben's scheme was not taken up, for it ran contrary to the sacred principle of extraterritoriality. However it had in common with Lacy's proposal the notion of re-arranging the army in stable groupings that would at once facilitate command on the larger scale, and promote cohesion and comradeship among the formations. These projects went far beyond the French essays (the first of their kind) in the divisional system, which were undertaken in 1758. In the event the only remotely comparable Austrian divisions did not appear in the field until 1799, and the corps not until 1809.

The March

We join the army at the moment the commander had agreed with his staff as to the time and destination of the next march. The *Generalquartiermeister* then set off with the officers of his staff, the company *Fouriers* and an appropriate escort to occupy and stake out the camp site; the routes for the individual columns were likewise flagged, and the pioneers assigned to improve the paths as necessary.[53]

Once all of these matters had been arranged, the *Generalquartiermeister* informed the army commander of what had been done, and which officers of the Staff had been assigned to guide the columns. These officers were in turn given instructions to provide against unforeseeable happenings on the march, since 'it often turns out that the generals, even of the highest rank, are in total ignorance of what the march is about, or at least its destination. The only people in the know are the officers of the General Staff who lead the columns'.[54]

It had long been the custom of the Austrians to thicken-up their outposts and prepare a meal on the evening before an intended march. Frederick took due note of the fires, and these practices continued until Daun saw the relevant section in the captured copy of the king's *General Principia* in 1760. 'That section on the signs of the enemy intentions is very useful to us,' wrote Daun, 'for now we will be able prevent the enemy detecting our movements'.[55] Armfeldt notes that the Austrians would set off at night or very early in the morning if there happened to be a particular reason, like stealing a march on the enemy, though they still liked to march only after the soldiers had had an opportunity to cook and eat a proper meal.[56]

There was no point in getting the soldiers to their feet if they were just to be left standing uselessly, weighed down by their knapsacks and equipment. 'Experience shows that if the army commander tells the generals of infantry and cavalry to set off at four in the morning, they will tell the colonels that the appointed time is two o'clock, and so it goes on down to the most insignificant functionary... It's just the same before a parade or a session of drill. Unless you are careful you will find that the regiment will be under arms three hours earlier than time actually ordered'.[57] The Prince de Ligne found that in summer time he could get the best from his men by setting out at three in the morning, marching with brief halts until ten, then allowing the troops to prepare their meals and sleep during the heat of the day; he then set them in march again at five in the afternoon, and continue until nine in the evening.[58]

According to the *Militär Feld-Regulament* of 1759 the leading regiment of each column signalled that it was setting off by beating the *Marsch-Streich* and three *Rufs-Schläge,* and this example was followed by the successive regiments down the length of the line; if silence were enjoined, the commander of each regiment had to watch carefully for the departure of the regiment immediately in front of him.

The number of columns, and their length, was determined to a great extent by whether the army was marching 'by lines' or 'by wings.' In the arrangement 'by lines' the army moved in two main columns, each corresponding to one of the lines of battle: the overall frontage was narrow (which might prove useful when traversing

GFWM. Joseph Count Ferraris, 1726–1814 (M. Militz, Military Academy, Wiener Neustadt). Ferraris had a keen eye for ground, and his exploits at Hochkirch gained him the M.M.T.O. After the war his great survey of the Austrian Netherlands (1770–7) represented a landmark in the history of cartography. He was still active in the war against the French Revolution, as is shown by the inscriptions.

difficult country), but the columns were of great length and would take a correspondingly long time to form into line of battle. In the march 'by wings' the army moved on a broad frontage in four main columns (one on either side for the wings of cavalry, and the other two in the centre for the wings of infantry), which brought the troops more quickly to their objective, but demanded plentiful routes and a wide tract of open terrain. If the *corps de reserve* were of any size, it would in any event form a further column on the side of the army furthest from the enemy. The heavy artillery was inserted between the columns of infantry – an awkward practice which impeded the march of the troops, and prevented the pieces from being brought into action with any speed (for these reasons the Prussians, who also marched by 'lines' or 'wings,' preferred to keep their heavy artillery train out to the side of the army nearest the enemy).

The *Militär Feld-Regulament* of 1759 emphasised the principle of keeping the individual columns as short and fat as possible. Thus the infantry were to march on a frontage of full tactical divisions, and adopt progressively narrower frontages of half-divisions and *Züge* only when they had to. A special order was required for the infantry to march by single file. The divisions or *Züge* normally marched in compact succession, which shortened the columns, but once in the presence of the enemy they opened the intervals to the full extent, and so won the space to swing into line by simultaneous quarter wheels. The cavalry marched in a column four files wide, which might be reduced temporarily to two files if the force had to negotiate a bridge or track through dense woodlands.

The column commander worked in close association with the officer assigned to him from the General Staff, and they kept an eye on the progress of the columns to either side. 'As far as possible they take care that the heads of columns keep station with one another, and enter camp in the same order. However that is not always possible, on account of hills, ravines, valleys or marshes, and because the army might number 60,00, 70,000 or up to 100,000 troops, and the marching columns often take up more than a *Meile* in breadth[59] (the *Meile* was the equivalent of about 7.5 km.).

In the event of a stoppage, the column commander rode to the spot to investigate the cause, and if necessary he ordered up specialised labour – the regimental *Zimmerleuthe* and the Corps of *Pioniere* – to clear paths or obstacles, repair existing bridges, or bring up the light *Laufbrücken*. Such work was given high priority.[60]

The infantrymen were forbidden to make detours around muddy stretches along the roads (such as were frequently found on the approaches to villages), but they were allowed to open up their files sufficiently to march freely, and to take off their neck stocks and undo some of the buttons of their waistcoats. The tents of the infantry were sent in advance to the camp sites on carts or pack animals, which was a further alleviation, but the soldier still had to carry his knapsack, water bottle, 60 cartridges and his bread for two or three days, and perhaps it might be his turn to be laden with the *Cameradschaft's* metal cooking-pot. The Prince de Ligne saw many soldiers collapse and die from heat exhaustion under the cruel constriction of the gaiters and the multiple straps, belts and slings,[61] and he confirmed the universal prejudice of the time when he asserted that it was most harmful for a soldier to lay aside clothing or take a cool drink.[62]

The *Militär Feld-Regulament* made specific provision for the march of the cavalry. Thus 'while fording a body of water the riders must never allow their horses to drink, for that invariably holds up the march; if a horse suddenly begins to make water and the rider cannot guide it to the side of the route, the others are not to halt, but instead carry on past him, leaving it to him to resume his place'.[63]

If any of the regimental wives of the infantry were unencumbered by children, they might be permitted to march with the column to retail spirits to the soldiers. Otherwise all the women, sutlers and walking stragglers were assigned to the baggage train, which was relegated to the tail of each column in the order of the component regiments, and kept in order by detachments from the main body. From 1758 the Staff infantry and dragoons took over the prime responsibility for escorting the baggage, which had hitherto absorbed an inordinate number of men from the regiments.

Austrian march security was of a high standard. Both Frederick and Armfeldt noted that it was impossible to catch the Austrians off their guard when they were on the move, for their routes took them through forests, marshes or secluded valleys, and they were further masked by the light forces which operated on their flanks.[64] The Austrians were equally circumspect when they were moving in small detachments. Rudolph Pálffy told his regiment of hussars that a corporal and six troopers must ride 15 minutes' distance in front of the main body; these men were not to comb the woods in a systematic way, but halt frequently to observe the behaviour of the peasants and listen for hoof beats. The officer coming up at the head of the main force was to have the woods investigated more closely, to uncover anybody who might still be concealed there.[65]

When he had the freedom to follow his preferred routine of march (above), the Prince de Ligne found that his troops could readily sustain a progress of 33,000 two-foot paces, or about 20 kilometres on each day of the march. Raiding corps could move somewhat faster. Hadik covered about 150 kilometres in six days in the course of his raid on Berlin in 1757, which makes a rate of about 25 kilometres per day. Lacy re-visited Berlin on behalf of the Austrians in 1760, and his corps marched a total of 334 kilometres over 10 days, or an average of rather over 33 to the day.

Even the cumbersome main force of the army could prove unexpectedly quick on its feet in an emergency, as Daun proved when he marched to the relief of Olmütz in 1758, and moved the 40 or so kilometres from Prodlitz and Dobromilitz to the heights of Gross-Teinitz in the 25 hours between four in the afternoon of 30 June and five in the afternoon of 1 July. The French observer Rutant de Marainville accompanied the army on this campaign (the first to be directed by the new General Staff) and he recorded how skilful the Austrians had become at reconnoitring routes and guiding the columns, at casting bridges over streams to enable the infantry to march by full tactical divisions, at sending their tents ahead to camp sites by pack animals, and keeping the baggage in order by their Staff infantry. The contrast with the disorders which had prevailed in 1757 could not have been more pronounced. 'Every detail is on a better footing. It is a pleasure to see how the march routes are prepared and opened up. The army can accomplish a march of three *Meilen* [about 22.5 kilometres] more speedily and easily than a march of one *Meile* last year.'[66]

Positions and their Place in War

At this period the predominant experience of warfare was not of fighting, or even or marching, but of spending longer or shorter periods in position. These were of two kinds – the temporary and cramped *'Nacht-'* or *'Marschlager,'* which were taken up when the army halted in battle order at the end of the day in the presence of the enemy, and the longer-term *'Standlager.'*

Prince Henry of Prussia had a keen eye for ground, and he repeatedly bid defiance to the *Reichsarmee* and the Austrians from his positions in Saxony, while Frederick ensconced himself in the fortified positions of Schmottseifen in 1759, Bunzelwitz in 1761, and again and again in the *Katzenhäuser* camp near Meissen. Daun noted concerning a relevant passage in the *General Principia*: 'In my opinion this article… is very good, and daily experience confirms the benefit which the King of Prussia derives from such positions'.[67]

However positional warfare was associated above all with the Austrians, for it minimised the inconveniences arising from their poor mobility at the minor tactical level, while playing to their strengths in quantity of troops and quality of artillery. Frederick wrote to his intimates in 1758 concerning the difficulty of drawing Daun, 'the old fox,' from the multitude of positions available to him in the broken country of Bohemia, Moravia and Saxony. It was not just that the Austrians were choosing positions that were strong in themselves, but they were deploying their forces in intelligent ways (below).[68] In this respect he conceded that the *General Principia* of 1753 no longer held good, 'for in the previous war the enemy had had no understanding of ground or tactics, and their artillery was pitiful and their infantry not much better'.[69]

Hadik tells us something of the Austrian perspectives when he describes the knowledge he had accumulated of the ground at Postelberg and other sites in north-western Bohemia. At the operational level, as we would now call it, the Postelberg position sat threateningly on the western flank of any Prussian force advancing on Prague, and:

> bearing in mind that we might be encamped there for some time, I chose the most convenient site in respect to the ground, the water and the stocking of provisions, and as far as possible I left... the peasants undisturbed in the growing season... the infantry encamped behind Postelberg on the far side of the river [Eger], and the cavalry on the near side in luxuriant and well-shaded meadows. Altogether this is just about the most convenient position I have encountered in my whole life. The troops liked it also, as you may deduce from the fact that 201 men had deserted on the march from Forchheim to Saaz, but not a single one during the whole of the month of June [1759].[70]

The immediate fighting position extended behind the Eger, for the ultimate qualification for a good camp site was its suitability as a defensive battleground.

The finest position had no virtue unless the defender knew how to exploit its potential. The Austrians liked to extend their camps not so much along the summits of hills, but on the lower slopes from where the ground fell away gently, like the glacis of a fortress. Frederick commented that 'this method is well thought-out, and is the fruit of experience, which shows that a grazing fire is more lethal than a plunging one. The soldiers standing on the crest of the glacis enjoy all the advantages of height without the inconveniences. The attacker, being exposed and advancing up the slope, is unable to inflict casualties by his fire, whereas the defender can lay down an effective and prepared cross-fire'.[71] The wings of the army rested on ravines, marshes, watercourses or other obstacles calculated to frustrate Frederick's favourite battle tactic of the outflanking march.[72] Some attention was also devoted to the question of communications:

> if the army is stationary for more than one night, and there happen to be streams, ravines or similar obstructions behind the camp, the *Generalquartierrneister* takes care to have bridges built... at least to the number of one for each wing... If there are detached corps thrown out to the left, right or front of the army, communications are duly opened with them as well... while the generals, who are detailed to support these corps if they come under attack, are not only under orders to reconnoitre the nearest and best routes, but to tell the regimental officers in charge of the relevant troops to do the same.[73]

In the Silesian Wars the Austrians had settled into their positions more or less in the same way as if they had been fighting in the open field, that is to say with their cavalry stationed on either flank, and the infantry across the middle. At Kolin Frederick noticed for the first time that the enemy had abandoned the conventional order of battle, and deployed the troops on the ground that best suited their modes of action. As for the artillery, the king observed that 'they take advantage of every slightly-projecting spur of ground to emplace pieces to fire obliquely, and thus build up as much of a cross-fire as they can. The result is that there is nothing to choose [in undesirability] between assaulting a fortress... and attacking an army which has prepared its ground in such a way'.[74]

It was not enough to overcome the first line. Frederick reminded his confidants that the Austrians were arranged in depth, with the successive positions representing so many ambushes, and held by forces that were earmarked for that purpose.[75] The Austrians held cavalry in their second line, ready to counter-attack if the infantry of their first line were giving way; some of the impetus of the Prussians was therefore already lost before they were faced with a new and terrible battle to overcome the second line, which the Austrians sustained by feeding up reinforcements from their third line [the *corps de reserve*].[76] Armfeldt states that it was the battle of Leuthen which convinced the Austrians of the need to array their forces in depth.[77]

Austrian digging never reached the extent caricatured by Tempelhoff and other Prussian writers. Prince Henry probably outdid the Austrians in the strength of his static defences, and indeed when the Austrians took over his old camp at Torgau in November 1760 they deprived the western flank of crucial protection when they plundered his abatis for firewood. The Austrians' own abatis were not always particularly strong, for they often neglected to fell the trees in such a way that the trunks fell across one another, and sometimes even the root ends were left facing the Prussians, and the branches projecting into the Austrian position.[78] Marainville noted that the Austrians, the Prussians and indeed the Germans in general made no use of the self-contained fortlets called 'redoubts,' which were popular in the French service, for the Teutons feared that they would be difficult to recapture if they fell into the hands of the enemy.[79] Among the Austrians Lieutenant-Colonel Rebain (Browne's engineer) was a lone advocate of this type of fortification; he knew that a good redoubt could be built by 600 men in just six hours, but 'we are not particularly fond of hard work, and shun the very notion'.[80] Again neither the Austrians nor the Prussians set much store by holding villages, which on this theatre of war were admittedly so flimsily-built that they had little defensive value.

No position could be called totally impregnable, and Armfeldt reckoned that in most of the camps he had seen the Austrians had left too little space in front of the camps to enable the troops to manoeuvre freely, and likewise insufficient gaps between the tents.[81] Frederick was on the alert to detect any kind of weakness, but he succeeded in taking a major Austrian position by direct assault only in one of the last actions of the war, which was at Burkersdorf on 21 July 1762, when he detected that the Austrian deployments were split in two by the Weistritz ravine; he therefore took the opportunity to concentrate his long-range artillery and his columns against the isolated eastern sector. Otherwise his only recourse was to try to manoeuvre the Austrians out of their positions by diversions and flank marches on the operational scale.

The vulnerability of the Austrian camps lay in other directions entirely. By living in a single position for any length of time the Austrians ran the risk of consuming all the fresh provisions of the neighbourhood, and so rendering themselves liable to scurvy, as Daun discovered during the long stalemate in the Silesian hills in 1762. Prolonged immobility caused an army not only to fall out of physical condition in this way, but to lose its edge in terms of morale; a defensive position could be tactically strong, and yet it might concede the psychological advantage to the enemy.[82]

We return to practical details. The first people to arrive on the scene of an intended camp were the *Generalquartiermeister* and his staff, their escort of Staff troops, and an officer and a couple of *Fouriers* from each regiment who proceeded to plant flagged stakes to mark out the lines of tents. The frontages corresponded to that of the lines of battle, allowing one pace for each file of infantry and each officer and NCO in the first rank, together with an interval of six or so paces between battalions, and four gaps of six paces each for the regiment's complement of artillery. Avenues at least 12 paces wide were left in front of and behind the regimental camps.

The officers down to first-lieutenant enjoyed the privilege of individual tents in marquee style, but the second-lieutenants and ensigns were consigned to communal ridge tents. Among the rank and file the tent *Kameradschaft* was the fundamental social unit, where authority exercised by a *Gefreyter* or another reliable old soldier. Here the infantry lived together half a dozen at a time, while the cavalry dwelt in groups of four or five.

The Austrian tents were inferior in quality to those of the Prussians, being made of thinnish unlined canvas, and lacking a canvas floor. This economy was misguided, since the Austrians had to be provided with longer coats to protect them from the cold and damp, 'and although is not considered an urgent camp necessity to be supplied as a matter of routine, we should bend our efforts to procure it and distribute it to the regiments if there is a question of encamping for any length of time in one place, or in adverse and cold weather'.[83]

The soldiers did their cooking in metal cauldrons which they suspended over fires 50 paces or so in front of their tents. Windfallen branches, hacked-down boughs and trees, uprooted palisades and fences, and ripped-out barn and house timbers all served to feed the flames, and Pietro Verri describes how early one morning outside Dresden the smoke from the camp fires hung so thickly that it was impossible for a man on horseback to see the ground.[84]

According to an inconvenient old custom the Austrians did not stack their muskets as in other arms under cover of the miniature tents called 'bells of arms'; they instead piled their muskets in open pyramids, or stacked them in wooden racks, which made a good show when freshly painted, but forced the soldiers to retrieve their muskets and place them in their tents in any kind of damp weather.[85]

The routine command of the army was invested in the rotating generals 'of the day' – one *FML*. each of infantry and cavalry, two *GFWMs* each from the infantry and cavalry, and a colonel, a lieutenant-colonel and a major from each wing. They were supposed to inspect the *Feldwachten* of the two lines and reserve at least once a day, and they had the responsibility of putting the army in battle array if the enemy made an unexpected appearance. In November 1758 Giuseppe Gorani

Camp scene (Austrian Army Museum). Sutlers are dispensing food and drink in the right and left foreground. The colour guard is in the centre foreground, and senior officers are dining in the marquee-style tent behind.

found himself with a detachment of 600 troops at the siege of Dresden, and he noted that 'these gentlemen fortunately visited us only in the daytime and forgot about us afterwards, apparently because it was not cold enough for them to need to warm themselves in our position, where the gunfire lasted all night'.[86]

The *Parole* was the most important ceremony of the daily routine. A selection of officers (the senior *G.d.C.* and *FZM.*, a *FML.* of infantry and another of cavalry from each of the wings, a *GFWM.* and a major from every brigade, and all the general-adjutants) assembled at headquarters to hear the challenge and the password (*Parole*) of the day from the commander-in-chief, and note any orders which the great man might care to deliver. The challenge was normally the name of a saint, and the response that of a town. Thus '*St. Florian!*' might be answered by '*Würzburg!*', or at least by bad language in a familiar voice. All of this was passed down the chain of command with the help of the general-adjutants, and ultimately transmitted to the individual *Feldwachten* when the troops on guard gathered in a circle around their captain. No particular time was fixed for the *Parole,* though it was normally pronounced at 11 in the morning if the army was due to march at four or five in the afternoon.[87]

The arrangement of the sentries and outposts was typical of an army of the time. The regimental *Wacht* comprised the men who were detailed to guard the officers' tents – usually three men on duty with their captain, and so onwards to the two NCOs and six men with the colonel. The troops assigned to such duties were notified the day before, so that they had the time to make themselves presentable. The colours of the infantry and the standards of the cavalry had their respective little *Fahnen Wachten* and *Estandart Wachten*. The regimental *Quartierwacht* was made up of posts of one corporal and three men each, deployed on either side of the regimental lines, and about 10 paces to the front and rear.

Special provision was made for the security of headquarters, where a company of grenadiers provided a super-large *Fahnen-Wacht,* and one or two companies of the *Staabs-Infanterie-Regiment* were quartered close at hand.

A triple layer of posts guarded the army as a whole. The *Piqueter* were substantial bodies of infantry, formed of some 210–220 men each from each brigade, and standing at the disposal of the infantry general of the day. The *Piqueter* of the first line were posted according to brigade one or 200 paces in front of the latrines, and those of the second line out to either flank of the army and 100 paces to the rear. Each brigade's worth of pickets deployed two sentries to its front and usually a couple of further sentries on the flanks, 'so that... the pickets can ensure that no suspicious or hostile people can worm their way as far as the army'.[88]

The *Bereitschaften* (from 24 March 1759 made up of two squadrons from each wing) were the corresponding bodies of cavalry, and took up station in front of the pickets of the first line; ahead of the *Bereitschaften* again stood the isolated cavalry *Feldwachten* (another four squadrons under the same arrangements).

All of these outposts were set out at six in the evening in summer, or at nightfall in winter. The pickets represented a heavy drain on the infantry and to no particular benefit, since the men were thrown together from different regiments and under unfamiliar officers, to the detriment of discipline and morale.[89] The cavalry benefited from a principle put forward at a Conference of 4 January 1758 when 'it pleased His Imperial Majesty to represent the great inconvenience which must necessarily arise from mixing small detachments drawn from various regiments'.[90] (This sensible notion of forming the *Bereitschaften* and *Feldwachten* from entire squadrons was made standard practice by the *Militär Feld-Regulament* of 12 March 1759). The vigilance of these people was seldom tested, since the army was screened by the watchful Croats, and by the roving corps which Frederick treated with such respect.

Winter cantonments were a form of dispersed encampment, whereby the troops sheltered from the season in billets among the civilian population on the theatre of war. This was in accordance with the ancient military maxim which held that the meanest hovel was to be preferred to the finest tent. As a measure of precaution the units were assigned assembly points in case of alarm, though the security of winter quarters depended primarily on the Croats, hussars and other suffering troops who were extended in cordon facing the enemy.

Der Kleine Krieg

> those men who are exposed continually, as if they were a species of humanity whose lives were of less account.[91]

'*Der kleine Krieg,*' '*la petite guerre,*' '*little war*' were the terms increasingly used in the 18th century to describe the kind of fast-moving, tactically irregular warfare waged by light forces – whether specially designated troops, or men whose calling or conditions of life made them peculiarly suitable for such activities. In the Austrian service '*der kleine Krieg*' was associated most immediately with the Croats and hussars, though dragoons, grenadiers and other suitable regular forces also had their place. For the historian the efficacy of '*der kleine Krieg*' can be as difficult to pin down as its practitioners, for it worked for most at the time on two quite separate planes – at the major operational level, by hitting at the enemy flanks and communications, and at a tactical level of a most basic kind.

In the period extending from the Silesian Wars and the War of the Austrian Succession until the middle 1750s the ascendancy of the Austrian light troops at '*der kleine Krieg*' was assumed to be near absolute, and a sure way of catching the Prussians at a disadvantage.[92] Frederick wrote in 1755 that the Croatian threat had forced the Prussians to throw out detachments to right and left to prevent their flanks being turned. He as yet had no genuine light infantry to pit against the Croats, and although he intended to form a couple of regiments from French deserters as an artificial substitute, he believed that the enemy would always hold the advantage.[93]

In the Seven Years War the Prussian regulars could still venture only at their peril into broken and unfamiliar country. The experience of the fine grenadier battalions of Billerbeck and Waldow will stand for many others. On 23 April 1757, two days after the Duke of Bevern's victory at Reichenberg in Bohemia, the battalions were pushing through difficult country towards an Austrian position. The valley floors were stuffed with Croats, hussars and Hungarian infantry, and the two Prussian battalions halted until Bevern could come up with the main force:

> When he arrived he ordered the advance guard to occupy the heights facing the hills held by the enemy. Our battalions were still short of the summit when the Croats fired a volley, which killed a fair number of our men. We stayed on that hilltop for three hours – it was extremely cold and we were buffeted by a violent wind. Towards evening the order came for the battalions to come down and occupy a belt of brushwood at the bottom of the hill... as we neared the bushes we were greeted by a fire which was all the more deadly because the Croats were lying prone and firing point blank at our grenadiers, and the officers in particular, whereas we could see nobody at all and were unable to exact our revenge. Our battalions stayed in that wood for more than 18 dangerous hours. At last on 24 April the Duke of Bevern allowed our battalions to fall back a little and pitch their tents. All the same the canvas was riddled with bullets in a matter of hours, and all through the night the camp was on constant alert, with sentries having their throats cut and bullets whistling about our ears.[94]

These were successes in the old style, but they were now counterbalanced by other engagements in which the Croats showed themselves at a needless disadvantage. The first and probably the most costly of the little disasters occurred at Schandau on 14 October 1756, just after *FM.* Browne had called off his attempt to rescue the beleaguered Saxons at Pirna. Under attack from Prussian horse a company of the Ottocaner grenadiers neglected to fix its bayonets, fell out of order and was wiped out. Kaunitz was distressed at the news, while Colonel Anton Losy von Losenau cited this episode when he wrote to Hadik on the shortcomings of the Croatian tactics. He added that he and Loudon had experienced much the same, as was illustrated by an incident during the Austrian retreat to Prague in April 1757, 'when my battalion [of Oguliner], which was standing under my immediate orders, disregarded every warning, and sallied forth in its usual state of fury and disorder to attack several squadrons of enemy cavalry in a plain; they lost a fair number of dead and wounded, and were lucky that most of them escaped with their lives.' Losy pointed out that the Croats were peculiarly vulnerable, for they were frequently deployed by isolated battalions as advance guards or rearguards, and had little protection against the Prussian cavalry. He proposed that they should be formed into self-protecting columns *a la Folard,* and kept under strict discipline to deter them from unravelling in their usual way.[95]

What had been going wrong? Losy's columns would have been shot up badly by artillery (despite arguments he advanced to the contrary), but he was not the only critic to call attention to the deplorable habit of many Austrians commanders of posting the light forces around the landscape in penny packets to lend security to the regulars, 'in such a way that we had, as usual, a little everywhere, but nowhere a formed whole'.[96] Such a dispersal of forces could be a sign of indecision on the part of the general, as the *Hofkriegsrath* indicated when it reprimanded the Prince of Zweibrücken on the subject in 1759.[97] Zweibrücken's successor as commander in Saxony, G.d.C. Serbelloni, incurred equal displeasure by frittering away his forces in pinprick raids. Maria Theresa objected to this practice on two accounts: 'On the one side these operations exhaust the troops and horses to the point of ruin, and cost the lives of many brave soldiers… whose loss we deplore. At the same time these undertakings do nothing of consequence to promote our main objectives, or dislodge the enemy from their positions'.[98]

The concerns of Maria Theresa were shared to the full by Kaunitz, who argued that:

> The Croats do not receive the credit which is their due. These men are the ones who are in the closest and most immediate contact with the enemy. They keep them in a state of constant unrest, they have to put up with more hardship and danger than the other troops… and they have to run rather than march. They are given the most exacting tasks as a matter of routine, and their losses are treated as being of no account.[99]

Although the Croats were supposed to receive pay and rations on the same scales as the 'German' forces, there were lengthy periods when they were left without any support, which encouraged them to take what they needed – and sometimes a little more – from the local population. It was never easy to distinguish between the bands which plundered out of necessity and those which plundered for criminal gain. Regular officers were inclined to take the uncharitable view, and regarded the habits of the Croats as an infection which corrupted all the troops with whom they came in contact.[100] Marauding was undeniably institutionalised among the hussars, but the Croats themselves were inclined to attribute the bad name of the *Grenzer* to the mercenary *NCOs* who appeared among them in wartime, and they had some unlikely advocates in the shape of Prussian townspeople who had seen them at close quarters. The Magdeburgers were struck by the gentlemanly conduct of the Croats who were accommodated among them as prisoners of war (see p. 240), while the citizens of Halle had expected the worst when their town came under occupation by the Austrians and troops of the *Reichsarmee* in the summer of 1759, and yet the officers kept the Croats under generally effective control, and even those who came into the town to plunder could be bought off with a trifle worth a few *Groschen,* whereas the hussars would be satisfied with nothing less than gold and valuables.[101]

Tactically, the little parties of hussars and Croats were exposed to repeated maulings by superior enemy forces, and became less and less inclined to show their faces.

> Although it is often asserted that the Croats are good in woodlands, the real reason why they like to fight there is that they find better concealment, and can make themselves scarce with less chance of being noticed. It is the easiest thing in the world to dislodge them from even the thickest woods and the highest hills, and when you call out to ask them why they do not stand fast, they reply that they have no officers with them, and so they are not obliged to fight. And in fact their officers are seldom to be seen, for they will have taken off already. In woodland the cowardly officer and soldier has plenty of opportunities to escape undetected, and so only a few brave souls hold out, and most of them are wounded or captured in the process.[102]

The Prince de Ligne points out that the woods themselves might offer only a marginal degree of protection against Prussians who were willing to venture into them. A wood might look impenetrable from the outside, 'but the Zieten Hussars taught me differently when I saw them working up and down one of these so-called forests, cutting down our brave Warasdiners at every passage'.[103] In the later years of the war the only warning usually had to come from the eyes and ears of the Croats themselves, for in Prussian Silesia and in Protestant Saxony the Austrians did not often have the *faveur du pays* at their disposal.

The tactical edge of the hussars and Croats was also being blunted by the process of regularisation, which by the time of the Seven Years War had progressed at once too far and not far enough – sufficient to deprive them of some of their useful savagery, but not enough to form them into trained light troops. Thus the Austrian hussars still performed feebly in all-out battle, yet lost their historic predominance in scouting, raiding and ambushes. In 1761 Daun had occasion to reprimand Hadik after a tactical debacle: 'I hope that the ambushes that you stake out in future will prove more successful than the one just now.'[104]

Again the Croats and especially the Warasdiners had done excellent service in Bavaria and Italy in the last war, at a period when they were still armed with their long Dalmatian muskets which shot accurately to 300 or 400 paces. Having done execution at long range they resorted to their main weapon, a sabre in the Turkish style, with which they rushed at the enemy. Now they had been told to abandon the charge with cold steel, and rely solely on fire with their new regulation muskets – a tactic they never succeeded in mastering.[105]

What was to be done? A run of reverses convinced Loudon that the courage of the Croats went for nothing when, having attained an objective, they were so scattered that they were unable to hold the ground they had conquered. Whereas Losy von Losenau identified a solution in his tightly closed-up columns, Loudon explained that his unit of 'Green Grenadiers' could be augmented with advantage into a full two-battalion regiment of 1,800 men to give the Croats immediate support by German-style infantry. He argued correctly that the free and adventurous life, the green uniforms and the designation 'grenadiers' would attract plenty of the right kind of men.[106] Loudon got his extra Green Grenadiers, who proceeded to act in close co-operation with the Croats in the way intended.

On the larger scale the hussars and Croats could come into their own when they came under the command of aggressive leaders who knew how to combine the potentials of light and regular forces. Not just Loudon, but a whole group of like-minded commanders – Beck, Brentano, Draskovich, Hadik, Jahnus, Kleefled, Luzinsky, Siskovics, Ried and Wied – used detached corps not in the manner of Zweibrücken and Serbelloni, but in a confident way which was first brought home to Frederick in his Moravian campaign of 1758. While he was laying siege to Olmütz in the central plain he found the Austrians closing in from all sides, and complained that Daun 'has his scoundrels on the large scale, who are concealing his movements, and also swarm upon swarm of little scoundrels who prevent our patrols from penetrating the woods and ravines where they have taken up their brigand-like abode'.[107] At the end of June Siskovics and Loudon cut across his communications with Silesia, and bushwhacked a vital convoy at Gundersdorf (28 June) and Domstadtl (30 June). Frederick abandoned his siege, and made his way back to Silesia by a circuitous route, taking heavy casualties from the Croats and *Jäger* on the way.

The wholesale use of detached corps became a characteristic of Austrian operations. It brought with it the danger of dispersal, and Armfeldt believed it was motivated primarily by plunder (see p. 234), but it was undeniably successful if we take as our measure the effect it had on the enemy. Frederick told his most trusted commanders:

> You are in combat with two kinds of armies – the heavy and the light. The Austrians have entrusted the command of these detachments to some very able officers, who have a particularly good grasp of ground. They have a habit of pitching their camps close to our armies, but they are careful to locate them on hilltops, in dense forests, or behind double or triple ravines. From these lairs they send out parties which strike when opportunity offers, and they emerge with the whole detachments when they have some important blow in mind.[108]

Joseph Prince Lobkowitz explained to Maria Theresa that the experience of working with the hussars accustomed the 'German' officers to fast-moving operations in dispersed order, and making up their minds in a hurry.[109] Cogniazzo makes the same point, and adds that the exploits of the mobile corps raised the morale of the troops as a whole.[110] Given the right leadership, therefore, the Austrian 'little war' may be counted a success at the operational level, despite the tactical shortcomings that were increasingly evident.

The big set-piece battles will claim out attention shortly, but it is perhaps worth pausing here to consider what contribution the Austrian light troops were capable of making to such affairs. The Austrian hussars (unlike their Prussian counterparts) were useless in the large-scale formal engagements, but the same was not entirely true of the Croats. Before the battle of Hochkirch (1758) the Croats stood in a security chain literally hand in hand, which prevented any deserters from reaching the Prussians with news of the impending attack.[111] Loudon, as we might have expected, made use of his Croats in a variety of settings, from the assault on Fouqué's camp at Landeshut in 1760 to the storming of the fortress of Schweidnitz in 1761.

Some episodes in Daun's victory at Kolin (1757) give some indication of what more could have been done. First the Banal Croats in the churchyard and earthwork at Krzeczhorz made such a fracas with their little 1-pounder artillery that Frederick turned his advance guard (Hülsen's division) aside from its grand flanking manoeuvre, and threw it into a frontal attack on the village. A little later the Prussian right wing, which should have been held back for further opportunities, was provoked by the sniping of Kleefeld's Croats into assaulting the village of Chozenitz and the ridge behind. Thus the battle degenerated into a contest of attrition which told against the outnumbered Prussians.

With hindsight we can see that the performance of the Croats at Kolin should have inspired the Austrians to investigate how the Croats and the regulars might interact in a systematic way on future battlefields. Such a development would have anticipated the way the French *tirailleurs* and formed troops worked together in the armies of the Revolution and Napoleon. There is no indication that the thought ever entered Daun's head. The Croatian infantry therefore reverted to a tactical role similar to that of the Red Indian auxiliaries of the English and French, while their useful little cannon were whisked away from them for no good reason.[112] When he drew up his proposed plan of campaign for 1761 Neipperg (who was well disposed towards the *Grenzer*) explained that when he added up the forces he took no account of either the Croats or the hussars, for their contribution in open battle was negligible.[113]

Battle

The Decision to Fight

Battle – combat in the open field on the largest scale – represented the ultimate standard by which an army could be judged. To put an army to this test for no cogent reason, and without a reasonable chance of success, was called in the 18th century '*Batailliren*,' or fighting for its own sake. Daun wrote to Maria Theresa concerning the relevant sections in Frederick's *General Principia*:

> No. 22. *On Battles*. In my opinion this article, on giving battle, is the one which demonstrates the king's ability most clearly. Thank God we have found the means of defeating him! But he is not to be underestimated, and we must bear two things particularly in mind – namely to exploit a victory with speed, and secondly not to be downhearted after a defeat, because losing three or five thousand men is of no great account (see p. 396).
>
> No. 23. *Why we should give battle*. This article indicates that the king has often fought without good cause. My opinion is that we should offer battle if we find that the benefit we derive from a victory is proportionately greater than the harm that would result from falling back or being defeated.[114]

Frederick's apparent '*Batailliren*' was in fact both necessary and possible: necessary because the king needed to bring affairs to speedy conclusions, and possible because the Prussian army was a responsive instrument, and owned great powers of recuperation. Conversely the Austrian army was not under the same urgent compulsion to fight, and, in spite of Daun's good intentions, it could be brought only with difficulty to exploit whatever favourable opportunities happened to come its way.

After his four campaigns with the Austrians, the Swede Armfeldt concluded that while the Austrians could be relied upon to put up a good fight on the defensive, 'to bring them to the attack they need to have great superiority of force, much time for debate, and very favourable circumstances.' But the passing moment could be decisive in warfare, and so their elaborately worked-out plans could be overturned in an instant.[115] The potential for accidents and misunderstandings were multiplied in a polyglot army like this. The Prince de Ligne noted how important it was to translate an order 'in terms that would be genuinely understood by the various nations composing this army, and then verify that the translation is accurate. I have seen so many people pretend that they know German, and by force of habit they end up by believing that they indeed know it'.[116]

Daun returned to the theme of battle in a further letter to Maria Theresa, in August 1761, this time in a more pessimistic mood than a year earlier:

> battles are uncertain, and their outcomes are more uncertain still. During this unfortunate war we have experienced victory and defeat alike, and in each case we have had to begin as if from the very start. The present state of affairs does not promise much better, and indeed our internal condition appears to have deteriorated considerably. To overcome this enemy we must be twice as strong as he is, bearing in mind his fortresses and the other advantages he owns on the theatre of war, as well as the assets represented by his personal character and the nature of his rule. We need to be able to put a force of 200,000 men into the field, made up of our own troops and those of our genuine allies – and not allies just in name like our present ones, who cannot put forth enough men to secure their own interests, let alone aid their partners.[117]

Battle Formations and Grand Tactics

If, in spite of everything, Daun or one of the other commanders had made up their minds to meet the enemy in the open field, they next had to determine the form of their grand tactics. The first stage of an offensive engagement, the approach march, was invariably conducted in columns, as these were much faster-moving and easier to control than lines; such columns could be arranged either 'by lines,' or in the bulkier formation of columns 'by wings,' as noted earlier.

At a few hundred paces' distance from the enemy the normal practice indicated that the army should re-arrange itself from columns into lines, as the formation best suited to bring to bear the greatest frontage of fire. Symbolism also played a part, for 'the elegance and discipline exemplified by magnificent troops in long, straight lines expressed the very spirit of enlightened despotism'.[118] The transition from column to line was usually accomplished by quarter-wheels of the sub-units according to a familiar routine (below), and the regulations have little to say about the procedure, apart from enjoining precision, speed and silence.

If we continue to assume that the army was fighting in the conventional style, in a unitary mass, then the resulting lines of battle corresponded with the current written Order of Battle, which laid down the sequence of the regiments and generals by strict precedence of seniority. The second line of battle formed up 500 paces behind the first, and third line or *corps de reserve* another 200 paces to the rear. Along the first line the intervals between the battalions were normally fixed at six paces. The battalions of the second line and reserve were spaced successively further apart. The same principle held true among the cavalry, where eight or 10 paces separated the squadrons of the first line, and 30 to 50 those of the second line, thus providing gaps through which any beaten squadrons of the first line could flee without causing disruption; if there were too many second-line squadrons to permit such intervals, they were deployed with the *corps de reserve*. Upon the army moving forward:

> the generals and all the senior regimental officers are to pay the greatest attention to preventing gaps opening up, or the troops veering out of the chosen direction, and they are to ensure that everyone advances in a straight, tightly closed-up line, and in silence and without any kind of outcry. In the same way the regimental guns and other attached artillery pieces must remain in their assigned stations… During the advance in question the infantry must keep their muskets shouldered close to the upright, and hold their fire until they are well within range of the enemy, the generals have given the appropriate order, and the method of fire has been ordained.[119]

To prevent the troops straying from the assigned course, the formation and unit

GFWM. Carl Baron Amadei, 1723–1796 (Dusch, Military Academy, Wiener Neustadt). He first made his name in a sortie (20 June 1757) in the defence of Prague, and led a number of further bold enterprises in the later campaigns of the Seven Years War. Through his skills as a planner and leader he exercised an important, if largely unrecognised, influence on Austrian grand tactics as they developed during the war.

commanders fixed on a church tower, a mill, a gallows hill, a rock, a tuft of grass or some other feature of the ground as their respective *points de vue*. In the experience of the Prince de Ligne the *points de vue* vanished at the first exchange of fire, and it was useless to continue to search for them or to attempt to maintain perfect alignment. All that mattered now was to come at the enemy in well-closed up lines.[120] This is confirmed by Cogniazzo, who maintains that the troops could march at the prescribed pace readily enough by platoons or even in full tactical divisions, but that regularity was impossible to sustain in any array larger than half a battalion, for then the component units lost step, drew out to the wings, or crowded together towards the centre.[121]

All of this applies to a unitary army which was fighting in the conventional linear formation. In the Seven Years War it took a Frederick and a Prussian army at their prime to make the system work well, which is perhaps why the Austrians chose to adopt a radically new procedure in their offensive battles, namely an attack by independent but converging columns. The Austrians first applied this grand tactic at Hochkirch (14 October 1758), apparently at the suggestion of Colonel Carl Amadei. Daun won his battle, though the victory fell short of his expectations. The plan was however put into effect with total success at Maxen (20 November 1759), where the main army and the corps of Brentano constituted the attacking formations, and the *Reichsarmee* and Kleefeld's Croats were thrown across the Prussian path of escape as a blocking force. The enemy were captured in their entirety, which made this victory the most complete to be attained by any combatant in the Seven Years War, not excluding the battle of Leuthen. At Liegnitz (15 August 1760) the Austrians strove to annihilate the royal army, and they might well have succeeded if Frederick had not changed his position overnight; the great blow by the main army and the corps of Lacy fell on thin air, while Loudon's outnumbered blocking force bore the full brunt of the battle.

Cogniazzo was present both at Hochkirch and the debacle at Liegnitz, and he identified the same shortcomings in both cases. He conceded that the scheme was 'annihilating and frightful' in concept, but he maintained that it demanded terrain free of obstacles, an uncharacteristically close and willing cooperation between generals who were usually divided by temperament and rivalry, and an enemy who stayed in position.[122] We may add that the formation commanders were men who had grown up in the era of linear tactics, and were therefore accustomed to seeing friendly formations extending endlessly on their own two flanks; they were now on their own, devoid of visible support, and it is hardly surprising that they did not always strike forward with freedom and confidence.

Cogniazzo's strictures are nevertheless exaggerated. Prince Henry of Prussia himself became a convert to the principle of the attack by converging formations. He applied it on a small scale on 12 May 1762 when he captured the greater part of the 2,500 troops of the Austrian *GFWM*. Johann Franz Zedtwitz at Dobeln, and then more ambitiously when he defeated the *Reichsarmee* and the supporting Austrians at Freiberg (29 October 1762), which proved to be the decisive battle of the war. The Austrians applied the converging attack well into the Revolutionary Wars, and they might have carried it into the new century if Bonaparte had not revealed where its inherent vulnerability lay – not in difficulties of terrain and timing as such, or even in a change of position on the part of the target, but in the danger of the columns being defeated in detail by a foe who was quick on his feet.

A second feature of the novel Austrian grand tactics, at least at Hochkirch and Maxen, was the employment of the closed column to overcome the enemy by a rapid succession of hammer blows (below). The resemblance to the French columnar formations of the Revolutionary and Napoleonic Wars is only superficial, for the Austrian columns were exclusively attacking formations, whereas the French variety were most commonly employed just as a means of arriving close to the enemy before deploying into line.

It will be evident that the Austrians were willing both to give offensive battles, and to explore new ways of fighting them. On the defensive, their well-known positions provided the main but not the exclusive foundation of their grand tactics. The Austrians were fully aware of the characteristic form of the Frederician attack that has since become known as the 'Oblique Order,' and which rested on the principle of marching the main force of the Prussian army at speed to bring an overwhelming concentration of force to bear against one or another of the enemy wings. For the Austrians to remain passively within their chosen ground would have exposed them to the danger of being outflanked; they therefore kept the Prussian movements under close observation, and once they had identified the intended point of the attack they moved to counter it by their combined corps of grenadiers (as at Prague), a designated *corps de reserve* (first employed at Kolin), or by reversing the entire frontage of their army (Torgau). Depth and mobility therefore proved to be the best answer to the Frederician attack, and not the simple expedient of prolonging the line, which led to a breakdown of control, and was employed for the first and last time at Leuthen.

The Infantry Battle

Our main source of reference concerning the tactics of the Austrian infantry is the printed *Regulament and Ordnung des gesammten Kaiserlich-Königlichen Fuss Volcks,* 2 vols., Vienna. As the first Prussian ambassador after the Second Silesian War, Count Podewils was unable to lay his hands on a copy, since every set was retained within the regiments under the most stringent conditions of secrecy. He learned indirectly that Maria Theresa had contributed material which she had learned from a former Prussian captain by the name of Doss, and that the Prussian drill had formed the chief model.[123] It is, however, difficult to reconstruct with any conviction exactly how the Austrian infantrymen fought in the Seven Years War, since (as in all armies and all periods) there were radical differences between what was put down on paper and what was done under field conditions. The text and illustrations were in any case largely outdated by the end of 1757, for the Austrians were abandoning the four-rank line of battle (which appeared in the *Regulament*) for a line of three ranks.

The fundamental tactical unit of the infantry was the battalion, whether the battalion of the combined companies of grenadiers, or one of the two component field battalions of the regimental fusiliers. The battalion was divided successively into:

Four divisions or companies (128 private soldiers each)
Eight half-divisions, each roughly equivalent to the large Prussian platoon (64 private soldiers each)
Sixteen *Züge* or platoons (32 private soldiers each)

The individual file was the equivalent of one two-foot pace, which put the battalion on a frontage of 145 paces (allowing for officers and NCOs) when drawn up four ranks deep according to the *Regulament* of 1749, but about 190 paces when arrayed in three ranks. In the latter case the first rank was made up of the tallest and best-looking men of the battalion; the second of the small and ugly, and the rearmost rank of solid and reliable men for the sake of stability.

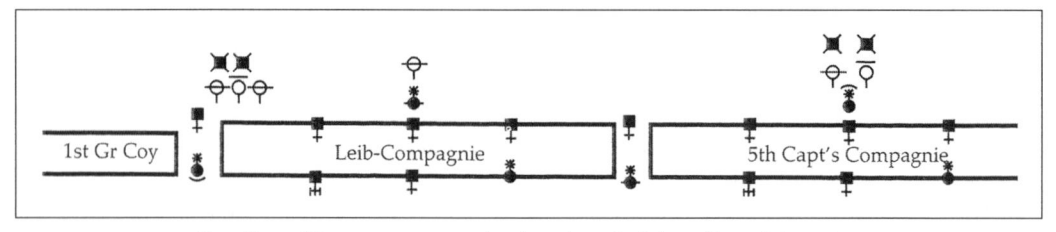

Battalion of four companies in battle order – Leib bataillon of the 1750s

The line three ranks deep was first taken up at Kolin (18 June 1757) as a matter of necessity. It seems to have been adopted formally in October of the same year, but it was still not universal use in 1758, when we hear an Austrian officer complaining that even then the troops were being ordered to convert from one to the other, and then back again. He wished that the generals would make up their minds, and he himself believed that the fourth rank served no useful purpose, being useless for fire. 'Moreover the fourth rank has no defensive value against the onset of cavalry, for once the first three ranks have been broken up and ridden down the victory of the horsemen may be regarded as complete, and all that the fourth rank does is to augment the disorder and destruction among our infantry'.[124]

It is perhaps useful to imagine the battalion and its sub-units as being enclosed by a light screen of officers and NCOs, who fulfilled three functions between them:

1. Command: exercised over the battalion as a whole by the major
2. Control of fire: by officers standing before the first rank
3. Cohesion and discipline: imposed, if necessary by lethal force, by the officers and NCOs who stood on the flanks and along the rear of the sub-units

In the Prussian infantry spatial direction was given by the colour party, which strode out ahead of the battalion, though it is uncertain whether such was the case in the Austrian practice.

The 'cadenced step' (marching in step) was introduced to 18th-century warfare by the Prussian army in the Silesian wars. Without the help of this device the columns used to set themselves in movement like the pleats of an accordion's bellows, drawing apart and bunching together without rhythm, and rendering any precision in tactics virtually impossible. The comte de Gisors observed the Austrians for up to a week at the camp of Kolin in 1754, when they were still trying to master the cadence, and he noted that it not yet working at all well, for the tempi were inconveniently fast or inconveniently slow.[125]

The *Regulament* of 1749 had laid down that when the soldier was marching 'his knee must always be kept stiff, without any bending; the foot must be raised a natural distance from the ground, and be set down smartly, though without stamping'.[126] The troops were trained respectively in the short *Chargirschritt* ('firing pace,' for loading and firing on the march, which was rarely put into practice), the longer standard *Marschirschritt*, and the fast *Doublirschritt* (for wheeling and the assault). The best aid to keeping step was not the regulation *Marschschlag*, which sounded like a confused rumbling, but simply by the drums beating time by the *Trupp*. In practice the maximum possible pace in proper alignment and cadence was 100 to the minute, and even this could not be prolonged to the end of a second minute without the precision falling apart.[127]

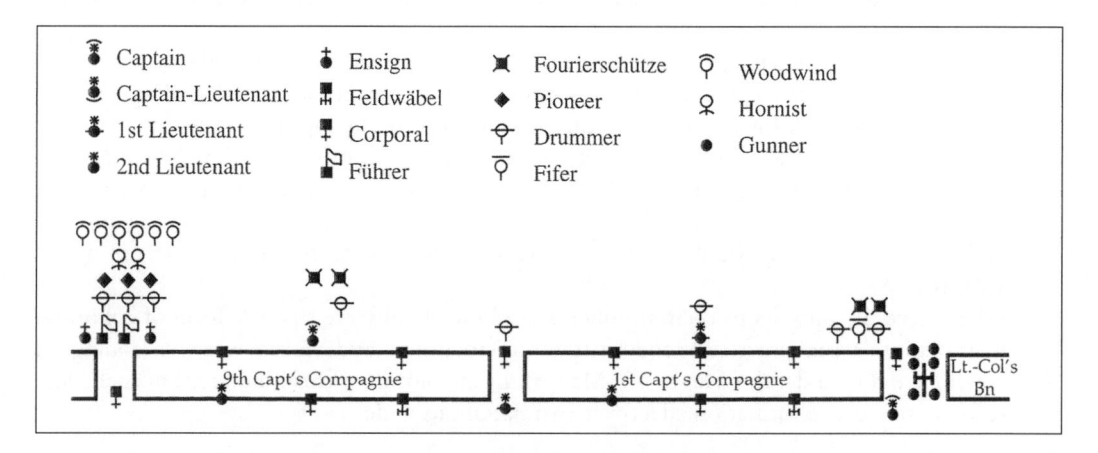

Arrangement of a company or full division — 1st Captain's Company, earlier Seven Years War

| 8th Platoon | 6th Platoon | 4th Platoon | 2nd Platoon |

4th Half Division | 2nd Half Division

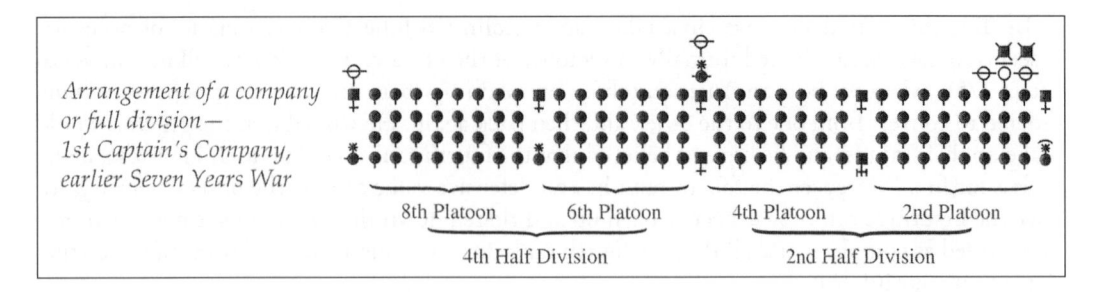

The greatest detail concerning the carriage of the individual soldier is to be found in the private code of the regiment of Joseph Esterházy (1747), where it was laid down that the soldier supported his musket by his left side by the four fingers of the left hand, with the thumb crooked around the lowest screw of the butt plate, and the trigger guard pressed hard against the body under the ribs so as to maintain the weapon in its near-vertical position; the right arm rested motionless by the side, without any swinging, for otherwise it would have been impossible for the men to march in their tightly-closed files. The head was to be turned to the right, though if the troops were marching past an officer they were to look him straight in the eye. The legs were to be kept stiff, without stamping, and the toes inclined slightly outwards. 'If the man fails to observe all of this on the march, he shows that he still has something of the peasant in him'.[128]

The *Regulament* of 1749 laid down that 'whenever a motion is to be made with the musket, it must appear sharp, short and hard, so that the noise rings out'.[129] On the last point the Prince de Ligne adds that it was easy enough to simulate precision and snap at drill and on the march. By making short steps, or even marking time on the spot, it was possible to keep a seemingly miraculously accurate step, while mistakes in unavoidably complicated movements, like a deployment, could be concealed by opening fire. Metal fittings on the musket could be loosened, to create a gratifying clatter, and a number of rings might be attached to the musket to make the sound carry further still.[130]

As regards the movement of formed bodies, we turn first to the much-disputed question of columns. To the Prince de Ligne columns smacked of the 'herd-like instinct' which drove mediocre troops together, and on the day of the battle he invariably had to break up columns of this kind with the flat of his sword, aided by his NCOs with blows of their sticks. He maintained that columns were particularly vulnerable to artillery, which could shoot down their length, and that two battalions advancing in column against two battalions drawn up in line would sustain 16 volleys (a theoretical 16,000 or so rounds), over the four minutes which passed between coming within effective range and closing with the enemy, and that even then the effect of 'shock' would prove illusory.[131]

Colonel Losy von Losenau asserted with equal confidence that columns moving at the double would deprive the artillery of an easy target, for the gunners were accustomed to dealing with the slow advance of troops in line, which gave them plenty of time to adjust their elevations to the closing ranges, whereas they would be likely to fire over the heads of troops who rushed them in column. His columns – 16 or at the most 32 files wide – would moreover present a narrower target than a line, and veer more easily out of the axis of artillery fire.[132] He proposed making an essay with his Croats, who usually fought in small formations which were all too easily overrun by the enemy cavalry.[133]

We shall leave the pundits to their arguments, and merely observe that the form of columnar assault, as put into actual practice by the Austrians at Hochkirch and Maxen, was on a frontage of one battalion, and on a depth of up to 12 (Maxen). Each column of this kind acted in such close association as to create a formation effectively two battalions wide.

OPERATIONAL AND TACTICAL DIMENSIONS 443

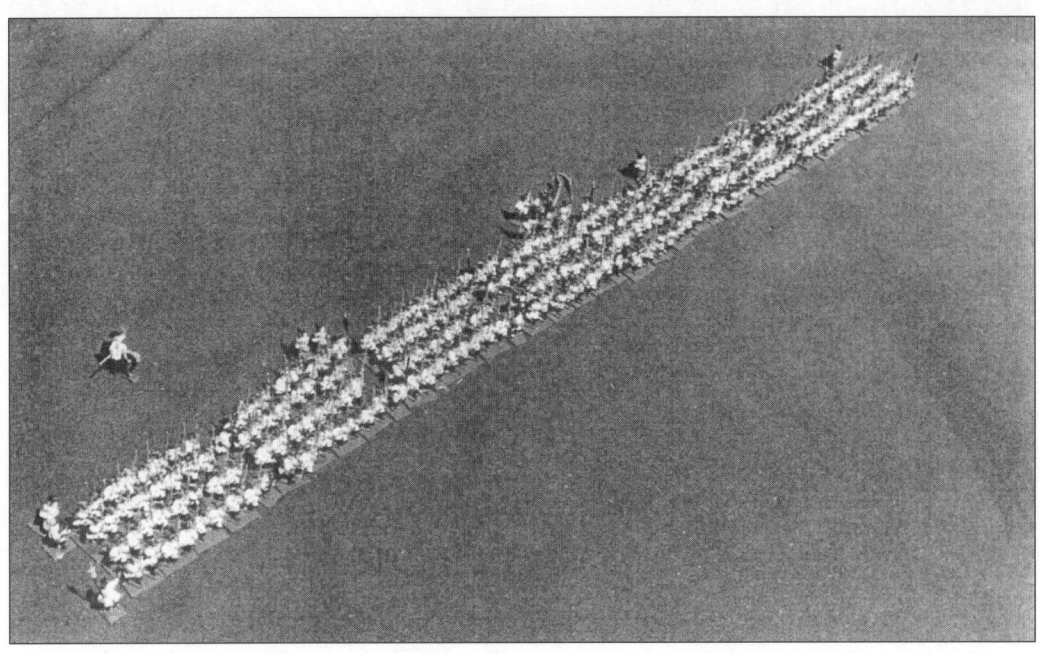

Two companies or full divisions in characteristic formations and evolutions. A (above). Line of battle in the four rank array.

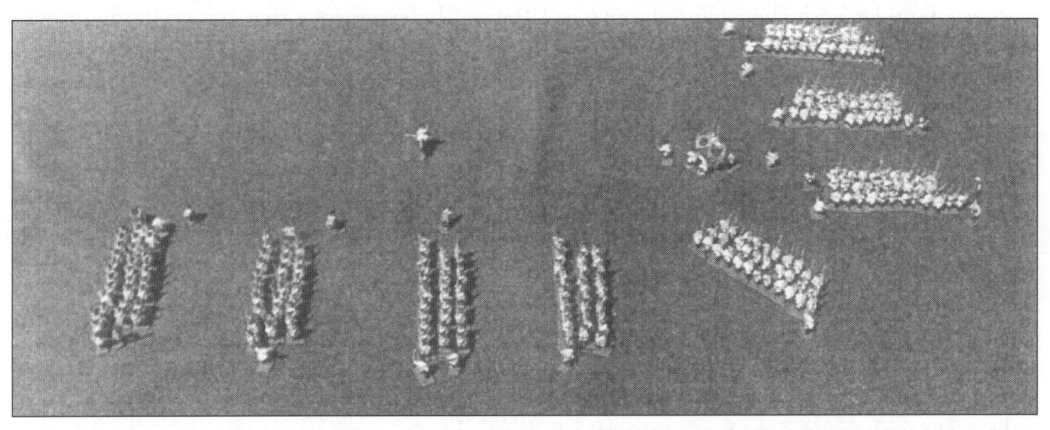

B (above). Formation of line from open platoon column (three-rank array) by the processional movement. The nearest four platoons are already marching along the chosen alignment. The fifth is executing a quarter-wheel to the right, and the remaining three platoons will follow its example. Once all eight platoons are marching in the same direction it will be possible to form the line of battle by simultaneous quarter wheels to the left.

C (below). The completed line of battle. The gain in length over the four-rank line (A) is striking.

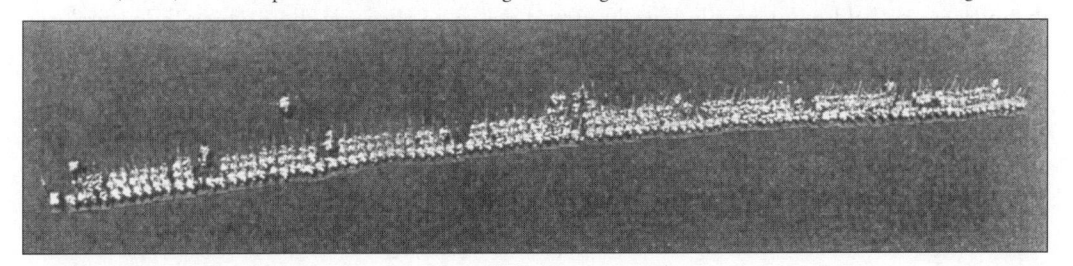

Whereas the columns of assault held on their course all the way to the enemy, the conventional columns converted into lines before coming within range of musket. These columns were most frequently in 'open' formation (that is, with the intervals between the component units corresponding with their intended frontages in line), and they finally transmuted themselves into continuous line by simultaneous quarter-wheels of the sub-units: 'executing the wheel is one of the things of which the foot soldier must have a fundamental understanding, because it is employed every time the men come on and off parade, on every kind of march, and frequently in action against the enemy'.[134] With practice the wheel could be accomplished with relative easy by *Züge*, half-divisions and full divisions. In theory regiments, brigades and even whole lines were capable of carrying out this evolution, but the effective limit was usually reached with the battalion. If we assume that the intervals had been judged correctly, then the principal complication arose from maintaining the alignment, for the troops nearest the pivoting flank did little more than mark time, while those nearer the swinging flank had to move successively faster – for those nearest the flank at a rate between the double and an all-out run.

In the Seven Years War the Prussians made some use of a 'deployment' into line from densely stacked-up closed columns. During the approach the formation bore a close resemblance to the Austrian column of assault; at a chosen distance, however, the leading sub-unit came to a halt, while the rearward-sub units fanned out from the column to come up in alignment on one or both sides. This they accomplished either by a perpendicular movements *en tiroir* (lit. like pulling out the drawers of a cabinet), or by executing an eighth-wheel to the left or right, then making directly to their assigned places in line by a diagonal movement. It cannot be established whether the Austrians made any use of this closed-column deployment during the Seven Years War, but Cogniazzo states that it was part of the pre-war training, and the Prince de Ligne writes as one who was familiar with the evolution, and had learned by experience that the preliminary one-eighth wheel for the diagonal deployment was unnecessary, for the soldier could simply take their muskets in their right hands and run: 'You are unlikely to find any soldier aged between 16 and 45 who is unable to run 300 paces or even 400. Besides, the companies which have to run the most are the flank companies, which are usually made up of the fastest, youngest and tallest of the men'.[135]

It was physically well-nigh impossible for regular infantry to load the 18th-century musket otherwise than standing up. When loading was complete, however, the first rank was supposed to sink to the right knee, thus clearing the way for the men of the second rank to level their muskets safely above them, while the muskets of the third rank poked between the heads of the men of the second rank. The troops were accordingly 'locked on' in staggered formation in such a way that the extended left foot of the man in the second rank reached almost to the left of the right knee of the corresponding man in the first, and the extended left foot of the man in the third rank to the right of the withdrawn right foot of the man in the first.

A number of details are not to be found in the official code. Thus, on the evidence of Armfeldt, the third rank never fired with fixed bayonets.[136] He was writing of the practice in the final years of the war, by when the fourth rank had disappeared altogether. The transition from four ranks to three confused the soldiers, who were now told to abandon the *Absetzen,* the movement whereby the musket was held momentarily upright after a volley, so that any shots which 'hung fire' (see below) and then went off would be likely to be discharged into the air instead of into the multiple ranks in front. The *Absetzen* was abolished entirely after the Seven Years War, but even then many veterans could not be weaned from their old ways.[137]

The Prince de Ligne claims that the kneeling of the first rank was confined largely to drills, when it was a favourite resort of officers who wished to make an impression on the spectators. It certainly looked good when a whole row of men crashed to the ground, but it was an excellent way of inducing ruptures, and few of the men would be eager to get to their feet again when bullets were flying about in real combat. The example was so contagious that the entire infantry might end up clambering about on all fours, as at the battle of Parma in 1734. It was often necessary to beat the men with the flat of the sword to get them moving again.

A great strength of the Prussian service was its practice of familiarising the infantry with a few simple procedures, which could then be applied in various combinations to meet all likely eventualities. In contrast the Austrian infantry *Regulament* of 1749 set out to perfect the troops in a multitude of separate drills. Most of the procedures were probably abandoned in combat, but they imposed a heavy burden on the officers and NCOs in peacetime.

Fire could be delivered by the whole battalion, or more commonly by divisions, half-divisions or the *Züge* (platoons). In that period of slow-loading weapons the purpose of such rolling fires by repartition was to maintain a rapid succession of volleys instead of one great blast, which would have to be followed by at least 15 seconds of re-loading, during which a whole major unit would be left defenceless against cavalry.

In the Austrian service the order of fire by the relevant sub-units ran from the flanks towards the centre. In addition there were a half a dozen special procedures:

Höcken-Feuer (hedge fire) was delivered by the ranks of the sub-unit in succession: 'This is employed when the enemy are concealed in hedges or brushwood, and posted in such a way that we cannot get at them from the flanks, or in any other way except frontally'[138]

Retranchement-Feuer was another form of fire by ranks, this time by troops spread out in open file to defend the breastwork or a fortification. There were variations for *Retranchement-Feuer* for night and day, to add to the elaborations

Doppeltes-Weeg-Feuer was the resort of a unit which was unlucky enough to be caught on the march in a sunken road or a dense wood, and was consequently unable to form into line. The troops at the head faced to their front, and those at the back to their rear, while the first and second ranks of the main body turned to their left, and the third and fourth to their right (a provision obviously outdated once the fourth rank was abolished). In theory no commander should have allowed himself to be taken at such a disadvantage, 'but we all know that in warfare we are not always at liberty to do what we know to be best, but only that which we are compelled to do'.[139]

Gassen-Feuer again supposed the men to be jammed together, this time in a street battle or when attacking a fortress. The troops came on by column of platoon, each platoon firing in succession, then dividing to allow the half-platoons to wheel respectively to right and left and retire to the rear of the column, and so make way for the platoon next in line. This principle was identical with that of the *Caracole* in 17th-century tactics

Brücken-Feuer was a drill whereby the grenadiers, a battalion, or a whole regiment threw itself against a bridge; if any pieces were available, they were to prepare the way by opening a cross-fire from the flanks

Squares were formed by one, two, three or four battalions at once. The procedures at the time of the Seven Years War were so slow and difficult as to be virtually inapplicable in a full-scale battle, and were attempted only *in extremis* when an isolated unit was in danger of being overwhelmed by cavalry during a retreat or in open country. Even then, wrote Cogniazzo, any trust which the troops might repose in this formation was likely to be misplaced, for unless they knew what it was like to be hit by a cavalry charge, they had no conception of how terrifying the experience could be.[140] An intelligent commander would instead manoeuvre in column and take advantage of any useful features of the ground to cover his flanks, front and rear.[141] More commonly the infantry faced the horsemen in lines up to six ranks deep, with the rearward ranks reversed if necessary if the cavalry came at them from behind.

In a rare instance of simplification the *Regulament* of 1749 reduced the basic fire orders to three commands:

'Man wird chargiren!' (*Prepare to fire!*)
'Macht euch fertig!' (usually abbreviated to *'Fertig!'*) ('Make ready!')
'Feuer!'

The regulations of 1769 added that 'although in action it is difficult to achieve the repartition of fire as exactly as on the parade ground, the officers and NCOs must as a general rule strive constantly to ensure that two adjacent units of fire do not discharge their muskets simultaneously'.[142]

The *Militär Feld-Regulament* of 1759 does not have much to say on the question of the effective range of musketry, except on the use of the soldier's dozen rounds of buckshot, which were to be reserved until the enemy infantry were within 100 paces. Against cavalry the troops must be arrayed 'immovably and in a tightly-closed up formation, and keep up a heavy fire with buckshot; as soon as the cavalry have closed to within 10 paces the first two ranks must present their bayonets to the horses' muzzles and stand firm, so as to alarm and confuse the animals, while the third rank fires at the riders'.[143]

The Prince de Ligne was more specific. He supported the general opinion that in combat against infantry a first volley delivered at close range would probably prove decisive, but he maintained that fire against cavalry had a worthwhile chance of hitting riders or beasts even at 500 or 600 paces, and that in this instance it was sensible to give way to the soldiers' natural inclination to open fire at long range.[144] A fellow-officer was of the same opinion, but adds that it was difficult to restrain the men from opening up at any kind of target, whether cavalry or not, and the result was to sacrifice the advantage of the first precious salvo, 'which ought to be the most forceful and damaging of all, and the one which commands the most respect'.[145]

The same officer had to concede that the Prussian infantry was the fastest-firing in Europe, which gave these troops 'an advantage which is astounding, but nevertheless attested by all impartial observers who have seen it with their own eyes, namely that they can get off three rounds to the Austrians' one'.[146] It is not easy to reconstruct what this signified in rounds per minute. Cogniazzo, who settled in Prussia after several years in the Austrian service, believed that it in battle conditions would be difficult for any infantryman to get off more than two shots a minute, for he was so weighed down by his field equipment, while the Prince de Ligne found that 30 rounds in succession, even if not fired particularly quickly, were enough to make the musket too hot to hold.[147] He nevertheless takes a rate of four rounds to the minute as the basis of his calculations (above).

The rate of sustainable fire was also influenced by the supply of ammunition. The Austrian practice at the beginning of the Seven Years War was for the first line of reserve cartridges to be held in the regimental ammunition carts (*Munitions-Karren*), from which the packets were handed out by the officers' servants and the fifers and drummers. The army reserves were held by the artillery, which assumed that each soldier had an initial allowance of 36 rounds of ball and 12 of buckshot. The existing arrangements proved to be inadequate at Kolin, where Prince Kinsky saved the hard-pressed regiment of Botta by commanding a cart-load of ammunition at pistol-point. At Leuthen a few months later the Prussian soldiers' ammunition pouches were refilled up to twice over by a systematic supply from extra ammunition carts; the Austrians probably learned by this experience, for the *Militär Feld-Regulament* of 1759 referred their infantry to the army's *Reserve Munitions Wagen* which were standing behind the second line of battle, and the regiments were ordered to detach six corporals from every battalion and one drummer and six men from each company to do the necessary fetching and carrying. By now 60 rounds per man were being allowed for a day of battle, though the Prince de Ligne believed that many of the cartridges were thrown away instead of being fired.[148]

Loading drill according to the infantry *Regulament* of 1749. Page 97 of this manual shows the firing of the musket, the useful *Absetzen* (to allow any round 'hanging fire' to discharge itself into the air), and the cocking of the hammer. On page 98 the fusilier reaches back to his cartridge pouch, bites off the end of the paper cartridge, and primes his pan with a little of the powder. On pages 99 and 100 we have the fusilier inserting the cartridge in the muzzle of his musket, removing the ramrod from under the barrel, and pushing it down inside. On page 101 he rams the charge firmly home, and finally on page 102 the ramrod is removed from the barrel and returned to its place. The weapon is then ready to fire.

This last comment shows that the lethality of musketry cannot be assessed simply by setting a list of casualties alongside one of rounds nominally 'expended.' Other evidence, marginally more reliable, may be derived from the practical experiments. Cogniazzo writes that target practice was common before the Seven Years War, and that the usual marks were representations of Prussian grenadiers painted on planks. 'We made our first essays at various ranges, when the soldiers shot as individuals, and then by whole ranks and platoons. It worked well. In the individual fire the soldier came to know his musket, and whether it carried high or low. The collective fire brought home to the men in a vivid way the force of fire by tightly closed ranks'.[149] The Prince de Ligne once had a whole 'company' of Prussians painted on a cloth screen, and drew up a large company of his regiment to shoot against it. The men had 10 cartridges apiece, which made 1,440 rounds in all, fired at ranges of 100, 150, 200, 250 and 300 paces. Altogether 270 rounds hit the cloth at this spread of ranges, but 'what I proved was that less than 30 of them would have been mortal, while more than 60 holed the cloth in the spaces between the arms and legs.[150] We may assume that in combat conditions the number of lethal hits would have been fewer still.

The *Militär Feld-Regulament* of 1759 specified that the troops were to aim at the centre of the body mass ('*wohl aufhalben Mann*'). In the course of the test just mentioned de Ligne found that at 100 paces the men had to aim at the knees, at 150 at the belt, at 200 at the chest, at 250 at the moustache, and at 300 one foot above the head. This was at variance with the target shooting as observed by Cogniazzo, which indicated that it was necessary to aim well below the mark in order to hit it, which made the practice of aiming at the middle of the man too high. Another officer attributed this effect to the kick of the musket, and both he and Cogniazzo commended the practice of the Prussian infantry, 'which shoots so low that the first rank aims at the ground 10 or 12 feet to its front, and the rearward ranks successively higher. The result is that most of the volleys exert their proper effect'.[151] The anecdotal and statistical evidence both indicate that a disproportionately large number of the Austrian wounded in the Seven Years War were hit in the legs and feet – which probably caused the Austrians more trouble than having their men killed on the spot.

The abiding image of 18th-century tactics is that of the regulated volley, as transmitted to us by artists and through the narratives of the battles. Upon closer examination, however, it transpires that almost the only troops who were capable of delivering controlled and continuous salvo fire were those who had been schooled in parade ground tactics over a number of years of peace, and who came to their first battle in effect 'not knowing any better.' The celebrated rolling volleys of the Prussians at Mollwitz (1741) offer one example. Austria's 'Mollwitz' was at the battle of Kolin (1757), which was actually fought on the favourite manoeuvre ground of the peacetime army. Out of all the battles which Cogniazzo had seen 'this was the first and the last in which I witnessed orderly and well-aimed volleys delivered by tightly closed-up ranks'.[152] This endowed the first, concerted discharge with all the greater importance, because it was normally followed by a general blazing-away. The *Regulament* of 1749, the post-war regulations of 1769, and the veterans de Ligne and Cogniazzo all assume or state outright that firing at will was the norm in combat. Certain procedures were nevertheless considered vital, and they called for constant repetition until they became unthinking responses.

The orders to open fire, and to cease fire, demanded unconditional obedience, even if the soldiers were left free to fire at their own best rates in the meantime. Strict attention also had to be paid to the details of weapon-handling:

> On the field of battle it is by no means as easy to take aim in the same accurate and composed way as in target practice. This is the result of the clouds of smoke which billow incessantly from the musketry and artillery, and from our habit of allowing our soldiers to open fire at long range, just so as to cheer them up. We must also be aware that there is a great deal of wild shooting by cowards who are trembling with fear, and by overenthusiastic men who get carried away. What counts in the critical moment of battle is the contribution made by those soldiers who by repeated drills have acquired an entirely mechanical skill in loading properly, seating the musket firmly on the shoulder, and aiming well.[153]

Close attention to such drills not only gave a better chance of killing the enemy, but spared many casualties among one's own comrades. In the noise and excitement of combat the man might not always be aware whether his musket had fired or not. In the case of a misfire the soldier might then load charges one on top of another, which might explode together and burst the barrel if a later priming took fire; little could be done against this evil apart from ordering the troops to pay attention to what they were doing. It was just as dangerous if the first priming was merely 'hanging fire,' that is waiting to touch off the main charge after a few moments' delay, when the shot was likely to kill the man in front. The old motion of the *Absetzen* was designed to lessen that risk, and Cogniazzo was not the only veteran to regret that it had been abandoned so as to save a little time.[154]

After he had torn open the paper cartridge and primed the pan with a little of the powder, the soldier compressed the closed end of the cartridge between thumb and index finger so as to retain the ball, emptied the rest of the powder down the muzzle, then closed the empty cartridge paper around the ball, poked it into the barrel, and rammed the whole firmly home. At the battle of Mollwitz the Austrians sought to answer the unprecedented speed of the Prussian fire by 'tap loading,' that is by dispensing with ramming altogether, and striking the butt of the musket on the ground in the hope of jolting the load to the bottom of the barrel. This parlous expedient deprived the round of much of its force.

Probably the most frequent and dangerous mistake was nevertheless to forget to withdraw the ramrod from the barrel when loading was complete; the round would then either burst the barrel, or propel the ramrod from the muzzle like a spear, skewering anyone who was in its path, and leaving the soldier with no proper means of re-loading his musket.

The Seven Years War supervened between two periods when pundits on infantry tactics set great store by 'cold steel' fighting by bayonet or sword rather than fire. Its proponents in the Austrian service had been *FM*. Ludwig Andreas Khevenhüller and *FZM* Adam Sigismund Thüngen, and it was perpetuated into the opening stages of the Seven Years War, when the command '*Marsch! Marsch!*' was supposed to send the troops doubling against the enemy with fixed bayonets.

There was much scepticism about the whole procedure. Our observers are adamant. 'On no occasion,' reported Armfeldt, 'did I see the Austrian infantry use the bayonet in the attack'.[155] De Ligne recalled only one instance, and that was the altogether exceptional case of the fighting on the Jäckelsberg at Moys on 7 September 1757, when Austrian and Prussian troops climbed opposite sides of the hill and ran into one another at the top. Otherwise it was 'virtually impossible to go out to attack an enemy force in open country without firing. The troops you are leading would be destroyed, it's as simple as that'.[156] It was true that the Russians prided themselves on the use of the bayonet against the Turks, but that was only because the Ottomans took an eternity to re-load.

The rearward rank of the grenadiers and the Hungarian infantry actually plunged after the Prussian infantry with drawn sabres in early encounters in the Seven Years War. This heroic procedure had little place after the thinned-out line of three ranks became the norm, and Cogniazzo doubted whether the tactic had ever been of much use. It was a risky undertaking at best, and 'if you wanted a perfect vision of chaos you only had to see this howling mob of bacchantes when they ran forward and back again in confusion'.[157]

The Austrian fusiliers (unlike the grenadiers and the Hungarian infantry) had no swords of any kind, which, as Cogniazzo had to admit, put them in some embarrassment if their muskets were broken. They were forbidden to fall back to the rear to pick up a musket from the casualties, and 'I have so often seen a fusilier standing defenceless, or at the most clutching his bayonet like a kitchen knife, and just because he could not at once lay his hands on a new musket'.[158]

The Austrian bayonets in themselves were good weapons (see p. 273), at least when fixed to the end of intact muskets, and came into their own when they formed a hedge of steel against cavalry.

The Cavalry Battle

Few of the Austrian cavalrymen were great writers, with an exception to be mentioned shortly, and what we know about their way of fighting comes mostly from observers among the infantry, from foreign military attachés, and from the prescriptions to be found in the two sets of cavalry regulations.

The *Regulament und Ordnung für gesammte Kaiserl.- Königlichen Cuirassier und Dragoner Regimenter* (two parts, 1749–51) contained details of riding instructions, and sections which laid down the organisation of the regiment and squadron, the ranks and their duties, the routines of camp and security, and tactics; we cannot imagine that the horsemen applied themselves with any great studiousness to the 54 pages detailing the dismounted drill, the four on how the mounted grenadiers were supposed to throw their grenades, or the 13 on the foot evolutions of the same grenadiers.

The companion instruction for the hussars was the *Regulament und Ordnung für Gesammte Kaiserl. Königl. Husaren Regimenter,* 1751. The provisions were identical with those for the German cavalry, except for the few passages concerning the distinctive Hungarian uniform and equipment, and the exhortation to the hussars to use their initiative in combat.

The author of the manuscript *Schreiben eines Officiers der Cavallerie an seinen Freund,* Königgrätz, 28 December 1756, almost the only analytical document of its kind, applauded the discipline which the various regulations sought bring to the mounted arm. The provisions for the attack were excellent,

450 INSTRUMENT OF WAR

and it should just be a question of putting them into effect. But there seems to be a sizeable obstacle in an inclination to depart from the rules as set down – indeed the spirit of contradiction has become a principle of deliberate obstruction... Again and again in the last campaign you would hear comments like: 'I haven't read a page of the regulations. I don't need them, and I don't want to know anything about them.' Talk of this kind would not be found in the other services, but here it is treated as normal, and it sets a very bad example, for it does nothing to raise the morale of the ordinary troopers when such ill-considered comments are made in their presence.[159]

Within the regiment of Austrian cavalry, the squadron formed the most important fighting unit. This force was normally ranged in three ranks, on a frontage of 44 files of troopers. The constituents of the tactical ranks are explained in the *Militär Feld-Regulament* of 1759, which laid down that the first rank should be made up of

> thoroughly good and reliable men, who should also be well mounted; the younger men and the recruits go to the second rank, but the third rank is composed of the most experienced and trustworthy troopers of all. In all such ranks... Each squadron is always... to be drawn up in three *Züge* [platoons], with central *Zug* three files (including the standard bearers) wider than the three flanking *Züge*.[160]

The squadrons of the first line of battle were placed between eight and 10 paces apart, and those of the second at 30 to 50 paces. Within the squadron the troopers were closed up knee to knee, or at least near enough to prevent enemy cavalry breaking between the files. The *Militär Feld-Regulament* observed that 'when the men are first being drawn up for battle they should take careful note of the man to their front and rear, and in what rank and file they were stationed'.[161] The successive ranks observed normal intervals of five paces, but they closed up when it came to wheeling or combat.

According to the regulations of 1749–51 the *Rittmeister* (captain of horse) and the cornet/ *Fähndrich* withdrew from in front of the squadron into the first rank in the event of combat, while the other officers were positioned down the two flanks of the squadron.[162] The author of the *Schreiben* explains that the concentration of the officers on the flanks was designed to compress the unit towards the centre, and it was all the more necessary because the Austrian cavalry was lightly

Dragoon of the regiment of Zweibrücken (Krauhse, Austrian Army Museum). Dark blue coat and breeches, red cuffs, lapels and turn-backs, light straw breeches.

officered, having only five officers to the squadron, or as little as two or three after detachments, as opposed to the 12 officers of the French squadron. Moreover 'the officers must not turn their attention from their men, let alone stare about them or chatter. The only man to speak must be the one who commands the squadron.'[163]

By the time of the *Militär Feld-Regulament* of 1759 the cuirassier cornets and the dragoon *Fähndrichs* had been designated *Unter-Lieutenants,* and the onerous responsibility of carrying the standard had been taken over by a new NCO rank, that of the squadron *Estandart-Führer,* 'and the most deserving and the bravest veteran of the squadron is to be promoted thereto. He is to bear the squadron standard on all occasions, and have it in his keeping.' The positions of the officers were re-assigned, now that there were effectively six of them instead of five. The senior captain was to station himself just in front of the centre of the unit, and even at the moment of shock he was to rein his horse only half-way back into the first rank, 'so as to keep himself visible to the squadron, and enable his orders to be heard more clearly.' The new *Estandart-Führer* was positioned immediately behind him in the second rank, and the second captain on the same central alignment but behind the third rank. One first-lieutenant and one of the newly-designated second-lieutenants took up station on each flank of the squadron.[164]

The cavalry was supposed to train in the frontal march, the countermarch by fours, forming of columns and wheeling from open column into line by quarter-wheels of squadrons, companies and *Züge;* the fan-liked *Deployiren* from closed column into line was not mentioned in the regulations, but seems to have been employed occasionally in practice.

Radicati's cavalry at Lobositz and that of Serbelloni at Kolin were both in the position of having to hold ground under fire with no immediate chance of hitting back, and there could have been no experience more harrowing for mounted troops. It was fortunate that the occasions were so rare. Otherwise the supreme test of the cavalry, and the cuirassiers and dragoons in particular, remained the attack.

According to the regulations of 1749–51 the cavalry were to approach the field of battle with sounding music and raised weapons, a practice which probably derived from the Turkish wars. All music ceased once the combat opened, and there was to be no shouting when the squadrons moved forward into the charge:

> On the attack the squadrons must not only maintain tightly closed-up ranks and files, but observe a common frontage with the rest of the regiment. When they come within about 200 paces of the enemy they are to advance against them at the trot, then at 20 or 30 paces attack them at the gallop… Every officer of cavalry must be firmly convinced that beating the enemy in combat comes down to two things – first to attack them with the greatest velocity and force, and second to strive to hit them from the flank.[165]

If the advance were tied rigidly to the flank of the line of battle, the cavalrymen had no alternative but to keep pace with the infantry, and rein in their mounts until they came within 20 paces of the enemy. As an alternative to the linear formation the regulations of 1749–51 recommended the use of columns of fours to win the enemy flank, and something of the sort was put into effect by *FML*. Stampach on the left wing of the main force of the Austrian army at Maxen in 1759. Frederick noted a further variation:

> In addition to their repository of skills they sometimes resort to ruses to lead the enemy general astray. They have a habit of pushing some of their cavalry forward, but I have observed that on a number of occasions that when they deploy an entire line they have no real intention of fighting. They are more in earnest if they array themselves in chequerboard formation.[166]

The Austrian cavalry were forbidden as a matter or principle to receive an attack at the halt. The Prussians undoubtedly had the capacity to be quicker off the mark (below), but experience taught Frederick to hold his cavalry in check at the beginning of an action, since the Austrians used to keep infantry waiting behind their first line of horsemen, ready to shoot up any Prussian cavalry which managed to break through.[167]

The Austrians gave no serious attention to fitting their hussars for combat in a full-scale battle, and the hussar regulations of 1751 merely commented that 'when the hussars are ordered to move against the enemy and bring them under attack, they are at liberty to resort to their time-honoured methods as indicated by the nature of the enemy and the ground, and other circumstances'.[168]

Until the last days of horsed cavalry much debate concerned the relative advantages of the two basic ways of dealing a blow with the sword – thrusting with the point (which was inherently the more lethal), or cutting with the edge, which was more instinctive. To the Prince de Ligne all the discussion was academic:

> Why talk of something which never happens? Has anybody witnessed these imaginary cavalry charges which take on the enemy by frontal attack?... All the wounded that you see are men who have been injured in the confused fighting which occurs when the victors and the defeated hit out at one another with their swords as they pass by... I have yet to see an all-out combat of cavalry against cavalry, and this must come from a lack of the necessary will on their part, for I know perfectly well that they could get at each other if they wanted to... What I have witnessed instead is two bodies of cavalry which come to a halt, as if at drill... they then ride on parallel courses for a couple of minutes, and finally part for ever. I am therefore persuaded that the best way to make use of your cavalry is to employ it against infantry instead.[169]

The Austrian cavalry was seemingly 'backward' in comparison with the best European practice, in that it still allowed an important place to fire from the saddle, which put it at a disadvantage when faced with horsemen trained in the school of Gustavus Adolphus, Marlborough and Seydlitz, who inculcated charging home with cold steel. Thus the regulations of 1751 suggested that the two flank squadrons of the regiment of hussars should push forward in dispersed order, 'and when they come to the scene of action all the hussars should fire as rapidly as they can, and not by volleys, because an irregular fire coming from all sides is the best way to reduce the enemy to confusion'.[170] The three remaining squadrons of the regiment could then exploit the situation in a variety of ways. The Prussian Field Marshal Schwerin could write of a skirmish near Königgrätz in May 1756: 'Our Austrian friends are very fond of shooting, and they lived up to their reputation in the action on the 22nd. They not only opened fire on our men, but to lend emphasis to their challenge they fixed bayonets on the muzzles of their carbines, and the first rank executed a mounted charge against our hussars. This was something of a surprise to our troopers, but they responded by falling on them with gusto'.[171] Armfeldt claimed that the penchant for mounted fire showed that the Austrians were unable to shake themselves free from the influence of their Turkish campaigns, where firearms were indeed effective.[172]

Considered as a whole, the Austrian cavalry in the Seven Years War scarcely maintained the standard of its showing in the Silesian Wars, and actually regressed in relative terms when measured against the much-improved Prussian horse as trained and led by Seydlitz and Zieten. The Austrians had fine horses and men, they were well equipped, and they stood up to artillery fire courageously, but in comparison with the Prussian cavalry they lacked speed, precision and boldness. Their fundamental drills were derived from the practice of the infantry, and their recruits were set on horseback without having been inducted into basic riding skills – a shortcoming which 'derives from the fact that most of the officers understand very little themselves'[173] (see p. 290).

The Austrians were poor at observing correct intervals, and, claims Armfeldt, 'without the slightest exaggeration I may assure you that, on the evidence of what I have seen a number of times, as soon as the Austrian cavalry sets itself in any rapid movement… it invariably disperses like the hussars. It can be brought back to order only at the halt, and then only after a long time'.[174] He noted that the generals were striving for something better, but there was little desire for improvement among the regimental commanders, 'the whole object of their attention being the kinds of trifles which are of no real use, but attract favourable attention.[175]

The Artillery Battle

Prince Liechenstein maintained boldly in 1753 that 'in the present way of making war the artillery branch (the soul of the army) has progressed so far that it determines the fate of our arms, and victory or defeat in battle (*Artillerie Systeme ab Anno 1753*). This promise was fulfilled in the course of the war that broke out three years later.

As has been described in an earlier chapter, the pieces of Austrian artillery were told off in combat as regimental or reserve artillery according to the way they were used, which did not always correspond with their calibre or type. Thus two of the 7-pounder howitzers (formidable pieces) were counted off for every two or three battalions of the first line, and grouped on the wings of the infantry. A corresponding number of 3-pounder cannon (light regimental pieces) were assigned to the reserve, from where they might be deployed in batteries of four pieces at a time (as witnessed by Gribeauval), or put at the disposal of Croats or detachments. At Torgau (1760) Daun assigned two 3-pounders to support Colonel Rudolph Pugnetti's flank march, and these pieces did considerable execution among the Prussian cavalry, to whom Frederick had neglected to supply any horse artillery.

Otherwise the roles of the light and heavy pieces were distinct. While the main purpose of the 3-pounder cannon was to complement the firepower of the infantry (which they supported by one piece per battalion), the true battle-winning potential of the artillery resided in the massed

Artillery in action. (Ottenfeld, 1898)

batteries of the heavier cannon and the 7-pounder howitzers. One or more batteries of 6- and 12-pounder cannon were placed in the centre of the line, and 7-pounder howitzers and further 6- and 12-pounders were stationed in the wings with the particular purpose of combating the enemy cavalry. 'The 12- and 6-pounder pieces represent a happy balance. The 12-pounders bolster the morale of the troops by firing at long range and anticipating the enemy, while the canister fire of the 6-pounders deranges the manoeuvres of the enemy by forcing them to form up, change front, deploy and so on'.[176] The Prince de Ligne advocated doing away with the 3-pounder altogether, for he maintained that seven or eight of these 'miserable' pieces took up as much space as two good 12-pounders, and had nothing like the same effect.[177]

The 7-pounder howitzer was a versatile weapon, for its heavy calibre (153 mm.) gave it a useful range with grapeshot (a heavier version of canister); when it fired shell the bombardiers were careful to elevate the barrel at such an angle that the missile described a number of bounds before it burst, in the hope that it would knock over a number of men by ricochet.

Leuthen (1757) was the only major battle in which the Austrians were heavily outgunned, for Prince Charles had arrived with only 43 heavy pieces on his hasty march from Breslau, and he scattered them in five batteries along his seven-kilometre front, whereas Frederick had 71 heavy pieces in action, and used them with great freedom. Otherwise the superiority of the Austrian artillery in the Seven Years War was convincing, though it had less to do with the number of their pieces than the manner in which they employed them (see p. 321).

The Austrians hauled their pieces as far forward as was tactically possible by their teams of horses, and then pushed and pulled them the rest of the way mostly by the main force of the infantry *Handlanger* or the Artillery Fusiliers. Little is known about the rate of fire of the Austrian pieces in action, for nearly all the data in this period derive from peacetime experiments,[178] however the artillery *Reglement* of 1757 states in general terms that 'we can attain a much higher speed of fire if we move the piece a fair distance, and stop to get off several rounds from the same location, rather than moving after every shot'.[179]

The opening rounds of the battery pieces were probably the greatest single resource at the disposal of an Austrian army commander, and so 'we recommend what has long been a practice in the Austrian service... namely that when the army forms up for battle a platoon of infantry is stationed in front of every pair of pieces in the first line, so as to conceal them from the prying eyes of the enemy... when the time comes to open fire the platoon duly marches off to left and right'.[180]

The timing was crucial. The Prussians, as the targets, knew that the fire of the Austrian artillery told to great effect as long as the gunners were out of musket range, but it became much less deadly thereafter.[181] This is confirmed by a passage of the *Militär Feld-Regulament* of 1759 which enjoined the artillery officers to 'take the greatest care to prevent the gunners and *Handlanger* from running away as soon as the small arms begin to play; they must instead direct a heavy fire of canister into the enemy, which will silence their musketry soon enough'.[182]

The censorious Armfeldt was not entirely acquainted with the circumstances. 'Whenever I saw the Austrian artillery in action its effect by far surpassed that of the Prussians, but I also observed that they preferred accurate fire to taking leisurely and accurate aim, and opened up at extreme range with both roundshot and canister. Experienced officers recognise this fault, and do what they can to remedy it'.[183]

Good horses, and a detachment of riding or mounted gunners could free artillery from the slow progress of the infantry pace, and enable it to give immediate support to the cavalry, and dash to favourable battery sites that would otherwise be out of reach. These principles were embodied in the batteries of 'horse' artillery which the Prussians brought into action from the middle of the Seven Years War. One of the Prussian batteries was captured when Finck surrendered at Maxen on 21 November 1759. Daun examined the trophies, and argued that the Austrians ought to set up a horse artillery of their own, which would consist of an initial 12 3-pounders, drawn by double teams of four horses each. Liechtenstein calculated that 120 *chevauleger-type* horses would make the pieces and their ammunition carts fully mobile,[184] and with his support the first Austrian horse artillery was ready for action in June 1760. The guns were deployed with the cavalry and with the artillery reserve, and in the following year the Russians helped Loudon to set up a further battery (of four 6-pounders) for service with his corps in Silesia. These two sets of artillery were still something in the nature of an experiment, and the horse artillery as such did not yet form a discrete branch of the corps.

The Battle of Wills

> a major gulf exists between a commander-in-chief – a general who leads the army as a whole or commands in a theatre of operations – and the senior generals immediately subordinate to him.
>
> (Karl von Clausewitz, *On War*, 1832).

Not the least of the travails of the leader of an army derived from the 'loneliness of command,' and the easiest way to alleviate the burden was to hold a council of war. When he saw what Frederick had written on the subject, Daun commented that he was 'at one with the king concerning councils of war. They are just the resort of commanders who are casting about for an honourable pretext to conceal their cowardice'.[185] This excellent principle did not prevent Daun from summoning as many councils as before. The reason was not indeed cowardice, but the lack of authority to impose his wishes on influential and self-willed generals (see p. 197).

Next to determination, *coup d'oeil* was probably the quality most prized in the 18th-century commander. It was understood to be the faculty of grasping the essentials of terrain and a military situation, and make a speedy and appropriate decision. Frederick's opinion on the matter drew a further comment from Daun: 'this is something which the greatest men recognise as being the most useful quality of all for a general. We would do very well to imitate what is written here'.[186] Daun once more fell short of his precepts, for time and time again the lengthy debates of the Austrians, and their desire to have the odds convincingly on their side, led to them neglecting the fleeting opportunity.[187]

Gunpowder had put an end to the kind of battle in which a leader could station himself on a hill and direct his army in person. The Prince de Ligne believed that the commanding general could still at least position himself a little in front of one of the wings, so that he could see along the frontage of the rival armies, and judge the progress of the battle from the density of the smoke. If the combat became more general, he should be in constant movement immediately behind the first line, and keep himself informed through his general-adjutants.[188] Daun was no galloper, but he had a gift for choosing excellent standpoints, as was displayed to particular effect towards the end of the battle of Kohn, at a time when Frederick was stuck on low ground near Chozenitz, and could have seen very little of what was going on. Daun was constantly up with the forward troops at Maxen, and again at Torgau, where his physical courage put him in the path of a bullet.

There remained endless possibilities for misunderstanding. Daun was much concerned with the authentication of orders, and he wrote in his *Militär Feld-Regulament* that the subordinate generals must learn to recognise the accredited bearers of messages, while the adjutants and staff officers who were dispatched with orders by the commanding general were to wear their sashes diagonally over their right shoulders.[189] Even when the order was carried by a properly-authorised individual, language difficulties might still cause it to be delivered in a garbled form.

All generals were supposed to display initiative in action, and there was a particularly heavy call for this quality when the army was sub-divided to carry out converging attacks from different directions, as at Hochkirch and Maxen. In conventional battles, however, it was rarely possible or even desirable for infantry commanders to move their divisions or brigades from their assigned place in the line of battle, and the opportunity for doing something grand and decisive fell only to generals who had a large and intact force of cavalry at their disposal, like Lucchese at Leuthen, or Loudon (more happily) at Kunersdorf.

Regardless of how they thought the day might end, the Austrians generals were under an obligation to put on a cheerful face, and ride up and down their wings or brigades before battle opened, urging the men to do their duty, and all the time keeping an eye on the doings of the enemy. The senior regimental officers were to follow this example, 'which is more likely to make a favourable impression… if the officers are already on easy speaking terms with the men'.[190]

The junior officers and NCOs were to tolerate no critical talk among the soldiers, or to indulge in any themselves. Demoralising language came all to easily when you were about to fight an enemy like the Prussians, 'and anyone who is heard speaking in that way ought to be punished. This might seem a trivial matter, but talk of this kind will heighten the fear of the enemy in the imaginations of a body of men, and perhaps even the army as a whole'.[191]

The troops were likely to be disturbed rather than cheered if the colonel called on the regimental *Pater* (often regarded as a bird of ill omen) to pronounce a short address and a general absolution.[192] In the effort to distract themselves from what was about to befall them, the men busied themselves with a compulsive cleaning of their weapons and other minor and self-appointed tasks.

Armies were bringing unheard-of quantities of artillery into the field, and 'at the beginning of a modern battle it seems as if somebody had upset a basket of tennis balls, for the ground is covered with leaping and bounding cannon shoe.'[193] Informed opinion held that in some respects the raw soldier, who knew nothing of combat and danger, was to be preferred to the veteran who knew what iron and lead could do to the human frame.[194] This first-time courage was illusory, for the inexperienced recruits were being held together by a cadre of long-serving officers and NCOs, and after their initial blooding the young soldiers could be steeled to face their second battle only through rigorous discipline and training.[195]

The horrors of action presented themselves in a variety of forms. The intensity of combat varied from battle to battle, and within the same engagement from one regiment to the next. The Prince de Ligne remarked that after most actions a regiment could reckon its wounded at about 50, but that there was no guarantee that it would not have 10 times that number in the next affray: 'Can you think of a battle when as many as 20 battalions have genuinely been under heavy fire?'[196] He was probably thinking of the experiences of his own regiment, which was lightly engaged even at Kolin, after which Daun commented that 'the battle lasted from two in the afternoon to eight in the evening, and the fighting was hot and bitterly-contested. I believe that nobody in the two armies had ever witnessed such a violent and continuous fire of artillery and small arms'.[197] The luck of the de Ligne regiment ran out at Leuthen, when it had to run from one extremity of the line to the other, and ended with terrible losses.

The perception of danger bore no direct relationship to the reality. Troops crossed bayonets very rarely indeed, and yet the glint of sunlight on the blades of an advancing enemy could erode courage more readily than the thud of a ball in a neighbour's body. The enemy's bullets, shot and shell were murderous enough in their own right, but in de Ligne's experience not as intimidating as the noise of one's own musketry and artillery.[198] The dust and smoke thrown up by both parties might be itself enough to reduce an army to confusion, as happened to the Austrians at Prague in 1757.[199]

Among the countervailing influences there was a place for realistic training. When troops were reduced to deliberate confusion in peacetime exercises, and told to put themselves back in order, they were better fitted to orientate themselves in the inevitable turmoil of combat (see p. 227). Selection of leaders could also play a part: 'If you came across a second-lieutenant who, under the heaviest fire, is managing to keep his platoon together, well closed-up and well-aligned, you ought to give him a company. If all the officers were capable of doing the same, victory would be ours'.[200]

Alcohol could help to steady unsettled nerves after a battle, but it seems to have figured little in heartening the Austrian soldier in combat. Cogniazzo was at pains to refute the charge that Loudon's troops were drunk when they stormed the Prussian positions at Landeshut in 1760. It would have taken a great deal of alcohol to intoxicate more than one-sixth of the 30,000 men engaged, and he could testify that he had accompanied a detachment of 600 troops in the assault and found them perfectly sober.[201]

When example and encouragement failed, the officers and NCOs were entitled to resort to coercion, as was made clear in the *Militär Feld-Regulament* of 1759: 'If one or other of the soldiers… is discouraging the others by demoralising talk, or looks around and leaves his rank and file to run away, such a man must be at once run through the body by the nearest officer or NCO'.[202]

The same stipulations extended to the cavalry, though they were probably applied less rigorously, since real or supposed failings of horses and equipment offered the troopers unchallengeable explanations for failing to close with the enemy. Conversely talk of 'honour' and motivation are to be heard more frequently among the cavalry than the infantry, whose way of fighting was dogged, mechanical and attritional.

Cavalry were to the fore in those small-scale outpost actions where success could implant a sense of superiority from the outset of a campaign.[203] Again the Austrian cuirassiers refused to part with the heavy and inconvenient iron breastplate, because it conveyed so convincingly the notion of armoured force. For the same reason *G.d.C.* Carl O'Donnell supported those officers who protested against the admission of under-sized men to the cuirassiers:

> we must bear in mind that just as a good outward appearance does a great deal to impose respect on the enemy, so the opposite would ensue from introducing so many unimpressive people among our ranks. In short, it would draw down the contempt of the enemy on the whole body of our cavalry, and such a superiority, once yielded up, would take a long time to win back.[204]

The opposing regiment in mounted combat could usually be identified by name, and victory was particularly sweet because a routed enemy would forfeit his drums, which could then be turned to one's use, and not consigned to a church or dusty hall like standards or colours. The captured drums of the Bayreuth Dragoons made the name of the Jung-Löwenstein *Chevaulegers*, just as those of the Jung-Platen Dragoons consolidated the reputation of the Austrian dragoon regiment of Kollowrat.

The Prince de Ligne devoted some thought to the question of courage among the officer class. For himself he claimed that it was no great ordeal to confront mortality in battle, when life could be taken so casually and ingloriously by a clumsy surgeon, a tile falling from a roof, a bolting horse, and when death came in the course of time to claim aged dandies, courtiers, churchmen and bureaucrats. Among his fellow-officers he had observed three types who could be described as courageous. First, those who were brave by temperament: there were very few of them, but their courage was unwavering. Men who were brave by reflection made up the second category. They were more praiseworthy in the moral sense, but they were subject to caution. Self-interest was the motive force of the rest, who could themselves be divided into two types. Those officers who tempered their ambition with honour were in the habit of counting the relative odds of advantage and danger, and they could be relied upon to keep their composure in the heat of action. The others could be 'distinguished so little from those who simply run away that they do little of any use in combat.' Their thought-processes were muddled, they wore gloomy expressions, and there was a lack of assurance in the way they held their swords'.[205]

Failure in a general was related less directly to physical courage, and Daun and Frederick agreed that a single unlucky moment should not be allowed to damn a commander who was otherwise blameless, and 'who has worked for many years to attain that respect which can be lost in an instant'.[206]

The Outcome

The issue of so many issues in the Seven Years War hung on a knife edge, like the outcome of the war as a whole. Kolin was won when Daun seemed to believe that it had been lost; he left the field of Torgau in the firm belief that he had gained the victory, and sent a courier to convey the news to Vienna – and was too late to call him back when he discovered that the Prussians had won after all; Adelsbach was one of the last Austrian successes in the war, and it was won because the commander of the Austrian grenadiers left his tent in the night to relieve himself. The Prince de Ligne suspected that the true turning point on many occasions was moral rather than physical, and that officers made up their minds for no particular reason that the thing had been lost, and then began to cast around for excuses, such as a flank being turned, or the troops running out of ammunition when there were still plenty of rounds available.[207]

Whether a retreat was justified or not, the *Militär Feld-Regulament* laid down that the manoeuvre was to be conducted 'slowly, without confusion, and in suitable order and without any kind of outcry... the pieces of the artillery, the colours and standards, the drums and the ammunition carts are to be defended to the utmost, and every conceivable effort devoted to saving them'.[208] Loudon carried out these prescriptions to the letter at Liegnitz in 1760, and wrested an expression of admiration from Frederick himself.

If the day had gone well, and the efforts had been crowned with victory, the emotional impact was as powerful in its way as a defeat. The senior generals made their way through the ranks of cheering soldiers to congratulate the commander-in-chief and hug the officers who had contributed the most to the outcome. 'My God, what a moment! The fanfares resound through the army... the wounded drag themselves along to see the general pass by... the army is brimming with confidence. Daring and activity! Collectively and individually we fear nothing... Let's jump on our hats! We have won our battle!'[209]

No accusation is levelled more widely, or more unfairly at 18th-century armies than the one that they failed to follow up their advantages. Battles were still fought most frequently in continuous lines, and any unit which ventured out of formation to follow up a local success was liable to be shot up or ridden down in the same style as the regiment of Haller at Kolin. Calculation as well as a sense of humanity induced Austrian commanders to do what they could to curb their soldiers' instinct to massacre or plunder their defenceless enemies. The *Militär Feld-Regulament* specified that towards the end of a victorious battle the pursuit was to be left to a couple of designated squadrons of cavalry, while the rest of the army 'advances in due order, slowly and to sounding music, and any man who leaves his rank and file without express order will pay for it with his life'.[210]

Regulations and custom laid down the formal celebrations, which were held one or more days after the victory. The singing of the *Te Deum* was followed by a double rippling *Lauf Feuer* by the muskets of the infantry and the carbines and pistols of the cavalry. A hard-riding officer was already well on his way to Vienna with the first notification of the triumph, and the commander-in-chief was now putting together a more considered version. The Prussians conceded that the Austrians were meticulous about giving credit where it was deserved, even to the most junior officer.[211]

A specially-favoured officer was appointed to carry the fully worked-up report, and the carriages of his cortege were piled with the trophies of the day. Outriders were awaiting him on the road, and they escorted him with blaring trumpets on the final stages of his journey to Court, where the shot-torn and bloody colours, standards and drums were arranged in artful display. Another harvest of the war was meanwhile being gathered in:

> I was one of the 26 officers designated to supervise the burial of the dead. Each of us had 30 soldiers and 100 peasants under his orders. We assembled the corpses in piles of 12 or 15 at a time, dug a pit beside each of the heaps, threw the bodies inside, and covered them with quicklime. We entered the numbers of the Prussian and Austrian dead on our lists. All men killed in battle are stripped instantly by the light troops and the sutler women, but we were able to tell them apart by the dressing of their hair...[212]

FM. Leopold Joseph Count Daun, 1705–66 (author's photograph, Austrian Army Museum).

Conclusions

Were the emerging states of modern Europe shaped by the requirements of forces capable of waging war in the period of the gunpowder revolution, or was it the other way around, that the regular armed forces were the product of the new bureaucratic states?[1] The matter is open to debate, but a little study has convinced the present writer that 'Austria' arrived comparatively late on the scene, and that the two processes, the building of the state and the army, went hand in hand. If this is accepted, some important consequences follow.

Most obviously, Maria Theresa and her advisers confronted a massive task. It is true that Maria Theresa's ancestors, the 'Baroque' Emperors, had cast at least an appearance of religious and cultural uniformity across the core of the Hereditary Lands, but the existence of a Habsburg monarchy in the social sense did not necessarily equate with a consciousness of belonging to a Habsburg-dynastic state (see p. 40), and an awareness of family rights and slights (today as strong as ever in the aristocracy of Central Europe) was as likely to shape the response to events as the allegiance of the moment. The changes of loyalty in the 17th century were a matter of fresh family record, and, simply because Austria took the strategic offensive in the Seven Years War, it is easy to forgot how close the Habsburg body politic had come to disintegrating as recently as 1741. If the Habsburg monarchy had truly been a despotism, then Maria Theresa would not have had to resort to persuasion to initiate changes in domestic affairs or foreign policy, nor would the direction of armies in the field have been a matter of negotiation between the commander-in-chief and his senior generals. This is what contemporaries had in mind when they termed the Habsburg rule a 'democracy,' and that is why the power still residing with local and particular interests was a greater obstacle to the unitary state than the more obvious diversities of nationality and religion.

The consistent and testimony of all well-placed observers – native, French and Swedish – indicates that the greater aristocracy engaged itself in the Austrian army, when it engaged at all, almost entirely on its own terms. It is significant that of the two areas in which the army made the greatest technical advances, the one, the evolution of the General Staff, was the least open to aristocratic influence, and the other, the artillery, provided one of the few cases in which a great magnate (Liechtenstein) was willing to commit his energies and fortune to the larger end.

Maria Theresa and her circle had a great deal to do if they were to bring their state and army into a fit state to survive in competition with Prussia. They also had a very short time in which to do it. The history of continuous domestic and military reform dates only from 1748, and it was overtaken by the new war in 1756, a war against a state which the House of Hohenzollern had been building on solid foundations since the time of the Great Elector's compact with his *Stände* in 1653; in other words, for every year which Maria Theresa had spent on consolidation the Prussians had been able to devote ten. Frederick could well afford to leave intact a system which was so well settled in all its parts. In the short time available to the Austrians, however, the process of military reform was disruptive as well as creative. Thus men of all ranks found it difficult to accommodate themselves to the complicated new drills, while *Kaisertreue* was less evident among the newly-regularised Croats than mass mutiny and the losing of the tactical advantage which they and the hussars had once enjoyed over the Prussians. The cuirassiers progressed marginally, if at all, and the undoubted advances among the infantry were surpassed by those among the already formidable Prussian foot soldiers.

It was much to the credit of the Austrians that the work of reform continued into the war, and was perhaps never more productive in the middle years, which saw the rise of the General Staff and its specialised supporting troops, the creation of the artillery fusiliers, and the emergence of the *chevaulegers*. These forward-looking and responsive forces were nevertheless the ones that were hit hardest by the financial retrenchments which were seen as inevitable towards the end of the war.

This was the army which had gone to war against an exceptionally potent enemy, led by a king who combined political and military authority, and is now numbered among the foremost commanders in history. On his side Kaunitz as a determined, far-sighted and resourceful statesman had assembled what seemed at the time as irresistible odds on the side of Austria in the war he engineered against Prussia. He knew very well that such a superiority depended on the active and direct assistance of French and Russian armies. In the event help in this form was not forthcoming, and Austria had to conduct war largely on her own account and from an inadequate financial base.

From the spring of 1758 the command of the main Austrian field army lay in the hands of Field Marshal Leopold Daun, who was at the same time the maker of his army and the man who had to risk it in battle (there are parallels with the case of General McClellan in the American Civil War). In Daun the proper sense of caution was coloured by a pronounced pessimism, and it was easy, and easier still with the elapse of time, to condemn him for his fundamentally defensive posture, and associate ourselves with Kaunitz, who urged him repeatedly to go over to the attack.[2]

There was a superficially attractive case for converting the grand strategic aim of recovering Silesia directly into action on the operational plane. One of Maria Theresa's advisers told her in 1760 that:

> My opinion, for what it is worth, has always been based on the principle that we are not waging war to defend our present possessions, but to recover that which has been snatched from us so unjustly. All of our combinations ought to be directed towards the offensive, and to succeed in that end there is no alternative but to seize the initiative in operations, and force the King of Prussia to conform to ours.[3]

The Austrian monarchy was nevertheless still unformed in many respects, which gave the army a unique value as Maria Theresa's only secular international institution. Daun therefore had more in his mind than just the possibility of being beaten in the field, for a second 'Leuthen' might bring down army and state together. Adapting the words which Winston Churchill applied to Admiral Jellicoe at Jutland in 1916, we may describe Daun as the man who could have lost the war for his country in an afternoon, and indeed more than just the war. Was it possible for Daun or any other commander to have been ignorant of the recent defection of the Bohemian nobles, of the absence of an identifiable military caste, or the lack of a modern and comprehensive fortress system? The work of military reform had only just begun, it was still in progress in the course of the war, and some of its most important achievements were going to be overturned by economies. Perhaps it was no more than common prudence which made Daun consider that it was in the vital interests of the monarchy to maintain an army 'in being,' to revert to naval images. In the Austrian context a comparison may be drawn with the situation of Archduke Charles after his victory at Aspern-Essling in 1809, when he declined to chase Napoleon across the Danube on the grounds that the army was 'the safeguard of the dynasty and could not be risked in battle'.[4] It took a Radetzky to draw the opposite conclusion in his campaign against the Sardinians, and convert a defensive posture into his fulminating counter-offensive of July 1848. The decision was not taken lightly, for, as Grillparzer proclaimed in his famous ode, the whole of Austria lay in his camp; in that sense she had also reposed in the camps of Archduke Charles and Daun.

The viewpoint of the Prussians also needs to be taken into account, when we bear in mind that the best course in war is usually to do that which is least welcome to the enemy. On the question of the offensive and defensive Frederick commented in the course of the Seven Years War that 'as long as we fail to drawn the enemy down to the plains we have no hope of attaining any substantial advantages over them. But if we can deprive them of their mountains, their forests and their broken country – which are so useful to them – their troops will no longer be capable of withstanding ours'.[5]

Such considerations do not necessarily justify Daun against Kaunitz and the Chancellor's fellow-spirit Loudon, but they do set out the context in which Maria Theresa and her commanders and statesmen had to make their decisions. Austria was in fact served well by the interaction between the detached corps of Loudon, and the measured proceedings of Daun, who committed his troops to offensive action only when the aspect of the stars seemed particularly favourable, but otherwise considered that he was doing well just to keep his army out of trouble.

In hindsight the outcome of the Second World War appears inevitable by the end of the second week of December 1941, by when the United States had entered the conflict, and the Soviets had mounted their first counter-offensive at Moscow. In contrast the issue of the Seven Years War in Central Europe remained in the scale until the final months of the conflict. The alliance was within almost literal heartbeat of victory at the outset of 1762, for the Prussians had lost their western provinces and East Prussia and Glatz, the Russians were overwintering in Pomerania, and Loudon had won the key fortress of Schweidnitz and thereby gained a firm footing for the Austrians in the Silesian plain. Frederick was saved in the first instance by the death of Elizabeth of Russia, a fact which was acknowledged widely. That war, however, had long been in the balance, and an unchallengeable decision could have been attained at almost any juncture in favour of one party or the other by a particular interaction of resources, calculation, passion or simple accident, which is another way of saying by force of arms:

> Chance selected this field out of so many, that low wall, this gentle slope of grass, a windmill, a farm or straggling hedge, to turn the tide of war and decide the fate of nations and creeds. Look on this scene, restored to its rustic sleep that was so rudely interrupted on that one day in all the ages; and looking, laugh at the 'science of History'! But for some honest soldier's pluck or luck in the decisive onslaught round yonder village spire, the lost cause would now be hailed as 'the tide of inevitable tendency' that nothing could have turned aside.[6]

List of Regiments (Designations as of 1759)

'German' Infantry Regiments

Name	Later numerical designation	Uniform (white coat with cuffs and lapels of)
Andlau	57	Red
Angern (Kheul -1758)	49	Red
Arenberg	21	Light blue
Baden-Baden	23	Blue
Baden-Durlach	27	Blue
Bayreuth	41	Red
Botta	12	Blue
Colloredo-Alt (Anton)	20	Dark blue
Colloredo-Jung (Carl)	40	Blue
Daun-Alt (Heinrich) (O'Kelly 1761–)	45	Red
Daun-Jung (Leopold)	59	Red
Deutschmeister	4	Dark blue
Gaisruck	42	Red, blue from 1757
Harrach	47	Red, blue from 1757
Harsch	50	Red
Hildburghausen	8	Red
Kaiser	1	Red
Kollowrat	17	Red
Königsegg	16	Blue
Lacy (Hagenbach -1757; Sprecher –1758)	22	Red
Lothringen	3	Red
Maguire (Tyroler Land- and Feld)	46	Red
Marschall	18	Red
Mercy	56	Blue
Moltke	13	Light blue
Neipperg	7	Blue
Pallavicini	15	Blue
Platz	43	Red
Puebla	26	Red
Salm	14	Black
Sincere	54	Red
Starhemberg	24	Dark blue
Thürheim (Piccolomini –1757)	25	Red
Tillier (Browne –1757; Kinsky 1761–)	36	Light blue
Waldeck	35	Red
Wallis	11	Red
Wied	28	Green

| Wolfenbüttel-Alt (Carl) (Loudon 1760–) | 29 | Blue |
| Wolfenbüttel-Jung (Ernst Ludwig) | 10 | Red |

Italian National Regiments

| Clerici | 44 | Red |
| Luzan | 48 | Green |

Netherlands National Regiments

d'Arberg	55	Red
de Ligne (Claude)	38	Rose red
Los Rios	9	Green
Sachsen-Gotha	30	Blue

Hungarian National Regiments

Name	Later numerical designation	Uniform (*white coat with distinctive*)
Batthyány	34	Yellow collar and cuffs, blue dolman and *Gatti-Hosen*
Bethlen	52	Light blue cuffs, dolman and *Gatti-Hosen*
Carl, Erzherzog (Ferdinand, Erzherzog 1762–)	2	Yellow cuffs, blue dolman and *Gatti-Hosen*
Esterházy, Joseph	37	Red cuffs, dolman and *Gatti-Hosen*
Esterházy, Nicolaus	33	Dark blue cuffs, dolman and *Gatti-Hosen*
Forgách	32	Dark blue cuffs, dolman and *Gatti-Hosen*
Gyulai	51	Dark blue cuffs, dolman and *Gatti-Hosen*
Haller	31	Blue cuffs, dolman and *Gatti-Hosen*
Pálffy, Leopold	19	'German' uniform*, with blue cuffs and lapels
Preysach (Pálffy, Johann –1758)	None	Red cuffs, dolman and *Gatti-Hosen*
Simbschen (recruited in Slavonia)	53	Red cuffs, turn-backs, dolman and *Gatti-Hosen*

* according to Bautzen Manuscript of 1762

'New Corps' of Infantry

Staabs-Infanterie-Regiment
(First Bn) — Blue coat, red collar and cuffs, blue breeches
(Second Bn) — Blue coat, red collar and cuffs, white turn-backs and breeches

Deutsches Feld-Jäger Corps — Bluish-grey coat, green collar, cuffs and turn-backs, bluish-grey waistcoat
(fully independent 1761) — waistcoat and breeches, black helmet
Volontairs Silesiens Beck — Green coat, buff cuffs and lapels, light green breeches

Grenadier-Bataillon Gran-Loudon — Mid-green coat, red cuffs and lapels, mid-green waistcoat and breeches

Jager-Corps Otto
Three Netherlands Free Battalions
Six companies of Netherlands *Gardes-Cotes* (possibly related to the above)
Anhalt-Zerbst battalion (1760–)

Auxiliary Infantry
Mainz regiment Lamberg
Regiments Blau- and Rot-Würzburg (later amalgamated)
Regiment Toscana

Cuirassier Regiments

Name	Later numerical designation	Uniform (white coat with red cuffs and turn-backs, and –)
Anhalt-Zerbst	None	Straw waistcoat and breeches (but jerkin and short jacket in last campaigns)
Anspach	33	White waistcoat, red breeches (but jerkin and short jacked in last campaigns)
Birkenfeld (Stampa 1761–)	23	White waistcoat, red breeches
Bretlach	29	Straw waistcoat and breeches
Buccow (Lucchesi –1758)	None	Red waistcoat and breeches
Daun (Benedict) (Radicati –1756; Löwenstein –1758)	27	White waistcoat, red breeches
Ferdinand, Erzherzog (Max, Erzherzog 1761–)	4	White waistcoat, red breeches
Kalckreuth (Prince Albert of Sachsen-Teschen 1760–)	22	Red waistcoat, straw breeches
Leopold, Erzherzog	3	White waistcoat, red breeches
Modena-Alt	None	N.B. blue cuffs and turn-backs, white waistcoat, blue breeches
O'Donnell	14	White waistcoat, red breeches
Pálffy, Carl	8	White waistcoat, red breeches
Portugal	6	Red waistcoat and breeches
Schmerzing (d'Ayasasa 1762–)	20	White waistcoat, red breeches
Serbelloni	12	Red waistcoat and breeches
Stampach	16	Red waistcoat, straw breeches
Trautmannsdorf	21	White waistcoat, red breeches
de Ville (Gelhay -1759)	None	White waistcoat, red breeches

Dragoon Regiments

Name	Later numerical designation	Uniform
Althann (Koháry -1756)	None	White coat, red cuffs, lapels and turn-backs, white waistcoat and breeches
Batthyány, Carl	7	Dark blue coat, red cuffs, lapels and turn-backs, dark blue waistcoat and breeches
Darmstadt, Hessen-	19	Red coat, light green cuffs, lapels & turn-backs, yellow jerkin (instead of waistcoat), straw yellow breeches
Joseph, Erzherzog	1	Dark green coat, red collar, cuffs and turn-backs (no lapels), dark green waistcoat, straw breeches
Kollowrat	37	Blue coat, red cuffs, lapels and turn-backs, blue waistcoat, red breeches

Name		Uniform
Liechtenstein	6	Blue coat, red cuffs, lapels and turn-backs, red waistcoat and breeches
Löwenstein, Jung- (*chevaulegers*)	18	Green coat, red cuffs and lapels, red waistcoat and breeches, black helmet
Modena, Jung-	13	Red coat, light blue cuffs, lapels and turn-backs, light blue waistcoat and breeches
Sachsen-Gotha	28	Red coat, light blue cuffs, lapels and turn-backs, straw breeches
St. Ignon (*chevaulegers*) (Netherlands) (Ligne, Ferdinand –1757; Daun, Benedict, 1758; Löwenstein-Alt, –1759)	None	Green coat, red cuffs and turn-backs, red waistcoat, straw breeches
Savoyen	9	Red coat, black cuffs, lapels and turn-backs, red waistcoat, red or straw breeches
Württemberg	38	Red coat, black cuffs, lapels and turn-backs, straw waistcoat and breeches
Zweibrücken	None	Blue coat, red cuffs and lapels, blue waistcoat, straw breeches
Staabs-Dragoner	None	Blue coat, red cuffs (no lapels), white turn-backs, red breeches

Hussar Regiments

Name	Later numerical designation	Uniform
Baranyay	30	Green pelisse and dolman, light blue leggings, kalpak with red or green bag
Bethlen (–1759 Morocz)	35	Light blue pelisse, dolman and leggings, kalpak with red bag
Dessewffy	32	Light blue pelisse and dolman, red leggings, black *mirliton*
Esterházy, Paul Anton (Luzinsky –1762)	24	Light blue pelisse and dolman, red leggings, kalpak with red bag
Hadik	16	Dark blue pelisse and dolman, dark blue or red leggings, kalpak with red bag
Kaiser	2	Dark blue pelisse and dolman, kalpak with dark blue bag
Kálnoky	17	Light blue pelisse and dolman, red leggings, kalpak with red or blue bag
Palatinal (or Török)	36	Light blue pelisse and dolman, red leggings, *mirliton* or kalpak with red bag
Nádasdy	11	Light green pelisse and dolman, dark blue leggings, kalpak with red or light green bag
Pálffy, Rudolph (Károly -1759)	16	Light blue pelisse, dolman and leggings, kalpak with red bag
Splényi (Esterházy, Emerich 1762–)	None	Light green pelisse and dolman, red leggings, kalpak with light green bag
Széchenyi (Festetics -1757)	None	Blue pelisse and dolman, kalpak with blue bag

Maintained Saxon Cavalry (Designations 1761)
Albert, Prinz
Bielack
Brühl
Carl, Herzog
Garde Carabiniers
Schiebel

Artillery and Technical Troops

Name	Uniform
Feld-Artillerie Haupt Corps	Greyish-brown coat, red cuffs, greyish-brown waistcoat and breeches
Netherlands Corps	Greyish-brown coat, red cuffs and lapels, greyish-brown waistcoat and breeches
Artillerie-Füsiliere-Regiment	Greyish-brown coat, red cuffs, greyish-brown waistcoat and breeches
Pontonier-Corps	Blue coat, red cuffs and lapels, bluewaistcoat and breeches
Sappeurs-Corps	Bluish-green coat, carmine red cuffs, collar, turn-backs, waistcoat and breeches; helmet
Ingenieur-Corps	Blue coat, red cuffs and lapels, red waistcoat and breeches

Croatian (Grenzer) Regiments

Name	Later numerical designation	Uniform
Carlstädter		
Liccaner	60	(Old) Red jacket, green dolman, red leggings (New) Semi German-style white jacket, green cuffs and turn-backs, green dolman, white leggings
Ottocaner	61	Red jacket, blue cuffs, light blue dolman, red leggings
Oguliner	62	Blue jacket, red cuffs, blue dolman, red leggings
Szluiner	63	Blue jacket, red cuffs, red dolman, red or blue leggings
Warasdiner		
Creutzer	64	Semi German-style white jacket, green cuffs and turn-backs, green dolman, green or white leggings
St. Georger	65	Semi German-style white jacket, green cuffs and turn-backs, green dolman, green or white pants
Slavonian		
Broder	66	Dark blue pelisse, dolman and leggings
Gradiscaner	67	Red jacket, light blue dolman, red leggings
Peterwardeiner	68	Dark blue jacket and dolman, light blue leggings

Banal
First	None	Dark blue jacket, red dolman and leggings
Second	None	Dark blue jacket, red dolman and leggings

Grenz-Husaren
Carlstädter	None	Dark blue pelisse, dolman and leggings, kalpak with red bag
Warasdiner	None	Red pelisse, dolman and leggings, kalpak with red bag
Slavonian	None	Light green pelisse and dolman, red leggings, kalpak with red bag
Banal	None	Dark blue dolman, red pelisse, dark blue leggings

Appendix I

Military Representation of Hungarian Counties and Transylvania

(1 percent and more only shown here)

Other Ranks, Regiments of Hungarian Infantry

Transylvania:	21.45
Trentschin:	7.63
Bihar:	5.14
Heves:	4.28
Neutra:	4.20
Borsod:	3.90
Pressburg:	3.59
Pest:	3.41
Zala:	3.29
Saros:	3.19
Zepeser:	3.10
Zemplén:	2.82
Féhérvar:	2.73
Abau:	2.71
Eisenburg:	2.46
Hont:	1.87
Baranya:	1.63
Szatmár:	1.59
Ödenburg:	.50
Gömer:	1.41
Somogy:	1.40
Veszprém:	1.37
Szabolcs:	1.34
Tolna:	1.20
Arva:	1.10
Neograd:	1.06
Komorn:	1.01

Other Ranks, Regiments of Hussars:

Pest:	7.50
Neutra:	7.42
Transylvania:	7.27
Pressburg:	6.00
Bihar:	5.37
Ödenburg:	5.20
Eisenburg:	4.88
Heves:	3.93
Zala:	3.51
Borsod:	3.32
Komorn:	2.94
Raab:	2.65
Zemplén:	2.46
Veszprém:	2.45
Hajdú towns:	2.27
Abau:	2.22
Féhérvar:	2.12
Neograd:	2.02
Sáros:	1.99
Tolna:	1.96
Jazygien:	1.83
Trentschin:	1.61
Gross Kumanien:	1.47
Csongrád:	1.44
Szabolcs:	1.39
Gran:	1.32
Hont:	1.29
Szatmár:	1.17
Bars, Wieselburg:	1.11 each
Szepes:	1.06

Officers, Regiments of Hungarian Infantry

Transylvania:	17.69
Pressburg:	7.40
Szepes:	6.58
Neutra:	5.86
Pest:	5.34
Eisenburg:	4.92
Heves, Ödenburg:	4.52 each
Raab, Zemplen:	4.11 each
Sáros, Trentschin:	3.70 each
Abau:	3.29
Komorn:	2.88
Féhérvar, Bihar, Gömer, Zala:	2.05 each
Bánát, Sohl, Szabolcs:	1.23 each

469

Officers, Regiments of Hussars

Eisenburg:	9.26
Pressburg:	8.14
Transylvania:	7.58
Neutra, Raab:	6.46 each
Ödenburg, Saros:	4.49 each
Heves, Pest:	3.93 each
Trentschin:	3.65
Comer, Szatmár:	2.52 each
Bars, Veszprém, Zala, Szepes:	2.24 each
Abau, Baranya, Bihar, Zemplén:	1.96 each
Féhérvar, Neograd, Tolna:	1.68 each
Borsod, Jazygien:	1.40 each
Komorn:	1.12

Appendix II

Religion in Hungary and Transylvania by Location

(As represented in whole army, as percentage of affiliation by county or principality; first 15 counties only in each category)

Other Ranks
Catholics
Wieselburg:	97.12
Neutra, Trentschin:	96.86 each
Jazygien:	95.02
Szepes:	94.87
Zala:	94.66
Pressburg:	93.37
Raab:	93.22
Ödenburg:	93.21
Eisenburg:	92.64
Gran:	91.82
Tolna:	88.56
Bars:	87.76
Csongrád:	87.50
Somogy:	86.73

Lutherans
Turócs:	29.26
Liptau:	26.74
Békés:	21.42
Gömer:	20.38
Neushol:	15.00
Komorn:	13.88
Sáros:	8.76
Transylvania:	8.44
Neograd:	8.36
Jász-Bereny:	7.14
Sohl:	6.73
Hont:	6.40
Veszprém:	6.38
Ödenburg:	5.91
Eisenburg:	5.28

Calvinists
Csanád:	72.73
Maros:	55.55
Bihar:	53.99
Gross Kumanien:	49.31
Szabolcs:	45.72
Szolnok:	41.93
Klein Kumanien:	40.96
Szatmár:	31.79
Borsod:	30.42
Bereg:	23.61
Veszprém:	19.14
Transylvania:	17.87
Békés:	17.14
Abau:	16.97
Pest:	16.06

Orthodox
Maros:	11.20
Máramaros:	2.53
Békés:	1.42
Bereg:	1.38
Transylvania:	.83
Arva:	.72
Gran:	.62
Bihar:	.43
All others:	Nil

Officers
Catholics
Abau, Bánát, Bereg, Csongrád, Féhérvar, Gran, Hont, Jazygien, Komorn, Somogy, Szolnok, Tolna, Torna, Turócs, Ugotsa, Ung, Wieselburg: all 100.00

Lutherans
Liptau:	100.00
Neusohl:	50.00
Sáros:	48.00
Szepes:	36.00
Szatmár:	33.33
Arva:	25.00
Ödenburg:	22.44
Veszprém:	22.22
Gömer	21.42

Calvinists
Hajdu towns, Gross Kumanien:	100.00 each
Szabolcs:	60.00
Bihar:	26.00
Transylvania:	20.00
Borsod:	14.28
Veszprém:	11.11
Zemplen:	5.58
Pest, Raab:	2.43 each
Pressburg:	1.58
All others:	Nil

Orthodox
Bács:	25.00
Baranya:	7.69
Pest:	4.87
Transylvania:	.11
All others:	Nil

Sects
Transylvania:	1.11
All others:	Nil

Appendix III

Origins of Netherlands Private Soldiers

(As percentage within regiments)

D'Arberg Infantry
Luxembourg:	29.90
Hainault and Tournai:	24.91
Flanders:	17.84
Brabant and Malines (excl. Brussels):	9.82
Antwerp:	5.92
Brussels:	4.71
Namur (province and town)	5.28
Limburg:	1.49

De Ligne Infantry
Luxembourg:	45.08
Flanders:	26.54
Hainault and Tournai:	11.55
Limburg:	10.64
Brabant and Malines (excl. Brussels):	2.40
Brussels:	1.94
Namur (province and town)	1.60
Antwerp:	0.22

Los Rios Infantry
Brabant and Malines (excl. Brussels):	27.50
Brussels:	21.09
Luxembourg:	16.17
Flanders:	11.71
Hainault and Tournai:	10.87
Antwerp:	7.15
Namur (province and town)	4.27
Limburg:	1.20

Sachsen-Gotha Infantry
Luxembourg:	45.42
Flanders:	16.43
Brabant and Malines (excl. Brussels):	10.50
Hainault and Tournai; Brussels:	6.80 each
Antwerp:	6.12
Limburg:	5.83
Namur (province and town):	2.04

De Ligne/ Benedict Daun/ St. Ignon Dragoons
Hainault and Tournai:	28.52
Luxembourg:	22.15
Flanders:	17.29
Brabant and Malines (excl. Brussels):	16.84
Limburg:	8.49
Namur (province and town):	4.70
Brussels:	1.06
Antwerp:	0.91

Netherlands Artillery Corps
Luxembourg:	53.30
Hainault and Tournai:	16.03
Brabant and Malines (excl. Brussels):	9.43
Brussels:	6.60
Namur (province and town):	5.66
Antwerp:	4.24
Limburg:	2.83
Flanders:	1.88

Netherlanders in the Rest of the Army
Luxembourg:	32.69
Flanders:	16.80
Hainault and Tournai:	16.00
Brabant and Malines (excl. Brussels):	13.60
Brussels:	7.90
Limburg:	4.76
Antwerp:	4.46
Namur (province and town):	3.74

Appendix IV

Origins of German Private Soldiers

All Arms
Swabia:	8.31
Bavaria:	7.37
Mainz:	6.97
Trier:	6.90
Saxony:	6.61
Palatinate, Lower:	5.49
Württemberg:	4.22
Würzburg:	3.00
Hessen-Cassel:	2.75
Cologne:	2.63
Bamberg:	2.52
Brandenburg:	1.99
Franconia:	1.96
Hessen-Darmstadt:	1.61
Ansbach:	1.56
Fulda:	1.55
Hamburg:	1.37
Bayreuth:	1.35
Palatinate, Upper:	1.32
Breisgau:	1.29
Black Forest:	1.25
Salzburg:	1.19
Westphalia:	1.23
Vorder-Österreich:	1.12
Nassau:	1.03

All other locations less than 1 percent

Infantry
(Total 10,676, highest 10 representations –)
Trier:	7.64
Swabia:	7.58
Mainz:	7.40
Bavaria:	6.68
Saxony:	5.87
Palatinate, Lower:	5.67
Württemberg:	4.69
Hessen-Cassel:	3.10
Cologne:	2.88
Würzburg:	2.82

Cuirassiers
(Total 1,278, highest 10 representations –)
Swabia:	15.33
Saxony:	14.08
Bavaria:	12.44
Würzburg:	5.08
Palatinate, Lower:	4.53
Franconia:	4.30
Mainz:	4.06
Palatinate, Upper; Black Forest:	3.67 each
Salzburg:	3.50

Non-combatant Supporting Staff
(Total 1,692, highest 10 representations –)
Saxony:	10.69
Bavaria:	10.22
Swabia:	8.92
Mainz:	5.79
Palatinate, Lower:	5.43
Brandenburg:	4.76
Franconia:	4.60
Würzburg:	4.13
Württemberg:	3.42
Bamberg:	2.95

NCOs
(Total 3,355, highest 10 representations –)
Bavaria:	11.35
Swabia:	10.76
Saxony:	7.63
Mainz:	6.08
Palatinate, Lower:	5.66
Franconia:	4.78
Württemberg:	4.67
Würzburg:	4.05
Bamberg:	2.77
Trier:	2.59

Appendix V

Wastage

Average Numbers and Percentages per Regiment by Type in the Course of the Seven Years War. Extracted from KA HKRA 1756 XIII 379, *Verzeichniss*)

	Total		Prisoner	KIA	Died of Wounds or Disease	Deserted	Missing or Invalided Out
Regular infantry	3,711.4	=	22.81%	11.35%	32.72%	21.73%	11.36%
'New Corps'							
Staabs-Inf	4,014	=	8.35%	2.59%	29.32%	40.03%	19.70%
Feld-Jäger & Pioniere:	920	=	27.50%	2.60%	40.65%	29.38%	Nil
Art.-Füsiliere	3,715	=	8.99%	1.96%	52.51%	33.86%	2.66%
Beck:	1,479	=	11.96%	17.10%	5.61%	58.89%	6.42%
Loudon:	2,211	=	20.94%	11.35%	3.39%	54.68%	9.63%
Anhalt-Zerbst	254	=	1.18%	Nil	44.48%	54.33%	Nil
Auxiliary infantry							
Mainz:	4,674	=	39.79%	3.29%	33.61%	21.60%	1.69%
Blau- & Rot-Würzburg:	4,757	=	24.95%	1.87%	30.52%	26.63%	16.01%
Toscana:	3,011	=	2.00%	4.71%	57.09%	28.46%	7.67%
Cuirassiers:	891.3	=	42.21%	18.53%	16.01%	12.26%	10.97%
Dragoons:	1,692.1	=	50.64%	13.23%	10.82%	9.00%	16.24%
Hussars:	2,775.8	=	56.30%	13.01%	5.34%	13.83%	11.50%
Grenz-Husaren:	311.5	=	63.39%	19.77%	11.71%	3.79%	1.31%
Feld-Artillerie:	4,315	=	Nil	6.48%	50.93%	21.08%	20.76%
Sappeurs-Corps:	64	=	29.68%	18.757	9.37%	42.18%	Nil
Ingenieurs:	32	=	65.62%	18.75%	15.62%	Nil	Nil
Croatian inf.:	1,554.1	=	39.74%	1.70%	43.44%	2.10%	12.99%

Rates of Annual Wastage, as Reconstructed from the Muster Lists
Rates of wastage may also be extracted on a different basis, from the periodic muster lists, which enter the numbers of men deficient from various causes from the time the muster last taken. The survival of muster lists was a matter of chance (see the relevant Bibliographical note), and hence the results are far less authoritative than the calculations of overall losses reproduced above. Moreover, the separation of categories of loss is by no means absolute. The value of the evidence however lies in the indication of the differing rates of losses experienced in different circumstances, and the minute (if frequently ambiguous) subdivisions of the categories.

Rates in Peace and War

	Peacetime	Wartime not on Campaign	Wartime, one or more Campaigns
Infantry:	6.66%	17.87%	38.76%
Cuirassiers & Dragoons:	4.50%	5.46%	14.44%
Hussars:	No musters processed	1.59%	28.94%
Feld-Artillerie Haupt-Corps:	No musters processed	No musters processed	11.42%

Rates by Cause (wartime, one or more campaigns)

Causes of wastage were entered (not very systematically) by an average of 15 main categories, many of which overlap in the usual annoying way. For convenience they are grouped here under three main headings:

'Routine'

	Released	Died or resigned	Died or executed	'Lost in hospital'	Released as Invalid
Infantry:	0.15%	5.75%	7.43%	1.40%	1.69%
Cuirassiers & Dragoons:	0.69%	2.66%	0.26%	0.09%	1.09%
Hussars:	0.85%	3.07%	0.51%	Nil	1.11%
Feld-Artillerie Haupt-Corps:	0.92%	1.28%	Nil	Nil	Nil

'Through Criminality'

	Deserted	Dismissed with disgrace	Executed	To Fortress labour	Released or Dismissed with disgrace
Infantry:	10.29%	0.001%	0.07%	0.27%	0.09%
Cuirassiers & Dragoons:	2.75%	Nil	0.05%	0.01%	0.17%
Hussars:	4.03%	0.01%	0.05%	0.009%	Nil
Feld-Artillerie Haupt-Corps:	3.02%	Nil	0.10%	0.31%	Nil

'Through Enemy Action'

	Lost in presence of enemy	KIA	Missing or otherwise lost	Captured
Infantry:	5.89%	2.02%	1.08%	2.62%
Cuirassiers & Dragoons:	2.06%	0.71%	0.32%	3.56%
Hussars:	3.35%	1.58%	0.25%	14.09%
Feld-Artillerie Haupt-Corps:	0.16%	0.49%	Nil	5.05%

The above entry for the artillery is useful, as giving a clue to the percentage of those who appear on the first list as 'Missing or Invalided' who were in fact prisoners. The Commissaries entered a variety of minor causes of wastage in a haphazard fashion. Thus it would appear that on campaign accidental drowning accounted for annual losses of 0.01% among the infantry, 1.22% among the cuirassiers and dragoons, and 0.06% in the *Feld-Artillerie Haupt-Corps*.

Appendix VI

Regimental Officers by Nationality

(omitting groups of less than 1 percent)

Regimental Officers as a Whole
Hungary:	18.02 percent
(20.00 with Transylvania)	
Reich:	17.84
Bohemia:	10.03
Lower & Upper Austria, Vienna:	9.46
Netherlands & Luxembourg:	8.85
Prussian Silesia:	5.34
Austrian Italy:	3.81
Italy (other):	3.31
Moravia:	3.16
Lorraine:	2.68
Ireland:	2.11
Transylvania:	1.98
Prussia (other):	1.41
Styria, Tyrol:	1.28 each

Ensigns, Cornets and Second-Lieutenants
Hungary:	16.52
(18.73 with Transylvania)	
Reich:	15.87
Bohemia:	11.66
Lower & Upper Austria, Vienna:	9.88
Netherlands & Luxembourg:	9.45
Austrian Italy:	5.07
Prussian Silesia:	4.91
Italy (other):	3.94
Moravia:	2.91
Lorraine:	2.48
Transylvania, Ireland:	2.21 each
Prussia (other):	1.19
Croatia (regular army):	1.07
Tyrol:	1.02

First-Lieutenants
Reich:	20.28
Hungary:	18.12
(19.48 with Transylvania)	
Bohemia:	9.70
Lower & Upper Austria, Vienna:	9.14
Netherlands & Luxembourg:	7.77
Prussian Silesia:	5.77
Moravia, Italy (other):	3.76 each
Lorraine:	2.80
Slavonia (regular army):	1.72
Austrian Italy:	1.52
Styria:	1.44
Transylvania, Ireland:	1.36 each
Tyrol:	1.20

Captain
Hungary:	19.61
(21.95 with Transylvania)	
Reich:	18.40
Netherlands & Luxembourg:	9.71
Lower & Upper Austria, Vienna:	9.54
Bohemia:	7.72
Prussian Silesia:	5.46
Austrian Italy:	3.90
Moravia:	3.12
Lorraine:	2.86
Ireland:	2.77
Transylvania:	2.34
Tyrol:	1.73
Italy, Prussia (other):	1.64 each
Styria:	1.04

Major
Hungary:	19.68
(21.25 with Transylvania)	
Reich:	18.11
Bohemia:	14.17
Lower & Upper Austria, Vienna:	7.87
Netherlands & Luxembourg:	7.08
Moravia, Styria, Austrian Italy, Prussian Silesia:	3.93 each
Lorraine, Prussia (other):	3.14 each
Vorder-Österreich:	3.07
Italy (other):	2.36
Transylvania, Swedish Pomerania:	1.57 each

Lieutenant-Colonel
Hungary:	25.00
(28.84 with Transylvania)	
Reich:	13.46
Bohemia:	9.61
Prussian Silesia:	7.69
Netherlands & Luxembourg:	6.73

Austrian Italy, Italy (other):   4.80 each
Lower & Upper Austria, Vienna;
  Transylvania; Ireland: 3.84 each
Lorraine: 2.88
Styria, Tyrol, Spain, Prussia (other): 1.92 each

Colonel Commandant
Reich: 21.15
Hungary: 16.34
  (no entries for Transylvania)
Lower & Upper Austria, Vienna: 12.50
Bohemia: 6.73
Prussian Silesia: 5.76
Italy (other):   4.80
Netherlands & Luxembourg: 3.84
Prussia (other):   2.88
Moravia, Tyrol, Lorraine, Ireland,
  Swedish Pomerania, Poland: 1.92 each

Steady regimental service and the large numbers of the relevant officers probably account for the striking consistencies up to and including the rank of captain, after which the smaller cohorts and the influence of privilege produce more and more aberrations.

Appendix VII

Age and Service of the Regimental Officer

Average Age

By Arms of Service
Infantry:	29
Cuirassiers:	30
Dragoons:	33.5
Hussars:	37
Artillery:	43
Pioniere, Mineurs, Sappeurs:	28
Croats & Regt. Simbschen:	27

By Rank
Ensigns, Cornets, Second-Lieutenants:	24
German infantry:	23
Hungarian infantry:	23
Netherlands infantry:	25
Italian infantry:	25
Cuirassiers:	29
Dragoons:	27
Hussars:	34
Others:	No records entered
First-Lieutenants:	32
German infantry:	30
Hungarian infantry:	31
Netherlands infantry:	34
Italian infantry:	34
Cuirassiers:	32
Dragoons:	33
Hussars:	38
Artillery:	43
Pioniers, Mineurs, Sappeurs:	35
Croats & Regt. Simbschen:	37
Captains:	36
German infantry	36
Hungarian infantry:	36.5
Netherlands infantry:	33.5
Italian infantry:	38
Cuirassiers:	36
Dragoons:	38
Hussars:	39
Artillery:	48
Pioniere, Mineurs, Sappeurs:	29
Others:	No records entered
Majors:	39
German infantry:	33
Hungarian infantry:	39.5
Netherlands infantry:	40.1
Italian infantry:	45
Cuirassiers:	35
Dragoons:	41
Hussars:	39
Artillery:	42
Pioniere, Mineurs, Sappeurs:	41
Croats & Regt. Simbschen:	42
Lieutenant-Colonels:	43
German infantry:	42
Hungarian infantry:	33
Netherlands infantry:	38
Italian infantry:	49.5
Cuirassiers:	46
Dragoons:	42.5
Hussars:	42
Artillery:	58
Pioniere, Mineurs, Sappeurs:	None of this rank entered
Croats & Regt. Simbschen:	37
Colonel Commandants:	43
German infantry:	43
Hungarian infantry:	38
Netherlands infantry:	38
Italian infantry:	48
Cuirassiers:	47.5
Dragoons:	49
Hussars:	39
Artillery:	38
Pioniere, Mineurs, Sappeurs:	36
Croats & Regt. Simbschen:	49

Average Service

By Arms of Service
Infantry:	10
Cuirassiers:	15
Dragoons:	13
Hussars:	15
Artillery:	23
Pioniere, Mineurs, Sappeurs:	5.5
Croats & Regt. Simbschen:	12.5

By Rank
Ensigns, Cornets, Second-Lieutenants:	5
German infantry:	3
Hungarian infantry:	3
Netherlands infantry:	6
Italian infantry:	2
Cuirassiers:	8
Dragoons:	11
Hussars:	13
Artillery:	15
Pioniere, Mineurs, Sappeurs:	3
Croats & regt. Simbschen:	None of this rank entered
First-Lieutenants:	12
German infantry:	10
Hungarian infantry:	11
Netherlands infantry:	13
Italian infantry:	14
Cuirassiers:	14
Dragoons:	12
Hussars:	16
Artillery:	23.5
Pioniere, Mineurs, Sappeurs:	2
Croats & Regt. Simbschen:	13
Captains:	16
German infantry:	16
Hungarian infantry:	16
Netherlands infantry:	15
Italian infantry:	17.5
Cuirassiers:	17
Dragoons:	18
Hussars:	17.5
Artillery:	24.5
Pioniere, Mineurs, Sappeurs:	5
Croats & Regt. Simbschen:	12

Majors:	18
German infantry:	19
Hungarian infantry:	20
Netherlands infantry:	18
Italian infantry:	22
Cuirassiers:	16
Dragoons:	21
Hussars:	17
Artillery:	22
Pioniere, Mineurs, Sappeurs:	None of this rank entered
Croats & regt. Simbschen:	None of this rank entered
Lieutenant-Colonels:	23.5
German infantry:	22
Hungarian infantry:	19
Netherlands infantry:	17
Italian infantry:	21
Cuirassiers:	27
Dragoons:	25.5
Hussars:	22
Artillery:	37.5
Others:	None of this rank entered
Colonel Commandants:	24
German infantry:	24
Hungarian infantry:	23
Netherlands infantry:	25
Italian infantry:	37
Cuirassiers:	29
Dragoons:	25
Hussars:	22
Artillery:	9
Pioniere, Mineurs, Sappeurs:	None of this rank entered
Croats & Regt. Simbschen:	33

Appendix VIII

Recruiting *Rayons* Designated for the Cavalry

(in the order presented in KA HKR Protocolle 1758 October 698, HKR to all regiments of cuirassiers and dragoons, 31 October)

Regiment	Place
Ansbach:	Bernburg, Furth, Rothenburg-an-der-Tauber
Brettlach:	Vörder Osterreich
Württemberg:	Heilbronn, Rothenburg-an-der-Tauber
Hessen-Darmstadt:	Frankfurt, Friedberg
Zweibrücken:	Worms, Speyer
Erzherzog Leopold, Erherzog Joseph, Erzherzog Ferdinand:	Lower Austria
Löwenstein:	Vienna and Prague
Kalckreuth:	Styria
Gelhay:	Upper Austria
Savoyen:	Principality of Jägerndorf (excluding Troppau)
Trautmannsdorf:	Troppau
Birkenfeld:	Principality of Tetschen
Serbelloni:	Circles of Znaim and Iglau
Liechtenstein:	Circle of Brünn
Schmerzing:	Circle of Hradisch
Pálffy, Carl:	Circle of Olmütz
Portugal:	Circles of Prerau and Czaslau
Anhalt-Zerbst:	Circle of Chrudim
Modena, Alt-:	Circle of Bechin
Stampach:	Circle of Saaz
O'Donnell:	Circles of Leitmeritz and Rakonitz
Althann:	Circle of Kaurzim
Buccow:	Circle of Pilsen
Daun, Benedict:	Circle of Elbogen and District of Eger
Kollowrat:	Circles of Bechin and Prerau
Modena, Jung-:	Circle of Königgrätz
Sachsen-Gotha:	Circle of Bunzlau

Appendix IX
Civilian Trades by Category

Textile
Bleacher (*Bleicher*), clothmaker (*Tuchmacher*), cotton spinner (*Baumwollspinner*), dyer (*Färber, Wollgerber*), lace-maker (*Posamentirer, Schnürrbortenmacher*), linen weaver (*Leinweber*), silk weaver (*Seidenwirker*), spinner (*Spinner*), wool spinner (*Wollspinner*), velvet maker (*Sammetmacher*), weaver (*Weber*), stocking knitter (*Stricker, Strumpfstricker, Strumpfwirker*)

Clothing and Footwear
Cobbler (*Schuster*), button maker (*Knopfmacher*), furrier (*Kürschner*), glove maker (*Handschuhmacher*), hatter (*Hutmacher*), leather worker (*Gürtler, Lederer, Riemer*), shoemaker (*Czischenmacher, Schuhmacher*), tailor (*Schneider*), tanner (*Rotgerber*), wig-maker (*Peruquier*)

Building and Furnishing
Brickmaker/ layer (*Ziegelmacher, Ziegelstreicher, Ziegler*), cabinet maker (*Schreiner, Tischler*), carpenter (*Zimmermann*), chimney sweep (*Kaminfeger*), glazier (*Glaser*), mason (*Maurer*), painter (*Mahler*), plasterer (*Stuckator*), stone-cutter (*Steinhauer, Steinmetz*), sculptor (*Bildhauer*), slater/ tiler (*Schieferdecker, Ziegeldecker*)

Food Processing
Baker (*Bäcker*), brewer (*Brauer*), butcher (*Fleischhacker, Metzger*), cellarman (*Kellner*), confectioner (*Zuckerbäcker*), cook (*Koch*), distiller (*Brandweinbrenner*), miller (*Müller*)

Metal
Bell foundryman (*Glockengiesser*), coppersmith (*Kupferschmid*), hammersmith (*Hammerschmid*), iron worker (*Eisenhauer*), iron foundryman (*Eisengiesser*), nailsmith (*Nagelschmid*), needle maker (*Nadelmacher*), pewterer (*Zinngiesser*), smith (*Schmied*), tinsmith (*Klempner, Spengler*), wire drawer (*Drahtzieher*). N.B. farrier (*Huffschmied*) entered under 'Transport,' and the more advanced metal-working trades under 'Manufacturing and Processing'

Mining
Miner (*Bergmann*)

Transport
Boatman (*Schiffmann*), cartwright (*Wagner*), father (*Hufschmied*), saddler (*Sattler*), wheelwright (*Rademacher*)

Manufacturing and Processing
Basket maker (*Korbmacher*), bookbinder (*Buchbinder*), candlemaker (*Wachszieher*), clockmaker (*Uhrmacher*), cooper (*Binder, Bittner*), glassmaker (*Glasmacher*), grinder/polisher (*Schleifer*), cutler (*Messerschmid*), goldsmith (*Goldarbeiter*), gunsmith (*Büchsenmacher*), jeweller (*Juwelier*), locksmith (*Schlosser*), paper maker (*Papiermacher*), printer (*Drucker*), potter (*Haffner*), powder maker (*Pulvermacher*), ropemaker, (*Seiler*), salpetre-boiler (*Saliterbrenner*), salt-boiler (*Salzsieder*), sieve maker (*Siebmacher*), soap-boiler (*Seifensieder*), swordsmith (*Schwerdfeger*), tobacco processor (*Tobakspinner*), toolmaker (*Zeugmacher*), toy maker (*Spielmacher*), trellice maker (*Spaliermacher*), turner (*Drechsler*)

Medical
Apothecary (*Apotheker*), barber surgeon (*Bader, Barbirer, Chirurgus, Feldscher*), physician (*Medicus*), tooth-puller (*Kieffer*)

Students
Student (*Student*)

Service
Clerk (*Schreiber*), gamekeeper (*Jäger*), gardener (*Gärtner*), merchant (*Kaufmann*), merchant's assistant (*Kaufmannsdiener*), musician (*Musicus*), runner (*Läufer*)

Appendix X

Age and Service of Private Soldiers

AGE STRUCTURE OF PRIVATE SOLDIERS

Regular Infantry

	Average Ages	Largest Single Age
1754:	27	27 at 7.40 percent
1756:	27	22 at 5.92
1757:	25	22 at 7.92
1759:	25	20 at 9.86
1760:	25	22 at 7.89
1761:	24	20 at 9.14
1762:	25	25 at 7.92
1763:	24	22 at 9.32

Age Grouping

	16–20	21–25	26–30	31–35	36–40	41–45	46–50	51–55	56–60	61–65	66–70
1754	26.57	25.65	31.23	17.48	8.29	5.93	2.68	1.46	0.54	0.06	0.06
1756	13.50	28.70	24.07	19.33	8.47	3.61	1.04	0.46	0.15	0.16	0.06
1757	11.91	34.07	28.46	14.53	6.42	3.08	0.98	0.47	0.04	–	–
1759	12.74	36.41	25.26	11.91	8.72	2.84	1.49	0.38	0.20	0.01	–
1760	12.44	37.04	23.71	13.28	7.93	3.38	1.57	0.44	0.13	0.02	–
1761	18.29	38.91	24.50	9.08	6.75	1.91	0.41	0.05	0.05	–	–
1762	9.56	35.6	27.82	11.23	8.09	4.40	2.21	0.64	0.29	0.09	–
1763	13.48	43.53	29.59	8.66	2.56	1.68	0.36	0.10	0.02	–	–

Specialised Infantry Average Ages

Staabs-Infanterie   1759: 20
'Artillerie-Füsiliere   1760: 23
Volontiers Silesiens   1760: 23
Feld-Jäger   1760: 26
Loudon Grenadiere   1761: 25

Cuirassiers

	Average Ages	Largest Single Age
1756:	30	31 at 9.62 percent
1759:	26	22 at 8.12
1760:	26	23 at 9.12
1762:	27	26 at 8.39
1763:	28	26 at 8.13

Age Grouping

	16–20	21–25	26–30	31–35	36–40	41–45	46–50	51–55	56–60	61–65	66–70
1756	10.50	16.41	21.00	30.63	7.65	7.22	4.59	1.96	–	–	–
1759	9.04	35.39	17.81	13.00	12.75	6.19	3.66	1.49	1.49	0.54	0.07
1760	7.33	37.75	17.11	14.40	11.00	5.09	3.44	2.20	1.42	0.09	0.04
1762	3.16	30.27	28.11	9.98	11.85	8.20	5.02	2.01	0.95	0.14	0.19
1763	6.28	23.63	33.69	12.57	10.47	6.37	3.18	2.76	0.83	0.16	0.09

Dragoons (excl. *Staabs-Dragoner*)

	Average Ages	Largest Single Age
1756:	24	21 at 9.35 percent
1759:	26	22 at 8.22
1760:	26	27 at 13.19
1762:	26	24 at 10.41
1763:	26	24 at 9.79

Age Grouping

	16–20	21–25	26–30	31–35	36–40	41–45	46–50	51–55	56–60	61–65	66–70
1756	20.83	38.76	20.07	9.46	4.04	3.40	2.14	0.63	0.37	0.12	–
1759	10.92	37.27	14.94	15.47	11.17	5.77	3.48	1.30	0.45	0.19	–
1760	7.23	38.24	22.45	13.15	9.95	5.01	2.54	1.11	0.20	–	–
1762	9.12	34.40	28.48	10.72	11.20	3.36	2.44	0.48	–	–	–
1763	5.86	39.23	30.18	10.41	7.48	2.86	3.18	0.68	0.12	–	–

Staabs Dragoner

	Average Ages	Largest Single Age
1762:	20	20 at 17.27 percent

Hussars (excl. *Grenz-Husaren*)

	Average Ages	Largest Single Age
1759:	24	22 at 14.41 percent
1760:	25	23 at 12.30
1762:	26	24 at 10.25

Age Grouping

	16–20	21–25	26–30	31–35	36–40	41–45	46–50	51–55	56–60	61–65	66–70
1759	11.29	48.76	15.56	7.60	10.40	3.86	1.64	0.49	0.19	0.07	0.04
1760	17.72	48.95	17.72	9.63	11.62	4.98	2.37	0.24	0.19	–	–
1762	8.25	44.25	35.87	6.12	4.57	0.62	0.25	0.25	–	–	–

Infantry Regiment Simbschen

	Average Ages	Largest Single Age
1756:	24	20 and 22 at 7.58 each

Slavonian Broder Croats

	Average Ages	Largest Single Age
1756:	24	23 at 10.28 percent

Age Grouping

	16–20	21–25	26–30	31–35	36–40	41–45	46–50	51–55	56–60	61–65	66–70
1756	21.29	33.64	19.72	13.57	6.78	3.34	0.93	0.44	0.14	–	–

Creutzer and St. Georger Warasdiner Croats

	Average Ages	Largest Single Age
1757:	26	23 at 9.94 percent

Age Grouping

	16–20	21–25	26–30	31–35	36–40	41–45	46–50	51–55	56–60	61–65	66–70
1757	11.38	34.00	30.88	14.88	6.55	1.50	–	0.61	0.05	–	–

Artillerie Haupt-Corps

	Average Ages	Largest Single Age
1762:	24	22 at 16.09 percent

Age Grouping

	16–20	21–25	26–30	31–35	36–40	41–45	46–50	51–55	56–60	61–65	66–70
1762	10.37	49.57	31.11	7.24	1.12	0.48	0.04	0.04	0.04	–	–

Netherlands Artillery

	Average Ages	Largest Single Age
1762:	27	23 at 9.34 percent

Age Grouping

	16–20	21–25	26–30	31–35	36–40	41–45	46–50	51–55	56–60	61–65	66–70
1762	10.37	49.57	31.11	7.24	1.12	0.48	0.04	0.04	–	–	–

(N.B. As mentioned in the main text, the only surviving muster lists for the two artillery corps date from late in the war, by when most of the veterans had wasted out)

Mineurs

	Average Ages	Largest Single Age
1762:	25	26 at 9.92 percent

Sappeurs

	Average Ages	Largest Single Age
1762:	26	24 at 10.14 percent

Pioniere

	Average Ages	Largest Single Age
1760:	25	22 at 7.36 percent

SERVICE STRUCTURE OF PRIVATE SOLDIERS

Regular Infantry

	Average Service	Largest Single Year
1754:	4	5 at 22.79 percent
1756 (under peacetime conditions):	5.5	6 at 11.87
1756 (under emergency conditions):	1	−1 at 37.17
1757:	5	7 at 10.34
1759:	1	1 at 27.01
1760:	1	1 at 25.91
1761:	1	1 at 37.10
1762:	2	3 at 18.54
1763:	2	1 at 19.27

Service Grouping

	−1–1	2–5	6–10	11–15	16–20	21–25	36–30	31–35	36–40
1754	10.98	54.83	27.06	5.18	1.32	0.39	0.06	–	0.06
1756 (under peacetime conditions):	15.30	29.71	37.03	15.26	1.75	0.57	0.11	0.06	0.06
1756 (under emergency conditions):	53.06	29.04	10.72	6.28	0.21	0.05	0.05	–	–
1757	15.17	31.76	34.39	15.89	2.12	0.96	0.06	0.05	0.02
1759	50.04	22.37	15.56	7.81	3.45	0.43	0.16	0.02	-
1760	44.24	33.04	10.24	8.56	3.22	0.49	0.12	0.03	0.02
1761	48.42	43.24	4.01	2.26	1.70	0.12	0.06	–	–
1762	30.64	47.80	8.06	4.94	6.38	2.00	0.02	–	0.02
1763	30.18	52.73	7.45	4.85	3.32	0.06	0.15	0.03	0.03

Specialised Infantry (where evidence available)
Average Service
Artillerie-Füsiliere 1760:	1
Volontiers Silesiens 1760:	1
Loudon Grenadiere 1761:	1

Cuirassiers

	Average Service	Largest Single Year
1756:	9.5	11 at 12.00 percent
1759:	4	2 at 15.98
1760:	3	3 at 19.02
1762:	5	4 at 11.83
1763:	6	5 at 12.84

Service Grouping

	−1–1	2–5	6–10	11–15	16–20	21–25	36–30	31–35	36–40
1756	17.46	13.75	22.24	31.21	4.12	5.13	4.57	0.42	–
1759	19.27	32.54	11.55	17.76	10.21	5.76	1.19	1.08	0.04
1760	17.04	40.42	9.01	16.14	7.44	4.51	2.59	1.79	0.14
1762	3.48	44.21	20.35	5.80	13.72	6.97	2.64	1.68	0.26
1763	13.09	27.10	30.91	8.87	11.65	3.16	3.50	1.07	0.08

Dragoons (excl. *Staabs-Dragoner*)

	Average Service	Largest Single Year
1756:	1	−1 at 33.16 percent
1759:	3	2 at 17.22
1760:	3.5	3 at 18.77
1762:	4	4 at 39.16
1763:	3.5	3 at 24.00

Service Grouping

	−1–1	2–5	6–10	11–15	16–20	21–25	36–30	31–35	36–40
1756	49.67	27.72	9.93	6.03	2.13	1.61	2.37	0.25	–
1759	26.09	30.05	7.31	20.18	8.25	5.37	1.45	0.81	0.12
1760	16.63	41.71	12.81	13.48	8.13	4.33	1.86	0.77	0.04
1762	23.24	39.16	17.17	9.20	8.25	1.58	1.08	0.15	–
1763	6.26	70.04	10.54	2.91	5.03	1.39	3.18	0.12	–

Hussars (excl. *Grenz-Husaren*)

	Average Service	Largest Single Year
1759:	2	2 at 44.21
1760:	2.5	3 at 32.16
1762:	3	5 at 42.03

Service Grouping

	−1–1	2–5	6–10	11–15	16–20	21–25	36–30	31–35	36–40
1759	19.18	53.74	1.61	11.82	10.04	2.14	0.64	0.29	0.02
1760	12.97	58.80	3.17	10.55	11.59	1.94	0.83	–	–
1762	24.83	74.88	0.24	–	–	–	–	–	–

Infantry Regiment Simbschen

	Average Ages	Largest Single Age
1756:	5	2 at 20.74 percent

Croats. No service entered on muster lists

Artillerie Haupt-Corps

	Average Ages	Largest Single Age
1762:	3.5	4 at 22.31 percent

Service Grouping

	−1–1	2–5	6–10	11–15	16–20	21–25	36–30	31–35	36–40
1762	14.09	61.32	22.22	1.47	0.78	0.03	–	–	–

Netherlands Artillery

	Average Ages	Largest Single Age
1762:	5	6 at 31.29 percent

Service Grouping

	−1–1	2–5	6–10	11–15	16–20	21–25	36–30	31–35	36–40
1762	7.73	30.69	50.63	2.24	0.32	–	0.32	–	–

Mineurs

	Average Ages	Largest Single Age
1762:	4.5	6 at 17.48 percent

Service Grouping

	–1–1	2–5	6–10	11–15	16–20	21–25	36–30	31–35	36–40
1762	14.68	41.94	25.14	6.25	4.17	9.96	–	0.69	–

Sappeurs (N.B. including service in other branches of the army)

	Average Ages	Largest Single Age
1760:	2	2 at 21.84 percent

Service Grouping

	–1–1	2–5	6–10	11–15	16–20	21–25	36–30	31–35	36–40
1760	27.66	47.55	10.16	11.14	2.9	–	–	–	–

Pioniere. No service entered on the muster lists

Appendix XI

Losses through Desertion

BY ARM OR SPECIALISED REGIMENT
(as percentage of average total loss per regiment in the Seven Years War)

Regular infantry:	21.73
Volontiers Silesiens:	58.89
Loudon Grenadiere:	54.68
Feld-Jäger & Pioniere:	29.23
Staabs-Infanterie:	40.03
Artillerie-Füsiliere:	33.86
Anhalt-Zerbst Bn.:	54.33
Mainz:	21.60
Blau- and Rot-Würzburg:	26.23
Toscana:	28.46
Cuirassiers:	12.26
Dragoons:	9.00
Regular hussars:	13.83
Feld Artillerie:	21.80
Ingenieurs:	No desertion
Sappeurs:	42.18
Croatian infantry:	2.10
Grenz-Husaren:	3.79

(N.B. It must be stressed that these figures are percentages of the *loss* per unit or formation, and must be understood in this perspective)

Numbers of Deserters per Regiment
(in descending order)

Regular Infantry

1	Salm:	1,779
2	Platz:	1,656
3	Deutschmeister:	1,169
4	Bayreuth:	1,125
5	Kollowrat:	1,099
6	Luzan:	1,078
7	Colloredo, Jung-:	1,073
8	Mercy:	1,068
9	Colloredo, Jung-:	1,063
10	Angern:	1,005
11	Pálffy:	1,002
12	Daun, Leopold	992
13	Ligne:	979
14	Clerici:	974
15	Esterházy, Nicolaus:	969
16	Arenberg:	960
17	Simbschen:	957
18	Haller:	925
19	Thürheim:	916
20	Pallavicini:	911
21	Erzherzog Carl:	910
	Lothringen:	910
22	Hildburghausen:	895
23	Baden-Baden:	881
24	Wied:	868
25	Neipperg:	846
26	Marschall:	845
27	Puebla:	823
28	Harsch:	794
29	Preysach:	780
30	Wolfenbüttel, Alt-:	775
31	Esterházy, Joseph:	762
32	Harrach:	752
33	Lacy:	719
34	Gaisruck:	710
35	Andlau:	703
36	Batthyány:	697
	Maguire:	697
37	Königsegg:	680
38	Moltke:	649
39	Bethlen:	645
40	Tillier:	627
41	d'Arberg:	623
	Waldeck:	623
42	Sincere:	617
43	Kaiser:	608
44	Wallis:	558
45	Giulay:	552
46	Daun, Heinrich:	540
47	Forgách:	429
48	Baden-Durlach:	442
49	Wolfenbüttel, Jung-:	421
50	Starhemberg:	398
51	Botta:	326
52	Sachsen-Gotha:	268
53	Los Rios:	224

'New Corps'

1	*Staabs-Infanterie:*	1,607
2	*Artillerie-Füsiliere:*	1,258
3	*Loudon Grenadiere:*	1,209

4	*Volontiers Silesiens:*	871
5	*Pioniere & Feld-Jäger:*	269
6	Anhalt-Zerbst Bn.:	138

Auxiliary Regiments

1	Blau- & Rot-Würzburg:	1,267
	(both regiments together)	
2	Mainz:	1,010
3	Toscana:	857

Cuirassiers

1	Stampa:	207
2	Kalckreuth:	166
3	Stampach:	142
4	Modena, Alt-:	137
5	Ville:	122
6	Buccow:	116
7	Schmerzing:	115
8	Ansbach:	114
9	O'Donnell:	111
10	Trautmannsdorf:	110
11	Anhalt-Zerbst:	108
12	Daun, Benedict:	98
13	Brettlach:	94
14	Pálffy, Carl:	80
15	Portugal:	71
16	Leopold, Erzherzog:	59
17	Ferdinand, Erzherzog:	55
18	Serbelloni:	47

Dragoons

1	Löwenstein, Jung-:	494
2	Sachsen-Gotha:	341
3	Württemberg:	311
4	Zweibrücken:	252
5	Joseph, Erzherzog:	249
6	*Staabs-Dragoner*:	227
7	Modena, Jung-:	183
8	Batthyány:	167
9	Darmstadt:	151
10	Liechtenstein:	133
11	Althann:	131
12	Savoyen:	124
13	St. Ignon:	93
14	Kollowrat:	91

Regular Hussars

1	Dessewffy:	614
2	Kaiser:	583
3	Hadik:	560
4	Baranyay:	482
5	Széchenyi:	447
6	Bethlen:	340
7	Pálffy, Rudolph:	317
8	Kálnoky:	311
9	Nádasdy:	256
10	Esterházy, Paul:	239
11	Splényi:	230
12	Palatinal (Török):	229

Feld Artillerie:	941
Ingenieurs:	No deserters
Sappeurs:	27

Croatian Infantry
(N.B., individual desertion, as opposed to unauthorised mass homeward departure)
Carlstädter
Oguliner:	24
Szluiner:	18
Liccaner:	13
Ottocaner:	11

Warasdiner
St. Georger:	36
Creutzer:	23

Slavonian
Peterwardeiner:	144
Gradiscaner:	21
Broder:	7

Banal
2nd	33
1st	30

Appendix XII
Background of the Personnel of the Field Artillery

Nationality
Nationality of Private Gunners
(*Büchsenmeister,* 2,787 individuals)
Bohemia: 62.68 percent
Lower and Upper Austria, Vienna: 8.82
Netherlands: 8.49
  (of which 4.01 Luxembourg)
Moravia: 8.07
Reich: 5.66
Prussian Silesia: 1.75
Hungary: 1.14
Other: 3.39

Nationality of NCOs
Bohemia: 67.57 percent
Reich: 7.57
Netherlands: 7.56
  (of which 3.63 Luxembourg)
Lower and Upper Austria, Vienna: 6.06
Moravia: 3.33
Hungary and Transylvania: 2.72
Other: 5.19

Nationality of Officers (nearest equivalent ranks)

Second-Lieutenants
Bohemia: 59.85 percent
Lower and Upper Austria, Vienna;
  Reich: 9.85 each
Hungary and Transylvania: 4.22
Netherlands and Luxembourg; Moravia: 3.52 each
Other: 9.15

First-Lieutenants
Bohemia: 48.14 percent
Netherlands and Luxembourg: 14.81
Reich: 11.11
Hungary and Transylvania; Austrian
  Italy: 7.40 each
Lower and Upper Austria, Vienna;
  Lorraine: 3.70 each
Other: 3.70

Captains
Bohemia: 44.10 percent
Lower & Upper Austria, Vienna: 14.70
Reich: 11.76
Netherlands and Luxembourg: 8.82
Other: 20.58

Majors
Bohemia: 66.66 percent
Other: 33.33

Lieutenant-Colonels
Bohemia: 80.00 percent
Other: 20.00

Origins of Bohemian Artillerymen by identifiable Circles
(all ranks, 1,855 individuals)
Saaz: 21.29 percent
Bechin: 15.74
Pilsen: 15.36
Leitmeritz: 10.13
Prague city: 7.33
Prachin: 6.36
Königgrätz: 4.74
Bunzlau: 3.71
Rakonitz: 2.91
Beraun: 2.64
Kaurzim: 2.53
Czaslau: 2.37
Chrudim: 2.04
Eger: 1.90
Elbogen: 0.86

Surnames of Bohemian Artillerymen (all ranks), by Type

	German	Czech	Not conclusively identifiable
Officers:	57.89	21.05	21.05
NCOs:	47.57	41.85	10.57
Non combatants:	58.33	25.00	16.60
Buchsenmeisten	49.02	40.78	10.18

Type of Former Civilian Trades of Artillery Personnel, All Locations (2,311 cases)

Textile:	8.39 percent
Clothing and Footwear:	23.66
Building and Furnishing:	11.68
Food Processing:	14.84
Metal (incl. Mining in this case):	3.59
Transport:	0.86
Manufacturing and Processing:	12.24
Medical:	3.20
Students:	9.38
Service:	12.11

Types of Identifiable Surnames of Bohemian Artillerymen (all ranks), by Circle or Large Town

Percentage of German Surnames

Elbogen:	87.50
Eger:	83.33
Saaz:	78.22
Budweis (town):	75.00
Leitmeritz:	59.04
Pilsen, excl. Pilsen town:	45.62
Rakonitz:	38.88
Czaslau:	38.63
Bechin, exc. Tabor:	38.16
Bunzlau:	36.23
Prague:	36.02
Königgrätz, excl. Königgrätz town:	33.33
Kaurzim:	29.41
Prachin:	28.81
Pilsen town:	27.27
Chrudim:	26.31
Königgrätz town:	23.07
Tabor (town):	22.22
Beraun:	20.20
Kolin (town):	Nil
Unidentifiable Bohemian locations:	50.62

Percentage of Czech Surnames

Kolin (town):	100.00
Kaurzim:	72.34
Königgrätz town:	69.23
Pilsen town:	68.18
Prachin:	66.10
Beraun:	62.26
Czaslau:	61.36
Königgrätz, excl. Königgrätz town:	58.66
Tabor (town):	56.55
Bunzlau:	56.52
Chrudim:	55.26
Rakonitz:	51.85
Prague:	50.00
Bechin, exc. Tabor:	49.23
Pilsen, excl. Pilsen town:	41.44
Leitmeritz:	29.93
Budweis:	16.66
Saaz:	14.68
Elbogen:	12.50
Eger:	8.33
Unidentifiable Bohemian locations:	41.25

Notes

Abbreviations used in the notes
(see Bibliography for details)
Armfeldt= Krigsarkiv, Sweden, Fromhold Armfeldt, *Remarquer öfvn k.k. Osterrikiska Arméen samt militarisk Dagbok*, Stockholm, 27 May 1763
Bratislava= Státny Ústredeny Archív SSR
Pálffy-Daun= Fond Pálfi-Daun
Rudolph Pálffy= C.K. Linia Pálffyovskéhor. Rudolf Pálffy (1719-1768)
Budapest, Military Institute-- Hadtörténeti Intézet és Muséum
HL= Hadik Levéltar
Budapest, State Archives= Magyar Országos Levéltár
HHStA= Haus- Hof- und Staaatsarchiv, Vienna
KA= Kriegsarchiv, Vienna
CA= Cabinettsakten
FA= Feldakten
HKRA= Hofkriegsrätliche Akten
HKR Protocolle= Protocols of the HKR (*Hofkriegsrat*)
M.M.T.O= depositions of candidates for the Military Order of Maria Theresa
Nostitz-Rieneck= papers of the Nostitz-Rieneck *Hofcommission*, 1791 etc
Vincennes A1 = Service Historique de l'Armée de Terre, Vincennes, correspondance générale

PART I THE FOUNDATIONS

1 Austrian Beginnings
1. Maria Theresa, *Kaiserin Maria Theresias Politische Testament*, 1952, 29–30

2 The Heart of the Monarchy
1. Francis Stephen, in Arneth, 1863–79, V, 495
2. Arneth, 1863–79, VII, 222
3. To Sylva Tarouca, February 1766, Kornauth, 1978, 8
4. Rousset, 1868, 101
5. Archenholtz, 1840, I, 116
6. Podewils, 1937, 48
7. KA CA 1760 XI 20, Montazet to Maria Theresa, 18 November
8. Podewils, 1937, 48
9. Budapest, Institute, HL 1762 X 558, Hadik to Prince of Stolberg-Gedern, 17 October
10. Armfeldt, 279
11. Ibid., 165–6
12. Gorani, 1944, 102
13. HHStA Kriegsakten 419, Kaunitz to Loudon, 18 August 1760
14. KA FA 1760 XIII 127, Loudon to Daun, 11 March
15. Budapest, State Archives, Habsburg Szalád Magyárovári Levéltár, Prince Albert of Sachsen-Teschen, *Mémoires de ma Vie*
16. Khevenhüller-Metsch, 1907–72,1V, 141
17. Podewils, 1937, 146
18. Ligne, 1927, I, 144
19. Podewils, 1937, 146

493

20 HHStA Staatskanzlei Vorträge 83, Kaunitz to Maria Theresa, 28 April 1758
21 Vortrag of 1767, quoted in Schilling, 1994, 348–9
22 Vincennes A1 3433, Montazet, Vienna, 29 June 1757
23 Personal communication from Professor Franz Szábo
24 HHStA Staatskanzlei Vorträge 82, Kaunitz to Maria Theresa, 22 June 1757
25 HHStA Staatskanzlei Vorträge 87, Kaunitz to Maria Theresa, 20 October 1760
26 Khevenhüller-Metsch, 1907–72, V, 14
27 HHStA Kriegsakten 413, Browne to Kaunitz, Kolin, 28 August 1756
28 HHStA Kriegsakten 418, Loudon to Kaunitz, Prossnitz, 7 March 1760; Loudon to Kaunitz, Zittau, 15 May 1760
29 HHStA Staatskanzlei Vorträge 87, Kaunitz's *Rapport à Sa Majesté l'Impératrice Reine contenant le Projet de l'Établissement d'un Conseil d'État pour les Affaires Interns des Pais Héreditaires de l'Allemagne,* 9 December 1760
30 E.g. KA CA 1760 V 19, Daun to Koch, 20 May; Budapest, Military Archives, HL 1762 I 93, O'Donnell to Hadik, 30 January
31 KA CA 1761 VI 6, Daun to Maria Theresa, 22 June
32 Arneth, 1863–79, IV, 99
33 KA CA 1761 VIII 7 D, Daun to Maria Theresa, 17 August
34 Arneth, 1863–79, V, 224
35 Walter, 1938, 347
36 Armfeldt, 129
37 E.g. HHStA Kriegsakten 87, Anon. *Verzeichniss deren vornehmsten und wichtigsten Vortheile, welche die Kayserl. Königl. Armeen, denen Königl. Preussischen zum voraus lassen,* ('Outline of the principal and most important advantages which the Austrian armies concede to the Prussian,'), undated. Hereafter referred to as '*Verzeichniss.*' See also Cogniazzo, 1788–91, II, 25–6
38 Arneth, 1863–79, VI, 246
39 KA HKRA 1759 VIII 8, HKR to Daun, 18 August
40 KA CA 1761 VIII 15, Daun to Maria Theresa, 28 August
41 KA CA 1761 IX 6, Daun to Maria Theresa, 11 September
42 KA CA 1761 VIII 7, Daun to Maria Theresa, 17 August
43 KA CA 1761 VI 5, Daun to Maria Theresa, 11 June
44 KA CA 1761 VIII 7, Daun to Maria Theresa, 14 August
45 KA FA 1757 XIII 467, Anon., *Réflexions sur la Campagne de l'Année 1757*. For a similar argument see Khevenhüller-Metsch, 1907–72, IV, 42

3 The Territorial Base
1 Budapest, Military Institute, HL 1761 II 1, *FML.* Guasco to Hadik, 1 February
2 Ligne, 1795–1811, II, 201–2
3 HHStA Staatskanzlei Vorträge 90, Van Swieten's *Note sur la prétensions des Ambassadeurs,* etc., enclosed in Kaunitz to Maria Theresa, 13 November 1762
4 Arneth, 1863–79, IV, 51
5 KA HKR Protocolle 1758 March 670, Directorium, 21 March; HKR Protocolle 1762 February 140, Bournonville to the HKR, 9 February
6 Khevenhüller-Metsch, 1907–72, IV, 138
7 Komlos, 1989, passim
8 Wimmer, 1991, 148
9 Amfeldt, 50
10 Küchelbecker, 1732, 101
11 De Luca, 1791, I, 437
12 Ligne, 1928, I, 246
13 Ibid., I, 60
14 KA HKR Protocolle 1759 August 330/5, Directorium to Maria Theresa, 13 August. See also in same file, *Nota,* 11 August; HKR to the Directorium, Würzburg and Zweibrücken, 13 August
15 KA HKR Protocolle 1762 July 565, in HKR to Maria Theresa, 21 July

16　HHStA Kriegsakten 419, *Beantwortung der dem General Lacy vorgelegten Puncten des gesammten Kriegswesens betreffend,* 1759. See also Riesebeck, 1784, I, 412–3
17　Hermann, 1781–3, III, 34
18　Ibid., III, 45–6
19　Straka, 1965, 47
20　Ibid., 60
21　Küchelbecker, 1732, 115
22　Dickson, 1987, II, 394
23　Hermann, 1781–3, II, 118–9, 125
24　Gorani, 1944, 96
25　Hermann, 1781–3, II, 129–30
26　Ibid., II, 137
27　Küttner, 1801, IV, 82
28　Lord Stormont, 1765, in Dickson, 1987, II, 395. See also Armfeldt, 50–1
29　KA HKR Protocolle 1760 February 414, HKR to the Directorium, 18 February
30　KA HKR Protocolle 1761 August 291, HKR to Colonel Caprara, 21 August
31　KA HKR Protocolle 1758 March 694, Maguire to the HKR, 26 March, and Wolckenstein to the HKR, undated
32　KA HKR Protocolle 1758 March 694, de Fürst to Neipperg, 15 January
33　KA HKR Protocolle 1758 March 694, HKR to Maria Thereesa, 16 March
34　Ligne, 1795–1811, 159–60
35　Bérenger, 1985, 443
36　HHStA Kriegsakten 393, Conference of 30 July 1756
37　Military Conference of 12 March 1757, in Khevenhülller-Metsch, 1907–72, IV, 317–8
38　Gorani, 1944, 114
30　Küchelbecker, 1732, 82
40　Keyssler, 1751, I, 288
41　Küttner, 1801, III, 86
42　Gorani, 1944, 86
43　Retzow, 1802, II, 290–1
44　KA Kriegswissenschaftliche Mémoires, 1760, II, 27
45　Guibert [1773], 1803, 87
46　Küchelbecker, 1732, 87
47　Marshall, 1772, III, 307
48　Ligne, 1795–1811, I, 66
49　Armfeldt, 50
50　Riesebeck, 1784, I, 412
51　Conference on 'Illyrian' affairs, 21 April 1756, Khevenhüller-Metsch, IV, 155
52　Armfeldt, 44–5
53　Archenholtz, 1840, I, 75
54　Frederick to Plotho, Frederick, Politische Correspondenz, 1879–1939, XV, 171, no. 9,102
55　HHStA Kriegsakten 413, Prince Charles to Maria Theresa, 9 August 1757
56　KA Staatskanzlei Vorträge 79, Kaunitz to Francis Stephen, 30 November 1756
57　Marczali, 1910, 32–3
58　Ligne, 1795–1811, I, 165
59　HHStA Kriegsakten 387, *Rangs and Conduits Lista,* Königgrätz, 10 March 1757
60　December 1765, quoted in Teuber, 1895, I, 113
61　Keyssler, 1761, II, Part 1, 279
62　Guibert, 1803, II, 18
63　KA FA 1761 XIII 16 A, *FML.* Engelhardt (commandant of Carlsburg) to Leopold Pálffy, Kaschau, 30 April
64　Küchelbecker, 1732, 46–7
65　Khevenhüller-Metsch, 1907–72, V, 46
66　Ligne, 1795–1811, I, 150

67 KA HKR Protocolle 1757 December 527, HKR to all regiments, 27 December
68 Donati, 1982, 553
69 Vienna, 18 May 1759, Verri, 1879, I, 11
70 See Maria Theresa's patent for Lieutenant Alexandre Franquet, KA M.M.T.O., file Franquet
71 Vortrag of 4 October 1755 on the Conference of 24 September, Volz and Küntzel, 1899, 176
72 Küchelbecker, 1732, 133–4
73 Khevenhüller-Metsch, 1907–72, IV, 165
74 Arneth, 1863–79, IV, 451
75 Ibid., IV, 450–1
76 Dorban, in Hasquin, 1987, 115
77 Ruwet, 1962, 38–9, 4102, 45, 88
78 Armfeldt, 78
79 Ligne, 1928, I, 261
80 Ligne, 1795–1811, X, 105
81 Ibid., XV, 15
82 Ligne, 1928, I, 7
83 Ibid., I, 58
84 HHStA Staatskanzlei Vorträge 84, Kaunitz to Starhemberg, 2 February 1759
85 HHStA Kriegsakten 399, Markgraf Friedrich to Colloredo, Bayreuth, 16 September 1762
86 Conference notes, 5 August 1756, Khevenhüller-Metsch, 1907–72, IV, 200
87 Vincennes A 1 3514, comte de Goertz to Choiseul, Bamberg, 29 April 1759
88 HHStA Kriegsakten 399, Duke Friedrich of Sachsen-Gotha to Francis Stephen, 11 January 1762. See also the printed *Wahrhaffte Geschichte-Erzehlung von dem Reichs-Gesetzwiedrigen Verfahren des Kayseri. Königl. Kriegs-Commissariats wieder das Reichs-Fürstenthum Altenburg.*
89 KA HKR Protocolle 1758 March 496, Behm to Maria Theresa, 15 April 1758
90 Ulfeldt's vote, 26 May 1756, Khevenhüller-Metsch, 1907–72, IV, 169
91 1 March 1753, Ibid., III, 357–8
92 Carl Eugen to Maria Theresa, 7 August 1757, Ibid., IV, 385–6
93 HHStA Kriegsakten 415, Maria Theresa to Prince Charles, 4 October 1757
94 Budapest, Military Institute, HL 1761 X 461 A, Cammer-Collegium to Hadik, 10 October
95 Vincennes A 3514, comte de Goertz to Choiseul, Bamberg, 29 April 1759
96 Warnery, 1785–91, II, 48–9
97 Guibert, 1803, II, 36
98 Arneth, 1863–79, VII, 25
99 Bratislava, Pálffy-Daun, XXXIV, no. 409. Hildburghausen to Queen Charlotte, Vienna, 2 March 1762
100 KA CA 1760 III 14, Daun to Maria Theresa, 14 March
101 Arneth, 1863–79, IV, 165
102 KA CA 1757 XI 21, Anon. *Réflexions sur le parti, que l'on pourroit peut-être tirer du grand nombre des prisonniers Prussiens,* Vienna, 26 November
103 HHStA Kriegsakten 413, Prince Charles to Maria Theresa, 18 August 1757
104 KA FA 1761 XIII 9 A, Lacy's letters
105 Armfeldt, 151
106 Armfeldt, 149
107 Taaffe, 1856, 33
108 Schmidhöfer, 1971, 136
109 Schmid, 1968, 497
110 O'Connell, 1892, I, 103

4 Finance

1 HHStA Kriegsakten 403, *Summarischer Ausweiss Was zu Verpflegung der Armee vor das 1758te Militar-Jahr an baaren Geldt erforderlich, dann was hierauf mit dem- den 17ten Decembris erfolgten Schluss des Monats Novembris würcklich eingegangen, und hierauf annoch ruckständig, oder aber mehr, als zurepartirt gewesen, angeführt worden*
2 Volz and Küntzel, 1899, 462

3   Khevenhüller-Metsch, 1907–72, V, 143
4   24 June 1757, Arneth, 1863–79, V, 146
5   Dickson, 1987, II, 408
6   HHStA Staatskanzlei Vorträge 84, Kaunitz to Maria Theresa, 9 March 1759
7   HHStA Staatskanzlei Vorträge 90, Kaunitz to Maria Theresa, 16 November 1762
8   Dickson, 1987, II, 389–90
9   KA CA 1759 XIII 43, *Empfang derer zu dem Militari gewidmeter Fundorum*
10 Janetschek, 1959, 121
11 Dickson, 1987,11, 388
12 Schilling, 1994, 350
13 Kriegsakten 403, Anon., *Feld-Erfordernüss vor das bevorstehende 1758te militar-jahr*
14 8 and 9 July 1756, Volz and Küntzel, 1899, 462
15 Dickson, 1987, II, 117–8
16 HHStA Kriegsakten 403, *État des Exigences extraordinaires qu'on a fait après la Catastrophe du 5. Decembre 1757, pour remettre les Armées de Sa Majesté l'Impératrice Reine en état d'opérer l'Anné 1758*
17 HHStA Kriegsakten 403, *Militar Erfordernuss pro Ao 1761*
18 KA Nostiti-Rieneck 1792 XVII 4, *Summarischer Haubt-Erforderniss Aufsaz ...*, 8 November 1761
19 HHStA Kriegsakten 403, Maria Theresa to the Bohemian Repräsentation und Cammer, 14 September 1758
20 KA HKR Protocolle 1759 July 420, HKR to Daun, Kollowrat and Serbelloni, 21 July
21 KA CA 1761 XIII 29, *Betrachtung des Herren Generalen Grafen Giannini,* undated
22 HHStA Staatskanzlei Vorträge 87, Kaunitz, *Rapport à Sa Majesti l'Impératrice Reine ...*, 9 December 1760
23 HHStA Staatskanzlei Vorträge 88, *Votum des Hof- und Staats Canzlern Grafens zu Kaunitz Rittberg,* 17 October 1761

5 Diplomacy
1   Schilling, 1996, 30
2   Opinion on the Barrier Treaty, 17 March 1751, Khevenhüller-Metsch, 1907–72, III, 331
3   *Vortrag,* delivered in the Conference of 21 August 1755, Volz and Küntzel, 1899, 155
4   KA CA 1759 VIII 13, Maria Theresa to Daun, 15 August
5   Kaunitz to Esterházy, 22 August 1756, Volz and Küntzel, 1899, 546

PART II THE ARMY

6 The Army as a Whole
1   Arneth, 1863–79, IV, 21
2   Braubach, 1965, V, 217
3   HHStA Staatskanzlei Vorträge 90, Kaunitz to Maria Theresa, 25 November 1762
4   Maria Theresa, *Kaiserin Maria Theresias Politische Testament,* 1952, 72
5   HHStA Staatskanzlei Vorträge 90, Kaunitz to Maria Theresa, 25 November 1762
6   Cogniazzo, 1788–91, II, 188. For comments on this interpretation of Austria's defeats see also KA Krieswissenschaftliche Mémoires 1756 11 24, *Schreiben eines Officers von der Cavallerie an seinen Freund,* Königgrätz, 28 December 1756
7   Cogniazzo, 1779, 24
8   Ibid., 25
9   Ibid, 21–2
10 KA HKRA 1756 XIII 384 D, report on the *Musterung* of October 1755
11 Eichel to Finckenstein, 23 November 1760, in Frederick, *Politische Correspondenz,* 1879–1939, XX, 107, no. 12,530
12 Cogniazzo,1788–91, II, 182
13 Yorke,1913, III, 224
14 3 May 1760, in Frederick, *Politische Correspondenz,* 18791939, XIX, 318, no. 12,057
15 Warnery, 1788, 498
16 KA CA 1762 1114, Anon., *Patriotisch- Und mit der unumschränkten Wahrheit begleitete, ouch ohne mindesten Eigennutz oder besonderen Absehen aufgesezte ohnmassgebliche Reflexionen über ein und andere Verfassungen,*

oder eingeschlichenen Missbrauchen bey der Kayl. König. Armee ('Patriotic Reflections on Various Usages of the Austrian army, or Abuses which have crept therein, motivated only by an Interest for the Whole Truth, and devoid of Any Prejudice or Private Aims'), 7 March 1761. Hereafter referred to as 'Patriotic Reflections.' See Also HHStA Kriegsakten 387, 'Verzeichniss,' and KA CA 1758 III 1, representation of Lieutenant-Colonel Rebain, Neisse. 19 March. Rebain (an associate of the late *FM*. Browne) had been captured at Leuthen, and had an unique opportunity to compare the Austrian and Prussian practices at first hand.

17   Thiébault, 1813, III, 222
18   Cogniazzo, 1788–91, II, 184
19   E.g. Captain Johann Michael von Kemptern to the HKR, in KA HKR Protocolle 1758 March 694, Maguire to the HKR, 22 March
20   HHStA Kriegsakten 387, *Rangs und Conduits Lista,* regiment of Erzherzog Carl, Königgrätz, 10 March 1757
21   KA CA 1758 XII 5, Paul Carl Pálffy, Pressburg, 8 December
22   Neipperg's *Betrachtungen,* 20 July 1756, Khevenhüller-Metsch, 1907–72, IV, 183
23   Ligne, 1795–1811, I, 12; Cogniazzo, 1788–91, II, 184
24   Podewils, 1937, 47–8
25   KA CA 1762 III 4, *Patriotisch-… Reflexionen*
26   HHStA Kriegsakten 387, *Verzeichniss,* 1758; KA CA 1758 XII 5, *FM*. Paul Carl Pálffy, Pressburg, 8 December; KA CA 1760 XIII 8, *FML*. Joseph Prince Lobkowitz to Maria Theresa, *Ansicht zur Herstellung des alten östreich. Waffenruhmes,* undated 1760
27   KA Nostitz-Rieneck 1762 VI 535, nos. 1–5, *Lieber die Grundsätzen zu Bestimmung der Stärke des bei einer Armee erforderlichen Transport Furhwesens*
28   Janson, 1913, 164
29   KA CA 1758 XIII 1 B, Anon.
30   KA CA 1759 XIII 35, Anon., *Nota,* undated
31   KA FA 1759 XIII 35, *Lettres de la Campagne 1759*
32   KA FA 1760 XIII 126, Loudon to Daun, Pirna, 4 March
33   KA FA 1760 XIII 81, Maria Theresa, possibly to Lacy, 26 January
34   KA CA 1761 X 4, Daun to Maria Theresa, 2 October
35   HHStA Staatskanzlei Vorträge 88, *Votum des Hof- und Staaats-Canzlern Grafen zu Kaunitz Rittberg,* 17 October 1761
36   HHStA Kriegsakten 417, Maria Theresa to Daun, 17 October 1761
37   KA CA 1761 X 10, Daun to Maria Theresa, 23 October
38   Armfeldt, 166
39   Cogniazzo, 1788–91, IV, 142–3
40   Ibid., IV, 144
41   Armfeldt, 127
42   Ibid., 165–6
43   Ibid., 167
44   Cogniazzo, 1788–91, 1, 193
45   HHStA Nachlass Lacy I 4, Lacy to Baron Koch, with the army in Saxony, 4 December 1761
46   KA HKRA 1762 IX 2 A, *Summarischer Extract pro Julio* 1762
47   Cogniazzo, 1788–91, IV, 144
48   HHStA Nachlass Lacy I 4, Lacy to Baron Koch, with the army in Saxony, 4 December 1761
49   KA CA 1762 III 2, Lacy to Maria Theresa, 21 March
50   KA Nostitz-Rieneck 1792 V no. 13, Nostitz, *Betrachtungen über die Österreichische Cavallerie … 1733 … bis 1792*
51   KA HKRA 1756 XIII 379, *Verzeichnus. Was von nachstehend. Kayl. Königlichen Generlitätat, General.- Staab, Artillerie, und Ingenieurs Corps, dann Infanterie- und Cavallerie-Regimentern seit dem Ausbruch des fürgewesten Kriegs jeglichen Jahrs an Staabs-Officiers, Staabs Partheyen, Ober-Officiers und von Feldwäbel oder Wachtmeister an bis Gemeinen von dem Feind gefangen, vor dem Feind geblieben, an Blessuren oder Kranckheiten in denen Spitallern gestorben, desertiret, ansonsten seind verlohren als Invaliden entlassen, und an Pferden vermüsset worden*
52   Ligne, 1795–1811, II, 11. See also Cogniazzo, 1779, 140
53   Richter, 1845, 141

54 Ligne, 1795–1811, II, 11
55 Meininger, 1961, 106
56 *Regulament und Ordnung des gesammten Kaiserlich-Königlichen Fuss-Volcks,* 1749, II, 7
57 Teuber, 1895, I, 84
58 Kaunitz (ed. Bleckwenn, H.) *Votum über das Militare* [1761], 1974, 35
59 Ibid., 37–8
60 Ligne, 1795–1811, I, 156
61 Ibid., II, 201
62 KA HKR Protocolle 1758 January 81, HKR to Daun, 5 January
63 Ligne, 1795–1811, I, 91
64 Kaunitz (ed. Bleckwenn, H.) *Votum über das Militare* [1761], 1974, 38
65 KA HKRA 1756 XDI 384 A, Commissary Lutter, *Haupt-Muster Relation,* Prague, 22 March. On the inspection of the regiment of Joseph Esterházy, October 1755
66 HHStA Staatskanzlei Vorträge 88, *Votum des Hof- und Staats-Canzlern Grafens zu Kaunitz Rittberg,* 17 October 1761
67 Ligne, 1795–1811, II, 177
68 KA HKR Protocolle 1759 September 129, Mannagetta to Engelshoffer, July and September
69 KA HKR Protocolle 1761 November 411/11, d'Aspremont-Lynden to Maria Theresa, 10 November, and Maria Theresa's ruling thereon
70 All the following citations are drawn from the Geheimes Archiv Preussischer Kulturbesitz, Berlin, Hauptabteilung L Rep. 96 Militaria, in this case No. 601 C, Gellhorn, 'Extract einiger Nachrichten,' enclosed in Winterfeldt to Frederick, Potsdam, 29 July 1750.
71 No. 601 C, undated report from Gellhorn, in Winterfeldt to Frederick, Potsdam, 12 August 1751.
72 No. 601 C, Winterfeldes 'Notata', in Winterfeldt to Frederick, Potsdam, 24 July 1750.
73 No. 601 C, Gellhorn to Frederick, Rogan, 26 December 1749.
74 No. 601 C, Gellhorn to Frederick, Rogan, 24 December 1749.
75 No. 601 C, Gellhorn to Frederick, Rogan, 24 July 1750.
76 No. 601 E, Gellhorn's 'Notata', in Winterfeldt to Frederick, Potsdam, 24 July 1750.
77 No. 601 C, Gellhorn's 'Relation über Östreichischen Umbstände, sowohl dem Militari, Civili, als Landt Mähren betreffendt,' in Winterfeldt to Frederick, Berlin, 29 July 1750.
78 No. 601 C, Winterfeldes 'Notata', in Winterfeldt to Frederick, Potsdam, 24 July 1750.
79 No. 601 E, Gellhorn's 'Notata', in Winterfeldt to Frederick, Berlin, 23 January 1754.
80 No. 601 C, Winterfeldes 'Notata', in Winterfeldt to Frederick, Potsdam, 23 July 1750.
81 No. 601 E, Gellhorn's 'Notata', in Winterfeldt to Frederick, Berlin, 23 January 1754.
82 No. 601 C, Winterfeldt to Frederick, Borschau, 10 July 1750.
83 No. 601 C, Gellhorn to Frederick, Rogan, 24 December 1750.
84 No. 601 C, Winterfeldes 'Notata', in Winterfeldt to Frederick, Potsdam, 24 July 1750.
85 No. 601 E, Gellhorn's 'Notata', in Winterfeldt to Frederick, Berlin, 23 January 1754.
86 No. 601 D, Wiedemann to Frederick, Potsdam, 12 October 1754.
87 No. 601 C, Winterfeldt's 'Notata, in Winterfeldt to Frederick, Potsdam, 24 June 1750.
88 No. 601 C, Winterfeldt to Frederick, Borschau, 10 July 1750.
89 No. 608 O, Warnery to Frederick, Oels, 25 June 1754.

7 The Rosenkavalier goes to War – The Austrian Officer

1 Ligne, 1795–1811, L 141
2 Cogniazzo, 1779, 109
3 KA CA 1762 DI 4 C, *Patriotisch-… Reflexionen*
4 Khevenhüller-Metsch, 1707–72, III, 162
5 KA CA 1762 III 4 D, *Patriotisch-… Reflexionen.* See also Fekete de Galantha [1787], 1921, 37–8; Berenhorst, 1798–9, II, 56
6 Lehmann, 1894, 11
7 KA CA 1761 III 4 C, *Patriotisch-…Reflexionen*
8 Ligne, 1795–1811, II, 149

9 Allmayer-Beck, 1967, 19
10 HHStA Nachlass Lacy I 3, *Zueignungs Schrifft* on the art of war, undated
11 Frederick to Keith, before Prague, 24 May 1757, Frederick, *Politische Correspondenz,* 1879–1939, XV, 75, no. 8,983
12 Ligne, 1795–1811, XVIII, 59
13 Esterházy, 1747, 401; *FM* Khevenhüller, quoted in Teuber, 1895, I, 80
14 KA HKR Protocolle 1757 April 213, Directorium to the HKR, 4 April
15 Verri, 1879, I, 32–3
16 KA CA 1762 III 4 C, *Patriotisch-… Reflexionen.* See also Ligne, 1795–1811, II, 148–9; Berenhorst, 1798–9, III, 146–7
17 Cogniazzo, 1779, 110–11
18 CA 1762 III 4 C, *Patriotisch-…Reflexionen;* Ligne, 1795–1811, II, 149
19 HHStA Kriegsakten 387, *Rangs und Conduits Lista,* Königgrätz, 10 March 1757
20 Gorani, 1944, 59
21 See the comment in Pichler, 1844, I, 5–6
22 Cogniazzo, 1779, 117
23 Teuber, 1895, I, 79
24 KA Nostitz-Rieneck 1792 II 21, *Note*
25 Vincennes A 1 3433, Montazet, Vienna, 29 June 1757
26 KA CA 1761 VIII 15, Daun to Maria Theresa, 31 August
27 HHStA Kriegsakten 416, *Species Facti,* in Daun to Kaunitz, Münchengratz, 4 April 1759
28 HHStA Kriegsakten 416, Daun to Kaunitz, 5 May 1759
29 KA CA 1759 XII 5, Daun to Maria Theresa, 6 December. See also the verdict of de Ligne, in Ligne, 1795–1811, II, 96–7
30 KA FA Korps Loudon VI 33 A, Kaunitz to Loudon, 13 June
31 KA CA 1762 III 4 D, *Patriotisch-… Reflexionen*
32 Gorani, 1944, 43
33 Ibid., 35
34 Ligne, 1795–1811,11, 4
35 HHStA Kriegsakten 384, Lacy to Matthias Kurländer, 18 April 1751
36 Gorani, 1944, 12
37 KA Neustädter Akten 1751 1, *Protocol Commissionis,* 28 November 1751
38 KA Neustädter Akten 1751 3, *Anfang, Wachstum und dermahlige Einrichtung des freyherrlich Chaosischen Stiffts zu Wienn*
39 KA Neustädter Akten 1754, Maria Theresa to Blümegen, 18 January 1754
40 Leitner von Leitnertreu, 1858, I, 75
41 Bever, 1762, 111, 114–5
42 KA Neustädter Akten 1751 1, Maria Theresa's note to the protocol of the first sitting
43 Printed *Benachrichtigung von der auf allerhöchste Anordnung Ihrer Kaiserl. Königl. Majestät, in der Wienerische Neustadt errichtenden Adelichen MilitarAcademie,* Vienna 1752, unpaginated
44 Bever, 1762, 113
45 KA Neustädter Akten 1751 1, Maria Theresa's note to the protocol of the first sitting
46 KA Neustädter Akten 1751 71, 72, *Verhaltung*
47 Armfeldt, 131
48 Bever, 1762, 114
49 KA Neustädter Akten 1751 71, 72, *Verhaltung*
50 KA Neustädter Akten 1753 9, Thürheim's *Pro Memoria,* Wiener Neustadt, 11 September 1753
51 KA CA 1760 VI 1, Daun to Maria Theresa, 2 June; KA CA 1760 IX 29, Daun to Maria Theresa, 29 September
52 Bever, 1762, 112
53 By an order of 24 November 1756, see HKR Protoccolle 1758 January 711, HKR to Colonel Commandant d'Aysasa of the Darmstadt Dragoons
54 HHStA Nachlass Lacy DI 2, Lacy to 'Angelo,' 9 November 1761
55 Guglia, 1917, II, 22

56 KA CA 1762 DI 4 D, *Patriotisch-...Reflexionen*
57 KA Nostitz-Rieneck 1792 DI 1, Francis Stephen, *idee qui mest venue pour trouver avec les fonts destine pour le militaire*
58 KA Kriegswissenschaftliche Mémoires 1756 II 24, *Schreiben eines Officiers von der Cavallerie an seinen Freund*, Königgrätz, 28 December 1756
59 Conference of 18 May 1757, Khevenhüller-Metsch, IV, 340
60 Gorani, 1944, 47
61 Ligne, 1795–1811,11, 148
62 KA HKR Protocolle 1762 April 295, HKR to Maria Theresa 25 April
63 Esterházy 1747, 334–5
64 Gorani, 1944, 59
65 Armfeldt, 60–1
66 Budapest, Military Institute, HL 1760 VII 155, *Puncta* for Colonel Sprung, 29 July
67 Armfeldt, 46
68 I-IHStA Nachlass Lacy III 2, *Receuil des lettres à des dames,* 25 April 1760
69 HHStA Kriegsakten 418, Loudon to Kaunitz, 28 July 1760
70 Khevenhüller-Metsch, 1907–72, IV, 103
71 KA M.M.T.O., file Bethlen, Bethlen to Kaunitz (?), 25 June 1758
72 Ligne, 1795–1811, I, 130–1
73 KA CA 1760 XIII 8, *FML*, Joseph Lobkowitz, *Ansicht zur Herstellung des alter östreich. Waffenruhmes;* KA CA 1760 III 4 D, *Patriotisch-... Reflexionen;* Armfeldt, 45–6; Ligne, 1795–1811, XXVIII, 59
74 Bratislava, Fond Pálffy-Daun, XXXIV, no. 414, Daun to Birkenfeld, 16 September 1759
75 KA Nostitz-Rieneck 1792 F IV no. 3, Baron de Vigneul, undated
76 KA CA 17621114 D, Patriotisch-... Reflexionen
77 KA CA 1762 VII 21, Wöber to Maria Theresa, July, undated
78 HHStA Kriegsakten 390, Liechtenstein's opinion on the plan of campaign for 1760
79 CA 1760 III 14, Daun to Maria Theresa, 14 March
80 *Generals-Reglement,* 1769, 68
81 Ibid., 70
82 Cogniazzo, 1788–91, III, 135
83 Armfeldt, 153–4
84 FA 1760 XIII 85, Maria Theresa to anon., undated
85 Cogniazzo, 1779, 109–10
86 Ligne, 1795–1811, I, 128–9
87 HHStA Nachlass Lacy I112, *Receuil des lettres à des dames,* 2 December 1760
88 HHStA Nachlass Lacy DI 2, *Receuil des lettres à des dames,* 2 December 1760. On the difficulty of promoting Beck out to turn to *FML.* see KA CA 1757 VII, Daun to Koch, 26 July
89 Ligne, 1795–1811, II, 68–70
90 KA CA 1760 XIII 6, d'Ayasasa to Daun, undated
91 Bratislava, Fond Rod Amade Üchtritz, *G.d.C.* Philipp Gottfried Wöllwarth, *Kurze Beschreibung meiner geleisteten Dienste*
92 Gorani, 1944, 83
93 Ligne, 1795–1811, I, 127–8
94 Bratislava, Rudolph Pálffy, Karton 11, Colonel J.J. Hintzmann, 22 January 1759
95 HHStA Staatskanzlei Vorträge 87, Kaunitz to Maria Theresa, 30 November 1760
96 KA CA 1762 111 4 D, C, *Patriotisch-... Reflexionen*
97. KA CA 1762 III 4 E, *Patriotisch-... Reflexionen*
98. KA CA 1759 XI 22, Daun to Maria Theresa, 24 November
99. KA Nostitz-Rieneck 1792 F 11 no. 8, Anon., *Gedanken über das Kauffen und Verkaufen der Chargen in der Armee*
100. Bratislava, Rudolph Pálffy, Karton 11, HKR to Colonel Commandant Revitzky of the Rudolph Pálffy Hussars, 11 February 1760
101 St. Paul, 1914, xxii

102 Archives de la Ville de Bruxelles, Portfeuille no. 55, Correspondance du Capitaine Pesser, anon. to Pesser, 12 January 1761
103 Bratislava, Rudolph Pálffy, Karton 11, Second-Lieutenant Huszty to Revitzky, 29 October 1760
104 Budapest, Military Institute, HL 1762 I 93, O'Donnell to Hadik, Dresden 30 January, communicating general order from Daun
105 KA HKR Protocolle 1762 March 855, HKR to Lieutenant-Colonel Strasser von Neudegg, 23 March; HKR Protocolle 1762 May 561, Daun to Maria Theresa, 12 May
106 Budapest, Military Institute, HL 1758 II 40, Hadik to Daun, Teplitz, 19 February
107 Khevenhüller-Metsch, 1907–72, III, 181
108 Ibid., V, 35
109 KA CA 1760 III 14, Daun to Maria Theresa, 14 March. On the weight given to Daun's advice see KA FA 1757 XIII 686 D, Colonel Müffling to FM. Seckendorf, Zittau, 2 August
110 E.g. Kunisch, 1983, 63
111 KA CA 1761 VII 4, Daun to Maria Theresa, 6 July
112 Kunisch, 1983, 60
113 KA CA 1761 4, Daun to Maria Theresa, 6 July
114 KA FA 1760 XIII 12, Lacy to Daun, 11 March; KA CA 1760 XIII 6, d'Ayasasa to Daun, June, undated
115 Armfeldt, 153
116 KA CA VII 21, Wöber to Maria Theresa, undated
117 KA HKRA 1756 XIII 384 D, report on the Bohemian *Musterung* of October 1755
118 Armfeldt, 169–70
119 Archives de l'État á Arlon, Fonds Van Eyll, Dossier no. 159, *Correspondence du comte Frédéric de Bryas, Capitaine de Carabiniers,* de Bryas to Comel, Reichenberg, 14 March 1760
120 Archives de l'État a Arlon, Fonds Van Eyll, Dossier no. 159, *Correspondence du comte Frédéric de Bryas, Capitaine de Carabiniers,* de Bryas to Comel, Freiberg, 21 November 1761
121 KA HKR Protocolle 1761 January 717, anon., *Gehorsamste Anmerkung. Das neue Sistem betreffend,* January, undated
122 Archives de la Ville de Bruxelles, Portfeuille no. 255, *Correspondence du Capitaine Pesser,* Mme. Pesser to Segura, 16 February 1765
123 Guibert [1773], 1803, II, 114, I, 256
124 *Regulament für die Röm.- Kaislerich-Königliche Infanterie, Cavallerie and Feld-Artillerie,* 1758, 88
125 KA CA 1762 III 4 F, *Patriotisch-… Reflexionen*
126 KA CA 1758 III 1, Lieutenant-Colonel Rebain, 10 March. See also CA 1760 XIII *FML.* Joseph Lobkowitz, *Ansicht,* undated; *Militär Feld-Regulament,* 1759, unpaginated
127 St. Paul, 1914, xxxviii
128 Archives de l'État á Arlon, Fonds Van Eyll, Dossier no. 159, *Correspondance du comte Frédéric de Bryas, capitaine de Carabiniers,* Bryas to Comel, County of Glatz, 28 February 1761
129 Gorani, 1944, 10
130 Sermage, 1923, 16 December 1758, 236
131 Gorani, 1944, 116
132 Verri, 1879, I, 97
133 Gorani, 1944, 130–1
134 Ibid., 13
135 Khevenhüller-Metsch, 1907–72, V, 17
136 Ortmann, 1759, 61
137 Lehndorff, 1910–13, I, 152
138 Lehndorff, 1907, 375
139 Lehndorff, 1910–13, I, 252–3
140 Gorani, 1944, 131
141 KA HKRA 1761 XII 1 Z, Gemmingen to Daun, citadel of Magdeburg, 30 October
142 Cogniazzo, 1788–91, IV, 100
143 KA HKR Protocolle 1758 February 365, HKR to Maria Theresa, 10 February
144 Lehndorff, 1910–13, I, 268

145 KA HKR Protocolle 1762 November 794, HKR to Fouqué, 38 November
146 Gorani, 1944, 161
147 Prittwitz, 1935, 175–6
148 Hülsen, 1890, 107
149 KA HKR Protocolle 1761 August 63, HKR Justiz Collegium, 4 August
150 HHStA Staatskanzlei Vorträge 82, Kaunitz to Maria Theresa, 17 March 1758, with Maria Theresa's marginal note
151 Khevenhüller-Metsch, 1907–72, V, 17
152 Gorani, 1944, 80
153 KA HKR Protocolle 1758 March 305, HKR to General Thurn, 12 March
154 KA HKr Protocolle 1761 November 794, Tückheim, 28 November
155 Archenholtz, 1840, II, 131
156 Ibid., 11,131
157 HHStA Staatskanzlei Vorträge 88, Kaunitz to Maria Theresa, 29 September 1761
158 HHStA Staatskanzlei Vorträge 88, *Antwort Schreiben des H. General Baron Loudon,* Vienna, 30 September 1761. The correspondence was later put into print in rival Prussian and Austrian versions, see KA HKR Protocolle 1761 May 456 /4, Kaunitz to the HKR. 16 May
159 Hülsen, 1890, 107
160 KA HKRA 1761 XII 1 LL, Finck to Neipperg, Kufstein, 10 December
161 Esterházy, 1747, 408
162 Bratislava, Rudolph Pálffy, *Pro Nota,* as supplement to his *Observations Puncten* of 8 May 1763
163 *Instruction für die Kriegs-Commissariatische Beamten,* 1749, 231
164 *Infanterie Regulament,* 1769, 46
165 KA CA 1757 XIII 4, anon. and undated testimonial
166 Verri, 1879, I, 104–5
167 KA CA 1757 III 1, Rebain, Neisse, 10 March
168 KA CA 1762 4 C, *Patriotisch-... Reflexionen*
169 *Militär Feld-Regulament,* 1759, unpaginated
170 Gorani,1944, 105
171 CA 1762 III 4 E, *Patriotisch-... Reflexionen*
172 Armfeldt, 41
173 Ibid., 115
174 Verri, 1879, I, 26, 30, 48–9
175 HHStA Kriegsakten 387, *Verzeichniss*
176 Armfeldt, 110–11
177 Vincennes A 13433, Champeaux, 17 June 1757
178 Ligne, 1795–05, II 197
179 Khevenhüller-Metsch, 1907–72, V, 88
180 KA CA 1762 III 4 D, *Patriotisch-... Reflexionen*
181 KA HKR Protocolle 1760 December 294, Maria Theresa to O'Donnell, Loudon and Hadik, 15 December
182 KA HKR Protocolle 1759 March 802, General Auditor Ignaz John, *Unterthünig-Gehorsamster Vortrag,* Prague, 6 March
183 KA CA 1759 VIII 14, Thomas Ignaz Pock to Maria Theresa, 17 August
184 KA CA 1763 DI 4 D, *Patriotisch-... Reflexionen*
185 Armfeldt, 101
186 KA CA 1763 III 4 D, *Patriotisch-... Reflexionen*
187 CA 1761 VIII 1, Daun to Francis Stephen, 3 August
188 CA 1762 DI 4 A, *Patriotisch-... Reflexionen*
189 Ligne 1795–1811, II, 98–100
190 Gorani, 1944, 81–2
191 Ibid, 122
192 KA CA 1762 III 4 D, *Patriotisch-... Reflexionen*
193 Esterházy,1747, 347–8

194 Gorani, 1944, 111
195 KA CA 1762 III 4 E, *Patriotisch-... Reflexionen*
196 KA CA 1758 HI 1, Rebain, Neisse, 1 March. See also HHStA Kriegsakten 387, *Verzeichniss*
197 Ligne, 1795–1811, II, 83. See also Cogniazzo, 1779, 51
198 Ligne, 1795–1811, II, 74–5
199 Vincennes A 1 3522, Choiseul to Montazet, Bautzen, 13 September 1759
200 KA CA 1762 III 4 E, *Patriotisch-... Reflexionen*
201 Gorani, 1944, 102. See also HHStA Kriegsakten 387, *Verzeichniss*
202 Warnery, 1788, 391
203 HHStA Kriegsakten 390, Liechtenstein on the plan of operations for 1760, undated. See also Budapest, Military Institute, HL 1761 XII 652, Albert Prince of SachsenTeschen to Hadik, 9 December
204 KA CA 1760 DC 10, Daun to Maria Theresa, 8 September
205 KA Kriegswissenschaftliche Mémoires 1760 II 27, Daun's comments on Frederick's *General Principia*
206 HHStA Kriegsakten 387, *Verzeichniss;* KA CA 1760 XIII 7, *FML.* Joseph Lobkowitz, *Ansicht,* undated; KA CA 1762 III 4 C, *Patriotisch-... Reflexionen*
207 KA CA 1759 IX 19, Daun to Maria Theresa, 18 September
208 Bratislava, Rudolph Pálffy, *Verhaltung überhaupts. Welche von denen unter meinen Brigade Stehenden Löbl. Houssaren Regimentern genauestens zu observiren seindt,* 14 November 1757
209 HHStA Nachlass Lacy III 2, Lacy to Daun, Dallwitz, 11 October 1761
210 VincennesA1 3433, Champeaux, 17 June 1757
211 HHStA Kriegsakten 389, anon., *Ohnmassgeblichste Gedancken über den dermaligen Stand des Kriegs,* undated
212 Waddington, 1899–1914, IV, 73, 74
213 KA CA 1761 11I 4 C, *Patriotisch-...Reflexionen*
214 KA HKR Protocolle 1757 March 6, Maria Theresa to Daun, 27 March
215 KA HKR Protocolle 1759 April 124, Daun to Maria Theresa, Münchengrätz, 3 April
216 KA HKR Protocolle 1760 March 154, HKR to the JustizCollegium, *Specification,* 27 March
217 KA HKR Protocolle 1760 December 294, Maria Theresa to O'Donnel, Loudon and Hadik, 15 December
218 KA HKR Protocolle 1761 January 520, *Eingaab,* undated
219 KA HKR Protocolle 1760 September 16, Colonel Waldstein to the HKR, 10 September
220 Budapest, Military Institute, HL 1761 III 131, Hadik to Colloredo, Cronach, 16 March; HL 1761 IV 224, Hadik to Colloredo, Cronach, 26 April
221 KA HKR Protocolle 1759 July 172, Zorn von Plobsheim to the HKR, Gorlitzheim, 23 July
222 Budapest, Military Institute, Hadik's Letter Book, O'Donnel to Hadik, 17 February 1762
223 KA FA 1758 X 181, on the promotion of officers after Hochkirch, from Lacys papers, with marginal notes by Daun
224 HHStA Kriegsakten 387, *Verzeichniss*
225 *Militär Feld-Regulament,* 1759, unpaginated
226 E.g. KA CA 1758 XIII 21, anon., *Très respectueuses Nottes. Par lesquelles j'ai l'honneur de recommender plusieurs bons sujets du corps de carabiniers et des grenadiers à cheval,* undated
227 HHStA Kriegsakten 387, *Rangs und Conduits Lista,* regiment of Erzherzog Carl, Königgrätz, 10 March 1757
228 Podewils, 1937, 48
229 Cogniazzo, 1779, 111–12
230 Broucek, 1982, 140–1
231 KA M.M.T.O., *Nota der Bohmisch-Österreichisch. Hofcanzley* to Kaunitz, 22 March 1760. The same applied to the Knights of the Military Order of Maria Theresa
232 Broucek, 1982, 135
233 See the applications of *GFWM.* Wied, 24 December 1760, and Colonel de Bosfort, 2 January 1761, KA M.M.T.O., files Wied, Bosfort
234 KA CA 1760 IX 29, Daun to Maria Theresa, 29 September
235 KA M.M.T.O., file Beck, Beck to Kaunitz, 23 January 1760
236 KA CA 1761 VIII 14, Daun to Koch, 24 August
237 Armfeldt, 134
238 Cogniazzo, 1779, 108

239 KA M.M.T.O., file Brunyan, Brunyan to Maria Theresa, undated
240 KA M.M.T.O., file de Ville, attestation of Draskovich, 23 February 1760
241 Ligne, 1795–1811, I, 138. See also Cogniazzo,1779, 108
242 Ligne, 1795–1811, III, 221–2
243 KA HKR Protocolle 1762 December 264, Gemmingen to the HKR, 2 December
244 Budapest, Military Institute, HL 1757 III 23, Browne to Hadik, Prague, 7 February
245 Ligne, 1928, I, 61
246 Bratislava, Rudolph Pálffy, Karton 9, Rudolph Pálffy, orders of the day, 12 June 1759
247 Verri, 1879, Lichtenau, 2 August 1759
248 Waddington, 1899–1914, IV, 31
249 KA HKR Protocolle 1760 September 16, Colonel Waldstein to the HKR, 10 September
250 Budapest, Military Institute, HL 1757 III 61 B, HKR to Browne, 8 March
251 Gorani, 1944, 56
252 Ibid., 121
253 KA Kriegsakten 387, *Rangs und Conduits Lista,* Königgrätz, 10 March 1757
254 Ligne, 1795–1811, I, 250
255 HHStA Kriegsakten 426, Daun to Kaunitz, 20 February 1759
256 Northumberland County Record Office, North Gosforth, Butler (Ewart) Mss ZBU B2/1, Count Henri Callenberg to Horace St. Paul, Brussels, 13 August 1757
257 Budapest, Military Institute, Hadik's letter book, Hadik to Colonel Sprung, 29 September 1761
258 KA HKR Protocolle 1758 March 388, as reported by Colonel Bender to the HKR, Görlitzheim, 7 August 1758
259 Gorani, 1944, 51
260 Ligne, 1795–1811, II, 221
261 Gorani, 1944, 110, 118
262 KA CA 1760 I 20, Daun to Maria Theresa, Dresden, 28 January
263 Marcus, 1927, 50
264 KA CA 1761 III 4 E, *Patriotisch-…Reflexionen*
265 Ligne, 1928, I, 221
266 Gorani, 1944, 157
267 KA HKR Protocolle 1758 March 690, HKR to Maria Theresa, 17 March
268 KA HKR Protocolle 1761 August 310, Resolution on the HKR's *Vortrag* of 12 August
269 KA HKR Protocolle 1759 March 560, HKR to Daun, 15 March
270 Gorani, 1944, 84
271 KA HKR Protocolle 1760, 32185/1, Gribeauval to the HKR, Dresden, 2 February
272 E.g. Conservatoire National des Arts et Metiers, 1956, 7
273 KA CA 1762 III 4 D, *Patriotisch-…Reflexionen.* See also Verri,1879, I, 96–7

8 Adam Bauer – The Austrian Private Soldier
1 Vincennes A1 3484, Stainville to Belle-Isle, 2 October 1758
2 Kaunitz, *Votum über des Militare,* 2 October 1761, Bleckwenn,1974, passim
3 Conference of 29 April 1757, Khevenhüller-Metsch, 1907072, IV, 362
4 Straka, 1965, 60–1
5 KA HKR Protocolle 1758 May 170, HKR to the Directorium and others, 5 May
6 KA HKR Protocolle 1759 November 199, Resolution on the Commissaries' report of 10 November
7 KA HKR Protocolle 1758 May 170, Vogtern to the HKR, Hermannstadt, 22 April
8 KA HKR Protocolle 1758 May 378, HKR to d'AspremontLynden, 13 May
9 KA HKR Protocolle 1757 November 474, HKR to the Directorium, 19 November
10 KA HKR Protocolle 1760 February 611, Directorium to the HKR, 23 February
11 KA HKR Protocolle May 170, Vogtern to the HKR, Hermannstadt, 22 April
12 *Instruction für die Kriegs-Commissariatische Beamten,* 1749, 6
13 KA HKR Protocolle 1761 November 291, HKR to Colonel Caprara, 16 November
14 KA CA 1761 X 13, Daun to Maria Theresa, 27 November

15 HHStA Staatskanzlei Vorträge 84, Kaunitz to Maria Theresa, 28 January 1759
16 HHStA Staatskanzlei Vorträge 84, Kaunitz to Maria Theresa, 9 March 1759
17 KA HKR Protocolle 1760 October 175, *Pro Memoria,* 11 October
18 HHStA Kriegsakten 405, Feld Kriegs Commissarius Weiss, *Pro Memoria,* Günzburg, 1 November 1758
19 KA HKR Protocolle 1760 March 591, HKR to Burmann, 25 March
20 KA HKR Protocolle 1760 December 229, *Reichs-Canzley* to HKR, 11 December; HKR Protocolle 1761 November 1 HKR to Burmann, 1 November
21 Ligne, 1795–1811, XXVIII, 60
22 KA HKR Protocolle 1761 August 320, Maria Theresa to Leopold Pálffy, 21 August
23 Esterházy, 1747, 311
24 Ligne, 1795–1811, I, 208
25 KA HKR Protocolle 1760 December 171 /1, Burmann to the Directorium, 18 December
26 Cogniazzo, 1779, 90
27 E.g. appeals of the mothers of Joseph Ohmann and Peter Szüllyö in KA HKR Protocolle 1758 September 434 and HKR Protocolle 1759 June 389
28 Ligne, 1795–1811, I, 207
29 KA CA 1758 XII 5, Pálffy, Pressburg 8 December
30 KA HKR Protocolle 1762 November 714, Maria Theresa's Resolution, dispatched 30 November
31 Corvisier, 1964, 643; Boios, 1990, 141
32 Komlos, 1985, 155–6
33 Cogniazzo,1779, 97
34 KA HKR Protocolle 1758 December 239, HKR to Daun, 13 December
35 KA HKR Protocolle 1761 January 406, HKR to Daun, the Directorium and Liechtenstein, 21 January
36 KA HKR Protocolle 1761 June 537, HKR to Daun, 19 June
37 E.g. KA HKR Protocolle 1760 December 344, HKR to Daun and the Directorium, 17 December
38 KA HKR Protocolle 1759 November 184, Cancellaria Intima Aulica to the HKR, 1 November
39 KA HKR Protocolle 1760 March 519, HKR to Burmann, 25 March
40 KA HKR Protocolle 1759 March 531, *Gehorsamster Vortrag,* enclosed in O'Donnell to Daun, Triebel, 21 August
41 KA HKR Protocolle 1762 December 489, HKR to Kollowrat, 16 December
42 KA CA 1761 X 4, Daun to Maria Theresa, 2 October
43 KA Musterungs Berichte 111 541, 31 January 1756
44 KA HKR Protocolle 1757 December 527, HKR to all regiments, 27 December
45 HHStA Kriegsakten 389, protocol of the Military Conference of 4 January 1758
46 KA HKR Protocolle 1758 April 177, Maria Theresa's Resolution of 1 April, and HKR's order of 3 April
47 HHStA Kriegsakten 405, Feld Kriegs Commissarius Weiss, *Pro Memoria,* Günzburg, 1 November 1758
48 Budapest, Military Institute, HL 1762 IV 352, O'Donnell to Hadik, 5 April
49 Budapest, Military Institute, HL 1761 IX 525, Daun to Hadik, Dresden, 9 November
50 Budapest, Military Institute, HL 1762 II 144, O'Donnell to Hadik, 15 February
51 KA Nostitz-Rieneck 1762 F DI no. 5, Moltke's *Puncten,* 29 February 1769
52 Cogniazzo, 1779, 120
53 See HHStA Kriegsakten 405, Feld Kriegs Commissarius Weiss, *Pro Memoria,* Günzburg, 1 November 1758; KA FA 1758 XIII E ad 177, *Instructions Puncten* for Gross
54 HHStA Kriegsakten 390, Daun to Maria Theresa, 6 October 1761
55 Budapest, Military Institute, HL 1762 II 98 B, Maria Theresa's Resolution on Rudolph Chotek's *Nota* of 22 January
56 Riesebeck, 1784, II, 137. See also KA HKR Protocolle 1760 January 534, on Colonel Colloredo to the HKR, Dresden, 20 January, on deserters from the regiment of Lacy
57 KA CA 1758 VIII 22, anon., *Articles Séparés, qu'on pourroit ordonner provisionellement pour la Campagne Prochaine,* undated
58 KA HKR Protocolle 1760 October 284, Würzburg, 14 October
59 *FM.* Khevenhüller's *Observations-Puncten* of 1722, in Wrede, 1898–1905, I, 98
60 *Instruction far die Kriegs-Commissariatische Beamten,* 1749, 6

61 KA FA 1759 XIII 467, anon., *Réflexions sur la Campagne de l'Année 1757*, undated
62 KA FA 1759 XIII 183, Loudon, *Allerunterthanig-Allergehorsamstes Pro Memoria*, undated
63 KA CA 1757 XI 2, anon., *Réflexions sur le parti, que l'on pourroit peut-être tirer du grand nombre des prisonniers prussiens*, 26 November. See also KA CA 1761 XIII 29, *Betrachtung des herren Generalen Grafen Giannini*, undated, 1761
64 KA HKR Protocolle April 269, HKR to Pachta and others, 17 April
65 KA HKR Protocolle 1760 October 175, HKR to Daun and others, 11 October
66 KA HKR Protocolle 1761 February 21/2, Maria Theresa's Resolution, 2 February. By the end of October 4,936 of the enemy natives were found to be serving in the army, of whom 4,665 had been enlisted in the infantry, with the largest single contribution (220) in the regiment of Carl Colloredo, see KA HKRA 1761 X 2 V, *Ausweis. Über die bey denen Kayl. Königl. Regimentern befindliche Königl. Preussische Unterthanen*, 30 October
67 KA Kriegsakten 300, *Sententia* of court martial, 11 February 1761
68 Ligne, 1795–1811, II, 196
69 Budapest, Military Institute, HL 1761 VII 327 A, HKR to Daun, undated; KA CA 1761 X 6, Daun to Maria Theresa, 6 October
70 Corvisier, 1964, 479
71 KA CA 1758 VII 22. Anon., *Articles Séparés, qu'on pourroit ordonner provisionellement pour la Campagne Prochaine*, undated
72 KA HKR Protocolle 1758, April 258, HKR to Daun and others, 7 April
73 HHStA Kriegsakten 405, Feld Kriegs Commissarius Weiss, *Pro Memoria*, Günsburg, 1 November 1758
74 HHStA Staatskanzlei Vorträge 80, Kaunitz to Maria Theresa, 22 June 1757
75 Esterházy, 1747, 315
76 KA Nostitz-Rieneck 1792 F VII no. 6., Hofrat J. Passelt, *Betrachtungen*, July 1790, describing the practice of the 1750s
77 Cogniazzo, 1788–91, DI, 303
78 *Regulament und Ordnung des gesammten KaiserlichKöniglichen Fuss-Volcks*, 1749, 15
79 *Regulament und Ordnung für gesamamte Kaiserl.-Königl. Cuirassiers und Dragoner Regimenter*, 1749–51, I, 3–4
80 Esterházy, 1747, 177
81 *Kurze Beschreibung und Heilungsart der Krankheiten, welche am öftersten in dm Feldlager beobachet werden*, 1758, 4
82 Ligne, 1795–1811, I, 109
83 HHStA Kriegsakten 387, *Verzeichniss*, 1758
84 Cogniazzo, 1788–91, DI, 5
85 Ligne, 1795–1811, I,107
86 *Instruction für die Kriegs-Commissaristische Beamten*, 1749, 49
87 Peeters, 'Desertie,' 1983, 388
88 KA HKRA 1756 XIII 384 D, *Kurtzer Auszug. Aus der Haupt-Muster Relation* (i.e. of 16 October 1755); KA HKRA 1756 XIII 383 A, *Haupt-Muster Relation*
89 KA HKR Protocolle 1758 October 461, HKR to Daun and the Directorium, 15 October
90 HHStA Staatskanzlei Vorträge 84, Kaunitz to Maria Theresa, 1 April 1759
91 Cogniazzo, 1788–91, III, 59. See also Budapest, Military Institute, HL Hadik's letter book, *FML*. Guasco to Hadik, 1 February 1761
92 Armfeldt, 41–2
93 Ibid., 105
94 KA Nostitz-Rieneck 1792 F VII no. 6, J. Passelt, *Betrachtungen*, July 1790, describing the practice of the 1750s
95 *Instruction far die Kriegs-Commissariatische Beamten,1749*, 108
96 KA CA 1762 III 4 C, *Patriotisch-… Reflexionen*
97 Ligne, 1795–1811, I, 190
98 KA CA 1758 XIII 22, anon., *Articles Séparés, qu'on pourroit ordonner provisionellement pour la Campagne Prochaine*, undated
99 *Militär Feld-Regulament*, 1759, unpaginated
100 Ibid.
101 Khevenhüller-Metsch, 1907–72, IV, 276

102 Ligne, 1795–1811, L 210–11
103 Budapest, Military Institute, HL 1761 IV 352, O'Donnell to Hadik, 6 April
104 Cogniazzo, 1779, 101
105 HHStA Kriegsakten 387, *Verzeichniss*
106 KA CA 1762 III 4 D, *Patriotisch-…Reflexionen*
107 *Regulament und Ordnung für gesammte Kaiserl.-Königlichen Cuirassiers und Dragoner Regimenter,* 1749–51, II, 44
108 Ligne, 1795–1811, I 175
109 KA HKR in Judicialibus, to an unnamed colonel, 19 April 1754
110 Cogniazzo, 1779, 123
111 Ibid., 120
112 Gorani, 1944, 94
113 Ibid., 94–5
114 *Regulament und Ordnung für gesamamte Kaiserl.-Königlichen Cuirassiers und Dragoner Regimenter,* 1749–51, II, 188
115 Ligne, 1795–1811, I, 145–6
116 Bratislava, Rudolph Pálffy, *Pro Nota,* as supplement to his *Observations Puncten* of 8 May 1762
117 Armfeldt, 107
118 Cogniazzo, 1779, 120
119 Armfeldt, 110
120 Ibid., 105
121 Ibid., 106–8
122 KA CA 1762 III 4 C, *Patriotisch-…Reflexionen*
123 Armfeldt, 109
124 KA HKRA 1756 XIII 379, *Verzeichnus*
125 Budapest, Military Institute, HL 1761 VI 246 A, copy of Maria Theresa's Resolution to the HKR
126 KA HKR Protocolle 1762 November 611, Vemeda to the HKR, Willsch, 24 October
127 KA HKR Protocolle 1762 November 611, Kerekes to the HKR, Reichenberg, 26 October
128 KA HKR Protocolle 1762 November 611, Altkirchen to the HKR, Cabitsch, 23 October
129 KA HKR Protocolle 1762 November 611, Eichholtz to the HKR, Eilenburg, 17 September
130 KA HKR Protocolle 1762 November 611, Zorn von Plobsheim to the HKR, 2 September
131 KA HKR Protocolle 1762 611, HKR to Maria Theresa, 6 November
132 Cogniazzo, 1779, 126
133 Ligne, 1795–1811, II, 199
134 *Exercitium für die sämmentliche K.K. Infanterie,* 1769, 58
135 KA HKR Protocolle 1762 June 146/2, Maria Theresa's Resolution, 6 June
136 Cogniazzo, 1779, 126
137 HHStA Kriegsakten 399, *Sententia,* 11 February 1761
138 Cogniazzo, 1779, 127
139 KA HKR Protocolle 1762 October 727, HKR to Daun and others, 23 September
140 KA Musterungs Berichte 111/118, June 1756
141 KA HKR Protocolle 1762 August 416, Daun to the HKR, Giersdorf, 8 August
142 Budapest, Military Institute, HL 1757 V 113, Daun to Hadik, 16 May. See also HL 1760 DI 89, Daun to Hadik, Pirna, 8 March
143 KA FA 1761 Korps Loudon X ad 15 A, testimony of Mandalieu, undated
144 Budapest, Military Institute, HL 1759 19 A, testimony of Gessler, undated
145 Ligne, 1928, I, 44
146 Bräker, 1852, 156
147 KA FA 1757 XIII 696 C, Colonel Müffling to FM. Seckendorf, Dux, 10 April
148 Gross, 1907, 83–5
149 Military Conference of 28 May 1757, Khevenhüller-Metsch, 1907–72, IV, 354
150 KA HKR Protocolle 1758 December 591, HKR to Serbelloni, 30 December
151 KA CA 1759 XI 22, Daun to Maria Theresa, 24 November
152 KA CA 1759 XII 5, Daun to Maria Theresa, 6 December

153 Schmutz, 1822, 60
154 KA HKR Protocolle 1758 March 672, HKR instruction, 21 March
155 Budapest, Military Institute, HL 1762 III 226 A, *K.K. Militär Oeconomie Hof Commission* to Burmütz, 13 August 1761
156 Fata, 1995,126–7
157 Boysen, 1795, II, 354–5
158 Prittwitz, 1935, 195
159 Archenholtz, 1840, II, 227
160 KA HKRA 1758 VII 17, Beck to the HKR, 12 July
161 KA CA 1759 XI 22, Daun to Maria Theresa, 24 November
162 Stephanie, 1771–87, III, 108–9
163 KA FA Hauptarmee 1762 VIII III E, captured letter, E. Flaminius to the Prussian captain Bone, *Relation von den durch die K.K. Kriegsgefangenen Croaten in Cüstrin den 1ten August 1762 erregten Auflauf*
164 KA HKR Protocolle 1758 January 148, HICR order, 7 January
165 Vincennes A1 3475, Boisgelin, Skalitz, 2 May 1758
166 KA FA Hauptarmee 1760 XI 5, *Aussage des auss der Preussischen Gefangenschaft ausgekommene Jägers*
167 Budapest, Military Institute, HL VII 430, Daun to Hadik, Seitendorf, 4 July
168 As above, see also FA Hauptarmee 1762 VII 26, HKR to Daun, 8 July
169 Lichtenau, 2 August 1759, Verri, 1879, I, 32
170 Ligne, 1794–1811, I, 244
171 Cogniazzo, 1779, 90–1
172 Anon., *Zuverlässige Nachrichten*, 1759, 7
173 Bratislava, Rudolph Pálffy, Karton 10, *Verhaltung überhaupts*, 14 November 1757
174 Bratislava, Rudolph Pálffy, Karton 10, Hadik, *Observations Puncten für mein unterhabenden Regiment, wie sich dasselbe in denen Kriegs Operationen zu verhalaten habe*, 1759
175 Cogniazzo, 1788–91, IV, 108
176 Cogniazzo, 1779, 131
177 KA HKR Protocolle 1761 August 20, Caprara to the HKR, Innsbruck, 8 July. For a similar case at Olmütz see KA HKR Protocolle 1760 April 144, HKR to the *Directorium,* 17 April; KA HKR Protocolle 1760 May 172, declaration of the Bishop of Olmütz, 10 May
178 KA Kriegswissenschaftliche Mémoires 1756 II 24, *Schreiben eines Officiers der Cavallerie an seinen Freund,* Königgrätz, 28 December 1756
179 KA HKR Protocolle 1762 July 827, HKR to Daun, 30 July
180 Ligne, 1795–1811, I, 140
181 Ibid., II, 87–8
182 Ibid., II, 86–7
183 KA CA 1762 III 4 C, *Patriotisch-... Reflexionen*
184 Ligne, 1795–1811, 1,150
185 KA CA 1762 III 4 C, *Patriotisch-... Reflexionen*
186 Ligne, 1795–1811, XII, 59
187 Cogniazzo, 1779, 139
188 Riesebeck, 1784, II, 141
189 Vincennes A1 3442, Marainville, 17 December 1757
190 Lloyd, 1781–90, II, vocvi.
191 Sonnenfels, 1783–7, III, 86
192 Ibid., III, 86
193 Stephanie, 1771–87, I, Introduction

9 The NCOs and the Unit Staffs
1 Budapest, Military Institute, HL 1760 VII 155, Hadik's *Puncta* for Colonel Sprung, 29 July
2 KA CA 1758 III 1, Rebain, Neisse, 10 March
3 KA Nostitz-Rieneck 1792 F IV no. 3, Vigneul, *Moyens d'attirer la bonne Bourgeoisie au service, de trouver là de bons officiers qui nous manquent*

4 KA CA 1762 III 4 C, *Patriotisch-... Reflexionen*
5 Esterházy, 1747, 425
6 Ibid., 409–10
7 KA CA 1758 XII 5, Carl Paul Pálffy, Pressburg, 8 December
8 Armfeldt, 47
9 KA HKR Protocolle 1759 April 583, Colonel Hrobschitzky, *Gehorsamste Nota*, 7 April
10 Gorani, 1844, 45
11 *Reglement für die sämmentliche K.K. Infanterie*, 1769, 108
12 KA HKR Protocolle 1759 June 166, Osterberg to the HKR, 13 May
13 Cogniazzo, 1779, 144
14 Archenholtz, 1974, 49
15 KA CA 1762 In 4 C, *Patriotisch-... Reflexionen*
16 Laukhard, 1930, I, 34

10 The Infantry
1 Esterházy, 1747, 259
2 Ligne, 1795–1811,11, 170–1
3 KA HKR Protocolle 1762 February 580, enclosed in Daun to Maria Theresa, 19 February
4 KA HKR Protocolle 1757 December 527, HKR to all infantry regiments, 27 December
5 Khevenhüller-Metsch, 1907–72, IV, 297. See also Armfeldt, 43
6 KA HKR Protocolle 1762 September 815, HKR to the regiments, 28 September
7 Armfeldt, 44, 50, 158
8 Ibid., 44–5
9 Khevenhüller-Metsch, 1907–72, V, 43
10 KA HKR Protocolle 1757 September 294, HKR to Károlyi and others, 14 September
11 KA HKR Protocolle 1758 February 175, HKR to the Directorium, 6 February
12 KA HKR Protcolle 1761 August 320, Maria Theresa to Leopold Pálffy, 18 August; HKR Protocolle 1761 December 359, HKR to Daun, 28 December
13 Warnery, 1788, 164
14 KA HKRA 1756 X 16 A, Charles to the HKR, Brussels, 28 October
15 Vincennes A1 3499, Champeaux, Czaslau, 12 June 1757
16 KA HKRA 1757 VIII 35, Dombasle to the HKR, Oldendorf, 6 August
17 Vincennes A1 3499, Champeaux, Schönberg, 11 September 1757
18 KA HKR Protocolle 1758 May 322, HKR to Daun, 10 May
19 KA HKR Protocolle 1758 May 322, Dombasle to the HKR, Würzburg, 8 June
20 KA HKR Protocolle 1762 July 565, HKR to Maria Theresa, 21 July
21 Ligne, 1795–1811, 11,173
22 HHStA Kriegsakten 390, Daun to Maria Theresa, 6 October 1761
23 Ligne, 1795–1811, II, 172–3
24 Kalckreuth, 1840, IV, 138
25 KA HKR Protocolle 1760 February 13, Directorium to the HKR, 31 January, and Maria Theresa's Resolution
26 Budapest, Military Institute, HL 1761 IV 197, *das samentliche Jäger Corps* to Hadik, Neustadtl, 9 April
27 KA FA 1759 XIII 183, Loudon, *Allerunterthänig-Allergehorsamstes Pro Memoria*, undated
28 Hanlon, 1998, 321–2
29 KA HKRA 1760 VIII 2 G, Loudon to Kaunitz (?), Gross Rosen, 17 August
30 Vincennes A1 3486, anon., *Mémoire sur les trouppes de Vurtenberg*
31 HHStA Kriegsakten 412, Fürstenberg to Colloredo, 16 August 1757
32 Vincennes A1 3486, anon., *Mémoire sur les trouppes de Vurtenberg*
33 Armfeldt, 27–8
34 KA HKR Protocolle 1757 August 616, Charles to Maria Theresa, enclosed in HKR to Charles, 27 August
35 KA HKR Protocolle 1762 January 147, HKR to Maria Theresa, 6 January, with Maria Theresa's note
36 Cogniazzo, 1779, 141–2
37 KA HKRA 1756 XIII 384 A, Commissarius Lutter, *Haupt-Muster Relation*, Prague, 22 March

38 KA CA 1758 III 1 B, Rebain, Neisse, 10 March
39 Cogniazzo, 1779, 143
40 Esterházy, 1747, 439–40
41 Armfeldt, 32–4
42 Cogniazzo, 1788–91, II, 184
43 *Regulament und Ordnung des gesammten Kaiserlich-Königlichen Fuss Volcks, 1749,* I, 1
44 Ibid., 138
45 Ibid., II, 22
46 Cogniazzo, 1788–91, II, 184. See also Armfeldt, 40–1; Ligne, 1795–1811,1, 12–13
47 Warnery, 1788, 126–7
48 Armfeldt, 157, 42
49 Ibid., 157–8

Chapter 11 The Cavalry
1 KA CA 1758 XII 5, Carl Paul Pálffy, 8 December
2 HHStA Kriegsakten 390, Daun to Maria Theresa, 6 October 1761 (copy in KA CA 1761 X 6)
3 KA HKR Protocolle 1762 December 833, HKR to Maria Theresa, 10 November, with Maria Theresa's Resolution
4 KA CA 1759 XI 22, Daun to Maria Theresa, 24 November
5 KA CA 1758 III 1 C, Rebain, Neisse, 10 March
6 KA HKR Protocolle 1759 March 569, HKR to Löwenstein, 22 March
7 KA HKRA 1760 VIII 1 V, Colonel Franz Pompeati to the HKR, Neumarkt, 18 July, on the delays experienced by the Sachsen-Gotha Dragoons
8 KA FA 1758 XIII 275
9 KA HKR Protocolle 1762 October 316, HKR to Maria Theresa, 2 September, enclosed in HKR to Liechtenstein, 12 October
10 *Regulament und Ordnung für die gesammte Kaiserl.-Königl. Cuirassiers und Dragoner Regimenter,* 1749–51, II, 9
11 Ibid., I, 7–8
12 KA CA 1758 XII 5, anon. memorandum with comments of Carl Paul Pálffy, 8 December
13 Ligne, 1795–1811, I, 28
14 KA CA 1758 XII 5, anon. memorandum, with comments of Carl Paul Pálffy to Maria Theresa, 8 December
15 *Kurze Beschreibung und Heilungsart der Kranckheiten welche am öftersten in dem Feldlager Beobachet werden,* 1758, 31
16 KA CA 1758 XII 5, Carl Paul Pálffy to Maria Theresa, 8 December
17 KA HKR Protocolle August 531, Colonel de Bosfort and others, *Gehorsamste Vortrag,* enclosed in O'Donnell to Daun, Triebel, 24 August
18 KA CA 1758 III 1 B, Rebain, Neisse, 10 March
19 KA CA 1758 XII 5, Carl Paul Pálffy to Maria Theresa, 8 December
20 KA CA 1758 III 1 B, Rebain, Neisse, 10 March
21 KA CA 1758 XII 5, Carl Paul Pálffy to Maria Theresa, 8 December
22 Armfeldt, 59
23 KA CA 1758 XII 5, Carl Paul Pálffy to Maria Theresa, 8 December. See also HHStA Staatskanzlei Vorträge, Protocol of the Conference of 21 January 1760
24 HHStA Kriegsakten 384, *GFWM.* Starhemberg to Kaunitz, Leitomischl, 5 March 1757
25 HHStA Staatskanzlei Vorträge 80, *Rimonta Contract,* 17 November 1756
26 KA CA 1757 XBI 13, anon. and undated memorandum; HHStA Kriegsakten 384, *GFWM.* Starhemberg to Kaunitz, Leitomisch, 5 Mary 1757
27 Cogniazzo, 1779, 152
28 HHStA Kriegsakten 389, Military Conference of 4 January 1758
29 Khevenhüller-Metsch, 1907–72, IV, 89 n.
30 Ligne, 1795–1811, L 33
31 Budapest, Military Institute, HL 1758 I 22, *Pro Memoria. Über das üble Verhalten im gegenwärtigen Kriege.* Full title below

32 Vincennes A1 3485, *Réponse au Mémoire,* October 1758; Ligne, 1795–1811, I, 33
33 KA FA 1760 XIII 81, Maria Theresa's conference notes
34 Cogniazzo, 1779, 69
35 KA Kriegswissenschaftliche Mémoires 1756 II 24, *Schreiben eines Officiers der Cavallerie an seinen Freund,* Königgrätz, 28 December 1756
36 KA CA 1758 XII 5, Carl Paul Pálffy to Maria Theresa, 8 December
37 KA Musterungs-Berichte 111 549, 31 January 1755
38 CA 1758 III 1 C, Rebain, Neisse, 10 March
39 Warnery, 1788, 128
40 KA Kriegswissenschaftliche Mémoires 1756 II 24, *Schreiben eines Officiers der Cavallerie an seinen Freund,* Königgrätz, 28 December
41 CA 1758 XII 5, anon. memorandum, quoted in Carl Paul Pálffy to Maria Theresa, 8 December
42 CA 1762 III 4 H, *Patriotisch-… Reflexionen*
43 HHStA Kriegsakten 417, Maria Theresa to Daun, 6 June 1762
44 KA HKR Protocolle 1758 January 85, HKR to the *Directorium,* 4 January
45 KA HKR Protocolle 1759 November 199, report of the commission of Leopold Pálffy to Maria Theresa, 10 November
46 HHStA Kriegsakten 390, Neipperg's plan of campaign for 1761, 27 December 1760
47 Teuber, 1895, I, III
48 KA HKRA 1757 XII 8, in HKR to Maria Theresa, 22 December
49 Bratislava, Rudolph Pálffy, Karton 10, *Kurze gefaste anmerckungs-Puncta. Weswegen Beschleunigung deren Housaren Werbung zur höchst nöthigen baldigen Allerhöchsten Dienstleistung,* undated. Herafter quoted as '*Kurz gefaste anmerckungs-Puncta*'
50 Budapest, Military Institute, HL 1758 I 22, *Pro Memoria. Über das denen Kayl. Königl. Housaren beymessenen üble Verhalten in gegenwärtigen Kriege, und in specie über die daraus entstehende Frage; warum sie sich in selbigen nicht solche Progressen wie in vormahligen Kriegen gemacht haben,* Vienna, 29 January. Herafter quoted as '*Pro Memoria*'
51 Bratislava, Rudolph Pálffy, Karton 10, *Kurz gefaste anmerckungs-Puncta*
52 KA HKR Protocolle 1760 November 199, Leopold Pálffy to Maria Theresa, 10 December
53 Ligne, 1795–1811, II, 162–3
54 KA HKR Protocolle 1757 June 27, *Allerhöchste-eigenheindige Erinnerung von I.K.K.M. vom 10ten Juny 1757,* with *Allerunterthänigste Auskünften hierüber*
55 Bratislava, Rudolph Pálffy, *Pro Nota,* as supplement to his *Observations Puncta* of 8 May 1762
56 *Regulament und Ordnung für gesammte Kaiserl.-Königlichen Husaren-Regimenter,* 1751, Anhang
57 Ibid.
58 Ligne, 1795–1811, II, 161
59 KA CA 1758 III D, Rebain, Neisse, 10 March
60 Armfeldt, 160
61 HHStA Kriegsakten 390, Neipperg's plan of campaign for 1761, 27 December 1760
62 KA FA 1761 XIII 9 A, Lacy to Hohenzollern, Übigau, 4 June
63 KA FA 1761 XIII 9 B, Lacy to Csedo, 19 September
64 Bratislava, Rudolph Pálffy, Karton 10, Lieutenant-Colonel Herberstein to Rudolph Pálffy, Pressnitz, 20 June 1759
65 KA FA 1762 XIII 91, *GFWM.* Wartensleben, *Mémoire. Pour accomoder le Systeme des Légions, au Service de Leurs Majestés Impériales, Royales, Apostoliques,* 20 December
66 Budapest, Military Institute, HL 1758 I 22, Hadik, *Pro Memoria,* Vienna, 29 June
67 KA FA 1761 XIII 66, *GFWM.* Bethlen, *Gehorsamstes Pro Memoria,* undated
68 KA FA 1761 XIII 9 A, Lacy to Hohenzollern, Übigau, 12 June
69 KA FA 1762 XIII 91, *GFWM.* Wartensleben, *Mémoire. Pour accomoder le Systeme des Légions, au Service de Leurs Majestés Impériales, Royales, Apostoliques,* 20 December
70 Budapest, Military Institute, HL 1758 I 22, Hadik, *Pro Memoria,* 29 January; HHStA Kriegsakten 387, *Verzeichniss,* 1758; KA CA 1758 III 1 D, Rebain, Neisse, 10 March
71 Warnery, 1788, 130–1
72 KA CA 1762 III 4, *Patriotisch-… Reflexionen*

12 The Artillery

1. Cogniazzo, 1788–91, II, 187
2. Armfeldt, 7
3. KA Nostitz-Rieneck 1792 F V no. 1, anon., *Vorgefallene Veränderungen in der K.K. Feld Artillerie nebst verschiedenen Betrachtungen*
4. Armfeldt, 13–14
5. Wrede, 1898–1905, IV, part 1, 64
6. KA Archiv des K.K. Artillerie Comite, *Artillerie Systeme ab Anno* 1753, Budweis, 23 October 1753. Hereafter quoted as '*Artillerie Systeme ab Anno 1753*'
7. KA HKR Protocolle 1760 March 288, Liechtenstein to the HKR, 9 March; KA HKR Protocolle 1760 April 358, HKR to Daun and others, 24 April
8. KA CA 1762 Ill 4 F, *Patriotisch-… Reflexionen*
9. KA HKR Protocolle 1761 December 6, Liechtenstein to the HKR, 28 November
10. Ligne, 1795–1811, II, 30
11. *Reglement für das Kaiserliche Königliche gesammte Feld-Artilleriecorps*, 1757, 3
12. KA HKR Protocolle 1761 December 6, Liechtenstein to the HKR, 28 November
13. *Reglement für das Kaiserliche Königliche Feld-Artilleriecorps*, 1757, 13
14. Ibid., 8–9
15. Armfeldt, 14
16. Ibid., 14–15. See also KA CA 1762 III 4 F, *Patriotisch-… Reflexionen*
17. Armfeldt, 7
18. *Reglement für das Kaiserliche Königliche gesammte Feld-Artilleriecorps*, 1757, 16
19. Cogniazzo, 1779, 25–6
20. Gribeauval, 3 March 1762, in Hennebert, 1896, 41
21. *Reglement für das Kaiserliche Königliche gesammte Feld-Artilleriecorps*, 1757, 131
22. HHStA Kriegsakten 393, *Protocoll der Zusammentrettung bey dem Fürsten Liechtenstein*, 24 January 1757
23. KA FA 1759 XIII 171, *Feld Aufsatz zur Campagne 1759*, 10 February; KA Nostitz-Rieneck 1792 F V no. 1, anon., *Vorgefallene Veränderungen in der Feld Artillerie nebst verschiedenen Betrachtungen*
24. KA *Artillerie Systeme ab Anno 1753*
25. KA Nostitz-Rieneck 1793–4, F XII no. 6, *Allerunterthünigste Protocoll*
26. KA FA 1759 XIII 171, *Feld Aufzatz zur Campagne 1759*, 10 February; KA Nostitz-Rieneck F V no. 1, *Vorgefallene Veränderungen in der Feld Artillerie nebst verschiedenen Betrachtungen*
27. HHStA Kriegsakten 390, O'Donnell, *Notata* for *FML*. Stampach, after the battle of Torgau
28. KA Nostitz-Rieneck 1792 F III, anon., *Einige Gedanken zum Dienst unserer Kayserlichen Majestät*, undated
29. Armfeldt, 18, 17
30. HHStA Kriegsakten 393, *Protocoll der Zusammentrettung bey dem Fürsten Liechtenstein*, 24 January 1757
31. HHStA Kriegsakten 390, Daun to Maria Theresa, 6 October 1761
32. KA Nostitz-Rieneck 1792 F V no. 1, *Vorgefallene Veränderungen in der Feld Artillerie nebst verschiedenen Betrachtungen*
33. KA Nostitz-Rieneck 1792 F V no. 1, *Vorgefallene Veränderungen in der Feld Artillerie nebst verschiednen Betrachtungen*
34. KA *Artillerie Systeme ab Anno 1753*
35. Quoted in Rousset, 1868, 100
36. KA *Artillerie Systeme ab Anno 1753*
37. Gribeauval, 3 March 1762, in Hennebert, 1896, 38
38. Ibid., 38
39. KA *Artillerie Systeme ab Anno 1753*
40. KA *Artillerie Systeme ab Anno 1753*
41. KA *Artillerie Systeme ab Anno 1753*
42. Armfeldt, 11–13
43. Gribeauval, 3 March 1762, in Hennebert, 1896, 40
44. Armfeldt, 11
45. Schmettau, 1806, I, 307
46. Public Record Office, London, SP 90/69, Mitchell, 29 June 1757
47. In his *Testament Politique* of 1758, Frederick, 1920, 200. See also Warnery, 1788, 126

13 The Engineers and Other Technical Support

1. KA HKR Protocolle 1760 May 386, Maria Theresa to Charles, 21 May
2. KA CA 1762 In 4 F, *Patriotisch-... Reflexionen*
3. KA HKR Protocolle 1758 March 78, HKR to the *Directorium,* 2 March
4. KA CA 1759 XI 22, Daun to Maria Theresa, 24 November
5. KA HKR Protocolle 1760 May 386, Maria Theresa to Charles, 21 May. For details of the implementation see KA HKR Protocolle 1760 June 255/4, 283, and KA HKR Protocolle 1760 December 128
6. KA HKR Protocolle 1761 March 446, Harsch to the HKR, 12 March
7. Vincennes A1 344(), Champeaux, Jauer,19 September 1757
8. HHStA Kriegsakten 415, Maria Theresa to Charles, 29 September 1757
9. Henri Callenberg to Horace St. Paul, Brussels, 16 November 1757, Northumberland Country Record Office, North Gosforth, Butler (Ewart) Mss. Z BU B 2/1
10. KA CA 1758 I 7, Daun to Koch, Vienna, 13 January
11. KA HKR Protocolle 1760 March 416, Harsch, *Gehorsamstes Pro Memoria,* Vienna, 12 February
12. KA HKR Protocolle 1760 March 416, Charles to Maria Theresa, 7 March
13. KA HKR Protocolle 1760 March 416, Charles to Maria Theresa, 7 March
14. KA CA 1762 III 4 F, *Patriotisch-... Reflexionen*
15. KA CA 1762 DI 4 F, *Patriotisch-... Reflexionen*
16. KA HKR Protocolle 1760 March 416, Harsch, *Gehorsamstes Pro Memoria,* Vienna, 12 February
17. KA HKR Protocolle 1760 March 459, HKR's *Nota,* 15 March
18. HHStA Kriegsakten 387, *Rangs and Conduits Lista,* Königgrätz, 10 March 1757
19. KA M.M.T.O., file 'Giannini
20. KA HKR Protocolle 1760 February 32, Gribeauval's memorandum, Dresden, 2 February
21. KA HKR Protocolle 1760 March 416, Charles to Maria Theresa, 7 March
22. KA HKR Protocolle 1760 February 32, Gribeauval's memorandum, Dresden, 2 February
23. KA CA 1762 III 4 F, *Patriotisch-... Reflexionen*
24. KA HKR Protocolle 1760 February 32, Gribeauval's memorandum, Dresden 2 February
25. Armfeldt, 20
26. KA CA 1762 III 4 F, *Patriotisch-... Reflexionen*
27. KA M.M.T.O., file Pawlowsky von Rosenfeld
28. Ligne, 1795–1811, XI, 124
29. KA HKR Protocolle 1760 February 32, Gribeauval's memorandum, Dresden, 2 February
30. KA HKR Protocolle 1760 March 549, HKR to all infantry regiments, 23 March
31. KA FA 1760 XIII 144, Gribeauval, *Mémoire pour le Corps de Sappeurs,* 20 April
32. KA FA 1760 XIII 144, Gribeauval, *Mémoire pour le Corps de Sappeurs,* 20 April
33. KA HKR Protocolle 1760 May 201, HKR to Liechtenstein and the *Directorium,* 11 May
34. KA HKR Protocolle 1760 August 32/1, HKR to Bechardt, 1 August
35. KA HKR Protocolle 1762 October 469, Bechardt, *Gehorsamstes Pro Memoria,* 20 October
36. KA HKR Protocolle 1762 October 469, HKR to Maria Theresa, 3 November
37. KA HKR Protocolle 469, Daun to the HKR, Ober Stein, 26 October
38. KA HKR Protocolle 1760 February 32, Gribeauval, 2 February
39. See Ligne, 1795–1811, II, 151; Catt, 1884, 414
40. KA HKR Protocolle 1757 July 799 /3, HKR to Hildburghausen and Colloredo, 24 July
41. KA Nostitz-Rieneck 1792 F V no. 1, anon., *Vorgefallene Veränderungen in der Feld Artillerie nebst verschiedenen Betrachtungen*
42. *Reglement für das Kaiserliche Königliche gesammte Feld-Artilleriecorps,* 1757, 108–9

14 The Croats

1. K.u.K. Kriegs-Archiv, 1896–1914, I, 142
2. De Saxe to Frederick, October 1745, Frederick, 1846–57, XVII, 301–2
3. KA HKRA 1759 II 4 N, Serbelloni to the HKR, Nuremberg, 5 February
4. KA HKR Protocolle 1761 October 198, Neipperg to Maria Theresa, 21 October
5. Khevenhüller-Metsch, 1907–72, IV, 144
6. Ibid., III, 50

7   KA M.M.T.O., file Liubibratich, Captains T. Lazarovich and H. Miloradovich to Kaunitz, undated
8   Guibert, 1803, II, 79
9   Kaser, 1997, 330
10 Editorial note by J. Matasovich, in Sermage, 1923, 18
11 KA HKR Protocolle 1758 October 490, *Gehorsamstes Journal* of the Temesvár-Bánát Land Administration, enclosed in HKR to the *Directorium,* 26 October
12 Guibert, 1803, II, 46, 74–5
13 KA HKRA 1760 III 11 G, Gefreiten Achim Dudukovich, Jovo Popovich and *Gemeiner* Sava Karan, petition *In Nahmen des gantzen Löblichen Szluiner Bataillons*
14 Archenholtz, 1840, II, 226
15 KA HKR Protocolle 1762 February 580, Mercy, *Gehorsamstes Pro Memoria,* Esseg, 6 December 1761
16 KA HKR Protocolle 1760 May 49, Commissarius Eichinger to the HKR, Trautenau, 6 April
17 Bratislava, Pálfi-Daun, XXIV, Siskovics to Daun, Szar Varos, 17 November 1764
18 KA HKR Protocolle June 647, Nenadovich to Maria Theresa, Carlowitz, 6 June (enclosed with the document below)
19 KA HKR Protocolle 1758 June 647, HKR to Daun, 24 June
20 Bratislava, Pálfi-Daun, XXIV, Nenadovich to Daun, Denna, 20 October 1758
21 HHStA Kriegsakten 417, Maria Theresa to Daun, 5 June 1762
22 HHStA Staatskanzlei Vorträge 89, Kaunitz to Maria Theresa, 7 June 1762
23 Bertling, 1912, 10
24 Guibert, 1803, II, 70–1
25 KA CA 1762 III 4 H, *Patriotisch-... Reflexionen.* See also Guibert 1803, II, 71
26 HHStA 419, *Auszug aus der Beantwortung der dem General Lacy vorgeletgen Puncten des gesammte Kriegswesens betreffend,* undated, 1760
27 KA HKRA 1760 VI 3 B, Petazzi to Maria Theresa, Carlstadt, 7 June
28 KA HKR Protocolle 1758 February 365, HKR to Maria Theresa, 10 February
29 KA HKR Protocolle 1758 July 307, Kleefeld's comments on Petazzi's proposals of 24 April
30 KA M.M.T.O file Liubibratich, Liubibratich to Kaunitz, *Unterthänigst gehorsambstes Pro Memoria,* 10 February 1762
31 Budapest, Military Institute, HL 1761 IX 623 A, Major Christoph Voikovich of the Banalisten to Hadik, 26 November
32 HHStA Kriegsakten 390, Loudon, *Allerunterthänigst Allergehorsmates Note,* undated, 1761
33 KA HKR Protocolle 1759 July 307, Kleefeld to Daun, 24 May
34 Lehndorff, 1910–13, I, 164
35 Sermage to his wife, Trautenau, 14 November 1758, Sermage, 1923, 222
36 Sermage to his wife, Nachod, 16 December 1758, Ibid., 236
37 KA HKRA 1759 II 4 K, Serbelloni to the HKR, Nuremberg, 4 February
38 KA HKR Protocolle 1760 April 49, Commissary Eichinger, *Gehorsamstes Beantwortung,* Trautenau, 6 April
39 KA HKRA 1759 II 4 A, forwarded by *GFWM.* Ried to the HKR, Zoppetten, 9 February
40 Archenholtz, 1840, II, 227
41 Guibert,1803, II, 76
42 KA CA 1758 III 1 C, Rebain, Neisse, 10 March
43 KA HKR Protocolle 1757 October 545, Neipperg to Maria Theresa, 30 September, with Maria Theresa's comments
44 KA HKR Protocolle 1760 July 382/3, HKR to Nádasdy and Petazzi, 19 July
45 KA HKR Protocolle 1762 February 580, Mercy, *Gehorsamstes Pro Memoria,* Esseg, 6 December 1761
46 Yorke, 1913, III, 224
47 Armfeldt, 49; Cogniazzo, 1779, 129
48 KA HKRA 1759 II 4 N, *GFWM.* Ried to the HKR, 12 February
49 Sermage to his wife, Trautenau, 14 November 1758, Sermage, 1923, 221
50 KA HKR Protocolle 1760 May 229, Kleefeld to *FML* Luzinsky, Gera, 5 May
51 KA HKRA 1760 VI 3, HKR to Maria Theresa, 4 May
52 KA HKRA 1760 VI 3 B, Petazzi to Maria Theresa, 7 June

53 KA HKRA 1760 VI 6 and 6 A, Daun to Maria Theresa, 9 April
54 KA HKRA 1760 III 11 G, Dudukovich, Popovich and Karan, *In Nahmen des gantzen Löblichen Szluiner Bataillons*
55 Military Conference of 7 November, Khevenhüller-Metsch, 1907–72, IV, 250
56 Budapest, Military Institute, HL 1762 IX 517, Hadik to the HKR, 14 September
57 KA HKRA 1760 III 11, HKR to Daun, 12 March
58 KA HKR Protocolle 1760 May 82, HKR to Zweibrücken, 2 May
59 Budapest, Military Institute, HL 1762 IV 365, Hadik to Wied, Freiberg, 9 April
60 KA HKRA 1762 IX 2 A, *Summarische Extract pro Julio 1762*
61 KA HKRA 1762 X 538, Hadik to Daun, Dresden, 3 October; HL 1762 X 645, Hadik to Daun, 14 November. For comparable experiences see HHStA Kriegsakten 390, O'Donnell's *Notata* for *FML.* Stampa, after the battle of Torgau; Budapest, Military Archives, HL 1761 529, Daun to Hadik, Dresden, 10 November
62 KA CA 1759 XI 22, Daun to Maria Theresa, 24 November
63 KA CA 1761 XIII 29, *Betrachtung des Herrn Generalen Grafen Giannini*
64 HHStA Kriegsakten 390, Daun to Maria Theresa, 6 October 1761
65 HHStA Staatskanzlei Vorträge 88, *Votum des Hof- and Staats Canzlern Grafen zu Kaunitz Rittberg,* 17 October 1761
66 Budapest, Military Institute, HL 1762 XI 611, Hadik to Maria Theresa, 3 November

15 Logistics
1 Armfeldt, 74
2 *Instruction für die Kriegs-Commissariatische Beamten,* 1749,
3 KA CA 1762 HI 4 I, *Patriotisch-… Reflexionen*
4 KA FA 1757 XIII 685 A, Colonel Müffling to *FM.* Seckendorf, Dux, 7 March
5 KA FA 1759 XIII 35, Lacy to Daun, Kolin, 27 March
6 Armfeldt, 119
7 KA Nostitz-Rieneck 1792 F 2, FM. Wallis, *Geschichte des Hofkriegsraths*
8 Khevenhüller-Metsch, 1901–72, IV, 142
9 Maria Theresa to Ulfeld, Ibid., IV, 399
10 KA Nostitz-Rieneck 1792 F 2, *FM.* Wallis, *Geschichte des Hofkriegsraths*
11 HHStA Staatskanzlei Vorträge 89, *Votum des Hof- und Staats-Canzlern über das Militar-Oeconomüe Weesen and Commissariat,* undated, January 1762
12 KA Nostitz-Rieneck 1792 F XVI no. 2, Passelt, *Geschichtliche Betrachtungen,* 6 November 1774
13 KA *Musterungs-Berichte* 111 307, 19 March 1755
14 HHStA Staatzkanzlei Vorträge 89, *Votum des Hof- und Staats-Canzlern über das Militar-Oeconomie Weesen und Commissariat,* undated, January 1762
15 KA HKR Protocolle 1762 August 764, *Rechen-Cammer* and *HKR in Commissariatics* to Maria Theresa, 26 August
16 E.g. KA HKR Protocolle 1759 January 18, HKR to Liechtenstein, 3 January; HKR Protocolle 1760 May 221, Directorium to Liechtenstein, 12 May; HKR Protocolle 1762 December 883, HKR to Liechtenstein, 30 December
17 IChevenhilller-Metsch, 1907–72, IV, 334
18 FIHStA Kriegskaten 389, Military Conference of 4 January 1758
19 KA HKR Protocolle 1762 December 833, HKR to Maria Theresa, 10 November, and HKR to Liechtenstein, 30 December
20 KA M.M.T.O., file de Piza
21 KA HKR Protocolle 1762 October 132, contract with Penzeneter, 16 October
22 KA HKR Protocolle 1762 December 833, HKR to Liechtenstein, 30 December
23 KA HKR Protocolle 1757 October 616, Metzberg, *Pro Memoria,* undated
24 KA HKR Protocolle 1762 July 461, Liechtenstein to Maria Theresa, 9 July
25 KA HKR Protocolle 1762 October 80, Liechtenstein's supplementary letter of 25 September
26 KA HKR Protocolle 1762 October 80, O'Donnells' report, 30 August
27 KA HKR Protocolle 1762 October 80/2, HKR to Liechtenstein, 4 October

28 KA CA 1762 III 4 I, *Patriotisch-... Reflexionen*
29 HHStA Staatskanzlei Vorträge 80, Conference *'in Betref der ferneren Militar-Veranstaltungen,'* 9 January 1757
30 KA Nostitz-Rieneck 1792 F II no. 29, Gomez, *Über die Grundsätzen zu Bestimmung der Starke des bei einer Armee erforderlichen Transport Fuhrwesens*
31 KA Nostitz-Rieneck 1792 F II no. 29, *Completter Stand der im Jahr 1758 im Feld gestandenen Kaiserl. Königlichen Armeen, sammt allen darzu gehörigen Branchen und ihrer Erfordernis an Brod und Haber, nach der damahligen Gebühr ausgeschlagen*
32 KA HKRA 1760 III 8 A, *Protocol Commissionis*, 26 February, on the supply of oxen. See also HHStA Staatskanzlei Vorträge 86, Conference of 21 February 1760
33 Vincennes A1 3485, *Réponse au Mémoire des raisons qui cherche à prouver que le Corps de 24 mille hommes ne doit être fourni en pain et en fourage par les Magazins des Impériaux*, October 1758
34 KA FA 1758 XIII 22, Carl Paul Pálffy, *Articles Séparés, qu'on pourrait ordonner provisionellement pour la Campagne Prochaine*, undated
35 KA HKR Protocolle 1760 September 168/4, Zweibrücken, *Project zur Bewegung nach Berlin*, Strehla, 5 September
36 Armfeldt, 71–2
37 KA CA 1761 VIII 16 C, Imperial Resolution on Grechtler's reports of 15 and 21 August
38 After the war Kaunitz reckoned that 6,007,224 florins had been laid our for *Naturalien* obtained from electoral Saxony from August 1758 to the end of January 1763, of which half had been made over on the spot, leaving the other half which must now be paid by the state. The provisions had been raised partly by contract, and partly by foraging in return for receipts. The relative cost of the items came to:

Oats: 51.13 percent
Hay: 40.25
Flour: 4.42
Baked bread: 2.05
Timber: 0.96
Other: 1.12

(HHStA Staatskanzlei Vorträge 91, Kaunitz to Maria Theresa, 2 March 1763)
39 KA HKRA 1762 IV 3 F, Proviant Commissarius Roser to *Hofrath* Hauer of the Directorium Prague, 1 May; HKRA 1762 IV 3 E, Grechtler to Johann Chotek, Fürstenstein, 11 May
40 Budapest, Military Institute, HL 1759 VI 72, *Ohnmassgebige Antrag. Wie die Fouragirung Ordnundmässig vorzunehmen wäre*, Gerlachsheim, 8 June
41 Armfeldt, 75, 77
42 Gorani, 1944, 67–8
43 Printed *Wahrhafte Geschichts-Erzehlung vom dem Reichs-Gesetzwiedrigen Verfahren des Kayserl. Königlichen Kriegs-Commissariats wider das Reichs-Fürstenthum Altenburg*, 1762
44 HHStA Kriegsakten 390, Daun to Maria Theresa, 6 October 1761
45 *Generals-Reglement*, 1769, 100
46 HHStA Kriegsakkten 403, *Summarischer Vorraths Rapport*, Zittau, 28 August 1757
47 HHStA Staatskanzlei Vorträge 80, Conference *'in Betref der ferneren Militar-Veranstaltungen,'* 9 January 1757
48 KA HKR Protocolle 1759 April 474, HKR to the *Directorium*, 20 April
49 Ligne, 1795–1811, I, 218
50 Nostitz-Rieneck 1793–4 F XII 36, *Allerunterthänigste Prothocoll*
51 KA Nostitz-Rieneck 1792 F XI no. 3, *Anmerckung über das in Siebenjährigen Preussischen Krieg bestehende ärarischen Furhwesen*, 1792
52 KA Nostitz-Rieneck 1792 F XVII no. 29, *Uber die Grundsätzen zu Bestimmung der Stärke des bei einer Armee erforderlichen Transport Fuhrwesens*, 1792
53 Armfeldt, 71
54 KA FA 1758 XIII 127, *Allerunterthänigste Nota*, undated
55 *Militär Feld-Regulament*, 1759, undated
56 Ligne, 1795–1811, 1, 171
57 *Regulament und Ordnung des gesammten Kaiserlich-Königlichen Fuss-Volcks*, 1749, II, 77

16 Body and Soul

1. KA HKR Protocolle 1758 May 391, Van Swieten, *Note sur la Relation d'Ollmütz par rapport aux plaintes du Staabs-Medicus Lackner,* 25 April
2. KA HKR Protocolle 1757 April 558, note by Van Swieten, 27 April
3. KA HKR Protocolle 1758 April 258, HKR circular, 7 April
4. Cogniazzo, 1779, 151–2
5. Bratislava, Pálfi-Daun, Karton 11, *nota* by Salburg, 4 March 1757
6. HHStA Kriegsakten 384, 'Verily Demill' (i.e. Brady) to Kaunitz, Prague, 29 October 1758
7. KA FA 1758 XIII 531, Wabst, *Allerunterthänigste Nota,* 9 April
8. KA HKR Protocolle 1759 October 351, *Instruction. Für die Kaysl. Königl. Regiments-Chyrurgos,* Olmütz, 12 June
9. KA 1-IKR Protocolle 1758 May 391, Van Swieten, *Note sur la Relation d'Ollmütz* (above). 25 April
10. Marginal note to the above
11. KA Musterungs-Berichte 111 1755
12. KA FA 1760 XIII 169, Graffenhuber, *Unterthänigste Nota,* undated
13. KA HKRA 1756 XIII 384 D, *Kurtzer Auszug. Aus der Haupt Relation, über die mit Ende Octobris 755 in dem Königreich Böheimb vorgenommenen Herbst Musterungen*
14. KA FA 1760 XIII 169, Graffenhuber, *Unterthänigste Nota,* undated
15. KA CA 1761 XIII 4 1, *Patriotisch-... Reflexionen*
16. KA HKR Protocolle 1759 October 357, Wabst, *Instruction. Für die Kayserl. Königl. Regiments-Chyrurgos,* Olmütz, 12 June
17. Warnery, 1785–91, IV, 83
18. Corvisier, 1964, 65
19. Vincennes A1 3433, Champeaux, Czalkowitz, 30 June 1757
20. Gorani, 1944, 108
21. Guillermand, 1982–4, I, 322–4
22. Barsewisch, 1863, 48–9
23. Archenholtz, 1840, I, 128. See also Ligne, 1795–1811, I, 177–8
24. KA Musterungs-Berichte 1755 111
25. Ligne, 1795–1811, I, 232
26. *Kurze Beschreibnung und Heilungsart der Krankheiten welche am öftersten in dem Feldlager beobachtet werden,* 1758, 31
27. Ibid., 72
28. KA FA 1760 XIII 157 B, *Protocollum Sessionis habitae die 22do Januari 1760*
29. *Kurze Beschreibung,* 1758, 31
30. KA FA 1761 XIII 153, *Gehorsambster Bericht. Über die dem 25ten January gehaltenen General Sanitäts Commission*
31. *Kurze Beschreibung,* 1758, 31
32. Ligne, 1795–1811, I, 68–9, 176–8
33. Donati, 1982, 543
34. Ligne, 1795–1811, I, 182–3
35. KA FA 1760 XIII 153 B, *Protocollum Sessionis,* 22 January
36. Budapest, Military Institute, HL Hadik's letter book, Hadik to Baron Ahsfeldt, 12 June 1762
37. KA FA 1760 XIII 167, Wabst, *Pro Memoria,* Liebau, 4 September
38. KA FA 1760 XIII 157 B, *Protocollum Sessionis,* 22 January
39. KA FA 1761 XIII 152, *Gehorsambster Bericht über die dem 25 January gehaltenen General Sanitäts Commission*
40. KA FA 1760 XI 76, report of du Creux, 6 December
41. KA FA 1758 XIII E 581, *Pro Memoria von S.E.H. Baron Netulizky,* undated
42. KA FA 1761 XBI ad 155, *Monathliche Commission,* Cosmanos, 25 April
43. KA FA 1760 XIII 157 B, *Protocollum Sessionis,* 22 January
44. KA FA 1760 XIII 157 B, *Protocollum Sessionis,* 22 January
45. KA FA 1760 XIII 157, Wabst, *Allerunterthänigstes Gehorsamstes Pro Memoria,* 4 September
46. KA FA 1760 XIII 157 B, *Procollum Sessionis,* 22 January

47 Ligne, 1795–1811, I, 183. See also KA FA 1758 XIII E 81, *Pro Memoria von S.E.H. Baron Netulizky,* undated, on the evacuation of the exposed hospitals in 1758
48 KA FA 1758 XIII E 555, Waldstein to Daun, 9 June
49 KA FA 1760 XIII 159, Graffenhuber, *Unterthänigst Gehorsambstes Pro Memoria,* Pirna, 14 February
50 KA HKR Protocolle 1759 October 357, *Instruction,* Olmütz, 12 June
51 Ligne, 1795–1811, I, 184
52 KA Musterungs-Berichte 1755 111
53 KA HKRA 1756 XIII 384, *Haupt Muster Relation* (of October 1755), Prague, 22 March
54 KA FA 1757 III 467, anon., *Réflexions sur la Campagne de l'Année 1757,* undated
55 KA CA 1757 XIII 13, anon. and undated report
56 Gorani, 1944, 81
57 KA HKR Protocolle 1758 May 391, Van Swieten, *Note sur la relation d'Ollmütz,* 25 April
58 Gorani, 1944, 82
59 KA HKR Protocolle 1758 September 557, *Nota* of the *Directorium* to the HKR, 22 September
60 KA CA 1760 III 14, Daun to Maria Theresa, 14 March
61 KA FA 1761 XI 1152, *Gehorsamster Bericht über die dem 25ten January gehaltenen General Sanitäts Commission*
62 Bratislava, Rudolph Pálffy, Karton 11, *Extract eines Schreibens aus dem Feld,* Bögendorf, 20 April 1762
63 KA HKRA 1756 XIII 379, *Verzeichnus*
64 Armfeldt, 78–9
65 Archives de la Ville de Bruxelles, Portfeuille no. 255, from the papers of Pesser
66 KA Nostitz-Rieneck 1792 F III no. 9, *Normale über die Invaliden-Versorgung und der Veṛpflegung der Soldaten Kinder,* 2 April 1772
67 KA HKRA 1756 XIII 384 D, *Kurtzter Auszug. Aus der Haupt Relation, über die mit Ende Octobris 755 in dem Königreich Böheimb vorgenommenen Herbst Musterungen*
68 KA HKRA 1756 XIII 384 D, *Kurtzer Auszug*

PART III WAGING WAR

17 Strategic Dimensions
1 Danish envoy Johann Hartwig Ernst Bernstorff to the duc de Choiseul, Koser, 1921–5, III, 161
2 John Rylands Library, Manchester, Bagshawe Muniments 3/21/18, Sir James Caldwell, *A Short View of the Present State of Austria and Prussia. Written in the Year 1763*
3 HHStA Staatskanzlei Vorträge 90, Kaunitz to Maria Theresa, 16 November 1762
4 Armfeldt, 167–8; Cogniazzo, 1788–91, I, 209–10
5 KA HKRA 1761 IV 6, Loudon to the HKR, Grafenorth, 27 March
6 HHStA Staatskanzlei Vorträge 87, *Kurz zusammengefasstes ohnmassgebliches Dafürhalten des Hof- und Staats Kanzlern über 10 Deliberations Puncten.* 30 December 1760
7 HHStA Staatskanzlei Vorträge 90, Kaunitz to Maria Theresa, 16 November 1762
8 Warnery, 1788, 214; Retzow, 1802, I, 53–4; Kalckreuth, 1840, II, 120; Naude, 1888, 235; Jany, 1901, III, 21; Lehndorff, 1907, 336; Lehndorff, 1910–13, I, 249
9 Kalckreuth, 1840, IV, 171
10 Ligne, 1795–1811, II, 42
11 Cogniazzo, 1788–91, I, 204
12 Bratislava, Pálfi-Daun, XXXIV, Schaffgotsch to Daun, 27 December 1758
13 Adams, 1804, 32
14 HHStA Kriegsakten 399, anon. memorandum, 15 March 1761
15 Ulfeld's vote, 26 May 1756, Khevenhüller-Metsch, 190772, IV, 169
16 HHStA Staatskanzlei Vorträge 86, *Mémoire remis par Mr. Le Comte de Choiseul,* 10 December 1759
17 HHStA Staatskanzlei Vorträge 86, *Réflexions impartiales sur l'État des Circonstances présentes,* undated
18 Khevenhüller-Metsch, 1907–72, V, 31
19 'Über die Liebe des Vaterlandes,' 1771, in Sonnenfels, 1783–7, VII, 7–9; Ligne, 1795–1811, X, 7–11
20 Archenholtz, 1840, II, 130. For attitudes in the army see KA CA 1762 HI 4 D, *Patriotisch-... Reflexionen;* Verri, 1879, I, 97
21 Guibert, 1803, II, 114, and I, 256

22 Klingenstein, in Ingrao (ed.), 1994, 200
23 Maria Theresa to Maria Antonia, 21 December 1758, in Maria Theresa (ed. Lippert), 1906, 34
24 Kaunitz's *Politische Erinnerungen* of 1776, in Kaunitz, (ed. Beer), 1872, 75
25 Porter, 1997, 426
26 Conferences of 16 and 30 January 1757, Khevenhüller-Metsch, 1907–72, IV, 284, 297
27 Warnery, 1788–91, 352–3, 534–5
28 HHStA Kriegsakten 415, Maria Theresa to Charles, 4 October 1757
29 HHStA Staatskanzlei Vorträge 85, Count Brühl to Count Flemming, Warsaw, 3 November 1759
30 HHStA Staatskanzlei Vorträge 85, Kaunitz's *Pro Memoria,* 17 November 1759
31 Vincennes A1 3434, Champeaux, Laukowitz, 19 July 1757
32 Cogniazzo, 1788–91, IV, 222
33 HHStA Kriegsakten 389, P. Mathei (of the Mainz military administration) to Kaunitz (?), Mainz, 19 January 1759
34 HHStA Kriegsakten 417, Maria Theresa to Daun, 22 December 1759
35 Budapest, Military Institute, HL 1757 IV 927, Hadik to Browne, 17 April
36 HHStA Nachlass Lacy II 2, Lacy to Daun, Vienna, 9 March 1762
37 KA HKRA 1760 VII 7 U, HKR to Marschall and others, 26 June, with Maria Theresa's note
38 KA HKRA 1761 II 2, O'Donnell to Maria Theresa, Dresden, 14 February, with enclosed *Specification*
39 HHStA Kriegsakten 400, Kaunitz to Francis Stephen, 17 January 1758
40 HHStA Kriegsakten 400, Rose to the Prince-Bishop of Würzburg, 15 March 1758; Prince-Bishop to Colloredo, Würzburg, 18 March 1758; Kaunitz to the Prince Bishop, 29 March 1758
41 Cogniazzo,1788–91, IV, 128
42 Ibid., IV, 129–31
43 KA HKR Protocolle 1762 December 689, HKR to Kaunitz, 23 December
44 Vincennes A1 3521, Rutant de Marainville, 21 August 1758
45 HHStA Staatskanzlei Vorträge 88, *Antwort Schreiben des H. General Baron Loudon an H. Markgrafen Carl von Preussen,* 20 September 1761
46 Salmon, 1752–3, I, 508
47 Vincennes A1 3475, Rutant de Marainville, Gewitsch, 31 May 1758
48 Frederick to Werner, Breslau, 13 April 1762, Frederick, *Politische Correspondenz,* 1879–1939, XXI, 368, no. 13,608
49 KA HKR Protocolle 1762 July 193/3, in HKR to Daun and Beck, 8 July
50 HHStA Nachlass Lacy III 2, Lacy to Loudon, 22 October 1758
51 KA FA 1761 XIII 78, d'Ayasasa to Daun, Vienna, 28 September
52 Kaunitz to Maria Theresa, 22 September 1756, Khevenhüller-Metsch, 1907–72, IV, 227–8
53 KA HKR Protocolle 1759 October 460, HKR to Daun, 25 October
54 *Circular-Rescript,* 1759, 26–7
55 KA HKR Protocolle 1762 May 456/4, Kaunitz to the HKR, 16 May
56 Cogniazzo, 1779, 13
57 Burgoyne, 1876, 76
58 Becker, 1798, 74
59 HHStA Kriegsakten 384, note from Friedrich Binder von Kriegelstein and enclosed memorandum, undated
60 KA Kriegswissenschaftliche Mémoires 1760 II 27, Daun to Maria Theresa
61 Loudon to *Hofrath* Elias Baron Hochstätter, Koniz, 11 May 1758, in Loudon (ed. Buchberger), 1872, 385–6
62 E.g. Cogniazzo, 1779, 57
63 KA CA 1757 XIII 13, anon. memorandum, undated, November
64 Quoted in Warnery, 1788, 217
65 Cogniazzo, 1788–91, IV, 90
66 KA HKRA 1756 XIII 379, *Verzeichnus*
67 Warnery, 1788, 533
68 Ligne, 1795–1811, II, 53
69 Northumberland County Record Office, North Gosforth, Butler (Swart) Mss. Z BU 2/1, Callenberg to St. Paul, Brussels, 16 November 1757

70 Vincennes A1 3521, memorandum presented at Vienna, 16 August 1759
71 Kaunitz's *Vortrag* of 24 January 1767, Khevenhüller-Metsch, 1907–72, VI, 470
72 Northumberland County Record Office, North Gosforth, Butler (Ewart) Mss. Z BU 2/1, Calleneberg to St. Paul, Brussels, 16 November 1757
73 Frederick, 'Réflexions sur la Tactique et Quelques Parties de la Guerre,' 23 December 1758, in Frederick, *Oeuvres,* 1846–57, XXVIII, 165
74 Choiseul, 1982, 151
75 Waddington, 1896, 155. Waddington's fundamental argument is still supported by Eckhard Buddruss, *Die französische Deutschlandpolitik 1756–1789,* Mainz 1995, passim
76 O'Brien, 1993, 145
77 HHStA Staatskanzlei Vorträge 82, Kaunitz to Maria Theresa, 28 April 1758
78 HHStA Staatskanzlei Vorträge 83, Kaunitz to Maria Theresa, 6 November 1758
79 KA CA 1760 IX 24, Daun to Maria Theresa, 25 September
80 KA CA 1759 IX 22, Daun to Maria Theresa, 24 November
81 Vincennes A1 3435, Courten, Vienna, 17 July 1757
82 Khevenhüller-Metsch, 1907–72, V, 88
83 Vincennes A1 3433, Montazet, Vienna, 29 June 1757; A1 3522, Montazet, Bautzen, 13 September 1759
84 KA CA 1760 IX 10, Daun to Maria Theresa, 8 September
85 *Mémoire du Chancellier … Kaunitz, exposant et justifiant la manière dont le traité secret d'alliance avec la France a été negocié,* undated, July 1756, Volz and Küntzel, 1899, 728
86 HHStA Staatskanzlei Vorträge 87, Kaunitz, *Kurz zusammengefasstes Dafürhalten des Hof- and Staats Kanzlers über 10 Deliberations Puncten,* 10 December 1760
87 HHStA Kriegsakten 431, St. André to Maria Theresa, Riga, 14 April 1757
88 HHStA Kriegsakten 431, St. André to Maria Theresa, Riga, 14 April 1757
89 Cogniazzo, 1788–91, III, 135
90 HHStA Staatskanzlei Vorträge 83, Kaunitz to Maria Theresa, 8 October 1758
91 Dirrheimer and Fritz, 1967, 68. See also KA HKR Protocolle 1759 August 259, HKR to Daun and Liechtenstein, 31 August
92 HHStA Nachlass Lacy I 3, Ehrensvard's *Mémoire Raisonné,* delivered to the Riksdag, 1761
93 HHStA Staatskanzlei Vorträge 93, *Anweisungs-Puncten* for Mednyansky, 1 July 1758
94 HHStA Nachlass Lacy I 3, Ehrensvard's *Mémoire Raisonné*
95 Vincennes A1 3523, Caulincourt, Pasewalk, 25 September 1759
96 Vincennes A 1 3523, Caulincourt, Pasewalk, 25 September 1759
97 HHStA Nachlass Lacy I 3, Ehrensvard's *Mémoire Raisonne*
98 Vincennes A1 3518, Caulincourt, Stockholm, 18 July 1759
99 HHStA Nachlass Lacy I 3, Ehrensvard's *Mémoire Raisonné*
100 E.g. KA HKR Protocolle 1760 February 553, Mednyansky to the HKR, 28 January
101 HHStA Nachlass Lacy I 3, Ehrensvard's *Mémoire Raisonné*
102 HHStA Kriegsakten 415, Maria Theresa to Daun, 4 August 1757
103 KA HKRA 1760 X 6 C, Lacy to Medyansky, Mariendorf, 9 October, and Mednyansky to Lacy, Werbelow, 13 October
104 Armfeldt, 355
105 Archenholtz, 1840, I, 44
106 KA HKR Protocolle July 799/3, HKR to Hildburghausen and Colloredo, 29 July
107 HHStA Kriegsakten 410, anon. to Hildburghausen, 26 November 1757
108 Budapest, Military Institute, HL IV 1759 43, Zweibrücken to Hadik, Bamberg, 8 April; Vincennes A1 3512, comte de Goertz, Bamberg, 12 April 1759; KA HKR Protocolle 1959 May 74, HKR to Zweibrücken, 4 May
109 KA HKR Protocolle 1757 July 799/3, HKR to Hildburghausen and Colloredo, 29 July
110 KA HKR Protocolle 1760 February 291, HKR to Daun, 12 February; HKR Protocolle 1760 February 660, HKR to Directorium, 29 February
111 HHStA Kriegsakten 411, Colloredo to Zweibrücken, 23 July 1759
112 HHStA Staatskanzlei Vorträge 86, Kaunitz to Maria Theresa, 5 February 1760
113 HHStA Kriegsakten 410, summary to Hildburghausen to Francis Stephen, 24 November 1757

114 KA FA 1760 XIII 127, Lacy to Daun, Vienna, 11 March
115 KA CA 1761 XIII 22, plan of *FM.* Batthyány, undated
116 KA HKR Protocolle 1761 June 228, Serbelloni to the HKR, Hof, 14 June
117 Vincennes A1 3512, Goertz, Bamberg, 12 April 1759
118 Armfeldt, 355
119 Warnery, 1788, 332
120 Conference of 7 August 1757, Khevenhüller-Metsch, 1907–72 IV, 200
121 Vincennes A1 3521, Rutant de Marainville, Leipzig, 21 August 1759
122 *Vortrag* of Kaunitz, 20 April 1757, Khevenhüller-Metsch, 1907–72, IV, 329
123 HHStA Kriegsakten 412, Fürstenberg to Colloredo, 16 August 1757
124 KA HKR Protcolle 1760 March 681, HKR to Daun and Harsch, 27 March
125 KA HKR Protocolle 1762, January 513, Resolution of 7 January
126 Vincennes A1 3428, de Vault, Vienna, 5 February 1757
127 HHStA Staatskanzlei Vorträge 85, Kaunitz to Maria Theresa, 30 September 1759
128 KA HKR Protocolle 1759 January 125, Baxeras to Maria Theresa, undated
129 KA HKRA 1759 III 4, Charles to Maria Theresa, Brussels, 12 March; HKRA 1759 III 4, Charles to the magistrates of the Flemish towns, Brussels, 7 March; HKRA 1759 III 4 B, *Règlement pour l'Établissement des Gardes Côtes;* HKRA 1759 DI 4 C, Maria Theresa to Charles, 24 March
130 KA HKRA 1757 XIII 3 B, Kaunitz, *Allerunterthänigste Pro Memoria. Die zur Defension des Litorals gegen die besorgende feindselige Unternehmungen der Englischen Flotte fürzukehrende Anstalten betreffend,* July, undated
131 KA HKRA 1757 XIII 3 B, Kaunitz, *Allerunterthänigste Pro Memoria.* Similarly HKRA 1757 VIII 3 A, Rudolph Chotek to Maria Theresa, 28 July
132 Szábo, 1994, 297
133 HHStA Staatskanzlei Vorträge 86, Kaunitz to Maria Theresa, 29 May 1760, with note of Maria Theresa
134 HHStA Staatskanzlei Vorträge 90, Kaunitz to Maria Theresa, 25 November 1762

18 Operational and Tactical Dimensions
1 HHStA Kriegsakten 388, anon. letter, Königgrätz, 21 December 1757
2 Vincennes A1 3433, Broglie, Vienna, 24 June 1757
3 Cogniazzo, 1788–91, III, 666
4 Vincennes A1 3522, Montazet to Choiseul, Bautzen, 13 December 1759
5 HHStA Kriegsakten 388, anon. letter, Königgrätz, 21 December 1757
6 Burgoyne, 1876, 69
7 Kleist to Hans Kaspar Hirzel, Maxen, 30 October 1758, Volz, 1926–7, II, 84
8 Lehndorff, 1910–13, I, 252–3
9 KA CA 1762 III 4 A, *Patriotisch-… Reflexionen*
10 KA Kriegswissenschaftliche Mémoires 1756 II 24, *Schreiben eines Officiers der Cavallerie an seinen Freund,* Königgrätz, 28 December 1756
11 Bratislava, Pálfi-Daun, XXXIX, Migazzi to Daun, 29 September 1758
12 Verri, 1 November 1759, Verri, 1879, I 78–9
13 Armfeldt, 131
14 Quoted in Küster, 1793, xi-xii
15 Budapest, Military Institute, HL 1761 III 149, Hadik to Colloredo, Cronach, 25 March
16 KA FA 1757 XIII 467, anon., *Réflexions sur la Campagne de 1757,* undated
17 Armfeldt, 80
18 KA CA 1758 1 7, Daun to Koch, 13 January
19 Armfeldt, 217
20 *Generals-Reglement,* 1769, 19
21 KA HKR Protocolle 1759 January 12, HKR to Daun, *Allerunterthänigste Vorschlag,* 3 January
22 KA M.M.T.O., file Giannini
23 KA HKR Protocolle 1759 January 12, HKR to Daun, *Allerunterhänigste Vorschlag,* 3 January
24 HHStA Nachlass Lacy II 2, *Receuil des Lettres à des Dames,* Lacy, Schurz, 9 May 1759
25 KA FA 1759 XIII 127, Lacy to Daun, Vienna, 11 March

26 HHStA Kriegsakten 384, Lacy to his regimental agent Matthias Kurländer, Leitomischl, 21 May 1758
27 *Generals-Reglement,* 1769, 21
28 KA CA 1761 X 6, Daun to Maria Theresa, 6 October
29 Keyssler, 1751, II, 288
30 HHStA Kriegsakten 384, Lacy to Kurländer, 4 May 1758
31 Budapest, Military Institute, Hadik's *Tagebuch,* 20 June 1759
32 KA HKRA 1756 VII 1, Browne to the HKR, 24 June
33 Vincennes A1 3427, d'Estrées, Vienna, 29 January 1757
34 KA HKRA 1759 VII 10 B, Fürstenberg, *Nota,* Prague, 17 June; HKRA 1759 VII 10 D, Kessler von Kestenach, *Ünterthanige Nota,* Prague, 26 June
35 KA FA 1761 XIII 9 A, Lacy to Daun, Übigau, 30 May
36 KA FA 1761 XIII 9 B, Lacy to Daun, Gross Dobritz, 1 August
37 Zimmermann, 1790, I 287–8
38 Frederick to Schwerin, Dresden, 15 January 1757, Frederick, *Politische Correspondenz,* 1879–1939, XIV, 204, no. 8,525
39 Hanoverian Kammerprasident G.A. Münchhausen to Finckenstein, 21 January 1759, Ibid., XVII, 56, no. 10,701; Frederick to Prince Henry, Bolkenhain, 4 April 1759, Ibid., XVIII, 150, no. 10,838
40 Retzow, 1802, I 108
41 KA FA 1761 XIII 160, *Beschreibung eines feindl. Espions*
42 Vincennes A1 3432, Champeaux, 2 June 1757; A1 3433, *Copie de deux lettres à l'armée à Krichnow en date du 21 Juin* 1757
43 KA CA 1757 XIII 467, anon., *Réflexions sur la campagne de l'année* 1757; Cogniazzo, 1788–91, II, 327–8
44 KA FA 1757 XIII 686, Müffling to Seckendorf, Jauer, 22 September 1757
45 HHStA Kriegsakten 417, Kaunitz to Daun, 14 April 1758. This document is a copy, retained in Vienna; Daun burnt the original on the instructions of Kaunitz
46 HHStA Kriegsakten 417, Kaunitz to Daun, 12 July 1758
47 HHStA Kriegsakten 418, intercepted letter from Berlin, 18 March 1760
48 KA Articles of the HKR, 30 January 1761
49 Ligne, 1795–1811, II, 213; Cogniazzo, 1788–91, IV, 59
50 KA CA 1757 XIII 28, *Pensées au sujet de la guerre presénte et de l'ouverture de la Campagne prochaine,* undated
51 HHStA Kriegsakten 419, *Auszug aus der Beantwortung der dem General Lacy vorgelegten Puncten des gesammten Kriegswesens betreffend,* undated, 1760
52 KA FA 1762 XIII 91, *GFWM.* Wartensleben, *Mémoire. Pour accomoder le Système de Légions, au service de Leurs Majestés, Royales, Apostoliques,* 20 December 1762
53 Armfeldt, 81–2
54 Ibid., 84
55 KA Kriegswissenschaftliche Mémoires 1760 II 27
56 Armfeldt, 86
57 Ligne, 1795–1811, 1,96
58 Ibid., I, 94
59 Armfeldt, 87
60 Armfeldt, 87
61 Ligne, 1795–1811, 1,177
62 *Kurze Beschreibung and Heilungsart,* 1758, 31
63 *Militär Feld-Regulament,* 1759, unpaginated
64 Frederick, 'Réflexions sur Ia Tactique,' 23 December 1758, Frederick, *Oeuvres,* 1846–57, XXVIII, 161; Armfeldt, 87
65 Bratislava, 'Rudolph Pálffy,' Karton 10, *Verhaltung überhaubts,* 14 November 1757
66 Vincennes A1 3475, Marainville, Gewitz, 27 May 1758
67 KA Kriegswissenschaftliche Mémoires 1760 II 27
68 Frederick, 'Réflexions sur la Tactique,' 23 December 1758, Frederick, *Oeuvres,* 1846–57, XXVIII, 155–6
69 'Testament Politique' of 1768, Frederick, 1920, 173
70 Budapest, Military Institute, HL Hadik's journal, 20 June 1759

71 Frederick, 'Réflexions sur la Tactique,' 23 December 1758, Frederick, *Oeuvres* 1846–57, XXVIII, 157
72 Armfeldt, 88
73 Armfeldt., 93
74 Frederick, 'Réflexions sur la Tactique,' 23 December 1758, Frederick, *Oeuvres,* 1846–57, XXVIII, 158
75 Ibid., XXVIII, 156
76 Ibid., XXVIII, 158
77 Armfeldt, 88–9
78 Ligne, 1795–1811, II, 107
79 Vincennes A1 3482, Marainville, Skalitz, 24 April 1758
80 KA CA 1758 III 1, Rebain, Neisse, 10 March
81 Armfeldt, 88–9
82 Cogniazzo,1788–91, III, 34–5
83 *Militär Feld-Regulament,* 1759, unpaginated
84 Verri, Dresden, 20 December 1759, Verri,1879, I, 99
85 Armfeldt, 91; Cogniazzo, 1779, 148–9
86 Gorani, 1944, 111–12
87 Armfeldt, 102–04
88 *Militär Feld-Regulament,* 1759, unpaginated
89 Ligne, 1795–1811, I, 80–1
90 HHStA Kriegsakten 389, Protocol of the Military Conference of 4 January 1758
91 HHStA Kriegsakten 389, anon., *idées sur la délivrance de la ville d'Ollmütz*
92 HHStA Kriegsakten 388, Jean Georges Pradatsch, *Plan d'opérations par la Lusace,* Prague, 4 April 1757
93 'Pensées et Règles Générales pour la Guerre,' 1755, Frederick, *Oeuvres,* 1846–57, XXVIII, 133
94 'Relation de l'affaire de Reichenberg. Par un officier Prussien, ' St. Paul, 1914, 83–4
95 Budapest, Military Institute, HL 1758 XII 333, Losy to Hadik, undated
96 Cogniazzo, 1788–91, IV, 220
97 KA HKR Protocolle 1759 May 218, Hadik to Zweibrücken, 10 May
98 KA HKRA 1762 VI 7 R, Maria Theresa to Serbelloni, 7 June
99 Military Conference of 1 November 1757, Khevenhüller-Metsch, 1907–72, IV,251
100 KA CA 1762 III 4 H, *Patriotisch-… Reflexionen*
101 Anon. pamphlet, *Zuverlässige Nachrichten von dem traurigen Schicksale der Stadt und Universität Halle,* Amsterdam, 1759
102 KA CA 1762 III 4 H, *Patriotisch-… Reflexionen*
103 Ligne, 1795–1811, II, 65
104 Budapest, Military Institute, HL 1761 VI 252, Daun to Hadik, 7 June
105 KA CA 1758 III 1, Rebain, Neisse, 10 March
106 KA FA 1759 XIII 183, Loudon, *Allerunterthänig-Allergehorsamtes Pro Memoria,* undated
107 Frederick to Keith, 3 June 1758, Frederick, *Politische Correspondenz,* 1879–1939, XVIII, 46, no. 10,032
108 Frederick to Fouqué, 'Réflexions,' 23 December 1758, Frederick, *Oeuvres,* 1846–57, XXVIII, 161–2
109 KA CA 1760 XIII 7, Lobkowitz to Maria Theresa, *Ansicht,* undated
110 Cogniazzo, 1788–91, III, 126–7
111 Armfeldt, 48; Küster, 1793, 5; Gorani,1944, 104–5
112 Ligne, 1795–1811, II, 166
113 HHStA Kriegsakten 390, Neipperg, 27 December 1760
114 KA Kriegswissenschaftliche Mémoires 1760 II 27
115 Armfeldt, 162–3
116 Ligne, 1795–1811, I, 229–30
117 KA CA 1761 VIII 7, Daun to Maria Theresa, 14 August
118 Lynn, 1984, 244
119 *Militär Feld-Regulament, 1759,* unpaginated
120 Ligne, 1795–1811, I, 66–7
121 Cogniazzo, 1779, 64
122 Cogniazzo,1788–91, III, 190–1

123 Podewils, 1937, 141
124 HHStA Kriegsakten 387, *Verzeichniss*
125 Rousset, 1868, 100
126 *Regulament und Ordnung des gesammten Kaiserlich-Königlichen Fuss-Volcks,* 1749, I 122
127 Ligne, 1795–1811, I, 110
128 Esterházy, 1747, 113–14
129 *Regulament und Ordnung … des Fuss-Volcks,* 1749, I, 90
130 Ligne, 1795–1811, I, 88–9; Cogniazzo, 1779, 39
131 Ligne, 1796–1811, I, 17, 18
132 Budapest, Military Institute, HL 1758 XII 332, Losy von Losenau to Hadik, *Unterthänig-gehorsamstes Beantwortung der Frage: Ob das Canonen feuer denen Colonnes nicht mehrer als denen ordinair rengirten Bataillons Schaden zufüge?* Undated
133 Budapest, Military Institute, HL 1758 XII 333, Losy to Hadik, undated
134 *Regulament und Ordnung … des Fuss-Volcks,* 1749, I, 243
135 Ligne, 1795–1811, I, 114–5
136 Armfeldt, 38
137 Richter, 1845, 41
138 *Regulament und Ordnung … des Fuss-Volcks,* 1749, I, 191
139 Cogniazzo, 1779, 56
140 Ibid., 45–6
141 Ibid., 47
142 *Exercitium für das sämmentliche K.K. Infanterie,* 1769, 229
143 *Militär Feld-Regulament,* 1759, unpaginated
144 Ligne, 1795–1811, I, 52, 70
145 HHStA Kriegsakten 387, *Verzeichniss*
146 HHStA Kriegsakten 387, *Verzeichniss*
147 Cogniazzo, 1779, 147; Ligne, 1795–1811, I, 68
148 Ligne, 1795–1811, I, 49
149 Cogniazzo, 1779, 32
150 Ligne, 1795–1811, I, 50
151 HHStA Kriegsakten 387, *Verzeichniss*
152 Cogniazzo, 1779, 31
153 Ibid., 33
154 Ibid., 30–2; Richter, 1845, 41
155 Armfeldt, 163
156 Ligne, 1795–1811, 1,47
157 Cogniazzo, 1779, 43–4
158 Ibid., 141–2
159 KA Kriegswissenschaftliche Mémoires 1756 II 24
160 *Militär Feld-Regulament,* 1759, unpaginated
161 Ibid.
162 *Regulament und Ordnung für Gesamte Kaiserl. Königl. Cuirassiers und Dragoner Regimenter,* 1749–51„ 318–9
163 KA Kriegswissenschaftliche Mémoires 1756 II 24
164 *Militär Feld-Regulament,* 1759, unpaginated
165 *Regulament und Ordnung für … Cuirassiers und Dragoner Regimenter,* 1749–51, II, 320, 322
166 Frederick, 'Réflexions,' 23 December 1758, Frederick, *Oeuvres,* 1846–57, XXVIII, 157
167 Ibid., XXVIII, 157
168 *Regulament und Ordnung für gesammte Kaiserl. Königl. Husaren-Regimenter,* 1751, 59
169 Ligne,1795–1811, I, 23–4, 25–6, 27
170 *Regulament und Ordnung für Husaren-Regimenter,* 1751, 60
171 Schwerin, 1928, 260
172 Armfeldt, 159
173 Ibid., 64

174 Ibid., 63
175 Ibid., 65
176 Ligne, 1795–1811, II, 120
177 Ibid., II, 123–4
178 Dolleczek, 1897, 202
179 *Regulament für das Kaiserlich Königliche gesammte Feld-Artilleriecorps,* 1757, 124
180 KA, Archiv des K.K. Artillerie Comite, *Artillerie Systeme ab Anno 1753*
181 Warnery, 1788, 429–30
182 *Militär Feld-Regulament,* 1759, unpaginated
183 Armfeldt, 17
184 KA HKR Protocolle 1760 February 191, Liechtenstein to the HKR, 2 February
185 KA Kriegswissenschaftliche Mémoires 1760 II 27
186 KA Kriegswissenschaftliche Mémoires 1760 II 27
187 Armfeldt, 162–3
188 Ligne, 1795–1811, II, 71–2
189 *Militär Feld-Regulament,* 1759, unpaginated
190 Ibid.
191 KA CA 1762 III 4 D, *Patriotisch-… Reflexionen*
192 Ligne, 1795–1811, I, 234–5
193 Ibid., II, 121
194 See e.g. Cogniazzo, 1788–91, III, 301
195 Ligne, 1795–1811, I, 167–8
196 Ibid., I, 255
197 HHStA Kriegsakten 387, Daun's report to Maria Theresa, 20 June 1757
198 Ligne, 1795–1811, II, 95
199 Bratislava, Fond Amade Üchtritz 101–12–067, XVI, G.d.C. Philipp Gottfried Wöllwarth, *Kurze Beschreibung meiner geleisteten Dienste*
200 Ligne, 1795–1811, II, 102
201 Cogniazzo, 1788–91, III, 152
202 *Militär Feld-Regulament,* 1759, unpaginated
203 Ligne, 1795–1811, 1,22
204 KA HICR Protocolle 1759 August 531, *Gehorsamste Vortrag,* enclosed in O'Donnell to Daun, Triebel, 24 August 1759
205 Ligne, 1795–1811, I, 236–7
206 KA Daun Kriegswissenschaftliche Mémoires 1760 II 27
207 Ligne, 1795–1811, I, 73
208 *Militär Feld-Regulament,* 1759, unpaginated
209 Ligne, 1795–1811, II, 62
210 *Militär Feld-Regulament,* 1759, unpaginated. For the experiences of Prussian officers who were maltreated or saved by the Ausrians, see Henkel von Donnersmarck, 1858, II, part 1, 90–1; Lemcke, 1909, 30–1; Prittwitz, 1935, 140–55
211 Wamery, 1785–91, III, 341
212 Gorani, 1944, 108, on the aftermath of Hochkirch

Conclusions
1 See the argument in Downing, 1991, passim
2 See the sage comment by Hans Delbrück 'Ein Nachwort zu Kosers Aufsatz über Friedrich des Grossen Kriegführung,' *Historische Zeitschrift,* Munich and Berlin 1904, 455
3 HHStA Kriegsakten 390, anon., *Observations sur la Campagne courante,* 1760
4 Quoted in Wawro, G., *The Austro-Prussian War. Austria's War with Prussia and Italy in 1866,* Cambridge 1996, 120
5 Frederick, 'Réflexions,' 23 December 1758, Frederick, *Oeuvres,* 1846–57, XXVIII, 164
6 Trevelyan, G., *Clio, Muse and other Essays,* London 1930, 157–8

The young Maria Theresa

Bibliography

MANUSCRIPT SOURCES
(in approximate order of degree of usage)

Vienna, Kriegsarchiv
Feldakten: Correspondence of commanders and officers in the field
Cabinettsakten: Personal correspondence between Maria Theresa and officers, esp. Daun; at once informal and highly informative. Dates wandering and globular script, his eccentric spelling, and his way of drifting between German and French have so far prevented his letters from being transcribed fully and accurately, with the result that his case has largely gone by default
Hofkriegsrätliche Akten: General correspondence of the HKR
Protocols of the HKR: Register of all documents sent and received by the main body of the HKR, with indications of contents, whether originals preserved (indicated with an 'a') or not. For the sake of convenience, the notes of the present book indicate both summaries and original documents by the Protocol number
Archiv des Militar-Maria Theresien-Ordens: For the depositions of candidates for the M.M.T.O; contains a wealth of tactical detail
Papers of the Nostitz-Rieneck Hofkommission, 1791 etc.: A commission consituted under *G.d.C.* Friedrich Nostitz to examine the reform of the army under 15 headings; many of the memoranda and the statistical summaries concern the period of the Seven Years War
Neustädter-Akten: Papers relating to the foundation of the Wiener Neustadt Military Academy
Kriegswissenschaftliche Mémoires: A number of private or semi-official papers on the art of war
Archiv des K.K. Artillerie Comite
(For the Muster-Listen please see the extended note at the end of the present Bibliography)

Vienna, Haus-Hof- and Staatsarchiv
Kriegsakten: A great rag-bag of documentation on numerous aspects of the Seven Years War
Staatskanzlei Vorträge: Esp. for the memoranda of Kaunitz to Maria Theresa, which are of fundamental importance for the state of political and military affairs.
Nachlass Lacy: The official and personal correspondence of Austria's first Chief of the General Staff, written and filed with characteristic neatness.

Stockolm, Krigsarkivet and Riksarkivet
Fromhold Armfeldt, *Remarquer öfun K.K. Osterrikiska Arméen samt Militärisk dagbok*, Stockholm, Military and State Archives, 27 May 1763. The report of the Swedish military attaché to his king, with his field diary of 1759–62. Both general aspects and specific detail are subjected to a searching analysis, making this the most important single document concerning the Austrian Army in the Seven Years War. His diplomatic counterpart was Nils Bark.

Budapest, Hadtörtenéti Intézet és Múzeum
Hadik Lévéltár: *G.d.C.* Hadik's military correspondence, diary and letter book, including more than 40 files from the Seven Years War. It is a considerable archive in its own right, and in addition to Hadik's own papers it holds official documentation which has survived nowhere else

Vincennes, Service Historique de l'Armée de Terre
Series A1 Correspondance générale: For the reports of the French attachés and observers. Most informative, though the superior tone adopted by those people is not always justified

Berlin, Geheimes Staatsarchiv Preussischer Kulturbesitz
Espionage papers in Hauptabteilung I, Rep. 96, Militaria

Bratislava (Slovakia), Státny Ústredeny Archiv
Fond Pálfi-Daun: Stray correspondence of the Field Marshal
C.K. Linia Pálffyovskehor. Rudolf Pálffy (1719–1768): The papers of a more than usually conscientious hussar commander
Fond Rod Amade Üchtritz, 101–12–067, XVI, *G.d.C.* Philipp Gottfried Wollwarth, *Kurze Beschreibung meiner geleisteten Dienste*: Mainly for the ironic account of the last battle of his long career, at Kolin

Budapest, Magyar Országos Levéltár
Albert Prince of Sachsen-Teschen, *Mémoires de ma Vie*: By a future son-in-law of Maria Theresa; shrewd and observant

Archives de la Ville de Bruxelles
Portfeuille no. 255, Correspondance du Capitaine Pesser: For everyday family life of a Netherlands officer without means or influence; a significant contrast to the accounts of the great men

Archives de l'État á Arlon (Belgium)
Fonds Van Eyll, Dossier no. 159, Correspondance du comte Frédéric de Bryas, capitaine des Carabiniers: Another useful corrective, this time telling of harsh living over extended periods in the field

Northumberland Country Record Officer, North Gosforth
Butler (Ewart) Mss., ZBU B series: For the many unpublished papers of the English volunteer Horace St. Paul and his correspondents, notably Henri Callenberg and the French observers Boisgelin and Rutant de Marainville; supplements the documents in the collection of St. Paul papers published in 1914 (below)

Public Record Office, Kew
State Papers 90/69, 72, 73, 74, 76: For the unpublished papers of Sir Andrew Mitchell, the British envoy to Frédérick of Prussia; again the printed set of correspondence (1850, below) is incomplete

John Rylands Library, Manchester
Bagshawe Muniments 3/21/18, Sir James Caldwell, *A Short View of the Present State of Austria and Prussia*. Written in the Year 1763.

Official Austrian Military Publications (all published in Vienna)

Instruction für die Kriegs-Commissariatische Beamten, 1749

Regulament und Ordnung des gesammten Kaiserlich-Königlichen Fuss-Volcks, 2 vols., 1749 (reprinted with introduction by Ortenburg, G., Osnabrück, 1969)

Regulament und Ordnung, für gesammte Kaiserl. Königl. Cuirassiers und Dragoner Regimenter, 2 vols., 1749–51

Regulament und Ordnung, für gesammte Kaiserl. Königl. Husaren-Regimenter, 1751

Reglement für die Rom. Kaiserlich-Königliche Infanterie, Cavallerie und Feld Artillerie, 1757

Reglement für das Kaiserlich Königliche gesammte Feld-Artilleriecorps, 1757

Kurze Beschreibung und Heilungsart der Krankheiten welche am öftersten in dem Feldlager beobactet werden, (also in French and Latin eds. Prague and Trieste), 1758

Militär Feld-Regulament, 1759. Largely a printing of sets of instructions already circulated by Daun in manuscript

Exercitium fur die sämmentliche K.K. Infanterie, 1769

Reglement fur die sämmentlliche K.K. Infanterie, 1769

Generals-Reglement, 1769

Documentary Collections; Memoirs, Letters and Commentaries of Contemporaries and near-Contemporaries

Adams, J.Q., *Letters on Silesia*, London 1804. Written by the future President of the United States, during his service as US Minister Plenipotentiary, 1800–1

Anon., *Zuverlässige Nachrichten von dem traurigen Schicksale der Stadt und Universität Halle*, Amsterdam 1759

Archenholtz, J.W., *Geschichte des Siebenjährigen Krieges in Deutschland*, 5th ed., 2 vols., Berlin 1840. Written 1791; Archenholtz had served as a Prussian subaltern in the Seven Years War

Archenholtz, J.W., *Gemälde der preussischen Armee vor und in dem siebenjährigen Kriege*, reprint, Osnabrück, 1974

Arneth, A. (ed.), 'Die Relationen der Botschafter Venedigs über Österreich im achtzehnten Jahrhunderts,' *Fontes Rerum Austriacarum*, XX, Vienna 1863

Becker, J.N., *Fragmente aus dem Tagebuch eines reisenden Neu-Franken*, Frankfurt and Leipzig, 1798

Barsewisch, C.F.R., *Meine Kriegs-Erlebnisse während des Siebenjährigen Krieges 1757–1763*, Berlin 1863

Berenhorst, G.H., *Betrachtungen über die Kriegskunst*, 3 vols., Leipzig 1798–9

Bever, S., *The Cadet. A Military Treatise*, 2nd ed., London 1762. Important for the early years of the Wiener-Neustadt Military Academy

Boysen, F.E., *Eigene Lebensbeschreibung*, 2 vols., Quedlinburg 1795

Bräker, U., *Der arme Mann im Tockenburg*, Leipzig 1852

Correspondance inédite de Victor-François Duc de Broglie avec le Prince Xavier de Saxe, 4 vols., Paris 1903

Political and Military Episodes ... derived from the Life and Correspondence of the Right Hon. John Burgoyne (ed. Fonblanque, E.B.), London 1876

Catt, H., *Unterhaltungen mit Friedrich dem Grossen. Memoiren und Tagebücher von Heinrich de Catt*, Leipzig 1884

Choiseul, *Mémoires du duc de Choiseul*, (ed. Guicciardini, J.-P, and Bonnet, P.), Paris 1982

Cogniazzo, J., *Freymüthige Beytrag zur Geschichte des östreichischen Militairdienstes*, Frankfurt and Leipzig 1779 (though 1780, according to Kunisch, J.)

—— *Gestandnisse eines östreichischen Veterans*, 4 vols., Breslau, 1788–91. Jakob Cogniazzo (there are many variations on his name) served in the Austrian army throughout the Seven Years War. He was nevertheless implicated indirectly in Brunyan's treason, and settled after the war in Prussia. His testimony is copious and indispensable, though must on occasion be treated with caution

Esterházy de Galantha, GFWM. J. (Joseph), *Regulament und unumanderlich-gebräuchliche Observations-Puncten,* Gavi, 1747. The last significant set of private infantry regimental regulations before the official version was issued in 1749

Fekete de Galantha, J., *Wien im Jahre 1787,* Vienna 1921

Frederick II, King of Prussia, *Oeuvres de Frédéric le Grand,* 31 vols., Berlin 1846–57

—— *Militärische Correspondenz des Königs Friedrichs des Grossen mit dem Prinzen Heinrich von Preussen,* 4 vols., Berlin, 1851–4

—— *Politische Correspondenz Friedrichs des Grossen,* 46 vols., Berlin 1879–1939

—— *Die Politischen Testamente Friedrichs des Grossen,* Berlin 1920

Gorani, G., *Mémoires de Gorani,* Paris 1944. Giuseppe Gorani became a subaltern in the regiment of Andlau. He was keen to do well, and judged events and conditions with an impartial eye – all of which marks him out from his countryman Pietro Verri (below)

Guibert, J.A.H., *Observations sur la Constitution Militaire et Politique des Armées de Sa Majeste Prussienne,* Amsterdam 1778

—— *Journal d'une Voyage en Allemagne, fait in 1773,* Paris 1803. Guibert harboured the typically jaundiced view of a Frenchman on Austrian military affairs. His comments on conditions among the Croats are useful, though confined to the unrepresentative Carlstadt Border

'Aus der Zeit des Siebenjährigen Krieges. Tagebuchblätter und Briefe der Prinzessin Heinrich und des Königlichen Hauses,' (ed. Berner, E., and Volz, G), *Quellen und Untersuchungen zur Geschichte des Hauses Hohenzollern,* IX, Berlin 1908. This was Princess Wilhelmine, wife of Prince Henry of Prussia

Militärischer Nachlass des Königlichen Preussischen Generallieutenants… Victor Amadeus Grafen Henckel von Donnersmarck, 2 vols., Leipzig 1858. Henckel von Donnersmarck (like Prince Henry himself) lived outside the Frédérick's charmed circle, and his testimony is all the more useful on that account

Benedikt Franz Herman's Reisen durch Oesterreich, Steyermark, Kärnten, Krain, Italien, Tyrol, Salzburg und Bayern, 3 vols., Vienna, 1781

Hülsen, C.W., *Ünter Friedrich dem Grossen. Aus den Memoiren des Aeltervaters 1752–1773,* Berlin 1890. Carl von Hülsen was a Prussian subaltern in the Seven Years War, and his vivid and detailed recollections are typical of the breed

Kalckreuth, F.A., 'Kalckreuth zu seinem Leben und zu seiner Zeit … Erinnerungen des General-Feldmarschalls Grafen von Kalckreuth,' *Minerva,* 1839, IV; 1840, II-IV, Dresden

Kaunitz, W.A., 'Denkschriften des Fürsten Wenzel Kaunitz-Rittberg' (Ed. Beer, A.), *Archiv für Österreichische Geschichte,* XLVIII, Vienna, 1872

—— 'Votum über das Militare' (ed. Bleckwenn, H.), *Zeitgenössische Studien über die altpreussische Armee,* in series *Altpreussischer Kommiss, offiziell, offiziös und privat,* XVIII, Osnabrück, 1974. Important on the ethos of the Austrian army

Keyssler, J.G., *Neueste Reisen durch Deutschland, Bohmen, Ungarn, die Schweiz, Italien und Lothringen,* 2 vols., Hanover 1751

Khevenhüller-Metsch, J.J. (ed. Schlitter, H, vol. XI by Breunlich-Pawlik, M., and Wagner, H.), *Aus der Zeit Maria Theresias. Tagebuch des Fürsten Johann Josef Khevenhüller-Metsch, Kaiserlichen Oberstbofmeisters 1742–1776,* 11 vols., Vienna 1907-72. The diary of a high court official, replete with the gossip and the observations which make it an indispensable source for the study of Maria Theresa's reign. Its value is enhanced by the lengthy official documents were are reproduced in the appendices. The numbering of the volumes is chaotic, and differs from catalogue to catalogue.

Kornauth, F., *Das Heer Maria Theresias. Faksimile-Ausgabe der Albertina-Handschrift 'Desseins des Uniformes des Trouppes LI. et R.R. de l'année 1762',* Vienna 1973. A beautifully produced and edited reproduction of an original set of uniform plates. Thümmler's admirable edition of the 'Bautzen' manuscript (below) makes a fitting companion piece.

Küchelbecker, J.B, *Allerneueste Nachricht vom Römisch-Kayserl. Hofe Nebst einer ausführlichen Historischen Beschreibung der Kayserlichen Residenz Stadt Wien,* Hanover, 1732

Küster, C.D., *Bruchstück seines Campagnelebens im Siebenjährigen Kriege,* Berlin, 1792

—— *Characterzüge des Preussischen General-Lieutenants von Saldern,* Berlin 1793. Küster was a Prussian *Feldprediger* in the Seven Years War, and his two studies hold a number of interesting insights

Küttner, C.G., *Reise durch Deutschland, Dänemark, Schweden, Norwegen und einen Theil von Italien in den Jahren 1792, 1798, 1799,* 4 vols., Leipzig 1801

Magister F. Ch. Laukhards Leben und Schicksale, 13th ed., 2 vols., Stuttgart 1930

Lehndorff, E. (ed. Schmidt-Lötzen, K.E.), *Dreissig Jahre am Hofe Friedrichs des Grossen,* Gotha 1907

—— *Nachträge,* 2 vols., Gotha 1910–13. Lehndorff was an official at the court of Frederick's unfortunate queen Elisabeth Christine, and had some enlightening conversations with Austrian officer prisoners of war

Lemcke, J.H. (ed. Walz, R.), 'Kriegs- und Friedenbilder aus den Jahren 1754–1759. Nach dem Tagebuch des Leutnants Jakob F. von Lemcke,' *Preussische Jahrbücher,* CXXXVIII, Berlin 1909. Typical Prussian junior officer memoirs; good value

Ligne, C.-J., *Mélanges Militaires, Littéraires et Sentimentaires,* 34 vols., Dresden 1795–1811. Prince Charles-Joseph de Ligne rose to the position of colonel-commandant in his father's regiment of Netherlands infantry in the Seven Years War. He threw together his 'Medley' with no regard for chronology, and little more for theme, but it remains the most informative published source on the life of the army of Maria Theresa

—— *Fragments de l'Histoire de ma Vie,* 2 vols., Paris 1928

Lloyd, H., *The History of the Late War in Germany between the King of Prussia and the Empress of Germany and her Allies,* 2 vols., London 1781–90. Dry, mechanistic and uninformative; as a veteran of the war he should have been in a position to do much better

Loudon, G.E., (ed. Buchberger, K.), 'Briefe Loudon's. Beitrage zur Geschichte des siebenjähigen Krieges,' *Archiv für Österreichische Geschichte,* XLVIII, part 1, Vienna 1872

Maria Theresa, *Briefe der Kaiserin Maria Theresia and ihre Kinder und Freunde,* (ed. Arneth, A.), 4 vols., Vienna 1881

—— *Kaiserin Maria Theresia und Kurfürstin Maria Antonia von Sachsen. Briefwechsel 1747–1772.* (ed. Lippert, W., Leipzig 1908

—— *Kaiserin Maria Theresias politisches Testament,* (ed. Kallbrunner, J.), Munich 1952

Marshall, J., *Travels… in the Years 1768, 1769, and 1770,* (vol. III, London 1772, for Central Europe)

Memoirs and Papers of Sir Andrew Mitchell (ed. Bisset, A.), 2 vols., London 1850

Ortmann, A.D., *Patriotische Briefe,* Berlin and Potsdam 1759

Pichler., C., *Denkwürdigkeiten aus meinem Leben,* 2 vols., Vienna 1844

Podewils, O.C., Graf v *Friedrich der Grosse und Maria Theresia. Diplomatische Berichte von Otto Christoph Graf von Podewils,* (ed. Hinrichs, C.), Berlin 1937. By the first Prussian ambassador to Vienna after the Second Silesian War; important evidence on the early stages of military and domestic reform

Prittwitz und Gaffron, C.W., *Unter der Fahne des Herzogs von Bevern. Jungenderinngerungen des Christian Wilhelm von Prittwitz und Gaffron,* Berlin 1935. Another good account by a Prussian junior officer

Retzow, F.A., *Charaktistik der wichtigsten Ereignisse des siebenjährigen Krieges,* 2 vols. Berlin 1802

Riesebeck, K., *Briefe eines reisenden Französen über Deutschland zu semen Bruder zu Paris,* 2 vols., Leipzig 1784

St. Paul, H., A *Journal of the First Two Campaigns of the Seven Years War,* Cambridge, 1914. From the papers of an English volunteer with the Austrian army during the Seven Years War, including many contributions from his contacts among the French attaches

—— *The Journal of Horace St. Paul,* (ed. Cogswell, N.), 4 vols., Guisborough 1997–8. The 4 vols were subsequently published as 2 vols by Helion 2016–18 as From *Lobositz to Leuthen: Horace St Paul and the Campaigns of the Austrian Army in the Seven Years War 1756–1757* and *From Olmütz to Torgau: Horace St Paul and the Campaigns of the Austrian Army in the Seven Years War 1758–1760.* A first-class new edition, with English translations of the French originals, together with new maps and topographical sketches, and meticulous editorial supporting apparatus. Further, unpublished papers of St. Paul are to be found in the Northumberland County Record Office (above)

Salmon, Mr., *The Universal Traveller,* 2 vols., London 1752–3

Schmettau, G.F., *Lebensgeschichte des Grafen von Schmettau,* 2 vols., Berlin 1806. Carl Christoph Schmettau left the Austrian service for the Prussian, where he rose to the rank of lieutenant-general; this is his biography by his son

Sermage, P.T., (ed. Matasovic, J.), *Die Briefen des Grafen Sermage aus dem Siebenjährigen Kriege,* Zagreb 1923

Sonnenfels, J., *Gesammelte Schriften,* 10 vols., Vienna 1783–7

Stephanie, G., *Stephanie des jüngern sämmtliche Lustspiele,* 6 vols., Vienna 1771–87

Memoirs of the House of Taaffe, Vienna 1856

Tempelhoff, G.F., *Geschichte des siebenjährigen Krieges in Deutschland,* 6 vols., Berlin 1783–1801

Thiébault, C., *Mes Souvenirs de Vingt Ans de Séjour à Berlin,* 4 vols., Paris 1813

Thielow, Adjutant, *Tagebuch eines preussischen officiers von der Königlichen Armee im Jahre 1760,* Cologne 1781

Thümmler, L.-H., *Die österreichische Armee im Siebenjährigen Krieg. Die Bautzener Bilderhandschrift aus dem Jahre 1762,* Berlin 1993. An excellent edition of the naive but most informative uniform sketches in the 'Bautzen' manuscript. See Kornauth (above) for the comparable 'Albertina' illustrations of the same year

Van Swieten, G., 'Ein Schreiben van Swieten's in Anglegenheit des Militär-Sanitätswesens,' *Mittheilungen des k.k. Kriegs-Archivs,* Vienna, 1885

Verri, P., *Lettere e Scritti Inediti di Pietro e di Alessandro Verri,* 2 vols., Milan 1879. A new edition, with comments by Zolezzi, N., was brought out as *Lettere Inedite di Pietro Verri,* Milan, 1965

—— *Pietro Verri,* (ed. Valeri, N.), Florence 1969. Verri's memoirs. Pietro Verri served in the regiment of Clerici as a captain in the Seven Years War; however his lack of military vocation together with his violent anti-Austrian prejudice (which grew with his re-working of his experiences) make him a less reliable guide than Giuseppe Gorani (above), who writes honestly of his life in the regiment of Andlau

Volz, G.B, Küntzel, G., 'Preussische und Österreichische Acten zur Vorgeschichte des Siebenjährigen Krieges; *Publicationen aus den Preussischen Staatsarchiven,* LXXIV, Leipzig 1899. A vast compilation

Warnery, C.E., *Herrn Generalmajor von Warnery sämtliche Schriften,* 9 vols., Hanover, 1785–91

—— *Campagnes de Frédéric II, Roi de Prusse, de 1756 a 1762,* Amsterdam 1788. Warnery served in the Seven Years War as a major of Prussian hussars. He was a friend of Seydlitz, and has much of interest to say on the relative performance of the Prussians and the Austrians

Yorke, P., (ed. Yorke, P.C.), *The Life and Correspondence of Philip Yorke Earl of Hardwicke,* 3 vols., Cambridge 1913. Major-General Yorke accompanied Frederick on the Moravian campaign of 1758, and noted the king's comments concerning the Austrians

Zimmermann, J.G., *Fragmente über Friedrich den Grossen,* 3 vols., Leipzig 1790

Secondary Sources

Albert, B., *Was uns der Becher des P. Andreas Faulhaber erzählt,* Glatz 1928. On the execution of the priest Faulhaber during the tyrannical rule of Fouqué in Glatz
Anon., 'Der hohe Adel im kaiserlichen Heere einst und jetzt,' *Mittheilungen des K.K. Kriegs-Archivs,* Vienna 1884
Anon., 'Die Ernährung und Leistungsfähigkeit der k.k. Truppen im Felde, von der Zeit des 30. Jährigen Krieges bis zur Gegenwart,' *Mittheilungen des k.k. Kriegs-Archivs,* Vienna 1885
Allmayer-Beck, J.C., 'Wandlungen im Heerwesen zur Zeit Maria Theresias,' in Heeresgeschichtliches Museum, 1967
—— (with Lessing, E.), *Das Heer unter dem Doppeladler. Habsburgs Armeen 1718–1848,* Munich 1981
—— 'The Establishment of the Theresan Military Academy in Wiener Neustadt,' in Rothenberg, Kiraly and Sugar, 1982
—— 'Die Armee Maria Theresias und Josephs II.; in Zöllner, 1983
—— 'Die friderizianische Armee im Spiegel ihrer österreichischen Gegner,' in Militärgeschichtliches Forschungsamt, 1987
—— *Friedrich der Grosse und das Militärwesen seiner Zeit,* Herford and Bonn 1987
Aretin, K.O., *Heiliges Römisches Reich 1776–1806. Reichsverfassung und Staatssouveränität,* 2 vols., Wiesbaden 1967
Arneth, A., *Geschichte Maria Theresias,* 10 vols., Vienna 1863–79. A classic. Unlikely to be displaced as the foundation of all studies of the reign
Augstein, R., *Preussens Friedrich und die Deutschen,* Frankfurt-am-Main, 1981
Bach, A., *Die Graffschaft Glatz under dem Gouvernement des Generals Heinrich August Freiherrn de la Motte Fouqué,* Habelschwerdt, 1885
Bachmann, P., Zeisler, K., *Der deutsche Militärismus vom 17. Jahrhundert bis 1917,* 2nd ed., Cologne 1986
Bangert, D.E., *Die russisch-österreichische militärische Zusammenarbeit im Siebenjärigen Kriege in den Jahren 1758–1759,* Boppard, 1971. Important
Barker, T.M., 'Armed Service and Nobility in the Holy Roman Empire. General Aspects and Habsburg Particulars,' *Armed Forces and Society,* IV, no. 3, 1978. Useful details
—— 'Military Nobility: The Daun Family and the Evolution of the Austrian Officer Corps,' in Rothenberg, Kiraly and Sugar, 1982
—— *Army, Aristocracy and Monarchy: Essays on War, Society, and Government in Austria, 1618–1780,* New York 1982
Baumgart, P., *Expansion and Integration: Zur Eingliederung neugewonnener Gebiete in den preussischen Staat,* Vienna and Cologne 1984
—— (with Schmilewski, U., eds.) *Kontinuität und Wandel. Schlesien zwischen Österreich und Preussen,* Sigmaringen, 1990
—— 'Die militärische Bedeutung Schlesiens und das Scheitern der österreichischen Rückeroberungsplane im Siebenjärigen Krieg,' in Baumgart and Schmilewski, 1990
—— 'Schlesien in Kalkül Konig Friedrichs II von Preussen und die europäischen Implikationen der Eroberung des Landes,' in Baumgart and Schmilewski, 1990
Bayer, F., *Andreas von Hadik und der kleine Krieg,* unpublished thesis, Graz 1977
Beales, D., *Joseph II. In the Shadow of Maria Theresa, 1741–1780,* Cambridge 1987
Benedikt, H., *Kaiseradler über den Apennin,* Vienna 1964
—— *Als Belgien Österrereichisch War,* Vienna 1965
Bérenger, J., 'Die Habsburgmonarchie als Ständestaat: Zäsur und Kontinuität zur Zeit Maria Theresias mit besonderer Berücksichtigung Ungarns,' in Österreichische Akademie der Wissenschaften, 1985

Bertling, M., *Die Kroaten und Panduren in der Mitte des XVIII Jahrhunderts und ihre Verwendung in den Friderizianischen Kriegen,* Berlin 1912
Billen, C., 'Une Révolution Agricole Introuvable?' in Hasquin, 1987
Black. J., A *Military Revolution? Military Change and European Society 1660–1800,* London 1991
Blanning, T.C.W., *Joseph II,* Harlow 1994
Bleckwenn, H., 'Die Regimenter der Kaiserin,' in Heeresgeschichtliches Museum, 1967
—— 'Uniformen und Ausrüstung der österreichischen Grenztruppen 1740–1769; in Heeresgeschichtliches Museum, 1973
Bled, J.-P., Faucher, E., Taveneaux, R. (eds.), *Les Habsbourg et la Lorraine,* Nancy 1988
Boehme, K.-R., 'Schwedens Teilnahme am Siebenjährigen Krieg; Innen- und aussenpolitischen Voraussetzungen und Rückwirkungen,' in Kroener, 1989
Boios, J.-P., *Les Anciens Soldats dans la Societé Française au XVIIIe Siècle,* Paris 1990
Boltek, J., 'Das k.k. Cavallerie Geschütz,' in *Mittheilungen des k.k. Kriegs-Archivs,* Vienna 1885
Bosl, K. (ed.), *Handbuch der Geschichte der böhmischen Länder,* 4 vols., Stuttgart 1967–74
Brabant, A., *Das Heilige Romische Reich teutscher Nation im Kampf mit Friedrich dem Grossen,* 3 vols., Berlin 1901–31. Lively and well-researched, though influenced by a pronounced anti-French bias. Reprinted at Bad Honnef in 1984. Vol. II was translated and edited by Sharman, A., and Cogswell, N., as *1758. The Campaign for the Liberation of Saxony,* 2 vols., Buchholz, 1998, with invaluable maps, topographical sketches and reference material
Braubach, M., *Versailles und Wien von Ludwig XIV bis Kaunitz. Die Vorstadien der diplomatischen Revolution im 18. Jahrhundert,* Bonn, 1952
—— *Prinz Eugen von Savoyen. Eine Biographie,* 5 vols., Munich and Vienna, 1965
Brinner, W., *Geschichte des k.k. Pionnier-Regimentes in Verbindung mit einer Geschichte des Kriegs-Brückenwesens in Oesterreich,* Vienna 1878
Broucek, P., *Der Geburtstag der Monarchie. Die Schlacht bei Kolin,* Vienna 1982. By the master of Austrian military documentation
Brüggemann, F., *Der Siebenjährige Krieg im Spiegel der zeitgenössischen Literatur,* Leipzig 1935
Bruneel, C., 'L'Essor Démographique,' in Hasquin, 1987
Buddruss, E., *Die französische Deutschlandpolitik 1756–1789,* Mainz 1995
Büsch, O., *Militärsystem und Sozialleben im alten Preussen, 1713–1807,* Berlin 1962
Butterfield, H., 'The Reconstruction of an Historical Episode. The History of the Enquiry into the Origins of the Seven Years' War,' in Butterfield, H., *Man on his Past. The Study of the History of Historical Scholarship,* Cambridge 1955
Carl, H., 'Les Meilleurs Ennemis du Monde? L'Occupation francaise en Allemagne pendant la Guerre de Sept Arts,' *Revue Historique des Armées. Mélanges,* I, Vincennes 1996
Collin, H., 'François-Étienne, dernier Duc de Lorraine (1729–1737) et premier Empereur de la Maison de Lorraine-Habsbourg (1745–1765),' in Bled, Faucher and Taveneux, 1988
Conservatoire National des Arts et Métiers, *La Voiture à Vapeur de Cugnot 1770,* Paris 1956
Corvisier, A., *L'Armée Française de la Fin du XVIIe Siècle au Ministere de Choiseul. Le Soldat,* 2 vols. with continuous pagination, Paris 1964. Inspired and inspirational
Csáky, 'La Contribution de Lorrains à la Formation de la Culture Autrichienne,' in Bled, Faucher and Taveneux, 1988
Dann, U., *Hanover and Great Britain 1740–1760,* Leicester 1991
Dickson, P.G.M., *Finance and Government under Maria Theresa, 1740–1780,* 2 vols., Oxford, 1987. Important, amongst other things, for the analysis of the distribution of power within the monarchy
Dikreiter, H.G., (ed.), *Altösterreichische Soldatengeschichten aus der Zeit Maria Theresias,* Breslau 1925
Dirrheimer, G., Fritz, F., 'Einhörner und Schuwalowische Haubitzen,' in Heeresgeschichtliches Museum, 1967
Dittfurth, F.W., *Die Historischen Volkslieder des Oesterreichischen Heeres von 1638–1849,* Vienna 1874

Dolleczek, A., *Geschichte der Österreichischen Artillerie von den frühesten Zeiten bis zur Gegenwart,* Vienna 1887. A very important study; at once humane and technically informative
—— *Monographie der k.u.k. Österr.-Ung. Blanken und Handfeuerwaffen,* (reprint) Graz 1970
Donati, C., 'Esercito e Società civile nella Lombardia del secolo XVIII: dagli Inizi della Dominazione austriaca alla Metà degli Anni Sessanta,' in *Società e Storia, XVII,* Milan 1982
Dorban, M., 'Les Débuts de la Révolution Industrielle,' in Hasquin, 1987
Downing, B., *The Military Revolution and Political Change,* Princeton, 1991
Duchesne, A., 'Le Souvenir que les Belges ont conservé de l'Impératrice Maria-Thérèse: Prosperité dans la Paix et Gloire darts la Guerre,' in Heeresgeschichtliches Museum, 1967
Englebert, G., 'La Compagnie des Grenadiers dans le Régiment des Dragons Wallons au Service d'Autriche,' *Revue Belge d'Histoire Militaire,* XVII, no. 5, Brussels 1968
—— *Wallonen in kaiserlichen Diensten,* (exhibition catalogue), Vienna 1978
—— 'Ridder Gaston D'Argout, Generaal-Majoor in Dienst van de Oostenrijkse Habsburgers,' *Revue Belge d'Histoire Militaire,* XXV, no. 1, Brussels 1983
—— 'Les Lorrains dans les Armées Impériales et XIX Siècles,' in Bled, Faucher and Taveneux, 1988
Evans, R.J.W., *The Making of the Habsburg Monarchy 1660–1711. An Interpretation,* Oxford 1979
Fata, M., 'Einwanderung und Ansiedlung der Deutschen (1686–1790),' in Schödl, 1995
Feigel, H., 'Die Auswirkungen der theresianisch-josephinischen Reformgesetzgeburtg auf die landliche Sozialstruktur Österreichs,' in Österreichische Akademie der Wissenschaften, 1985
Gabriel, R.A., Metz, K.S., *A History of Military Medicine,* 2 vols., New York 1992
Gooch, G.P., *Maria Theresa and Other Studies,* London 1951
Grosse, O., *Prinz Xaver von Sachsen und das sächsischen Korps bei der französischen Armée. 1758–1763,* Leipzig 1907
Grosser Generalstab (German), *Der Siebenjährige Krieg,* 13 vols., Berlin 1901–14
Guglia, E., *Maria Theresia, ihr Leben und ihre Regierung,* 2 vols., Munich 1917
Guillaume, G., *Histoire des Régiments Nationaux des Pays-bas au Service d'Autriche,* Brussels 1887
Guillermand, J. (ed.), *Histoire de la Médicine aux Armées,* 2 vols., Paris 1982–4
Gürtler, A., *Die Volkserzählungen Maria Theresias und Joseph II 1753–1790,* Innsbruck, 1909
Hackl, O., *Die Vorgeschichte, Gründung and frühe Entwicklung der Generalstäbe Österreichs, Bayerns und Preussens,* Osnabrück 1997
Hanlon, H., *The Twilight of a Military Tradition. Italian Aristocrats and European Conflicts, 1560–1800,* London 1998
Hasquin, H. (ed.), *La Belgique Autrichienne, 1713–1794,* Brussels 1987
Hausmann, F., 'Die Feldzeichen der Truppen Maria Theresias,' in Heeresgeschichtliches Museum, 1967
Heeresgeschichtliches Museum (ed.), *Maria Theresia. Beiträge zur Geschichte des Heerwesens ihrer Zeit,* in the series *Schriften des Heeresgeschichtlichen Museums/Militärwissenschaftliches Institut,* III, Graz 1967
—— *Die K.K. Militärgrenze. Beiträge zur ihrer Geschichte, Schriften,* VI, Vienna 1973
Henderson, W.O., *Manufactories in Germany,* Frankfurt-am-Main, 1985
Hennings, F., *Und sitzet zur linken Hand. Franz Stephan von Lothringen, Gemahl der selbstregierenden Königin Maria Theresia und Römischer Kaiser,* Vienna 1961
Hennebert, Lieutenant-Colonel, *Gribeauval,* Paris 1896. Esp. for Gribeauval's report on the Austrian artillery, 3 March 1762
Hirtenfeld, J., *Der Militär-Maria Theresien-Orden und seine Mitglieder,* 2 vols., Vienna 1857. A great storehouse of information
Hock, C., Bidermann, H.I., *Der österreichische Staatsrat,* Vienna 1879
Hoensch, J.K., *Geschichte Böhmens. Von der slavischen Landnahme bis ins 20. Jahrhundert,* Munich 1987

Horn, D.B., 'The Diplomatic Revolution,' chapter in the *New Cambridge Modern History*, VII, Cambridge 1966
Hudemaim-Simon, C., *La Noblesse Luxembourgeoise au XVIIIe Siècle*, Paris and Luxembourg 1988
Ingrao, C.W., *The Habsburg Monarchy 1618–1815*. Cambridge 1915
—— (ed.) *State and Society in Early Modern Austria*, West Lafayette (Indiana) 1994
Janetschek, *Die Finanzierung des Siebenjährigen Krieges*, unpublished thesis, Vienna 1959
Janko, W., *Loudon's Leben*, Vienna 1869
Janson, A., *Hans Karl von Winterfeldt, des Grossen Königs Generalstabschef*, Berlin 1913. Esp. for intelligence operations in Austrian territory
Jany, C., *Geschichte der preussischen Armée vom 15. Jahrhundert bis zum Jahre 1914*, (reprint), 4 vols., Osnabrück 1967. An invaluable source of reference; one of the few studies to give proper weight to the French designs on Hanover
Kaindl, F., 'Die K.K. Militärgrenze - zur Einführung in ihrer Geschichte,' in Heeresgeschichtliches Museum, 1973
Kann, R.A., 'Reflections on the Causes of Eighteenth-Century Warfare in Europe,' in Rothenberg, Kiraly and Sugar, 1982
—— 'Ideengeschichtliche Bezugspunkte der Aussenpolitik Maria Theresias und ihrer Söhne (1740–1792),' in Österreichische Akademie der Wissenschaften, 1985
Kaplan, H.H., *Russia and the Outbreak of the Seven Years War*, Berkeley 1968
Kaser, K., *Freier Bauer und Soldat. Die Militarisirung der agrarischen Gesellschaft an der Kroatisch-slawonischen Militärgrenze*, Wiesbaden 1997
Keep, J.L., 'Die russische Armée im Siebenjährigen Krieg,' in Kroener, 1989
Kennett, L., *The French Armies in the Seven Years War. A Study in Military Organization and Administration*, Durcham (North Carolina) 1967
Kerner, R.J., *Bohemia in the Eighteenth Century*, New York 1932
Kessel, E., (ed. Kunisch, J.), *Militärgeschichte und Kriegstheorie in neuerer Zeit: Ausgewälte Aufsätze*, Berlin 1987
Klima A., 'Probleme der Proto-Industrie in Böhmen zur Zeit Maria Theresias,' in Österreichsiche Akademie der Wissenschaften, 1985
Klingenstein, G., *Der Aufstieg des Hauses Kaunitz. Studien zur Herkunft und Bildung des Staatskanzlers Wenzel Anton*, Göttingen 1975
—— 'Modes of Religious Tolerance and Intolerance in Eighteenth-Century Habsburg Politics,' *Austrian History Yearbook*, VGV, Minneapolis, 1993
—— 'Between Merchantilism and Physiocracy. Stages, Modes, and Functions of Economy Theory in the Habsburg Monarchy, 1748–63,' in Ingrao, 1994. Esp. for the influence of French economic ideas on Habsburg thought and practice, revealing the wider basis of the Austro-French alliance —(with Szabo, F., eds.) *Staatskanzler Wenzel Anton von Kaunitz-Rietberg, 1711–1794: Neue Perspektiven zu Politik und Kultur der europaischen Aufklärung*, Graz 1995
Koci, J., 'Die Reformen der Unterthänigkeitsverhältnisse in den Böhmischen Ländern unter Maria Theresa und Joseph II,' Österreichische Akademie der Wissenschaften, 1985
Komlos, J., *Nutrition and Economic Development in the Eighteenth-Century Habsburg Monarchy: An Anthropometric History*, Princeton 1985
Kosáry, D., *Culture and Society in Eighteenth-Century Hungary*, Budapest 1987
Koschatzky, W., Krasa, S., *Herzog Albert von Sachsen-Teschen 1738–1822. Reichsfeldmarschall und Kunstnäzen*, Vienna 1982
Koser, R., *Geschichte Friedrichs des Grossen*, 4 vols., Stuttgart and Berlin 1921–5, reprinted Darmstadt 1963. Still the standard biography

Kotasek, E., *Feldmarschall Graf Lacy: Ein Leben für Österreichs Heer,* Horn 1956. Sympathetic and reliable, and a useful corrective to generations of Loudon-worship. The original thesis (1945), with full documentary references, is to be found in the Library of the Vienna Kriegsarchiv

Krajsich, P., 'Die Militärgrenze in Kroatien,' in Heeresgeschichtliches Museum, 1973

K.u.K. Kriegs-Archiv, *Österreichischer Erbfolgekrieg, 1740–1748,* 9 vols., Vienna 1896–1914

Kroener, B.R., 'Wirtschaft und Rüstung der europäischen Grossmächte im Siebenjährigen Krieg,' in Militargeschichtliches Forschungsamt, 1987

—— 'Die materiellen Grundlagen österreichischer und preussischer Kriegsanstrengungen 1756–1763,' in Militärgeschichtliches Forschungsamt (ed. Kroener, B.R.), Munich 1989

Krones, F., *Ungarn und Maria Theresia und Josef II,* Graz 1871

Kunisch, J., 'Feldmarschall Loudon: Jugend und erste Kriegsdienste,' *Archiv far Österrereichische Geschichte,* CXXVIII, no., 3, Vienna 1972

—— *Der kleine Krieg. Studien zum Heerwesen des Absolutismus,* Wiesbaden 1973

—— *Das Mirakel des Hauses Brandenburg. Studien zum Verhältnis von Kabinettspolitik und Kriegführung im Zeitalter des Siebenjährigen Krieges,* Munich and Vienna 1978

—— Staatsverfassung und Mächtepolitik: Zur Genese von Staatenkonflikten im Zeitalter des *Absolutimus,* Berlin 1979

—— 'Feldmarschall Loudon oder das Soldatenglück,' *Historische Zeitschrift,* CCXXXVI, Munich 1983

—— 'Friedensidee und Kriegshandwerk im Zeitalter der Aufklärung,' *Der Staat,* XXVII, no. 4, Berlin 1988

—— 'Die grosse Allianz der Gegner Preussens im Siebenjährigen Krieg,' in Militärgeschichtliches Forschungsamt, ed. Kroener, 1989

Küntzel, G., 'Friedrich der Grosse am Ausgang des siebenjährigen Krieges und sein Bündniss mit Russland,' *Forschungen zur Brandenburgischen und Preussischen Geschichte,* XIII, Leipzig, Munich and Berlin 1900

—— *Fürst Kaunitz-Rittberg als Staatsman,* Frankfurt-am-Main 1923

Leitner von Leitnertreu, *Geschichte der Wiener Neustädter Militär-Akademie,* 2 vols., Vienna 1852

Lenders, P., 'Vienne et Bruxelles,' in Hasquin, 1987

Lesky, E., 'Österreichisches Gesundheitswesen im Zeitalter des aufgeklärten Absolutismus,' *Archiv für Österreichische Geschichte, CXXIL* part 1, Vienna 1959

Liebel-Weckwicz, H., 'Auf der Zuch nach neuer Autorität: Raison d'Etat in den Verwaltungs-und Rechtsreformen Maria Theresias urtd Josef II., in Österreichische Akademie der Wissenschaften, 1985

Link, E.M., *The Emancipation of the Austrian Peasant 1740–1798,* New York 1949

Loehr, A.O., 'Die Finanzierung des Siebenjährigen Krieges,' *Numismatische Zeitschrift,* LVIII, Vienna 1925

Longworth, P., *The Making of Eastern Europe,* Basingstoke and London 1992

Lotz, L., *Kriegsgerichtprozesse des Siebenjährigen Krieges in Preussen. Untersuchungen zur Beurtheilung militärischer Leistungen durch Friedrich II.,* Frankfurt-am-Main 1981. On the courts martial of senior officers. Contrasts the leniency of the Austrian proceedings with the strict accounting in the Prussian army

Lynn, J., *The Bayonets of the Republic: Motivation and Tactics in the Army of Revolutionary France 1791–94,* Urbana and Chicago 1984

McGill, W., 'The Roots of Policy: Kaunitz in Italy and the Netherlands, 1742–1746,' *Central European History,* I, Atlantic Highlands (New Jersey), 1968

—— 'The Roots of Policy: Kattnitz in Vienna and Versailles, 1749–1753,' *Journal of Modern History,* XLIII, 1971

Marcus, H., *Friedrichs des Grossen literarischen Propaganda in England,* Brunswick, Berlin and Hamburg 1927
Masslowski, D., *Der siebenjährige Krieg nach Russischer Darstellung,* 3 vols., Berlin 1889–93
Marczali, H., *Hungary in the Eighteenth Century,* Cambridge 1910
Mediger, W., *Moskaus Weg nach Europa. Der Aufstieg Russlands zum Europäischen Machtstaat im Zeitalter Friedrichs des Grossen,* Brunswick 1952
Meininger, A., *Rastatt als Residenz, Garnison und Festung,* Rastatt 1961
Melton, J. Van H., *Absolutism and the Eighteenth-Century Origins of Compulsory Schooling in Prussia and Austria,* Cambridge (Massachussetts) 1988
—— 'The Nobility in the Bohemian and Austrian Lands 1620–1780,' in Scott, 1995
Mikoletzky, H., *Kaiser Franz I. Stephan und der Ursprung des habsburgisch-lothringischen Familienvermögens,* Vienna 1961
Militärgeschichtliches Forschungsamt (ed.), (with Kroener, B. ed.) *Europa im Zeitalter Friedrichs des Grossen. Wirtschaft Gesellschaft, Kriege,* Munich 1989
Memoirs and Papers of Sir Andrew Mitchell (ed. Bisset, A.), 2 vols., London 1850
Mortier, R., 'La Littérature de la Langue Française,' in Hasquin 1987
Mozzarelli, C., 'Sovrano, Società et Amministrazione locale nella Lombardia teresiana 1749–1758,' in *Saggi,* no. 220, Bologna 1982
Naude, A., 'Aus ungedruckten Memoiren der Brüder Friedrichs des Grossen. Die Entstehung des siebenjahrigen Krieges und der General von Winterfeldt,' *Forschungen zur Brandenburgischen und Preussischen Geschichte, I,* Leizpig, Munich and Berlin 1888
Nitsche, G., *österreichisches Soldatenthum im Rahmen Deutscher Geschichte,* Berlin and Leipzig 1937
Novotny, A., *Staatskanzler Kaunitz als geistiger Persönlichkeit. Ein österreichisches Kulturbild aus der Zeit der Aufklärung und des Josephinismus,* Vienna 1947
O'Brien, C.C., 'The Wrath of Ages. Nationalism's Primordial Roots,' *Foreign Affairs,* LXII, no. 5, New York 1993
O'Connell, M.J., *The Last Colonel of the Irish Brigade. Count O'Connell and Old Irish Life at Home and Abroad 1745–1833,* 2 vols., London 1892
Österreichische Akademie der Wissenschaften (ed.), *Österreich im Europa der Aufklürung. Kontinuität und Zäsur in Europa zur Zeit Maria Theresias und Josefs* Vienna 1985
Otruba, G., 'Schlesien im System des österreichischen Merkantilismuys. Die Auswirkungen des Verlustes Schlesiens für die österreichische Wirtschaft,' in Baumgart and Schmilweski, 1990
Parisse, Michel, 'Réflexions sur les Origines des Habsbourg-Lorraine,' in Bled, Faucher and Taveneux, 1988
Parker, G., *The Geopolitics of Domination,* London 1988
Peball, K., 'Das Generalsreglement der Kaiserlich-Königlichen österreichischen Armée vom 1. September 1769. Versuch einer Quellenanalyse,' in Heeresgeschichtliches Museum, 1967
—— 'Aspekte der Forschung zum Kriegswesen der Zeit Maria Theresias und Josefs II.,' Österreichische Akademie der Wissenschaften, 1985
Peeters, B., 'Desertie uit de Nationale Regimenten van de Oostenrijkse Nederlanden in die 18de Eeuw,' 'De Ronseling van Recruten voor de Nationale Regimenten in de Oostenrijkse Nederlanden,' and 'Wie waren ze in feite, de Recruten van de Nationale Regimenten in de Oostenrijkse Nederlanden?', *Revue Belge d'Histoire Militaire,* XXV, no. 1, Brussels 1983
Pesendorfer, F., *Feldmarschall Loudon. Der Sieg und sein Preis,* Vienna 1989
Pollard, S., *Peaceful Conquest. The Industrialisation of Europe 1760–1970,* Oxford 1981
Porter, R., *The Greatest Benefit to Mankind. A Medical History of Humanity from Antiquity to the Present,* London 1997
Prinz, F., *Böhmen und Mähren,* Berlin 1993 (in series *Deutsche Geschichte im Osten Europas,* ed. Conze W., etc.)

Rauchensteiner, M., 'The Development of War Theories in Austria at the End of the Eighteenth Century,' in Rothenberg, Kiraly and Sugar, 1982

Regele, O., *Der österreichische Hofkriegsrat 1556–1848,* Vienna 1949

Richter, A.F., *Historische Bemerkungen über den k.k. österreichischen Militärdienst in allen seinen Zweigen,* 2nd ed., Pressburg 1845. Esp. for the difficulties of habituation to the infantry drill of 1749

Richter, H.M., *Österreichische Volksschriften und Volkslieder im Siebenjährigen Kriege,* Vienna 1869

Riley, J.C., *The Seven Years' War and the Old Regime in France. The Economic and Financial Toll,* Princeton 1986

Roider, K.A., *Austria's Eastern Question,* Princeton 1982

Rothenberg, G.E., Király, B.K. Sugar, (eds.), *East Central European Society and War in the Pre-Revolutionary Eighteenth Century,* New York 1982

Ruwet, J., *Soldats des Régiments Nationaux au XVIIle Siècle. Notes et Documents,* Brussels 1962

Schasching, J., *Staatsbildung und Finanzentwicklung. Ein Beitrag zur Geschichte des österreichischen Staatskredites in der 2. Hälfte des 18. Jahrhunderts,* Innsbruck 1954

Schieder, T., *Friedrich der Grosse. Ein Königtum der Widersprüche,* Frankfurt-am-Main, 1983. Accepted as the best of the later biographies; should be read in association with Koser

Schilling, L., *Kaunitz und das Renversement des Alliances. Studien zur aussenpolitischen Konzeption Wenzel Antons von Kaunitz,* Berlin 1989. Persuasive and highly readable

Schimert, P., 'The Hungarian Nobility in the Seventeenth and Eighteenth Centuries,' in Scott (ed.), 1995

Schmid., L., 'Irish Doctors in Bohemia,' *Irish Journal of Medical Science,* 7th series,L no. 11, Dublin 1968

Schmidhöfer, E., 'Das irische, schottische und englische Element im Kaiserlichen Heer,' unpublished thesis, Vienna 1971. Important

Schmidchen, V., 'Der Einfluss der Technik auf die Kriegführung zur Zeit Friederichs des Grossen,' in Militärgeschichtliches Forschungsamt, 1987

Schmitt, R., *Prinz Heinrich von Preussen als Feldherr im siebenjährigen Kriege,* 2 vols., Greifswald 1885

Schmutz, K., *Historische-topographisches Lexikon von Steiermark,* Graz 1822

Schödl, G. (ed.), *Land an der Donau,* Berlin 1995. In series *Deutsche Geschichte im Osten Europas,* (ed. Conze, W. etc.)

Schünemann, K., *Österreichs Bevölkerungspolitik unter Maria Theresia,* Berlin 1936

Schwarze, K., *Der Siebenjährigen Krieg in der zeitgenössischen deutschen Literatur. Kriegserleben, und Kriegserlebnis in Schrifttum und Dichtung des 18. Jahrhunderts,* Berlin 1936

Scott, H.M. (ed.), *The European Nobilities in the Seventeenth and Eighteenth Centuries,* for vol. II, *Northern, Central and Eastern Europe,* London 1995

Seeger, K., *Marschallstab und Kesselpauke. Tradition und Brauchtum in der Deutschen und Österreichisch-Ungarischen Armee,* Stuttgart 1939

Shanahan, W.O., 'Enlightenment and War, Austro-Prussian Military Practice, 1760–1790,' in Rothenberg, Kiraly and Sugar, 1982

Showalter, D.E., *The Wars of Frederick the Great,* London 1995. It is difficult to think of a book better calculated to awaken interest in the subject

Stolz, O., *Wehrverfassung und Schützenwesen in Tyrol von den Anfdngen bis 1918,* Innsbruck 1960

Storrs, C., Scott, H.M., 'The Military Revolution and the European Nobility, c. 1600–1800,' *War in History,* no. 1, London 1996. The authors demonstrate how very well the old nobility adapted itself to the gunpowder revolution in warfare

Straka, M., 'Die Rekrutierung für den Siebenjährigen Kriegs aus der Steiermark,' *Zeitschrift des Historischen Vereins Steiermark,* LVI, Graz 1965. This is one of the several references which I owe to Dr. Grete Klingenstein

Subtelny, O., *Domination of Eastern Europe. Native Nobilities and Foreign Absolutism, 1500–1715,* Kingston and Montreal 1986

Szabo, F.A., 'Unwanted Navy: Habsburg Naval Armaments under Maria Theresa,' *Austrian History Yearbook,* XVII–XVIII, Minneapolis 1981–2
—— *Kaunitz and Enlightened Absolutism, 1753–1780,* Cambridge 1994. The first volume of a valuable work
Taveneux, R., 'La Lorraine, les Habourgs et l'Europe,' in Bled, Faucher and Taveneux, 1988
Teuber, O., illustrated by Ottenfeld, R., *Die Österreichsische Armee von 1700 bis 1867,* 2 vols., Vienna 1895, reprinted Graz 1971. The lack of obvious scholarly apparatus has sometimes led to this fine work being dismissed as a coffee-table book
Thüna, L., *Die Würzburger Hilstruppen im Dienste Österreichs 1756–63,* Würzburg 1893, reprinted Buchholz-Sprötze 1996. Thüna provides much useful detail, but does not address the central question of why these particular troops were so good
Thürheim, A., *Von den Sevennen bis zur Newa,* Vienna 1879. For the visit to Vienna of Count Valentin Esterházy, an Hungarian in the French employ
Tremel, F., *Wirtschafts und Sozialgeschichte Österreichs,* Vienna 1969
Urbanski, H., 'Prince Charles de Lorraine, ' in Bled, Faucher and Taveneux, 1988
Valsecchi, F., *La Lombardia,* vol. II of *L'assulutismo illuminato in Austria e in Lombardía,* Bologna 1934
Waddington, R., *Louis XV et le Renversement des Alliances: Préliminaires de la Guerre de Sept Ans, 1754–6,* Paris 1896. Waddington's attributes the woes of France to the unequal treaties of Austrian alliance, without giving due weight to the narrower interests of the French in continental Europe
—— *La Guerre de Sept Ans,* 5 vols., Paris 1899–1914. A massive work, based solidly on archival research and packed with information
Walter, F., *Die Geschichte der Österreichischen Zentralverwaltung in der Zeit Maria Theresias (1740–1780),* I., no. 1 of *Die Österreichische Zentralverwaltung,* ed. Kretschmayr, H., Vienna 1938
—— *Männer um Maria Theresia,* Vienna 1951
—— *Die theresianische Staatsreform von 1749,* Vienna 1958
—— Feldmarschall Leopold Joseph Graf Daun und Feldmarschall Gideon Ernst Freiherr von Laudon,' in Hantsch, H. (ed.), *Gestalter der Geschicke Österreichs,* Innsbruck and Vienna 1962
Wandruszka, A., Urbanitsch, P. (eds.), *Die Völker des Reichs,* II, no. 1 of *Die Habsburger Monarchie 1848–1918,* Vienna 1980
Wandycz, P.S., *The Price of Freedom. A History of East Central Europe from the Middle Ages to the Present,* London and New York 1992
Wangermann, E., *The Austrian Achievement 1700–1800,* London 1973
Wellmann, I., 'Kontinuität und Zäsur in Ungarns Bauernleben zur Zeit Maria Theresias,' in Österreichische Akademie der Wissenschaften, 1985
Wilson, P.H., *War, State and Society in Württemberg, 1677–1793,* Cambridge 1995
—— *German Armies. War and German Politics, 1648–1806,* London 1998. Fresh information and stimulating insights
Wimmer, J., *Gesundheit, Krankheit and Tod im Zeitalter der Aufklärung. Fallstudien aus den habsburgischen Erbländern,* Vienna and Cologne 1991
Wolf, G., *Die Vertreibung der Iaden aus Bömen im Jahre 1744 und deren Rückkehr im Jahre 1748,* Leizpig 1869
Wrede, A., completed by Semek, A., *Geschichte der k. and k. Wehrmacht. Die Regimenter, Corps, Branchen und Anstalten von 1618 bis Ende des XIX. Jahrhunderts.* 5 vols., Vienna 1898–1905. The fundamental work of reference
Wright, W.E., *Serf, Seigneur and Sovereign: Agrarian Reform in Eighteenth-Century Bohemia,* Minneapolis 1966
Zimmermann, J., *Militärverwaltung and Heeresaufbringung in Österreich bis 1806,* in *Handbuch zur deutschlen Militärgeschichte,* I, Munich 1965

Bibliographical Note – The Muster Lists (KA *Musterlisten*)

Most of the tables in the present book are derived from the details of 140,000-odd regimental personnel of all ranks up to and including lieutenant-colonel, entered on the muster lists that were compiled by the officials of the *Commissariat* on their periodic visitations. The information is presented in a standard style, which sets forth the individual's full names, age, religion, marital status, civilian trade (if any) and length of service; a number of entries also concern personal history (e.g. 'captured deserter') or or the nature of any disabling illness or injury. Appearance goes without comment, apart from that unfortunate soldier singled out as 'ugly,' and the muster lists of this period do not as yet give any indication of height.

I chose 1759 as the preferred sample year, for it was the middle year of the war, it showed a mixture of types of recruits (the new short-service Capitulants as well as men originally engaged for life), and it registered the Staabs Infanterie-Regiment. However only a relatively small proportion of the muster lists have survived, which made it necessary to look for the best remaining sets closest to the target date. Although it was not my original intention, the result was a range of documentation which made it possible to register a number of significant changes over a spread of time. Inevitably a few of the chosen lists stand outside the period of the war. After some cogitation I decided to include those of the infantry regiments of Platz and Salm (entered late in 1754), but to exclude that of the infantry regiment of Arenberg, not so much on account of its remoteness (1753) but because it had a heavily Protestant and north German character which would almost certainly have been diluted beyond recognition by the middle of the war. In processing the muster lists of the regiments (the great majority) which stood on the war establishment, I included the field battalions and squadrons, but omitted the garrison and depot units.

My sets of figures are therefore the product of a number of a number of subjective decisions. The reader should also bear in mind that the original material falls short of modern statistical standards. The limitations have been described in various places in my text, where they happen to be relevant, and I will just mention here that in respect of age, for example, we could think of many reasons why a soldier should have been represented as younger or older than he really was, and not least because many people in that period were genuinely unaware of their age.

For some time I pondered whether to present my findings at all, let alone down to two decimal places, out of concern that I might be be ranked in the tribe of cliometricians (about whom some hilariously shocking tales could be told). Historical statistics invite justifiable scepticism on account of their apparently 'scientific' nature (good for research funding), and because it can take years of work to challenge them, which is not the case with documentary references. I was persuaded to go ahead when I recalled the range of information which has survived in the muster lists, and nowhere else, and by the truly massive bulk of that information; after all, 'quantity has its own quality.' We will probably not go far astray if we are content to regard the evidence of the muster lists as the equivalent of anecdotal evidence of a high standard.

The following regimental muster lists were processed in the preparation of this book:

Infantry
1754: Platz; Salm
1756: d'Arberg; Bayreuth; Botta; Gyulai; Lothringen; Simbschen
1757: Andlau; Erzherzog Carl; Deutschmeister; Forgách
1759: Baden-Durlach; Batthyány; Daun, Heinrich; Esterházy, Joseph; Esterházy, Nicolaus; Gaisrugg; Haller; Kaiser; Kollowrath; de Ligne; Los Rios; Moltke; Neipperg; Pallavicini; Sachsen-Gotha; Waldeck; Wallis; Wolfenbüttel, Ludwig

1760: Angern; Clerici; Colloredo, Alt-; Colloredo, Jung-; Daun, Leopold; Harsch; Harrach; Königsegg; Lacy; Luzan; Maguire (the four relevant companies only); Preysach; Sincere; Starhemberg; Thürheim; Tillier; Wied
1761: Baden-Baden
1762: Bethlen; Marschall; Mercy
1763: Hildburghausen; Loudon; Pálffy, Leopold; Puebla

'New Corps'
1759: *Staabs-Infanterie Regiment*
1760: *Artillerie Füsilier-Regiment; Feld-Jäger; Volontiers Silesiens Beck*
1761: *Grenadier Regiment Loudon*

Cuirassiers
1756: Gelhay
1759: Anhalt-Zerbst; Daun, Benedict; Erzherzog Ferdinand; Kalckreuth; Portugal; Serbelloni; Trautmannsdorf
1760: Anspach; Birkenfeld; Pálffy, Carl
1762: Brettlach; Buccow; Modena, Alt-
1763: Althann; Erzherzog Leopold; Stampach

Dragoons
1756: de Ligne (chosen in this case as the nearest list preceding its great day at Kolin)
1759: Hessen-Darmstadt; Liechtenstein; Savoyen; Württemberg; Zweibrücken
1760: Batthyány; Erherzog Joseph; Kollowrath; Modena, Jung-
1763: Löwenstein, Jung-

New Unit
1762: *Staabs-Dragoner-Regiment* (by then wasted down to squadron strength)

Hussars
1759: Baranyay; Dessewffy; Esterházy, Paul; Kaiser; Károly; Morocz; Nádasdy; Széchenyi
1760: Hadik; Kálnoky; Splényi
1762: Török (Palatinal)

Grenz-Husaren
1756: Slavonian
1757: Warasdiner

Artillery and Technical Corps
1760: *Sappeurs-Corps*
1762: Artillery *Haupt Corps* and Netherlands Corps; miner companies

Croatian Infantry
1756: Slavonian Broder
1757: Warasdiner Creutzer; Warasdiner St. Georger

Index

Adams, John Quincy, 386
Aides-de-camp, 162
Aix-la-Chapelle (1748), Peace of, 19, 25
Albanians, *see* Croats
Albert of Sachsen-Teschen, Prince, 23, 98, 194, 278
Alfson, Adolph Nicolaus, 300, 305, 320
Allgauer horses, 286
Alsace: contribution to Austrian war effort, 102-103, 224, 254, 368
Alt-Colloredo IR, 108, 153, 207, 221, 262, 367
Alt-Löwenstein Chevaulegers-Regiment, 281
Alt-Wolfenbüttel IR, 182, 379
Altenburg, 95, 236, 359
Amadei, Carl, Baron, 90, 438-439
Ammunition, 31, 301, 306-309, 314-316, 318-321, 345, 349, 353-354, 377, 391, 446, 455, 458
Amsterdam, bankers of, 113
Andlau IR, 52, 61, 82, 108, 160, 162, 168, 176, 209, 233, 255, 262, 370, 377
Anhalt-Zerbst battalion, 93, 98, 119, 147, 259, 270, 278, 281
Anhalt-Zerbst, Prince Friedrich August of, 96, 269, 412
Ansbach, 95-96, 99-100, 128, 384, 412
Anton, Paul, 77, 179, 291, 295
Apraksin, Stephan Fedorovich, 404
Aranjuez, Treaty of (1752), 123
Arcieren-Garde, 20
Arenberg, Charles Duke of, 90, 187, 208, 390
Arenberg, Leopold-Philippe, Duke of, 90, 211
Armfeldt, Fromhold, 68, 103: on Bohemian troops, 64; on Netherlands troops, 88; an isolated Daun, 276; compares Prussian and Austrian infantry, 276; on artillery ammunition, 320; on the artillery train, 310; on Austrian camps, 430; on Austrian preference for defensive, 437; on artillery, 454; on bayonet attacks, 449; command, 455 on cavalry tactics, 452; on marching, 426-428; on mounted fire, 452; on the new staff, 419; on Austrian officers, 192; on Austrian generals, 197; on Colonels-Commandant, 170; on Daun, 192; on general's income, 182; on M.M.T.O., 203; on care for the troops, 229; on savage punishments, 233; on foraging, 358; on supply trains, 328; rates *Reichsarmee*, 410; on engineers, 327; on Reduction, 144
army German, 38, 150
army, *see* Austrian army
Artillerie-Füsilier-Regiment, 117, 143, 301
artillery, *see* Austrian artillery

Auditor, regimental rank, 251, 257
Auersperg, family: 37, 44, 58, 157, 178
Austria: origins, 15; income, 119; limited war, 387; reprisals, 391; excessive conciliation of Saxony, 389
Austrian army: lack of will to win, 388; reform, 135; discipline, 133; drills and manoeuvres, 132; ethos, 147; length of service, 219; marriage, 230-231; military traditions, 148-149 motivation and honour, 242; organisation, 424; responsive to command, 416; Austrian style of war, 416; in battle, 436-437, 454; General staff created, 419; grand tactics, 438-439; horse artillery, 454-455; meticulous about giving credit, 458-459; morale, 456-457; on the march, 425; extraterritoriality, 150-151, 229-230; pay, rations and accommodation, 228-229
Austrian artillery, 299-321; an assessment, 320-321; ammunition, 319; at work, 306-307; compared to Prussian, 310-311; gun carriages, 316-317; horse artillery, 454-455; life in the Corps, 303-304; ordnance stores, 307-308; organisation, 301; personnel, 302-303; recruits, 304-305; specifications of individual field pieces; in battle, 453-455; age of gunners, 231-232
Austrian cavalry, 278-298: in battle, 449-453; tactics, 449, 457-458; considered backward, 452-453; organisation, 279-280; training, 290-291; remounts, 285-286
Austrian infantry: as described by Gellhorn, 153; in battle, 439-449; 'German' Infantry, 261-262; musketry, 444-447; tactics, 440-441; tradesmen and specialists within the regiment, 255-256
Austrian Italy, *see*, Italy (Austrian)
Austrian Netherlands, *see*, Netherlands (Austrian)
Austrian prisoners, 186-187, 189-190, 241-242
Austrian strategy: 383; limited war, 387-388; reprisals, 391-392; excessive conciliation of Saxony, 389-390
Auxiliary Troops, 139, 269
d'Arberg, 87-88, 90-91, 265-266
d'Aspremont-Lynden, 92, 103, 151, 215, 281, 289
d'Averna, Joseph Lucchese, 28, 104-105, 298
d'Ayasasa, Joseph-Charles comte, 20, 91, 176, 393, 465

Bánát of Temesvar, 16, 36, 69, 72, 117, 150, 289, 334, 338, 414
Bark, Nils, on ambitions of Kaunitz, 396
Barnabite brothers, 162
barracks, 154, 230-231, 351, 366

544

INDEX

Barrier Fortresses, 25, 85, 154
Batthyány family, 39, 77, 79, 85, 101, 141, 152, 218, 235, 410
Batthyány, Carl Paul, 335, 337
Bavaria, 72, 93, 97, 108, 121, 334, 385, 435; threat from, 18; contingent in Austrian service, 246, 259, 270, 409, 411
Bayreuth, Principality of, 93, 95-96, 98-99
Beaulieu de Marconnay, Jean-Pierre baron, 91
Bechardt, Johann, 328-329
Beck Volontiers Silesiens, 266
Beck, Philipp Levin, 186, 268
Behm, 95
Belgrade, capture of, 16-17; loss of, 214, 334, 384, 414
Beltrame, Count Cristiani, 81
Berlin and Austrian prisoners, 186-190, 241-242
Bernis, Abbé, 127, 397, 400
Bestuzhev, Aleksei Petrovich, 26, 125, 402
Bethlen, Adam Joseph, Count, 79, 156, 172
Bettoni, 82
Bevern, Duke of, 433; prisoner of the Austrians, 188-189, 240
Bülow, Ferdinand Friedrich, 196
Birkenfeld, Count, 172
Bischoff, Heinrich Nicolaus, 95
Blau-Würzburg IR, *see* Würzburg IRs
Blümegen, Heinrich Cajetan, Count, 82, 213
Bohemia, 36; description of, 59-62; serfs of, 41-42, 63-64; industrialisation, 61-62; nationalism, 58; loyalty of, 63-64; unmilitary nature of nobility, 61; recruiting, 216-217; becomes Habsburg possession, 15-16; the cost of war, 395-396; preponderance in the artillery, 304-305
Bohemian *Stände*, 16, 18, 385-386, 421
Bohn, Paul Ferdinand, 322-324, 326
Bornstedt, Colonel, 68
Botta IR, 104-105, 108, 151, 153, 262, 271, 446
Botta, Antonio, 104
Brady, Dr, 364-365
Brand, Johann Christian, 91
Brandenburg-Schwedt, Markgraf Carl of, 190, 392-393
Brandt, Baron, 194-195
Breisgau, 57, 96, 99, 167
Brentano-Cimarolli, Joseph, 82
Breslau (1757), battle of, 160, 185, 188-189, 203, 222, 246, 311, 351, 454
Bretlach, General Johann Franz, 96
Britain: policy, 123, 125, 127; possible war with, 386, 400, 413-414; subsidy to Prussia, 121
Broglie, French general, 399
Browne IR, 95, 108, 153, 191, 271
Browne, Field-Marshal Maximilian, 27-28, 78-79, 107-108; on manoeuvres, 132-133; as defender of Bohemian interests, 60; compares Austrian and Prussian hussars, 294-295; concentrates the grenadiers, 260-261; corresponds with Keith, 389-390
Browne, Ulysses, 107-108, 389

Brünn, 36, 65, 172, 239, 334, 360
Brunyan, Conrad Emanuel Count, 99-100, 194, 204, 422
Büchsenmacher, regimental rank, 256
Büchsenmeister, artillery rank, 301-304, 306-307, 319
Budweis, 36, 61-62, 305-306, 359
Bülow, Ferdinand Friedrich, 100, 186, 196
Burgoyne, Sir John, 394, 416
Burmann, GFWM, 217-218, 221
Butler, 106, 180
Buturlin, Aleksandr Borisovich, 404-405

Callenberg, Henrich Count, 396
Calvinism in Hungary, 67, 74, 78
Cameradschaft, 175, 222, 252, 285
Campitelli, 105, 180
Canzleydeutsch, 37
'Cap' Party in Sweden, 406
Caprara, Aeneas Count, 244
Captain, rank of, 172, 178
carbines, cavalry, 237, 243, 280, 283-284, 295, 299, 309, 328, 353, 452, 458
Carinthia, 36, 40, 114, 167, 215-216, 224, 248, 333, 335, 338; description of, 45, 48, 50-51; becomes Habsburg possession, 15
Carniola, 45, 114, 150, 164, 167, 224, 226, 254, 286, 331-332, 352; description of, 36, 40, 51-52, 333; becomes Habsburg possession, 15
Castiglione, Principality of, 80, 104-105
Catholic religion, 85, 99, 189, 213, 339
Cavalry, *see* Austrian cavalry
Cavriani, Franz Carl Count, 165
Champeaux, French attaché: on Austrian officers, 193; on isolation of Daun, 199; on medical services, 370
Chancellery of Foreign Affairs, *see* Staatscanzley
Chancellery of the German Empire, *see* Reichscanzley
Chaplains, 43, 48, 50, 52-53, 55, 57-58, 64-67, 77, 79-80, 83, 92, 101-102, 104, 207, 241, 258, 340, 379-380
Charles Albert, Elector of Bavaria, 18, 21, 60
Charles of Lorraine, 19, 27-28, 96-97, 132-133; character of, 24; organises Walloon contingent, 264-265; and engineers, 322-324; as governor-general of the Netherlands, 83-84
Charles V, Emperor, 16, 38
Charlotte, Queen of England, 98
Chernyshev, Zakhar, 340, 405
chevaulegers, 104, 108, 139-141, 145, 239, 267, 278-279-281, 285, 298, 353, 391, 457, 461
Chevaulegers-Regiment Löwenstein, 278, 457
Choiseul, duc de, Étienne-François comte de Stainville, 211, 383, 386, 396, 398-400
Chotek, family of, 18
Chotek, Johann, Count, 29, 141, 152, 351
Chotek, Rudolph, Count, 41, 112, 141, 152, 163, 356, 388
Chotusitz (1742), battle of, 19, 289, 299
Church: small contribution of, 38, 111-112

Civilian Trades, 43, 48, 51-57, 62, 65, 67, 77, 79-80, 83, 86, 224-225, 331
Clary, Count, 357
Claude de Ligne IR, 87, 176, 220, 265-266, 271, 456
Clerici IR, 81-82, 88, 192-193, 216, 220, 235, 264-265
Clerici, Antonio Giorgio Marquis, 41, 81
Clermont, French general, 399
Cobenzl, Johann Carl Philipp, 65, 85, 387
Cogniazzo, Jacob, 55-56, 72-73, 159-160, 175, 1201-202; on Austrian generals, 197-198; as Brunyan's messenger, 203-204; on escaped officers, 187; on attempt to kidnap Frederick, 390-391; on Croats, 220-221; on failure in drill, 227-228; on military justice, 232-233; on pay, 229-230; on plunder, 243-244; on soldier's height, 218-219; on doctors, 365; on infantry *regulament*, 276; on musketry, 446-448; on the new tactics, 439-440; on use of columns, 444-445; on *kleine Krieg*, 433-434; on 1752 manoeuvres, 132-133; opinion on 1761 Reduction, 144-145
Colloredo, Carl, 400
Colloredo, Rudolph Joseph, Count, 54, 92, 397
Colloredo-Waldsee, Rudolph Count, 30
Cologne, 93, 99-100, 217, 287
Colonel Commandant, rank of, 95, 99, 153, 157, 160-162, 168, 170-172, 177, 193-194, 200, 207-208, 230, 236, 244, 251, 255-257, 276, 296, 352, 379-380
Colonel Proprietor (*Inhaber*), rank of, 61, 90, 96, 98, 106, 167, 171, 173, 175, 178, 180, 182, 207, 209, 212, 233, 251, 273, 280-281, 284, 293-295, 299, 359, 412, 421
Commissariat Hofcommission, see Commissariat
Commissariat, 29-30, 32, 181, 216, 222, 289, 349-362, 365, 375
Commissaries, evils of, 219
Conferenz in Mixtis, 30
Conferenz, 29-30, 122-124, 132
Constanz, 57
Convention of Stockholm, 127
Cornets, 63, 167-170, 181, 184, 208, 279, 285, 451
Corporals, 43, 48, 50-58, 61-67, 77, 79-83, 89, 92, 101-104, 136, 157, 165, 218, 251, 253-254
Corvisier, André, 369-370
Council of State, *see Staatsrath*
Counter-Reformation, 38, 412
Court Council of War, *see Hofkriegsrath*
Crimean Tartars, 392
Croatia: becomes Habsburg possession, 15; description of, 40, 77, 79-80, 140, 147, 167, 215, 334-335, 343
Croatian Military Borders, 27, 31, 131
Croats, 333-334; confused with Pandours, 334-335; contribution declines, 346-347; grievances, 336; Guibert's inspection, 338; history, 301; military commitment, 340; mutineers, 345-346; NCOs, 343-344; nobility, 343-344; officers, 341-342; organisation, 335; promotion, 342-343; embittered by Prussian prisons, 392-393; & *kleine Krieg*, 433-435; prisoners of war, 240; opinion in Magdeburg, 240; plundering, 343-344; Slavonian grenadiers, 260-261; opposition of Inner Austrian, 334-345; domestic life, 357
Cugnot, Nicolas-Joseph, 210-211, 323-325
cuirassiers, 278-279; assessment, 289; recruiting for, 218-219; problem of under-sized men, 457-458
currency, debasement of, 113, 118-120, 145, 186, 189, 339, 346, 407
Cüstrin, Croat prisoners, 240-242
Czernin, family of, 18, 39, 60

Dalmatia: description of, 54, 81, 224
Danes, serving in the Austrian army, 105
Daun, Leopold Joseph von 32-33, 35, 132-151-152, 161-162, 171-172, 198-199, 205; and Kaunitz, 28-29; on 1761 Reduction, 141-142; in Prussian eyes, 152-153; and ADCs 196-197; Wiener-Neustadt Military Academy, 165-166; grandmaster of M.M.T.O., 203-204; on factions & generals, 198-199; and Infantry *Regulament* of 1749, 274-275; on light troops, 266; complains soldiers subject to commissiaries, 350-351; on Commissariat, 351-352; on discipline, 234-235; on recruiting, 221-222; on recruits, 219-220; on Frederick's General Principia, 417-418, 436-437; choice of positions, 428-429; hindered by need for constant reports, 418; leads from the front, 455-456; on test of battle, 455-456; too defensive, 417-418; Netherlands flavour to his staff, 90-91; on Irish officers, 108-109
debasement of Prussian currency, *see* currency debasement
Demographic Revolution, 36
desertion, 20, 68, 88, 136, 154, 220, 223, 229, 233, 235-237, 244-245, 264, 289, 295, 340
Dessau, Prince Dietrich of, 95
Dessau, Prince Eugen of, 95
Dessweffy Hussars, 177, 291, 295
Dettingen (1743), battle of, 19, 90
Deutsches Feld-Jäger Corps, 267, 274
Deutschmeister (IR No. 4), 20, 246-246, 260, 262, 271
Dickson, Peter, 115-116
Dietrichstein family, 39, 65, 157, 185, 246, 299
Diplomatic Revolution, 123, 126, 324, 386, 398, 414
Directorium in Publicis et Cameralibus, 29, 60, 132
discipline, 132, 134-135, 151, 154, 158, 160, 162, 166-167, 170, 192-193, 198-200, 207, 228, 232-236, 240, 242, 244-246, 252, 256-257, 296, 327, 334, 336, 341, 349, 351, 362, 374, 376, 407, 425, 432, 434, 438, 441, 449, 456
disease, 207, 327, 235, 346, 364, 367, 371-373, 377, 408
Dombasle, Charles-François, comte de, 102-103, 265-266
Donati, Claudio, 82
Donauschwaben, 36

INDEX 547

Dönhoff, Friedrich Ludwig Count, 98
dragoons: assessment, 289; recruiting for, 209, 218-219, 224, 231, 259, 289
Draskovich, Joseph, 79, 204, 263, 343, 435
Dresden (1748), peace of, 19, 122
Dresden, 39, 97, 106, 185-186, 196, 204, 207, 210, 242, 359-360, 367, 387-388, 391-392, 411, 417, 431-432 ; as winter quarters, 185, 327-328, 377
drill, 124, 153, 160, 162, 166, 170, 192-194, 213, 227-228, 232, 245, 275-276, 284, 304, 306-307, 341, 372, 409, 426, 440, 442, 445, 447, 449, 452
Drummers, Trumpeters and Fifers, 183, 225, 251, 255, 446
duelling, 284
Dutch, serving in the Austrian army, 90, 92, 111, 121, 123, 217

East Frisia, 93, 100, 121-122
Ehrensvärd, Augustin, Swedish general, 406
Eichinger, Count, 339, 344, 349
Elisabeth of Brunswick-Wolfenbüttel, Princess, 17
Elizabeth, Empress of Russia, 26, 125, 401-405, 462
Elmpt, Philipp, 98
Engel, Dr, 364
Engelhardt, Christoph Baron, 323
Engineers, 136-137, 163, 210, 304, 329-331, 407, 421; history, 322-323; humiliation, 322-323, 326-327
English, serving in the Austrian army, 105, 174, 178, 353
Ensigns, 63, 65, 157, 167-168, 181, 184, 193, 199
Epirot volunteers, 394
Erzherzog Carl (IR No. 3), 73, 134, 160, 193, 200-201, 206, 209, 263, 325, 366
Erzherzog Ferdinand Cuirassiers, 17, 200, 219
Erzherzog Leopold Cuirassiers, 244, 283, 355
d'Este, Duke Francesco III, 269
Esterházy family, 39, 68, 77, 79, 156
Esterházy, Nicolaus Joseph Prince, 77
Esterházy, Paul Anton Prince, 77, 179
d'Estrées, French general, 69, 265, 400
États of the Netherlands, 40
Eugene of Savoy, Prince, 16-17
extraterritoriality, 150, 230, 425

Fabri, Friedrich August von, 423
Fähndrich, regimental rank, 149, 168, 450
famine, 42
Faulhaber, Catholic priest, 385-386
Felbiger, 22, 248
Feld Artillerie-Corps, maintains own hospitals, 376
Feld Proviant-Amt, 356
Feld-Artillerie Haupt-Corps, 301
Feld-Artillerie Staab, 301
Feld-Jäger Corps, see Jager Corps
Feldwäbel, regimental rank, 160, 165, 241-242, 248, 252-253
Feldzeugamt, 301-302
Ferdinand I, Emperor, 32
Ferdinand of Brunswick, 133, 399-400

Ferdinand, Austrian Archduke, 14-15, 17
Fermor, Villim Villimovich, 403-404, 407-408
Feuerstein von Feuerstein, Anton Ferdinand Baron, 57
Feuerstein von Feuersteinsberg, Andreas, 300
Finck, Prussian general, 82, 133, 187, 190-191, 239, 276, 377, 454
Fiume: becomes Habsburg possession, 15; description of, 15, 45, 54, 73, 413
Flags, 274, 285; cavalry standards, 432
Flemming, Count, 389, 397
FM (*Feldmarschall*), rank of, 173
FML (*Feldmarschall Lieutenant*), rank of, 173
Fontenoy (1745), battle of, 25, 91, 163
Forgách IR, 235-236, 263-264
Fouqué, Heinrich de la Motte, religious persecutor, 186, 189-190, 384-385, 417
Fourier, regimental rank, 218, 256, 325
France: defrays cost of Saxon corps, 23-24; threat from 18; conduct of war, 397-403; influence on Austria, 387-388; prefers to fight Hanover rather than Prussia, 399-400; subsidy, 112-115, 127-128, 400-401; joins alliance against Prussia, 127; recruitment of Hungarians, 68-69; recruitment from, 102-103
Francis III Stephen of Lorraine, Duke of Lorraine, 17; as Grand-Duke of Tuscany, 24, 102
Franquet, Emanuel-Alexandre Baron, 90, 195
Frederick II of Prussia, 18; opinion of Maria Theresa, 21; intent to overthrow Habsburg dynasty, 385-386; kidnap attempt on, 390-391; attempts alliance with Turks & Tartars, 392-393; on weakness of opposing alliance, 396-397; displays petty malice, 392-393; attempted assassination of, 390; on Austrian artillery, 321; on Austrian cavalry tactics, 451; on Austrian light troops, 435-436; on Austrians in battle, 429-430; annexes East Frisia, 122; debases currency, 118-119; financial skills, 120; sharp practise on prisoner exchanges, 189; meets Austrian officers, 185; threatens to split *Reich* along religious lines, 92-93; nearly captured by coup de main, 101-102
Free Corps, 139, 268, 281, 334, 392
Freemasonry, 208
Freiburg, 57, 92, 99
Freicorps Béthune, 268
Freicorps Kuhwein, 268
Freicorps Le Bon, 268
French attachées, 161, 398-401, 423
French officers: tradition of Austrian service, 401
French subsidy, 38, 111-115, 401
Freudenthal, Koschinna von, 350
Freyenfels, Johann Baron, 66, 173, 182-183
Frie, Johann, 38
Fuchs, Countess Charlotte, 17, 152
Führer, regimental rank, 170, 251-252, 279, 285, 451
Fulda, Bishop of, 217
Fürstenberg, Ludwig Egon the, Landgraf of, 422
FZM (*Feldzeugmeister*), rank of, 28, 173, 175, 409

GdC (*General der Cavallerie*), rank of, 173
Gallas, family of, 18
Garrison Battalions, 136, 140, 143, 227, 261
Gefreyter, regimental rank, 252, 430
Geheime Conferenz, 29-30
Gelhorn, 422
Gemmingen, Colonel von, 153
Gemmingen, Reinhard Baron, 97-98
General Officers, 173
General Staff created, 133
General-Kriegs-Commissariat, 349
Genoa: Austrian influence in, 103-104, 112-113; bankers of, 113
George II of Great Britain, 399-400
Gerl, Matthias, 165
'German' Infantry, 259
German language: use of, 191
Germans in Hungary, 412
GFWM (*General Feldwachtmeister*), rank of, 173
Giannini, Ernst Friedrich Alexander, 104-105: as Loudon's chief of staff, 420; on Croats 346-347; on debasement of the currency, 118-119
Glatz, County of, 19, 122-123, 375, 384-385, becomes Habsburg possession, 19
Goethe, Johann Wolfgang von, 95
Golden Fleece, Order of, 26, 41, 202-203
Gomez, 137-141, 145, 361-362
Gorani, Giuseppe, 82, 160-161, 170-171, 176, 196-197; on education, 162-163; on freemasonry, 208-209; on gambling, 206; as prisoner of war, 186; ringleader of escape, 187; in a bad way, 184; on religion in Bohemia, 62-63; on medical services, 369-370; on evils of foraging, 359-360
Gorizia, becomes Habsburg possession, 15
Görz and Gradisca, as source of officers, 41, 54
Görz, 15; description of, 81, 108, 114, 158, 167, 337; Jews in, 39
Gotschee, language island, 36
Gradisca, 38; description of, 45, 53
Graffenhuber, Wolfgang, 364, 366-367, 376
Grassalkovich, Anton Count, 77, 263
Graz, 36, 48, 50, 52, 316, 333-335
Grechtler, Johann Georg Baron, 33, 180, 358
Grenadiers, 98, 101, 105, 117, 119, 153, 168, 191, 219, 222, 226-237, 246, 259-261, 265, 268, 270, 272-276, 279, 283, 285, 342, 345, 347, 354, 391, 395, 412, 432-435, 440, 445, 447, 449, 458
Grenz-Husaren, 79-80, 136-139, 147, 223, 288, 292, 335, 339, 341
Grenzer, see Croats
Gribeauval de Vaquette, Jean-Baptiste, 324; and sappers, 324, 326, 328-330
Gröller, Dionys Ferdinand, 32
Guasco brothers, Franz & Peter Alexander, 38, 104-105, 108, 419
Gugliemi, Gregorio, 23
de Guibert, Jacques-Antoine de: tours Croat settlements, 337; compares Austrians and Prussians, 98, 342, 387

Guicciardini, Joseph, 336
Gumpendorf Academy, 325
Gylau von Maros-Németh und Nadaska, Samuel, Count, 79

Habsburgs, 15-17, 25, 38-41, 58, 66, 68, 72, 77-78, 82, 84, 92, 96, 103, 108, 120-121, 202, 333, 340, 383, 385-386
Hadik, Andreas, 28, 38, 69, 73, 79, 171, 179, 200, 203, 205. 207, 209, 243, 251, 268, 291, 293, 296-297, 346, 348, 396, 408, 411, 419, 421, 424, 428-429, 434-435
Hainault, as source of officers, 89-91
d'Hallot, Ludwig Johann, 323
Hamilton, Gustav David, Swedish general, 406, 408
Hanover, 19, 93, 96, 100, 121, 123-125, 127-128, 265: French ambitions on, 399-400, 413
Harrach family, 39, 44
Harrach, Johann Joseph Harrach, 32, 132, 156
Harsch, Ferdinand Philipp, 197, 211, 323-325, 330
Hastenbeck (1757), battle of, 265, 400
'Hat' Party in Sweden, 127
Haude, Gottfried Fabian, 151, 414, 424
Haude/Rexin, 414-415, 422
Haugwitz, Friedrich Wilhelm, Count, in Prussian eyes, 384; his 'System', 110, 116, 119, 152, 181; spurs reform programme, 151-152, 230, 350
Hausartillerie, 301
heimweh, 45, 52
Hennersdorf (1745), battle of, 19
Henry of Prussia, Prince: the 'new' tactics, 360, 411, 423, 428, 439
Hessen-Cassel, Erbprinz Friedrich of, 93
Hessen-Cassel, Landgraf Wilhelm III of, 93
Hessen-Darmstadt, Landgraf Ludwig VIII of, 96
Hildburghausen, *see* SachsenHildburghausen
Hofburg, palace, *Hofcanzley* (Bohemian), 17, 20, 30, 32, 203
Hofcanzley, 45, 60, 81, 131, 240
Hofkriegsrath, 16, 22, 28-34, 44, 48, 56, 106-107, 118, 131-132, 135, 138, 144, 150, 159, 165, 170-175, 177, 181, 187, 189, 195, 199-200, 206-210, 215-221, 223, 231-232, 236, 240, 244, 255, 257-258, 261, 264, 271, 281, 292, 299, 303, 322, 324, 328-329, 335, 340, 343-344, 346, 349, 351-352, 355, 364-366
Hohenfriedberg (1745), battle of, 19, 97, 289, 391
Hohenzollerns, 92-93
Holstein, Duchy of, 96, 287-288, 402
horse artillery, 453-455
horses, 38, 69, 74, 97, 117-119, 134, 137-147, 150, 154, 182, 184, 198, 218, 238, 252, 255-256, 280-281, 285-293, 295, 303, 309-310, 313-318, 321, 327, 334, 339, 349, 351, 354, 356-358, 361-362, 370, 405, 418, 421, 427, 434, 446, 452, 454-457; feed, 280, 288, 294, 356, 358
hospitals, 23, 31, 116, 220, 287, 364-367, 370, 374-368

INDEX 549

Hungarian Infantry, 18, 42, 48, 51, 55, 57-58, 64, 66-68, 72-73, 77, 79-80, 83, 92, 101, 136-137, 159, 161, 209, 215, 224, 231, 253-254, 263-264, 271-273, 293, 354, 433, 449
Hungarian Noble Leibgarde, 20
Hungary, 41-42; contribution to the war effort, 67-68; description of, 66-78; religions, 38, 67-68, 73-74; economy, 74-77; loyalty, 67-68; magnates, 72-73, 76-77; nationalities, 71-72; French recruitment from, 68-69; becomes Habsburg possession, 15-16; Rebellion, 17; loyalty of magnates, 18; & recruiting, 214-215; soldiers prone to desertion, 235-236; national myth of hussars, 292-293; financial contribution, 112-114
Hussars, 290-291; uniforms, weapons and equipment, 293-294; assessment, 294-295; plundering, 243

Iglau, 36, 65, 226, 287, 351-352, 360; language island, 65
illiteracy in Carinthia, 51
Infantry, 259-277; organisation, 259-260 assessment, 274-275; Austrian compared with Prussian 276
Invalids, 183, 239, 244, 301, 349, 370, 374, 378-379, 413
iodine deficiency in Styria, 50
Irish: serving in the Austrian army, 106-109, 174
Istria, County of: description of, 15, 45, 53-55, 81, becomes Habsburg possession, 15
Italian troops: description of, 81; infantry, 42, 48, 50-51, 53-58, 67, 77, 79-83, 92, 101, 136, 209, 231, 253-254
Italy (Austrian), 36; description of, 79-80; peasantry of, 41-42; unhealthy garrisons, 373-374; recruitment from 103-104

Jäger-Corps, 108, 259, 267; origin in Sappers, 119
Jäger Corps Otto, 267
Jäger rifles, 267, 274
Jahnus von Eberstädt, Franz Maximilian Baron, 99
Jesuits, 163-164, 343, 398
Jews, 222; status of, 39
Joseph Esterházy IR, 263-264, 272, 274-275, 291, 295, 442
Joseph, future Emperor Joseph II, 418
Jung-Löwenstein Chevaulegers, 278-281, 285, 457
Jung-Modena Chevaulegers, 104, 108, 281
Junkers, compared to equivalent Austrian class, 27
Justiz-Collegium, 195, 199, 233-234

Kaiser IR, 32, 133, 195, 242, 255, 274, 293, 367, 379
Károly family, 68, 77, 79
Károly, Alexander Count, 68
Károly, Franz Anton Count, 263
Kaunitz-Rietberg, Wenzel Anton Count, 20-21, 64-66; family background, 60; experience of the Netherlands, 84-85; and Hessen-Cassel, 93-95; writing style, 36; and the Jews, 39-40; problem of Serbian emigration, 68-69; and military reform, 131-132; on recruiting, 213-214; character of, 25-26, views on Croat troops, 26-27, 337-338, 347-348,434-435; and espionage, 423; creates the *Staatsrath*, 416; on Croats, 434-435; on *Commissariat*, 351; fear of Turkish War, 279-280, 354; motivation, 384-385; on French policy, 400-401; alarm at Russian success, 401-402; as publicist, 392-393; berates Prussian conduct, 393-394; as coalition leader, 396-397; influenced by French styles, 387-388; on value of German contingents, 410-411; on Austrian military culture, 148-149; in Prussian eyes, 152-153; & M.M.T.O., 202-203; diplomacy, 121-128; early career, 121; Diplomatic Revolution, 123-124; reassesses value of provinces, 115; & the financial crisis of 1761, 118-119; & currency debasement, 118
Kaunitz-Rietberg family, 39; claims to East Frisia ignored, 122-123
Kesselsdorf (1745), battle of, 19
Khevenhüller, Field-Marshal Ludwig Andreas, 19, 32, 275, 449
Khevenhüller-Metsch, Hans Joseph, Count, 185-186, 194, 263
Kinsky von Chinitz und Tettau, Joseph & Franz Ulrich, Counts, 61, 64
Kinskys, family of, 18, 39, 60, 156
Kleefeld von Hnogek, Wenzel Matthias Baron, 99
kleine Krieg, 433
Kleist, Ewald von, 416
Kleist, Friedrich Wilhelm, 'Green', 189-190, 392-393
Kollowrat family, 18, 39, 60-61, 156
Königsberg, attempted mass escape from, 187-188
Königsegg IR, 108, 156, 262
Königsegg, Baron, 39, 199
Kopf, Ferdinandus, 189
Krammer von Obereck, Adam Ferdinand, 101
Krems, hospitality to Prussians, 188
Kriegelstein, Frederick Binder von, 31
Kufstein, 187, 190-191
Kunersdorf (1759), battle of, 396, 403, 405, 408

Lackner, 366
Lacy, Franz Moritz, 36,106-108, 172-173, 350-351; on regimental command, 171-172; rapid promotion, 176; on Candola & Carinthia, 48; advocates divisional system, 425; dismayed by Reduction, 142-145; in Prussian eyes, 153-154; founding father of the pioneers, 330-331
Laimgrube Preparatory School, 163-164
Landeshut (1760), battle of, 243, 420, 436, 457
Language in the Habsburg Monarchy, 44-45, 48-51, 53-55, 64-67
Lanthieri, 54, 82, 180
Lantingshausen, Jakob Albrecht, Swedish general, 406
Latin, use of, 38, 73, 210, 215
Leghorn (Livorno), bankers of, 113
Lehndorff, Count, 186, 417
Leopold I, Emperor, 16, 78, 164
Leopold Pálffy IR, 263-264

Leppert und Till, Baroness von, 422
Lessing, Gotthold Ephraim, 247, 249
Leuthen (1757), battle of, 91, 117, 147, 184-185, 196, 274, 357, 362, 378, 419, 430, 439
Liechenstein, Joseph Wenzel, Prince, 19, 22, 33, 65-66, 105, 131, 156, 299-321, 453-455; and Russian guns, 405-406; and swords, 354; responsible for arms & ammunition, 352; on recruiting, 213
Liechtenstein family, 39, 65-66, 299
Liège, Archbishopric of: 84, 88, 103, 353, recruitment from, 88, 103
Liegnitz (1760), battle of, 105, 421
Lieutenant-Colonel, rank of, 95
Lieutenants, rank of, 185
light infantry, 27, 266, 292, 433
de Ligne Dragoon Regiment, 87, 105, 265
de Ligne IR, Claude, 87, 220, 265
de Ligne, Prince Charles Joseph, 25, 156,158, 193-194, 208-209; description of, 90-92; on language in the army, 38; on the Netherlands soldier, 87-88; on the Hungarian soldier, 72-73; on Austrian generals, 197-198; childhood, 162-163; on officers & faith, 207-208; on gambling, 206; on officers off-duty, 204-205; rebukes old generals, 193-194; disapproves of promotion by seniority, 176; on field hygiene, 373-374; disapproves of specialised troops, 260-261; faces light infantry, 266; lack of engineering support, 327-328; on musketry, 445-446; bayonet attacks, 449; on columns, 444-445; on musketry, 447; on infantry tactics, 442; on marching, 427-428; on fighting in woodland, 434-435; on orders for a multilingual army, 437-438; on sword play, 452-453; on drill, 227-228; on leave, 231-232; on Prussian deserters, 223-224; on soldier's motivations, 244; on limited war, 395-396; patriotism, 386-387; complains of civilian control, 150-151
linear tactics, 439
Linz, 36, 45, 222, 287
literary accounts of Austrian soldiers, 393, 418
little war, *see kleine Krieg*
Lloyd, Henry, 193, 246, 418
Lobkowitz, Joseph Maria Carl Prince, 61; on *kleine Krieg*, 63
Lockhart, Captain Jakob Count, 105
Logistics, 349-363; contracters default, 358-359; direction of, 349-350; failure before Leuthen, 351; fraud, 356-357; magazines, 359-360; magazines captured by Prussians, 360-361; political restrictions, 358-359; procurement, 352; Prussian advantages, 357-358, 360-361
Lombards in the Austrian service, 82
Lorraine, Duchy of: contribution to Austrian war effort, 102
Lorraine, Prince Charles of, *see* Charles of Lorraine
Los Rios IR, 87-88, 91, 178, 182, 265-266, 271
Losy von Losenau, Colonel, on columnar tactics, 434-435, 439, 442

Lothringen, Carl, IR, 102, 266
Loudon 'Green' Grenadiers, 117, 142-143
Loudon free battalion, 117, 119, 142-143, 237, 268, 347
Loudon, Gideon Ernst, 27-28, 181: rapid promotion, 176, 179; on regimental command, 171-172; a Muscovite, 180-181; commends Prussian administration, 384-385; no quarter at Landeshut, 391-392; on peasant support in Moravia, 394-395 and plunder, 243-244; reports to Vienna, 419; skill at retreat, 358-359; use of Croats, 436-437; on Irish officers, 108; raises his Green battalion, 268-269
Louis XV of France, 124, 127, 399-401
Löwenstein-Wertheim, Christian Wilhelm Prince, 280
Lower Austria, 36, 39-40, 44-45, 110, peasantry of, 42, 225 ; and recruitment, 72, 114, 216, 293
Luise Ulrike, Queen of Sweden, 127, 406
Lutheranism in Hungary, 67, 74, 78, 339
Luxembourg, Duchy of, 83-89
Luzan IR, 81, 216, 235, 264-265, 271

M.M.T.O. (Militärischer- Maria TheresienOrden), 27-28, 44, 202-203; for miners, 331-332; for sappers, 329-330; for artillerymen, 305-306; for Croats, 342-343
Magdeburg, and Austrian prisoners, 187, 191, 240, 424, 434
Maguire von Inniskillen, Johann Sigismund, 335
Magyar language, 38, 73
Mainz: and recruiting, 99, 147
Mainz Regiment, 93, 96, 216, 259, 269-270, 410, 412
Mainz, Bishop of, 98
manoeuvres, 21-22, 132-133, 248, 411, 418, 454
Mantua, Duchy of, 80-83; Jews in, 39
maps, 33, 297, 330, 419, 421, 424
Marainville, Rutant de, French attaché, 401, 428
Maria Theresa, 83-84, 159-160; youth of, 17; founds military academies, 163-164; on rewards, 201-202; and Khevenhüller-Metsch, 194; displeased with officers, 194; and Hungary, 67-68; on Jews, 38; & the nobility, 41-42; and medical services, 365; & military reform, 131-132; & Reduction of 1761, 141; unpopular according to Gellhorn, 151-152; absenteeism, 387-388; appeals to the public, 392-393; belated hardening of attitude, 389-390; hatred of Frederick, 385-386; motivation, 384-385; impressed by Liechtenstein, 299; Political Testament, 131-132, on Prussian desertion, 222-223, 239; escaped POWs, 242; on desertion, 234-235; on schools for soldiers' children, 230-231; opposes requisitions, 358-359; parity of Hungarian regiments, 262-264; on uniforms, 270-271; character of, 20; concern for soldiers, 21
Maria Wilhelmina Josepha, Princess of Auersperg, 32
Marie-Therese, widow of Duke Emanuel of Savoy-Carignan, 163
marriage in Austrian service, 171, 208-209, 230-231

Marschall von Biberstein, Ernst Dietrich Count, 99
Mecklenberg, Prince Ernst of, 87 Mecklenburg, duchy of, 98
Medical Services, 364-380; decline in health after 1761, 377-378; dismal quality, 366; *Directorium* competes with *Hofkriegsrath* for control, 364; mortality, 368-369; personnel, 367-368; superior Prussian arrangements, 374-375
Mednyansky, 406, 408
Mercy, Anton Ignaz, 339
Meyern, 180
Milan, Duchy of, 81
Militärischer- Maria Theresien-Orden, see M.M.T.O.
Military Academy at Wiener-Neustadt, *see* Wiener-Neustadt
Military *Conferenz*, 30
military music, 255
Military Order of Maria Theresa, *see* M.M.T.O.
Military Reform Commission, 132, 158, 259
Military Reform, 131, 133, 152, 201, 275, 349, 460-461
Minenburg, Waldhütter von, 79, 159
Mineurs, 331-332
mining, proceeds from Hungary, 114
Ministry for Internal Affairs, *see Directorium in Publicis et Cameralibus*
Modena Contingent, 259, 269
Mohács (1526), battle of, 15, 67, 333
Moltike, Philipp Ludwig, 221
Montazet, Antoine-Marie de Malvin, comte de, French attaché, 21, 161, 197, 324, 357, 401, 419; on Austrian generals, 197
Moravia, 36: becomes Habsburg possession, 15; military contribution, 64--66; description of, 64-66; serfs of, 41-42; protestantism, 62-63; the cost of war, 395-396
Motivation and Honour, 242
Motte-Fouqué, *see* Fouqué
muskets, 133, 153, 173, 183, 219, 226, 253, 260, 264, 267, 271, 273-274, 308-309, 344-345, 353, 391, 413, 431, 435, 438, 444, 446, 449, 458; and musketry, 274, 299, 446-448, 454, 456

Nádasdy, Franz, 68, 79, 88, 153, 203, 270, 291-293, 298, 337
Naples: tradition of Austrian service, 105
nationality: in the Habsburg Monarchy, 36, 62, 363, 460; of the troops, 104, 258, 331, 367
Navarro, Lieutenant-Colonel, 196
NCOs, 251-258: compared with Prussian, 251
Neipperg, Reinhard Wilhelm, Field Marshal, 18,32, 56-57, 134, 137-138, 153-154; praises Croats, 334; puts down 'Warasdiner rebellion', 336; on garrison battalions, 261-262; on uniforms, 270-271
Neny, Patrick Francis de, 85, 109
Netherlands (Austrian) 36; condition of peasantry, 41-42; description of, 83-91; substantial contribution to war effort, 84-85; recruitment, 88-89; unexpected scale of contribution, 115; defensive arrangements, 412-413; as source of engineers, 322
Netherlands Infantry, 55, 57-58, 67, 80, 83, 90, 92, 101, 208-209, 231, 253-254
Netolitzky von Eisenber, Wenzel Kasimir, 213, 250
Nettine, Louise Barbe, banker, 113
Nettolitzky, Count, 152
Neugebauer, Franz Ludwig Baron, 101
Niederländische National-Artillerie, 302
Nobility, power of, 56, 58, 73
Normann, Ernst Baron, 98
Norwegians, serving in the Austrian army, 105, 368
Nostitz family, 39, 60
Nostitz-Rieneck reform commission, 356, 361
Nugent von Westmeath, James, 109, 417

O'Donnell Cuirassiers, 355
O'Donnell, Carl Claudius, 106, 457-458; on height of recruits, 219-220; on swords, 355-356; on cavalry recruits, 283-284
O'Donnell, Johann, 107
O'Kelly, 108-109, 180, 262
O'Leary, Ellen, 109
O'Sullivan, Abigail, 109
Obereck, Krammer von, 101, 175
Ödenburg, County of, 36, 73, 75-76, 79
Officers: accountability, 199-200; encouragement and reward, 200-201; commissioned upstarts, 159-160; private conduct and relationships, 204; professional conduct, 191; promotion, 179; social class, 156; discipline, 199-200; killed by own men, 192; & bad women, 207
Olmütz, a dogged defender of, 105, 325, 343
Ordnance Stores, 308
Orthodox Christianity in Hungary, 73-74
Otto Jägers, *see Jäger Corps Otto*
Ottoman, Ottomans, *see* Turks

Pabliczek, Joseph, 331
Palatinate, 72, 93, 99-100
Pálffy family,
Pálffy Hussar Regiment, 291
Pálffy, Carl Paul, 134 218-219; on cuirassiers, 278-279; on uniforms, 281-282; on swords, 283-284 on the cuirass, 283
Pálffy, Leopold, 263-264, 292-293, 296, 352
Pálffy, Nicolaus, 293
Pálffy, Rudolph, 234, 243, 291, 293, 428
Pallavicini-Centurioni, Johann Lucas Count, 81
Pan-Slavism, 340
Panduren-Corps von der Trenck, 263
Paper Money, 112-113, 407
Patriotic Reflections, 177, 192-193, 244-246 251, 290-291 296-297, 350-351, 356-35, 417
Pawlowsky von Rosenfeld, Wenzel, 327
Pay, Rations and Accommodation, 228-229
Peace of Westphalia, 68, 93, 106, 127, 406
peasantry, 82, condition of 39,
Pest, 34

Petazzi, Benvenut, 335-336, 342-346
Peter III of Russia, 146, 340
Philip of Spain, 124, 128
Piacenza (1746), battle of, 17, 19, 81, 299
Piedmont-Sardinia: 25, 123, agreement with Austria, 25, 123; recruitment from, 217
Pionier-Corps, 267, 330; disbanded, 143
Pitt, British Prime Minister, 26, 400
Piza, Franz de, 281, 353
Plobsheim, August Zorn von, 102, 200, 236
Plundering, 88, 118, 177, 183, 243
Plunkett, 109, 180
Podewils, Count, Prussian ambassador, 385, 423, 440
Political Testament of Maria Theresa, 131
Pompadour, 26, 123, 127, 207, 397
Pontoniers, 330-331
Pope Clement XIII Rezzonico, 386
Portugal Cuirassier Regiment, 200, 278
Pragmatic Sanction, 17
Prague, 36, 61; Jews in, 39, 271
Preiss, Joseph Baron, 102, 352
Princes and Grandees, 39, 41, 90, 107, 156-157, 159, 299
prisoners of war (Austrian), 186-190, 241-242; escapees, 187-188, 241-242; Prussian view of, 186
prisoners of war (Prussian), 188-189, 222-223, 237, 239-240, 347
Privy Council, *see Geheime Conferenz*
Profos, rank of, 251, 257
Protestants: position of, 38, 63, 68, 106, 160, 224, 270, 339, 379-380, 384, 386, 409, 411; in Moravia, 63; in officer corps, 38, 95, 202
Proviantmeister, regimental rank, 251, 256
Prussian deserters, in Austrian service, 215-217, 220-223, 235-238, 265-269, 329, 342, 387, 423; in Austrian service, 222-223
Prussian Espionage, 151, 421
Prussians in the Austrian officer corps, 98-99
punishment, 63, 69, 178-179, 190, 200, 218, 233, 236, 243-244, 253, 255, 257, 265, 289, 293, 336, 340-341, 366, 387, 407

Rabenbach, 117
Radicati Cuirassier Regiment, 105, 278, 281, 289, 298, 451
Ragip Pasha, 415, 422
rations, 119, 133, 180-182, 228-2229, 233, 288, 296, 349, 356-360, 362, 375, 378, 412, 434
Ravizza, Anton, 44, 175
Rebain, 251, 322, 430-431; on dragoons, 279-280; on swords, 283-284; compares Prussian and Austrian officers, 191; on Croat uniforms, 344-345
Rebentisch, Lt-Col., Prussian spy, 151, 153
recruitment: artillery, 304-305; by the Local Estates, 214; systems of recruitment, 213; voluntary enlistment, 216; qualifications, disqualifications & conditions, 218; bounties, 221-222; undesirables, 221-222; for cuirassiers, 282-283; for hussars, 292-293; the limits, 387-388; of doctors, 365

recruits: height, 218-219; age, 219-220; background, 48, 245
Reduction of 1761/2, 141-145; damage of, 145
regimental baggage, 362
regimental officers, 31, 40, 44, 54, 89, 95, 99, 108, 134, 161, 165, 168, 172-176, 182-184, 191-192, 196, 209, 234-235, 248, 290, 328, 352, 362, 403, 429, 438, 456
Regiments-Quartiermeister, rank of, 257
Regulament, 132 148-149, 417-418, 444-445; for infantry, 274-275, 439-440; cavalry, 449; of 1759, 426, 446-448; for engineers, 322; flags, 274-275; the Prussian view, 153-154; cuirassier and dragoon, 228-229
Reich, 15; comes to Austria's aid, 128; contribution to war effort, 115; war effort, 408-409; and the Austrian war effort, 91-92; threat of secularisation, 97-98
Reichs-Executions Armee, see Reichsarmee
Reichsarmee, 30, 93, 97, 145, 187, 210, 216-217, 267, 313, 331, 350, 358-359, 391, 396, 409-411, 434, 439; at war, 409-411
Reichscanzley, 30, 219
Reichstag, 92-93, 115, 409
Reintrie du Pin, Henri Baron de la, 287
Religion: in the Habsburg possessions, 38; danger of Reich fracturing on religious lines, 92-93; of the troops, 223-224; Silesia religious battleground, 385-387
Reluition (substitution money), 44-45, 214-217, 221-223
remounts, 117, 143, 154, 256, 268, 285, 287-288, 293, 349, 388
Révay, spoiled Franciscan brother, 69, 79
Rexin, Carl Adolph von, 414-415, 422
Richthausen, Johann Conrad, Baron von Chaos, 325
rifles, 267, 274
Ritterakademien, 163
Ritterschaft, 41, 58
Riverson, 324, 401
Robot, 42, 56
Romanians, *see* Wallachians
Rosen, Fredrik, Swedish general, 406
Roth-Würzburg IR, *see* Würzburg IRs
Rothschütz, Georg Sigismund Baron, 99
Rouvroy, Joseph Theodor, 300, 305
Russia: army, 402-403; artillery, 404-405, 454-455; conduct of the war, 401-407; cossack depradations, 391-392; diplomacy of, 125-127; encouraging emigration of Serbs, 71-72; lack of will to win, 388-389; subverts Croats, 340
Russian auxiliary corps, 144, 146
Rüstungs Commission (Mobilisation Commission), 29, 112, 116
Ruwet, Joseph, 87

Sabbioneta, Principality of, 80
Sachsen in Hungary & Transylvania, 72
Sachsen-Gotha IR, 87-88, 98, 265-266

Sachsen-Gotha, Duke Friedrich of, 95
Sachsen-Hildburghausen, Joseph Friedrich, Prince of, 22, 97-98, 131: commands *Reichsarmee*, 408-410; with Croats, 333-337
Sachsen-Teschen, Prince Albert of, 23, 98, 163
Saint-Severin, 122
Sala, Bishop Baron de, 215
Salburg, Franz Ludwig Count, 132, 165, 216, 349
Salm IR, 236, 271, 413
Saltykov, Petr Semenovich, 34, 199, 404-405
Salzburg, 48, 99; and recruiting, 96, 99-101
Salzburg, bishop of, 96, 217, 386
Sanitäts Commissionen, 367
Sappeurs-Corps, 139, 143, 147, 223, 327
Saxons of Hungary, 77-78
Saxony 92-93; cavalry, 238-239, 278-279; in the Seven Years War, 96-98; invaded, 126-127; as winter quarters, 184-186; lack of commitment, 388-389; troops, 237-238, 411-412; near-despotic powers of Wilczek, 350; supply problems, 358-359
Saxony, Friedrich August (Augustus the Strong'), Elector of, 96
Schaffgotsch, Philipp Gotthard, 385-386
Schmerzing Cuirassiers, 200, 278, 386
Schmettau, Karl Christoph, 321, 391
Schönbrunn, Palace of, 20-21, 23, 188
Schröder, Gottfried Johann, 99
Schröder, Wilhelm Baron, 98
Schwachheim, Joseph Peter, 415
Schwarzenberg family, 44, 60, 157
Schweidnitz: defence of (1762), 159-160, 331-332; storm of (1757), 90-91, 101-104; storm of (1761), 241, 243-244
Schwerin: on Austrian use of mounted fire, 452
Scots, serving in the Austrian army, 105-106, 174
Second Enserfment, 41-42
secularisation in the Reich, 97, 384, 386
Serbelloni, Giambattista, 82, 409
Serbian emigration, 69
Serbs, 15, 69, 72, 334, 337, 340; *see also* Croats
serfdom, 41-42, 78, 335, 338
Sergeants, 251
Shuvalov, Petr Ivanovich, 402-402, 405
Silesia (Austrian), 36: description of, 66-67
Silesia (Prussian): contribution to Austrian war effort, 100-102; treatment of civilians, 394-395; ideological battleground, 385-386; Austrian loss of, 383-384; outstanding source of NCOs,251-252
Simbschen IR, 80, 136-138, 209, 231, 253-254, 259, 263-264, 334; origins, 138
Slavonia, description of, 40, 79-80, 133, 337-340
Slavonian, *see* Croats
Slovaks in Hungary, 72, 74
soldiers: life, 226-227; age & service, 231-232, desertion, 223-224, 234-235; discipline, 232-233; leave, 231-232; nationality, 223-224; punishment, 232-233; religion, 223-224
Sonnenfels, Joseph von, 209, 246-249, 387
Soor (1745), battle of, 19, 289

Soubise, French general, 396, 399
Spain: agreement with Austria, 15-16, 123-124, 148, 385; recruitment from, 79, 81-82, 103-104, 224, 254
St. André, Friedrich Daniel, 403-404
St. Ignon Dragoons, 281
St. Paul, Horace, 105, 162, 178, 183-184
Staabs-Dragoner-Regiment, 143, 231, 421
Staabs-Infanterie-Regiment, 139, 143, 219, 259, 330, 420, 432
Staabs-Pioniere, 421, *see also* Pioneers
Staatscanzley, 29-32, 111
Staatsrath, 25, 30-31, 81, 113, 119, 240, 416
Staff officers, 170, 235, 403, 417, 423, 455
Stampa, Cajetan Count, 82-83, 180, 193, 278
Stampach, Lt General, 153, 200, 278, 289, 451
Stände, 16, 26, 39-40, 40, 44, 50, 52, 56, 78, 110-112, 132, 143-144, 159, 163-164, 201, 213-231, 236, 242, 261, 267, 283, 303, 327, 333-335, 350-351, 358, 350, 362, 376, 378-379, 387, 460; admission to, 41, 50; Bohemian, 18, 60, 216, 229, 327, 385, 421; recruiting, 44, 143, 214-215, 387
Standrecht, regimental rank, 257
Starhemberg family, 39, 44, 286
Starhemberg, Emanuel Michael, accused of corruption, 25, 121
Starhemberg, Georg Adam Count, 124-128, 189, 398
Starhemberg, Maria Ernestine von, 25, 121
Starhemberg, Winulph, 189
Steenhalt, A. De, 85
Stephanie, Johann Gottlieb, playwright, 210, 241, 248-249
Sternberg, family of, 18, 60
Stolberg, Christian Carl, 409, 411
Styria, 36; becomes Habsburg possession, 15; description of, 47-48; languages, 48-50; peasantry of, 41-42; unmilitary reputation, 48-50; and recruiting, 214-215
supply, 29, 31-33, 95, 108, 118, 132, 135, 138, 139, 144, 218, 257, 288, 296, 327, 344, 349, 351, 354-356, 358, 374-375, 388, 395, 403, 406, 409, 417, 421-422, 446; artillery, 303, 308, 324, 410, 453; horse feed, 287, 389;
'Subsistence', 42, 116-117, 184, 208, 245, 338, 408; *see also* Logistics
sutlers, 170, 205, 207, 231, 257, 361-363, 427, 431
Swabians in Hungary, 72
Sweden: conduct of the war, 405-409; Austria needs support of, 386-387; diplomacy of, 126
Swedes, serving in the Austrian army, 396, 406
Swedish Pomerania, 99, 105, 224, 406-407
Swieten, Gerhard Van, 39, 364-367, 372-373
Swiss, serving in the Austrian army, 105, 217, 238
swords, 18, 161, 183, 187, 200, 206, 273, 284, 308, 336, 344, 353-355, 369, 393, 449, 452, 457
System of 1716, artillery, 314
System of 1753, artillery, 314-320
Szatmár (1711), Treaty of, 17, 68, 72-73, 76, 79
Székely, Michael, 68. 78-79
Szelders, 77-78

Taaffe, Count, 101
Taaffe, Nicholas, Sixth Earl of Carlingford, 106
Taaffe, Viscount Francis, Third Earl of Carlingford, 107
tactics: answer to Frederick's oblique order, 439-440; battle, 437-438; closed columns, 439-440; infantry, 440-441; the 'new' tactics, 438-439; columnar, 442; tactics: infantry *regulament*, 275-276
Tamzi, Giuseppe, banker, 113
Tanner, Rittmeister, 422
Tax Burden, 51, 60, 110, 112, 383, 407
Terzi, Ludovico Baron, 171, 177, 209
Teuffel, Baron, 56
Teutonic Order, 97, 248
Theresianisch-Savoyische Ritterakademie, 163-164
Thirty Years War, 17, 25, 58, 60, 124, 200, 214, 333, 384
Thüngen, Adam Sigismund, 449
Thürheim, Franz Ludwig, 44, 165-166, 186, 262
Thurn, Count, 131
Thurn-Valsassinas, family of, 54
Tillier, Johann Anton Baron, 104-105
Tillier, Joseph Maximilian Baron, 104
Tilsit, mass escape from, 187, 188, 208, 241
Torgau (1760), battle of, 21, 61, 101-102, 242, 276, 300
Toscana IR, 105, 259, 269
Trabanten-Garde, 20
tradesmen and specialists within the regiment, 195, 251, 256-257, 302, 305
transport, 43, 48, 51-58, 65-67, 79-80, 83, 95, 110, 117, 137-141, 183, 211, 265, 275, 285, 296, 309-310, 317, 325, 349, 356-362, 370, 375, 389
Transylvania: description of, 36, 67-68, 72-74, 78, 111, 114, 150; religions, 38, 75-78; and recruitment, 77, 79, 215, 223-224, 235, 239, 253-254, 339, 368
Traun, Field-Marshal, 19, 81
Trautmannsdorf, Franz Carl, Count, 61, 165
Trenck, Franz von der, 104, 163, 334: *see also PandurenCorps von der Trenck*
Trieste: description of, 53-54; Jews in, 39-40
Turks, 71-72; earlier wars with, 279-280; threat of war, 354
Tuscany, 17, 102, 105
Tyrol: peasantry of, 41-42, 56; description of, 45, 55, 57; becomes Habsburg possession, 15
Tyroler Land- und Feld-Regiment, 56, 216, 244, 262, 267

Ulfeld, Corfiz Anton Count, 25, 123
undesirables, 222
Ungern-Sternberg, Mathias Alexander, Swedish general, 406
uniforms: cost, 352-353; Croat, 344-345; cuirassier & dragoon, 280-281; hussar, 293-294; Hungarian, 264; infantry, 270-271; generals', 183
Upper Austria: description of, 36, 40, 42, 354; peasantry of, 41-42, 287

Upstarts, 159, 179
d'Ursel, Charles-Elizabeth duc, 90-91

Vaduz, territory of, 299
Valentiniani, Francesco, 192, 265
Verneville, Chevalier de, 161
Verri, Pietro, 81-82; on Daun, 205; on fellow officers, 191: on Henry Lloyd, 417-418
Versailles, Treaties of, 115, 125-127, 397-401
Vienna, 36, 42-45; as artillery depot, 307-308; sits in judgement on the generals, 392-393
Vienna Stadt Banco, 111-113
Vigneul, baron de, 251
Vocaillovich, Thomas, 187, 342
Voghtern, FML Immanuel, 78, 100, 215
Volontiers Silesiens Beck, 268
Vorarlberg, 57
Vorder-Österreich; peasantry of, 41; description of, 18, 57, 72, 111, 114
Vorontsov, Mikhail Ilarionovich, 125

Wabst, Christian Xaver, 364-368, 371, 373, 376
Wachtmeister, regimental rank, 251-253
Wagenmeister, regimental rank, 251, 256, 309-310
Waldenau, Ignaz Walther von, 44, 175, 203, 300, 302, 305
Waldhütter, First-Lieutenant Michael, 79, 159
Waldstein family, 18, 39, 58-61, 157, 200, 376
Wallachian Border, *see* Croats
Wallachians: in Hungary, 78; in Transylvania, 177, 215
Wallis, Michael Johann, 107
Wallis, Olivier, Baron Carighmain, 107
Walloon infantry, 265
War of the Austrian Succession, 19, 32, 81, 85, 216, 351, 399, 433
War of the League of Augsburg, 121
War of the Polish Succession, 17, 102
War of the Spanish Succession, 16, 56, 103, 121
Warasdiner 'rebellion', 337
Warkotsch, Count, 102
Warkotsch, Gottfried Baron, 390-391
Warnery, Charles-Emanuel, 154, 276, 297, 395
Wartensleben, 296, 425
Wastage, 35, 50, 143, 147, 280, 292, 295, 310, 346, 356-357, 367
Weapons: infantry, 133, 228, 256, 270, 274, 293, 345, 352, 355, 445; cavalry, 238, 270, 274, 281, 285, 355; hussar, 270, 274, 294, 297, 355
Weiss, Gottlieb, 195, 210
Werner, Johann Paul, 68, 390
Westminster, Treaty of, 125
Wetzel, 422
White Mountain (1620), battle of the, 17, 60
Widmann, Johann Wenzel Baron, 93
Wiedemann, 153-154
Wiener Neustadt Military Academy, 104
Wiener-Neustadt & Prussian prisoners, 190
Wilczek, Joseph Maria, 350-351

Wilhelm of Brandenburg-Ansbach, Margrave Carl, 95, 190
Williams, Sir Hanbury, 124-125
Windish (Slovenian) in Styria, 48
Winterfeldt, Hans Carl, founder of Prussian espionage, 137, 151-157, 296, 298, 385, 395, 422
Wöber, August Thomas, 32-33, 44
Wöber, Augustin, 132
Wolckenstein, Count, 56
Wolff, Christian, 122
Wöllwarth, Gottfried Baron, 176
Württemberg troops, 96, 246, 259, 270, 281, 409, 411-412, 422
Württemberg, Duke Carl Eugen of, 96, 270, 412
Württemberg, Prince Friedrich Eugen, Prussian general, 389
Württemberg, Prince Louis of, Austrian general, 389
Württemberg: princes of, 98, 408; support needed by Austria, 386
Würzburg IRs (Blau- and Roth-Regiments), 93, 98, 259, 270
Würzburg, Bishop Adam Friedrich of, 98; and recruiting, 217
Würzburg, GFWM, 217-218

Xaver August of Saxony, Prince, 238

Zenta (1697), battle of, 16
Zeughaus in Vienna, 48, 308
Zimmermann, regimental rank, 150, 256
Zinzendorf, Ludwig Count, 113
Zweibrücken, Pfalz-, Friedrich Michael Prince, 409
Zwittau, language island, 65